The
LONGMAN HANDBOOK
for
UIC
WRITERS AND READERS

Chris M. Anson
University of Minnesota

Robert A. Schwegler
University of Rhode Island

 LONGMAN

An Imprint of Addison Wesley Longman, Inc

New York • Reading, Massachusetts • Menlo Park, California • Harlow, England
Don Mills, Ontario • Sydney • Mexico City • Madrid • Amsterdam

Manager of Addison Wesley Longman Custom Books: Caralee Woods
Production Administrator: Rohnda Barnes
Cover Design: Zina Scarpulla

The LONGMAN HANDBOOK *for*
UIC WRITERS AND READERS

ISBN: 0-201-45657-5

98 99 00 3 2 1

Contents

Preface for Students and Instructors

All writers, whatever their skills and experience, need at least occasional advice, and sometimes even more. We have designed *The Longman Handbook for Writers and Readers* as a resource both for times when you are looking for the answer to a specific question and for times when you want extended help.

You can turn to the handbook for advice about writing strategies and critical reading; for questions about grammar, punctuation, and style; and for help in making research, analysis, and documentation an effective part of your writing. You can also use it for advice in dealing with a variety of audiences and kinds of writing—academic, professional, and personal—all of which make different demands on writers and readers.

Over the past two decades, composition teaching has changed dramatically in response to contemporary research and theory. Classroom activities now give students greater responsibility for their own learning. Teaching has taken on more supportive roles. Work on syntax, grammar, usage, and style now rests on a deeper understanding of the causes of error and the remedies. Yet composition handbooks, with their roots in earlier modes of teaching, have often lagged behind these advances. We have written *The Longman Handbook for Writers and Readers* out of a sense that composition teaching will benefit from an innovative approach to handbooks, one that responds directly to recent developments in theory and practice.

Throughout the handbook, we draw on contemporary research and practical knowledge to provide direct, specific answers and advice. At the same time, we recognize the need for flexibility. The writing and reading strategies appropriate for one task or audience may be inappropriate for another, and there are many ways to correct punctuation or grammar errors and design effective sentences. We know, too, that even if a handbook is detailed and comprehensive, it has little value unless its users can quickly and easily find the information they need.

The Longman Handbook is at once authoritative and flexible, balancing comprehensiveness with conciseness and ease of use. It presents detailed examples and specific writing strategies rather than broad generalizations. It provides concrete techniques for recognizing and revising errors instead of abstract, inflexible rules.

To achieve these ends, we have extended the familiar and successful composition handbook format with a number of innovative approaches. First, *The Longman Handbook for Writers and Readers,* as the name suggests, takes full account of the crucial role an understanding of readers and reading can play in the composing process and in editing writing for correctness and clarity. Second, the handbook treats writing and reading as social, collaborative processes, which may vary considerably according to setting and purpose. Third, the handbook reflects a belief in the importance of concrete, specific writing strategies and ease of reference. These and other special features deserve extended discussion both in their own right and as a way of understanding how to make the best use of the resources in *The Longman Handbook.*

Paying Attention to Readers

Writing often takes place in private—in our minds, at our desks, on our computer screens—so we may tend to think of it as something that takes shape in the absence of readers. This perspective, however, is a mistake. Because writing is a form of communication, our real or potential readers are present (or ought to be) from the earliest stages of writing to the final editing and proofreading. Even in writing for ourselves in order to discover and explore ideas (see Chapter 2 on keeping a journal), we engage in a process that enables us to "read" our own thinking.

In *The Longman Handbook,* we emphasize the importance of readers and reading in a number of ways.

- **Making Reading Part of the Writing Process.** Throughout Part 1 of the book, "Writing and Reading," we stress the many important roles that critical reading and awareness of audience play in the writing process. Of special interest here are the paired Chapters 2 ("Strategies for Active Writing") and 3 ("Strategies for Active Reading"). In addition, Chapter 6 ("Considering Your Readers") is filled with practical advice for making your audience part of your writing. Other chapters, such as Chapters 8 ("Revising"), 13 ("The Editing and Proofreading Process"), and 44 ("Locating Sources and Reading Critically"), highlight reading skills of particular use at different times in the writing process and with different kinds of writing. Much of Part 4 ("Writing Strategies") as a whole is devoted to developing an awareness of specialized kinds of audiences and the ways they are likely to read your writing.
- **Considering Your Readers.** Chapter 6, "Considering Your Readers," focuses on the importance of keeping your readers in mind as you shape your text. Elsewhere in the book we emphasize the need to consider readers' expectations and patterns of perception as you create paragraphs (Chapters 9 and 10), sentences (Chapters 11 and 12), and various kinds of academic and professional writing (Chapters 43 to 53).

- **Collaboration and Feedback.** Perhaps the best way to understand how readers respond to a text and to learn how to view your own writing as readers do is to collaborate with other writer-readers. Many writing courses recognize the importance of collaboration by making use of peer response groups and similar activities. For these classes and for writers who wish to develop an ability to read others' work analytically and helpfully, we offer special, practical advice about giving and receiving constructive criticism during revision (8c, "Using Feedback Constructively") and about editing for style and correctness (13b, "Collaborative Editing"). We go far beyond this, however, by including a collaborative activity in virtually every set of exercises in the text because we believe that developing an awareness of readers and learning how to read both your own and others' work critically takes considerable practice and experience.
- **Critical Thinking and Reading.** Beyond the handbook's cohesive, integrated view of writing and reading, we have focused throughout on the critical reading and thinking skills needed for success in college. Techniques for effective reading are related not only to paraphrase and summary but also to higher-level research and writing skills such as synthesis, interpretation, and evaluation. Critical thinking skills are treated directly in Chapter 50, which focuses on reading and argument, and in Chapters 51 and 52, which treat various kinds of academic discourse, including reading and writing about literature.
- **Reader's Responses.** Problems in sentence or paragraph structure and violations of the conventions of grammar, punctuation, mechanics, and style will confuse, distract, and irritate readers—sometimes to the point where they begin to reject or ignore what a writer has to say. Throughout the text, and especially in our discussions of grammar, sentence problems, punctuation, word choice, and mechanics, we explain errors and writing conventions in terms of their negative or positive effects on readers. In addition, we provide numerous Reader's Responses to illustrate how particular kinds of errors mislead or irritate readers. We believe that this approach helps explain the importance of writing conventions and highlights the consequences of errors without excessive preachiness or overly technical discussion.

Writing and Reading as Social Processes

We believe that writing and reading are social processes, characterized by constant transactions between writers and readers and by the context within which these transactions occur.

- **Purpose and Form.** To emphasize the importance of audience and social setting in writing, the seven chapters in Part 1 of the text ("Writing and Reading") highlight the role of audience and social setting in shaping the purposes of effective writing and in determining which forms of expression are likely to be most useful. Along with Part 2 ("Revising and Shaping Your Writing"), these chapters provide numerous practical strategies for shaping writing as a response to audience and setting and for writing in ways that are likely to have an effect on readers' outlooks and actions.

- **Correctness.** Correctness in writing—employing the conventions of expression appropriately—is to a considerable extent a matter of social awareness. Following or failing to follow conventions in grammar, sentence structure, punctuation, and style can help determine the way readers respond to your writing.

  Research tells us that conventions of grammar and expression vary greatly over time and from group to group. These variations are clear to any contemporary reader of Shakespeare and to anyone who notices the differences in language use in different settings, such as a college classroom and a dormitory. At the same time, the members of any particular community are likely to place considerable importance on following certain conventions. Businesspeople and professionals are justifiably concerned with the negative impression left by misspellings and careless punctuation; academics have good reasons for paying special attention to the conventions of documentation and for avoiding confusing uses of pronoun reference. It is also easy to understand why educated readers generally expect clear, logical, and consistent use of verb tense and subject-verb agreement.

  Effective writers are aware both of the importance of following conventions and of the ways in which conventions are likely to vary. Throughout the handbook we try to develop this dual awareness. In Did You Know? boxes, we provide historical and research-based perspectives on the way conventions have developed or changed and on their importance for writers and readers. In Writer's Tips, Writer's Alerts, and informative boxes, we highlight those conventions most likely to cause problems for writers and those where errors are most likely to have serious consequences. In Part 3, "Editing and Proofreading," we use Strategy sections to offer practical suggestions for recognizing and revising errors.

  Above all, Part 3 of the text offers firm answers about correctness in grammar, sentence structure, word choice, punctuation, mechanics, and spelling—a firmness that is balanced by clear discussions of the flexible options writers often have as a result of shifting conventions and different audiences.

- **Different Audiences, Different Forms of Expression.** One of our main goals in the handbook is to help develop an awareness of the way communities of readers and writers share habits of thought and expression that distinguish them from other groups. For this reason, we provide extensive discussion of different forms of writing, the settings in which they frequently appear, and the purposes they serve.

These discussions introduce most of the kinds of writing students encounter in college courses in the humanities, social sciences, and natural sciences as well as much of the writing used in business, the professions, and civic life. Of particular interest is our innovative use of the categories point-driven writing (Chapter 50) and informative writing (Chapter 52) to distinguish kinds of writing with markedly different purposes and writer-reader relationships.

Practical Advice

We believe that writers turn to a handbook most often for concrete advice: for ways to accomplish a writing task, for answers to questions about grammar and punctuation, or for ways to document a source. Even when they want to know about a relatively general subject, such as how to write a research paper or the most useful ways to revise and edit, writers are often best served by learning about specific strategies they can employ.

- **Strategies.** *The Longman Handbook* places special emphasis on concrete, practical strategies that writers and readers can employ in their work. One innovation in the text is the use of Strategy sections to present techniques writers and readers can apply immediately. The Strategies are detailed and specific, and they suggest ways to employ the general advice offered in the more general discussions that precede them.
- **Recognize and Revise.** We believe that knowing the definition of an error such as a sentence fragment, a problem with pronoun reference, or misused punctuation is often not sufficient. Writers need to be able to recognize such errors as they draft, revise, and edit, and then they need to be able to correct mistakes. Each of the reference chapters in Part 3 of the handbook ("Editing and Proofreading") is built around a recognize-and-revise pattern and offers concrete suggestions for identifying errors and avoiding or revising them. Many of the Strategy and Writer's Tip sections in these chapters pay special attention to common errors that readers find particularly distracting or confusing. In addition, the innovative Chapter 13, "The Editing and Proofreading Process," offers useful advice for recognizing errors and other problems.

Organization of the Text

Because it is organized around the process actually used by writers, this handbook shows students how to become successful writers, how to correct and improve their writing, and how to follow conventions expected by readers. One important feature of the text is that it treats recognizing and revising errors as an integral part of the writing process (Part 3, "Editing and Proofreading"), not as an activity only loosely related to the process.

In Part 1, "Writing and Reading," we introduce strategies you can use as a writer and a reader, including the journal and the dialogue journal. We then explain how to develop a paper, moving from planning strategies to defining a purpose, considering readers, and drafting.

Part 2, "Revising and Shaping Your Writing," first explains and illustrates the process of revision, both major and minor. The next four chapters focus on ways to develop effective paragraphs and sentences and to revise these elements so that they successfully link writers and readers.

Part 3 treats editing and proofreading as part of the writing process. Chapter 13 gives an overview of the process with concrete suggestions for keeping readers in mind. Part 3 then includes five full sections: "Editing for Grammar" (Chapters 14–18), "Editing for Sentence Problems" (Chapters 19–26), "Editing for Word Choice" (Chapters 27–30), "Editing for Punctuation" (Chapters 31–36), and "Proofreading for Mechanics and Spelling" (Chapters 37–42). These reference chapters concentrate first on how to recognize a problem and then on how to revise, edit, or proofread to solve it.

Part 4, "Writing Strategies," devotes seven chapters to the research process, emphasizing the writer's role as a researcher; search strategies; library, field, and electronic resources; critical reading; and documentation using the MLA, ACW, APA, CBE, and CMS systems. The next four chapters explore the purposes and conventions of other kinds of writing, including argument and other forms of point-driven writing (Chapter 50), writing about literature (Chapter 51), informative writing (Chapter 52), and business writing (Chapter 53). Included in these chapters are discussions and illustrations of some of the kinds of writing students are most likely to encounter in their college courses.

Ancillary Package

The ancillary package for *The Longman Handbook* is designed to bring helpful resources to both instructors and students.

For Students

The Writer's Workshop Interactive Software Program with Papers In Progress, prepared by the Daedalus Group, "pops-up" over any commercial word processing program (IBM or Mac) to provide writing prompts specifically designed to accompany *The Longman Handbook for Writers and Readers*—invention heuristics, revision strategies, and writing techniques—for students while they compose their papers. In addition, this software includes the Paper-in-Progress feature from the handbook, which allows students to explore various stages of the writing process by interacting with annotated online student papers.

The Writer's Workshop also includes *The Longman Handbook for Writers and Readers* online (IBM or Mac) and the Documentor feature, which helps students put their citations in correct MLA or APA form, updated to include ACW guidelines for electronic sources.

For online research, the *Electronic Library* is a powerful and easy-to-use researching tool, coproduced by Longman and Infonautics and available through Prodigy. Students input their research topic in the *Electronic Library* CD, and Prodigy performs the key word search on a large base of texts, primarily newspapers and magazines, which are updated daily. The first month is free for all those who purchase the *Electronic Library* with *The Longman Handbook for Writers and Readers.*

The *Documentation Guide* with sample student papers is a fast and easy reference for students writing research papers in the humanities and sciences. Adapted from the research writing chapters in *The Longman Handbook for Writers and Readers,* the guide provides coverage of MLA, ACW, APA, CMS, and CBE styles in a pocket-sized format. The Documentation Guide includes a full sample MLA paper and a full sample APA paper.

The Longman Workbook for Writers and Readers to accompany the Longman Handbook is designed to give students extra practice in problem areas. Prepared by Karen Weekes of the University of Georgia, it is useful for students who need extra practice in editing as well as planning, drafting, revising, and writing papers. The organization of the workbook follows that of the handbook and includes solitary and collaborative exercises. There is an answer key in the back of the workbook.

The ESL Workbook for Writers and Readers is written by Ellen Bitterman of the State University of New York, The College at New Paltz, who also prepared the ESL Advice sections in the handbook. This workbook is directed at the growing population of ESL writers in college composition classes. With additional coverage of topics that are challenging for nonnative speakers of English, *The ESL Workbook's* clear grammar explanations, examples, and exercises are targeted specifically to ESL students' needs. There is an answer key in the back of the workbook.

Using Word Perfect in Composition and *Using Microsoft Word in Composition,* prepared by Marcia Peoples and Karen G. Druliner of the University of Delaware, are brief guides that assume no prior knowledge of *WordPerfect* or *Microsoft Word.* Each guide begins with word-processing basics and gradually leads students through more sophisticated functions. From logging on to a network to using a spelling checker, these user-friendly manuals introduce students to word-processing capabilities in the context of the writing process. The *WordPerfect* guide covers both DOS and Macintosh versions of the program; the *Microsoft Word* guide addresses Macintosh and IBM-Windows versions.

80 Readings, compiled by Longman editors, is a thematic collection of professional and student essays—written to perform, persuade, or inspire—with an alternate rhetorical table of contents.

Reading Critically, by Judith Olson-Fallon of Case Western Reserve University, helps students become more analytical readers.

Learning Together and the *Student Manual for Peer Evaluation,* both by Tori Haring-Smith of Brown University, are student guides to collaborative learning. *Learning Together* discusses the advantages and varieties of collaborative work, including numerous exercises and suggested paper topics. It provides information on how to work effectively in groups, how to revise with peer response, and how to coauthor a paper or report. The *Student Manual for Peer Evaluation* offers forms to guide students' peer critiques, including general guidelines and specific forms for different stages in the writing process and for various class emphases.

An *Answer Key* providing answers to the exercises in *The Longman Handbook for Writers and Readers* is available separately.

The *Oxford American Dictionary,* a desktop-sized hardcover dictionary, is available with *The Longman Handbook for Writers and Readers.*

For Instructors

The *Instructor's Resource Manual,* prepared by the authors with Charlotte Smith of Adirondack Community College, is an excellent resource for both new and experienced instructors. Besides containing chapter-by-chapter coverage of *The Longman Handbook for Writers and Readers,* the *Resource Manual* includes a discussion of course design, sample syllabi, transparency masters, answers to the exercises, additional exercises and assignments, ideas for collaboration, and suggestions for using *The Longman Handbook.*

Newly revised by Josephine Koster Tarvers, *Teaching in Progress: Theories, Practices, and Scenarios,* introduces both the basics and the latest trends in composition theory. Besides presenting a variety of composition theories and approaches to teaching, this new edition adds special "Teaching in Progress" sections, brief cases or scenarios that illustrate the issues involved in practical application. Topics covered include organizing a course, conducting classes, designing assignments, using appropriate teaching strategies, and evaluating papers and the course. *Grades,* a software program for IBM-DOS compatible computers, comes shrink-wrapped in every copy to help instructors with grade keeping and classroom management by maintaining data for up to two hundred students. This companion to the *Instructor's Resource Manual* is designed for the training of new instructors; it can offer more experienced instructors new perspectives and ideas.

Teaching On-Line: Internet Research, Conversation, and Composition, an introduction to Internet resources for teaching writing, was prepared by Daniel Anderson, Bret Benjamin, Chris Busiel, and Bill Paredes-Holt, all of the University of Texas. *Teaching On-Line* is accessible to instructors who have never surfed the net, offering in each chapter basic definitions, numerous examples, and detailed information about finding and using Internet resources. *Teaching On-Line* shows you how and why to use the Internet in your classroom; how to use *e-mail* and *Listservs;* how to use Usenet newsgroups to emphasize critical reading; how to use *MOO* and *IRC* to link conversation and composition; how to browse Gopher and the World Wide Web to begin a research project and learn how to evaluate sources; how to use *HTML* to expand your audience, publish Web pages, and use graphics and imagemaps. Chapter-end case studies and a sample research paper show numerous applications of online composition, conversation, and research. *Teaching On-Line* is available in both printed and DOS and Mac disk formats.

Writing and Designing Documents, written by Margaret Batschelet of the University of Texas at San Antonio and Maxine Hairston of the University of Texas at Austin, is a collection of sample designs for documents including academic, extracurricular, business, and personal applications. Chapters on planning documents, working with print, and working with visual elements precede 28 specific projects you can tear out and share with your students.

Teaching Writing to the Non-Native Speaker, developed by ESL specialist Jocelyn Steer, examines issues that arise when nonnative speakers enter the first-year composition classroom. It includes profiles of international and ESL students and the factors that influence second-language acquisition. Also covered are how to teach writing to ESL students, how to respond to ESL writing, and how to manage a multicultural classroom. Each chapter includes a summary of key information and examples of effective teaching methods.

Model Research Papers from Across the Disciplines, edited by Charlotte Smith of Virginia Polytechnic Institute and State University and Albert C. DeCiccio of Merrimack College, is a collection of student-written research papers that illustrate discipline-specific variations in format and documentation styles for the humanities and sciences. The collection has been completely updated to reflect the most recent revisions to the major documentation styles.

Teaching Composition in the 90s: Sites of Contention, edited by Christina G. Russell of Texas Christian University and Robert L. McDonald of the Virginia Military Institute, is a collection of papers that explores the current debates on teaching composition and was inspired by the Second Annual Symposium on the Teaching of Composition held at Texas Christian University. Participants in this lively and informative discussion include Gwen Gong, Jim Corder, and James L. Kinneavy.

Video: Writing, Teaching, and Learning: Incorporating Writing Throughout the Curriculum, produced by David A. Jolliffe of DePaul University, is a 24-minute color video demonstrating techniques that help students produce good writing in any field. Classroom examples are drawn from political science, sociology, and advanced math.

Video: Writing Across the Curriculum: Making It Work, produced by Robert Morris College and the Public Broadcasting System, features faculty presenters from science, business, and math at the 1992 WAC Video Conference. They share their experiences in analyzing their course objectives and in developing writing activities to meet the needs of students in their disciplines.

TestMaster, a computerized testing program, allows instructors to customize any of the questions contained in the TASP, CLAST, Diagnostic, and Competency Profile tests that are available with *The Longman Handbook for Writers and Readers.*

Quizmaster, an extension of *TestMaster,* allows instructors the opportunity to offer their *TestMaster* tests online to their students. It will also generate test scores.

Diagnostic and Editing Tests, prepared by Sarah Harrold of Southwestern Oregon Community College and John Feaster and Edward M. Ueling of Valparaiso University, is a collection of diagnostic tests to help instructors assess students' competence in standard written English for purposes of placement and to gauge progress. The diagnostic tests are keyed to *The Longman Handbook for Writers and Readers* and are available in reproducible sheets or on disk.

Competency Profile Test Bank, prepared by Judith Olson-Fallon of Case-Western Reserve University, is a series of objective tests (with an accompanying answer key) that covers ten general areas of English competency. Each test is available in remedial, standard, and advanced versions and comes in reproducible sheets or on disk.

80 Practices is an additional collection of photo-reproducible, 10-item exercises that provide additional practice for specific grammatical usage problems, such as comma splices, capitalization, and pronouns. It includes an answer key.

CLAST Test Package, developed by Helen Gilbart of St. Petersburg Junior College, consists of two 40-item objective tests to evaluate students' readiness for the CLAST exams. Strategies for teaching CLAST preparedness are included. It is available in reproducible sheets or on disk.

TASP Test Package, prepared by Judith Olson-Fallon of Case Western Reserve University and Carolyn Comeaux of Lamar University, consists of twelve practice pre-tests and post-tests that assess the same reading and writing skills covered in the TASP examination. It is available in reproducible sheets or on disk.

Acknowledgments

This handbook has taken many more years and much more work to complete than either of us anticipated. We have incurred debts we can never repay, and these few words are simply acknowledgments of them.

First of all, we wish to thank those who contributed directly to the writing of some of the chapters in the book. In particular, we wish to acknowledge the work of Ellen Bitterman (State University of New York, The College at New Paltz) in the ESL sections and the work of Charlotte Smith and Eric Pappas (Virginia Polytechnic Institute and State University) in Part 4 of the book. We wish to thank Nancy Newman Schwegler for contributing her skill as a writer and her professional knowledge of research techniques, library and resource organization, reference materials, and online information at a time when we were unable to bring order to several important chapters.

In addition, many of our colleagues have advised us, reviewed our drafts, and tested the prototype edition of the handbook in their classrooms at institutions across the country. Our special thanks go to the following people:

David L. Anderson, Butler County Community College (Pennsylvania); Lois Ascher, Wentworth Institute of Technology; James Barcus, Baylor University; Dennis Baron, University of Illinois at Champaign/Urbana; Rebecca Bell-Metereau, Southwest Texas State University; Robin Benny, Chicago State University; Wendy Bishop, Florida State University; Peggy Broder, Cleveland State University; Robin Brown, University of Minnesota; Norman E. Carlson, Western Michigan University; Tami Carmichael, University of Georgia; Caryn Chaden, De Paul University; Jo Chern, University of Wisconsin at Green Bay; Patricia E. Connors, University of Memphis; Patricia Davis, Pima Community College (Arizona); Susan X. Day, Illinois State University; Janet Eber, County College of Morris (New Jersey); Nancy Enright, Seton Hall University; David C. Estes, Loyola University; Faun Bernbach Evans, Chicago State University; Jim Farber, Vernon Regional Junior College (Texas); Mary Finley, California State University, Northridge; Michael Flanigan, University of Oklahoma; William Handley, University of California at Los Angeles; Jeannette Harris, University of Southern Mississippi; Vicki Hay, Arizona State University, West; David Jolliffe, De Paul University; Kathleen Kelly, Northeastern University; Kristen Kennedy, University of Rhode Island; Jeannette Kent, University of Illinois; Douglas Krienke, Sam Houston State University; David M. Kvernes, Southern Illinois University; Scott Lamascus, University of Oklahoma; Rebecca Lartigue, University of Illinois; Sarah Liggett, Louisiana State University; Diane Lourey, Eden Valley–Watkins High School, Eden Valley, Minnesota; Daiva Markelis, University of Illinois at Chicago; Bruce Maylath, University of Memphis; Terry Miller, Indian River Community College (Florida); Mike Moran, University of Georgia; Kim Moreland, The George Washington University; Guy Moyer, University of Illinois; James S. Mullican, Indiana State University; Justin O'Connell, University of Minnesota; Mary Ellen Pitts, University of Memphis; Mary Prindiville, University of Wisconsin at Green Bay; Linda Redelsheimer, Champlin Park High School, Brooklyn Park, Minnesota; Nedra Reynolds, University of Rhode Island; Liv Rosin, Mounds View High School, St. Paul, Minnesota; Donald Ross, University of Minnesota; Carol Rutz, University of Minnesota; Barbara Saez, University of Rhode Island; Mary Sauer, Indiana University–Purdue University at Indianapolis; Linda

K. Shamoon, University of Rhode Island; John S. Shea, Loyola University of Chicago; Alice E. Sink, High Point University; Beverly Slaughter, Brevard Community College (Florida); Barbara Sloan, Santa Fe Community College (Florida); Charlotte Smith, Virginia Polytechnic Institute and State University; Susan Smith-Nash, University of Oklahoma; Joyce Smoot, Virginia Polytechnic Institute and State University; Rita Speltz, Central High School, Red Wing, Minnesota; Jocelyn Steer; Sandra W. Stephen, Youngstown State University; Robert C. Stiepock, University of Rhode Island/Harvard University; Rick Straub, Florida State University; Lida Strot, University of Minnesota; Anne Tanaka, University of Illinois; Mara Thorson, University of Arizona; Allysen Todd, Community College of Allegheny County (Pennsylvania); John Trimbur, Worcester Polytechnic Institute; Pamela Turley, Community College of Allegheny County (Pennsylvania); Paul Tuttle, University of Louisville; Andrea Van Vorhis, Bowling Green State University; Patricia Webb, University of Illinois; Karen Weekes, University of Georgia; Lance E. Wilcox, Elmhurst College; James D. Williams, University of North Carolina at Chapel Hill; Judith Younk, Watertown Mayer High School, Watertown, Minnesota; and Peter T. Zoller, Wichita State University.

We have had the help, support, and patience of an extraordinary team at Longman. Our sponsoring editor, Lisa Moore, has used her sharp insights into handbook design and use to encourage us to make this book serve its users' needs. Her assistant, Lynn Huddon, has helped us in countless ways, sharing her knowledge of teaching and of rhetoric and composition studies. Our project editorial manager, Bob Ginsberg, has never failed to exceed our expectations in his contributions to the content and design of this book. Marcia Muth, our extraordinary development editor, has guided us with tact and commitment to the task, encouraging us to go one step beyond again and again when we thought no more steps were possible.

Chris Anson gives heartfelt thanks to Geanie, Ian, and Graham for their love, encouragement, and unabated endurance over the many years it took to create this book. No project has ever seemed to them so arduous. He admires them for their patience and is grateful for their unstinting support.

Bob Schwegler thanks Brian for sharing his insights, experiences, writing ability, and anthropological perspective, and he thanks Tif for keeping him honest, sort of. And for Nancy Newman Schwegler, who once observed that in terms of its effect on a family, "writing a handbook is like building a B-2 in the living room," Bob wants everyone to know that in the words of the classic, "This is dedicated to the one I love."

A Guide to Using
The Longman Handbook
for Writers and Readers

Finding What You Need

A handbook is of little use unless you can turn quickly to the page containing the information you need and then locate it on the page without confusion. *The Longman Handbook* offers you a variety of ways to locate the information and advice you need.

- **Index.** The detailed index at the end of the text covers all the topics, large and small, discussed in the book and gives the page number on which the discussion appears. The index also indicates related topics that may be of interest or use, introducing them with the phrase *See also*. As an additional resource, the index also includes terms that may be familiar to you from other places, such as high school courses or other textbooks. For example, the term *run-on sentence* is widely used, though it seldom appears in college handbooks. It is included in the index, however, followed by the suggestion *See Comma splices; Fused sentences*.

Topic ——→ Telnet sites, sources from, MLA style, 694 ←—— *Page*
Tense. *See* Verb tense ←——————————— *Cross reference to another*
Tense sequence, **247**–248, G-45   *index entry*
Tentative/draft thesis statement, **634**–635,
    G-45 ←——————— *Bold faced page reference*
Main term ——→ Text analysis, **812**–826, G-45 ←—— *to definition*
    elements of, 825–826
Subtopics ——→ sample papers: focus on meaning, 817–822; *Cross reference to*
       focus on technique, 813–817, 822–825 *Glossary entry*
than, in comparisons, 221–222
than, then, 560, G-45
that
    as demonstrative pronoun, 179, 204, 275
    with direct quotations, 462
    matching to antecedent, 328–329
    misplaced modifiers and, 335
    parallel clauses with, 374
    pronoun reference and, 319, 322–324

- **Table of Contents.** The table of contents at the front of the book outlines the four sections into which the book is divided: Part 1, "Writing and Reading"; Part 2, "Revising and Shaping Your Writing"; Part 3, "Editing and Proofreading"; and Part 4, "Writing Strategies." It also indicates the topic and major sections of each of the chapters.

  The table of contents appears in detailed form on pages iii–x and in summarized form inside the front cover.

Brief Table of Contents (inside front cover)

Full Table of Contents

- **Revision and Editing Symbols and Reader Response Symbols.** Inside the back cover, on the left, is a list of correction symbols commonly used by instructors commenting on a paper. You can use this list to locate relevant sections of the handbook. On the right is a list of reader response symbols, shortcuts for responding to another writer's paper.

Revision and Editing Symbols

abbrev	incorrect abbreviation, 41	**no ¶**	no new paragraph, 10
agr	error in subject-verb or pronoun-antecedent agreement, 17	**p**	error in punctuation, 31–36
		punc	error in punctuation, 31–36
Abbreviation	lack of (or incorrect) possessive apostrophe, 33	⌃	comma, 31a–31i *Name of problem or issue*
		no ⌃	no comma, 31j
art	article used incorrectly, 14a	;	semicolon, 32a
awk	awkward construction	:	colon, 32b
cap	capital letter needed, 37	⸝	apostrophe, 33 ← *Handbook section*
		" "	quotation marks, 34

- **Recognize and Revise Ten Serious Problems.** This chart, located just before the Revision and Editing Symbols, illustrates ten significant problems, identifies each problem, and directs you to the appropriate section of the handbook for advice.

Recognize and Revise Ten Serious Problems

Sample sentence illustrating problem

Recognize	Revise *Name of problem*
1. The heavy rain turned the parking area to mud. *Which meant that thousands of cars would get stuck.*	fragment, 19
2. The promoters called *the insurance company they discovered* their coverage for accidents was limited.	fused sentence, 20 *Handbook section*
3. After talking with the grounds keeper, the security chief said *he* would not be responsible for the safety of the crowd.	unclear pronoun reference, 21 *discussing problem*

- **Glossary.** The "Glossary of Usage and Terms" (pp. G-1 to G-48, just before the index) provides concise definitions of key terms and concepts, along with cross-references to chapters and sections with extended discussions of the topics. The terms explained in the glossary are in boldface type in the text so that you can easily turn to the glossary if you need to check the meaning of a term. In addition, the glossary answers commonly asked questions about word choice and correct usage, including definitions of frequently confused words such as *accept* and *except*.

- **Tabs, Titles, and Abbreviations.** On the pages of the text, headings on the top left supply the chapter titles and those on the top right describe the specific topics covered in the section. Tabs at the sides of the pages identify the chapter and section numbers so that you can quickly thumb through and find a particular section. Abbreviations of topics appear within the tabs and also in the brief table of contents. The ESL notation above some of the tabs marks sections particularly useful for students whose native language is not English. Throughout the text, cross-references link sections and will lead you to related or more detailed explanations.

Finding Information on a Page

Each page of your handbook includes a heading at the top of the page, a tab, and other features to help you find material quickly.

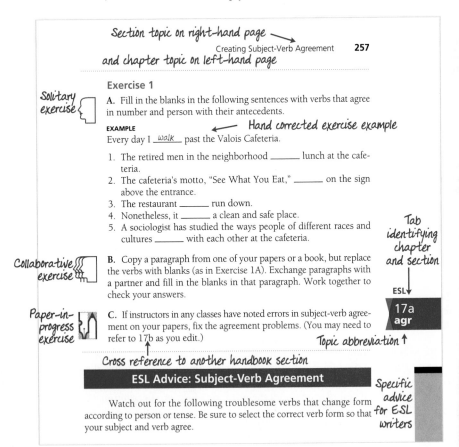

Section topic on right-hand page
Creating Subject-Verb Agreement   **257**
and chapter topic on left-hand page

Exercise 1

Solitary exercise

A. Fill in the blanks in the following sentences with verbs that agree in number and person with their antecedents.

EXAMPLE   ← *Hand corrected exercise example*
Every day I __walk__ past the Valois Cafeteria.

1. The retired men in the neighborhood _____ lunch at the cafeteria.
2. The cafeteria's motto, "See What You Eat," _____ on the sign above the entrance.
3. The restaurant _____ run down.
4. Nonetheless, it _____ a clean and safe place.
5. A sociologist has studied the ways people of different races and cultures _____ with each other at the cafeteria.

Collaborative exercise

B. Copy a paragraph from one of your papers or a book, but replace the verbs with blanks (as in Exercise 1A). Exchange paragraphs with a partner and fill in the blanks in that paragraph. Work together to check your answers.

Tab identifying chapter and section

ESL
17a
agr

Paper-in-progress exercise

C. If instructors in any classes have noted errors in subject-verb agreement on your papers, fix the agreement problems. (You may need to refer to 17b as you edit.)

Topic abbreviation ↑

Cross reference to another handbook section

ESL Advice: Subject-Verb Agreement

Specific advice for ESL writers

Watch out for the following troublesome verbs that change form according to person or tense. Be sure to select the correct verb form so that your subject and verb agree.

Your handbook also supplies headings, and special features throughout each chapter so that you can refer to information efficiently.

Chapter number and section letter

Heading for main topic

22a Recognizing and editing misplaced modifiers

Boldfaced term explained in Glossary

If you do not make the relationship between a modifier and its headword clear and specific, you may mislead or confuse readers. To recognize a **misplaced modifier,** look for a word that fails to modify its intended headword and instead appears to modify some other word or phrase in the sentence. Sometimes a misplaced modifier even modifies *both* the word before it and the word after.

**22a
mm/dm**

↑ Explanation emphasizing first recognition and then editing alternatives

Strategy with specific technique for immediate application

Strategy

To correct a misplaced modifier, either move it closer to its headword or rewrite the sentence so the connection between modifier and headword is clear.

Reader's Response showing how a reader might respond

MISPLACED MODIFIER

After you have finished talking about the assignment, write the directions for the students on the overhead projector.
READER'S RESPONSE: Are the students on the overhead projector?

MOVED NEXT TO HEADWORD

After you have finished talking about the assignment, write the directions **on the overhead projector** for the students.

MISPLACED MODIFIER

People who abuse alcohol frequently have other problems.
READER'S RESPONSE: Does *frequently* refer to the rate of alcohol abuse or the likelihood of problems?

REWRITTEN

People who abuse alcohol tend to have other problems as well.

Labels for problems and solutions

**44g
source**

Writer's Tip ⟵ *Writing advice or caution*

Don't launch into field research without doing some background reading and developing a plan. Begin your research in the library, especially if the subject is unfamiliar.

Did You Know? providing information about writing

Did You Know?

**9a
¶ foc**

In English, readers expect paragraphs to have a specific focus, and we often look to a topic sentence for guidance. In other languages, however, paragraph conventions can take quite different forms. For example, Hindi paragraphs need not focus on a sharply defined topic; they do not require a clear topic sentence; and they often contain discussion of loosely related ideas or information. Paragraphs in other languages, such as Thai, also differ from English paragraphs. Consequently, learning to write in a sec-

Special Features

The following special features appear throughout the handbook, emphasizing valuable and engaging information for student writers. As you use your handbook, look for the special features that supply the help you need.

- **Writer's Tips** and **Writer's Alerts** highlight advice and cautions, including practical suggestions for students writing with computers.
- **Reader's Response** notes link writer and reader by supplying reader reactions to unedited examples.
- **Strategy** sections identify specific techniques that student writers can immediately apply in their own writing.
- **Did You Know?** boxes supply lively historical, comparative, or research-based insights about language and composition.
- Icons set off the **solitary, collaborative,** and **paper-in-progress exercises,** emphasizing the social context for writing.

 Solitary exercises, designed as individual work, supply thematically linked discourse for immediate reinforcement and practice.

 Collaborative exercises translate the writer-reader relationship into activities for pairs and small groups of students.

Paper-in-progress exercises apply chapter topics directly to the student's current writing project.

- **Integrated ESL sections** by Ellen Bitterman of the State University of New York, The College at New Paltz, are tailored for students whose first language is not English.
- **Paper-in-Progress** sections follow one student through planning, drafting, revising, and editing a paper.
- **Research-in-Progress, Argument-in-Progress,** and **Informative-Writing-in-Progress** sections use student examples to illustrate key phases of the research and writing processes for these special assignments.
- MLA, APA, CBE, and CMS styles are explained. Two **sample research papers** illustrate MLA and APA styles.
- Five **sample student papers** (three complete plus selections from two others) illustrate argumentative and other forms of point-driven writing.
- Selections from sample student papers illustrate seven types of informative writing.
- Three student papers illustrate the analysis of literary texts (a poem, a short story, and a film).

1

WRITING AND READING

CHAPTER

1

On Being a Writer and Reader

In an introductory writing course at a large university, the students spent some time discussing their feelings about reading and writing. Here are some of their comments.

PAULA WORLEY: I've always liked writing poetry and stories. People who read my work tell me I'm a pretty good writer, but I can never seem to write easily. I read a lot, but I don't understand how great writers can just pour their ideas right onto the page.

JODY CORBO: I only read what I have to, and I don't write much, either. I figure I wasn't born with the knack for writing. I've just never been too good at it, and I guess I never will be.

ALONSO DIAZ: I wouldn't worry about it. I mean, most of us won't be doing much writing after college anyway, so what's the big deal? My mother's secretary reads her mail and does most of her memos for her.

Paula Worley, Jody Corbo, and Alonso Diaz are all writers and readers, whether they want to admit it or not. They all bring some common beliefs and attitudes to their literacy. Worley, who likes to read and write, wonders why her own writing takes so much work. Corbo is anxious and frustrated. And Diaz doesn't see a place for reading and writing in his life. When these students begin a reading or writing assignment, their beliefs and experiences affect their behaviors. Worley tries to write faster and more easily (assuming that's what great writers can do), but she finds that good writing still takes effort. Corbo gets writer's block and leaves her assignments until the very last minute. And Diaz puts little time into his reading and writing, resigning himself to mediocre grades.

Before they discussed their feelings in their writing class, these three students had not thought much about the place of reading and writing in their lives. They hadn't seen how their beliefs about literacy influenced their experiences—whether they found reading and writing easy or hard, frustrating or effortless, painful or fun.

1a   How good writers clear a path to success

Let's consider some of the issues raised by Worley, Corbo, and Diaz.

1 Do good writers have a "knack"?

Corbo said she dislikes writing because she wasn't born with the knack. Yet every healthy person is born with the potential to write and, with enough determination, can become a respectable writer. Not everyone, of course, will walk away with a Pulitzer Prize or even become the company "writing expert," but neither will every avid golfer end up winning the U.S. Open.

But why resign yourself to mediocrity just because you're not wildly successful each time you write? On reflection, that seems a rather odd reaction. In speaking, you've made all sorts of social blunders, used ungrammatical constructions, and created confused or garbled statements —sometimes getting unfavorable reactions from your listeners. But you didn't stop talking.

At times, it may seem as though all your hard work isn't yielding any improvement. Don't expect each new writing project to flow along more smoothly and more effortlessly than the last; remember that every assignment not only draws on skills you've already developed but also poses fresh challenges. Becoming a good writer takes time. It's like watching the hands of a clock—nothing much seems to happen at any one moment, but over a semester or an academic year, your writing will become stronger. (Just compare your present writing with some papers you wrote two or three years ago.)

2 Can people be successful without writing?

Diaz thinks he won't need to write well to be successful in his career. But most people in business and industry testify that good writers have a better chance of being successful on the job than poor writers. They'll tell you that each step in a career requires more sophisticated writing skills. Although Diaz's mother may be turning over short memos to her secretary (whose own career likewise depends on being able to write well), she herself is probably drafting complex reports and proposals.

Partly because writing takes hard work and concentration, many students breathe a sigh of relief when a course doesn't require any writing. Yet everything we know about the writing process shows that *writing actually creates knowledge*. Writing makes you examine ideas more fully, react to new concepts, and push your learning further into your memory. The more energy you put into your writing, the more effectively you'll learn.

3 Do good writers have it easy?

Although she's never watched a professional writer at work, Paula Worley has the impression that good writers can "pour" their intelligent, witty, well-reasoned thoughts right onto the page, in elegant, sophisticated prose. But studies of successful writers reveal that they spend *more* time on their writing as they get better. In contrast, students who have the most trouble writing spend the *least* time planning, drafting, and revising. Worley enjoys success as a writer partly because she works at it. Yet she still believes writing should be easier for her. What keeps good writers going if they work harder than poor writers?

First, good writers are motivated. Worley already knows from experience that writing is hard work; she spends time on her writing because she considers more options, tries out more alternatives, and reworks her drafts more extensively than many other students do. Sometimes she wrestles with her writing, becomes frustrated, bites her lip over the tiniest decisions. At other times she becomes immersed in her ideas and ends a drafting session surprised at how long she's worked.

Instead of wondering why writing isn't always effortless, "flowing" right onto the page the first time around, Worley needs to understand that her tough decisions, false starts, and crossed-out paragraphs are healthy—the necessary rehearsals for a good performance. Those rehearsals also lead to interesting digressions as she conjures up new ideas that may significantly change her final product.

Good writers approach their tasks hopefully. They assume that time spent thinking about their writing, immersing themselves in a draft, and carefully revising it will, in fact, pay off. No matter how murky their initial thoughts may be, no matter how anxious they are about the task at hand, they know that time and attention will always yield a better product than will a hurried, last-minute effort.

Finally, successful writers have learned how to allocate their resources. Instead of trying to finish an entire paper in one sitting, they may map out their ideas one evening and then produce a tentative draft the next, only to take it through three revisions over the weekend. Studies of authors' early and later drafts show this sort of deliberate, tentative working and thinking, sometimes over weeks, months, and years. Whenever possible, such writers give themselves ample time to explore and develop their ideas.

Exercise 1

A. Take some time to jot down your own experiences and thoughts about writing. What sorts of successes and problems have you had as a writer? What has writing been like for you in school? Have you done any writing outside of school? What are some of your own beliefs about writing? Write quickly and informally, perhaps working from an initial list of ideas. Then reflect on your experiences and attitudes as we did with those of Paula Worley, Jody Corbo, and Alonso Diaz.

B. Get together with a group of two or three other students and share your writing histories. Try to find common beliefs or experiences about writing, especially any that might explain what sometimes makes writing hard. Generate a short list of statements in your group to complete the phrase "Writing is ———." Then discuss the statements, focusing especially on those that not everybody agrees with.

1b
write

Did You Know?

A survey of several hundred business employees in a sample of Fortune 500 companies found that 58 percent thought writing was of "critical" or "great" importance to their work. Another 36 percent thought that writing was of "some" importance. In other words, the vast majority (94 percent) implied that being a good writer is linked to being a successful employee. Even more remarkable, about half the employees said they spent between eight and forty hours of each workweek writing!

Paul V. Anderson, "What Survey Research Tells Us About Writing at Work," *Writing in Nonacademic Settings,* ed. Lee Odell and Dixie Goswami (New York: Guilford, 1985) 3–83.

1b Reading as a writer, writing as a reader

Reading as much and as carefully as you can may in itself improve your writing. Being a good reader exposes you not only to various types of writing but to new ideas as well. If you've read widely about avalanche disasters at European ski resorts, you'll probably write more fluently about the topic. An account of your family's decision to move your grandfather into a nursing home may ring with greater clarity and insight if you've read an article on the issue of aging in the United States or an anthropological account of how the Eskimo treat their elders.

In addition to exposing you to many views, ideas, and experiences, reading helps you to learn the "rules," or conventions of language, on which readers and writers agree in order to communicate through print. Some people mistakenly write "It's a dog-eat-dog world" as "It's a doggy-dog world" because they lack the experience of *seeing* the phrase in print. If you were learning to write in Spanish, how could you know that questions begin with an upside-down question mark and end with a right-side-up version unless you had seen this practice followed consistenly in print? Similarly, it's much easier to remember that the phrase *a lot* consists of two words (not *alot*) if you've passed your eyes over this phrase hundreds or thousands of times as a reader.

Finally, reading helps you to understand, even if only indirectly, the effects of writers' choices. And when you discuss the effect of these choices with the writer of a paper in progress, *both* of you will learn about writing in ways not possible when you work alone.

1 Do all readers define "good writing" the same way?

KIM GRAFF: When I worked for a while as an intern in my father's company, a lot of what I had learned about writing in school didn't sit too well there. Most of the things I read didn't have a thesis statement the way my papers in English had to.

During her internship, Graff discovered an important principle about the relationship between reading and writing: *What counts as good writing for readers in one setting may not work as well for readers in another setting.* Some characteristics of writing, especially correctness, are almost universal; a spelling mistake screams out as loudly in an advertisement as it does in a corporate report or a major term paper. But other concerns—such as how long or short a document should be, how meandering or direct, how literary or bureaucratic in style, how explicit in the beginning or summative at the end—all vary from place to place, from one set of readers to another. Graff's contribution to her high school yearbook won't resemble the term paper she will write in her art history class. In fact, it won't even look like a distant relative.

2 Do students need to know all forms of writing?

If readers' expectations are so varied, how can you learn all the different forms of writing? Right now, you don't have to. Eventually you'll need to master the conventions of writing in specific *fields:* client profiles in psychology, literary criticism in English, museum catalogs in art history, lab reports in mechanical engineering. You'll be concerned with how readers define good writing in your chosen profession.

Mastery of these more specialized forms will come in due time, as you gain the expertise and knowledge required in your major field of study and as you move into your career. For now, it's more important to master the conventions of **general academic writing,** of the sort written and read in introductory classes across the college curriculum. This typically takes the form of reports, abstracts, term papers, essay exams, argumentative analyses, and syntheses of articles. Your concern now should be how readers (especially teachers) define good writing in general college courses.

Even general academic writing, of course, won't always take the same form. Graff's paper for an introductory class in U.S. history may require her to interpret several accounts of an incident—the Battle of Chickamauga, for example—and then analyze how those accounts could be so different. Her next paper in an American literature course, however, might ask her to discuss "Chickamauga," Ambrose Bierce's Civil War story, without reference to other people's ideas or even the historical circumstances of the battle itself. Both assignments will encourage her to do some good, hard thinking, but the two papers will differ considerably in form, style, organization, and content.

The fact that readers' expectations vary in different settings also suggests the importance of **adaptation.** Adapting your writing means being flexible in style, organization, and language, just as you adapt your speech to the different situations you face each day. Thinking too rigidly about your writing may lead to frustration, as Kim Graff would have discovered had she tried to write a business report using the five-paragraph essay model she learned in high school.

1b
write

Exercise 2

A. Make a list of all the types of writing you've done in different situations. Describe some of the characteristics that distinguish good writing from bad for each type of writing you list. Which characteristics of good or bad writing are common to all the types? Which are particular to one type?

B. In a small group, create a combined list from your responses to Exercise 2A. If two or more of you listed the same type(s) of writing, compare your descriptions of what counts for "good" and "bad" writing. What might account for your descriptions?

3 Is it fair to get help from a reader?

LEWIS BROWN: One of my teachers said it was cheating to have someone else read your paper before you turned it in, but then the next year I had a teacher who actually had us do that in class.

The contradiction that puzzles Brown shows again how we are affected by our views of reading and writing. His first teacher saw writing as a solitary act performed by individuals with no help from others, perhaps as a test of a student's achievement. In contrast, his next teacher assumed that writers should try out ideas and rough drafts on each other. For one, help was cheating. For the other, help was part of the writing and learning process.

How and when you can work with others will depend on your situation. It's a rare teacher who would allow you to talk to other students while you write an in-class essay exam. In such a situation, you're not "learning what to say" as much as you're "saying what you've already learned."

When you write papers in order to learn course material more effectively or practice your skills at composition, however, enlisting the reactions of peers can make you more sensitive to the possible responses of your intended readers. Instead of trying to write your papers in secrecy, you invite people in and ask for their advice and reactions. When it comes time to turn in your final, polished paper, your audience may differ in some ways from your helpers, but your paper will stand a better chance of success. Other people's opinions not only help you to write more effective papers—they also improve your writing in general by making you more sensitive to the concerns that readers are likely to raise.

Another social relationship that you enter into when you write involves a set of agreements between you and your intended readers. Your reader brings certain expectations to your writing. To be successful, your writing needs to fulfill those expectations. By way of analogy, consider the sort of cooperation required in visiting an aquarium. Some group of people has set up the aquarium for the delight and edification of the general public. People who pay admission to tour the aquarium expect various species of fish to be displayed in an attractive, educational way, perhaps organized into different clusters of tanks representing areas of the world. They want order to their experience, as well as some color and uniqueness. For their part, the managers of the aquarium expect the visitors to behave civilly, not tapping on the glass. The designers and managers of the aquarium (writers) and the people who visit it (readers) have certain expectations of each other—a sort of unwritten agreement.

From a reader's point of view, this agreement contains at least five expectations of the writer.

EXPECTATION 1   I'll do my best as a reader to understand what you're trying to say in your writing, but remember that I become bored, tired, and confused very easily.

EXPECTATION 2   If you make lots of errors in your writing, I'll become frustrated and may stop paying attention to what you're saying. Please try not to distract and annoy me.

EXPECTATION 3   If we disagree about something, it would help our relationship if you would at least acknowledge my opinions from time to time and give them some thought. Please respect me.

EXPECTATION 4   I have a large capacity for interesting and entertaining ideas. But tell me the obvious, or talk in circles, or try to dazzle me by making simple ideas sound complicated, or wander around in generalities, and I may put your writing into the recycling bin. Please remember that I'm a busy person.

EXPECTATION 5   I like to think and learn. Teach me something or show me something new. Give me another angle on something old. But don't just trot out the first cliché that occurs to you.

Working with others as you plan, draft, and revise your writing gives you a *social* context for your work. In this context, you can negotiate your writerly decisions with trial readers who bring all the usual expectations to bear on your prose and do so constructively.

Exercise 3

A. Describe in a brief paragraph the different ways in which other people have been involved in something you wrote (as helpers, readers, editors, or listeners). How did they help you? How did their comments affect your writing?

B. In a small group, compare your responses to Exercise 3A. Then collectively make a list of all the ways in which other people can influence the development, progress, and outcome of a piece of writing. Consider the different situations of your group's writing. Were there some situations when it seemed more natural to write together than alone?

CHAPTER 2

Strategies for Active Writing

Most people assume that the purpose of writing and reading is to communicate. It may seem unnatural to use writing for ourselves as a way to think and learn. Yet history shows us that many famous scientists, philosophers, politicians, inventors, and artists considered writing for themselves to be an indispensable part of their intellectual lives. They found it useful—sometimes even essential—to keep a journal or logbook or sketch pad of personal speculations so they could record their thoughts, explore their ideas, and prepare for writing something more formal, such as a scholarly book, speech, or article. Consider this short excerpt from Charles Darwin's personal journal, written in 1837.

> I should expect that Bears & Foxes &c. are same in N. America and Asia; but many species closely allied, but different, because country separated since time of extinct quadrupeds;—same argument applies to England. Mem. Sh[r]ew mice.
> Animals common to South and North America? *Are there any?*
> Rhinoceros peculiar to Java and another to Sumatra. Mem. Parrots peculiar, according to Swainson, to certain islets in East India archipelago. . . . Gnu reaches Orange River and says: so far will I go and no further. — CHARLES DARWIN, *Notebooks on Transmutation*

Although Darwin's journals are now published and widely read, this excerpt was not originally intended to communicate anything to anyone else. Instead, Darwin used his journal as a place to record thoughts, explore ideas, reflect on other people's work, make connections and observations—in short, to write for *himself,* in order to think and learn.

2a How to think about a journal

An **academic journal** is a place to think and write about what you are learning. In a writing course, you might use it to explore concepts, experiment with your prose, write rough drafts, and reflect on the principles of writing. Your entries may be dated and may involve sequential observations, though they don't always have to be chronological. An academic journal, however, is not a diary. Diaries record people's daily activities, thoughts, and personal lives. Nor is it a set of lecture notes, simply transcribing someone else's words.

A good way to define the academic journal is to contrast it with the formal academic paper.

Formal academic paper	Journal
Used to communicate	Used to think and learn
Directed to an audience	Written for oneself
Will be evaluated	Not usually evaluated
Reflects final opinion	Reflects thinking process
Is carefully organized	Can be unstructured
Is grammatically correct	May have informal grammar, spelling, and usage

Unlike a carefully crafted paper, your journal serves as a clearinghouse for ideas, speculations, first starts, notes and jottings, drawings and doodles, plans, occasional insights—anything that helps you to learn more fully and begin writing. By its very nature, a journal is often messy, exploratory, tentative, and loosely structured. It reflects a raw kind of thinking, an initial attempt to explore a thought or discover new ideas. A formal paper, in contrast, reflects the *outcome,* the end product, of thought.

Journals are used in college courses for two main reasons: (1) to learn and explore new material, without an eye to writing anything formal; and (2) to engage in the many processes that go into a final, polished, written document. In the following excerpt, first-year student Jessica White uses her journal in a course on short fiction in order to clarify her thinking about a story.

"Birthmark" by Hawthorne. 3rd person. Theme is mortality & life/death, meddling with nature. Evident in Georgiana's death, but also relates to contemporary issues like being preoccupied w/ physical appearance. Characters don't seem well developed, but is this necessary for the focus on Aylmer's obsession? I think the story is really getting at power (esp. in 19th cen.) and fear, too, of our growing knowledge and ability to manipulate nature with science, and the obsession to make a perfect world through our own intervention. After all, G. is perfect except for the one little birthmark (shaped like a hand? definitely significant). Then A. "meddles" with nature to try to remove it. And poof, she dies.

Notice in this entry how White gropes for possible meanings in the story. Although she might at some point decide to write a paper on "The Birthmark," she uses her writing here mainly for the purpose of *thinking,* which she couldn't do nearly as well without seeing her ideas on the page.

The result is a better memory of details, a sharper analysis for an in-class essay exam, and a deeper understanding of the story's themes.

In a second excerpt, White is preparing to write a narrative about her experience winning the state high school basketball tournament. This time, she uses her journal to begin brainstorming ideas for her paper.

> I was co-captain of the cheerleading team and I loved basketball. I put a lot of work into the season of our victory. Also important, and I hope to bring this out in the paper somewhere, was the camaraderie the team felt, even with the cheerleaders involved on the sidelines. They stood behind the team from start to finish and led our families and fans to great enthusiasm and spirit, which I believe had a tremendous effect on our team. I want to get at this sense that whenever you have a team, it's not just the individual or even the collective ability that leads to a victory but something in your heart, the motivation to win.

Notice that even at this early stage, White explores the possibility of a main point or thesis for her paper. Her journal writing anticipates the beginning of a more formal draft of her narrative.

Did You Know?

The word *journal* came into the English language via Old French from Latin *diurnalis* or "daily." As a written document, the journal originally referred to a sort of log where daily records could be kept: the stages of a route or other information for travelers, commercial transactions and accounting, official events, a ship's course, the progress of drilling in a mine, or even the day's performance at battle in a war. The word is related to *journey,* which originally referred to a single day's travel or work. The connection between the two words precisely defines the use of the academic journal—a point of departure for various intellectual journeys (whether over one day or many).

2b How to keep a journal

At first, keeping a journal may feel strange or artificial. After all, you're writing mainly to and for yourself, with no concern about your spelling, no worry that you're using the first person pronoun (*I*) when you're not sure whether this is acceptable. After years of writing formal papers, keeping a journal may take some adjustment. Here are some suggestions for getting started.

1 What kind of journal should you get?

The actual shape and size of your journal is less important to its success than what you do in and with it. It helps to have a journal from which you can remove pages; you can circulate them or turn them in to your teacher, then reinsert them into your journal. An inexpensive, slim three-ring binder may work best in these circumstances.

After you begin keeping a journal, you may find that you want to create separate sections for different sorts of writing. One section might become a place where you write to think and learn; other sections might include material leading up to a specific writing project. Many avid journal writers like to keep several different notebooks, each for its own purpose.

2 How much and how often should you write?

The more you write, the greater the chance to think about the material in your course. The length of each journal entry will (and should) differ. Working half a day in the library on a term paper might yield ten or fifteen pages of notes, speculations, quotations, and references, but an idea that occurs to you late at night might yield just a few lines of drowsy prose sufficient to jog your memory the next morning. Be disciplined, but don't hold yourself at gunpoint in order to scratch something out on the page.

The "rhythm" of your journal writing will depend largely on your schedule and how comfortable you are writing at certain times of the day. If you miss a day, don't despair, especially if on some occasions you find yourself writing more than you expected to. The mind is a curious organism: sometimes it becomes increasingly stimulated by its own thinking. At such a moment, you may find that an hour has passed, you're energetically scribbling at the bottom of your fifth page, and you hardly feel tired. On other occasions, the thought of opening your journal may feel like beginning a marathon in lead shoes. But at all costs, *write regularly.* Journals abandoned for more than a day or two soon wither up and die from lack of nourishment.

3 What should you write?

Most classes that require academic journals have informal assignments designed to help you learn and think about course material, perhaps in preparation for class discussion. You may also be asked to write entries on your own, with no prompting from an assignment. If you're at a loss for words, try freewriting (see 4a and 4b). When all else fails, simply summarize your new knowledge. *Test* your own versions of what you're learning. Use the journal as an informal but intellectually stimulating place to carry on an internal conversation about your academic studies.

Exercise 1

A. For your first journal entry, choose something that stands out in any of your course work—a controversial assertion, an opinion you disagree with, an especially difficult concept, or a general theoretical statement that begs for an example of some sort. For ten or fifteen minutes, write informally about what you've chosen, but do so in a way that challenges and extends your thinking. Try generating *new ideas* and *new perspectives*.

When you've finished, review your entry and circle three or four new ideas or thoughts you discovered while you wrote. If you can't come up with that many ideas, continue writing or repeat the exercise with another concept or assertion.

B. Share your entry with two or three other students in a small group. What common characteristics do you notice about your writing? How does it differ from formal academic prose? What differences do you see in your personal journal-writing styles? How did you feel about the process of journal writing?

C. Begin an assignment by writing a page or two in your journal, perhaps exploring ideas for a focus. See how far you can take your ideas into productive material for your paper.

2C How to use a journal to think and learn

Journal writing is a state of mind. Once you begin to see its benefits, journal writing will seem quite natural. The following paragraphs discuss some specific ways to use your journal for deeper, richer learning.

1 Translate your new knowledge

Most new knowledge comes to you prepackaged, in someone else's words. Your journal can help you translate this new knowledge into your own terms, so that it will make sense to you. To practice this, look through your class notes from another course (or skim the textbook) and locate a concept, term, or idea that is difficult to understand. Imagine you're writing to someone (perhaps a younger sibling) about this new knowledge. Try explaining what it means in your own words. As you do so, two things are likely to happen: first, you'll be forced to *speculate* about the meaning of the information at those places where you're most confused; second, you'll often *clarify and resolve* your confusions in the process of writing.

2 Generate ideas for a paper

Instead of staring at a blank piece of paper, waiting for perfect sentences to roll off your pen or keyboard, use your journal for **brainstorming.** When you brainstorm, you think associatively, letting one idea lead to another or exploring the connections among ideas. Because your journal is by its very nature exploratory, messy, and tentative, it's an ideal place to work through your thoughts in preparation for writing a draft of a paper. (See Chapter 4.)

3 Extend your thinking

Imagine that you learn this fact in a sociology course: Human aggression increases in hot weather. Recording such an observation in your journal may take a few seconds. But imagine *extending* this idea a little, seeing its implications, wondering about possible solutions. Are people more aggressive in hot regions than in cold regions? If discomfort in general causes aggression, why doesn't aggression also rise during the winter, when people feel very cold? Are workers in steel plants more aggressive because of the heat there? Do Northerners feel more aggressive when they vacation in the South during the winter? Does "heat aggression" relate to social or economic class? Writing about such questions is a way to extend and expand upon new information.

4 Relate new ideas to your own experience

You can also use your journal to personalize your learning, relating new ideas to your own experience. Suppose that the worst fight you ever had with a member of your family occurred in the middle of the summer on one of the hottest days of the year. Writing about what you learned in your sociology course might give you some special insight into the causes of this fight and help you understand the sociological concepts.

5 Take issue with ideas

Although your journal may feel comfortably informal, it can also be an excellent place to argue with someone else's point of view or criticize a position. Many writers at first react in a combative way to ideas or beliefs that challenge their own. Their journals let them "have it out" with an opponent without risking actual confrontation. The result can be a more balanced view of the controversy.

6 Avoid procrastination

No doubt at some point you have suffered from the awful realization that the deadline for a piece of writing is looming, but for days you've been doing the most unpleasant things to avoid facing the blank page—folding the laundry, tidying your room, running errands. Such a strategy may divert you from the increasing panic, but it won't get your writing done.

To avoid procrastination, try writing *about* the topic for your paper; this will yield some preliminary thoughts or ideas that could blossom into something usable. At this point, no one will fault you for not knowing what you want to say, for writing an illogical sentence, or for creating a disorganized paragraph. More important, you will have *begun* to write, if only half a page of hastily scribbled notes.

7 Explore confusions and let off steam

Learning can be frustrating. Confusion, ambiguities, and difficult terminology can exasperate you. The journal can be a good place for you to puzzle out problems in learning and even to give vent to some frustration. The chances are also good that you'll gain more insight into the source of your confusion.

Exercise 2

A. The following journal entry was written by Kelly Odeen, a student in a course on literacy in America. Read Odeen's entry, and then identify specific functions for which she is using her journal. What characteristics of her entry suggest these functions?

Reading on the Amish community left me with very mixed feelings—not sure what to make of them yet. I really admired the family support of Eli's literacy development. Sounded like the older family members did just what we've been encouraged to do as tutors. They gave him positive feedback, etc. Focused on accomplishments rather than failures. But the setting looked sort of ideal. Everyone in Eli's family reads and writes, even more than in my family. I don't think it's possible to make learning totally individualized in the public school system. Choices have to be made that are better for some children than others. I don't have a solution, but I think the author is being too idealistic to think there can be this match like the Amish have. I'd like to look into this more for my project, maybe. Because I do agree that there are many ways of perceiving literacy, each valid, and we have to be sensitive to where kids are coming from *compared* with the school system they're going into.

B. Should animals be used in laboratory experiments for the advancement of scientific, medical, and behavioral knowledge? Write a page or two in your journal on this question, considering as many issues and angles on the topic as you can. Then compare your journal writing in a small group. What ideas did the writing yield? How helpful was it? How would you describe the style, organization, and other characteristics of your writing? Which of the purposes described in the preceding section did your writing serve?

2d How to write in a journal

Like taking a walk alone, you write in a journal mainly for *yourself.* Your pace can be fast or slow, meandering or purposeful. You can wear sneakers or work boots. You can stop along the way to examine something more fully or pass it by or return later. Here are some tips for finding a comfortable voice and style in your journal.

1 Use the personal voice

Many academic assignments require you to remove yourself from your writing. Use your journal writing to express your own beliefs, opinions, and reactions. Speculate. Instead of writing in abstract terms and formal language, go ahead and use a more **personal voice.** Use phrases like "I wonder if. . . ," "I think it's wonderful that. . . ," or "I can't understand why. . . ."

2 Be conversational

In formal writing, you're advised not to use colloquial expressions, not to sound "talky." In your journal writing, try a chattier kind of language, as if you're carrying on a conversation with yourself. A sentence like "Hmmm . . . I guess I never figured a senator could get so ticked off about something so silly" would cry out for a revision in a formal paper. In a journal, you can feel safe using such a casual tone.

3 Use shortcuts

Try writing quickly. Use abbreviations, if you're sure you will remember what they mean. Don't worry at this point about underlining titles, correcting commas in a series, or looking up the spelling of every difficult word. (Remember that Darwin's journal contained abbreviations, sentence fragments, and other personal shortcuts.)

4 Be subjective

Feel free to express your own reactions using adjectives, emphatic statements, or exclamation points. Sentences like "Wow! I was *flabbergasted* by MacAndrews' research," which would call for major surgery in an academic paper, are quite normal in a journal. Use such subjective statements to probe deeply into the subject. *Why* is the research interesting? *What is it* in the research that made you react this way? What *assumptions* about research did you bring to your reading?

5 Experiment with language

Journals encourage the free play of language and thought. Let the poetry emerge, if you wish, from your writing. Be as expressive as you want. Try out ideas that may at first seem outrageous, or write in a style you've never used before. Try imitating or parodying other writers. All such experimentation not only helps you explore your thinking but makes you more flexible as a writer.

Writer's Tip: Using a Computer

Computers allow you to insert new ideas into the middle of a journal entry, something impossible to do in a handwritten journal except in the margins. You can return to your journal entries and add to them or even splice usable material into a more formal project. Most computers, however, are not portable, which takes away some of the spontaneity of journal writing. If you keep a computer journal, it's a good idea to have a small notebook as well, so you can capture ideas any time during the day. You can easily transfer your notebook writing to your computer later on. Journal writing can also be a good way to learn how to use a computer or word processor.

Exercise 3

A. Choose a short reading about a current controversy. First, try writing a journal response to the reading, following the suggestions in the preceding section. Next, write a brief letter to the editor of a local or campus newspaper about the same controversy. Try *converting* your journal writing into more formal prose suitable for a general audience.

B. In a small group, discuss your "journal conversions" from Exercise 3A. What information carried over from your journal writing into your letter? On what basis did you select the information? In what ways, if any, did you make changes in style, word choice, sentence structure and rhythm, organization, and the use of evidence to support your assertions? What uses can you see for such "conversions" in writing papers for your courses?

Did You Know?

In a study comparing two groups of students in a high school science course, the group that wrote about their learning remembered more than the group that didn't keep a journal. Similar findings have been reported in several other studies.

Robert Tierney, "Using Expressive Writing to Teach Biology," *The Teacher-Researcher*, ed. Miles Myers (Urbana: National Council of Teachers of English, 1985) 149–66.

CHAPTER

Strategies for Active Reading

If you're seeing these words on the page, you're a reader. Yet reading may still be difficult for you. For example, you may not understand reading material at the level you want to. Opening a textbook may soon lead you to frustration, boredom, or sleep. You may read with one response, but your teacher wants another. You may wish you could find out what you need to know quickly without plowing through every paragraph.

What can you do to improve your reading and make the process more useful and enjoyable? You may have already tried some strategies, such as paying better attention as you read, underlining important passages, or searching out quiet places where you can work. All these may have helped you. But the key to better reading is found in a *systematic* approach to the reading process, an approach in which you practice particular strategies before, during, and after reading.

3a How to become an active reader

1 Before reading

If you're like most people, when you sit down to absorb a complicated college textbook or journal article, you just open to the first page and start reading. Without "warming up," however, you may soon lose concentration or feel bewildered. Instead of launching right into your reading, try some **prereading strategies** first.

Preview the Organization of the Text. Try prereading books and long works by skimming their tables of contents to see how they are organized. What appears first, second, third? In journal articles and readings without tables of contents, look first for any headings or subheadings; these road maps tell you where the reading will take you and help you to plan your time. If you have only half an hour to read before you need to do something else, knowing that the first section of a journal article ends on page 9 might help you to plan your time accordingly.

Examine the Context. By taking a few minutes to ask yourself some questions about the nature of your reading material, you can prepare yourself for the information to follow. Is the reading by a single author? If the reading is an article, what journal or periodical did it appear in? (Knowing that an article is published in a highly conservative or liberal magazine can often tell you a lot about how to interpret its contents.) Who is the intended reader? When was the reading published? If you're reading a book, how many printings or editions has it gone through? (This is a good measure of the book's popularity.) What can you learn about a book from the inside front and back covers?

Sample Some Words and Terms. Look for groups of words in your reading that are related in meaning or reference. By scanning through the text first, you can activate your own knowledge. If you encounter terms that seem unfamiliar, you will be better prepared to interpret these new words in their proper context. If a few words stand out as incomprehensible, you might look them up in the dictionary or the book's glossary before you actually begin reading. Consider the following excerpt from an investment document.

> *The Stock Account.* The **Stock Account's portfolio** includes **stocks** listed on the **New York Stock Exchange, securities traded** on othe **national stock exchanges,** the **National Association of Securities Dealers Automated Quotation (NASDAQ) system** and other **over-the-counter markets,** and **foreign securities.**

This document contains a group of terms associated with the world of finance and investment. By glancing through the reading first and taking note of such words as *NASDAQ,* you'll be less likely to stumble when you reach them later, and you'll gain a sense of what the reading is about.

Make Predictions. Sample some paragraphs or sentences, and try to predict what you think the reading is about and where it will take you. Do your samples imply a particular direction? Look for examples and illustrations, which can help you prepare for your reading more effectively than abstract assertions.

Learn Some Background. If your prereading suggests that a chapter or article will stump you no matter what you do, consider doing some background reading first. An encyclopedia entry on the topic might introduce some key terms and concepts. If you feel overwhelmed reading an article entitled "Stem Cell Collection and Bone Marrow Purging," you might start with some background reading in a good medical reference guide on the nature and functions of human bone marrow and on recent bone marrow transplantation technology. You might also talk to people who know something about the subject.

Exercise 1

A. Locate a short reading that has no overt structure—no headings, chapter divisions, or other organizational devices. Then make up headings or divisions for different parts of the reading.

B. Compare your structural prereading in Exercise 1A with the work of two or three classmates. How successful, generally, was this strategy in helping you to read and understand your chosen article?

2 While reading

You've probably had the experience of reaching the end of a passage in a book or article and realizing that you haven't been paying any attention to it. Most good readers can literally "read" a text—that is, pass their eyes over it—without comprehending it. To avoid this problem, try the following strategies.

Pause and Assess. When you reach a place where you can stop reading without interrupting a line of reasoning or a crucial narrative, put the reading aside for a moment. Where are you? What have you learned so far? What do you think? What still confuses you? Jot down answers to these questions in your journal or on a piece of paper. Then skim what you've read. If you're uncertain about something, reviewing the text can sometimes clarify it.

Share Interpretations and Insights. If you're reading a common text in a class, stop and share your ideas with some of your classmates. If you're assigned the first two chapters of a ten-chapter book, get together in a small group and discuss what you notice so far about the content or language of the reading. Compare your responses with those of your fellow readers. Are there differences? Did you miss something? Do any of the other readers' responses puzzle you? Skim back over the reading to see how they might have arrived at their interpretations.

Summarize in Chunks. After reaching a natural stopping point, you might also write an abstract or summary of what you've read to that point, glancing back over what you've read if necessary. This can help you to monitor your comprehension. What's the main point or gist so far? Can you guess or predict where the reading will go next? If you're unsure about the meaning at this point, your overall understanding will suffer later.

Highlight Important Information. If you've ever bought a used textbook, you've probably seen someone else's bright yellow or pink highlighting. Often there's so much highlighting on each page that you wonder how the student could separate the important from the unimportant material.

If you're an avid highlighter *while* you read, try to change your style. Don't spend lots of time attending to tiny details the first time through your reading. Instead, read to capture the essential points of the piece. This will let you see a "bigger picture," a set of organizational or argumentative structures, without constantly trying to focus on minutiae and perhaps getting lost among them. Go back a second time and write notes in the margins of your reading or use your highlighter to outline what's *really* important.

3 After reading

Finally, when you've finished your reading assignment, don't just close the book or magazine and forget about what you just read. Remember that you want to lodge the material deeper into your memory; you want to interpret it more fully; you want it to *create* new thoughts. Simply "reading" won't accomplish those goals very well.

Write Annotations in Your Text. In the old days, students were often punished for writing in books (even their own copies). If a book isn't yours, of course, don't write in it; make a photocopy of relevant material and write on the copy. (Consider reducing the copy, if possible, to give you more marginal space for your notes.) If you own the book, annotate in the margins. The **annotations** can be especially useful later on when you want to remind yourself of what you were thinking at the time.

Good annotations can include the following types of responses.

* Interpretations: what does the author or speaker mean?
* Confusions: at what points do you become puzzled?
* Questions: what more do you need to know?
* Objections or counterarguments: where do you disagree?
* Restatements: how can you say it in your own words?
* Evaluative statements: what do you like or dislike about the passage or section of the reading?

After reading, you might also consider taking a 3" × 5" or 5" × 7" file card and writing down some of the main ideas from the reading, or doing the same in your journal. These records are especially useful when you are creating research papers or short documented papers; they offer a convenient way of reviewing several readings without leafing through dozens of pages of photocopies or books.

> # Did You Know?
>
> During the normal reading process, your eyes are moving only about ten percent of the time. The rest of the time they are fixating on a specific word, word group, or letter. In other words, when you read, your eyes are more often standing still than moving, even though you may have the impression that your gaze is flowing smoothly across every word on the page.
>
> Irving H. Anderson and Walter F. Dearborn, *The Psychology of Teaching Reading* (New York: Ronald, 1952).

Jot Down Some Notes in Your Journal.   What do you already know or think about the topic at hand? If the article takes a strong position, spend some time jotting down your own views about the topic. You'll be better prepared to think about and weigh someone else's arguments. You'll do some critical thinking of your own, so that you won't simply allow the author to "brainwash" you.

Highlight Significant Passages.   Now is the time to take out your highlighter, if you use one, and mark passages or sentences that strike you as important. But go lightly. Think of your highlighter as an attention-getter for when you review the article later. The more highlighter you use, the harder it will be to pull out the most significant points from the text.

Reread and Review.   If you're learning sophisticated concepts or working through difficult arguments, you may need to read the material more than once in order to perform well on tests. Every time you read something again, you'll find more information or new ideas.

    Rereading doesn't have to take the same shape as the initial reading. Try reviewing, skimming the reading more quickly, and then sampling some of the passages you highlighted on your first post-reading pass through the text. The idea is to read from different perspectives—once from afar, once closely. Skim the material quickly once, then study it meticulously.

Exercise 2

A. Find a relatively challenging reading, or choose one that you've already been assigned, perhaps in a course such as physics or history. Then try each of the prereading strategies outlined in this section. Don't begin reading until you've accumulated as much information as you can about the piece and have made several predictions about it. Jot these down. Then read the text.

B. Share your observations and readings in a small group. In what ways do you think the prereading activities helped your reading? How did the knowledge you brought to the text help you to interpret it?

3b How to discuss readings in a dialogue journal

Writing *about* your reading can help you to think about and learn the material much more fully than passively absorbing it as a reader. There are many strategies for using writing to focus on your reading. An especially valuable one is known as the **dialogue journal.** Keeping a dialogue journal means that instead of writing "solo" about your reading, you share your thoughts and speculations with another person in an ongoing written conversation. Like solo journals, dialogue journals can serve many purposes. Their greatest benefit in college classes, however, is their way of encouraging more active, critical reading of course materials and related sources. Unlike an oral conversation, a dialogue journal leads to deeper and more careful thought because your ideas (and those of your partner) are committed to paper, where you can mull them over.

A dialogue journal takes the form of regular "swapped" installments separated by a day or more. The gaps between installments give you crucial time to reflect on your partner's entries and then respond in turn. It's like starting a conversation with someone you don't yet know—you will almost always begin a dialogue journal a bit haltingly until each of you has written a few entries. Writing a solo entry can often "get the ball rolling." Soon your entries will feel much more comfortable, as reflected in the following excerpts from a successful dialogue journal between two students discussing an article in a psychology course.

TERRA: Hi, Michael. I know you liked Kruger's article, so I won't dwell on it, but I don't get this line: "Mystique encircles the paranormal; the abnormal concerns deviations within the sphere of what we believe to be normal. . . ." Huh? So, a grocery list that contains "fuses, gunpowder, detonation device, paper for evil plan" is *normal* while a list that contains "bird innards for ritual, candles, hair, toenails," and stuff like that is *paranormal?* I still don't get it.

MICHAEL: Terra—I wasn't really puzzled by the difference. I think what she's getting at is that abnormal is sort of the flip side of normal, because it's explained *in terms* of what's normal, whereas what's paranormal can't be explained using the usual laws of nature, physics, etc. If I suddenly did something weird (like telling you something about yourself that only *you* know), you'd try to explain it rationally (you forgot you'd told someone who must have told me, and so on).

Notice how Terra and Michael's journal seems informal but never loses sight of the reading in their course. Later on, they began writing in the margins of each other's entries. This variation of dialogue journals works especially well when you're discussing complex, multifaceted readings.

Dialogue journals may be unfamiliar to you. Try the following strategies to keep your dialogue going.

1 Respond to your partner

Some dialogue journals are not successful because neither writer ever responds directly to what the partner is saying. This type of dialogue turns into a series of exchanged solo entries, instead of being conversational, interactive, and social. Acknowledge your partner from the start, and you'll be off to a stimulating academic friendship.

2 Don't feel you must respond to everything

The participants in a good conversation don't have to follow up on every single remark anyone else makes. Nor should you feel it necessary to answer every query, take up every line of speculation, or consider each idea put forth by your partner. Sometimes an entry will retreat into a kind of solo domain, and it will be clear that you're not explicitly invited in. In such cases, simply write on another topic.

3 Beware of wasting time

Journals are supposed to support your learning. If at any point you feel that your conversation with your partner has strayed from this goal into a time-wasting exchange of trivia, change the topic. Wrench yourself and your partner back into the subject at hand: the readings and topics in your course.

4 Help each other

Two heads are, as the saying goes, better than one. Dialogue journals provide a context for collaborative learning. If you don't understand something, the worst thing you can do is hide your confusion for fear of being embarrassed in front of your partner. Once both of you have humbly revealed your humanness in the face of academic trial, you'll find that your journal entries will reflect mutual (mis)understandings and a spirit of cooperation.

Writer's Tip: Using a Computer

Computers networked or linked by modem are becoming increasingly popular. If you have access to such systems, consider keeping your dialogue journal electronically. The computer gives you a much faster and more efficient way to respond to your partner(s), and your exchanges will seem even more conversational. You can also save your entries and send them at a time convenient for your partner or just try swapping computer disks to respond to each other's entries.

Exercise 3

Write a journal entry in response to your next reading assignment, and then exchange entries with a partner in your class. Read your partner's entry, and write a second entry, this time addressing your partner directly and responding to what he or she wrote about the reading. Ask questions about what your partner wrote, react to his or her assertions, or connect the entry to your own experience.

Now, with your partner, reflect on the nature of your interaction. What happened after you exchanged entries? How did the exchange change your understanding of the reading? How did the features of your writing differ from any solo entries you have already written? What benefits and problems can you imagine for dialogue journal writing?

CHAPTER

4

Planning

In practically any creative endeavor, you need to discover and "rough out" your ideas before you can really get started. Imagine trying to build a house without a plot of land, without a tentative structure or design in mind, and without a store of raw materials. Yet many students begin even major papers and essays without taking any time to think and plan *before* they launch into a full-fledged (and often final) draft.

Planning before writing—often called **prewriting**—reduces anxiety, self-doubt, and writer's block. Considering your ideas first or discovering inconsistencies in your thinking means that you won't have to make all your decisions *as* you write (which can lead to halting sentences, slashed-out paragraphs, and the frustration of a dozen crumpled first starts).

Planning strategies are many and diverse. Some work well at the earliest stages of writing; others can help you later on as you fill gaps in your knowledge, work out patterns and relationships among ideas, and make some tentative decisions about structure.

4a Generating ideas

Whatever the writing task, from a personal narrative in a composition class to a corporate report in a large business, you will want to ask, "What do I know about what I'm writing, and what else do I need to know?" Before you can write anything, you need to call up from your memory sufficient ideas or knowledge to string words together on a page.

It's dangerous to assume, however, that starting to write means pulling from your mind well-formed capsules of thought and then laying them out on the page in stylish sentences. Research shows that when writers begin jotting down ideas on a page, the very act of stringing words together leads to the **invention** of new ideas. This phenomenon is best expressed in a famous saying attributed to E. M. Forster: "How can I know what I think until I see what I say?"

The academic journal, presented in Chapter 2, is an ideal environment for practicing invention. Because journals are by their very nature informal, speculative, and messy, your first few words about a topic may be halting and jumbled. But those first few words will *get you started.*

1 Try freewriting

In **freewriting,** you put your pen to a blank sheet of paper and then begin writing as quickly as possible. You should concentrate entirely on *writing without stopping,* even if you think you have nothing to say. In such a case, simply writing "I'm stuck, I'm stuck" will at least force you to begin writing. Curiously, such empty or rambling prose will soon begin to bore you, and you'll find yourself almost magically slipping into more interesting ideas. The result is often the start of something good.

2 Try focused freewriting

Focused freewriting can help you develop an idea you already have in mind. Your first few sentences could start, "I don't know what to say about euthanasia. I can't think of anything to say, except I'm in favor of it generally." As you continue to write, you'll again find yourself exploring what you know or feel about the topic.

Most focused freewriting involves a free association of ideas, especially if you begin with a general topic. If you can state your topic as an assertion, however, you can systematically question that assertion, anticipating a spark that ignites your interest.

Eric Sannerud began a paper by freewriting on the very broad, general topic of recycling. After one freewriting episode, he discovered that he wanted to focus on the problem of waste batteries. He wrote the following assertion in his journal.

> People should be fined for putting household batteries into the regular trash.

The very act of writing this statement got Sannerud thinking about what it implied. His focused freewriting, some of which follows, suggested lots of interesting questions on his topic.

> Who will enforce the fine? Won't that enforcement cost a lot of money? Also, how will anyone know that a small battery is buried somewhere in someone's weekly garbage? I'm sure this happens all the time. People dump their old car oil down the sewer drain. And who can prove guilt beyond doubt? Wouldn't all the extra legal stuff clog up the courts? And yet without a

*punishment, will we ever clean up the chemicals in our
environment?*

Having asked these questions, Sannerud then began discovering gaps in his
knowledge that gave him ideas for what he needed to investigate.

*What exactly do batteries do in landfills? A garbologist
found perfectly preserved guacamole from 1968 in a landfill,
so what difference do the batteries make? I also wonder
how many small batteries are thrown out each year. Maybe
visit the 46th Street fire station and ask how many
people drop off batteries in their collection drum. Also I'd
like to know if there are alternative, safer types of
batteries. How many types of batteries are rechargeable?*

Note that each question raised during a focused freewrite can, in turn,
become the grist for further freewriting. In a related stategy called **looping,**
you can look over your freewriting, select good phrases or ideas, and then
produce freewriting on those. Several cycles of looping can yield many useful details for your paper.

Did You Know?

Freewriting has been practiced for many years, but it was not
widely used until the 1960s. In the 1920s, several members of a
group of avant-garde creative people known as "Dadaists" exper-
imented with a strange form of freewriting that had its roots in
theories about unleashing the subconscious in free association
activities. Instead of using freewriting for the more academic,
focused goals advocated in this chapter, the Dadaists wanted to
explore strange and surreal ideas, emotions, and images submerged
beneath layers of "rational" thought.

Writer's Tip: Using a Computer

Freewriting and other quick invention exercises work
well on computers because typing can be much faster and less
fatiguing than handwriting. *Remember, though, that the more formal look of typed prose can make you pause or backtrack to revise
sentences.* Keep pushing forward, even if you've made lots of
typographical mistakes. Consider darkening or turning off the
screen. The point is to work with ideas first. You can always
fiddle with the usable prose later.

Exercise 1

A. Think of something you'd like to persuade someone or some group to do. In your journal, write an assertion like Eric Sannerud's, assuming that your assertion might be the start of a persuasive paper for your class. Then simply *consider* your assertion. First, write at least five questions about your assertion. Then review your questions and decide which of them you could answer by doing some sort of research, such as reading, observing your subject, or interviewing someone.

B. In your focused freewriting, note any cases in which writing one question *led to* another question. Bring your samples to class, and share them in a small group of three or four students.

C. Use the freewriting technique to explore some ideas for your paper. If you have already developed a topic, use the focused freewriting technique to generate ideas or information you might use in the paper. Then circle or put an asterisk next to any potentially useful material.

4a
plan

3 Use listing

Listing can help you in two ways: it draws out knowledge already in your mind, and it *creates* new ideas through association. Write your topic at the top of a piece of paper and then list ten thoughts, facts, or ideas about the subject.

Sandy Carrell's first list for his paper, "The Endangered Panda," looked like this.

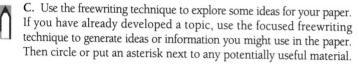

Pandas
1. Bamboo is primary diet
2. Nixon got 2 as gifts from Chinese government
3. Classification questionable—closer to bears or raccoons?
4. Hard to breed in captivity; artificial insemination failed
5. Sing-Sing sat on her baby and killed it
6. "Opposable thumb"
7. Toy industry exploits "cuteness" of pandas
8. Babies cling to mother's fur—danger?
9. Extremely shy; won't mate in presence of humans
10. Very popular (National Zoo)

In the five minutes it took him to produce this list, Carrell created several ideas for writing. Of course, such a general list wasn't much use until he began exploring the more specific angles. To do this, he continued cycling through the listing process, each time trying to think of ten items. His first idea ("Bamboo is primary diet") yielded five more ideas, some of which took the form of questions for research.

Bamboo Is Primary Diet
1. *Bamboo forests in China shrinking*
2. *Pandas endangered primarily because of diet*
3. *Zoos need constant supply of expensive bamboo*
4. *Pandas destructive to bamboo forests—which to protect?*
5. *Possibility of synthetic foods*

Notice that Carrell knew pandas eat large quantities of bamboo, but his listing led to a more complex questioning of that fact and its implications.

Exercise 2

A. Pick any topic that interests you, or simply search at random for an idea or term, such as *smokestack industry, world food supply, severe-storm warning systems,* and so forth. Then try out the listing procedure. Begin by listing ten things you know about your chosen topic. Then choose one item, and generate another sublist beneath it. If you can, keep going to a third or fourth level.

B. In a group of three, exchange *topics* only. Try to generate a list of ten ideas for each partner's topic. If you have time, generate sublists of five items from one of the original ten items in each list. Then compare your lists as a group, and see which items overlapped and which were unique.

C. Generate a list of ten items for your paper in progress. Choose one of the ten items, and generate a sublist of at least five more items. Try the procedure with as many main items as you can.

4 Tease out the details

Good writing is very often *detailed.* A narrative written as a stark outline of events won't engage your readers, nor will a lab report that lacks specific observations and procedures. Such writing needs detail to help a reader envision what you mean, what you did, or what you saw.

Like listing and sublisting, searching for details to particularize general statements can lead you to new ideas and associations. For every idea, make a **detailing list** of specific details beneath it. You may find yourself listing your own impressions first. Label these personal impressions; *then* make a list of the specific features that led to each impression. You'll find that once you have written down the specific features, you no longer need to state the impression—you've already reproduced it for your readers to experience.

Consider the following excerpt from Heather Strong's draft about a trip to the Grand Canyon.

> When we first looked out over the Grand Canyon we were just amazed. What a beautiful sight! It was like nothing we had seen before—so impressive and marvelous. It was simply incredible to gaze out over such a spectacle of nature.

This paragraph cries out for *specifics*. Figure 4-1 shows part of a detailing list Strong created to help her develop her ideas. Note how she systematically questions the general impressions in the original paragraph, each time adding a more specific level of detail.

Contrast the generalized prose of Strong's draft with her revision, written with the help of her detailing list.

> The view from the North Rim was just as breathtaking as when we first set eyes on this spectacle of nature. From Tiyo Point we could see Shiva Temple. To its east was the flat-topped formation of Budda Temple, with its red sandstone lit up like a flaming torch by the sun. Across the canyon, we could make out the limestone-capped Brahma Temple. The effect of these varied red, brown, and gold formations is almost religious. It felt as if we were standing in a cathedral of stone, looking down into a million years of statuary, spires, and domes, all bathed in soft, stained-glass hues of light.

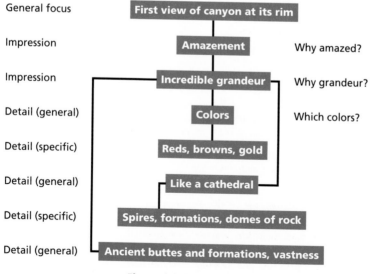

Figure 4-1 Detailing list

Detailing lists need not always lead to cause-effect relationships like those in Figure 4-1. They can also fill in gaps in chronologies, give spatial details, or provide specific examples for generalizations.

5 Ask the journalist's questions

Some forms of prewriting can help you not only to pull information from your memory but also to think about what *new* information you need to gather. One such strategy is the familiar set of **journalist's questions:** *who, what, where, when, why,* and *how.* To use this technique, write each question on a piece of paper, and then freewrite or list an answer to it. Ignore any questions that don't apply to the situation.

In prewriting for his paper arguing why the city council shouldn't allow a high-rise apartment to be built adjacent to a public park in his home-town, Brian Corby began by answering the journalist's questions. Under the fifth category ("Why"), he listed further ideas. As he did so, he realized that he was listing "whys" in *favor* of the construction, so he created a new category, "Why Not," and brainstormed a list for that.

Who   Granger Construction; city council; residents

What   Proposed high-rise apt., 18 stories, 102 units plus 3 penthouses

Where   Tower will overlook east side of Piedmont Park between Sunrise Ave. and Claremont St.

When   Proposal approved by Feb.; planning by Feb. next yr.; groundbreaking by June; finished structure by Aug. of following year

Why   Developers' profit
- Brings jobs to Lake Walton
- Raises property tax base, which is supposed to funnel money back into the city and parks
- Provides medium-cost housing in growing area
- Develops ugly vacant property by park

How   Council approval; plans for construction; construction and completion

Why Not
- "Citifies" one of the few green patches in Lake Walton
- Increases traffic, crime rate, park use
- Adds to waste; pollution from proposed garbage incinerator in building
- Opens the door to other high-rise development because of new zoning ordinance

6 Create a dialogue

Any conversation about a subject will usually yield at least some new ideas. The **dialogue journal** (see 3b) can be a productive place to try out ideas with someone else or explore a subject in preparation for writing a paper. When you need to work alone, however, creating an **internal dialogue** in your journal can be a suitable substitute.

To create an internal dialogue, imagine that you're talking about your topic with someone else. It helps to give your imaginary partner an identity (perhaps someone you know or a well-known figure). Then simply create a written dialogue, as if you were recording a conversation with the person (as Jodi Hakes-Smith does here with a researcher whose work she has been reading for a paper).

4b plan

Me: I think literacy really is tied to socioeconomic background.

Dr. Bowman: Oh, so you mean race, huh. What you really mean is something insidious like genetic predisposition. Well, let me tell you something about . . .

Me: No, that's not what I mean. I mean that when you look at the households of poor people, you're likely to find lower levels of literacy.

Bowman: And why do you suppose that's the case?

Me: Well, for one thing, people with little money can't afford magazine subscriptions, daily newspapers, books . . . they often don't have cars to take them to the local library.

Bowman: I see. You think simple money will help? . . .

In writing dialogues, don't be afraid to "dominate" the discussion. You're not, after all, trying to write a conversation; you're trying to use conversational tactics to produce your own writing.

4b Using techniques for finding patterns

The prewriting strategies described in 4a will help you to generate abundant material for a piece of writing. There comes a point, of course, when simply *generating* material for the sake of getting started will begin to feel either useless or overwhelming, as if a convoy of trucks keeps delivering more and more lumber, cement blocks, wire, and shingles to a construction site, but no one ever starts actually building the house.

The following additional prewriting strategies may enter into even the earliest stages of writing a paper. But because these conceptual maps suggest ways of *grouping ideas* or *seeing relationships,* they can be especially useful later on as you approach the drafting stage of writing.

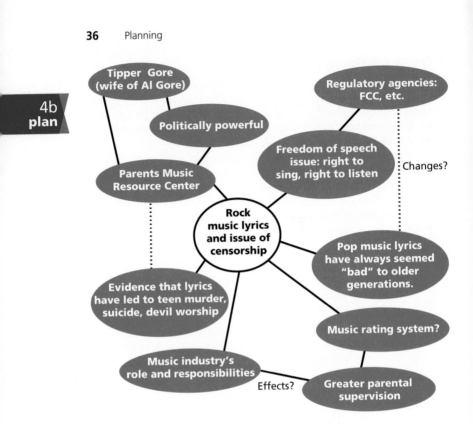

Figure 4-2 A simple conceptual cluster

1 Draw clusters

When you create a *cluster*, you produce a group of ideas related to a kernel topic and link these ideas with lines to display how they are associated. **Clustering** encourages the interconnection of ideas. A single idea may develop into several seemingly unconnected nodes, but on further reflection these may suggest some other connections you hadn't yet considered.

Begin by writing a concept, idea, or topic in the center of a page, and circle it. Then, as in listing, randomly jot down associations with this central idea, circling them and connecting them with lines to the center, like the spokes of a wheel. As you continue to generate ideas around the central focus, think about the interconnections among subsidiary ideas, and draw lines to show those. After a few minutes, you'll probably have something like the cluster in Figure 4-2, written by Marianne Kidd. As you can see from Kidd's cluster, she's already produced a wealth of ideas to consider developing in her paper.

You can also create clusters in cycles, each subsidiary idea becoming the central focus on a new page. As when you work with layers of lists, you'll soon find that some clusters begin petering out once you've exhausted your fund of knowledge. Stand back and assess what you have. Is there enough to go on, without further consideration? If so, you may be ready to start some harder, more critical decisions about your paper's direction. If not, perhaps further work will open up additional ideas. In her original cluster, for example, Kidd could pull out a subsidiary idea, such as a music rating system, and then subject it to further clustering.

4b
plan

2 Create tree diagrams

Tree diagrams resemble clusters, but their branches tend to be a little more linear, with fewer interconnections. Tree diagrams rely on the notion of subordination: each larger branch can lead to smaller and smaller branches. For this reason, tree diagramming can provide a useful way to visualize the components of your paper. You can even "revise" a tree diagram into a sort of preliminary outline to use when deciding what to place in each paragraph of your paper.

In Figure 4-3, Bill Chen has used a tree diagram to discover a tentative structure for his paper on the possible uses of virtual reality, a new technology in which a computer can simulate a "virtual" world in three-dimensional space and allow a viewer to enter this world and move around in it. In this case, each main branch of the diagram ended up as a separate main section of Chen's paper. Most of the smaller branches turned into para-

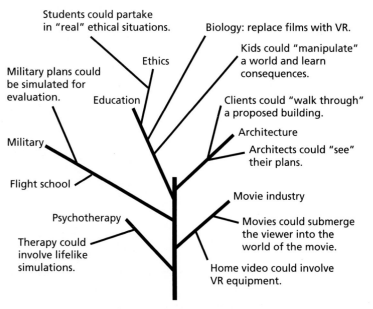

The Uses of Virtual Reality

Figure 4-3 A simple tree diagram

graphs, although in a few cases two or three branches were consolidated into a single paragraph. If Chen were to broaden his topic to include a section on how virtual reality works, he might create another tree (parallel with the first) labeled "How Virtual Reality Works." Yet another section might provide a history of virtual reality's development.

Exercise 3

A. Choose a simple topic you know well. Then try creating a cluster or a tree diagram. Does the result suggest a possible structure for a paper? What problems might arise in "translating" the cluster or diagram into an outline for the paper?

B. In a small group, describe your cluster or tree diagram and explain its nodes or branches. Then collaboratively try generating more branches for each writer's diagram.

C. For your paper in progress, choose one idea created from earlier prewriting strategies, and then create a cluster and a tree diagram for the idea. Circle or star any ideas that seem potentially useful.

3 Build time sequences

If you're writing a paper organized chronologically or involving sequences of time, you may find a **time sequence** technique useful. Begin by framing each event along a line. Then, if you wish, draw vertical lines of thicker or thinner widths depending on how closely connected one event is with the next. In a paper on the early life of Haydn, for example, Carol Schmidt created the time sequence shown in Figure 4-4.

In her first draft, Schmidt used each part of her timeline for a section of her paper discussing the progress of Haydn's musical career. In order to move beyond a simple chronology and look for connections between particular events and certain aspects of Haydn's music, however, Schmidt couldn't rely solely on the time sequence. Instead, she took each section of the sequence and listed possible influences on Haydn's work. The two most interesting were his uncle's influence and his service to Prince Anton Esterhazy. These became the focus of Schmidt's paper.

4 Create problem-solution grids

Some of your writing, especially persuasive papers or editorials, will outline a problem of some sort and then propose various workable solutions or show the advantages of one solution over another. This is called a **problem-solution sequence.**

In this type of writing, you can use a simple but powerful technique for exploring ideas and revealing organizational options for your paper: a

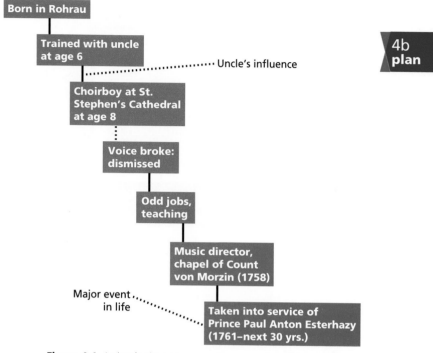

Figure 4-4 A simple time sequence for a narrative history

problem-solution grid. Begin by writing a phrase or sentence illustrating the problem at hand. Box it off; then draw several vertical lines to subsidiary boxes and label these "solutions." Extend your thinking about each solution by branching downward to further problems the solution might create (or dimensions of the solution that need to be considered).

In Figure 4-5, Paula Masek identified three possible temporary solutions to the problem of hunger among the homeless: more shelters that serve meals, distribution of fresh food, and an "invite a homeless person to dinner" program that would recruit volunteers to feed someone a meal once a month. Each solution led to one or more problems which in turn begged for solutions. Using this grid to guide her structure, Masek discussed each boxed item in a separate section or paragraph of her draft.

5 Draw principles and look for generalizations

If you are writing analytical or interpretive papers that require moving from particulars to generalizations (or, for that matter, from generalizations to particulars), you may want to try out the following strategy. First, list as many facts about your subject as possible, using the listing technique

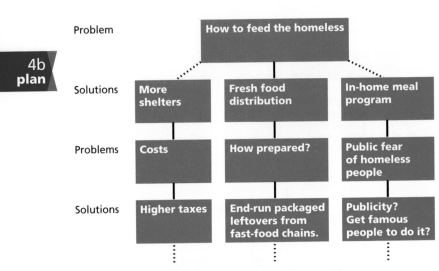

Figure 4-5 A problem-solution grid

described in 4a. Then ask yourself whether you can derive some principle or generalization from those facts.

This strategy is illustrated in Tim Pagenhart's planning for a paper on teenage boys' gang membership.

- Most teenagers who join gangs are from fatherless homes.
- Joining a gang involves rituals intended to prove the new member's manhood or toughness.
- Gangs seek new members in poverty-stricken areas.
- There is a strict hierarchy within the gang, which leads the new member to take outrageous risks in order to impress those in power and gain their favor.

Taken together, these facts suggested to Pagenhart that gangs thrive on recruiting members who lack strong male role models at home and desperately need a way to build self-esteem. Once he made that generalization, he could then look for other facts to support it. (See Figure 4-6.)

6 Invent outlines

The best-known traditional prewriting technique is the trusty **outline,** complete with Roman numerals. Unfortunately, the traditional outline doesn't do much to help writers *generate* ideas before they decide how these ideas should be arranged.

As a true prewriting technique, however, the **working outline** can be useful. The trick is to use the outline to generate new categories of infor-

4b
plan

Fact:

> **Most teenagers who join gangs are from fatherless homes. (Harris, 1989)**

Fact:

> **Joining gang involves rituals intended to prove manhood or toughness. (*Book of Gangs*)**

Fact:

> **Gangs seek new members in poverty-stricken areas such as ghettos and barrios.**

Fact:

> **Gangs have a hierarchy; new members take risks to impress leaders and gain favor.**

Generalization:

> **Gangs survive by recruiting members who lack strong male role models at home and need ways to build self-esteem. Normal activities that help build self-esteem may not be available in poor and crime-ridden areas, so young recruits look to gang leaders as authorities and protectors.**

Figure 4-6 Generalizations from particulars

mation rather than to label ones you've already thought up. If you begin with a simple topic as the main heading of an outline, for example, you might commit yourself to three second-level subheadings by writing the letters *A, B,* and *C* beneath the main topic (leaving a lot of space in between). Then try filling in the blank subheadings. Once you've "discovered" three main subheadings, commit yourself to three third-level headings by writing 1, 2, and 3 beneath *each* of your letters *A, B,* and *C.* Then try filling those in, as Mitch Weber did in the following example (see also 45c-4).

    I. Influence of Caxton's printing press [main topic]
       A. On literacy
          1. How-to and self-help industry
          2. Books in the schools
          3. Dictionaries and grammars
       B. On politics
          1. Pamphlets and political treatises
          2. Circulation of laws and regulations
       C. On commerce
          1. Early advertising
          2. Book industry itself (flourishing of printing)
          3. Early news industry

Note that Weber simply couldn't think of a third item under "Politics." In further brainstorming, he might well come up with one. But maintaining an exact three-part balance is obviously not crucial to writing a good paper on this topic. Note also that Weber could further expand each third-level item in his outline into three more specific bits of information. In this sense, outlining is a kind of structured listing.

Did You Know?

A study of planning discovered that older, experienced writers made complex, condensed, often diagrammatic notes they later expanded in their drafts. In contrast, younger, less experienced writers made notes that were simply first drafts of their compositions. These observations suggest that certain kinds of planning, especially brief references to larger, complex chunks of information, may help writers more than just trying to write out the text.

P. J. Burtis, Carl Bereiter, Marlene Scardamalia, and Jacqueline Tretoe, "The Development of Planning in Writing," *Explorations in the Development of Writing,* ed. Barry M. Kroll (New York: Wiley, 1983) 153–74.

Writer's Tip: Using a Computer

Some newer word processing programs come with a special outlining function. You can give invisible "heading" commands to various titles and sentences and then use these headings as an outline. You can also create an outline and then, as you write each section of your paper, import the new headings you've created. If you wish, you can move your headings around in your outline, view the entire document, and see how those moves affect your overall organization. The outlining feature works especially well for speeches and other oral presentations when you want to talk from notes instead of reading a prepared document.

Exercise 4

A. Create a list of five topics, issues, or problems. Choose the one that most interests you. Then briefly try out three of the planning techniques discussed in 4b. After experimenting with them, jot down some notes about which one(s) worked worst and best for you. Why do you think this was the case? What sort of topic did you choose, and how did the technique you used affect its development?

B. Compare your general impressions of your three chosen planning techniques in a small group. Which ones seemed to work best for everyone? Were certain strategies more useful for certain topics?

C. Choose at least two planning techniques in 4b to apply to the material you have already invented for your paper. Work through the strategies; then go back and see if any organizational patterns are beginning to emerge from your material. Which ideas seem likely to produce a paragraph or a section of your paper?

4C Planning: Paper in progress

Rachel Ritchie's first assignment in her composition class required her to find specific examples, cases, or illustrations to support general ideas or statements. After generating possible topics for her paper, Ritchie finally settled on a generalized subject: the effects of TV violence on children. She decided to do some preliminary listing to see what specific illustrations she could find to support her generalized topic (see 4a-3). Here is her list.

- Kid who brought gun to school in my hometown
- Logan (boy I baby-sat for)—Power Rangers made him violent
- Media—drive-by shootings (my friend Paula was wounded)
- England (kids killing kids and recent case in U.S.)
- Growth in gun sales and more kids using guns
- Portrayal of violence on TV (we think it's normal)
- Accidental suicide (with guns especially)
- Gangs (Kim)

Exercise 5

A. Study Rachel Ritchie's planning list. What questions would you ask Ritchie about the items on her list relative to the generalized topic she has chosen to illustrate with examples? What advice would you give her for either elaborating her list or choosing specific items on it to include in her paper?

B. In a small group, compare your responses to Exercise 5A. Work together to generate a list of additional particulars that Ritchie could use to develop her topic.

Defining Your Purpose

College writing fulfills at least three *general* purposes: (1) it helps you to learn new ideas and information; (2) it helps you to practice the craft of writing; and (3) it communicates your thoughts to various readers, including your teacher and classmates. Classrooms are unique because they encourage you to write for all three of these purposes at once. A typical assignment, given to you for the purpose of practice, will almost always involve some exploration and learning. You'll also direct your writing toward some real or imagined reader, as well as to your teacher.

Each paper you write, moreover, will fulfill *specific* rhetorical purposes related to the task at hand. If you're writing in order to entertain your readers with a rich, interesting description of a personal experience, this purpose will help you choose an appropriate structure, style, and content. If, instead, you're trying to persuade your readers of a position on a controversial issue, your choices for these features may be quite different. Thinking about your specific purposes for writing a paper can help you to develop a clear thesis, or main point, and to make appropriate choices as you plan, draft, and revise your writing.

5a Analyzing the purpose of your assignment

In many writing situations, someone else hands you a task or assignment, and it's your job to produce a decent piece of prose from your available resources. In the business world, almost no one escapes having to complete such writing tasks, whether they're actually assigned ("Please reply to this request for information about our product X") or whether the tasks are simply assumed as part of the job.

In college courses, your main **purpose** for writing is usually to fulfill just such a task—a teacher's assignment. That assignment may be designed to help you think through a problem or an issue, to teach you about some principle of writing, to increase your awareness of different audiences, or to encourage you to grasp some principle or knowledge more fully. But these educational goals are usually achieved in a paper designed to communicate information to other people.

One of your early steps in planning for any writing assignment, therefore, should be to analyze the assignment itself, taking time to figure out what you're being asked to do. Most writing assignments will include some reference to the type of writing (such as a narrative, an argument, or a summary) and the intellectual activity the writing should involve.

1 Locate the topic of the assignment

The **topic** of an assignment refers to its content or focus—what subject you will be writing about and any specific treatment or angle you must take. Locating and analyzing the topic in your assignment can help you to begin planning your paper by narrowing your many options.

Strategy

Look for any nouns or noun phrases in the assignment, and underline them. In your planning notes, write these nouns and then, by freewriting or creating conceptual maps (see 4a and 4b), begin inventing possibilities for your paper's contents.

In analyzing a writing assignment in his first-year English class, Dennis Buehler underlined a key noun phrase.

> Everyone is an expert at something—car repair, sewing, babysitting, baseball history, roofing, raising prize heifers. For your third assignment, be the expert. In three or four pages, tell a nonexpert audience (the rest of our class) <u>something interesting about the subject of your expertise.</u>

The underlined topic can be stated more simply as *something you know about or can do well.* This assignment leaves the topic very much open but seems to value something of high interest.

After underlining the key topic in the assignment, Buehler wrote the following planning notes to help him explore possible directions for his paper.

> <u>Something interesting about the subject of your expertise.</u> This probably doesn't make me an "expert," but last year I lived for the entire summer with a family in Amsterdam. I got to know the city really well, so that after a month or so I didn't even need a map to get around. I saw just about everything. I also learned a lot about how to get along

in the Dutch culture, how to have a good time without spending a lot of money, and what to watch out for. I could write a mock travel guide for someone just visiting for a few days. This could include the best sights, tourist hazards, and "must-eat" restaurants.

Buehler knew that he could write enough as an "expert" about Amsterdam to complete his paper, but he developed a plan that could also fulfill the assignment's purpose of maintaining the reader's interest.

2 Locate the action statement in the assignment

Every assignment will also contain directions that specify the type of writing you should do and the *processes* you should go through to complete the assignment. Such directions often take the form of an **action statement**—a verb or verb phrase. Sometimes these statements are very specific; other times they are vague and undefined, giving you more room to define the assignment as you wish.

Strategy

Underline any verbs or verb phrases in your assignment that can tell you what to *do* in your paper. Then, as with topic nouns, use one or more planning techniques to generate material for your paper from the verbs. (See Chapter 4.)

In analyzing her second writing assignment, Corinth Malletas found several different directions expressed in verb phrases. She underlined two phrases that seemed to get to the heart of the assignment.

> Assignment 2: Find an advertisement that catches your attention in a popular magazine. Then analyze the ad for its hidden cultural assumptions, being sure to describe exactly what is happening in the ad, including techniques of camera angle, coloration, focus, and so on, and paying attention to what is in the ad versus what is cut off, not shown, or partially shown. Be sure to go beyond plain description and into analysis, showing how features of the ad reflect our selves and our cultures.

Once Malletas had found an appropriate ad, she spent much of her early planning process listing descriptive details about the ad and then freewriting short interpretations of these details.

Some of the more common verbs used in writing assignments follow, along with brief definitions and examples.

Describe. Show how something looks, feels, smells, sounds, or tastes; paint a picture in words.

EXAMPLE "Describe the French Quarter in New Orleans."

Analyze. Divide or break something into its constituent parts so you can **analyze** their relationships. Begin with careful description and observation.

EXAMPLE "Analyze the relationships between form and color, light and shadow, and foreground and background in one of Titian's paintings."

Synthesize. Combine separate elements in a **synthesis**, producing a single or unified entity.

EXAMPLE "Synthesize this list of disparate facts about energy consumption."

Evaluate. Reach conclusions about something's value or worth. Substantiate all **evaluations** with evidence based on careful observation and analysis.

EXAMPLE "Evaluate the effectiveness of camera technique and sound in Alfred Hitchcock's *The Birds*."

Argue. **Argue** to prove a point or **persuade** a reader to accept or entertain a particular position. (See 48a.)

EXAMPLE "Write a letter to the editor arguing your position on the campus-wide ban of indoor smoking."

Inform. Discuss some facts, views, or phenomena to **inform** your reader.

EXAMPLE "Write an informative paper about the hazards of lead paint in older homes."

Extend. Take an idea or concept and **extend** it—apply it more extensively.

EXAMPLE "Extend Darwin's concept of 'survival of the fittest' to life in the inner city."

Trace. Map out some history or chronology, or **trace** the origins of something.

EXAMPLE "Trace the development of Stalinism."

Discuss. Provide an intelligent, focused commentary when you **discuss** your topic.

EXAMPLE "Discuss the limitations of Skinner's view of human behavior."

Show. Demonstrate or provide evidence to **show** something.

EXAMPLE   "Show how Pip, in his later years, is influenced by Joe's upbringing and working-class values in Dickens's *Great Expectations*."

Exercise 1

A. Examine the following writing assignments. Locate the topic noun(s) and the action statement(s) in the assignments. Then analyze the purposes implied in the assignments. Paraphrase the assignments if you need to.

Sample Assignment 1. Everyone at some time recognizes a prejudice against another person or group. These prejudices usually come from stereotypes—inaccurate generalizations we make on the basis of limited experience, rumor, or things other people tell us. Choose some past action in your life that came out of a prejudice. What was the cause of the action? If the same circumstances arose today, would you behave differently?

Sample Assignment 2. For a paper of four to six pages, choose two opposing views on a controversial social issue. Present these views objectively, and then critique each position to reach a conclusion about which is more valid.

B. Compare your analyses in a small group. What aspects of the task do you agree on? Where do you differ? How might you go about writing each of these papers?

C. Using the Strategies outlined in this section, analyze an assignment you are now working on or preparing to work on, either in your writing course or in another course you're taking.

Did You Know?

In a study of legislative analysts' writing, when the researchers substituted single words in the writers' documents and then asked them whether these changes were acceptable, the writers often agreed or disagreed with the substitutions on the basis of what they were trying to *do* with their writing. This research reveals how often writers' purposes guide even the smallest of decisions as they compose.

Lee Odell, "Beyond the Text: Relations Between Writing and Social Context," *Writing in Nonacademic Settings,* ed. Lee Odell and Dixie Goswami (Ne York: Guilford, 1985) 249–80.

5b Using rhetorical purposes to guide decisions

Once you've analyzed the general purposes implied in an assignment, you can begin considering more specific **rhetorical purposes** for your paper. When you think about your rhetorical purposes, you're anticipating certain effects on your reader. You might want your first paragraph to grab your reader's attention, or you might want a middle section of your paper to show that you do, in fact, understand the position you're arguing against. Rhetorical purposes refer to what you want your writing to *do* at each stage.

1 Rough out a purpose structure

As you think about how you want to affect your reader, it helps to begin planning a very general **purpose structure** for your paper's contents. This is far more primitive, at this early stage, than an outline or detailed description of parts; it's merely a general blueprint to help you get started.

In planning to write a paper arguing the benefits of living off campus in an apartment or house, Carol Stotsky first defined her general purpose (to argue a point and to help people to understand the advantages of living on one's own while in college). But then she needed to become more specific. What is it, exactly, about living off campus that makes so much sense? How should she present her points, and for what reasons?

For her beginning, Stotsky decided to describe why the idea of living off campus is so controversial that someone would want to write a persuasive paper about it.

> Beginning: Map Out the Controversy

Stotsky decided that after showing why this topic is controversial and needs examination, she would discuss each housing option in detail, analyzing the advantages and disadvantages of each. She planned to have the middle section of her paper *explore* the issue in depth.

> Middle: Explore Housing Options in Detail

She then decided to have her final section move toward a resolution of the controversy by making claims for the advantages of living off campus. Since she'd already analyzed the various options, she stood a better chance of demonstrating her point.

> Ending: Argue for Benefits of Off-Campus Housing

This sort of planning from her purposes gave Stotsky a tentative order for her explorations.

2 Particularize your purposes

You can further particularize each of the rhetorical purposes that have led to a sense of your essay's parts, listing possible ways in which that purpose can be developed. Carol Stotsky decided, for example, that the beginning of her paper on housing options would explain the controversy for readers who may not understand why it's an important topic. She listed four possibilities.

1. I could begin with a true-to-life description of someone's day off campus: "Joanne awakens to the smell of hot coffee coming from her automatic coffee maker in the kitchen of her small apartment on the outskirts of campus."
2. I could begin with a string of quotes from parents concerned about their children's welfare off campus.
3. I could begin with the story of the woman who was raped in her off-campus apartment last year, and then follow that with the story of the student who was thrown (fell?) from his dorm window last winter after a drinking party.
4. I could begin with the results of the study by Breland on differences in autonomy and self-esteem among students who lived off campus or in dorms at American universities.

Having listed these options to fulfill the rhetorical purpose of explaining the controversy, Stotsky could choose one and start her paper, or try loosely drafting several of her alternative beginnings and then see which one most clearly fulfilled her purpose.

Exercise 2

According to an article in *Smithsonian,* Great Basin National Park in eastern Nevada is the newest national park in the United States. Amid the stark beauty of this deserted stretch of basin and rangeland lives the bristlecone pine, a tree that has survived in the arid, rocky terrain of this region for over 4,000 years. The oldest living tree known to humankind was not long ago continuing to eke out its existence in the bristlecone forest. It had survived for over 4,900 years until a researcher, before the Great Basin was protected as a national park, cut it down to study its growth rings.

Imagine that you have ample information about the history of Great Basin National Park, the nature and habitat of the bristlecone pine tree, and the circumstances of the oldest bristlecone being cut down by the researcher. Decide on a main purpose for a paper on the bristlecone. Then try to plan a three-part structure for your paper based on this purpose.

Did You Know?

Many academic assignments already define your main purpose for you. It's hard to imagine, for example, some purpose other than what's actually stated in the assignment "Write a letter to your senator arguing your position on gun control." Yet in a case study of four first-year writers, the students made more of the tasks, for themselves, than anyone would have thought from simply looking at their final papers. They used the writing assignment to interest themselves and to learn new ideas in the process of communicating.

Chris M. Anson, "Composition and Communicative Intention," diss., Indiana U, 1984.

5c Defining a thesis

Because most college writing is relatively short, your papers will focus sharply on particular issues, events, processes, or ideas. A three-page paper can't even scratch the surface of a broad topic such as pollution, genetic engineering, U.S. involvement in foreign disputes, or abortion rights. Trying to write about such a topic without developing a specific point about it yields an extremely general and often boring paper.

One way to avoid such bland, general writing is to develop a specific thesis that you then explore, support, or illustrate in your paper. A **thesis,** from the Greek word meaning "to put or set down," is the **controlling idea** in a paper; it controls the rest of the information presented. Most of your papers will contain a **thesis statement,** usually a single sentence, that appears somewhere early in the text, often at the end of the first full paragraph. (Sometimes, however, the thesis of a paper may be more subtle, implied rather than stated overtly.) Your thesis acts as a kind of internal statement of purpose for your paper, telling your reader what you're trying to demonstrate or argue. It's a map to help your reader interpret the details in the body of your paper.

Depending on the nature of your writing process, you may begin drafting a paper with a clear thesis in mind. If you're using the drafting process as a way to explore ideas, you may instead discover your thesis later on and revise your draft accordingly. You may also begin with a clear thesis and then modify it as you look for evidence or **supporting ideas** to back up your assertions.

1 Turn topics into theses

When you begin a paper, you may think about large domains of knowledge or experience that often take the form of nouns or noun phrases:

the death penalty, conservation versus jobs in the timber industry, animal rights.
Developing a thesis means *narrowing* one of these topics into something
much more specific and verbal, some statement of principle, action, or belief.

To develop a thesis from a topic, first try **narrowing** the topic to
some specific angle or perspective. Then begin turning the topic from a
noun (a "thing") into a statement that contains a verb, as Lynn Scattarelli
did in her paper on the death penalty.

Vague topic	The death penalty
Still a topic	Hanging as a death penalty
Still a topic	Cruelty in hanging as a death penalty
Rough thesis	Hanging is a cruel way to impose the death penalty.

The topic became sharper in the second and third versions, but Scattarelli
brought the fourth version to life by expressing some belief about it, seeing
it from a specific perspective.

2 Complicate or extend your rough thesis

Early thesis statements often beg for some clarification or elaboration.
In Scattarelli's rough thesis, it's not clear whether she is arguing against the
death penalty by using the example of hanging or whether she is arguing
only against hanging as a method of execution. Answering this question led
her to a more complex and interesting thesis.

FINAL THESIS   Although the death penalty remains an acceptable means of
punishment, the process of hanging represents unusual cru-
elty and should be abolished in favor of more merciful means
of execution.

Scattarelli complicated her final thesis by accepting the death penalty in
principle. The main point (that hanging is cruel punishment) *qualified* or
extended her rough thesis.

More complex theses often lead to papers your readers will find interesting and enlightening. In working on a personal experience paper, Stephanie
Cox turned a vague topic into a complex thesis by connecting the dress
code at her school with the concept of social competition.

TOPIC   The dress code we had at Morgan County Middle School

ROUGH THESIS   Our dress code at Morgan County Middle School was successful.

COMPLEX THESIS   Our dress code at Morgan County Middle School helped us
to focus on our learning by lessening the competition for
appearance and the display of wealth.

3 Use a thesis to sort out your ideas

The thesis offers your reader a way to organize the information in your paper in chunks, fitting subsidiary paragraphs and sections into the larger statement of purpose. But *you,* as writer, need to decide on these ideas in the first place. If you develop a clear thesis early in your work, many of your decisions about the supporting ideas in your paper will be much easier to make.

A simple but illustrative model is the **five-paragraph theme.** In this form of student writing, the first paragraph leads into a sharp thesis statement. The next three paragraphs, each beginning with a **topic sentence,** offer three different perspectives, supporting arguments, or illustrations of the thesis. The final paragraph then sums up, usually by repeating the thesis more conclusively, and sometimes doles out some food for further thought. Although this rather mechanical model is seldom found outside of school and is today considered a relatively unsophisticated formula for essays, the five-paragraph theme still can be useful when you take a timed essay test, since the teacher will be looking for organized, succinct answers to difficult questions.

Beginning with a five-paragraph format can also help you to structure your rough drafts around specific rhetorical purposes, as Joel Kitze found in his paper on CD-ROM reference tools.

THESIS	In spite of the popularity of CD-ROM encyclopedias, computers will never take the place of books as the primary medium of written literacy.
SUPPORTING IDEA 1	Books will always be more democratic, since only the middle and upper middle class can afford personal computers.
SUPPORTING IDEA 2	Books can be transported and enjoyed anywhere—on a bus, on the beach, in bed.
SUPPORTING IDEA 3	Children enjoy the physical comfort of reading with adults, a comfort harder to achieve with computers.

Each idea formed a kind of "minithesis" for its paragraph or section, guiding the ideas and focus of that paragraph. At the same time, each idea also provided support for the overall thesis of Kitze's paper.

4 Modify your thesis

Sticking too strictly to a preplanned thesis can sometimes shut down the chance to rethink your ideas. At some point during your planning, writing, or revising, you will probably find yourself entertaining other ideas, especially those that seem to contradict your thesis statement.

In such cases, your paper will seem more interesting if you can modify your earlier position or perspective and revise your thesis and its supporting ideas. For example, in searching for good reasons to favor books over CD-ROM disks, Joel Kitze thought of some distinct advantages of CD-ROM technology as well, including its ease of storage (much smaller than books), its huge memory (hundreds of pages per disk), and its ability to be updated without the cost of reprinting and republishing (disks are cheaper than books). Newer systems can show color graphics and pictures, weakening the argument about the visual appeal of books. After thinking about four or five supporting reasons like these, Kitze went back and modified his thesis, making it more complex and subtle.

ORIGINAL THESIS   In spite of the popularity of CD-ROM encyclopedias, computers will never take the place of books as the primary medium of written literacy.

MODIFIED THESIS   Although CD-ROM technology allows masses of information to be stored on small, easily shelved discs, it will never replace the bound book as the most convenient, affordable, and magical medium for print.

Kitze's revised thesis acknowledged that CD-ROM discs have certain advantages, yet he still made a case for books. Readers of this new thesis had more to think about than in the earlier version.

Exercise 3

Turn each of the following topics into two different thesis statements. Be as inventive as you like.

EXAMPLE

TOPIC   Saw-blade sabotage in the timber industry

THESIS   Spiking trees to sabotage the saw blades of timber workers is both illegal and extremely dangerous but should be understood as a subversive act to stop the further depletion of virgin forests.

THESIS   Protests that include the illegal spiking of trees to sabotage the saw blades of timber workers actually help the timber industry by suggesting to the public that conservationists are less concerned about safety and human life than about trees.

Topic 1: UFOs
Topic 2: Phone sex on 900 numbers
Topic 3: On-site day-care centers in corporations
Topic 4: Fur coats
Topic 5: American fast-food restaurants in Europe

Did You Know?

Good writing that explains or argues makes frequent use of comments that guide a reader. In English, words and phrases like *for example, I believe, on the other hand, in the discussion that follows,* and *the evidence suggests* alert readers to important ideas and information while pointing out the ways you have organized a discussion. Other languages and cultures use expressions with similar purposes, though the wording of the comments and the frequency with which they are used differ from language to language and from culture to culture. Consequently, writers for whom English is a second language need to pay attention to comments like *however* and *for instance* as they read, so they can learn where and when to use them.

Avon Crismore, Raija Markkanen, and Margaret S. Steffensen, "Metadiscourse in Persuasive Writing: A Study of Texts Written by American and Finnish Students," *Written Communication* 10 (January 1993): 39–71.

5d   A word about discovery

Clearly, defining your purpose can be a useful way to *plan* before you begin drafting. Knowing where you want to go with your writing and why, you can make wise decisions about the most effective route. The writing process, however, doesn't always work in a structured, linear way. Toward the end of the process, when you're putting the final touches on a paper, a reader's astute response might send you back into an earlier stage, such as inventing ideas, to think of ways to get around a problem that you didn't recognize before. The same goes for purpose. Many writers *discover* purposes for their writing late in the process, and this discovery makes them reconsider much or all of what they're written. If you find yourself redefining your purpose or questioning decisions you made early on, go ahead and make even substantial changes.

Considering Your Readers

Imagine that you're writing a short article for one of the in-flight magazines found in the seat pockets of most commercial airlines. What and how you write for such a magazine will depend on your knowledge of its readers—people locked in a pressurized cabin thirty-five thousand feet above the earth. What do you know already about such readers, at least generally?

- Your readers are likely to be reasonably well educated and not poor, since air travel is expensive.
- Your readers are likely to include travel-minded vacationers and businesspeople.
- Your readers' physical circumstances (restrained in a seat, stressed by travel) may make them bored, tired, or uncomfortable.
- Your readers are likely to be impatient to get somewhere.

Potentially bored, tired, and impatient readers will not warm to a deeply theoretical reading. They'll want short, lively pieces they can read in ten or fifteen minutes, preferably on human-interest topics or geography. Since some passengers enjoy flying about as much as perching on the edge of a fifty-story building, they're not likely to be entertained by a graphic account of the last major jet crash. Yet they'll certainly want to be informed and entertained, if only as a distraction.

Already you can see how just a few thoughts about your readers can help to limit the infinite choices you face when you write—choices of style, content, or length. In most of your writing, as in the preceding example, you should plan to spend some time consciously focusing on your **readers.** Such analysis will eventually become second nature to you.

6a Defining your reader

Many writing experts use the term **audience** to refer to actual or implied readers. An audience may be one person, such as the city official you address in a letter complaining about the poor condition of the neighborhood sidewalks; or it may be dozens, hundreds, or thousands of people, such as the readers of the newspaper that publishes your letter about the same problem.

Your first question in any analysis of audience will be "To whom am I writing?" Is your audience a flesh-and-blood person you know intimately? Or is it a shadowy, unknown reader, with only a faint silhouette to guide your thinking? Is your audience a single person or a large group?

To begin answering these questions, study Figure 6-1. This illustration shows an audience continuum, beginning with the most intimate reader on one end (yourself) and ending with the remote and amorphous "general community of unknown readers" on the other.

The Self. Writing for the self can be an excellent way to learn and to plan for formal writing (see Chapter 2). In more formal writing, the self can also act as a critic or interested reader.

The Specific, Intimately Known Reader. Close friends and relatives make up an audience very different from people you've never met. Letters directed to intimately known readers usually don't have to be very formal, yet you can still carry on an "academic conversation" with such readers.

The Specific, Personally Known Reader. Individuals you know well but not intimately include teachers, supervisors or other employees, and acquaintances. Your knowledge of these people accumulates through a social, scholastic, or occupational relationship. Just as your conversation with such a person might be a little more formal than a talk with a close friend or relative, the style and tone of your writing will also be less casual and chatty.

The Specific Community of Known Readers. *Groups* of readers often can be characterized socially or geographically. Although you can no longer describe this audience's unique personality, you can think of it as a *community* of readers whose members may not all think, act, dress, or live exactly the same way but are bound together by some shared situation. Your writing class is an excellent example of such a community.

The Specific, Publicly Known Reader. You come to know public audiences indirectly through news, gossip and rumor, speeches, interviews, or published works. You don't personally know someone like Oprah Winfrey, but you do know *of* her; you may have seen her on her TV talk show, watched her act in one of her TV or movie roles, or read one of her books. What you know of her largely depends on what's been made available for you to know.

The Specific, Unknown Reader. This reader lives in the shadows. Often you know only his or her name and affiliation: Mr. Ed Walters, director of personnel; or Sondra Teisch, president, local chapter of Mothers Against Drunk Driving. What you know of such readers usually comes not from

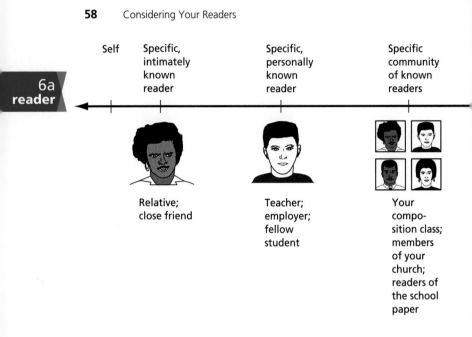

Figure 6-1 The Audience Continuum

any specific actions, words, or direct experience but from what they *do,* what *context* they're in when you write to them. Because you know these people neither personally nor publicly, you should usually address such an audience using a formal style.

The Specific Community of Unknown Readers. The larger the group, the less direct knowledge you'll have of its individual members. It might take only a few weeks to get to know the members of a school club, sorority, or fraternity, but it might take months or years to become acquainted with everyone who reads the school paper or alumni magazine. Yet even the hundreds or thousands of undergraduates at your college or university share the same social and academic context and are tied together by mutual goals, circumstances, and knowledge.

The General Community of Unknown Readers. At this end of the continuum is the most abstract and faceless audience of all. When you decide to write for conservative voters, collectors of classic cars, or vegetarians, for example, you can only generalize about their shared characteristics. For many opinions or characteristics you might assign to such a group, you'll be able to find members who don't share them.

Audiences themselves can also shift positions over time. An acquain-

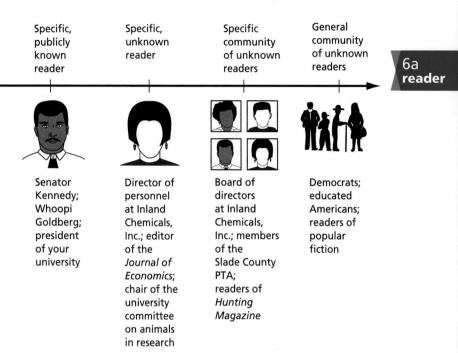

Specific, publicly known reader	Specific, unknown reader	Specific community of unknown readers	General community of unknown readers
Senator Kennedy; Whoopi Goldberg; president of your university	Director of personnel at Inland Chemicals, Inc.; editor of the *Journal of Economics*; chair of the university committee on animals in research	Board of directors at Inland Chemicals, Inc.; members of the Slade County PTA; readers of *Hunting Magazine*	Democrats; educated Americans; readers of popular fiction

tance, whom you might address formally at first, can become a friend, then a close friend. Some specific, personally known readers might, by virtue of their position or your relationship, be addressed more casually than others.

Exercise 1

A. Imagine that you're living on a small estuary along the coast of Florida. A favorite winter vacation spot, the area boasts some excellent shelling beaches. But now, after years of intensive beachcombing, fewer shells appear at low tide, and the area is attracting a more limited variety of birds and other wildlife. The local city council has proposed a general ban on beachcombing and plans to pass an ordinance that would require visitors to obtain a permit, at a cost of $20, to use the public beaches. The money will be channeled back into the study and preservation of the local environment.

You're planning to write a position statement on the proposed ordinance for *The Castaway*, a local monthly newspaper distributed free all around the area. *The Castaway* is read by local residents as well as many visitors. It even has a small out-of-state circulation to retired people who migrate to the area from northern states during the winter months.

Referring to the audience continuum, analyze the audiences (local businesspeople, residents, and so forth) for your position statement. Take a position on the issue, and consider which readers will disagree with your position and why. Write a short letter to the editor expressing your position.

B. Compare your letters in a small group. Discuss the ways in which your audience analysis influenced your letters.

C. For your paper in progress, locate your audience on the continuum, and freewrite about your knowledge of and relationship with that audience. (For freewriting strategies, see 4a.)

6b Characterizing your readers

Although you might identify actual people as readers (your mother, your teacher, the First Lady, the owner of the gas station down the street), at some level your writing is shaped by how *you* think of your audience. Constructing audiences also draws on your knowledge of **social context.** If you know very little about feminism, for example, and you write to an audience of feminists, you may stereotype them in misguided ways. Knowing that there are many varieties of feminism complicates your audience, but the result is a richer and more accurate picture that leads to a better informed and more incisive piece of writing.

Use the following list to think critically about the nature of your readers to help you plan and revise your writing.

1. **Size and Relationship.** How large is your audience, and how generalized? How intimately do you know your audience? What sort of relationship do you share with your audience?
2. **Prior Knowledge.** How much does your audience know about the subject of your writing? Are its members complete novices or just short of being experts? Do they share your prior knowledge of the subject? Are they young or old? Are they worldly-wise or inexperienced and naive?
3. **Physical Context.** Where are your readers situated geographically? Is it possible to pinpoint their location? If not, can you generalize about their location (Florida State University, San Francisco, Capitol Hill)?
4. **Social Context.** What characterizes your audience socially and culturally? Are its members educated? Poor? Middle-class? Do they spend their time watching TV or reading books? Do they listen to Brahms? Do they go to tractor pulls? Do they spend time at singles bars or PTA meetings?

5. **Intellectual Disposition.** How would you characterize your audience way of thinking? Are these people highly conservative? Radical? Apathetic? Where would they stand on certain major issues? Are they more likely to read and enjoy the *National Enquirer* or the *National Review? Science* or the *Christian Science Monitor?*

6. **Conditions of Reading.** Under what conditions will members of your audience be reading your writing? Will they be at home? At school? At the office? At the breakfast table? Will they be studying your work closely, poised over a desk beneath a bright light, or reclining in an easy chair after a good meal? Will they be busy or distracted? Will time be on their side, or will they be wishing they could buy a few extra hours?

In specifying these characteristics, be aware that you're dealing with *tendencies.* Sitting on any given airplane, for example, may be a relaxed person deeply engrossed in a dense philosophical treatise or a complex analysis of trends in computer programming. But usually this person will be the exception.

Exercise 2

A. Imagine that your longtime next-door neighbors take a temporary position in another country and rent their house. Soon after the renters move in, they begin piling up the yard and driveway with junk cars, old refrigerators, tires, and other debris. The situation becomes intolerable, so you decide to write to your neighbors overseas, calling attention to the problem. You also decide to write to the local city inspections office, which is responsible for enforcing various codes on yard debris.

Write the two short letters, addressing the first to John and Susan Valentine and the second to Ms. Betsy Lewis, City Inspections Office.

B. In a small group, compare the style, tone, and contents of your pairs of letters. In each case, you were writing to a specific audience. How did their positions on the audience continuum influence your decisions? What general principles can you draw about the relationship of audience analysis to certain choices in your writing?

C. In planning or revising your notes for your current paper, list each of the six specific characteristics of audience (size and relationship, prior knowledge, physical context, social context, intellectual disposition, and conditions of reading). Beneath each characteristic, list as many facts and details about your audience as you can.

6c
reader

Did You Know?

In a recent study, one group of students was assigned specific audiences to write for, and another group was not. Students in the audience group were more interested in the assignment, put more effort into the work, and used more audience-based writing strategies than students in the "nonaudience" group.

Theresa M. Redd-Boyd and Wayne H. Slater, "The Effects of Audience Specification on Undergraduates' Attitudes, Strategies, and Writing," *Research in the Teaching of English* 23 (1989): 77–108.

6C Adapting your content, structure, and style

Imagining readers of your writing means more than gathering isolated facts about them (average age, occupation, likes and dislikes, and political positions). In analyzing your audience, stopping at facts is like lining up the pepper, oregano, and basil without knowing which spices you should add to the stew. You need to know what to do with the ingredients once you've lined them up on the counter.

Analyzing an audience can influence many decisions you make as you plan and revise your writing. At least three characteristics of your writing will vary according to the way you analyze your audience: *content, structure,* and *style.*

1 Consider your content

The specific ideas or information you select to present in your writing will depend in part on your audience. Imagine that you are an interior designer commissioned to plan the redecoration of someone's living room and to estimate the work involved. Your reader will be expecting something akin to a proposal, not a poem or an editorial. The **content** of that proposal will probably assess the present design and its limitations; propose a redecorating plan with details about wallpaper, furniture, and lighting; and estimate the work involved and the expense of carrying it out. It would be inappropriate to include other kinds of information, such as instructions for hanging wallpaper (since your reader is hiring you to arrange this) or a description of your own living room (since your reader doesn't expect a comparative analysis).

2 Shape your structure

How you arrange and organize your ideas—your **structure**—will likewise depend on your audience. Imagine that you're an investment banker explaining to your clients that their stock has tumbled and their assets are now worth a fraction of the original value. You might want to lead up to your main point slowly, perhaps by explaining the circumstances of the loss first. Or imagine that you're writing an essay for a professor of philosophy who doesn't like unsupported generalizations. You can establish some points first to lessen the risk of the professor's marginal comment, "How do you know this?"

3 Adjust your style

How you think about your audience will influence the **style** of your writing. Anticipating the possible responses of your intended readers, you can decide how informal or formal your writing should be, how clinical or emotional, how friendly or hostile, how embracing or adversarial. For example, most anthropology teachers reading a final essay in their course will not accept sentences like "Leakey's stuff makes a lot of sense" or "Margaret's theories have been disproved" (when referring to Margaret Mead). Nor would you say, when asking a stranger where your bus is headed, "Whence goeth this too solid and unyielding monstrosity of yellow steel?"

Exercise 3

A. Susan Sisk, a college student, was driving to a party in the car her parents had bought her when she ran a red light and was struck by a pickup truck. She wasn't hurt, but her right rear door was dented. Sisk's insurance agent asked her to write a letter explaining the accident, and to attach three written estimates from auto repair services. She did so and then wrote a letter to her parents explaining what had happened. Here are the first few lines of each letter.

Dear Ms. Pellerino:

Thank you very much for your advice concerning my September 7 accident in my 1996 Toyota Camry, which is insured at Manassas Mutual. My policy number is HCR 5530 36. This is a family policy issued to Howard Sisk, and I am the primary driver of this car. I am attaching the three estimates for repairs, as you requested. I would appreciate it if you could mail the claim reimbursement directly to me since I intend to have the repairs done here in Tallahassee.

Dear Mom and Dad,

I feel like such an idiot! But the worst that could happen has. (Actually it could have been a lot worse, but I'm OK and everything is under control.) I know, I know, you're thinking, "Get to the point, Susan," and by now you've guessed the bad news. I had an accident in the Toyota.

Compare these excerpts from Sisk's letters on the basis of content, structure, and style. What features of Sisk's different readers might account for the differences in her two letters?

B. In a small group, compare your responses to Sisk's letters. Then share any situations in which you've written two letters about the same thing to different readers. How did your readers influence the content, structure, and style of each letter?

C. At the top of three pieces of paper in your planning notes, write the words *content, structure,* and *style.* Then, on the basis of the characteristics of your intended audience, make some tentative decisions about each of these aspects of your paper. What do you want to include and exclude? How will your arrangement affect your reader? What preliminary decisions about style can you make on the basis of your audience?

Did You Know?

Audiences from different countries can vary in what they consider desirable traits in writing. In one study, 84 percent of U.S. students and 75 percent of Finnish students preferred essays with a personal approach while only 60 percent of Australian students did so. In addition, Australian students and U.S. students tended to prefer simple language and sentences while Finnish students preferred language using metaphors and other figures of speech.

R. Elaine Degenhart and Sauli Takala, "Developing a Rating Method for Stylistic Preference: A Cross-Cultural Pilot Study," *Writing Across Languages and Cultures* (Newbury Park: Sage, 1988) 79–106.

6d Addressing academic readers

Although it may seem as though your academic audience is almost always a teacher, the college community provides a rich assortment of readers for your writing. A particular college or university consists of a loose confederation of scholars and teachers, students, administrators, and people serving in many public and private capacities. However, unless you're assigned to write for a specific, clearly defined reader, you can safely assume a "default" readership of your *teacher, self, peer group,* or *general academic readers.* In some circumstances, you may need to address or think of more than one of these readers, which complicates your task.

1 Writing for the teacher

A common first-day activity for most students is figuring out the teacher. Is she tough or undemanding, rigorous or relaxed? Does she expect flawless, highly polished papers, or is she more concerned with the messy, exploratory side of writing? Does she seem to welcome diverse views, even if they don't match her own?

As part of audience analysis, these questions are certainly reasonable; after all, you'll be spending ten or fifteen weeks in this class, and your teacher will regularly assess your work. Knowing what she's like may help. Guessing, however, may be less useful than getting concrete details.

Strategy

Always attend to the specific guidelines for a paper. If these are provided orally, write them down carefully. Reread all directions several times. Above all, *ask questions*. Teachers generally dislike being asked "What do you want in this paper?" because such a question is too broad and implies that the point is simply a "regurgitation" of learning. But most teachers are willing to elaborate on their expectations for a paper. Their answers often tell you what they are like as readers (and, perhaps more important, as evaluators of your writing).

2 Writing for yourself

Writing for yourself can help greatly in formulating or exploring new knowledge (in other words, in writing to *learn*). Your teacher knows full well that your paper summarizing early psychoanalytic readings of *Hamlet* may fall short of reflecting what he already knows about those readings, but being able to "outdo" the teacher isn't really the point. The teacher has asked you to look into something he already knows well just so that you can learn it. In reading your paper, your teacher isn't so much expecting you to tell him something new or brilliant as he is hoping that your paper will reflect your own learning in an intellectually rich and carefully organized way. If you end up informing him of something new, so much the better. But most of your writing will be written to an expert from the position of an apprentice.

Strategy

Ask yourself what the assignment is designed to do for *you*. What sort of learning is implied by its design? How can you maximize your own interest in the subject? What will *you* get from your efforts?

3 Writing for your peer group

Many writing classes today use **peer groups** as a way to encourage more diverse responses to your writing than you might get from your teacher alone. Peer groups can give you support during stages when you're uncertain about your writing, and they can provide valuable "test runs" to determine audience response after you've completed a rough draft. You can also ask a peer group to read *as if* they were a specific audience, testing how well you've achieved your purposes. (For more on peer groups during revision, see Chapter 8.)

Sometimes a writing assignment may call for you to write *for* your peers in the classroom, that is, to have as your primary audience the other members of your class. Because you know something about the group, you're not exactly writing for a generalized academic audience. But your teacher may ask you to write for your class precisely because it's a microcosm of the wider academic community. This situation involves all four of the audiences described in this section: yourself (as learner and intellectual explorer), your peers (as readers in your class), the general academic audience (as represented by your peers), and your teacher (who will gauge how effectively you've juggled all three of the others).

Strategy

During the planning stages of your writing, discuss your ideas with members of a peer group, and then ask them to role-play your intended audience.

---

4 Writing for the general academic audience

A rather murky and ill-defined audience, but one often alluded to in directions for or evaluations of writing assignments, is the general academic audience. Although it is difficult to define this audience very clearly, it usually refers to members of an academic or intellectual community—for example, most people in your college or university. Many teachers favor the undefined, general academic audience for classroom writing for the very reason that its members' opinions will vary widely—so your work will require more thought, hence, deeper learning.

Readers in the general academic community tend to be educated, well informed, and interested in the pursuit of knowledge (often for its own sake). They have incisive, critical minds; they like to be entertained with new and stimulating ideas; and they read more than the general public.

In reading your writing, teachers often allude to this generalized academic audience with statements like "How would the audience for this piece react to so radical a statement?" or "Are you sure you've considered the opposing views that your audience might raise here?" Such statements assume an audience of educated readers much like members of your college community. Teachers often read as one member of that setting, using their own reactions as representative of what a more general reaction might be.

►◄ Strategy

In your planning notes, circle any assertions or points that a reader in your academic community could challenge. Then brainstorm to develop several responses to the challenges. Are the challenges well reasoned—that is, would they seem outrageous to other members of your community? If not, consider acknowledging or incorporating them in your paper.

6e Forgetting about readers

Thinking carefully about your reader can lead to many important decisions for your writing. You might need to make substantial changes later on if you have not thought about who you're writing for. Sometimes, however, if you become too conscious of readers in the early stages of your writing, paralysis may set in. Tough-minded audiences can make you so self-conscious that hardly a line will emerge from your pen that you don't immediately scrutinize and send to the wastebasket. The result is frustration, procrastination, and anxiety.

Audience analysis is not something you do once, in planning your writing, and then put aside during the later stages. While drafting and revising, you will want to continue to think sharply about your reader. Once you've marked the general outlines in the clay, you can continue to define the features more sharply as you work your way toward finished sculpture.

Exercise 4

A. Pick a specialized magazine with which you are very familiar (such as *Road and Track, Bon Appétit, Runner's World,* and so on). Get a recent copy of the magazine and glance through it, noting the topics, lengths, and formats of its articles; its advertisements; its layout; and its writing style. Then, using the advice outlined in this chapter, select one method for analyzing the magazine's audience. If you can't answer a question definitively, make as educated a guess as possible, and state what further information you'd like to have.

B. Join a group of three or four other students. Briefly describe and compare your magazines, and then discuss your audience analyses. What issues surface about the relationship between the writing and the audience? What problems or questions about audience would you like to discuss? Jot these down.

CHAPTER

7

Drafting

Drafting means stringing words together into sentences and paragraphs that together will begin to make some sense to a reader. All the planning, purpose setting, and audience analysis you do for a piece of writing will prepare you to write. But don't be too optimistic, expecting to sit down and draft a smooth, coherent paper simply because you've accumulated a lot of material. The process of pulling your information together and *writing* will always be intellectually challenging. Nothing can change the fact that drafting is hard work.

When you write a **rough draft,** you try to create something that begins to resemble a fully elaborated text, tentative though it may be at first. If planning can be likened to thinking up the outline and script for a movie, then drafting means getting to work and actually filming it, always realizing that later on you may want to retake entire scenes, add new material, and let lots of footage fall to the cutting-room floor.

7a Moving from planning to drafting

Your use of various planning strategies, such as freewriting, listing, and drawing tree diagrams or clusters, should produce more than enough material to begin drafting. By the time you feel ready to write a first draft, you should be wondering how you'll get *so many* ideas into your paper, not how you'll ever be able to reach your required page length. The problem you face at this stage is knowing how and where to begin writing your draft. You need to assess what you have and start turning your material into sentences that make sense and move your ideas forward.

1 Draft in manageable parts

Outlines of various sorts (topic sequences, maps, tree diagrams, or clusters) do more than simply help you generate ideas. A good cluster, for example, will also show you relationships among connected ideas and ways you might think about organizing your paper.

The various parts of your outline or your planning materials will usually suggest some specific chunks of information that you can draft fairly efficiently in one sitting. A ten-page term paper on the increasing abuse of the elderly by younger family members may seem daunting, but a two-page section describing three specific cases of such abuse may seem far easier to tackle.

Strategy

Return to your planning notes and look for specific ideas that suggest paragraphs or sections of your paper. Then choose one idea and generate some material about it, either in draft form or in the form of lists, notes, or sentences.

In a cluster Amy Burns drew for her paper on superstition, one of the nodes branching from "cases of superstition" was "rabbit's foot." As she reviewed the cluster, she realized that she knew enough about the superstition of the rabbit's foot to write some ideas about it.

> A rabbit's foot—common lucky charm. Omen of good fortune. Brasch says thumping noise from hind paws = communication. Thought to possess magical powers. Newborns brushed with foot to chase evil spirits.

Burns's cluster gave her a way to organize the drafting process into a manageable task—a series of simple phrases. She could then expand these phrases and ideas into a full paragraph.

2 Develop a general structure

The kind of paper you're writing may determine the way you organize it. A narrative, for example, will probably be arranged *chronologically* (each event following the previous event in time); an argument may be organized *logically,* by paragraphs supporting some assertion. Whatever you're writing, you need to have in mind at least some sense of what should come first, second, and third in your paper.

Most academic writing will contain at least three parts: an **introduction,** a **body,** and a **conclusion.** This simple anatomy of your writing can help you to make some preliminary decisions about how to group your ideas.

Strategy

Look through the material you've generated from your planning activities. Although you probably won't use all this material, try to group specific ideas, topics, or terms into one of the three categories of introduction, body, and conclusion. Tentatively organizing your ideas in this way will help you to develop a stronger focus when you begin writing any part of your essay.

By thinking about this three-part organizing scheme, Amy Burns was able to generate some ideas for her paper on superstition and develop a preliminary structure.

INTRODUCTION   Fear; people who believe in superstitions; origins

BODY   Examples of superstitions (black cat, #13, crossing fingers, ladder, rabbit's foot)

CONCLUSION   Truth and falsity of superstitions; mystery surrounding them; concepts of reality

When she began drafting her paper, Burns used the ideas from this preliminary plan to write an introduction about how superstitions originate in a fear of the unknown.

Many people are superstitious, or at least practice some of the bizarre rituals of superstition, but very few know why or have thought about the reason. A lot of people practice superstitions without realizing that what they are doing is superstitious. The biggest percentage of people practice superstition because of a fear of the unknown. You might have heard some superstitions from parents or grandparents, been influenced by school or religion, or perhaps even read about them in books. However or wherever you heard of them, you practice superstitions because you are afraid of what will happen if you do not.

Although this first attempt underwent considerable revision, Burns could continue drafting because she had found a way and a place to start.

Writer's Tip: Using a Computer

If you use a computer, try opening separate files so that you can work on shorter parts of your paper, one section at a time. You can later cut and paste these separate files together into a single text, using block moves or file imports. Moving paragraphs or sections of your paper in this way can help you to see larger organizational possibilities.

3 Assess your purpose and redraft

Once you've drafted some material for your paper, you may want to stand back from it and think about whether it's achieving your general purposes for writing (persuading someone of a position, telling a story, explaining how to do something) or your more specific purposes for different parts of your paper (providing information, livening up a paragraph with an anecdote, illustrating a point with an extended example). These rhetorical purposes can help you assess your early material and begin refining your direction even before you've written a full draft.

Strategy

Read through the material you've drafted and assess whether it's accomplishing your general and specific purposes (see Chapter 5). Extend, cut, or redraft your early material to more adequately reflect your intended purposes.

In her paper on superstition, Burns did not generate a thesis but rather a broad purpose for her paper—to inform her readers about the nature of superstition and to encourage some enjoyable reflection. Her first specific purpose statement was "I want to grab my readers' attention and get them thinking about the nature of superstition." From this statement, she realized that her original introduction was informative but too dull. She drafted some new sentences and then followed them with her earlier material.

> Do you knock on wood after making a prediction? Shiver when a black cat crosses your path? Consider the number 13 unlucky? If so, then you have already been swept into the fantasy world of superstitions. Many people are superstitious, or at least practice some of the bizarre rituals of superstition, but very few know why or have thought about the reason.

Exercise 1

A. Thinking about all your own experiences as a writer, give some advice about drafting to an imaginary audience of high school students. Feel free to include personal experiences, tips, and specific techniques. You might, for example, give advice about the best times to write, how to get started, what to avoid, or how to handle difficult writing tasks.

B. Share your "advice papers" in a small group. Are any behaviors typical? Is any advice consistent?

C. Apply at least one of the Strategies discussed in 7a to your paper in progress. Then assess how useful the Strategy was in helping you to write a draft.

Did You Know?

The word *draft,* used in the sense of creating a preliminary form of a written document, comes from a word originally related to *draw*. A drafter is a professional drawer, planner, or sketcher—someone skilled in designing. When you draft a document, you're essentially being your own designer or sketcher, roughing out the basic ideas and contents, which you can later refine into an effective text. Many related senses of *draft* suggest a sort of drawing out, in which something is extracted or pulled out from a larger mass: cattle from a flock or herd, chips from a mason's stone, or, for that matter, ideas from a writer's head.

7b Using strategies for drafting

What makes drafting so challenging? Partly, it's the need to get a complicated job done, finding the right words for the ideas in your head while you're still figuring out where to begin. Partly, the challenge also comes from dealing with apprehensions, such as feeling the direction slipping away from you as you write, or looking back a few lines and thinking your writing isn't working, or perhaps finding that you're revising every sentence instead of moving quickly ahead.

The challenge of drafting can be made much less daunting if you practice some useful techniques for getting words down on the page.

1 Write about your writing

Worrying about your writing probably won't ever go away—even the best of the pros do it. Worrying yourself into avoidance or confusion, however, won't help you get your paper written.

A very common fear is the deadline. Strangely, many writers react to deadlines by putting off the writing until the specter of doom is practically breathing down their necks (often in the few late-night hours before the writing is due). For these procrastinators, just about any other task, even the most onerous, will take precedence over sitting down and actually starting to write. Because there isn't the time, *right now,* to finish an entire paper, smaller tasks (doing the dishes, feeding the cat) begin to beckon. This reaction is an excellent way to clean up your life, but it won't get your paper written.

Strategy

Begin drafting not by writing your paper but by writing *about* it. What's foremost in your mind about your paper? What do you hope to do with it? What possible ways might you start it? As you make notes to yourself, you'll soon find yourself a little less anxious about starting it—after all, you *have* started it. As your anxiety lessens, you'll find yourself more willing to take some risks and try out a few lines of a beginning.

2 Draft quickly

Another source of frustration during drafting comes from the struggle to find the right words for your ideas. Sometimes every sentence seems to tangle you in a mess of thoughts and contradictions, until you're no longer sure what you want to say. In this situation, you want to gain momentum, to feel that your ideas are smoothly giving way to words.

Strategy

Draft quickly. As you begin, don't worry too much about writing perfect sentences and paragraphs. Just aim to get as much material on paper as you can, right from the start. Writers often find that when they write quickly, they feel a momentum developing, a kind of "flow." A computer can encourage this momentum by helping you to write quickly without worrying about small details.

3 Semidraft

Writing a first full draft in one sitting, especially of a major paper, may be too ambitious, and you will need to divide the task into several drafting episodes. Some writers, however, can't seem to continue drafting anything for more than a few minutes before they stall out and want do something else. Stalling out happens when you can't come up with the words to describe a particular idea, often because you're tired or haven't thought very much about a point you write down in your draft.

> ## Did You Know?
>
> In a study of college students with serious writing problems, Mina Shaughnessy found that the more they worried about the correctness of their prose while writing, the more paralyzed they became and the less coherent their drafts turned out to be. "Some writers," Shaughnessy wrote, "inhibited by their fear of error, produce but a few lines an hour or keep trying to begin, crossing out one try after another until the sentence is hopelessly tangled."
>
> Mina P. Shaughnessy, *Errors and Expectations* (New York: Oxford UP, 1977) 7.

Strategy

Semidrafting refers to the process of writing full sentences until you feel you're about to stall out. At that point, you can simply write the word *etc.* in place of the full text and then continue into your next point. Or you can insert a brief direction to yourself in brackets, telling you what to do when you return to the draft to push that section a little further along.

In a paper on the histories of "wild children" (lost and raised by wolves or other animals in the woods), Kavita Kamal semidrafted the following paragraph.

> The first case to be examined was that of Victor, the "Wild Boy of Aveyron." Victor first appeared in a village in southern France in January 1800. His age was estimated to be about eleven or twelve years. [Explain how he was adopted by Jean-Marc Gaspard Itard and Madame Guerin; discuss their subsequent studies.] People assumed that he was a mute when they first dealt with him because he did not speak. Nor did he show any evidence of hearing. [Now go into the stuff from Roger Shattuck's *The Forbidden Experiment* on the fact that he had no malformation of the tongue, mouth, etc., then into Itard's paper in 1801 on Victor.] This selective deafness lasted until January of 1801, when Victor showed the first signs of hearing human voices.

Notice how Kamal suspends what may amount to several paragraphs or even pages while she pushes her draft forward into new areas. This gives her a sense of its form—a kind of flow—without forcing her to flesh out every detail. It's then far simpler to fill in the missing information than it would have been to return to the draft without knowing what points to make next.

Writer's Tip: Using a Computer

Although drafts may be expendable, they are also perishable. In these days of computer technology, power outages or damaged disks can spell the end of all your labor on a draft. *Always* make copies of files and disks if you use a computer. Also frequently save your file while drafting to avoid losing new material.

---

4 Talk it out or write to a friend

Sometimes nothing works. You simply can't, at that moment, put coherent sentences together on the page, and your frustration can cause you to lose interest in the project.

Writing is not like breathing, something you do as a matter of course. It's more like eating, which depends on your appetite. If you simply can't write, no matter how many techniques you try, then don't. Put off your writing until a little later. But don't just *put it off*. Set a time to return to the task, preferably on the same day, but no later than the same time the next day. In the meantime, try out these final Strategies to keep going.

Strategy

If you feel stuck, try talking about your writing project with someone you know well. Explain what you're trying to do. You may find that expressing your concerns helps to alleviate tension and may even show you some solutions. Your listener may also have ideas and suggestions to help you get started.

You might also try writing to a friend. Imagine the most sympathetic listener you can. Then tell him or her about the topic of your paper. You don't have to be flip or overly casual, but you may feel less intimidated if you pretend to write to an interested friend than if you imagine a critical reader looking over your shoulder as you write.

Exercise 2

A. Try out any one of the Strategies for drafting described in this chapter. Jot down some notes about how well it worked to get you started drafting and keep you moving forward.

B. Compare the results of your experiment in a small group. What worked? What didn't? How could you modify or add to the Strategy to make it work better for you? What other problems did you encounter as you drafted, and how might you solve them in the future?

7c draft

C. Put any of the Strategies in this chapter into actual practice, applying them in drafting your current paper.

7C Drafting: Paper in progress

After Rachel Ritchie listed possible examples to support her generalization about the effects of TV violence on children (see 4c), she decided to try freewriting for a few minutes on selected items in her list. Here is her freewriting passage on the item "Logan (boy I baby-sat for)—Power Rangers made him violent."

> *Most TV shows are incredibly violent. When I baby-sat for Logan he watched Power Rangers after school. I think this show has a definite effect on him. It's like he absorbs it. This is a 4-year-old boy that is already being exposed to violence by the TV set.*

Exercise 3

A. Examine Ritchie's freewriting. At this point, she had not yet written a full first draft of her paper, but she wanted to use some ideas in her freewriting as she planned her drafting. What advice would you give her about the ideas she has begun to explore here? What other details on the subject of Logan could she include in her rough draft? Is there anything in the freewriting that suggests a good place for this passage in her paper (beginning, middle, or end)?

B. In a small group, compare your responses to Exercise 3A. What did the members of your group agree could be profitably expanded from the freewriting as Ritchie drafts her paper? Was there any consensus in your group about where to place this section of the paper?

2

REVISING AND SHAPING YOUR WRITING

Revising

Because so much of what we read is in a final, published form, we often forget how much work went into its creation. Invisible to us are the hours the author spent revising—considering and reconsidering the content and structure of the writing, tearing out whole sections and redrafting them, honing and refining the paragraphs, polishing the style, and finding just the right words to express a thought.

The word **revision** means, literally, "seeing again" (*re* + *vision*). However, re-seeing can mean many different things to different people—a quick glance in passing; a short stare; a long, studied look; or a series of close inspections. Some people think that revision is **editing,** a fine tuning for style, grammar, and problems with sentences and wording. Others think that revision means **proofreading,** a final-stage of cleaning up typographical errors or a search for missing commas and apostrophes. People who view revision as editing or proofreading often write a rough draft in one sitting, then scan it quickly for any noticeable mistakes. Their first draft becomes, essentially, their last.

When accomplished writers use the word *revision,* they don't mean the sort of superficial changes implied in the old elementary school phrase "Copy it over in ink." Revision doesn't even mean writing your paper over again. It means *reading* your draft carefully in order to make principled, effective changes in the existing text. It means stepping outside the draft you've created; assessing its strengths and weaknesses as if you were a reader seeing it for the first time; and deciding what parts of the draft need to be expanded, clarified, elaborated, illustrated, reworded, restructured, modified—or just plain cut. The kind of work you do during the revision process takes concentration, determination, and, at times, a sort of ruthlessness with your prose that comes from knowing you can always find new and better words to express your ideas.

8a Making major revisions

When you begin revising your prose, you may be tempted to start tinkering with words and sentences—a process of minor revision. Try not to do this yet. Minor revisions are relatively specific, local changes that don't usually affect the overall purpose, organization, and content of your paper. Spending lots of time playing around with these smaller matters may be fruitless if later you decide to throw out the whole paragraph or section.

Instead, concentrate your first revision on more major concerns. A **major revision** is a large-scale, global change in your draft. For example, if you decide that the tone of your paper is too sarcastic, you may end up changing its introduction, deleting a negative paragraph, or adding several paragraphs exploring more sensibly a position you had earlier trivialized. Or if you've left out a major point, you may need to draft some new material and change your conclusion.

8a
revise

When you make major revisions, you'll perform at least four large-scale operations on your draft: *redrafting, reorganizing, adding,* and *deleting.* Each of these types of revision is illustrated on the following pages in Jessica White's narrative about cheerleading for her team during the state high school basketball championship. In each case, her revisions helped her to produce a more effective piece of writing.

1 Redraft unworkable material

When you read and reread your rough draft carefully, thinking critically about its content, structure, tone, style, appeals to audience, and purpose, some part of the draft may seem inappropriate, illogical, or unworkable. No matter how hard you try to salvage what you've written in such a section, the writing still doesn't seem to improve. In cases like these, you may find yourself **redrafting** the unmanageable part entirely.

Strategy

Read through your draft as if you were a reader seeing it for the first time. As you read, place a question mark next to any paragraph or section that seems confusing or garbled. When you're done, go back to each place where the writing seems to lose its vitality, sense, or style, and place an opening bracket there. Then move forward to the place where the writing picks up again, and add a closing bracket. Ask yourself just what it is that you're trying to accomplish in that section. Then take out a clean sheet of paper, and try to say it again. Don't even look back at your previous draft unless you think that some small part of it can be salvaged.

The first draft of Jessica White's introduction seemed to lie on the page like a corpse. She tried to give it life by changing a few words but finally realized that she was taking the wrong approach entirely, providing information instead of engaging her readers through a well-described scene. Here are the original and redrafted paragraphs.

ORIGINAL DRAFT

    I was a cheerleading captain and I loved basketball. I put a lot of work into my cheerleading season. We had a great team spirit between the cheerleaders and the teammates. We stood behind our team from the beginning to end. We led our crowd to great enthusiasm and spirit which I believe had a terrific effect on our team.

REVISED DRAFT

    There we were, a bunch of cheerleaders packed into Rebecca's car. Everyone's spirits were soaring; we had won the quarter-final game of the state basketball championship. It was a bitterly cold night, but none of us felt the chill. Surrounded by blaring music, we laughed, joked, and endlessly replayed the highlights of the game. Talk then turned to the upcoming finals. Would the team keep up its level of intensity? What were our chances of winning? What would we do if we lost?

Note the differences in style and content of these two versions. When White shared her first draft with some classmates, they felt that the first paragraph didn't capture much tension and excitement. She simply discarded her first paragraph and rewrote it. Although she continued to work on her introduction, this first revision helped her to begin engaging her readers.

2 Reorganize poorly arranged paragraphs or sections

Structural problems are also common in early drafts. Maybe something you've said later in the draft would fit better earlier on, or vice versa. Often you find that you've written your way "into" your main point, discovering what you want to say in the process of drafting. It may be more graceful or logical to move that later material right up front, into your introduction. Or you may recognize that two different paragraphs or sections are making the same point and should be consolidated.

Strategy

Number each paragraph in your draft. Then, on a clean piece of paper, explain in a phrase or a single sentence what each numbered paragraph says—its main point. When you've finished, look back at your list of statements. Could any paragraphs be consolidated? Are any paragraphs ineffectively ordered? Could you arrange the paragraphs or parts of the paper to yield a clearer, smoother flow of ideas?

After White labeled the paragraphs of her draft, she noticed that two of them seemed chronologically mixed up. The first was supposed to describe the rising tension and excitement just seconds before the end of the final game, but parts of it referred to the game as a whole. The other paragraph was supposed to describe the moment of victory, but the earlier paragraph seemed to dull the effect. (White's revision statements follow each paragraph.)

8a
revise

FIRST DRAFT

The crowd was just psyched. We, the cheerleaders, were going to give our team as much support as possible. Constant cheering and yelling came from the fans. I remember looking up into the stands and seeing hundreds of faces painted orange and black. Nobody sat during the entire game. We had twice as many fans as our opponents in all the games of the tournament.

This paragraph describes the very end of the game, but it also refers to the entire game.

"Five, four, three, two, one!" The crowd roared! It had happened—the Smithtown Orioles Basketball Team won the state championship! We were number one. The road had been a long one with a lot of hard work and dedication. But all of our efforts had finally paid off.

This paragraph describes the moment of victory.

In her restructuring, White consolidated her two paragraphs into a single paragraph that captured both the crowd's enthusiasm and the excitement of the game's final moments. Some of her dull statements disappeared, yielding a description that more artfully reflected the moment.

REVISED VERSION

"Five, four, three, two, one!" The crowd roared. It had happened—the Smithtown Orioles Basketball Team won the state championship! We were number one. The stands were a sea of orange and black waves as the fans screamed their support for the team, knowing how much hard work and dedication had gone into this victory.

3 Add new material

Because you may write your first draft quickly, just to get it down on the page, you may find various places where something is missing. Added material can enliven a dull description, clarify or extend a point, or provide

---

Writer's Tip: Using a Computer

If you use a computer, make a backup copy of your early draft so you can keep an original version. Open the copy, and experiment with broad, global revisions. You can, for example, mark, cut, and move large chunks of your writing to see how major organizational changes might work. Any sections you cut can be pasted into an auxiliary file so that you can still recover them if your cuts were too drastic.

8a
revise

essential information that your readers will need in order to make sense of your ideas.

Strategy

As you reread your paper, look at how your sentences and paragraphs relate to each other. Mark any cases when a paragraph doesn't connect clearly enough to the one before it. Also note any gaps (in information or detail) within and between paragraphs. Try making a detailing list if you need to add information to your draft (see 4a-4).

In this excerpt, White added some material to her second draft.

All of a sudden we weren't rookies anymore. The Smithtown Basketball Team had been rated number two in the state before the season even began. **The year before, we had been fourth-place finishers, but now three of our best players were returning starters and the other two players had started in half the previous year's games.** Good things were expected from our players this year and everyone felt it. **And here it was the first weekend of the regional tournament.**

White made these additions to clarify just why the team was ranked highly at the start of the season, information that helped to explain the expectations the coaches, players, and fans had for the year.

4 Delete unnecessary or redundant material

Too much prose can be just as distracting or frustrating to a reader as too little. But cutting can be hard. You've invested time and energy producing sentences and paragraphs, and once they're on the page they seem almost sacred. Don't be afraid to slash away large portions of your draft if it's clear that they're unnecessary, distracting, illogical, or redundant. Treat them like so many weeds crowding out the real splendor of the garden, and use the sharpest shears you can find.

Strategy

Reread your draft as if an editor has accepted it for publication in a magazine with the stipulation that you trim at least ten percent of the fat. What can you cut? Could some paragraphs be eliminated altogether, perhaps by merging just the essential material from them into another paragraph?

In another part of her draft, White decided to cut several sentences because they didn't add anything useful or descriptive.

**8a
revise**

> Once we were inside the arena it all started to seem real. For the next half hour the place was a hayday. ~~Everyone seemed so excited, just bubbling over with anticipation of the game. It was great. I had never seen such excitement and confusion.~~ People tried to squeeze into their right school section and then fought for the best seats, spilling popcorn on each other. Cheerleaders ran around trying to figure out where they were going to stand. Occasional chants were already coming from various corners of the arena. ~~I was so impressed with the whole scene. It's almost difficult to describe what we were feeling.~~

Note that White is not yet focusing *deliberately* on details of style and usage, even though such matters may be revised in passing. She doesn't change the word *heyday,* for example, which is both misspelled and used incorrectly. Later, if that sentence even survives her larger revisions, she will need to check the dictionary definition of *heyday* to see whether this is the best word she can use to describe the atmosphere in the arena. Right now, she has larger concerns to worry about.

Exercise 1

A. Compare the following first-draft and revised versions of Maureen Lagasse's paper on racism. Describe the nature of Lagasse's changes— did she redraft, reorganize, add, or cut? What do you think motivated her revisions?

FIRST DRAFT

In setting out to write this paper my concept to explain was racism, and in doing some reading and thinking, I realized that racism can't be defined or explained in one simple definition. In the dictionary the definition of racism is "the practice of racial discrimination, segregation, etc." Although this is what racism is, this definition doesn't fully explain racism. What exactly are races, and how do people actually develop these discriminations against people of different races?

REVISED DRAFT

Have you ever wondered why people view interracial relationships as unacceptable? Have you wondered if there really is a difference between you and someone of another race? In the dictionary the definition of racism is "the practice of racial discrimination or segregation." Although this is a legitimate definition, it doesn't fully explain racism.

**8b
revise**

B. In a small group, compare your responses to Exercise 1A. Were there any revisions you didn't notice? What other major revisions might you suggest for Lagasse's first paragraph?

C. Apply all four Strategies for major revision to your draft in progress. Then analyze what you decided to change and why. How much needed redrafting? Reorganizing? Adding? Cutting?

Did You Know?

In a study of skilled versus unskilled writers, the skilled writers spent more of their time in various kinds of revision than the unskilled writers, who tended not to look back over their drafts when they had finished writing them. This suggests that, contrary to popular myths about writing, better writers spend *more* of their time, not less, revising.

Nancy Sommers, "Revision Strategies of Student Writers and Experienced Writers," *College Composition and Communication* 31 (1980): 378–88.

8b   Making minor revisions

Minor revisions are fairly small changes, mostly in the individual sentences of your prose. Here you're not rebuilding the entire structure of your text; you're scraping and repainting the siding. You will usually do this work on a *later* draft—not the first attempt (which will need a good deal more than a new color on the shutters and trim).

Like major revisions, minor revisions involve redrafting, reorganizing, adding, and cutting, but now at a more specific level. You're no longer asking questions about the direction, organization, or main thrust of your paper. Instead, you're refining and polishing. Most of the time, you'll make minor revisions for three reasons: *sense* (how clear and understandable is your prose?), *style* (how elegantly and smoothly does your prose read?), and *economy* (how much can you say in the least space?). Paul Tichey's paper on the environmentally threatened wild mustangs of Nevada illustrates these three types of minor revision.

1 Revise for sense

Too full an immersion in your writing can sometimes make you forget what your reader *doesn't* know or think, and that can lead to illogical, contradictory, or puzzling statements.

**8b
revise**

────▶◀────
Strategy

Read each sentence of your paper individually and test its clarity: Does the statement *make sense* in the context of the paper? Don't let your mind float back into your own construction of ideas; instead, imagine yourself as your intended reader. If you have peer readers, ask them to place question marks next to any statement or group of statements they find confusing or garbled.
────▶◀────

The following three sentences in Tichey's second draft struck several of his peer readers as somewhat confusing.

SECOND DRAFT

The Air Force was partly responsible for the reduction in the number of wild mustangs on the Tonopah missile range. The Air Force is part of a team that also includes the Bureau of Land Management and a group of wild-horse preservationists. All three groups have banded together to help the wild mustangs in this period of drought and dehydration.

In these sentences, it's unclear whether the Air Force is helping or harming the wild mustangs. Tichey recognized this problem and made the following minor revisions for clarity.

REVISED VERSION

The Air Force , which was partly responsible for the ~~reduction in the~~ demise
the
~~number~~ of wild mustangs on the Tonopah missile range. ~~The Air~~ has now
joined forces with
~~Force is part of a team that also includes~~ the Bureau of Land

Management and a group of wild-horse preservationists. ~~All three~~
~~groups have banded together~~ to help the ~~wild~~ mustangs ~~in this period~~ ^save^ ^from dehydration^
~~and death during the duration~~ of the ~~drought~~o
~~of drought and dehydration.~~ ^and death during the duration of the^ ^drought~~to~~^

2 Revise for style

When you revise for style, you're concerned with the way your prose
"sounds"—that is, with its rhythm, complexity, and diction or word choice
(see 12b, 12c, 27b, and 27c). When you read a rough draft, some parts will
usually sound better to you than others. Use your intuition as a reader.

8b
revise

Strategy

Place an asterisk next to any paragraph of your paper that strikes you
as less than polished. Then go back and place a +, ✓, –, or ? next to specific sentences within these marked paragraphs to indicate whether you feel
positive, neutral, or negative, or aren't sure about it. Concentrate first on
the sentences you don't like; chances are your reader won't like them either.
When you get to the questionable ones, try rephrasing them or choosing
different words. If you're still uncertain, ask one or more readers to give
you their impression. *When in doubt, try an alternative.*

Tichey placed an asterisk next to the same paragraph he had already
revised for sense. Something still bothered him about the paragraph, but
he wasn't able to identify it until he could look carefully at each sentence
in it. Finally he placed a minus sign next to the following sentence in the paragraph.

SECOND DRAFT

The Air Force, which was partly responsible for the demise of
the wild mustangs on the Tonopah missile range, has now joined
forces with the Bureau of Land Management and a group of wild-
horse preservationists to help save the mustangs from dehydration
and death during the duration of the drought.

Tichey liked the clarity of his revision, but the end of his new sentence
seemed awkward because so many words began with a *d* ("dehydration and
death during the duration of the drought"). He also thought that "during
the duration" seemed redundant. Here's his further revision.

THIRD DRAFT

The Air Force, which was partly responsible for the demise of
the wild mustangs on the Tonopah missile range, has now joined

forces with the Bureau of Land Management and a group of wild-horse preservationists to help save the mustangs from **fatal** dehydration ~~and death during the duration of the drought.~~**while the drought persists.**

3 Revise for economy

Human thinking involves a great deal of inference. In a given passage of text, much more is usually left out than included. To revise for economy, read your writing and think about what you can cut from it *without causing it to lose sense or coherence.* Cut away the deadwood. Economize. Make your writing lean.

In the middle of Tichey's paper, one of the paragraphs included too much material. He decided that half of it could be painlessly cut.

8b
revise

SECOND DRAFT

A serious problem confronting groups who want to manage wild mustangs on military sites in Nevada is the relative inaccessibility of the sites, since many require security passes or are fenced off, and environmentalists can't come and go as they please, as they can on public or even some private land. It's simply harder to study or help horses on restricted military installations. Open rangeland has easier access, and inspectors can simply move in and out at will.

THIRD DRAFT

Restricted access to Nevada military sites presents a serious obstacle to successful horse management. In contrast to open rangeland, where inspectors can come and go as they please, military sites are often fenced off and require security clearance.

In the revised paragraph, Tichey said essentially the same thing in 38 words that he had said before in 78—a cut of over 50 percent! Note, however, that he had to reword the sentences remaining after his first cuts.

Exercise 2

A. Examine the following paragraphs from Anita Jackson's paper on Buddhism. Then characterize the sorts of minor revisions Jackson made in the paper. Did she revise for sense, style, or economy? What sorts of changes did she make?

EARLY DRAFT

The man who became the first Buddha was named Siddhartha. Siddhartha was a prince in northern India who lived in a large palace. His father didn't allow him outside the palace, because he wanted to spare Siddhartha from the miseries of the world.

Siddhartha became curious and one day he went riding outside the palace. What he saw would forever change his life and influence the lives of many thereafter. That which Siddhartha saw has since been named the Four Sights.

REVISED DRAFT

The man who became the first Buddha was Siddhartha, a pampered prince of northern India who lived in a lavish palace. Yet for all his riches his father would not allow him to venture beyond the castle walls because he wanted to spare Siddhartha the miseries of life. Siddhartha grew extremely curious about the outside world and one day went riding beyond the limits of the palace. What he saw that day would forever change his life and influence the lives of many thereafter.

What Siddhartha saw has since been named the Four Sights. . . .

B. In a small group, compare your analyses of Jackson's revisions. How successful were her changes? Why?

C. Apply the three techniques for minor revision to your paper in progress. Then analyze your changes. How much did these methods help you to improve your earlier draft?

8c Using feedback constructively

We tend to think of writing as a solitary activity, done in the cloistered privacy of a study or dorm room. *Collaboration* sounds to many people like cheating. But professional writers rarely produce a good piece of writing without getting responses from many readers along the way, especially after they've written a rough draft.

Whether or not you have opportunities in your classroom to work with other students on your writing, *make sure to ask at least one other person you respect to read your papers and give you some honest feedback, and promise you'll do the same in return.* Here are a few tips for getting and giving helpful feedback in **collaborative revision.**

1 Respond helpfully

When you're reading someone else's writing in order to offer constructive criticism, remember that your most helpful role is not as proofreader or editor but as real, warm-blooded *reader.* But because you may not be a part of the intended audience for your partner's work, you need to get some background information before you start.

- Find out the writer's purpose for the piece. What is the writer trying to accomplish? What sort of paper is this?
- Who is the writer's intended reader?
- What are the writer's main concerns at this point? What would the writer most like to find out from you?

Once you have reasonable answers to these questions, read the paper through, jotting down some comments in the margins and keeping track of your thoughts and impressions as a reader.

When you convey your responses to your partner, remember that you'll need to balance praise with helpful criticism. Don't simply say, "I liked it. It was really good." But don't come out with a list of spelling errors, either. You're not a proofreader; you're a reader. The writer will take your response into account when revising. If you feel compelled to offer some advice, do so tentatively and diplomatically. Don't say, "You should move this paragraph up to page 3," but rather ask, "What would happen if you moved this paragraph?" or suggest, "I wonder whether that paragraph would fit better on page 3."

8c
collab

2 Make the most of response

The suggestions in 8c-1 for giving feedback should work in reverse for receiving it. You're not out to collect a dozen pats on the back for a job well done; you want the most useful, constructive commentary you can get from astute, honest readers. This will mean accepting even hard-hitting reactions and suggestions with grace and diplomacy. If you react defensively to a peer reader's criticism of your description of your grandmother, that person is not likely to keep giving you much feedback. If a reader questions something you especially like in your draft, *remember that no one can force you to make a change.* All that people can do is tell you how they feel. You have the final say.

Take note of these tips.

- Give your readers a list of specific concerns you have about your draft. What do you want them to comment on? Tone? Style? Structure? Logic?
- Keep your apologies to a minimum. You may feel anxious about sharing a first draft with your classmates, but as writers you're all facing the same situation.
- If you and your group members are short on time, consider giving them each an inexpensive cassette tape for their reactions. You'll get far more response than if you ask for something in writing. A group meeting, of course, is always preferable. If all of you are working on papers at the same time, forming a writer's group and spending time on each of your drafts can be an especially valuable experience.

- Using your readers' responses, *spend some time planning your changes.* If no one liked the description of your grandmother, do you want to change it? If so, how? Do you want to delete it completely, or find another way to describe her, or show what she's like by portraying her more completely in the action of your narrative? A few minutes planning your revisions may save you lots of time experimenting.

Exercise 3

A. If you haven't done so, form a small revision group, and circulate rough drafts of your papers in progress. Using the tips in this section as well as the techniques for major and minor revision described in 8a and 8b, comment on your partners' drafts. Then meet in a revision group to discuss your drafts. Keep track of the group's comments on your own paper.

B. Analyze your group experience. What was helpful? What comments will lead (or have led) to specific revisions? What comments did you choose not to act on? Why?

8d
revise

8d Revising: Paper in progress

After freewriting several paragraphs about items on her list of particulars, Rachel Ritchie was prepared to write the following rough draft of her generalization paper.

First Draft of Violence Paper

Rachel Ritchie

Every night while watching the television or reading the newspaper, I see the rise in violence, a drive-by shooting one night, a kid killing another kid the next. As the amount of violence on TV goes up so does the amount of violence around us. The amount of violence involving kids around us has sharply risen.

More kids are being able to buy guns' and more are bringing them to school. Only last year did an 11-year-old 6th grader in my hometown bring a loaded rifle to school and threatened to shoot the principal, because he was given a night of detention. What was going through his mind? I only wish I knew so I could understand his logic.

Every night there are television shows about gangs, killings and crimes. And now we see all these stories on the news too!

Not long ago, a twelve year old boy strangled a 3-year-old in the woods near there houses. A similar occurence happened a few months earlier when two boys in England kiddnapped a boy from a shopping mall and killed him. These are young kids killing babies. These killers are not even teenagers yet They haven't even started high school.

8d
revise

Some of the most popular television shows are police shows, which in the end the "bad guys" are caught and sent to jail, but the violence is incredible. Gangs fighting gangs and drive-by shootings are often topics on these types of shows. The television producers exaggerate the violence while trying to make it realistic.

A friend of mine lived in Los Angelos for a year and witnessed a drive-by shooting. She told me she remembered seeing the gun and hearing shots. She got up and ran. After her adrenalen rush was over, she realized her knee was burning. She looked down and saw blood, she had been shot. A bullet went right through her knee. Now she has a hole in her knee cap and scars from surgery.

Another friend of mine who grew up in Chicago was in a gang. Her parents sent her to live with her brother in Maine because they were afraid she would be killed. A few of her friends had been killed by rival gangs and her boyfriend had been killed by a police officer while fleeing a crime scene.

Not all violent shows are geared for older kids. Afternoon cartoons are violent too! One of the most popular is the Power Rangers, the title tells all. A little boy I baby-sat for watches it religiously. After the show is over he runs around the house with play swords, kicking things and sometimes people while yelling, "I'm the red ranger!." This is a four-year-old boy that is already being exposed to violence by the television and reacting to it.

8d
revise

The growth in gun sales is horrible too! And the more guns on the street, the more planned killings and the more accidental shootings occur. Last television season, Beverly Hills 90210 had a show where a friend of the group was cleaning a gun and accidentally killed himself. This type of violence on television is good. It showed what accidents can and does happen when people mess around with guns.

So the next time you watch the news or read a newspaper, take notice of the amount of violence in the world. Then watch television and figure out where all the ideas come from. Then look at the kids around you and wonder where their ideas are coming from.

Exercise 4

A. Study Ritchie's first draft. (You may wish to look back at her planning list in 4c.) Assuming that Ritchie drafted with a loose structure in mind, how would you describe that structure? What is your impression of the draft as a whole, and what suggestions would you make for its organization and its supporting points relative to the main generalization that TV violence affects children?

B. In a small group, compare your analyses of Ritchie's first draft, and try to reach some consensus about what she should focus on in her revision.

8d
revise

CHAPTER 9

Effective Paragraphs: Focusing and Linking Ideas

Every time you indent to begin a new **paragraph,** you give readers a signal: Watch for a shift in topic, a different perspective, or a special emphasis. In this way, skillful paragraphing can guide readers through the parts of an essay while focusing attention on specific ideas and details.

To create an effective paragraph, you need to call attention to its topic or perspective, giving it focus (unity) as you write and revise. You also need to create coherence, linking sentences and ideas in ways that make their relationships clear. (Your paragraph also needs adequate development of details and ideas, a process discussed in Chapter 10.)

If you fail to provide focus and coherence in a paragraph, readers may find it hard to identify your topic or main point and may have difficulty following your line of reasoning, as in this example.

LACKING FOCUS AND COHERENCE

The caffeine in popular beverages comes from natural sources: coffee beans (coffee), coca leaves (hot chocolate), tea leaves (tea), evergreen leaves (maté), and kola nuts (colas). Tea comes from the leaves of bushes native to Asia. Maté comes from a South American shrub similar to holly. More caffeine is found in coffee or tea than in maté. Tea and maté are made in similar ways except that the water for maté is heated in a gourd. People often drink the beverage through a straw stuck into the gourd. In Paraguay, Argentina, Chile, and the southern regions of Brazil, many people find refreshment in a maté-filled gourd.
READER'S RESPONSE: What is the topic of this paragraph: Tea and coffee? Caffeine? Caffeinated beverages? Maté? Every time one sentence focuses on a topic, the next sentence suddenly changes direction.

Even paragraphs that are focused, coherent, and effective do not stand alone. They need to be linked into clusters that support an essay's purpose.

By making the relationship among paragraphs clear, you can help readers keep track of a line of argument or the logic of an explanation.

9a Focusing paragraphs

By making a paragraph's topic, main idea, or perspective evident and by maintaining this focus throughout, you can create a paragraph that is focused or unified. A **focused paragraph** is effective because it does not confuse or mislead readers by straying into unrelated or loosely related details and statements. A **unified paragraph** is one in which all the sentences are clearly and directly related to the main idea, as in the following selection.

> Values are changing, too. Solid majorities of both women *and* men now believe that when a woman works for pay, household responsibilities should be shared. The idea that a woman's hours of employment are irrelevant for the distribution of household work no longer holds the power it once did. Of course, old habits die hard and many men who "believe" in sharing housework are not actually willing to take on much of this often-unrewarding work. Twenty-four percent of employed wives are still saddled with *all* the household work, and an additional 42 percent do "the bulk" of it. However, things are improving, especially among young people. It is likely that the future holds more, not less, household equality.
>
> — JULIET SCHOR, *The Overworked American*

Schor unifies this paragraph by making sure all its parts develop and support the main idea: people are beginning to view housework as a responsibility shared by women and men. The opening two sentences introduce the topic and main idea while giving some evidence of the change in attitudes. The third sentence provides a more precise definition of the values in question while suggesting that the transformation is by no means complete. The fourth and fifth sentences explore current resistance to change, and the last two sentences look to a future in which shared responsibility for housework will increase—a future that the writer endorses by saying that "things are improving."

1 Recognizing unfocused paragraphs

Many paragraphs do not start out tightly focused, even in the hands of experienced writers. For example, as you concentrate on presenting detailed information, you may temporarily lose sight of a paragraph's main point. Or you may become intrigued by the fresh insights that emerge during drafting and then create unfocused paragraphs that pull your readers in more than one direction.

Strategy

Use the following questions to help identify unfocused paragraphs and to guide your revisions.

- What is my main point (or topic) in this paragraph?

  For a paragraph lacking a central theme, decide on a focus.

- How many different topics does this paragraph cover?

  For a paragraph with many possible centers of interest, decide which one you will emphasize.

- Have I announced my focus to readers? Where? How?

  Look for sentences or phrases announcing the focus or clearly implying it. Add such statements if necessary.

- Do statements in the paragraph elaborate on the main idea? Do details fit within the topic?

  Look for material not directly related to a paragraph's focus, and decide whether it undermines the unity or adds interesting variety.

Here is how one college student, Jeanne Brown, used such questions to analyze an unfocused paragraph.

UNFOCUSED

Another color to look at is the color red. Red is often considered a very fast and sporty color when used for cars. Porsches that are red are likely to be chosen over blue ones. Red ties are often called "power ties." Red can also be considered a very daring color to wear. A woman who wears a long red dress and has painted fingernails to match is not a shy woman. She is going to be noticed and will revel in the attention.

- My topic and my main point?

  I want to talk about the strong effects red can have on people. I don't think that the focus on red's power or its possible effects is clear now.

- Main point announced to readers?

  Not really. I need to say that the color affects people who wear or own something red and that it attracts attention.

- Statements elaborate on main idea?

  No, not very well. I need to help readers understand how each example explains my view of red's effect on moods and attitudes.

In revising, Brown gave the paragraph a specific focus and unified it around the main idea.

REVISED

　　Red is another color that can affect how people feel and react. Red makes heads turn, and the person associated with the color often ends up feeling important and influential. A red Porsche draws more attention than a blue one. A red tie, or "power tie," can be bold and assertive. Worn with a blue or gray suit, the touch of red makes the wearer stand out in a crowd and helps build self-confidence. A woman wearing a long red dress with nails painted to match is probably not shy. She is going to be noticed and will revel in the attention because it will reinforce her positive self-image.

9a
¶ foc

Exercise 1

A. Revise the unfocused paragraph presented at the beginning of this chapter (p. 94) to create focus and appropriate emphasis on ideas and supporting evidence. Combine sentences, cut irrelevant information, or draw on your own knowledge for specifics that contribute to the paragraph's focus and effectiveness.

B. Working in a group, draw on the different versions group members wrote for Exercise 1A, and create *either* a single version of the paragraph, representing agreement on the best way to revise, or two versions, providing different patterns of emphasis. Be ready to explain how the two versions differ.

C. Exchange essays with another writer, and select one paragraph from your partner's work that might benefit from revision. Suggest to the writer three ways in which he or she might improve the focus, emphasis, and clarity of the paragraph.

2 Using topic sentences

　　One way to help your readers recognize a paragraph's focus is to state your topic and your main idea or perspective in a single sentence, a **topic sentence.**

The mambo, the samba, and the tango combine dance steps and music in ways that please both dancers and observers.
Sentence introduces paragraph topic and main idea.

From an environmental perspective, however, the project poses several difficult engineering problems.
Sentence highlights a new and contrasting stage in the argument.

By the next morning, we felt accustomed to the thin air of the high altitude and began surveying the challenges of the glacier-filled valley that was the next step in our climb.
Sentence indicates changes in time and place.

As you write, you can use a topic sentence as the focal point for the other sentences in a paragraph. When you revise, you can often easily improve an unfocused paragraph by adding a topic sentence, placing it in an effective position in the paragraph.

Topic Sentence at Beginning.   When you want readers to grasp the point of a paragraph right away, state it in a topic sentence at the beginning. In the following paragraph, the author uses the topic-sentence-first strategy to comment on life in rural New England during the Great Depression.

9a
¶ foc

Topic
sentence

Supporting
examples

Most families carried their thrift to great extremes and often deposited quantities of dilapidated items in their sheds and lofts, hoping that someone would find a use for them. Our shed chamber, as the attic was called, contained large boxes of completely worn-out shoes and mismatched gloves full of holes. Several barrels of dry corncobs stood in one corner to be used for smoking meat, although we might use only eight or ten cobs each year. Neatly spaced were boxes of hopelessly rusted nails, rotten leather harness straps, broken window glass, and many pieces of heavy string that were too short or too far gone for any possible uses.
— LEWIS HILL, "Waste Not, Want Not"

Topic Sentence Plus Limiting or Clarifying Sentence.   If you are covering a broad topic or offering much detailed information, you can give a paragraph a sharper focus by creating a **limiting** or **clarifying sentence** (or two) following the topic sentence. The added sentence tells readers which specific aspects of the topic you will discuss or clarifies your point of view.

Topic sentence

Limiting or
clarifying
sentence

Children on soap operas are secondary. Because they serve largely as foils for the adult characters, their development does not follow the slow, steady pattern of the rest of the action. Their growth is marked by a series of sudden and unsettling metamorphoses as new and older juvenile actors assume the role. On Tuesday, little Terence is cooing in his cradle. On Monday next, he is the terror of the Little League. By Thursday, his voice begins to change. Friday night is his first date. He wakes up on Monday a drug-crazed teenager, ready to be put to use creating heartbreak and grief for his devoted mother and her new husband. He stays fifteen years old for about two to five years (more if he managed to get into lots of scrapes), and then one day he again emerges from the off-camera cocoon transformed into a full-fledged adult, with all the rights, privileges, pain, and perfidy of that elite corps. And so the cycle continues.

— Donna Woolfolk Cross, *Sin, Suffer, and Repent*

Topic Sentence at End. If you place your topic sentence at the end of a paragraph, it can summarize or draw conclusions from the information that comes before. This strategy can show how your perspective grows logically from the evidence, and it can tie together details with a forceful generalization.

Here is an example from my own experience, a story that I blush to recount. A few years ago, at an international conference held in an exotic and luxurious setting, a prestigious professor invited me to his room for what he said would be an intellectual discussion on matters of theoretical importance. So far, so good. I showed up promptly. But only minutes into the conversation—held in all-too-adjacent chairs—it emerged that he was interested in something more substantial than a meeting of minds. I was disgusted, but not enough to overcome 30-odd years of programming in ladylikeness. Every time his comments took a lecherous turn, I chattered distractingly; every time his hand found its way to my knee, I returned it as if it were something he had misplaced. This went on for an unconscionable period (as much as 20 minutes); then there was a minor scuffle, a dash for the door, and I was out—with nothing violated but **Topic sentence** my self-esteem. I, a full-grown feminist, conversant with such matters as rape crisis counseling and sexual harassment at the workplace, had behaved like a ninny—or, as I now understand it, like a lady.

— Barbara Ehrenreich, "What I've Learned from Men"

Topic Sentences at Beginning and End. You can "frame" the information in a paragraph by opening with one topic sentence and closing with another offering a somewhat different perspective. For instance, you might move from a problem to a solution or from a generalization to its extension or modification, as in this example.

Topic sentence Men and women speak different languages of love, but in psychotherapy, research, and popular lore, the female language has become the dominant one. Women appear to be better than men at intimacy because intimacy is defined as what women do: talk, express feelings, and disclose personal concerns. Intimacy is rarely defined as sharing activities, being helpful, doing useful work, or enjoying companionable silence. Because of this bias, men rarely get credit for the kinds of loving actions that are more typical of them.

Topic sentence

— CAROL TAVRIS, *The Mismeasure of Woman*

9a
¶ foc

Did You Know?

In English, readers expect paragraphs to have a specific focus, and we often look to a topic sentence for guidance. In other languages, however, paragraph conventions can take quite different forms. For example, Hindi paragraphs need not focus on a sharply defined topic; they do not require a clear topic sentence; and they often contain discussion of loosely related ideas or information. Paragraphs in other languages, such as Thai, also differ from English paragraphs. Consequently, learning to write in a second language involves becoming familiar with paragraph conventions.

Robert Bickner and Patcharin Peyasantiwong, "Cultural Variation in Reflective Writing," and Yamuna Kachru, "Writers in Hindi and English," *Writing Across Languages and Cultures,* ed. Alan C. Purves (Newbury Park: Sage, 1988) 160–74, 109–37.

Topic Sentence Implied Rather Than Stated. At times a paragraph's content may make the main point so clearly that you do not need to restate it in a topic sentence. Instead, you can rely on readers to recognize an implied topic sentence. This strategy is useful when you wish to divide a long paragraph for easier reading, knowing that readers will easily see that the topic sentence in your first paragraph continues to apply to your second. It is also useful when an explicit topic sentence might distract from examples and details.

Whenever we went to my grandfather's house, he would lead the three of us to the closet stocked with toys, saying "I bought these especially for you" as his crystal blue eyes twinkled. I can remember playing with the toys outside on the lawn and running through the sprinkler he set up for me and my brothers on sunny days. Just when we started getting tired and hot, he would call us in for a lunch of hot dogs or tuna sandwiches with plenty of potato chips and soda pop. And there were always popsicles for dessert.

— CAREY BRAUN, College Student

READER'S RESPONSE: Your grandfather seems like a person who understands children and knows how to make them feel cared for and loved.

Writer's Tip

In an essay with effective topic sentences, you can often trace the explanation or argument quickly by scanning paragraphs and reading just the topic sentences. This works best when the majority of topic sentences begin paragraphs. You can also look at your own draft essays this way to check for paragraphs with missing, misleading, or inadequate topic sentences. When you find such paragraphs, decide whether they also need revision for focus. In addition, this is a good way to identify paragraphs that take the discussion in misleading or irrelevant directions.

9a
¶ foc

Exercise 2

A. Identify any topic sentences and clarifying or limiting sentences in the following paragraphs. Analyze how the paragraphs make use of these sentences to create focus and emphasis.

Kids are in the mall not only in the passive role of shoppers—they also work there, especially as fast-food outlets infiltrate the mall's enclosure. There they learn how to hold a job and take responsibility, but still within the same value context. When *CBS Reports* went to Oak Park Mall in suburban Kansas City, Kansas, to tape part of the hour-long consideration of the mall, "After the Dream Comes True," they interviewed a teenaged girl who worked in a fast-food outlet there. In a sequence that didn't make the final program, she described the major goal of her present life, which was to perfect the curl on top of the ice-cream cones that were her store's specialty. If she could do that, she would be moved from the lowly soft-drink dispenser to the more prestigious ice-cream division, the curl on top of the status ladder at her restaurant. These are the achievements that are important at the mall.
— WILLIAM SEVERINI KOWINSKI, "Kids in the Mall: Growing Up Controlled"

It is the traditional role of men to dominate life outside the home. Indeed, we expect this of men. Through centuries of mutual agreement between the sexes, men have been granted the world at large as their special territory. It is only recently that the occupation of different spheres of activity by men and women has become a competitive issue. The world outside the home has continued to enlarge, offering more and more opportunities for the development of social and cognitive capacities. The world inside the home has shrunk to minute, unsatisfying proportions that leave little room for the critical manipulation of things and people. Despite the battle over women's (and minorities') rights to participate in the world of men, the current trends are still dictated by expectations so old that they are no longer conscious. It is completely in accordance with these expectations that white men take first prize for college development on predominantly white campuses.   — JACQUELINE FLEMING, *Blacks in College*

 B. After you have examined the paragraphs in Exercise 2A to see how they use topic, clarifying, or limiting sentences for focus and emphasis, work in a group to reach consensus on the ways each paragraph employs these strategies.

 C. Look over the paragraphs in the body of an essay you are writing. Use the Strategy in 9a-1 to identify any paragraphs that lack focus. Revise them, eliminating irrelevant information, developing relevant details and generalizations, or adding topic sentences.

9b Making paragraphs coherent

Even if your paragraphs are tightly focused (see 9a), they will still be hard to read unless you pay attention to their **coherence.** A paragraph is coherent if each sentence leads clearly to the next or if the sentences form a recognizable, easy-to-understand arrangement.

1 Recognizing incoherent paragraphs

Paragraphs may lack coherence for several reasons. In some, sentences may be out of logical order. In others, the movement from sentence to sentence may be so abrupt that readers have a hard time following the train of thought. By checking for logical order and sentence-to-sentence relationships, you should be able to spot incoherent paragraphs needing revision.

Strategy

Use the following questions to help identify paragraphs lacking adequate coherence.

- Does the paragraph highlight and repeat words naming the topic and main points? (See 9b-2.)
- Do transition words alert readers to relationships between sentences? (See 9b-3.)
- Do parallel words and structures highlight similar or related ideas? (See 9b-4.)
- Are ideas and details arranged in ways that clarify their relationships? (See 9b-5.)

Note how these questions help reveal why the following paragraph lacks coherence.

Lacks
coherence

Captain James Cook discovered the island of Hawaii in 1779. Mauna Kea, on Hawaii, is the tallest mountain in the Pacific. Cook might have noticed the many mountains on the island as he sailed into Kealakekua Bay. The island also has five major volcanoes. Mauna Loa, another mountain on the island, is a dormant volcano that last erupted in 1984. Kilauea is the most active volcano on earth. It continues to enlarge the land that makes up this largest island in the Hawaiian chain. The volcano sends forth lava continuously.

READER'S RESPONSE: This paragraph provides a good deal of information, especially about the volcanic mountains of Hawaii, yet it doesn't direct attention to this topic through repeated words or parallel structures. The paragraph is also a bit hard to follow because the information isn't very clearly arranged and no transition words point out links among the details and ideas.

9b
¶ coh

You can also use the questions to identify revision strategies, like the ones employed in the following praragraph.

Revised

Paragraph arranged in logical order: question to answer

In 1779, Captain James Cook sailed into Kealakekua Bay and discovered the island of Hawaii. As he entered the bay, did Cook **notice** the many **mountains** on the island? Perhaps he **noticed** Mauna Kea, the tallest **mountain** in the Pacific. Perhaps he **spotted** one or more of the five major **volcanoes. One of these,** Mauna Loa, is a dormant **volcano** that last erupted in 1984. **Another,** Kilauea, is the most active **volcano** on earth. It sends forth lava continuously. **In addition,** it keeps adding to the land mass of what is already the largest island in the Hawaiian chain.

Repeated words

Parallelism in sentence openings

Transition words

2 Repeating words and phrases

By repeating words and phrases that refer to your topic and main point, you keep readers aware of a paragraph's focus and link sentence to sentence. Synonyms and related words can also be part of a pattern of effective repetition, as in the following paragraph.

"**Childhood is the kingdom where nobody dies**" is a line, from the poem by Edna St. Vincent Millay, that has stuck in my mind ever since I first read it, when I was in fact a **child** and **nobody died.** Of course **people did die,** but **they** were either very old or **died** unusual **deaths, died** while rafting on the Stanislaus or loading a shotgun or doing 95 drunk: **death** was construed as either a "blessing" or an exceptional case, the dramatic instance on which **someone else's** (never **our own**) story turned. Illness, in that **kingdom** where I and **most people** I knew lingered long past **childhood,** proved self-limiting. Fever of unknown etiology signaled only the indulgence of a week in bed. Chest pains, investigated, revealed hypochondria.   — JOAN DIDION, "After Henry"

9b
¶ coh

Writer's Tip

If you wish to use repeated words to link sentences in a paragraph, you need to place the words in prominent positions, often near the beginning or end of sentences. When you bury repetition in the middle of a sentence, its effect is weakened, and each sentence in a passage may seem to address a new topic.

INEFFECTIVE REPETITION

According to recent research, the facial features of people married for a long time often become similar. Younger couples display only chance resemblances between their faces. Sharing emotions for many years, however, leads to similar expressions for most older couples.

REVISED

According to recent research, **people married for a long time** often develop similar **facial features. Younger couples** display only chance resemblances between their **faces.** Because **they** share emotions for many years, however, most **older couples** develop similar **expressions.**

---

3 Supplying transitions

You can use **transitional expressions** like *in addition, therefore,* and *on the other hand* to alert readers to relationships among sentences and ideas. You can also make your paragraphs easier to understand by using such words to highlight a paragraph's design and purpose. (See p. 106)

Note how the lack of transitions makes the following paragraph difficult to read.

LACKING TRANSITIONS

Many people still consider the choice of college the most important career decision you can make. Graduate school is the most important choice. The competition for all kinds of jobs has gotten fiercer. Business positions at the entry level often go to people with MBAs and law degrees. Many good jobs require advanced training and skills. Employers pay attention to more than the presence of an advanced degree on your résumé. They look at the program of study. They consider the quality of the school. Think about going to graduate school. Choose your school carefully.

REVISED

> Many people still consider the choice of college the most important career decision you can make. **These days, however,** graduate school is the most important choice **because** the competition for all kinds of jobs has gotten fiercer. **For example,** business positions at the entry level often go to people with MBAs and law degrees. **In addition,** many good jobs require advanced training and skills. **Moreover,** employers pay attention **not only** to the presence of an advanced degree on your résumé **but also** to the program of study **and** the quality of the school. **Therefore,** think about going to graduate school, **and** choose your school carefully.

9b ¶ coh

Did You Know?

When asked to restore paragraphing to a text from which paragraph indentations had been removed, readers looked for major shifts in topic as places to begin new paragraphs. To identify topic shifts, the readers relied most heavily on content words (nouns) and the pronouns referring to them, paying special attention to words appearing in the beginnings of sentences.

Sandra J. Bond and John R. Hayes, "Cues People Use to Paragraph Text," *Research in the Teaching of English* 18 (May 1984): 147–67.

---

4 Using parallel structure

You can link elements within a paragraph by using **parallelism**—repeating the same parallel grammatical structures to highlight similar or related ideas (see also 25c). Note how the parallel words and phrases in the following paragraph serve to create coherence.

> I have a place on the West Coast **where** my relatives still farm, **where I heard** the stories of feuds and backbiting, and **where I saw** that people **survived and flourished** because fundamentally they **trusted and relied** upon one another. **A death in the family** is not just **a death in a family;** it is a **death in the community. I saw people** help each other with money, materials, labor, attention, and time. **I saw men** gather once a year, without fail, to clean the grounds of a ninety-year-old woman who had helped the community **before, during,** and **after** the war. **I saw her** remembering them with birthday cards sent to each of their children.
>
> — Kesaya E. Noda, "Growing Up Asian in America"

Transitions	
TIME AND SEQUENCE	next, later, after, while, meanwhile, immediately, somewhat earlier, first, second, third (firstly, secondly, thirdly), shortly, thereafter, in the future, over the next two days, concurrently, subsequently, as long as, soon, since, finally, last, at that time, as soon as
COMPARISON	likewise, similarly, also, again, in the same manner, in comparison
CONTRAST	in contrast, on one hand . . . on the other hand, however, although, even though, still, yet, but, nevertheless, conversely, at the same time, regardless, despite
EXAMPLES	for example, for instance, such as, specifically, thus, to illustrate, namely
CAUSE AND EFFECT	as a result, consequently, since, accordingly, if . . . then, is due to this, for this reason, as a consequence of
PLACE	next to, above, behind, beyond, near, across from, to the right, here, there, in the foreground, in the background, in between, opposite
ADDITION	and, too, moreover, in addition, besides, furthermore, next, also, finally
CONCESSION	of course, naturally, it may be the case that, granted, it is true that, certainly
CONCLUSION	in conclusion, in short, as a result, as I have demonstrated, as the data show
REPETITION	to repeat, in other words, once again, as I said earlier
SUMMARY	on the whole, to sum up, in short, to summarize, therefore

5 Using patterns of arrangement

You can also make paragraphs more coherent by organizing details to emphasize relationships such as spatial order, chronological order, and logical order.

Spatial Order. A **spatial** organization guides readers through the details of a scene, a work of art, a person's appearance, or a complex mechanism in an easy-to-follow order such as left to right, top to bottom, inside to outside, or some combination of these. Paragraphs developed with descriptive details often employ a spatial arrangement (see 10b-2).

Chronological Order. **Chronological** organization works well for the events in a narrative, the steps in a set of instructions, or the stages in a process. Presenting the elements in time sequence, first to last, is the clearest arrangement. Simple rearrangements, such as flashbacks or the presentation of simultaneous events, are not likely to confuse readers as long as you signal the shifts with words and phrases like *much earlier, at the same time, next, later,* and *earlier.* (See 10b-4 for a paragraph developed in this manner.)

Logical Order. When you pose a question, readers generally expect you to provide an answer. When you present a problem, they expect you to consider a solution. Consequently, you can use **logical order,** arranging a paragraph's details and generalizations according to a **question-answer pattern** (as in the next example) or a **problem-solution sequence.** This way you create an order that readers can readily recognize and understand.

9b
¶ coh

Question   Why is buying a good running shoe such a difficult job for many athletes? Lack of choice certainly isn't the answer.
Unlikely answer   The walls and counters of sporting goods stores are covered with the latest products from the top manufacturers, with designs ranging from basic to high tech and prices ranging
Reasonable   from reasonable to absurdly expensive. The real answer lies
answer plus   in our desire to find the ideal shoe, one that feels comfort-
support   able, helps prevent injuries, aids performance, and offers high quality for a reasonable cost—and suits the peculiarities of our feet and running styles. Seldom, however, do runners encounter shoes that offer just the right combination of qualities, and they often end up having to choose between the most comfortable shoe and the one with expensive high-performance features. They may even have to settle for a pair that feels great on the right foot but not quite as good on the left.   — ALEXIS BRADY, College Student

There are two other common strategies. In the **general-to-specific pattern,** you offer broader generalizations and examples first and then move to more specific statements and details. In the **specific-to-general pattern,** you follow a reverse order, moving from specific examples, details, and statements toward a generalization about them.

Exercise 3

A. As you work through the following activities, increase coherence and readability by repeating words, adding transitions, using parallel structures, following a pattern of arrangement, and making any other changes necessary.

1. Rewrite the following paragraph, increasing its coherence.

> Heart attacks have many causes. Some heart attacks occur because a blood clot closes a coronary artery. Sometimes a mass of fatty substances (plaque) has the same effect. Heart attacks with these causes are the most frequent. A spasm in an artery may also close it and prevent blood from reaching the heart. Smoking, hypertension, and diabetes can create conditions that keep blood from reaching the heart. The blood-starved tissue may die. This will cause permanent damage to the heart's ability to pump blood. A dead portion of the heart is called a myocardial infarction.

2. Rewrite the following sentences to create a coherent paragraph. Feel free to add information or to retain the wording.

> Fajitas originated in Mexico.
>
> They are one of the most popular foods in Mexico, and their popularity in the rest of North America is growing.
>
> Fast-food restaurants in the United States and Canada began serving fajitas around 1985.
>
> The first restaurant in the United States to serve them may have been Pharr's Roundup Restaurant, which added them to the menu in 1972.
>
> The Mexican style of preparing fajitas was modified when they were introduced into fast-food restaurants.
>
> The fast-food restaurants designed fajitas that are somewhat similar to tacos.

 B. Copy a paragraph from one of your own essays, scrambling the order of the sentences, and then exchange scrambled paragraphs with a fellow student. Rewrite and strengthen your partner's paragraph by putting the sentences in the most effective order and revising to increase coherence among sentences.

 C. Look up some recent medical, technical, or scientific advances in science magazines written for a general audience. Then prepare a coherent and clear paragraph explaining one of the advances in detail.

9c Linking paragraphs

The paragraphs in an essay should work together to form a coherent whole. Typically, an essay will have several sections, each consisting of one or more paragraphs or clusters of paragraphs. To guide readers through an essay, you need to clarify the relationships among the paragraphs in a cluster or even an entire section.

Strategy

As you draft or revise, think about the many possible connections among the ideas and information you are discussing; then decide which connections you wish to highlight for readers. Draw on the following techniques to link paragraphs in ways that emphasize connections and that call attention to your line of reasoning.

- Announce your purpose.
- Provide transition words and boundary statements.
- Create transition paragraphs.

1 Announce your purpose

When you announce your purpose and organization near the beginning of a cluster of paragraphs, you help readers anticipate the line of reasoning you will use to develop and support ideas. Some readers may consider a direct statement of your purpose desirable; others may prefer a more indirect approach. You can usually decide on an appropriate strategy by checking with members of your intended audience or reading a number of selections addressed to a similar audience.

DIRECT STATEMENT The next section looks at the new generation of situation comedies that has taken over the top of the ratings chart in the last two years.

LESS DIRECT STATEMENT Advertisers have developed sophisticated ways to identify the tastes, purchasing power, and needs of consumers. Each of these tactics needs to be examined in detail.

INDIRECT STATEMENT Most paintings from the period show the influence of the new artistic techniques and a growing emphasis on realism.

Statements like these can be helpful as you draft or revise because they are promises you need to fulfill through carefully organized and developed paragraphs (see Chapter 10).

2 Use boundary statements

Sometimes a single word or a short phrase like *and, but,* or *in addition* can link paragraphs effectively, especially when an explanation or argument is not very complicated (see the transitions listed on p. 106). To help present detailed reasoning or information, however, consider using opening paragraphs with a **boundary statement**—a sentence at the start of a paragraph that acts as a bridge from the paragraph before. A boundary statement begins with a reminder of material covered in the preceding paragraph (or paragraphs). It then presents the topic sentence of the paragraph to come. In the following example, the writer begins by briefly mentioning the subject he has just finished discussing ("the rise of the Sunbelt"), then highlights the main point of the paragraph itself ("the decline of rural America").

<table>
<tr>
<td>Boundary
statement</td>
<td>**The rise of the Sunbelt** in recent years has been accompanied by **the decline of rural America.** Until 1920, a majority of Americans lived in small towns and on farms. Today, 77 percent of Americans are packed into metropolitan areas of more than 100,000 people. Meanwhile, many tightly knit city neighborhoods and ethnic enclaves have disintegrated as a result of urban renewal, crime, and suburbanization. The steady growth of new suburbs, with their malls and fast food joints, symbolizes the rootless pattern of American life.</td>
</tr>
</table>

> — BRAD EDMONDSON, "Making Yourself at Home"

9c
¶ link

3 Use transition paragraphs

In short essays, simple transitions or boundary statements (see 9c-2) generally provide adequate guidance for readers. In longer essays or complicated discussions, you may need to give readers extra guidance with one- or two-sentence transition paragraphs. Brief transition paragraphs come in several kinds.

Signal paragraphs alert readers to a major change in direction or the beginning of a new section of the discussion.

> While the American automobile manufacturers were producing an almost unbroken string of successes, developments halfway around the world were laying the base for a new center of power in the industry.   — BEN SANTOS, College Student

> Despite all the cast's grumbling, my father decided that he was going to like working for Howdy Doody. Shortly thereafter, my sporadic visits to Doodyville became more regular pilgrimages, a routine that would continue for the next four years.
> — STEPHEN DAVIS, *Say Kids! What Time Is It?*

Brief **summary paragraphs** can mark the end of a discussion or help readers remember main points.

Drug prices are therefore likely to remain a source of conflict. Responsible people will continue to point out that pharmaceutical companies need to make a healthy profit, and equally responsible people will argue that keeping drug prices as low as possible is essential for public health. — GENISA WASHINGTON, College Student

In their impact and personal dramas these five Black men led basketball flying, faking, blocking, and dunking into the present.
— NELSON GEORGE, *Elevating the Game*

Short **planning paragraphs** near the beginning of an essay or the start of a section help readers understand the arrangement of a discussion and aid comprehension.

The three main concerns are quality, appearance, and cost. Each needs to be examined in detail, especially the question of financing and long-term expenses.

Highlight paragraphs call attention to important ideas and information.

The result over time is a series of distinct cohort-groups that includes everyone ever born. Each of these we call a "generation," and each of these possesses what we call a "peer personality."
— WILLIAM STRAUSS AND NEIL HOWE, *Generations*

Exercise 4

A. Look at one of the sample student research papers in Chapters 46–49, and analyze the way the writer links paragraphs.

B. Working with a group of fellow writers, examine articles in a popular magazine, concentrating on those presenting detailed information or arguing in support of a generalization. From among the articles, choose two clusters of paragraphs and identify the different strategies used to link paragraphs within the clusters. As a group, decide what makes the clusters effective, and try to suggest ways they might be improved.

C. Working with a partner, exchange drafts of essays that you are writing. Choose a cluster of paragraphs from your partner's essay and rewrite the cluster, linking the paragraphs in a different way than your partner did. After you have both completed your revisions, share the new versions and assess the effectiveness of each. Now go back to your paper and work again on your paragraphs, strengthening each cluster.

Effective Paragraphs: Developing Ideas

You will disappoint readers if your paragraphs fail to provide enough information, detail, or support for your conclusions.

LACKING DEVELOPMENT

A good résumé can greatly increase your chances of getting a job you want. You should pay attention to both the content and appearance of your résumé.

READER'S RESPONSE: Exactly what kinds of information should I include? What kind of headings should I use? What kind of paper or printing style will impress an employer? I need specific suggestions.

You can improve flawed paragraphs like this by adding supporting details and by explaining your ideas.

REVISED

A good résumé can greatly increase your chances of getting a job you want. You should pay attention to both the content and appearance of your résumé. Books on job hunting and business communication can tell you what to include on a résumé and how to present the information on the page. Word processing programs frequently offer patterns for résumés that are easy to read and understand. Desktop publishing programs can help you enhance the appearance of your document. Copy centers offer professional-looking printing at low cost—including special paper that will make your résumé stand out in the pile of applications an employer receives.

10a Developing paragraphs

Suppose you encountered the following paragraph in an essay on pets. How would you react?

> Dogs and cats make wonderful pets, but certainly not trendy ones. Exotic animals of all kinds, including Vietnamese pot-bellied pigs and llamas, have begun appearing in living rooms and backyards.

You would probably respond that the paragraph has a clear main point and a potentially interesting example but seems skimpy and uninteresting. Without supporting details, the paragraph is neither informative nor convincing. **Paragraph development** provides the examples, facts, concrete details, explanatory statements, or supporting arguments that make a paragraph informative and support your ideas and opinions.

1 Recognizing poorly developed paragraphs

10a
¶ dev

Short paragraphs are not always underdeveloped, nor are long paragraphs always adequate—yet length can be an important cue. Generally, more than two sentences are necessary for a paragraph to explore a topic and support a generalization. Even though the following paragraph provides some support for the writer's opinion, most readers are likely to find the brief presentation unconvincing.

UNDERDEVELOPED

> Recycling is always a good idea—or *almost* always. Recycling some products, even newsprint and other paper goods, may require more energy from fossil fuels and consume more valuable natural resources than making them the first time.

READER'S RESPONSE: I'd like to know more before I agree with this point of view. Which products is this writer talking about? How much energy does it take to recycle them? What natural resources do they consume and how much?

Strategy

Use these questions to help identify paragraphs that need to be developed more fully.

- Does the paragraph present enough new material to be *informative* to readers?
- Does the paragraph provide *adequate support* for any generalizations being offered?

In using this Strategy to analyze a paragraph, you may wish to shorten the questions to a few words: "Informative?" "Adequate support?"

Informative? A well-developed paragraph presents readers with fresh, interesting, or useful information. As you try to decide whether you have presented enough information in a paragraph, remember that readers probably know less about the subject than you do. They may require detailed explanations, and you may need to tell them what information is new or unusual and what is general knowledge. Remember, too, that a careful mix of old and new informs readers without overwhelming them with novelty.

Adequate Support? Effective paragraphs provide statements and facts to support a generalization. To spot underdeveloped paragraphs, look for statements that simply repeat the generalization or that fail to explain how the information being presented supports the main point. Look also for incomplete, vague, or unconvincing information. In narrative and descriptive writing, make sure your paragraphs are rich enough in description of sights, sounds, and other sensory details so readers will be able to share the experience you are presenting. (See also 4a-4.)

The following paragraph lacks development in several areas, as the marginal comments indicate.

10a
¶ dev

About how much do they spend? What do they spend it on?

Be more precise about number of years?

Many prescriptions have two boxes for the doctor to check, one marked "Dispense as Written" and the other "Substitution Allowed." The substitution usually is a generic drug. Generic drugs are in most ways just like brand name drugs only they cost less. Pharmaceutical companies spend a lot of money on brand name drugs and, therefore, charge more for them. After a certain amount of time, however, other pharmaceutical companies are allowed to make the drugs and to sell them under their scientific names. These generic drugs are much the same as the drugs with brand names. Getting your doctor to check "Substitution Allowed" can save you a lot of money.

"Most ways" is rather vague! Just how much lower is the cost of generics?

Repeats the third sentence.

Did You Know?

As Craig Carver points out, the word *paragraph* and the paragraph symbol, ¶, have been in use a long time.

A break in a narrative or discourse where a new idea or argument begins was marked in ancient Greek manuscripts with a short horizontal stroke, also used to mark off the different speeches in a play. Because it was written in the margin or beside the running text, this mark was called a *paragraphos*, from *para* (by the side of, beside) and *graphos* (written). . . . Besides a horizontal stroke, the Greek scribe sometimes used a wedge-shaped

> mark, the ancestor of the reversed P indicating a paragraph break, sometimes called a *pilcrow*. This symbol had been in common use in Middle English manuscripts and was retained by early printers before indenting the first line of a paragraph became standard practice.
>
> Craig M. Carver, *A History of English in Its Own Words* (New York: HarperCollins, 1991) 89–90.

2 Adding details and statements

Fully developed paragraphs give readers an in-depth picture of a subject by mixing general statements that provide an overview with specifics that provide support and explanation. For variety in development, effective paragraphs use examples, concrete detail, facts and statistics, and supporting statements. Don't expect to create varied, fully developed paragraphs all at once, especially during drafting. The task is complicated and is often best accomplished through revision.

Developing Paragraph Content

EXAMPLES
Use brief, specific examples or an extended, detailed example.

CONCRETE DETAIL
Re-create sights, sounds, tastes, smells, movements, and sensations of touch.

FACTS AND STATISTICS
Offer precise data from authoritative sources, perhaps in numerical form.

SUPPORTING STATEMENTS
Provide your own interpretive statements or include quotations from other people whom readers are likely to trust.

Examples. Examples, whether brief or extended, help you clarify difficult concepts. They support a generalization by showing how plausible or widespread something is. They provide good reasons for readers to agree with your opinion. And they are often easy for readers to understand because they are specific and concrete rather than general and abstract.

Here is the underdeveloped paragraph from page 113 developed with brief examples.

Topic sentence
Dogs and cats make wonderful pets, but certainly not trendy ones. Exotic animals of all kinds, including Vietnamese

Brief examples   pot-bellied pigs and llamas, have begun appearing in living rooms and backyards. About the size of beagles, the pigs are affectionate and easy to care for. Llamas require more room and care, but these gentle animals are now in demand as well—at least among people who can afford the one or two thousand dollars needed to buy one. Ferrets, Amazon parrots, pygmy goats, and dwarf rabbits have been finding places in fashionable homes as well. People who want to keep well ahead of the crowd might consider Old World chameleons or dart-poison frogs (the source of poison for blowdarts used by jungle hunters).

**10a
¶ dev**

In contrast to brief examples, an extended example helps a reader see an idea in action and understand its consequences. An extended example can draw a reader into an event and create emotional responses that make a paragraph convincing and interesting to read.

Extended example   One day in 1957, the songwriter Johnny Mercer received a letter from Sadie Vimerstedt, a widowed grandmother who worked behind a cosmetics counter in Youngstown, Ohio. Mrs. Vimerstedt suggested Mercer write a song called "I Want to Be Around to Pick Up the Pieces When Somebody Breaks Your Heart." Five years later, Mercer got in touch to say he'd written the song and that Tony Bennett would record it. Today, if you look at the label on any recording of "I Wanna Be Around," you'll notice that the credits for words and music are shared by Johnny Mercer and Sadie Vimerstedt. The royalties were split fifty-fifty, too, thanks to which Mrs. Vimerstedt and her heirs have earned

Topic sentence   more than $100,000. In my opinion, Mercer's generosity was a class act.   — JOHN BERENDT, "Class Acts"

Concrete Detail.   Concrete details of sight, sound, smell, taste, touch, and movement make a paragraph more vivid and enjoyable. They enhance a reader's understanding of objects, situations, and events. They also make examples more persuasive and facts easier to remember.

Some rapids, like one called Hermit, seem more dangerous than they are and give us great roller-coaster rides. Others—Hance, Crystal, Upset—seem less spectacular, but are technically difficult. At Crystal, our boat screeches and twists against its frame. Its nose crumples like cardboard in the trough; our boatman makes the critical move to the right with split-second timing and we are over a standing wave and into the haystacks of white water, safely into the tail waves. The boatman's eyes cease to blaze.

— BARRY LOPEZ, "Gone Back into the Earth"

Facts and Statistics. Facts and statistics provide the particular evidence that many readers find convincing proof for generalizations or opinions. Besides being interesting and informative in their own right, facts and statistics can also help readers understand complicated social and natural phenomena.

Topic sentence

Facts and
statistics

Though the ozone depletion can't be blamed for the present epidemic [of skin cancer], it's bound to contribute in coming years. According to the latest projections, a 1 percent decrease in ozone heralds a 2.6 percent increase in basal and squamous cell cancers. With an annual total of 600,000 diagnoses in the United States, that would mean if the ozone over our heads permanently thinned by one percent starting this year, there will be an additional 156,000 cases a couple of decades down the line.

— MARY ROACH, "Sun Struck"

10a
¶ dev

Supporting Statements. When you use examples, details, facts, and statistics, you can make them more persuasive and easier to understand by including interpretive statements that link them to a paragraph's main point. Give reasons for accepting a generalization, and use direct or indirect quotations from authorities on the subject; these can also be effective as supporting statements.

Interpretive
statement

Breakfast cereals can differ radically in serving size even though most cereal boxes define a single serving in the same way, as a one-ounce portion. A one-ounce serving of Cheerios is $1^1/4$ cup, for example, while a one-ounce serving of Quaker 100% Natural Cereal is $^1/4$ cup. Weight measurements can disguise the differences between products; measurement by volume reveals the contrasts. For dieters, volume can be as important a measure as the number of calories per serving because the volume indicates how much cereal you will have to appease your appetite: two bites or a bowlful. — SARA BRILLIANT, College Student

Exercise 1

A. First, examine the paragraphs in Exercise 2A in Chapter 9, and identify the various strategies of development used by the writers. Which seem particularly effective, and why? Which, if any, seem ineffective?

Next, for each of the following topic sentences, explain which kind or kinds of supporting information (examples, concrete details, facts and statistics, or supporting statements) you believe would create the most effective paragraph.

1. Money to pay for college costs can come from many different sources.
2. I realize that I am probably the only person you know who watches and enjoys [*name of television program*], so I want to tell you what you are missing.
3. Making exercise part of a busy schedule may be difficult, but it is essential.
4. What makes a town a good place to live?
5. [*Name of artist*] is perhaps the best performer on the contemporary music scene.

10b
¶ dev

B. Working in a group, compare your responses to Exercise 1A. Record both agreements and disagreements about the paragraphs in Exercise 2A in Chapter 9. Then continue to work together to develop one of the topic sentences into a paragraph. Be ready to explain why you chose to develop the paragraph in the way you did. Feel free to revise the topic sentence.

C. First, look over a draft essay you are working on, and identify any paragraphs needing further development. For each of these paragraphs, decide on one or more strategies for adding details and statements that you might employ in revising, and identify the kinds of information and ideas you might add.

Next, do some reading and research to discover facts and statistics you can use to develop a paragraph for a paper you are working on. Then write the paragraph, making sure it has a clear topic sentence.

10b   Using patterns of development

Your writing may often require you to do a familiar task such as explain a process, isolate cause and effect, or construct a definition. To accomplish these tasks efficiently in a paragraph (or paragraphs), you can turn to patterns of development that help you develop and organize your writing. Because readers will be familiar with patterns like comparison-contrast, classification, and definition, they will find it easier to recognize a paragraph's purpose and arrangement.

1 Narrating

You will often turn to **narration** to present events in the past, the present, or even the imagined future. Your narrative may focus on the facts, as, for example, in presenting historical background. It may re-create an experience for readers, as in a personal essay, or tell an anecdote to introduce a discussion or to illustrate a point. Or it may envision images of the future, as in a proposal for a new policy or project.

Patterns for Paragraph Development

TASK	DEVELOPMENT STRATEGY
Tell a story; re-create events; present an anecdote.	Narrating
Provide detail of a scene or object; portray someone's character; evoke a feeling.	Describing
Explore similarities or differences; evaluate alternatives.	Comparing and contrasting
Provide directions; explain the operation of a mechanism, procedure, or natural process.	Explaining a process
Separate a subject into parts; explore the relationships among parts.	Dividing
Sort things or people into groups; explain the relationships among the groups.	Classifying
Explain the meaning of a term or concept; explore and illustrate the meaning of a complicated concept or phenomenon.	Defining
Consider why something happened or might happen; explore possible causes and consequences.	Analyzing causes and effects

---

10b
¶ dev

Suddenly the ground thundered, and, as if called, a train caught up with Uncle Clark. It slowed only a little, but not enough to be caught, even by my uncle, strong and sleek as he was. Undaunted, Uncle Clark let out a piercing whistle. Out of the black square shadow of one boxcar shot a long arm. In a flash my uncle grabbed it and was hoisted inside the wide door. We never saw the other hobos; we only heard them laughing at the show they'd given us townies.

— BRENDA PETERSON, "Vaster Than Empires and More Slow"

2 Describing

You can create images of a place or object, sketch a person's character, or provide images that evoke and share a feeling through paragraphs developed by **description.** Depending on whether you are writing a personal essay or a scientific or technical report, you may choose to emphasize the emotional impact of scenes (**subjective description**) or to stick to the physical details (**objective description**).

With its shed roof sloping north, the cabin sits low and compact in the snow, a pair of moose antlers nailed above a window in the high south wall. There are four dog houses to the rear of it, each of them roofed with a poke of snow-covered hay. A meat rack stands to one side, built high between two stout spruces, and a ladder made of dry poles leans against a tree next to it. A hindquarter of moose hangs from the rack; it is frozen rock hard and well wrapped with canvas to keep it from birds. Just the same, I see that camp-robbers have pecked at it and torn a hole in the canvas. Nothing else can reach it there seven feet above the ground.   — JOHN HAINES, "Three Days"

3 Comparing and contrasting

You can employ paragraphs built around **comparing** and **contrasting** to evaluate alternative policies or products. You can examine pros and cons or contrasting qualities of ideas and experiences or compare your arguments and explanations with those offered by other writers.

In arranging comparison paragraphs, you can employ a **point-by-point organization,** examining each comparable feature for first one subject and then the next.

Topic sentence	But biology has a funny way of confounding expectations. Rather than disappear, the evidence for innate sex-
Feature 1	ual differences only began to mount. In medicine, researchers documented that heart disease strikes men at a younger age
Feature 2	than it does women and that women have a more moderate
Feature 3	physiological response to stress. Researchers found subtle neurological differences between the sexes both in the brain's structure and in its functioning. In addition, another gen-
Feature 4	eration of parents discovered that, despite their best efforts to give baseballs to their daughters and sewing kits to their sons, girls still flocked to dollhouses while boys clambered into tree forts. Perhaps nature is more important than nurture after all. — CHRISTINE GORMAN, "Sizing Up the Sexes"

Or you can use a **subject-by-subject organization**, considering each subject in its entirety, as in the next example.

Topic sentence	For everyone, home is a place to be offstage. But the comfort of home can have opposite and incompatible mean-
Subject 1	ings for women and men. For many men, the comfort of home means freedom from having to prove themselves and impress through verbal display. At last, they are in a situation where talk is not required. They are free to remain silent.

Subject 2 But for women, home is a place where they are free to talk, and where they feel the greatest need for talk, with those they are closest to. For them, the comfort of home means the freedom to talk without worrying about how their talk will be judged.

— DEBORAH TANNEN, "'Put Down That Paper and Talk to Me!'"

Did You Know?

Since the time of the ancient Greeks and Romans, patterns of development like the ones described here have been regarded as useful ways to think about a subject and to communicate with an audience. Some scholars believe that patterns like comparison, cause and effect, process, and description reflect basic patterns of thought. If this is true, we can assume our readers share our knowledge of the patterns.

Frank D'Angelo, *A Conceptual Theory of Rhetoric* (Cambridge: Winthrop, 1975).

10b
¶ dev

4 Explaining a process

You may need to provide readers with **directions** or explain how a mechanism or procedure works. To explain such processes effectively, label the steps or stages clearly, and present your **explanation** in chronological order or in another logical arrangement.

DIRECTIONS

Cooking a country ham requires some strength, a bathtub, and a large pot, but little skill. First, scrub the ham well with a stiff brush under cold running water to remove any mold. Do this in the bathtub. Then fill the tub with cold water to cover the ham; let it soak twenty-four hours. Don't try to get the salt out by soaking longer; you'll need a bath, and extended soaking will destroy the texture of the ham. Finicky cooks will soak the ham in a large pot.

— BILL NEAL, "How to Cure a Pig"

EXPLANATION

Stage One sleep is very light—just the other side of wakefulness. Stage Two (which makes up about half our total slumber time) is a transitional phase into either slow-wave or REM sleep, while stages Three and Four are slow-wave sleep. In slow-wave, or deep, sleep, brain activity slows to a crawl. In REM, or dreaming sleep, on the other hand, the brain bursts into high activity virtually identical to being awake—though the muscles are temporarily paralyzed from the neck down.   — ROYCE FLIPPIN, "Tossing and Turning"

5 Dividing and classifying

When you divide a subject, you split it into parts. A **division paragraph** offers you a chance to explain a subject in detail and to highlight the relationships of its parts.

> Sunglasses should be more than cheap plastic frames with dark lenses. A good pair has three important features: it protects, adds a touch of style, and costs a lot more than $1.99. Eye-damaging ultra-violent rays make protection essential. Your sunglasses should guard against both UV-A rays and the shorter, more damaging UV-B rays. The racks of sunglasses, many sporting designer names, offer styles from wraparound to wire frames, from amber tints in red rims to gray on gray. You can create almost any impression: debonair, retro, sexy, athletic, Hollywood, even owlish and scholarly. Yet trendy appearance and effective protection come at a price. Be ready to pay at least $20 for a pair of sunglasses coated to protect from all the harmful rays and ten times as much (or more) for designer styles from this year's collection.   — MEGHAN TUBRIDY, College Student

When you classify, you sort several subjects into groups based on their similarities. A **classification paragraph** is an opportunity for you to explore similarities *within* groups and explain the differences and relationships *between* groups.

> Men all have different styles of chopping wood, all of which are deemed by their practitioners as the only proper method. Often when I'm chopping wood in my own inept style, a neighbor will come over and "offer help." He'll bust up a few logs in his own manner, advising me as to the proper swing and means of analyzing the grain of the wood. There are "over the head" types and "swing from the shoulder" types, and guys who lay the logs down horizontally on the ground and still others who balance them on end, atop of stumps. I have one neighbor who uses what he calls "vector analysis." Using the right vectors, he says, the wood will practically *split itself.*
> — JAMES FINNEY BOYLAN, "The Bean Curd Method"

6 Defining

When you need to introduce a term or concept to your readers, you may need to write just a phrase or sentence to define it, or you may need to create a definition paragraph if the term is complicated. In creating a paragraph-length definition, you have the space to contrast your definition with those of other writers. Or you can take a term or concept with multiple meanings and stipulate the one it will carry in your essay.

> When they hear the word *crystal,* many people think of a mineral dug from the ground. But the lead crystal used to make beautiful plates, glasses, and vases does not come from this source. The crystal in these objects—artworks, actually—is glass with a high lead content. The glass is made from a mixture of sand and other ingredients like potash (potassium) or soda that help the mixture melt. The various minerals also affect the color and clarity of the glass. Lead crystal must contain at least 30 percent to 35 percent lead oxide (by weight) in its ingredients. The resulting material is easier for artists to work with as they grind intricate facets into the surface to create designs that sparkle and intrigue like a finely cut diamond.
>
> — ANDREA HERRMANN, College Student

10b
¶ dev

7 Analyzing causes and effects

When you wish to explain why something has occurred, you might devote a paragraph to causes. When you want to explore consequences, you might focus on effects. Or you might combine causes and effects, as in the following paragraph.

> Of all the habits I have, there is one my friends simply cannot understand. I always set my clock ahead fourteen minutes. "What for?" everyone asks when they notice that my clock is running so far ahead. The habit started in my first year of high school. I was so nervous about being late for the first day of "real" school that I moved the clock hands ahead—fourteen minutes ahead. When I got into bed, I had a secure feeling that everything would work out fine. Since then, I feel rushed and hurried every time I set my clock to regular time, but relaxed and secure when I set it to my time, fourteen minutes fast.
>
> — KRIS LUNDELL, College Student

Exercise 2

A. Choose one of the following pairs of topics. Drawing on your own knowledge, develop each topic into a paragraph, using the pattern of development indicated in brackets.

1. A paragraph on an unusual sport or hobby [process] *and* a paragraph on an unusual or memorable pet [description or narration]
2. A paragraph examining different ways of studying [classification]

and a paragraph telling how an average college student spends his or her leisure time [division]

3. A paragraph exploring a common problem students face in studying for tests and proposing a solution [division] *and* a paragraph identifying the reasons some students do well (or poorly) on tests [cause-effect]

4. A paragraph exploring different outlooks about the relationships of parents and children [comparison-contrast] *and* a paragraph defining what it means to be a parent in the 1990s [definition]

5. A paragraph examining some common behavioral differences between men and women [subject-by-subject comparison] *and* a paragraph identifying differences in life-style and behavior between people holding different kind of jobs (restaurant manager and doctor, for example, or teacher and chemical engineer) [point-by-point comparison]

10b
¶ dev

B. Working in a group, identify the patterns of development in the following paragraphs. The paragraphs may have a single dominant pattern or use more than one. Explain the way each pattern or combination is used.

At Spotted Tail Agency the body of Crazy Horse was wrapped in his blanket and placed on a scaffold of four posts, the red and white calfskin cape he wore into battle laid over him. Some say that his golden pinto was shot there beside the scaffold, but others insist that this would have been against the man's unostentatious ways. Certainly there were none of the gaudy accoutrements to blow in the wind for awhile and then be laid aside for posterity. Beyond the little blue stone tied behind his ear and the occasional lone feather of his chieftainship in his hair, Crazy Horse had worn no adornment.

— MARI SANDOZ, "The Burial of Crazy Horse"

None of the foreign geologists had ever encountered anything quite like the disaster at Lake Nyos. Our earliest hypotheses seemed to be almost as numerous as the scientific teams present. Some workers, impressed by the accounts of survivors who reported smelling rotten eggs or gunpowder and hearing explosions, were convinced that a volcanic eruption beneath the lake had released sulfurous gases. Others, including me, suspected that the gas had come from within the sediments on the lake bed. Eventually, though, geological and chemical investigations made it obvious that the lake had released carbon dioxide from within its own waters—independent apparently of any other process. Like an enormous bottle of soda water, it belched and fizzed gas from its depths.

— SAMUEL J. FREETH, "Incident at Lake Nyos"

C. Look over a paper you are writing, and identify a paragraph that would benefit from further development. Rewrite it, using one of the patterns in 10b to develop its content and make it structurally clearer.

10c Using special-purpose paragraphs

Beginning an essay, concluding it, and presenting dialogue are challenges you can meet with some useful special-purpose paragraphs.

1 Creating introductory paragraphs

In the opening paragraphs of an essay, you invite readers to learn about a subject, explore ideas, share an experience, or examine a line of argument. You need to build a relationship with your readers so they will want to continue reading.

To attract and hold your readers' interest, your introductory paragraphs generally need to answer three questions in a clear and interesting manner.

- What topic (problem, issue) will this paper address?

  Be precise, and provide adequate information. A broad or vague topic may not encourage readers to pay attention to what you are saying.

- Why should readers be interested in this topic?

  Let your readers know why they should spend time and energy reading about the topic.

- What is the main idea or purpose of this paper?

  If you plan to support a generalization or argue for an opinion, stating it in your opening is generally a good idea. If you plan to present information, explore ideas, or re-create experiences, make sure you convey your purpose clearly.

To answer these questions, you can use strategies like those listed in the chart on the next page.

Here are examples of introductory paragraphs employing different strategies. In each case, the writer tries to create interest in the subject and builds toward a statement of thesis or purpose.

ANECDOTE   It was advertised as the biggest non-nuclear explosion in Nevada history. On October 27, 1993, Steve Wynn, the State's official "god of hospitality," flashed his trademark

10c
¶ dev

Strategies for Introductory Paragraphs

PROVIDE BACKGROUND
Provide background information on a topic or problem; present an issue in context; give the history of the subject.

TELL A STORY
Open with a brief **anecdote** or story.

EXPLAIN AN ISSUE
Present the different sides of an issue, along with any particularly well-known or controversial events relevant to the topic.

OFFER A DEFINITION
Define an important concept or term that will recur throughout the paper.

ASK A QUESTION
Present provocative questions or opinions that require further discussion.

USE AN EXTENDED EXAMPLE
Start with an extended example related to the topic and main idea.

PRESENT A QUOTATION
Quote from an authority or from someone whose opinion leads into the topic or highlights key ideas.

MAKE A COMPARISON
Highlight the importance of a topic or issue by comparing it to another situation, historical period, subject, or issue; offer an intriguing analogy.

PROVIDE STATISTICS
Supply facts and statistics that introduce the topic or that help define an important issue or problem.

DESCRIBE A MYSTERY
Present a mysterious or interesting phenomenon worth exploring or explaining.

---

smile and pushed the detonator button. As 200,000 Las Vegans cheered, the 18-story Dunes sign, once the tallest neon structure in the world, crumbled to the desert floor.

— MIKE DAVIS, "House of Cards"

Davis introduces the environmental threat posed by Las Vegas culture.

DEFINITION   It used to be that a diner was a lowly place to eat. It was known as a greasy spoon, a hash house, or—in trucker lingo—a choke and puke. Diners were where the city's fallen angels went for a cup of mud (coffee) and a sinker (a doughnut) beneath fluorescent lights; where night hawks and wandering hoboes whiled away the wee hours. As for the food at diners, it was strictly for the crude of palate—heavy on the starch, grease, and gristle.

— JANE STERN AND MICHAEL STERN, *Roadfood*

The Sterns are about to review a different kind of diner: clean, with good food and more fashionable customers.

QUESTIONS AND OPINIONS

Many times, after I have finished a lecture on the decline of American farming and rural life, someone in the audience has asked, "What can city people do?"

"Eat responsibly," I have usually answered. Of course, I have tried to explain what I meant by that, but afterwards I have invariably felt that there was more to be said than I had been able to say. Now I would like to attempt a better explanation.

Statement of purpose

— WENDELL BERRY, "The Pleasures of Eating"

Berry appropriately splits this paragraph in two so that the change in speakers is clear. (See 10c-3.)

10c
¶ dev

Strategies to Avoid in Introductory Paragraphs

AVOID OBVIOUS GENERALIZATIONS

An opening filled with a series of obvious statements doesn't suggest that the essay will offer fresh or worthwhile insights.

AVOID APOLOGIZING

If you seem unsure about the value of your ideas, information, or conclusions, why should readers pay attention to them?

AVOID SHOPWORN PHRASES

Readers certainly won't expect anything new or interesting from an essay that begins with worn-out phrases like *An important subject facing us today, From the beginning of time,* or *In today's society.*

AVOID REFERRING TO YOUR OWN TITLE

Readers already know what the title says. Referring to it or repeating it doesn't add anything new or useful to the discussion.

Exercise 3

A. Revise the following introductory paragraphs to make them more effective. Use whatever strategies you think best.

1. I used to work in a restaurant. Waiting on tables was a terrible job, but I got to learn a lot about different kinds of people.
2. In elementary school, many children, boys and girls alike, are fas-

cinated with dinosaurs. Dinosaurs aren't cuddly, and learning about them takes a good deal of effort—at least for a third grader. Why, then, are kids so interested in the big lizards?

3. Some people view AIDS as a serious epidemic that is not different in kind from the challenge earlier generations faced from tuberculosis, smallpox, and polio. Other people think that AIDS creates new and terrible challenges. Some people even think it is a special punishment from God.

B. Working with a group of writers, exchange draft essays and review each other's introductory paragraphs. Discuss each paragraph, and suggest possible revisions.

10c
¶ dev

C. Draft two possible introductory paragraphs for a paper you are currently writing. Use a different strategy for each paragraph.

2 Creating concluding paragraphs

Paragraphs that conclude essays should generally remind readers of key ideas and encourage them to think about information you have presented or actions you have proposed. Here are strategies you may find useful for concluding paragraphs.

Strategies for Concluding Paragraphs

SUMMARIZE MAIN POINTS
Review the main points briefly; a detailed summary will seem repetitive.

RESTATE THE THESIS
Put the thesis in different words to drive home the essay's main point.

PREDICT FUTURE EVENTS OR SPECULATE
Look at relatively clear consequences, not those requiring explanation; keep speculations interesting but not so provocative that they require extensive discussion.

USE A QUOTATION
Provide a quotation that makes key ideas memorable or supports your conclusions.

OFFER A STRIKING EXAMPLE, ANECDOTE, OR IMAGE
Supply a mental picture or brief narrative to reinforce an essay's message.

ECHO THE INTRODUCTION
Use this echo to create a sense of completion.

The following paragraphs illustrate two of the strategies to use in concluding paragraphs.

SUMMARY OF MAIN POINTS

So if it's any consolation to those of us who just don't manage to fit enough sleep into our packed days, being chronically tired probably won't do us any permanent harm. And if things get desperate enough, we just might have to schedule a nap somewhere on our busy calendars.   — DANIEL GOLEMAN, "Too Little, Too Late"

QUOTATION

Abigail Adams, a pistol if there ever was one, wrote in the famous "Remember the ladies" letter to her husband, John, the second president: "While you are proclaiming peace and good will to men, emancipating all nations, you insist upon retaining an absolute power over wives." It was a young country then. In some ways it still hasn't grown up.   — ANNA QUINDLEN, "The Two Faces of Eve"

Strategies to Avoid in Concluding Paragraphs

AVOID APOLOGIZING
By pointing out weaknesses in your presentation, you undermine your essay's effectiveness. Pointing out limitations or areas for further study can be a useful strategy, however.

AVOID SIMPLY REWORDING YOUR THESIS STATEMENT
If you restate your main point, do so in a fresh way.

AVOID INTRODUCING NEW IDEAS
You will not be able to discuss new ideas or issues adequately, and they are likely to draw attention from your main points.

AVOID OVERSTATEMENT
Keep your conclusions within the limits of the evidence and explanations you provided in the essay.

---

3 Using dialogue paragraphs

You can help readers keep track of two or more people in a conversation by beginning a new paragraph for every change in speaker.

We had been walking for ten minutes. When my grandfather turned to me, his face was dead white. I was shocked. He knelt until the pails touched the ground and then shrugged from under the yoke.

He sat on the ground and I thought he was going to be sick. "Might be," he said.

"Are you all right?" I asked.

"Don't worry," he said. "Don't worry." His face gradually relaxed and color returned to his cheeks.

"It's my turn to carry the yoke," I said. "My hands hurt from the wire handles of these buckets, and anyway, I want to learn how to carry the yoke."   — DONALD HALL, *String Too Short to Save*

Exercise 4

A. Revise the following concluding paragraphs to make them more effective.

I have explained that learning to repair your own car is not difficult and that it can save you considerable money. I have also tried to show how it can help you spot problems before your car breaks down on a dark rainy night. Perhaps you should buy a book on auto repair or sign up for a course soon.

I probably have left out some of the arguments for and against gun control, though I think I have covered the main ones. The point I really want to stress most is that gun control is a difficult question. Simple proposals such as banning all handguns or getting rid of all regulations won't work. We need new ideas that balance the rights of gun owners with the right to be free from violence and crime. Though I have not explained it in detail, we probably need a program like the national registration and education system that has been recently proposed. And we certainly need to do something about the many handguns readily available to teenagers.

B. Have each of the members of a writing group bring in a popular magazine containing relatively long articles. As a group, examine the articles, and choose three openings and three conclusions that you consider successful. Identify the strategies used in each.

C. Examine the introductory and concluding paragraphs in a paper you are currently drafting. Look over the advice on strategies to use and avoid (see 10c-1 and 10c-2), and identify ways you might revise either paragraph.

Creating Clear Sentences

Most people would find the following sentences hard to read and understand.

> My cousin did not, because he was embarrassed by his lack of camping experience, sign up for the college's Outdoor Orientation for first-year students.
> **READER'S RESPONSE:** This sentence seems complicated even though what it says is simple.

> It is suggested that employee work cooperation encouragement be used for product quality improvement.
> **READER'S RESPONSE:** Who is suggesting this? What is "employee work cooperation encouragement"?

You can make sentences like these easier to read by using clear subjects and verbs or by creating simple and direct sentence structures.

CLEAR
> We will try to improve the quality of our products by encouraging employees to work cooperatively.

SIMPLE AND DIRECT
> My cousin did not sign up for the college's Outdoor Orientation for first-year students because he was embarrassed by his lack of camping experience.

11a Making subjects and verbs clear

Generally, the clearest sentences readily answer the question "Who does what (to whom)?" To create such sentences, you need to pay special attention to subjects and verbs.

CLEAR
>   subject   verb   object
> The research team investigated seizure disorders in infants.
>   who?   does what?   to whom (or what)?

subject   verb

CLEAR   The seizures often become harmful.

who?   does what?

Of course, many sentences in good writing are more complicated than those that move directly from subject to verb (to object). You can create complex yet clear sentences by making the main elements—especially subjects and verbs—easy for readers to identify.

UNCLEAR   One suggestion offered by physicians is that there is a need to be especially observant of a child's behavior during the first six months in order to notice any evidence of seizures.

CLEAR   Physicians suggest that parents watch children carefully during the first six months for evidence of seizures.

**11a
clear**

1 Use significant subjects

Sentences whose subjects name important ideas, people, topics, things, or events are generally easy for readers to understand.

> **The authors Jayne Gackenbach and Jane Bosveld** argue that we can control our dreams.

> **Lucid dreaming** is a way of confronting hidden thoughts and desires during sleep.

> **This technique** resembles transcendental meditation in a number of ways.

You can create sentences with significant subjects by asking, as you write, "Who (or what) am I talking about in this sentence?" and "Is this the subject I want to emphasize?" You can also use these questions to identify and revise sentences whose subjects are not significant. Consider this sentence from an essay entitled "Should You Try to Get a Tan?"

UNFOCUSED   You run the greatest risk if you expose yourself to a tanning machine as well as the sun because both of them can damage the skin.
        READER'S RESPONSE: I thought this essay was about the dangers posed by sunbathing and tanning salons. Why are these subjects buried in the middle of the sentence?

**POSSIBLE
REVISION**   Either **the sun or a tanning machine** can damage the skin, and you run the greatest risk if you expose yourself to **both** of them.

2 Avoid unnecessary nominalizations

When you create a noun from some other kind of word, the result is called a **nominalization** (from *nominal,* meaning "pertaining to nouns"). You can turn a verb like *complete* into a noun like *completion* or turn an adjective like *happy* into a noun like *happiness.* Some nominalizations play important roles in effective sentences; others act as stumbling blocks for readers.

Nominalizations may name ideas and issues essential to a discussion. As subjects, they can serve as focal points for clear sentences.

USEFUL NOMINALIZATION **Distractions** like television, the VCR, and electric lights (for reading or conversing) keep us up at night, robbing us of the hours of sleep previous generations enjoyed.
Distractions, a nominalization, comes from *distract,* a verb.

USEFUL NOMINALIZATION **Sleepiness** causes many accidents at work and on the highway.
Sleepiness, a nominalization, comes from *sleepy,* an adjective.

Used inappropriately, however, nominalizations may obscure important information from your readers or cause you to omit it entirely.

Strategy

As you write or as you review a draft, pay special attention to the following problems.

- A nominalization that draws readers' attention away from a sentence's proper focus
- A nominalization that leads to vague sentence subjects or objects
- A nominalization that causes you to leave important information out of a sentence

Revise sentences with these nominalization problems by making sure every sentence indicates clearly who did what (to whom). To do this, replace an inappropriate nominalization with a word indicating a clear and significant subject (or object), and name the sentence's action (did what?) in the verb.

DISTRACTING Stimulation of the production of serotonin by a glass of milk or a carbohydrate snack causes sleepiness.
This sentence from an essay entitled "How to Get a Good Night's Sleep" draws a reader's attention to the nominalized word *stimulation* rather than to *milk* and *snack,* the important "how-to's."

REVISED **A glass of milk or a carbohydrate snack stimulates** the production of serotonin and causes sleepiness.
The nominalization *stimulation* becomes the action verb *stimulates.*

**11a
clear**

VAGUE   Dissatisfaction among employees frequently leads to shoddiness in products.
Nominalizations created from adjectives often lead to vague statements, as is the case with *dissatisfaction* and *shoddiness* in this sentence.

REVISED   Dissatisfied employees make shoddy products.
The new verb, *make,* specifies the action more clearly.

INFORMATION OMITTED   An examination of the effects of too little sleep on college grades is going on now.
READER'S RESPONSE: Who is doing the study? Where?

REVISED   The psychologists at our counseling center are now examining the effects of too little sleep on college grades.

**11a
clear**

Writer's Tip

Spotting nominalizations can be difficult at first, but you can quickly turn this search into a useful habit. Words ending in *-tion, -ence, -ance, -ing,* and *-ness* are often nominalizations. Here is a list of some common nominalizations to watch for.

Noun	Verb	Adjective
analysis	analyze	
beginning	begin	
convenience		convenient
delivery	deliver	
denial	deny	
flight	fly	
guidance	guide	
investigation	investigate	
length		long
loneliness		lonely
meditation	meditate	
opening	open	
openness		open
preference	prefer	
redness		red
solution	solve	

---

3 Consider using *I, we,* and *you* as subjects

I, we, and *you* are often inappropriate in academic or professional writing. As a result, writers may fail to recognize the many settings where *I, we,* and *you* can act as clear subjects (or objects) in effective sentences. For example, memos, letters, reports, personal essays, and even an occasional academic text can benefit from careful use of *I, we,* or *you.*

VAGUE AND WEAK	The project succeeded because of careful cost control and attention to the customer's needs.
CLEAR AND FORCEFUL	The project succeeded because **we** controlled costs carefully and paid attention to **our** customers' needs.

Using I. When you are the subject of an essay, when you are speaking directly to readers, or when you are reporting on your own investigations or conclusions, *I* is an appropriate subject.

> In designing the survey, **I** avoided questions likely to embarrass respondents.

On the other hand, adding statements like *I think* and *I feel* when you are already clearly stating your point of view makes your writing more wordy but not more effective.

Using We. *We* is appropriate when you use it to report the actions of a group or to discuss experiences you as a writer share with most readers.

> **We** [North Americans] consume a large portion of the world's resources.

Using You. *You* is appropriate when used to mean "you, the reader." Use *people, individuals,* or a similar word to refer to people in general.

APPROPRIATE	Before asking a large number of people to complete the survey, **you** should test it on a few individuals to identify any major flaws in the design.
INAPPROPRIATE	According to an article in *Healthtime* magazine, **you** were less likely to die from an infectious disease thirty years ago than **you** are now.
	READER'S RESPONSE: Because I've been alive for only twenty years, this sentence seems silly to me, though I realize the author is probably writing about people in general.
REVISED	According to an article in *Healthtime* magazine, **people** were less likely to die from an infectious disease thirty years ago than **they** are now.

4 Be careful with strings of nouns

In a **noun string,** one noun modifies another.

Noun	Noun		Noun	Noun	Noun
sleep	deprivation		hip	joint	replacement
jet	lag		computer	network	server

Or nouns plus adjectives modify other nouns.

Adjective	Noun		Noun	Noun
triple	bypass		heart	surgery

Familiar noun strings can help you create concise yet clear sentences.

WORDY   To resolve conflicts, companies and unions often set up committees that investigate employees' grievances.

MORE CONCISE   To resolve conflicts, companies and unions often set up **employee grievance committees**.

Unfamiliar noun strings, however, can make sentences hard to understand. Readers may have trouble deciding which noun in a string represents the focal point.

CONFUSING   The team did a ceramic valve lining design flaw analysis.
READER'S RESPONSE: Did the team analyze flaws or use a special feature called flaw analysis? Did they study ceramic valves or valve linings made of ceramic material?

One way to avoid unclear noun strings is to turn the key word in a string (usually the last noun) into a verb. Then turn other nouns from the string into prepositional phrases.

REVISED   The team **analyzed** flaws **in** the lining design **for** ceramic valves.

Another strategy involves turning a noun from the string into the sentence's subject.

REVISED   **Flaws** in the lining design for ceramic valves were analyzed by the team.
This version highlights the subject being analyzed.

....

Exercise 1

A. Revise the following sentences to create clear subjects and make the sentences easier to understand.

EXAMPLE

~~Our expectation is that~~ athletic shoes, ~~will~~ look good as well as feel comfortable.
We expect   *to*

1. Thirty years ago, purchase of only two styles of sneakers, high or low cut, in only two colors, black or white, was possible.

2. Today, athletic shoe manufacturer representatives boast of their companies' many different products.
3. Competition between companies is on the basis of price, appearance, features, and advertising "sizzle."
4. Labeling of athletic shoes generally indicates the activities for which they have been designed, either running, walking, basketball, tennis, or fitness.
5. Choice of shoe is usually on the basis of style, however.

 B. In a group, collaboratively revise each sentence in Exercise 1A in two ways. Then decide which (if either) is better, and why.

 C. Identifying sentence subjects and recognizing nominalizations are important steps in revising for clarity. Select two paragraphs from a draft of a paper you are writing. Circle each sentence subject (for help in identifying subjects, see 14b-1). Underline each nominalization. (You may wish to exchange papers with another writer to check your identifications.) Next, revise the paragraphs by creating significant subjects where needed and eliminating unnecessary nominalizations.

**11a
clear**

5 Use clear and specific verbs

Clear, specific verbs can make sentences forceful and easy to understand.

WEAK   Our agency is responsible for all aspects of disaster relief.

STRONGER   Our agency **plans**, **funds**, **delivers**, and **monitors** disaster relief.

Overuse of the verb *be* (*is, are, was, were, will be*) can lead to weak sentences. You should always consider replacing forms of *be* with more forceful verbs. Pay special attention to sentences that provide lists or enumerate qualities.

WEAK   Some of the programs included in the software package **are** a word processor, a spreadsheet, and a database program.

STRONGER   The software package **includes** a word processor, a spreadsheet, and a database program.

Look for predicate nouns (nominalizations) you can turn into clear, specific verbs (see 11a-2).

WEAK   The new molding process is a **money saver**.

STRONGER   The new molding process **saves money**.

Eliminate general verbs (*do, give, have, get, provide, shape, make*) linked to nouns by turning the nouns into verbs.

WEAK   Our company **has done a study** of the new design project and **will provide funding** for it.

STRONGER   Our company **has studied** the new design project and **will fund** it.

6 Keep subjects and verbs clearly related

Clear subjects and verbs play key roles in effective sentences. When subject and verb are separated by long phrases, readers may have trouble identifying these key elements and may find the sentence difficult to understand.

CONFUSING   The veterinary association, **in response to concern about the costly facilities required by new guidelines for animal care and disposal of medical waste**, has created a low-cost loan program for its members.

REVISED   The veterinary association has created a low-cost loan program for its members **in response to concern about the costly facilities required by new guidelines for animal care and disposal of medical waste**.

Separating the parts of a verb (verb phrase; see 14a-3) can also make sentences difficult to read.

UNCLEAR   Manufacturing companies **can,** if they wish to improve product quality, cost, and reliability, **contact** the university's Design for Assembly program.

REVISED   If they wish to improve product quality, cost, and reliability, manufacturing companies **can contact** the university's Design for Assembly program.

Exercise 2

A. Rewrite the following sentences, using clear verbs to make them easy to understand.

EXAMPLE

Speaking in public, is a frightening experience for many people.

frightens

1. Public speaking, regarded by many experts as an important element in successful business careers, especially on the executive level, is no longer a required course at many colleges.

2. Included among the programs offered by our consulting company is a course in public speaking.
3. We also give demonstrations of how to prepare effective graphics for a presentation.
4. Our consultants can, if a company wishes, provide training for both small and large groups.
5. The training program is a confidence builder for many people.

 B. Work with several other writers to turn the sentences in Exercise 2A into a clear, forceful paragraph that a consulting company might include in a pamphlet advertising its services. Add material if necessary to produce an effective paragraph, and combine or rearrange sentences as appropriate.

11b
clear

 C. Circle all the *to be* verbs in a draft paper; then revise any that need to be clearer and more specific.

11b Using expletive constructions sparingly

Generally, your readers will find direct sentence structures clearer and more concise than indirect sentence structures. A direct sentence structure moves from subject to verb (to object). An indirect sentence structure uses an **expletive construction** (*there is, there are,* or *it is*) to control the arrangement of the words.

	subject	**verb**	**object**
DIRECT	In this case, the man	bit	the dog.
	who?	did what?	to whom?

INDIRECT **This is** the case in which the man bit the dog.

An expletive construction does not name the subject until well into a sentence. Much of the time, expletive constructions make your sentences wordy and hard to understand.

EXPLETIVE **It is important for us to raise** more capital in order to continue developing new products.

DIRECT **We must raise** more capital in order to continue developing new products.

An expletive construction may also enable you to withhold information about the doer, the person or thing responsible for an action. You need to decide whether the lack of information is appropriate, given your context and purpose, or whether an expletive construction has led you to omit details important to your readers.

DOER NOT NAMED   There was considerable debate over whether to charge the brokerage house with insider trading and conspiracy to defraud investors.

In rewriting, you can replace an expletive construction with a significant sentence subject.

DOER NAMED   **Lawyers in the federal prosecutor's office** debated whether to charge the brokerage house with insider trading and conspiracy to defraud investors.

MORE SPECIFIC   **O'Neill, Brown, and Cappuzzo, the three lawyers in charge of the investigation,** debated whether to charge the brokerage house with insider trading and conspiracy to defraud investors.

Strategy

Review something you have written, looking for expletive constructions (*there is, there are, it is*). Decide which are justified and effective. Rewrite to eliminate any that are needlessly wordy, vague, or confusing.

You can sometimes use expletive constructions to good effect. By waiting until late in a sentence to name the subject, you can create suspense and surprise.

There were at least **four more sudden, loud explosions**.

And you can use expletives to introduce topics that will be taken up in following sentences.

There are at least **four good reasons** why the legislature should restore funding for education.
By withholding the subject, "the legislature," this writer focuses a reader's attention on the promise to discuss "four good reasons" in upcoming sentences.

A sentence with an expletive construction may also be the clearest and most precise way to make a statement.

Historians used to believe that a sudden invasion by shepherding tribes caused major changes in the region's culture. Now, however, **there is** new archaeological evidence that the "invasion" was actually a gradual resettling that took about a century.

11c Using passive voice with care

When a sentence's verb is in the active voice (see 16d), the doer (or agent) is also the subject of the sentence.

>   doer   action   goal
> The outfielder caught the towering fly ball.
>   subject   verb   object

When you choose the **passive voice** (16d) for the verb form, you turn the sentence's goal into the subject and make naming the doer optional.

11c
clear

>   goal   action   [doer]
> The towering fly ball was caught [by the outfielder].
>   subject   verb   [prepositional phrase]

Using the passive voice, you de-emphasize the doer by placing it in a prepositional phrase or by dropping it altogether. In addition, you create sentences that are generally wordier than corresponding versions in the active voice. Note how emphasis and length differ in active and passive versions of the following sentence.

ACTIVE VOICE
                doer (subject)
       The Centers for Disease Control interviewed three thousand people affected by the toxin.

PASSIVE VOICE
            subject
       Three thousand people affected by the toxin were inter-
                           doer
       viewed by **the Centers for Disease Control.**

Strategy

Review your writing, looking for sentences that use verbs in the passive voice (see 16d). Recast in the active voice any sentences that are unnecessarily wordy or that create inappropriate emphasis. Consider naming the doer in any sentences that fail to provide this information.

If you wish to emphasize the *doer,* use the active voice. If you wish to draw readers' attention to the goal or outcome of an action rather than its doer, consider using the passive voice.

ACTIVE
            Poorly trained contract workers caused the explosion and fire at the refinery.
            Subject emphasizes cause.

PASSIVE   **The explosion and fire** at the refinery were caused by poorly trained contract workers.
Subject emphasizes result.

You can also use the passive voice to highlight significant elements in a discussion.

Refineries are potentially dangerous workplaces. **Most accidents** can be prevented, however, by careful training of workers.
Passive voice in the second sentence keeps attention on the dangers.

11c
clear

Did You Know?

Advice on using the passive voice has changed radically during the last hundred years. According to Dennis Baron, experts on grammar and writing style during the eighteenth and nineteenth centuries had few objections to sentences using the passive voice. By the middle of the twentieth century, however, they had begun criticizing the passive voice for encouraging wordiness, vagueness, and even deception (by allowing writers to avoid naming the person or group responsible for an action). Now, editors and writing teachers regularly advise writers to eliminate passive voice whenever possible.

Dennis Baron, "The Passive Voice Can Be Your Friend," *Declining Grammar and Other Essays on the English Vocabulary* (Urbana: National Council of Teachers of English, 1989) 17–22.

You can choose whether or not to name the doer in a sentence written in the passive voice.

Requirements for the term paper were distributed in all sections of the psychology course [by the individual instructors].

When the doer is unknown or unimportant, you can appropriately omit it.

Federal income tax forms will be mailed on January 1.
By the IRS, of course.

But when leaving out the doer would omit important information or mislead readers, include it.

Consumers were not informed of their right to sue for damages.
The sentence doesn't say who withheld the information.

Exercise 3

A. Revise the following sentences to eliminate expletive constructions and passive voice.

EXAMPLE

Grocery stores sell
~~There are~~ _many different kinds of ice cream~~, sold by grocery stores~~_.

1. It is the superpremium brands that many people choose from the ice cream freezers in their supermarkets.
2. Superpremium ice cream is blended with more butterfat and less air than regular ice cream contains.
3. The high fat content ought to be considered before the ice cream is purchased.
4. There are new frozen dessert products that are challenging the rich, tasty ice creams.
5. Frozen yogurts with candy and nuts mixed in have been heavily promoted.

11c
clear

B. Working in a group, use revised versions of the sentences in Exercise 3A to create a paragraph. You can draw on your knowledge and experience to add information or to create sentences of your own to fill in any gaps in the explanation. Make sure that the sentences you add are clear and effective.

C. First, do some research on different kinds of ice cream and other frozen desserts, and create a short essay of your own explaining the different kinds or exploring recent tastes and trends in the frozen-dessert industry. Make sure the sentences in your essay are both detailed and clear.

Next, review a draft of a paper you are preparing. Circle any expletive constructions, and underline any sentences containing verbs in the passive voice. Revise the draft to eliminate any unnecessary uses of the passive voice or expletive constructions.

Creating Emphatic and Varied Sentences

The best writing offers sentences that go beyond correctness and clarity. It uses sentence strategies that guide readers by creating appropriate emphasis while at the same time intriguing and pleasing with variety and style. You can sometimes create such sentences as part of an initial draft. They are more likely to take shape during revision, however, as the products of your careful attention and effort.

Sentences in the following passage, for example, provide variety, forceful emphasis, and even surprise.

> Water is at the heart of the system. It feeds the Biscayne Aquifer, the gigantic underground cavern that supplies fresh water to Miami and other thirsty coastal towns. And it has given life to a magnificent array of creatures. When the first Spaniards arrived in 1513, an estimated five million alligators lived in the Glades, along with uncounted crocodiles; this lush habitat is one of the few on earth where these cousins exist together. The sloughs (freshwater rivers running through the saw-grass prairies) were thick with largemouth bass and bluegills. There were herds of deer, thousands of raccoons, opossums, otter, mink, and black bear and fox, along with the beautiful Florida panther. There were twenty-six kinds of snakes. In the bays and rivers you could see the manatee, huge and homely and shy. In Florida Bay, there were stone crabs, dolphins, sharks, and barracuda. And always, there were the birds. — PETE HAMILL, "The Neverglades"

The sentences vary in length from six words to thirty-five. They vary in detail, from plain statements to extensive lists. And they vary in strategy: from simple, direct statements; to clusters of details; to arrangements that withhold surprising (or upsetting) information until the end ("There were twenty-six kinds of snakes").

12a Creating emphasis

Your readers will not automatically notice the most important ideas and information in a sentence. In revising, you can highlight significant material by making it the subject of a sentence, by placing it at a sentence's beginning or end, by repeating it, or by presenting it in a special sentence pattern.

1 Pay attention to sentence subjects

The information you place in a sentence subject often gets the most attention. Note how each version of the following sentence offers a different focus according to the writer's choice of subject.

**12a
sent**

> **The portfolio** should contain those essays that represent your achievement as a writer.

> **Your achievement as a writer** should be represented by those essays contained in the portfolio.

> **The essays contained in the portfolio** should be those that represent your achievement as a writer.

2 Use sentence beginnings and endings

A reader's attention gravitates toward sentence beginnings and endings. You can take advantage of this phenomenon by shifting the material you wish to emphasize to a sentence's opening or closing.

UNEMPHATIC   Gases produced during the cheese-making process by the "eye former," a bacterium, create the holes in Swiss cheese.

REVISED   **The "eyes,"** or the holes in Swiss cheese, are created during the cheese-making process by gases produced by a bacterium, **the "eye former."**
    Words at the beginning and end emphasize the unusual names. The verb shifts from active to passive voice (see 11c).

REVISED   **Called "eyes" and produced by gases from a bacterium called the "eye former,"** the holes in Swiss cheese are created during the cheese-making process.
    Phrases at the beginning emphasize the names.

3 Employ repetition

By repeating words and ideas within a sentence or within a cluster of sentences, you draw attention to them. Note how the following unemphatic passage gains focus and direction when the writer revises it to add repetition.

UNEMPHATIC   The original Egyptian hieroglyphs were pictures of things. Later they became symbols, so that a leg could also mean *run* or *fast*. Next they came to indicate sounds in the spoken language and then syllables of words. Finally, they began representing the sounds of single letters.

REVISED   The original Egyptian hieroglyphs were **pictures** of things. Later they became **idea pictures,** so that a leg could also mean *run* or *fast*. Next, **sound pictures** indicated **sounds** in the spoken language and then syllables of words. Finally, the **pictures** turned into symbols representing the **sounds** of single letters.

**12a
sent**

Repetition has dangers, however. Too much repetition calls attention to itself, not the writer's ideas. Unless it focuses on key words and ideas, repetition may make a passage hard to read, as in the following example.

CONFUSING   The **Phoenicians** were not the first **people** to invent an **alphabet,** but they were the **people** responsible for spreading the **alphabet** to other **peoples** of the Mediterranean.
READER'S RESPONSE: I think the contrast between *inventing* and *spreading* is the most important idea here, though other things in the sentence seem to draw more attention.

4 Create emphatic sentence patterns

Inverted sentence order, climactic order, periodic sentences, and cumulative sentences all offer ways to create emphasis. These patterns may be somewhat unfamiliar to you as a writer—though you have undoubtedly encountered them in reading. You are therefore more likely to find them useful as revision strategies you can use consciously to add or vary emphasis.

Inversion. By inverting the normal subject-verb-object/complement word order, you can shift the focus of a sentence. **Inverted sentence order** often calls attention to itself and to the element you have moved to the initial position.

INVERTED   **From the darkness near the rear of the auditorium thundered the director's voice** with criticisms of our acting.

NORMAL   **The director's voice thundered** from the darkness near the rear of the auditorium with criticisms of our acting.

Because inversion creates emphasis in part by disrupting a reader's expectations for sentence order, overuse of it or other exotic sentence orders will confuse or irritate readers.

Climactic Order. Using **climactic sentence order**—sentences that build to a climax—can create powerful emphasis, especially on the last element in a series.

> What every truly modern home has, she said, is a dishwasher, a gas grill, a Jacuzzi, **and a divorce.**

Periodic Sentences. A **periodic sentence** piles up phrases, clauses, and words at the beginning, delaying the main clause of the sentence. The suspense casts a spotlight on the main clause.

> Because she knows that inspired designs often spring from hard work, because she loves perfection yet fears failure, and because she believes that risk-taking does not eliminate attention to detail, Jennifer is working eighteen hours a day on her fall clothing collection.

12a
sent

The risk, of course, lies in delaying so long that the reader loses track of the meaning, as in the following example.

CONFUSING   Having begun the business as much to escape from boredom as to make a profit, and also suffering from a lack of skill in accounting and an unwillingness to listen to the good advice of the professionals they hired to review the management and recordkeeping procedures that were causing dissension among employees, Sheila and Stefan decided to declare bankruptcy.

Did You Know?

Readers are not likely to notice the style of a piece of writing or to consider it emphatic and memorable unless the author takes some chances and goes beyond everyday ways of constructing sentences. As Ronald Carter and Walter Nash point out, "One of the most widespread definitions of style is that we recognize it because it stands out in some way. You notice a distinctive way of doing things, whether this is a particular style of fashion or a style of playing tennis, because it is *marked* in relation to the more standard or *normal* ways of doing it."

Ronald Carter and Walter Nash, *Seeing Through Language* (Oxford: Blackwell, 1990) 3.

Cumulative Sentences. To build a **cumulative sentence**, you start with the main clause, then add details and statements in the form of modifying phrases, clauses, and words. The main clause provides a firm base to which you can add details and ideas, bit by bit.

A cumulative sentence allows you first to emphasize the main clause, then the successive words, phrases, and clauses that work cumulatively to build a detailed picture, an intricate explanation, or a cluster of ideas and information.

Main clause	Varna stumbled down the stairs,
Details	the flowerpot falling from her grip,
Details	spilling dirt into the air,
Details	shattering on the linoleum floor just seconds before she landed among the shards of pottery and fragments of geranium,
Details	the loud thud bringing everyone in the house to attention.

12a
sent

Sometimes you may wish to combine periodic and cumulative sentence strategies, as in the first sentence of the following example. Or you may wish to use the strategies alone, as in the second sentence, where the author presents details cumulatively.

In "the library," inside the mission-style bookcase with its three diamond-latticed glass doors, with my father's Morris chair and the glass-shaded lamp on its table beside it, were books I could soon begin on—and I did, reading them all alike and as they came, straight down their rows, top shelf to bottom. There was the set of Stoddard's Lectures, in all its late nineteenth-century vocabulary and vignettes of peasant life and quaint beliefs and customs, with matching halftone illustrations: Vesuvius erupting, Venice by moonlight, gypsies glimpsed by their campfires.   — EUDORA WELTY, *One Writer's Beginnings*

Writer's Tip

If one of the elements following the main clause in a cumulative sentence is another main clause—a clause that can stand on its own as a sentence—your cumulative sentence will become hard to read, illogical, or ungrammatical.

CONFUSING   Shauna jammed the documents into the express mail package, hurriedly, with trembling fingers, **her eyes were barely focused,** worried about the consequences of her actions, which she nonetheless completed because she felt morally obligated.

The independent clause "her eyes were barely focused" makes Shauna's eyes, rather than Shauna herself, "worried about the consequences."

To keep your cumulative sentences from becoming loose and ungrammatical, make sure none of the elements you add following a main clause can stand on its own. (See 14c.)

REVISED	Shauna jammed the documents into the express mail package [main clause],
	    hurriedly,
	    with trembling fingers,
	    eyes barely focused,
	worried about the consequences of her actions,
	which she nonetheless completed because she felt morally obligated.

Exercise 1

A. Combine the following statements into sentences that provide appropriate emphasis. Add or eliminate words as necessary.

EXAMPLE

To keep from making mistakes in your work and to avoid accidents as you drive, ʌYou need to be alert and wide awake during the day. ~~You need to be alert to keep from making mistakes in your work. You also need to be wide awake to avoid accidents as you drive.~~

1. Sleep researchers study patterns of being awake and being asleep. They have been studying napping.
2. Truck drivers, medical interns, and security guards need to stay alert while on the job. They often get sleepy while working.
3. Some research studies indicate that naps can help prevent sleepiness while working. Naps can make a person more alert. They can improve a person's mood.
4. Afternoon naps are particularly helpful. They can help overcome the effects of too little sleep at night.
5. Napping patterns vary from culture to culture. Working and eating patterns vary as well.

B. Examine the following passage carefully, and identify the strategies the author uses to create emphasis.

There was a time when people who wanted to keep the peace and keep the crockery intact held to a strict dinner-table rule: Never argue about politics or religion. I don't know how well it worked in American dining rooms, but it worked pretty well in our schools. We dealt with religion by not arguing about it.

Children who came out of diverse homes might carve up the turf of their neighborhood and turn the playgrounds into a religious battlefield, but the public classroom was common ground. Intolerance wasn't tolerated.

In place of teaching one religion or another, the schools held to a common denominator of values. It was, in part, the notion of Horace Mann, the nineteenth-century father of the public-school system. He believed that the way to avoid religious conflicts was to extract what all religions agree upon and allow this "non-religious" belief system into schools.

I wonder what Mann would think of that experiment now. Was it naive or sophisticated? Was it a successful or a failed attempt to avoid conflict in a pluralistic society?

— ELLEN GOODMAN, "Religion in the Textbooks"

Working with a group of fellow writers, try to agree on answers to these questions about the Goodman passage: Which sentence strategies do you think add to the effectiveness of the passage, and why? Which, if any, detract from its effectiveness?

C. Choose two paragraphs from a draft of an essay you are writing, and revise them to add emphasis, using the techniques discussed in 12a. Then repeat the process with two more paragraphs at a time until you have revised the entire paper.

12b   Creating variety

Too many sentences of similar length, type, and structure can create unemphatic writing that bores readers. Variety, carefully constructed, can make your writing more lively. Many of the strategies that create emphasis (see 12a) can also create variety, and the two qualities often go together.

1   Vary sentence length

Making your sentences all the same length—short, medium, or long— is a recipe for monotony. Revision is a good opportunity to pay attention to varying the length of sentences. Try variety. Use short sentences for dramatic contrast and for emphasis. Create longer sentences to explore relationships among ideas and to add rhythmic effects to your prose. Use middle-length sentences as workhorses, carrying the burden of explanation and description, but don't use too many of them at once.

Note how variety in sentence length helps make this explanation easy to read and interesting.

The real country ham may or may not be smoked after curing. Smithfield, Virginia, hams are smoked over hardwood or hardwood sawdust. Unscrupulous producers use smoke flavoring. But Mac Pierce, who runs the country's largest retail pork market, Nahunta Pork Center in Pikeville, North Carolina, says less than 1 percent of his hams are smoked, and most of those are bought by northerners. "Smoke masks a good ham's flavor," says Mac.

— BILL NEAL, "How to Cure a Pig"

Strategy

Vary sentence length as you revise. Combine some draft sentences to highlight relationships; compress others to emphasize ideas. Cut or add words and ideas as appropriate.

12b
sent

DRAFT   Political conventions used to be occasions for selecting among rival candidates. They are no longer serious contests. The likely winners are known well in advance. Conventions are now simply places for political strategists and campaign workers to meet. They are also ways of getting attention from the media.

REVISED   Political conventions used to be occasions for selecting among rival candidates, but no longer, for the likely winners are now known well in advance. They are now simply meeting places for political strategists and campaign workers. They are media events.

2 Vary sentence types

It's easy to get into the habit of using only **declarative sentences,** sentences that make statements (see 14d on sentence types). This is especially true in expository and argumentative writing, where your purpose is to present, explain, and support ideas or information. An occasional exclamation (**exclamatory sentence**), a mild order (**imperative sentence**), or a question (**interrogative sentence**) can vary the pace of your prose effectively, making it more lively and memorable.

DRAFT   Some of the less familiar sports offer good opportunities for entertainment and exercise. Soccer games, lacrosse matches, and bicycle races can provide you with fast-paced and often thrilling events. A rugby team, a badminton class, or a squash league can offer you strenuous exercise and vigorous competition. All you have to do to benefit from these activities is to take the simple step of getting involved.

REVISED   Some of the less familiar sports offer good opportunities for entertainment and exercise. Are you looking for fast-paced, thrilling events? Go see a soccer game, a lacrosse match, or a bicycle race. Do you want strenuous exercise and vigorous competition? Sign up for a rugby team, a badminton class, or a squash league. To benefit from these activities you need only take a simple step: Get involved!

A **rhetorical question** is one that requires no answer or that you plan to answer yourself in the course of an essay. Rhetorical questions can be especially useful in expository and argumentative writing.

These are all ways you can get more time for sleep, even in the midst of a busy schedule. **But is it really important for most of us to get more sleep?** It is, and staying healthy and staying alert aren't the only good reasons for doing so.

12b
sent

3 Vary sentence structures and patterns

You can create variety by blending sentence structures in your writing (use simple, compound, and complex sentences; see 14d) and by varying the kinds of coordination and subordination you employ (see Chapter 26). You can also create variety by using periodic and cumulative sentence patterns (see 12a-4).

By trying different sentence openings or inverting sentence order (see 12a-4), you can make sure your sentences vary in arrangement.

INVERSION	The house paint we bought no one liked.
PHRASE	**To our neighbor's eyes,** the house looked like it belonged somewhere else.
PHRASE	**Looking for a bargain,** we bought the paint at a discount store.
PHRASE	**The paint having been cheaply made,** the house began peeling within a year and a half.
DEPENDENT CLAUSE	**If you want to be happy with a paint job,** spend the money for quality materials.
TRANSITIONAL EXPRESSION	**In addition,** choose the color carefully.

Exercise 2

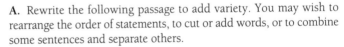

A. Rewrite the following passage to add variety. You may wish to rearrange the order of statements, to cut or add words, or to combine some sentences and separate others.

Psychologists have been studying what events people remember. People from middle age on remember events from their early years more clearly than they remember more recent events. People in their seventies have clear memories of their thirties but less clear memories of their fifties. Most of us remember very little about childhood. Almost no one remembers events from before four years old. Researchers think that we tend to remember events that are new or exciting to us and to forget routine events. Memorable events are most likely to occur early in life. Infants probably have not developed the mental abilities necessary to create memories, however.

 B. Compare your rewritten version of the passage in Exercise 2A with those produced by other writers. Working in a group, produce one version of the passage that draws on the best parts of the individual versions.

12c sent

 C. Count the words in three paragraphs of a draft essay of your own in order to discover the average number of words per sentence. If most of the sentences are close to this average length, rewrite the paragraphs to add variety. Following this, rewrite the rest of the draft to introduce variety in sentence length when appropriate.

12c Creating surprise

Good writing often takes risks and employs strategies that surprise readers by creating intriguing and pleasing patterns. Sentences that change direction—or seem to—are particularly effective.

1 Use summative modifiers

A **summative modifier** summarizes the preceding part of a sentence, then sends it off in a new direction.

To protect your vegetables against harmful insects, you can use soap sprays, scatter insect-repelling plants among the beds, or introduce "friendly" insects like ladybugs and praying mantises—**three techniques** that will not leave a harmful chemical residue on the food you grow.

2 Use resumptive modifiers

A **resumptive modifier** extends a sentence that appears to have ended, adding new information or twists of thought.

People who are careful about what they eat may lead healthier lives, **healthier,** though not necessarily longer.

The advertising campaign is a surprising failure, **surprising** because it worked so well with test audiences.

3 Create antithesis

Antithesis—the use of parallelism to emphasize contrast—can be witty, dramatic, cynical, ironic, or memorable.

To err is human, to forgive divine. — ALEXANDER POPE

Can an honest politician be smart, or a smart politician honest?

12c
sent

Exercise 3

A. Browse through the current magazines at the library, looking for one that contains relatively long essays with varied and often surprising writing style. You might look at *Vogue, Esquire,* the *New Yorker, GQ, Vanity Fair,* the *Utne Reader, Commentary, Details,* or *Tikkun.* Choose two paragraphs whose style you admire, and identify in them as many as you can of the sentence strategies discussed in this chapter. Be ready to discuss why the sentences can be considered effective in communicating the author's ideas.

B. Choose an everyday activity, and write a paragraph about it that uses emphasis and variety in sentence strategy in such a way that the activity seems interesting, enjoyable, and worth doing. Create at least one sentence with a summative modifier and one with a resumptive modifier. You may want to write about repotting a plant, fixing a problem on a car, or even writing a paper for class.

C. Read your paragraph aloud to a group of fellow writers, and then listen to their paragraphs. When you are finished listening, exchange paragraphs with another group member. Read your partner's paragraph. Underline the sentence you like best, and suggest a revision for the sentence you like least. When you are finished, explain your responses to your partner.

EDITING AND PROOFREADING

The Editing and Proofreading Process

After making major and minor revisions in your writing (see Chapter 8), you can turn your attention to editing. **Editing** means fine-tuning your work for a reader—adjusting sentences and words for clarity, for precise meaning and effect, and for correctness. It means identifying problems in grammar and sentence structure as well as glaring omissions or repetitions. And it means looking for consistency in style, punctuation, word usage, and tone.

Finding and changing such problems should not be confused with proofreading. When you proofread a paper, you hunt for distracting or careless errors such as misspelled words, transposed letters, and incorrect hyphenation or word division. Proofreading is your last chance to make sure that errors in presentation do not distract and annoy your reader.

The ability to edit and proofread is a valuable and marketable skill—so valuable, in fact, that it makes up an entire profession. In college, some students pay professional editors to look over their papers. But shirking the responsibility of learning how to edit your own writing won't serve you well when the resources of an editor aren't available to you—and that will be most of the time. You will need to rely on your own editing and proofreading skills, along with some help from your peer readers, to improve your drafts.

To develop your editing skills, begin recognizing errors or areas of your writing that need improvement. Relevant sections of this handbook will help you to locate recurring problems in your drafts, thus improving the specific paper you are working on. This process will improve your overall writing ability so that your papers are stronger from the start.

13a   Editing your own writing

To edit successfully, you first must learn to read your writing with an editor's eyes. Good editing demands that you focus hard on a text and read carefully and slowly. You simply can't edit well if you are skimming a paper twenty minutes before class.

Editing for style and correctness calls for a special kind of reading, one that shifts away from content (what's being said) and toward form (how it is being said). Once you've restructured confusing paragraphs or garbled sentences through major and minor revision, you can then take a magnifying glass to each sentence and scrutinize it for smaller stylistic concerns, grammar, and punctuation. Problems, inconsistencies, and errors will emerge, and you *must* repair them before your paper can be considered finished.

Often, editing requires you to hold in mind a certain concern (commas, for example, or sexist language) while you scour your entire text for specific cases. If you look for too many different problems at once, the demands on your editing process may be too great. Sometimes you may need to read your text four, five, six, or more times, holding in mind a different cluster of concerns for each reading.

**13a
edit**

1 Final editing for economy and style

Even after major and minor revision have tightened the focus and eliminated inessential or repetitive sections (see Chapter 8), most papers can still profit from some final cosmetic surgery. If any part of a sentence adds little or nothing to style or meaning, eliminate it during a final check for redundancy or excess verbiage.

NEAR-FINAL DRAFT	In actual fact, the team's jubilation, happiness, and joy lasted only as long as they were victorious winners. **READER'S RESPONSE:** This seems repetitive and tiring.
EDITED	~~In actual fact,~~ **T**he team's jubilation~~, happiness, and joy~~ lasted only as long as they were victorious. ~~winners.~~
NEAR-FINAL DRAFT	After the city of Chambers built the new public library, my parents decided to take my brother and me there to introduce us to literature and give us a chance to read great works of fiction. **READER'S RESPONSE:** The sentence says the same thing twice.
EDITED	After the city of Chambers built the new public library, my parents decided to take my brother and me there to introduce us to **great** literature. ~~and give us a chance to read great works of fiction.~~

Strategy

To edit for final trimming and styling, ask yourself the following questions about your draft.

- Are my sentences reasonably easy to read?

  Try reading your sentences (even out loud) from the perspective of a reader unfamiliar with their content and purpose. Whenever you stumble over a phrase or a whole sentence, try rearranging the structure for easier reading.

- Do any words stand out as odd or inappropriate for my purpose?

  Try to choose a more appropriate word. Consider turning to a dictionary or thesaurus for help (see Chapter 28).

- Have I used some sentence structures too often?

  Try varying sentence structures. For example, do almost all sentences begin with nouns or with a pronoun like *I*? Then try starting some sentences with prepositional phrases or subordinate clauses.

- If I had to cut ten words from each page, which ones could I eliminate?

  Cut the excess if you can do so without creating new problems in style (for example, short, choppy sentences).

13a
edit

Exercise 1

A. In a brochure-writing assignment, Kim Francis wrote the following draft paragraph for a pamphlet describing tourist attractions and accommodations near her Wisconsin home. Read the paragraph once for meaning and then a second time for editing. During the second reading, focus on editing for economy and style. Ask some of the questions listed in the Strategy in 13a-1. Then edit the paragraph to make it more effective.

After spending a day exploring the countryside, rest and relax at a quaint country inn, relaxing by the fire and sipping on some mulled wine. After spending a quiet night in a room decorated with beautiful old antiques, wake up to a country breakfast. Then after your pleasant stay at the inn, explore the quaint towns and roads that have made Door County, Wisconsin, such an attractive vacation destination for people who like to escape and get away from it all.

B. Meet with some fellow writers and share your edited versions of this paragraph. Next, work as a group to prepare a single edited version of the paragraph. If you wish, make use of the individual versions produced by group members.

C. Apply the Strategy in 13a-1 to your paper in progress, being sure that you have reached an appropriate stage for editing after taking the draft through one or more major and minor revisions.

2 Editing for grammatical problems

Editing your writing for grammatical problems will challenge you in two ways. First you must *identify* the problem, then you must *edit* your prose to alleviate the problem. Many writers spend too little time identifying problems and simply correct those few they spot while quickly skimming their drafts. But if you leave it up to your reader to find errors that you missed, the entire force of your paper will be compromised.

You will be able to identify some problems in your writing immediately because you simply "slipped" while you were more engaged in your thoughts than your expression. Other problems may be less obvious but still identifiable because you have a "sense" that you've made an error or because you know you have difficulty with that feature. Still others may be errors that you're not conscious of making or that you don't know how to spot. You may need to try different strategies in each of these situations.

13a
edit

Identifying Known Errors. All writers make identifiable mistakes in grammar, word choice, and other editing concerns while immersed in their thoughts during the writing process. These are the easiest problems to spot because you already know what's wrong. Editing gives you the chance to focus on whether your writing is grammatically correct and conforms to all your reader's expectations.

Strategy

Read your paper slowly from start to finish. Resist becoming too immersed in your ideas. Instead, look carefully and deliberately at each paragraph, circling or marking any errors in grammar, punctuation, and sentence logic. If you can quickly correct an error along the way, do so. If you're not certain how to correct the error, wait until you've finished identifying problems, then refer to the appropriate sections in this handbook or other reference tools for advice.

"Before" and "after" paragraphs from Jim Tollefson's paper on the Endangered Species Act show his circled errors (labeled in the margins) and his edited version.

DRAFT WITH ERRORS IDENTIFIED

Critics of the endangered species act *caps* think it is too broad. Because some specie's *fragment / apostrop* may be less vital to environmental balance than others. They want to protect species *Who?* selectively, however, scientists still do not *comma splice* know which species are more important.

EDITED

Critics of the Endangered Species Act think it is too broad because some species may be less vital to environmental balance than others. These critics want to protect species selectively. However, scientists still do not know which species are more important.

13a edit

Here is a list of errors that many instructors are likely to consider quite serious because they confuse or irritate readers. Refer to the chapter or section listed in parentheses for more information on these topics.

Sentence fragments (Chapter 19)
Comma splices and fused sentences (Chapter 20)
Pronoun reference (Chapter 21)
Subject-verb agreement (17a and 17b)
Comma usage (Chapter 31)
Lack of parallelism (Chapter 25)
Misplaced, dangling, and disruptive modifiers (Chapter 22)
Mixed sentence structures (24a)
Problems with verb form and tense (Chapter 16)
Spelling (Chapter 42)

You may wish to begin your editing by focusing on problems like these and then continue by checking other areas of sentence structure, word choice, spelling, and punctuation that interfere with the relationship between you and your reader.

Identifying Suspected Errors. Other kinds of problems in your writing that require editing will be somewhat less obvious to you. For example, you may suspect that you've made an error but may not be completely sure. In such cases, *don't take a risk* by failing to follow the lead. Check the rule or convention to be sure, and edit accordingly.

Strategy

Circle or mark all suspected problems or errors in your paper. Then check appropriate sections in this handbook or another reference work, and edit those that are, in fact, errors. Ignore any circled problems that turn out not to be errors. If any suspected errors are still unresolved after a thorough check, ask a teacher, editor, or knowledgeable peer or friend to help you. Use any actual errors to help build your editing checklist.

Create your own editing checklist of problems or errors that you often encounter in your writing. Apply the checklist to each paper you write. Begin by analyzing your own papers and by giving some samples of your writing to a teacher or expert writer. Ask that person to identify *patterns* of error in your writing, and also look for them on your own. Using this handbook, study the errors and try to identify their causes. Then create your own strategies for recognizing the errors, and turn these into a personalized editing checklist for your papers and other writing. As you get better at recognizing and repairing these problems, you can delete strategies you no longer need and add new ones. This process can be especially useful as you learn to write in more diverse and sophisticated settings.

13a
edit

After thoroughly editing her paper on the effects of loud music, Carrie Brehe put three more items on her editing checklist.

1. A lot—sounds like one word but is actually two. Think of an entire "lot" full of whatever. From the noise paper: "Alot of teenagers have no information about how their hearing works." Search for all cases of alot.
2. If they would have known. I say this a lot (ha!). I'm still not sure what the subjunctive means, but this problem shows up when I write "if." Correct to if they had or if they were. Search for all cases of "if + would." From the noise paper: "If they would have known what the concerts were doing to their eardrums, they might have stopped going."
3. Their vs. there. Sound the same. I usually write "there" for "their" when I make this mistake, but not the reverse. "Their" is possessive only, and "there" is location. From the noise paper: "Most people are not even aware that there hearing can be damaged by lawn mowers, chain saws, and even jets taking off." Search for all cases of there/their.

Identifying Unknown Errors. A final category of mistakes consists of those you have no idea you're making. These are the most frustrating kind because in most cases you need to learn them through experience. Writing courses and tutoring services are designed to help you identify and edit such errors so that you can eventually avoid them in the first place. Studying handbooks and reading as much professional prose as you can may help; but by far the best strategy is to work with your own writing.

Strategy

Read your writing, preferably aloud. Sometimes this will help you to locate problem spots intuitively. Or you may recognize them because you encounter difficulty reading a passage. Circle everything you question; then use the strategy on page 161 for checking suspected errors.

Ask someone to read your paper and to mark or circle any problems he or she encounters. Your reader doesn't need to be a grammarian to call attention to problems with sentences, usage, and the like. Good readers will spot errors intuitively. Since they're not as close to the text as you are, these readers may find some problems you might overlook yourself. (See 13b for more on collaborative editing.)

As you discover them, add *all* previously unknown errors to your editing checklist. Refer to your checklist when you edit all future papers. You can remove these items from the checklist when you are sure you handle these problems correctly.

13a
edit

Exercise 2

A. Working from a paper that your instructor has commented on (or that you have asked another teacher or expert writer to examine), begin creating your own editing checklist.

B. Share checklists with a group of your fellow writers, and create a checklist for the entire group. Do you all have the same problems? Try to explain why particular features cause difficulties for writers in the group, and try to arrive at strategies for identifying and overcoming the problems. Then create an editing checklist for your entire class.

C. Keep adding to and revising your editing checklist throughout the term, applying it to your papers in progress. At the end of the term, review your checklist along with the various changes you have made in it. On the basis of the checklist, prepare a brief report highlighting the things you have to be alert for as you edit. Also summarize any changes in your writing habits that the checklist revealed during the term.

13b Collaborative editing

When you edit collaboratively, you identify and talk about specific problems in a paper with one or more "consulting readers," usually friends or peers. The value of collaborative editing lies not just in ridding an individual paper of errors but in learning to identify and correct errors on your own. Every time someone points out an error to you, focus on it and its effects on your reader. Identifying problems takes only a few minutes of hard, conscious attention, and the investment in time will pay off for the rest of your writing life.

Collaborative editing, like the more central practice of collaborative revising, takes some practice. When you are the consulting reader and one of your partners or group members is the writer, you might try some of the following suggestions for providing the best advice. Use the same principles for gleaning advice from your own consulting readers.

- When someone asks you to read his or her paper for editorial feedback, be sure the paper is finished enough for this kind of work. If the paper still requires attention to matters of content and organization, explain to the writer that until these matters are dealt with, surface editing will be a waste of time. (You can also provide feedback for larger revisions, as explained in Chapter 8.)
- Try to use familiar language and symbols for your comments so the writer will readily understand them. The terminology used in this handbook is generally accepted in education and business. As you learn to identify errors in your writing, attach the appropriate labels to them. This will make it easier to help other writers to locate appropriate explanatory or corrective material for their own patterns of error.
- If you're uncertain about a feature, such as a possible spelling error, just note your uncertainty. Let the writer use a reference source (a dictionary, a style guide, or this handbook—see Chapter 28) to identify and correct the problem.
- Avoid "taking over" the writer's draft. Identify outright errors, but don't rewrite whole sentences and paragraphs. Rewriting is the author's job.
- If the draft is clearly in need of major revision rather than editing, it's not worthwhile to spend lots of time tinkering with small details. You might offer more global feedback instead.
- If you think that a writer has been unnecessarily sloppy, hoping that you'll clean up the mess, don't spend much time working on the paper. The draft you're editing should be as clean a version as the writer can produce.
- Comments about style are always more helpful when they're specific. Marginal comments like "awkward," "good," or "I like this" won't always help the writer know specifically what works or doesn't work.

**13b
edit**

If something is good or bad, tell why. But don't spend time writing long explanations.

- Try to identify patterns of error in the writer's prose. If the writer repeats the same mistakes, point the repetition out.

Exercise 3

 On the day your teacher returns drafts or finished papers with comments, look for any errors he or she has noted or identified. Working in groups of three or four, read each other's papers, looking for patterns of error. Compare these patterns and, as a group, try to write "rules" explaining how to fix them. In creating the rules, feel free to use your own terms and ways of explaining. Add any new cases to your editing checklist.

13c Shortcut editing

Editing has its share of "quick fix" remedies. Among the most attractive are computer programs that "read" a piece of prose and then tell you how to correct or improve it. Before buying such a program, learn something about what it can and can't do.

1 What computer editors can do

Each year, programs that claim to identify problems in your writing become more sophisticated. Some can be useful, depending on your goals and your writing situation. Professional contexts, for example, often encourage the use of needlessly complex or jargon-filled prose. Some editing programs can identify features like the average length of sentences and instances of the passive voice. They can also provide a "jargon index" of words not in the vocabulary of most readers. You can then use this information to edit your prose.

When examining an editing program, see whether it will meet your specific needs. Use the following questions as a guide.

- Does the program identify errors in spelling, punctuation, capitalization, and usage?
- Does it identify incorrect sentence structure?
- Does it allow you to design your own rules and add them to the program, tailoring it to meet your editorial needs?
- Will it alert you to unclear sentences, problems with subject-verb agreement or modifiers, sexist or discriminatory language, and vague expressions?

- Is it linked to a spelling checker, thesaurus, dictionary, synonym finder, or other utility?
- Will it identify clichéd or vague expressions and commonly misused words?

2 What computer editors can't do

Although they may claim to answer most of your writing problems, most computerized editing programs are no match for human readers and editors. Most programs will alert you to a potential problem but leave you to identify and repair it yourself. Grammar and style checkers also take a lot of time for what they deliver, and they can check only material that has been typed into the computer. The programs provide few options for different kinds of writing or for audiences that differ in sophistication and background knowledge. Beware, therefore, of blanket pronouncements from the program. They may be inappropriate for your writing situation.

Of course, *anything* that responds to your writing can be useful, if only in increasing your awareness of the features in your text. Go ahead and try some programs. If they work for you, so much the better. But remember, computers can't do what human readers can. The hard work of editing is probably here to stay.

13d
proof

Did You Know?

A recent study suggests that the activities of writers, readers, and editors are quite different. When you engage in one of the activities, it's very hard to engage in the others, because each requires a certain way of thinking and a different way of perceiving the text. Although you may be able to do all three activities fairly well, it's hard, if not impossible, to do them at the same time. This and related studies show how important it is to set aside time for each activity.

Karen M. Petit, "Communication as a Function of Writers Writing, Readers Reading, and Editors Editing," diss., U of Rhode Island, 1993.

13d Proofreading

Finally, after you've made as many conscious decisions about your writing as possible and are ready to submit it, it's time for **proofreading**, looking for errors you may have missed during the editing process. No writer produces an absolutely flawless document every single time. This book, for example, has undergone extensive scrutiny to be sure that *every* word is spelled correctly and that *every* punctuation mark is in the right place. And still, after everything the authors did, after every one of the numerous reviewers had spotted mistakes, after every editor worked on the project, there were tiny flaws only an astute proofreader's eye could find. (We hope, of course, that all of them were found, but published books often contain at least one *erratum,* a trivial mistake overlooked by the entire crew working on the project.)

You may wonder why there is so much fuss about editing. Every time a reader encounters even a tiny error, the author looks slightly less in control. One or two insignificant mistakes have little impact, especially if the work is otherwise powerful. But as the slips accumulate, the author's credibility sinks in the reader's mind.

In college, when teachers read your writing, loss of credibility can ruin the effectiveness of your ideas and lead to a poor assessment of your work. Surprisingly, many students skip proofreading, one of the simplest of all the processes a paper needs to go through before it's finished. Before you turn in a piece of writing, submit it to a meticulous reading. Focus consciously on every word of your document. Don't let your eyes blur. Instead, move from word to word, fixing your eyes on each word to be sure it doesn't contain transposed letters, typographical errors, and the like. Or try reading your writing out loud. Treat every error you identify as if it were a prize catch, raising the credibility of your ideas.

13d proof

Exercise 4

A. Two versions of a paragraph follow—one in an unedited form, the other partly edited. Without looking at the edited version, read the unedited draft like an editor. Scrutinize the passage as ruthlessly as you can, making any corrections you wish and explaining these in a notebook. Then compare your editing with the changes made in the second paragraph. What differences do you find between your own editing and the writer's editing?

UNEDITED DRAFT

At the start of her career, historian Barbara Smithey, felt forced to choose between a life of: public service vs. research. As curator of the Westville Museum of New England culture in Westville, Ct, she was passionately devoted to preserving or restoreing old houses in disrepair and seeing to it that they were entered if they qualified into the National Register of Historical Places. At the same time, she had a kean interest in research on the town of Westville which had been settled in the early 17th-Century. She manfully seized control of all public documents on the area, that were not already protected and got them housed in the local historical archives. These included, some early notes about the Indian savages that the White men encountered when they settled the land. Also some personal diaries lady settlers kept.

EDITED DRAFT

At the start of her career, historian Barbara Smithey felt forced to choose between a life of public service ~~vs.~~ *and* research. As curator of the Westville Museum of New England culture in Westville, ~~Ct,~~ *Connecticut,* she was passionat*e*ly devoted to preserving or restor*e*ing old houses in disrepair and seeing to it that they were entered if they qualified into the National Register of Historical Places. At the same time, she had a ke*e*n interest in research on the town of Westville, which had been settled in the early ~~17th-Century.~~ *seventeenth century.* She ~~manfully~~ seized control of all public documents on the area that were not already protected and ~~got~~ *had* them *placed* ~~housed~~ in the local historical archives. These included some early *settlers'* notes about ~~the Indian savages that the White men encountered when~~ *local Native Americans, as well as* ~~they settled the land. Also~~ some personal diaries ~~lady settlers kept.~~ *of women settlers.*

13e edit

B. Compare your editorial changes to those of a small group of your peers. Did you all notice the same things? Did you all make the same changes? Does each member of the group have a different editing style? Prepare a brief report summarizing differences and similarities among the ways members of the group edited the paragraph. Share your report with other groups in class.

13e Editing and proofreading: Paper in progress

Before revising her rough draft (see 8d), Rachel Ritchie received comments from both her instructor and her peer group. All these readers agreed that Ritchie had presented some strong examples of violence in our culture, both from news sources and from personal experiences. However, her readers thought that some of her material didn't directly illustrate her generalization about the relationship between TV and violence in children. They suggested that she test each example in her paper against her generalization and then consider how much she actually could show about the causal relationship between TV watching and violence among children. After thinking about this issue and redrafting sections of her paper, Ritchie decided to change the focus of her paper so that it didn't imply a causal relationship between TV and violence. Instead, she provided examples to support the generalization that crime among children and adolescents is on the rise. After writing the following second draft, Ritchie was ready to do some careful editing, then prepare the final version and turn it in.

Second Draft of Violence Paper

Rachel Ritchie

Every night while watching the news or reading the newspaper, I see the rise in violence, a drive-by shooting one night, a kid killing another kid the next. The amount of violence around us, involving kids, has sharply risen.

More kids are being able to buy guns' and more kids are using them. A friend of mine lived in Los Angelos for a year and witnessed a drive-by shooting. She told me she remembered seeing the gun and hearing shots. She got up and ran. After her adrenalen rush was over, she realized her knee was burning. She looked down and saw blood, she had been shot. A bullet went right through her knee. Now she has a hole in her knee cap and a scar from surgery: a constant reminder of youth violence.

Another friend of mine who grew up in Chicago was in a gang. Her parents sent her to live with her brother in Maine because they were afraid she would be killed. A few of her friends had all ready been killed by rival gangs and her boyfriend had been killed by a police officer while fleeing a crime scene.

Not all violence occurs in large cities' like Los Angelos and Chicago. Last year an 11-year-old

6th grader in my hometown brought a loaded rifle to school and threatened to kill the principal, because he was given a night of detention. What was going through his mind? I only wish I knew so I could understand his logic.

A few months ago a twelve year old boy strangled a 3-year-old in the woods near there houses. A similar occurence happened a few months earlier when two boys in England kidnapped a boy from a shopping mall and killed him. These are young kids killing babies. These killers are not even teenagers yet. They haven't even started high school.

Violence is not only seen in older kids. Mild forms of violence is also seen in young kids. One of the most popular television cartoons is "Mighty Morphin Power Rangers." A little boy I baby-sat for watches it religiously. After the show is over he runs around the house with play swords and knives, kicking things and sometimes people while yelling, "I'm the red ranger!." This is a four-year-old boy that is already being exposed to violence and reacting to it.

13e edit

So the next time you watch the news or read the newspaper, take notice of the amount of violence in the world. Then take notice of how many of the violent crimes are being commited by kids.

Exercise 5

A. Edit Ritchie's paper. Identify every error in the paper that you can. Look also for specific sentence- or word-level concerns that Ritchie could address as part of her editing process before turning in the final paper. Review this chapter or relevant sections in this handbook if necessary. (Even though some errors such as misspellings would be caught during final proofreading, assume that Ritchie is trying to produce a flawless draft.)

 B. In a small group, compare all your suggestions for editing. Make the most complete list of editorial suggestions or corrections that you can.

13e
edit

EDITING
FOR GRAMMAR

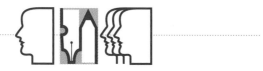

Identifying Sentence Elements and Sentence Patterns

To draft a sentence, you need not be consciously aware of its different parts. Careful revising and editing depend on such awareness, however, because they require you to change the relationships between sentence elements or to choose between alternative sentence patterns. You may occasionally be able to edit flaws in simple sentences without formal knowledge of sentence grammar. Most of the time, however, you need a basic understanding of grammatical concepts and terms in order to spot difficulties in your writing, to correct them, or to find the information in a handbook that will help you make a correction.

Admittedly, discussions in this handbook limit use of technical language so you can locate and benefit from the advice even if you know relatively little about grammatical terms and concepts. Some knowledge is essential, however, and this chapter provides a basic introduction to the features of sentence grammar, along with tips for identifying and using them.

14a Using words

Being able to identify the category to which a word belongs is an important step in understanding its role in a sentence. At the simplest level, sentences consist of different types of words, often called *parts of speech:* nouns, pronouns, verbs, adjectives, adverbs, prepositions, conjunctions, and interjections.

1 Using nouns and articles

You can generally recognize nouns by keeping in mind this familiar definition: A **noun** is a word naming a person, place, idea, or thing.

Crescent Dragonwagon writes **books** for **children.**
The **pictures** capture the **beauty** of **Lake Louise.**

Nouns often require an **article:** *the, a,* or *an* (*a* before consonants, *an* before vowels).

The book I like best tells **a** story about **a** young girl and **an** owl.

You can often rely on word endings to distinguish the singular and plural forms of nouns. Most nouns add *-s* to the singular form to make the plural: *cow* + *-s* = *cows; cake* + *-s* = *cakes.* Some nouns ending with *s*-like sounds (*s, z, j,* for example) add *-es* for the plural: *gas* + *-es* = *gases; base* (silent *e*) + *-es* = *bases.* Some nouns don't follow this pattern; their plural forms are irregular.

Singular (base) form	Plural form
child	children
deer	deer
fish	fish
goose	geese
mouse	mice
ox	oxen

In writing and editing, you often need to treat count nouns, mass nouns, and collective nouns in different ways. **Count nouns** indicate individual items. That is, they are nouns that can be *counted,* for example, two *chairs,* four *cups,* or a hundred *beans.* **Mass nouns** (or **noncount nouns**) indicate material that can't be counted, for instance, *flour, water, steel.* **Collective nouns** generally take a singular form but refer to a unit composed of more than one individual or thing, for instance, *group, board of directors, family,* and *flock.* They may be singular or plural in meaning.

GROUP   The audience showed **its** approval in the form of applause.

INDIVIDUALS   The audience clapped **their** hands.

Did You Know?

Modern packaging makes it possible for many mass nouns to act as count nouns. *Milk* is generally considered a mass noun. You can't say "six milk." Yet when milk comes in half-pint containers, the word becomes a count noun, as in "I drank three milks at lunch yesterday."

You also need to treat common nouns and proper nouns differently. **Proper nouns** refer to specific people, places, titles, or things. They are capitalized: *Miss America; Tuscaloosa, Alabama; Tierra del Fuego;* and *Microsoft.* All other nouns are called **common nouns** and are not capitalized (see 37b).

Nouns indicating possession (**possessive nouns**) are easy to identify because they usually add an apostrophe and *-s* (see 33a).

Common	Proper	Possessive
school	Tollgate School	school's, Tollgate School's
coffee	Sanka	coffee's, Sanka's

ESL Advice: The Articles *A, An,* and *The*

In using the **indefinite articles** *a* and *an,* or the **definite article** *the,* you can follow some rules and guidelines, but you need to pay attention to the many exceptions to these rules. Make sure you notice articles as you read. This will also help you to achieve a greater facility with articles. Most important, remember that the basic meaning of your sentence will still be communicated even if you choose the wrong article or if you forget to use one.

ESL

14a
gr

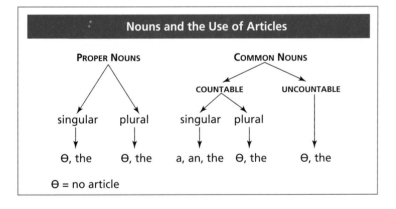

Singular and plural proper nouns

Proper nouns use either no article or *the.* Proper nouns are capitalized and include names of people, places, religions, languages, courses of study, mountains, and rivers. (See 37b-1.)

Singular proper nouns generally use no article, and plural proper nouns usually use *the.*

NOT APPROPRIATE The Sir Francis Drake was a famous English sea captain.
(SINGULAR)

CORRECT   **Sir Francis Drake** was a famous English sea captain.
(SINGULAR)

NOT APPROPRIATE Everglades have abundant wildlife and tropical plants.
(PLURAL)

CORRECT   **The Everglades** have abundant wildlife and tropical plants.
(PLURAL)

Singular count nouns

Singular **count nouns** use *a, an,* or *the*. Remember, these nouns cannot stand alone.

NOT APPROPRIATE Pig is a very intelligent animal.

CORRECT   **A pig** is a very intelligent animal.

CORRECT   **The pig** is a very intelligent animal.

ESL

14a
gr

Plural count nouns

Plural count nouns use either no article or *the*. You should use no article to show a generalization.

NOT APPROPRIATE The books are the best teachers.

CORRECT   **Books** are the best teachers.

You should use *the* with plural count nouns to refer to something specific.

NOT APPROPRIATE Books on his desk are from the library.

CORRECT   **The books** on his desk are from the library.
                 The prepositional phrase makes the noun specific.

Noncount (mass) nouns

Noncount (mass) nouns use either no article or *the*. They are never preceded by the singular article *a* or *an*.
General mass nouns sometimes stand alone.

NOT APPROPRIATE A laughter is good medicine.

CORRECT   **Laughter** is good medicine.

With specific mass nouns, use *the*.

NOT APPROPRIATE Laughter of children is good medicine.

CORRECT **The laughter** of children is good medicine.
The prepositional phrase makes the noun specific.

Strategies for choosing *a*, *an*, or *the*

- How do you know if you need to use *a* or *an*? When you are talking about a nonspecific, singular count noun, you use the indefinite article *a* or *an*. This means you are not referring to any specific person or thing. *A* is used before a consonant sound. *An* is used before a vowel sound.

I need to have **a car** to go to work.
The car is unknown or nonspecific. It is any car.

- How do you know if you need to use *the*? When you are talking about a specific, singular noun, you use the definite article *the*. This means you know the exact person or thing to which you are referring.

ESL

14a
gr

I need to have **the car** to go to work.
The car is a specific, known car.

Mr. Frank was sitting on **a beach. The beach** had sand that was unusually white.
The beach is first unknown, so the writer uses the indefinite article *a*. Then the beach is known because it has already been mentioned, so the writer uses the definite article *the*.

- Should you use *the* with plural nouns? Plural and mass nouns do not usually require any article.

COUNT **Airline tickets** to Florida are at half price.

MASS **Information** about flights to Florida is available.

- Should you use *the* when a plural noun is followed by a modifier? All plural count nouns and mass nouns are specific when they are followed by modifiers, and you need to use *the*.

COUNT **The** airline tickets that you bought are at half price.

MASS **The** information that you received about flights to Florida has changed.

In each of these sentences, the adjective clause makes the noun specific.

2 Using pronouns

A **pronoun** is a word like *them, she, his,* and *it.* To recognize a pronoun, look for a word that takes the place of a noun (generally a noun that appears earlier in the sentence or passage) and that can play the same roles in a sentence as the noun. In editing your writing, keep in mind that by using a pronoun in place of a noun, you can avoid repeating the noun.

NOUNS REPEATED   **Jim** changed **Jim's shirt** after spilling gravy on the **shirt.**

PRONOUNS   Jim changed **his** shirt after spilling gravy on **it.**

Because a pronoun's meaning depends on the noun to which it refers— its **antecedent**—you need to check during editing that this relationship is clear to readers.

> antecedent   pronoun
> **Jean** presented **her** proposal to the committee.

(For detailed help making pronoun-antecedent relationships clear, see 17c, 21a, and 21b.)

Pronouns usually take the place of nouns, but you can also use them as adjectives modifying a noun or another pronoun.

> **This** part has been on order for four months, and **that** one for ninety days.

Pronouns change form to indicate the **number** (singular or plural) or **gender** (masculine, feminine, or neuter) of the noun to which they refer. Pronouns also change form according to their role in a sentence—subject, object, or possessive (see 15a). To keep from confusing readers, check pronoun form carefully as you edit. Note that each of the following kinds of pronouns is used in different ways and may take different forms.

14a
gr

Personal Pronouns. Use **personal pronouns,** such as *I, you, it,* and *they,* to designate persons or things.

SINGULAR   I, me, you, he, him, she, her, it

PLURAL   we, us, you, they, them

When you use a personal pronoun as a subject or object in place of a noun, check that you have chosen the appropriate form, or **case,** reflecting its role in the sentence (see 15a on case of personal pronouns).

> Jorge told the members of the class that **we** had completed the training program and invited **us** to the graduation ceremony.

Possessive Pronouns. Use a **possessive pronoun** to show ownership.

SINGULAR   my, mine, your, yours, her, hers, his, its

PLURAL   our, ours, your, yours, their, theirs

Some possessive pronouns take one form when they stand for nouns (*mine, yours, hers, ours, theirs*) and another when they act as adjectives (*my, your, her, our, their*).

noun
substitute   adjective
Kim bought **hers** at **her** cousin's store.

Relative Pronouns. You can use the **relative pronouns** *who, whom, whose, which,* and *that* to introduce subordinate clauses that modify or add information to a main clause (see 14c-5).

> Cost-conscious consumers are the kind of people **who** shop at this store regularly.

> I gave Kim the coffee pot **that** I had used during four years of college.

The clauses you create with relative pronouns are known as **relative clauses.** They act as **adjectives** modifying a noun or pronoun and answering the questions "What kind of?" and "Which one?" *Who* takes different forms (*who, whom* or *whose*) depending on its role within the clause (see 14c-5).

When you use *who* and *which* to introduce questions, they are known as **interrogative pronouns.**

> **Who** bought the new minivan?
> **Which** dresser should I use?

Reflexive and Intensive Pronouns. You can use pronouns ending in *-self* or *-selves* as **intensive pronouns** to add emphasis to a sentence.

> They **themselves** did all the work on the new barn.
> They did all the work on the new barn **themselves.**

Or you can use them as **reflexive pronouns,** which enable the subject or doer to be also the receiver of an action.

> He paid **himself** for the work.

Indefinite Pronouns. An **indefinite pronoun** refers to people, things, and ideas in general rather than to specific antecedents. Indefinite pronouns include *all, any, anybody, anything, anyone, another, both, each, every, every-*

body, everyone, everything, either, few, fewer, many, neither, nothing, nobody, no one, none, one, several, some, somebody, someone, and *something.*

> **Nobody** has done anything to clean up the mess.
> **All** of us have a chance to win at this game.

Demonstrative and Reciprocal Pronouns. A **demonstrative pronoun** (sometimes called a **demonstrative adjective**)—*this, that, these,* or *those*—points out or highlights an antecedent. You can use it to refer to a noun or a pronoun or to sum up an entire phrase or clause.

> **That** <u>copier</u> breaks down about once a week.
>
> I want **these** <u>shiny</u> ones arranged in a circle.
>
> <u>She was late for the meeting</u>. **This** surprised me because she is usually punctual.

A **reciprocal pronoun** (*one another, each other*) enables you to refer to individual parts of a plural antecedent.

> The two kinds of birds compete for territory by destroying **each other's** nests.

**14a
gr**

....

Exercise 1

A. Underline each noun in the following selection *once* and each pronoun *twice.*

> Seconds later the Help Desk received a call from another user with the same problem. The switchboard lit up. There were callers from all over the company, all with the same complaint: their computers were making odd noises. It might be a tune, one of the callers added helpfully, coming from the computer's small internal speaker. The sixth caller recognized the melody. The computers were all playing tinny renditions of "Yankee Doodle."
> — Paul Mungo and Bryan Clough, "The Bulgarian Connection"

B. Exchange papers in progress with another writer, and identify all the nouns and pronouns in a relatively long paragraph of your partner's work. Then return the essay and point out where you agree or disagree with your partner's identification of nouns and pronouns (or lack of identification).

C. Choose a paragraph from a paper you are preparing, and identify all the nouns and pronouns it contains. Revise the paragraph wherever appropriate by substituting pronouns for nouns (for conciseness) and nouns for pronouns (for clarity).

....

3 Using verbs

To identify **verbs,** look for words that express actions (*jump, build*), occurrences (*become, happen*), and states of being (*be, seem*). A **main verb** can stand alone or be accompanied by one or more helping verbs (or auxiliary verbs).

main verb
Toy companies **create** many new products each year.

helping main
verb   verb
New toys **must compete** for space on store shelves.

You change a verb's form to signal relationships in time (**tense**).

PRESENT TENSE   They **stack** the boxes.

PAST TENSE   They **stacked** the boxes.

You also use verb form to indicate **person** and **number** (see 17a)**.**

PERSON   She **restores** antique furniture.
She **restore** antique furniture.

NUMBER   The song **makes** me sad.
The songs **make** me sad.

Choice of **voice** (active or passive; see 16d) and **mood** (16b) also requires changes in form.

ACTIVE VOICE   The pump **cleans** the water.

PASSIVE VOICE   The water **is cleaned** by the pump.

INDICATIVE MOOD The key **was** in the drawer.

SUBJUNCTIVE   If the key **were** in the drawer, I would have found it.
MOOD

Because verbs play a central role in sentence meaning, you should pay considerable attention to verb form as you edit. (Verb tense and the roles of number, person, mood, and voice are discussed in detail in Chapter 16. For passive and active voice, see 11c and 16d.)

The **helping** (or **auxiliary**) **verbs** include the different forms of *be*, *do*, and *have*. You can also use **modal auxiliary verbs** as helping verbs but never as main verbs. They include *will/would, can/could, shall/should, may/might, must,* and *ought to.* (See 16b.)

> helping   main
> verb   verb

The tourist agency **is planning** to make a video of the local attractions.

> modal   main verb

They **might decide** to include our restaurant.

A **verb phrase** consists of a main verb plus a helping verb.

> verb phrase   verb phrase

I **am hoping** that the renovations **can be done** in time for the video-taping.

Use **action verbs** to indicate an action or activity, for example, *swim, analyze, dig, turn,* or *negotiate.*

Chris **turned** the main valve.
The company and the union **negotiated** a new contract.

Use **linking verbs** (also known as **state-of-being verbs**) to express a state of being or an occurrence: *is, seems, becomes, grows* (see 14b-2).

Flowers **remain** my favorite decoration.
 subject   verb   complement renames subject

The flowers **smelled** musky.
 subject   verb   complement describes subject

Marigolds **became** popular during this century.
 subject   verb   complement describes subject

14a
gr

Some verbs, known as **phrasal verbs,** consist of a verb plus a closely associated word that seems like a preposition but is known as a **particle,** as in *run along* (depart), *run down* (exhaust), or *look up* (improve). These verbs differ from verb-plus-preposition combinations, whose meanings are clearly the sums of their parts, such as *run up* (*run* = action; *up* = direction). The meaning of phrasal verbs differs considerably from the meanings of the separate words: for example, *run by* means "consult," *fall off* means "decline," and *put up* means "preserve."

Phrasal verb	Verb + preposition
I **ran** the idea **by** the committee.	I **ran by** the house.
Profits are **falling off.**	My cousin **fell off** the deck.
Did you **put up** tomatoes this year?	Did you **put** the mixer **up** on the shelf?

4 Using verbals

You can employ the verb parts known as **verbals** as nouns, adjectives, or adverbs—but never ask them to stand alone as verbs. (Word groups built around a verbal rather than a verb and punctuated as sentences are fragments; see 19c-2.) There are three kinds of verbals: infinitives, participles, and gerunds. To identify an **infinitive** look for *to* plus the base form (see 16a) of a verb: *to play, to analyze, to reduce.* Even though you use it in a different sentence role, an infinitive retains some of the active force of a verb.

AS NOUN | **To play** in a major orchestra is my dream.

AS ADJECTIVE | *The Naked and the Dead* is an intriguing novel **to analyze.**

AS ADVERB | The air filtering system helps **to reduce** allergic reactions.

You can choose between two forms of participles: present and past. To recognize a **present participle** look for the *-ing* form of a verb (see 15a), such as *slipping, irritating,* or *carving.* To recognize a **past participle** look for the *-ed* form of a verb (or its equivalent for an irregular verb), for instance, *estimated, repaired,* and *shrunken.* Participles (present and past) act as adjectives to modify nouns and pronouns.

PRESENT PARTICIPLE | The **slipping** belt on the car's engine made an **irritating** noise.

PAST PARTICIPLE | The **estimated** cost for a **repaired** engine was more than my **shrunken** checking account could bear.

To identify a **gerund** look for the *-ing* form of a verb that is acting as a noun.

> **Running** can be enjoyable.
> The doctor tells me to restrict my **eating** to low-fat foods.

A gerund is identical in form to a present participle, but you use it as a noun rather than an adjective.

> gerund (noun)   participle (adjective)
> **Swimming** can be a **relaxing** exercise.

(See 14c-4 for discussion of verbal phrases.)

**14a
gr**

Exercise 2

A. In the following sentences, underline each main verb once and each helping verb twice. Circle each verbal.

EXAMPLE

The new construction in Maple Valley <u>has</u> <u>created</u> some (challenging) problems.

1. Looking for the best way to bring electricity to the new development, the power company's engineers began studying a map of the area.
2. Because the area is heavily wooded, they thought about using underground cables.
3. A field test revealed a large rock ledge, so the engineers decided that underground lines would be too expensive.
4. They proposed cutting a path through the woods for the power lines, but the contractor claimed that potential homebuyers might not like the effect on the scenery.
5. They solved the problem by stringing the power lines on poles following the main road into the development.

B. Exchange papers in progress with a fellow student. Choose a relatively long paragraph, and underline all main and helping verbs once. Underline each verbal twice. For all verbals ending in -*ing,* indicate whether the verbal is a present participle or a gerund.

C. Working with a draft paper of your own, choose two paragraphs and revise them by adding verbals as appropriate to create sentences that provide readers with detailed ideas and information. Exchange papers with another student, and evaluate the results of each other's revisions.

**14a
gr**

5 Using adjectives

You can use **adjectives** to modify nouns, pronouns, or word groups acting as nouns. They help you describe more precisely or limit your meaning by answering questions like "How many?," "What kind?," or "Which one?"

The **three** chairs need upholstering.
   how many?

My brother is the **tall** one.
   which one?

The report they submitted was **unacceptable.**
   what kind?

Adjectives come in three degrees of comparison: *high, higher, highest; crooked, more crooked, most crooked* (see 18c).

ESL Advice: Adjective Forms

Adjectives in English never use a plural form.

NOT APPROPRIATE Santo Domingo is renowned for beautifuls beaches.

CORRECT   Santo Domingo is renowned for beautiful beaches.

6 Using adverbs

You can use **adverbs** to modify verbs, adjectives, other adverbs, and entire sentences. They enable you to describe or limit your meaning by answering such questions as "When?," "Where?," "Why?," "How often?," "Which direction?," "What conditions?," and "What degree?"

He ran **yesterday.**
When? Adverb modifies verb.

The **very** tall woman is a runner.
What degree? Adverb modifies adjective.

I use the microwave **quite frequently.**
How often? Adverb modifies adverb; adverb modifies verb.

ESL

14a

gr

By adding *more* or *less* and *most* or *least* to many adverbs, you can describe comparative levels: *more quickly, less frequently, most unfortunately, least openly* (see 18c).

You can recognize many adverbs easily because they consist of an adjective plus *-ly: quickly, blindly, unfortunately, frequently, characteristically.* Others do not take this form, including such common words as *very, too, tomorrow, not, never, sometimes, well,* and *so.* In addition, some adjectives end in *-ly,* including *neighborly, slovenly,* and *lovely.* The surest way to distinguish an adverb from an adjective, therefore, is to see whether the word modifies a noun or pronoun (it's an adjective) or a verb, adjective, or adverb (it's an adverb).

                                                    adverb   adjective
In the afternoon it rained **heavily,** yet by evening we had **lovely** weather.

You can use **conjunctive adverbs** such as *however, moreover, thus,* and *therefore* to indicate logical relationships. (For advice on using conjunctive adverbs, see 20b.)

They did not like the new administrative guidelines; **nevertheless,** they promised to implement the policies.

The commissioners approved the plan for a trash incinerator; they could not decide where to build it, **however.**

Did You Know?

Since the 1700s, adverbs like *frankly, strictly, regretfully,* and *basically* have been used to modify entire sentences, for example, "Sadly, they could not raise enough money to keep the bank from repossessing the farm." Clark Gable uses one of these **sentence adverbs** in *Gone with the Wind*: "Frankly, my dear, . . ." and they appear frequently in the work of highly regarded writers such as John Ruskin and T. S. Eliot. Nonetheless, some readers may react negatively to *hopefully* (meaning "let us hope" or "I hope") used as a sentence adverb.

QUESTIONABLE   Hopefully, the tests will be finished today.
ACCEPTABLE   I hope the tests will be finished today.

As Robert Burchfield points out, the ban on *hopefully* is recent but quite forceful: "Suddenly, round about 1968, and with unprecedented venom, a dunce's cap was placed on the head of anyone who used just one of the [-*ly* adverbs]—*hopefully*—as a sentence adverb."

Robert Burchfield, *Points of View* (New York: Oxford UP, 1992) 85.

**14a
gr**

Exercise 3

A. In the following passage, underline all adjectives once and all adverbs twice.

Back in Chicago, Sereno's analysis of his new dinosaur's skeleton convinces him it is indeed more primitive than *Herrerasaurus*. It lacks a flexible jaw that let *Herrerasaurus* and later carnivores snag and trap struggling prey. Thus Sereno believes this new creature is the closest fossil we have to the first dinosaur.

"I call it 'Eoraptor,'" he says. "Eos was the Greek goddess of dawn. Raptor means thief. It was a light-bodied little rascal. And it may have been a thief, dashing in to grasp scraps of someone else's kill."

— RICK GORE, "Dinosaurs"

B. Expand the following sentences by adding details and information in the form of adjectives and adverbs.

EXAMPLE

generally   *deep, extended*
The term *coma*ʌrefers to aʌstate of unconsciousness.

1. Accidents leave people in comas.
2. Comas are serious medical problems.
3. Newspapers contain reports of people awakening from comas.
4. Long comas are dangerous.
5. They cause irreversible damage.

 C. Revise an essay of your own by adding adjectives and adverbs as appropriate (or by cutting them).

7 Using prepositions

When you combine a **preposition** with a noun or pronoun, you create a modifying phrase known as a **prepositional phrase.** You can use prepositional phrases to add information that makes sentences detailed and precise.

Most prepositional phrases act as adjectives or adverbs.

PREPOSITIONS
of   through   with   of

PREPOSITIONAL PHRASES
of grilled onions   through the window
with the musty air   of the dungeon

PREPOSITIONAL PHRASES USED AS MODIFIERS

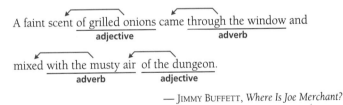

A faint scent <u>of grilled onions</u> came <u>through the window</u> and
             adjective   *adverb*

mixed <u>with the musty air</u> <u>of the dungeon</u>.
        adverb   *adjective*

— JIMMY BUFFETT, *Where Is Joe Merchant?*

Common Prepositions				
about	at	despite	near	to
above	before	down	of	toward
across	behind	during	off	under
after	below	except	on	until
against	beneath	for	out	up
along	between	from	outside	upon
among	beyond	in	over	with
around	by	into	past	within
as	concerning	like	through	without

14a
gr

Occasionally, a prepositional phrase may act as a noun.

Among friends is where I want to be.

Exercise 4

A. Underline all the prepositions in the following sentences. Circle all the prepositional phrases.

EXAMPLE

(At eighteen minutes)(after one o'clock,)the emergency number received a call(from Mrs. Serena Washington.)

1. From its station near city hall, the rescue truck drove to Briar Brook Avenue.
2. Along the way, it narrowly missed colliding with a bread truck that failed to pull to the side of the road.
3. Despite the near accident, the rescue team arrived at the Washington's home in less than five minutes.
4. Mr. Washington was complaining of pain in his chest and back and displaying other symptoms of a heart attack.
5. By its quick response to the emergency call, the rescue team may have saved a life.

ESL

14a
gr

B. For each of the following word groups, create two sentences, one using the words as a verb plus preposition, the other using the words as a phrasal verb (see 14a-3). Then rewrite the sentence that contains the phrasal verb, substituting another word or words for the phrasal verb.

EXAMPLE: tear out
Brian tore out the old shelving.
Brian tore out the door.
Brian hurried out the door.

cut down	hang around	run up
fill in	put up with	call up

ESL Advice: Prepositions

Using prepositions in English may be difficult for you, and sometimes you will need to memorize which preposition to use. However, these guidelines can help you remember which preposition to choose.

Prepositions of time, place, and location

Prepositions of Time: *At*, *On*, and *In*.

Use *at* for a specific time.

Brandon was born **at** 11:11 a.m.

Use *on* for days and dates.

He was born **on** Monday.
My new job began **on** August eighteenth.

Use *in* for nonspecific times during a day, a month, a season, or a year.

He was born **in** the morning.
My new job began **in** August.
The weather becomes cooler **in** autumn.
The book was first published **in** 1980.

Prepositions of Place: *At*, *On*, and *In*.

Use *at* for specific addresses.

He works **at** 99 Tinker Street.

Use *on* for the names of streets, avenues, and boulevards.

The White House is **on** Pennsylvania Avenue.

Use *in* for the names of areas of land—counties, states, countries, and continents.

He works **in** Washington, D.C.

Prepositions of Location: *In*, *At*, *On*, and No Preposition			
IN	**AT**	**ON**	**NO PREPOSITION**
(the) bed*	class*	the bed*	downstairs
the bedroom	home	the ceiling	downtown
the car	the library*	the floor	inside
(the) class*	the office	the horse	outside
the library*	school*	the plane	upstairs
school*	work	the train	uptown

*You may sometimes use different prepositions for these locations.

Order of prepositional phrases

Use prepositional phrases in this order.

PREPOSITIONAL PHRASE OF PLACE + PREPOSITIONAL PHRASE OF TIME

place   time
The runners will be starting **in the park on Saturday.**

Writer's Alert

When you express the idea of going to a place, use the preposition *to.*

NOT APPROPRIATE I am going work.

CORRECT   I am going **to** work.

NOT APPROPRIATE I am going the office.

CORRECT   I am going **to** the office.

In the following cases, use no preposition.

NOT APPROPRIATE I am going **to** home.

CORRECT   I am going home.

CORRECT   I am going downstairs (downtown, inside).

ESL

14a
gr

For and *since* in time expressions

Use *for* with an amount of time (minutes, hours, days, months, and years).

I have lived in upstate New York **for** many years.

Use *since* with a specific date or time.

I have lived in upstate New York **since** 1974.

Prepositions with nouns, verbs, and adjectives

Some noun-plus-preposition combinations are often found together.

noun + preposition
He has a strong **appreciation of** music.

Noun + Preposition Combinations		
approval of	fondness for	need for
awareness of	grasp of	participation in
belief in	hatred of	reason for
concern for	hope for	respect for
confusion about	interest in	success in
desire for	love of	understanding of

Some verb-plus-preposition combinations are also common.

verb + preposition
Parents **worry about** many things.

ESL

14a
gr

Verb + Preposition Combinations		
apologize for	give up	prepare for
ask about	grow up	study for
ask for	look for	talk about
belong to	look forward to	think about
bring up	look up	trust in
care for	make up	work for
find out	pay for	worry about

Likewise, some adjective-plus-preposition combinations are often used together.

adjective + preposition
Life in your country is **similar to** life in mine.

Adjective + Preposition Combinations		
afraid of	fond of	proud of
angry at	happy about	similar to
aware of	interested in	sorry for
capable of	jealous of	sure of
careless about	made of	tired of
familiar with	married to	worried about

8 Using conjunctions

Conjunctions help you join words and groups of words. They enable you to signal relationships among these words and word groups.

Coordinating Conjunctions. Use the **coordinating conjunctions** (*and, but, or, nor, for, yet,* and *so*) to link grammatically equal elements such as parts of compound subjects, verbs, objects, and modifiers; phrases; and clauses.

WORDS   Analyze **and** discuss
Orange juice **or** grapefruit juice

PHRASES   Through the door **and** up the stairs

Determined to cut costs **yet** worried about harming the quality of service

CLAUSES   They put down their rackets, **and** they went to the side of the court for a cold drink from the thermos.

Subordinating Conjunctions. Use a **subordinating conjunction** such as *because, although, while, if,* or *since* to create a subordinate or modifying clause (see 14c-5; see 26b-2 for a list of subordinating conjunctions).

> **Because** they were tired, they did not notice that the pot was boiling over.

Remember that because the clause created by a subordinating conjunction is a modifying clause, it cannot stand on its own as a sentence. Instead, attach it to a **main (or independent) clause** that it qualifies or limits in some way.

>   main clause   subordinate clause
> The blender still works, **although** the cord needs repairing.

(See 14c for discussion of main clauses and subordinate clauses; see Chapter 26 on coordination and subordination.)

Correlative Conjunctions. **Correlative conjunctions** come in pairs, including *not only . . . but also, either . . . or, neither . . . nor, both . . . and, whether . . . or,* and similar combinations. You can use them to join sentence elements that are grammatically equal. (See 25b-2 on parallelism with correlative conjunctions.)

14a
gr

Exercise 5

A. Underline all the conjunctions in the following passage. Indicate whether each is a coordinating, subordinating, or correlative conjunction.

Thirty-five years ago, E. R. Guthrie and G. P. Horton described an experiment in which cats were placed in a glass-fronted puzzle box and trained to find their way out by jostling a slender vertical rod at the front of the box, thereby causing a door to open. What interested these investigators was not so much that the cats could learn to bump into the vertical rod, but that before doing so each animal performed a long ritual of highly stereotyped movements, rubbing their heads and backs against the front of the box, turning in circles, and finally touching the rod. The experiment has ranked as something of a classic in experimental psychology, even raising in some minds the notion of a ceremony of superstition on the part of cats: before the rod will open the door, it is necessary to go through a magical sequence of motions.   — Lewis Thomas, "Clever Animals"

B. Working with a group, rewrite the passage in Exercise 5A by employing different conjunctions (or kinds of conjunctions) than those in the original. Try to retain the general sense of the original, but feel free to add your own emphasis or perspective in the revision. Reword as necessary.

C. Revise a paper of your own by combining sentences and ideas with the help of coordinating, subordinating, or correlative conjunctions.

9 Using interjections

You can use an **interjection** to convey a strong reaction or emotion, such as surprise (*Hey!*) or disappointment (*Oh, no!*). Interjections often stand on their own or as elements only loosely related to the rest of a sentence.

> **Wow!** Did she really say that?
> All of a sudden, **worse luck,** I realized that my contact lens had torn.

14b Creating sentence parts: Subjects and predicates

In English, each sentence you create needs to be built around a subject, naming the doer or the thing talked about, and a predicate, indicating an action, a relationship, the consequences, and any conditions.

1 Creating sentence subjects

In a sentence **subject** you indicate the doer or the topic being addressed. A **simple subject** consists of one or more nouns (or pronouns) naming the doer or the topic.

simple subject
Cellophane was originally made from wood fiber.

A **complete subject** consists of the simple subject *plus* all its modifying words or phrases.

A subject may be singular, plural, or compound (linked by *and* or *or*).

SINGULAR **She** put the monitor on the desk.
SUBJECT

PLURAL SUBJECT **Trucks** cannot use this bridge.

COMPOUND **John and Chifume** are medical students.
SUBJECT

In an imperative sentence expressing a request or command, the subject is *you*, generally implied but not stated (see 14d-2).

[**You**] Put the insulation around the edges of the doorframe.

Subject-Verb Order. In most sentences, the subject comes before the verb.

subject verb
Dinosaurs lived in this valley millions of years ago.

By beginning a sentence with expletive constructions such as *there is (are)* or *here is (are),* you can delay the subject until after the verb (see 11b).

verb subject
There **were dinosaurs** living in this valley millions of years ago.

By inverting sentence structure for emphasis or dramatic effect, you also alter the position of subject and verb (see 12a-4).

verb subject
In this valley, millions of years ago, **grew plants** whose leaves are recorded in fossils.

Questions frequently place the subject between the helping verb and the main verb (see 14a-3).

helping main
verb subject verb
Did dinosaurs live in this valley millions of years ago?

2 Creating sentence predicates

In a sentence **predicate** you indicate the action or relationship expressed in the sentence, and you may also specify the consequences or

14b
gr

conditions. A **simple predicate** consists of only a verb or a verb phrase (see 14a-3).

VERB	The car **stopped.**
VERB PHRASE	The car **might stop.**

The verb may be single or compound (linked by *and* or *or*).

SINGLE	The customer **slipped.**
COMPOUND	The customer **slipped and fell.**

A **complete predicate** consists of a verb or verb phrase *plus* any modifiers and other words or word groups that receive the action or complete the verb. The elements you can include in a complete predicate depend on the kind of verb you choose: intransitive, transitive, or linking.

If you choose an **intransitive verb,** you cannot include either objects or complements in the predicate. When you use a **transitive verb,** you can add objects and object complements. With a **linking verb,** you can join a subject with a subject complement. (See the following discussion of objects and complements.)

**14b
gr**

Object Patterns. When you build a sentence around a *transitive verb,* you often include in the predicate a **direct object** that tells *who* or *what* receives the action.

    subject   predicate

The bank officer approved the loan application.

            verb   direct object

Sentences built around transitive verbs can be either active or passive, depending on whether the verb is in the active or passive voice (see 16d).

ACTIVE	The bank officer approved the loan application.
PASSIVE	The loan application was approved [by the bank officer].

In a sentence with a transitive verb you can also include an indirect object. An **indirect object** is a noun or pronoun that lets readers know *to whom* or *for whom* the action is undertaken.

                    indirect   direct

    subject   verb   object   object

The Marine Corps Reserve gives needy children toys.

                           to whom?

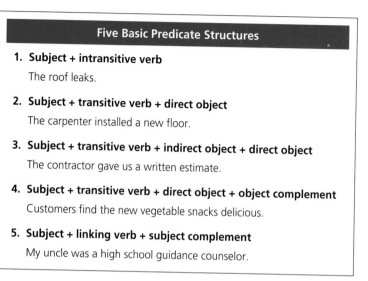

		Five Basic Predicate Structures

1. **Subject + intransitive verb**
   The roof leaks.

2. **Subject + transitive verb + direct object**
   The carpenter installed a new floor.

3. **Subject + transitive verb + indirect object + direct object**
   The contractor gave us a written estimate.

4. **Subject + transitive verb + direct object + object complement**
   Customers find the new vegetable snacks delicious.

5. **Subject + linking verb + subject complement**
   My uncle was a high school guidance counselor.

<pre>
                      indirect
subject verb   object   direct object
Nicole made her friends a bowl of spaghetti and meatballs.
                      for whom?
</pre>

**14b
gr**

You can add information to a predicate with an **object complement,** a word (noun or adjective) that renames or describes the direct object.

ADJECTIVE   Critics judged the movie **inferior.**

NOUN   His co-workers elected Jim **project leader.**

Subject Complement Patterns. When you build a sentence around a linking verb, such as *is, seems,* or *feels* (see 14a-3), you can also include a **subject complement.** A subject complement "completes" the linking verb by describing the subject or renaming it.

<pre>
                           subject
  subject   verb   complement
The new store seems successful.
</pre>

<pre>
                        subject
  subject verb   complement
The plan is too complicated.
</pre>

Intransitive Verb Patterns. An intransitive verb does not take either an object or a complement; the verb does not require them in order to complete its meaning.

Our team **lost.**

Last week, the ferryboat **sank.**

The picture tube **faded out.**

Fade out is a phrasal verb (see 14a-3).

Exercise 6

A. In each of the following sentences, circle the complete subjects and draw a wavy line under the complete predicates.

EXAMPLE

⟨Stories about Mount Everest⟩ often mention people known as Sherpas.

1. The Sherpas are well-known guides for mountain-climbing expeditions in the Himalayas.
2. They are a group of about 35,000 people who live in the country of Nepal.
3. The Sherpas, who are primarily Buddhists, live in a country dominated by Hindus.
4. Before the early 1900s, most Sherpas did not attempt to scale the mountains in their homeland.
5. In the early part of this century, however, Westerners wishing to climb the mountains gave many Sherpas jobs as guides and laborers.

B. Exchange papers in progress with another writer. Choose two paragraphs, and identify which of the five predicate patterns (listed in the chart in 14b-2) the writer uses in each sentence. Then suggest revisions that vary the predicate patterns in order to provide appropriate emphasis and variety. When you are finished, work together to identify those suggested revisions most likely to improve each paper.

C. Review a draft paper of your own, looking for ways to add emphasis and detail by varying predicate patterns. Pay particular attention to sentences that might be made more effective through the addition of objects and complements.

14c Creating phrases and subordinate clauses

When you write sentences, you use many groups of words that cannot stand on their own as sentences yet act as contributing word groups within sentences. Such word groups may be either phrases or subordinate clauses.

A **main clause** (also called an **independent clause**) is a word group that includes a subject and a verb and can act as a complete sentence (see 14b). A **phrase** is a word group that lacks one or more elements needed to make a complete sentence. (For example, the phrase *will be climbing* lacks a subject; *the man running across the field* lacks a predicate; and *under the sink* lacks both.) A **subordinate clause** (14c-5) is a word group that contains both a subject and a predicate yet cannot stand on its own as a sentence because it begins with a subordinating word such as *because, since, although, which,* or *that* (see 14a-8; see 26b-2 for a list of subordinating conjunctions).

1 Creating prepositional phrases

A prepositional phrase has two parts. To identify a prepositional phrase, look first for a preposition—a word like *at, for, in, to, according to, instead of,* or *under* (see 14a-7). Then identify the **object of the preposition**—the noun, pronoun, or word group that follows the preposition.

Preposition	Object of preposition
to	the beach
near	her
after	a falling out

You can use a prepositional phrase as an adjective. In this role it almost always follows the noun or pronoun it modifies.

The coupons **in the newspaper** offer savings **on groceries.**

When you use a prepositional phrase as an adverb, you may place it next to the verb being modified or elsewhere in the sentence.

Her electronic wristwatch started beeping **during the meeting.**
During the meeting, her electronic wristwatch started beeping.

2 Creating absolute phrases

An **absolute phrase** includes (1) a noun, a pronoun, or a word group acting as a noun; (2) a present or past participle and any modifiers (*the deadline approaching quickly*). You can use an absolute phrase to modify a sentence as a whole rather than a word or element within the sentence.

Their lungs burning from the acrid smoke, the firefighters pressed ahead into the burning building.

It took them many minutes to reach the fire, **the dense smoke slowing their efforts.**

**14c
gr**

3 Creating appositive phrases

In using an **appositive** you rename a noun in order to add information to a sentence. An **appositive phrase** consists of an appositive (generally a noun) along with its modifiers. You may wish to introduce an appositive phrase with words like *for example, that is, namely,* or *in other words.*

> Ken Choi and Stephanie Almano, **my classmates,** won an award for their innovative packaging design.

> They used "environmentally conscious" materials, **for example, recycled paper and soy-based ink.**

You can sometimes use an appositive to restate an adjective.

> I was tired, **not upset.**

4 Creating verbal phrases

Several kinds of phrases are built around the verb forms known as **verbals.** A verbal may be an infinitive, a present participle, a past participle, or a gerund (see 14a-4).

A **verbal phrase** consists of a verbal plus its modifiers, object, or complements.

> present
> participle   object   adverb
> sanding the tabletop with care

> infinitive   object   modifying (prepositional) phrase
> to bury the roots under an inch of soil

You can use verbal phrases as adjectives, adverbs, or nouns. Do not treat them as complete sentences; they cannot stand alone, because they lack subjects and because verbals are not verbs (see 14a-3).

Verbal phrases come in three kinds: participial, gerund, and infinitive. You can use each type for a different role in a sentence.

Participial Phrases. A participial phrase is built around the *-ing* (present participle) or *-ed/-en* (past participle) forms of a verbal. You can use participial phrases as adjectives to modify or limit a noun or pronoun.

> Most people **watching the show** did not notice the commotion in the lobby.

> The chef chose a cake **flavored with orange peel.**

14c
gr

Gerund Phrases. A gerund phrase is built around the *-ing* form of a verbal (*present participle*). You can make a gerund phrase act as a noun in a subject, object, or subject complement.

                                                                    object of
       sentence subject   **preposition**
Closing the landfill may be necessary to keep it from **polluting the groundwater.**

Infinitive Phrases. An infinitive phrase uses the *to* form of a verbal. You can use an infinitive phrase as an adjective, adverb, or noun.

           noun (sentence subject)
To live in the mountains of Montana was his goal.

                                                           adverb
He used several books on organic farming **to help plan his garden.**

Exercise 7

A. First, identify all the phrases in the following passage, and tell whether each is a prepositional, verbal, absolute, or appositive phrase.

Without electricity, we would perish. We could learn to do without the flow of electrons that power VCRs and food processors, but the currents inside our bodies are vital. The brain needs electricity to issue its commands from neuron to neuron. When these signals reach a muscle, they set up a wave of electrical excitation in the fibers, which in turn triggers the chemical reactions that make the fibers contract or relax. The most important muscle is the heart; it shudders under a wave of electricity about once each second.

— CARL ZIMMER, "The Body Electric"

Next, combine the following sentences to create a paragraph that might follow the one above. Try to create a variety of phrases.

The heart has an electric field. The field radiates into the chest cavity. The field sends clues. The clues are about the heart's function. The clues go toward the skin. Cardiologists can get a peek at the heart. They are taping electrodes. The electrodes are taped to a person's torso. Each electrode produces a familiar squiggle. The squiggles are on an electrocardiogram. The electrocardiogram shows how the voltage changes at that single point. The point is on the body. Cardiologists spend years learning. They learn to infer heart function from these signals. They learn to recognize the telltale signs. The signs are in EKG readings. The signs tell of dangerous heart conditions.

B. Share your revised paragraph from Exercise 7A with a group of fellow writers in order to decide which versions are the most effective.

 C. Choose several paragraphs from a draft paper of your own, and combine sentences and ideas by creating phrases.

ESL Advice: Gerunds and Infinitives

Gerunds and infinitives are verbals (see 14a-4).

Gerund	**Infinitive**
verb (base form) + *-ing*	*to* + verb (base form)

Verbs followed by either gerunds or infinitives

You can follow some verbs with either a gerund or an infinitive, though the meaning of some of these verbs may change slightly.

ESL

14c
gr

GERUND
subject + verb + gerund
People   like   **socializing**   with friends.

INFINITIVE
subject + verb + infinitive
People   like   **to socialize**   with friends.

Common Verbs Taking Either Gerunds or Infinitives

begin	intend	regret
can't stand	learn	remember
continue	like	start
forget	love	stop
hate	prefer	try

Writer's Alert

The meaning of some verbs will change depending on whether you use a gerund or an infinitive. For example, these forms of *remember, forget,* and *stop* have different meanings.

GERUND   I **remembered** meeting your friend.
I recall an event in the past.

INFINITIVE   I **remembered** to meet your friend.
I did not forget to do something in the past.

GERUND	I never **forget** visiting the Statue of Liberty.
	I recall a past event.
INFINITIVE	I never **forget** to study for exams.
	I remember to do something.
GERUND	I **stopped** smoking.
	I do not smoke anymore.
INFINITIVE	I **stopped** to smoke.
	I paused to smoke.

Verbs followed by gerunds

You can use only a gerund to follow some verbs.

subject   +   verb + gerund
GERUND   Children enjoy **reading** fairy tales.

ESL

14c
gr

Common Verbs Taking Gerunds		
admit	deny	mind
anticipate	discuss	miss
appreciate	dismiss	postpone
avoid	enjoy	practice
can't help	finish	quit
consider	imagine	recommend
delay	keep	suggest

Idiomatic expressions using gerunds

You must use gerunds with some idiomatic expressions.

• After the word *go* (in any tense)

subject + *go*   +   gerund
I   **go**   shopping on Saturday.
I   **went** swimming.

• After the expression *spend time.*

subject + *spend time*   +   gerund
Students **spend** a lot of **time** writing papers.
Teachers **spend** a lot of **time** reading papers.

* After the expression *have* + noun

subject   +   *have* + object   +   gerund
Pilots   **have** difficulty   <u>flying</u> in bad weather.
Shopkeepers **have** fun   <u>decorating</u> their stores.
Music lovers **have** a great time <u>going</u> to concerts.

* After a preposition

preposition + gerund
Veterinarians are interested **in**   <u>helping</u> animals.
Farmers sometimes worry   **about** <u>having</u> an early frost.

ESL

14c
gr

Writer's Alert
In the following examples, the phrase beginning with *to* is not an infinitive. *To* acts like a preposition in each sentence and must be followed by a gerund ending in *-ing*.

I am looking **forward** to <u>living</u> abroad.
He is **accustomed** to <u>spending</u> time alone.
Adults are **used** to <u>taking</u> care of children.

Verbs followed by infinitives
After some verbs, you must choose an infinitive instead of another verb form.

subject   +   verb + infinitive
Some students **need** to work part time.

Common Verbs Taking Infinitives		
agree	hope	pretend
ask	intend	promise
choose	manage	refuse
decide	need	seem
expect	offer	venture
fail	plan	want

Verbs followed by an object and the infinitive

You must use an object and then the infinitive to follow some verbs.

subject +   verb +   object + infinitive
Parents often **advise** their children to eat well.

Common Verbs Taking an Object + Infinitive			
advise	encourage	need	teach
allow	expect	permit	tell
ask	force	persuade	urge
convince	help	require	want

Writer's Alert

The verbs *make, let,* and *have* follow a different model.
Use the infinitive without *to* (the base form).

subject + { *make* + object + base form
          let
          have

She   { **made**   me   clean my room.
         let
         had

ESL

14c
gr

Adjective expressions followed by infinitives

Use infinitives after certain adjectives.

subject + verb + adjective + infinitive
I   **am**   delighted to know you.
It   **is**   easy   to understand the lesson.
They **are**   pleased   to help.

5 Creating subordinate clauses

A subordinate clause contains both a subject and a complete verb,
yet it cannot stand on its own as a complete sentence because it begins with
a subordinating word. This word (usually a subordinating conjunction like

because, although, or *if* or a relative pronoun like *who, which,* or *that*; see 14a-8 and 14a-2) signals that the clause is merely a sentence element—acting as an adjective, adverb, or noun—and not a sentence in itself. For this reason, subordinate clauses are sometimes called **dependent clauses;** that is, they "depend" on the main clause to which they are attached.

SUBORDINATE CLAUSE	**because** I was very busy
AS PART OF A SENTENCE	**Because I was very busy,** I forgot to call the car dealer for a service appointment.

If you mistakenly punctuate a subordinate clause as a sentence, you will create a sentence fragment (see 19a-2).

Subordinate Clauses as Adjectives. You can use a subordinate clause to modify a noun or a pronoun.

> Many people **who live in Foxwood Estates** came to the zoning board meeting.

> They had questions about the industrial park **that the county plans to create near their homes.**

To identify an adjective clause, look for a subordinating word, either a relative pronoun (*who, which, that,* or *whom*) or a relative adverb (*when* or *where*). Then check that the clause it introduces modifies a noun or pronoun. (Adjective clauses generally come right after the words they modify.)

Subordinate Clauses as Adverbs. You can use subordinate clauses as adverbs to modify verbs, adjectives, or adverbs. An adverb clause begins with a subordinating conjunction such as *because, although, since,* or *while* (see 14a-8).

> **As the speaker droned on,** Jeanelle began feeling very sleepy.
> The clause is an adverb answering the question "When?"

> She had come to the lecture **because she was interested in learning about tax deductions for small businesses.**
> The clause is an adverb answering the question "Why?"

Subordinate Clauses as Nouns. You can use subordinate clauses in the same sentence roles as nouns: subject, object, or complement. Noun clauses begin with *who, whom, whose, whoever, whomever, what, whatever, when, where, why, whether,* or *how.*

14c
gr

sentence subject
Whoever is interested in a career in accounting ought to attend
the information session on Thursday.

direct object
You should pack **what you need for the weekend** as quickly as
possible.

Exercise 8

A. Underline all subordinate clauses in the following passage.

Because the tax laws have gotten more complex recently, we have
published a guide to tax preparation that highlights new features of the
tax code. In addition, the guide provides step-by-step instruction for
tax forms, which should be helpful even if a person has considerable
experience filling out the forms. Anyone who plans to file taxes for a
small business will be interested in the special section on business tax
laws. Although many professionals and businesspeople rely on accountants when tax time arrives, they will nonetheless find that the guide
provides money-saving advice.

B. Working with another writer, revise the passage in Exercise 8A
by combining ideas and word groups in different ways and by using
different supporting words. Retain the general sense of the passage, but
feel free to add your own ideas and perspective.

C. Choose several paragraphs from a draft paper of your own, and
combine word groups and ideas by creating subordinate clauses.
Choose subordinating words that indicate relationships between ideas.
Add details and ideas to make the paragraphs more interesting and
effective.

ESL

14c
gr

ESL Advice: Adjective, Adverb, and Noun Clauses

Adjective, adverb, and noun clauses are subordinate clauses that combine with other sentence parts to form complex sentences.

Adjective clauses

Adjective clauses (also called **relative clauses**) work like adjectives
in complex sentences because they modify or add more information to

nouns. You also can use them to combine simple sentences and form complex sentences, thus creating a more compact writing style.

In order to form a relative clause, use a relative pronoun: *who, whom, that, which,* or *whose. Who, whom, that,* and *whose* are used to modify people. *That, which,* and *whose* are used to modify animals, places and things. In spoken American English the use of *whom* generally is optional, but it is always used in formal writing.

Use *who, that,* or *which* to replace a **subject pronoun** with a relative clause.

SIMPLE SENTENCE Mahatma Gandhi led India to independence.

           subject pronoun
SIMPLE SENTENCE **He** was called the father of modern India.

COMBINED Mahatma Gandhi, **who** was called the father of modern India, led India to independence.

Use *who, whom, that,* or *which* to replace an **object pronoun** with a relative clause.

SIMPLE SENTENCE Gandhi was a political and spiritual leader.

                        object pronoun
SIMPLE SENTENCE People admired **him.**

COMBINED Gandhi was a political and spiritual leader **whom** people admired.

Use *whose* to replace a **possessive pronoun** with a relative clause.

SIMPLE SENTENCE He was a great leader.

                        possessive pronoun
SIMPLE SENTENCE People appreciated **his** simple way of life.

COMBINED He was a great leader **whose** simple way of life people appreciated.

Use a preposition plus *who, whom, which,* or *whose* to replace the **object of a preposition** with a relative clause.

SIMPLE SENTENCE Gandhi believed in the independence of India.

                     object of preposition
SIMPLE SENTENCE He worked tirelessly **for it.**

COMBINED Gandhi believed in the independence of India, **for which** he worked tirelessly.

> ### Writer's Alert
>
> *Where* (place), *when* (time), and *why* (reason) are sometimes used to form adjective clauses.
>
> | | |
> |---|---|
> | **PLACE** | My hometown is a place **where** I long to be. |
> | **TIME** | The late evening is the time **when** he writes a lot. |
> | **REASON** | Safety is the reason **why** seat belts are required. |

Use a quantifier plus *who, whom, which,* or *whose* to replace the *object of a quantifier* with a relative clause.

SIMPLE SENTENCE	Gandhi also worked for equality for all people in India.
	object of quantifier
SIMPLE SENTENCE	**Many of them** were very poor.
COMBINED	Gandhi also worked for equality for all people in India, **many of whom** were very poor.

ESL

**14c
gr**

Place the relative clause as close as possible to the noun (the antecedent) that it modifies.

DRAFT	The <u>professor</u> is excellent **who teaches microbiology.**
REVISED	The <u>professor</u> **who teaches microbiology** is excellent.

The relative pronoun may be dropped from the sentence if it is not the subject of the adjective clause. Either form is correct.

INCLUDED	The apartment **that** we rented was very lovely.
OMITTED	The apartment we rented was very lovely.

Adjective clauses can be changed to **adjective phrases** when the relative pronoun is the subject of the adjective clause. To change a clause with a *be* verb to a phrase, omit the relative pronoun and the *be* verb.

	x x
CLAUSE (WITH *BE*)	He is the man **who is studying German.**
PHRASE	He is the man **studying German.**

To change a clause with another verb to a phrase, omit the relative pronoun and change the verb to the present participle form.

	x
CLAUSE (WITHOUT *BE*)	He is the man **who wants to study German.**
PHRASE	He is the man **wanting to study German.**

Adverb clauses

Adverb clauses work like adverbs in complex sentences because they modify or add more information to verbs. Adverb clauses give information about time, reason, contrast, and condition.

TIME	**When** the weather changes, people tend to catch the flu.
	Senior citizens choose to get flu shots **before** they get sick.
REASON	**Since** the weather has turned colder, many people have gotten sick.
	It is difficult to get an appointment at the doctor's office **because** flu season has started.
CONTRAST	**Although** some people choose to get flu shots, others do not.
	Some people choose to get flu shots **while** others do not.
CONDITION	**If** you are unaccustomed to winter weather, you can get an inoculation to protect yourself.
	You may catch the flu **unless** you dress in warm clothes.

Some Words to Introduce Adverb Clauses

TIME		REASON	CONTRAST	CONDITION
while	when	because	although	if
before	whenever	since	though	even if
since	as soon as	as	even though	only if
until	after	now that	while	unless
once	as		whereas	provided that
				as long as

Noun clauses

When you combine the three types of **noun clauses** with other sentence parts to form complex sentences, these clauses work like nouns in the sentences.

THAT CLAUSE	I believe **that** life exists in other solar systems.

Writer's Alert

The word order of a *wh-* question noun clause may vary. Note how this works.

- The word order changes when the question includes a form of *be* and a subject complement.

QUESTION	Who **are** your friends?
NOUN CLAUSE	I wonder who your friends **are.**

- The word order changes when the question includes a modal.

QUESTION	How **can** I meet them?
NOUN CLAUSE	Please tell me how I **can** meet them.

- The word order changes when the question includes the auxiliary *do, does,* or *did.*

QUESTION	When **do** you plan to introduce us?
NOUN CLAUSE	Let me know when you plan to introduce us.

- The word order changes when the question includes the auxiliary *have, has,* or *had.*

QUESTION	How **have** you met so many people?
NOUN CLAUSE	I'm interested in how you **have** met so many people.

ESL

14c
gr

***YES/NO* QUESTION CLAUSE**	I wonder **if** life exists in other solar systems.
	I wonder **whether** life exists in other solar systems.
***WH-* QUESTION CLAUSE**	I wonder **where** signs of other life may be found.

This third kind of noun clause is formed by a question that is embedded into the sentence as a statement. It is introduced by a question word such as *who, whom, what, where, when, which, why, how, how much,* or *how many.* Sometimes the noun clause follows an introductory clause, and then the word order of the noun clause does not change. It remains the same as the word order in the original question. Note how this works.

QUESTION	Who discovered the fire?
NOUN CLAUSE	Do you know **who discovered the fire?**
QUESTION	What started the fire?
NOUN CLAUSE	Did anyone see **what started the fire?**
QUESTION	How much damage was caused?
NOUN CLAUSE	The company knows **how much damage was caused.**
QUESTION	Which fire fighters came to help?
NOUN CLAUSE	He knows **which fire fighters came to help.**

14d Creating different sentence types

You can create **sentences** with a variety of structures: simple, compound, complex, and compound-complex. You can also give them different purposes: declarative, interrogative, imperative, and exclamatory.

1 Building sentence structures

Your sentences vary in structure according to the kind and number of clauses you include.

Simple Sentence. A sentence with one main (independent) clause and no subordinate (dependent) clauses is a **simple sentence.**

> The community development program sponsored several construction projects in the city.

> The director of the program and her two assistants visited the senior center and answered questions about the proposed expansion.

Compound Sentence. A sentence with two or more main (independent) clauses and no subordinate (dependent) clauses is a **compound sentence.**

> main clause
> Most people in the audience seemed pleased with the plans,

> main clause
> yet some complained about the relatively small space allotted for the library.

Complex Sentence. A sentence with one main (independent) clause and one or more subordinate (dependent) clauses is a **complex sentence.**

> subordinate clause
> Because people complained about the lack of library space,

> main clause   subordinate clause
> the architect revised the plans. When the new plans were ready,

> main clause
> the director came back to the senior center to discuss them,

> subordinate clause   subordinate clause
> even though she was sure that most people would be
> pleased with them.

Compound-Complex Sentence. A sentence with two or more main (independent) clauses and one or more subordinate (dependent) clauses is a **compound-complex sentence.**

> subordinate clause   subordinate clause
> Because he wanted to make sure that work on the extension did not

> main clause
> damage the existing building, the architect asked the contractor to

> main clause
> test the soil for stability, and he examined the frame of the older structure himself.

2 Choosing sentence purposes

You can create different kinds of sentences according to the relationship you want to establish with readers. A **declarative sentence** makes a statement. An **interrogative sentence** poses a question. An **imperative sentence** makes a request or command. An **exclamatory sentence** makes an exclamation.

DECLARATIVE   The motor is making a rattling noise.

INTERROGATIVE   Have you checked it for overheating?

IMPERATIVE   Check it again.

EXCLAMATORY   It's on fire!

14d
gr

CHAPTER

15

Case of Nouns and Pronouns

As you write, you use changes in pronoun form to guide readers through sentences and highlight your meaning. In the following sentence, for example, the forms of pronouns indicate their functions.

> Aretha Franklin started making recordings in the 1960s, and **she** has kept on releasing **them** during the four decades of **her** career.

15
case

As you read the pronouns in this sentence, you probably noticed, quickly and unconsciously, that *she* is a pronoun indicating a subject, *them* is a pronoun indicating an object, and *her* is a pronoun indicating possession.

In writing, for the most part, you choose appropriate pronoun case as quickly and unconsciously as you recognize case forms during reading. At times, however, you may have to struggle with choices between *we* or *us, her* or *she,* and *who* or *whom.* The wrong choices can mislead readers.

CONFUSING Dr. Landova criticized the report. The other team members liked it better than **her.**

READER'S RESPONSE: *Her* makes the sentence say that the team members liked the report more than they liked Dr. Landova. It's possible that the writer means this, but I don't think so.

EDITED Dr. Landova criticized the report. The other team members liked it better than **she.**

READER'S RESPONSE: This sentence makes more sense. They liked the report better than she liked it.

Moreover, some errors are likely to irritate readers and create a negative image of you as a writer.

INCORRECT **Him** and **me** will make a strong management team.

READER'S RESPONSE: *Him and me* sounds careless and uneducated. It's a lot easier to trust the judgment and leadership of someone who writes more carefully and precisely.

EDITED **He** and **I** will make a strong management team.

15a Choosing pronoun case

Because a pronoun's form can signal its role in a sentence, you need to choose forms that accurately reflect your meaning. Pronouns change form according to their role in a sentence. A pronoun in the **subjective case** acts as a subject. A pronoun in the **objective case** acts as an object. And a pronoun in the **possessive case** indicates possession or ownership.

SUBJECTIVE CASE   **He** designs furniture for Herman Miller Company.

OBJECTIVE CASE   The modular furniture we are using was designed by **him.**

POSSESSIVE CASE   **His** design team created the dividers forming work spaces in the sales office.

When your sentences follow a familiar order, such as subject-verb-object (see 14b-1 and 14b-2), pronoun case merely highlights roles that will also be obvious to readers from the sentence's arrangement.

> subjective   objective
> case   case
> Tanika helped them.
> subject   verb   object

When you use complicated sentence structures, your readers will depend even more on case to grasp your meaning.

> With Jim, **her,** and Susan, **you** have hired three people **who** are better able to work together than **we.** In addition, as industrial engineers, **they** always pay attention to a product's ease of assembly as well as **its** appearance.

I, we, he/she, it, you, and *they,* the **personal pronouns,** take additional forms to provide readers with other kinds of information, as the chart on page 214 indicates. **First person** pronouns (*I, we*) tell who is speaking. **Second person** (*you*) tells who is being spoken to. And **third person** pronouns (*he/she, it, they*) tell who or what is being spoken about. Pronouns can also indicate **number** (*I, we, he/she, they*) and **gender** (*he, she, it*).

Other kinds of pronouns (**relative, interrogative,** and **indefinite** types—see 14a-2) change form only to indicate case.

In English, nouns vary in form only for the possessive case: *the study/the study's conclusions.* Thus the present chapter looks primarily at pronoun case.

1 Choosing subjective case

Deciding to use a pronoun's subjective form is relatively easy if the pronoun is the subject of all or part of a sentence.

15a
case

Case of Pronouns

PERSONAL PRONOUNS

	SUBJECTIVE		OBJECTIVE		POSSESSIVE	
	SINGULAR	PLURAL	SINGULAR	PLURAL	SINGULAR	PLURAL
First person	I	we	me	us	my	our
					mine	ours
Second person	you	you	you	you	your	your
					yours	yours
Third person	he		him		his	
	she	they	her	them	her	their
					hers	theirs
	it		it		its	

RELATIVE AND INTERROGATIVE PRONOUNS

SUBJECTIVE	OBJECTIVE	POSSESSIVE
who	whom	whose
whoever	whomever	
which	which	
that	that	
what	what	

INDEFINITE PRONOUNS

SUBJECTIVE	OBJECTIVE	POSSESSIVE
anybody	anybody	anybody's
everyone	everyone	everyone's

She wants to know why the orders have not been filled.

Often, however, you need to choose the subjective case for pronouns play-ing other roles. (See 14b for discussion of subjects, complements, and other sentence parts.)

▶━◀ Strategy

As you edit, check whether a pronoun is acting as a subject within some part of a sentence. Check also whether it renames or restates a subject. If it plays either role, use the word's subjective form.

subject of subordinate clause
Because **they** were unable to get a loan, the business failed.

subject of relative clause
Atco Manufacturers will be hiring people **who** are willing to work the night shift.

subject of implied verb
I attend class more regularly than **he** [does].

complement renames subject
The new auditor is **he,** the person at Sandi's desk.

appositives rename subject
Two of the people in the group, **she** and **I,** have experience with desktop publishing.

---

2 Choosing objective case

When you make a pronoun the direct (or indirect) object of an entire sentence, you need to use the word's objective form.

direct object
The police arrested **them** for disturbing the peace.

indirect object
The company bought **her** a spreadsheet program.

In addition, you need to choose the objective form for pronouns playing a number of other roles in a sentence. (See 14b for definitions of objects and other sentence elements.)

**15a
case**

Strategy

As you edit, check whether a pronoun is acting as an object within some part of a sentence. Check also whether it renames or restates an object. If it plays either role, choose the word's objective form.

object of preposition
The rest of **them** had to wait several months for the software.

object in relative clause
An accountant **whom** the firm hired helped her out.

object in gerund phrase
Mr. Pederson's research for the report included interviewing **them.**

object in participial phrase
Having interviewed **us,** too, Mr. Pederson had a lot of material to summarize.

The report contained interviews with the two dissatisfied work-
appositive renames object
ers, **her and him**.

You may sometimes find that pronouns used with infinitive phrases are tricky, so keep the following example in mind.

Mr. Pederson asked **us** to read the summaries of the interviews.

You might be tempted to treat *us* as the subject of the infinitive phrase *to read the summaries of the interviews. Us* is the direct object of the sentence, however (*Mr. Pederson asked us*), and the objective form is correct.

3 Choosing possessive case

When you use a pronoun to show possession, choose the possessive case. Remember that the particular form of the possessive you use depends on whether you use the pronoun *before a noun* or *in place of a noun.*

BEFORE NOUN   The Topeka office requested a copy of **her** report.

REPLACING NOUN **Hers** was the most thorough and up-to-date study available.

You should also use the possessive form before a gerund.

gerund
Their requesting a copy of the report pleased our boss.

Choosing Possessive Forms		
BEFORE A NOUN		**IN PLACE OF A NOUN**
my problem	=	mine
your problem	=	yours
her problem	=	hers
their problem	=	theirs
our problem	=	ours
	BUT	
his problem	=	his
its problem	=	its

Writer's Tip

Do not use an apostrophe with a possessive pronoun. Readers will notice the error. (See 33a.)

INCORRECT   your's, her's, it's, their's

CORRECT   yours, hers, its, theirs

Use *it's* only as a contraction meaning *it is.*
Form possessive nouns with an apostrophe: *Luis's, cat's, Barbara's, government's.*

Did You Know?

In the 1300s and 1400s the pronoun *it* (neuter) took these forms: *hit* (subjective), *his* (possessive), and *hit* (objective). By the 1600s, *hit* lost the *h* to become *it,* but *his* remained the possessive form. As a result, one of Shakespeare's characters says, "How far that little candle throws his beams," instead of "throws *its* beams." During the seventeenth century, however, people began using several substitutes for *his* as a neuter possessive, finally accepting *its,* the form we use today.

Albert C. Baugh, *A History of the English Language,* 2nd ed. (Englewood Cliffs: Prentice, 1963) 293–95.

Exercise 1

A. In each of the following sentences, pick the correct pronoun from the pair within parentheses. Then name the case of the pronoun you have chosen.

EXAMPLE

Ruth and (*I*/*me*) are planning to open a children's clothing store.
subjective

1. The design for the new store was prepared by (*she/her*).
2. The city requires (*we/us*) to submit plans for remodeling the store we plan to rent.
3. Having interviewed Ruth and (*I/me*) about our marketing plan, the bank's officer approved our loan.
4. The person who will choose the stock for our store is (*she/her*).
5. I will supervise the salespeople (*who/whom*) we hire.

Next, revise the following sentences by correcting any errors in pronoun case.

EXAMPLE

The foundation sent copies of the grant proposal to ~~she~~ *her* and me.

1. Her and three other people worked for three weeks preparing the grant proposal.
2. The original grant-writing team included two other people, Kristen and she.
3. Because I spent more time working on the grant, I think I ought to get more credit for its success than him.
4. It is me who will have to supervise research work done under the grant.
5. Responsibility for budgeting the grant money is your's.

15a
case

B. Working with a group of writers, choose a draft paper one of the group has written, and examine two paragraphs carefully. Identify all pronouns in the subjective, objective, and possessive cases, and check to see that they are used correctly. Then suggest revisions for the paragraphs, drawing on some of the sentence and pronoun patterns illustrated in 15a and 15b.

 C. Using the charts in 15a as a reference, edit a draft paper of your own to eliminate any problems with pronoun case.

15b   Solving common problems with pronoun case

All writers struggle at times with pronoun case. Many of your troubles are likely to occur at predictable places. Compound subjects and objects often cause confusion, for example, as do comparisons beginning with *than* or *as.* As you edit, therefore, pay attention to the following troublesome sentence constructions.

1 Choosing pronoun case in compound subjects and objects

When you use a compound subject or object containing a pronoun, such as *the committee and I* or *Jim and me,* you need to decide on the proper form for the pronoun. The rule is simple enough: Use the same case for pronouns in compounds that you would use for single pronouns playing the same role.

COMPOUND SUBJECT	Denise or (*he/him*) should be responsible for creating the new database.
USE SUBJECTIVE CASE	Denise or **he** should be responsible for creating the new database.
COMPOUND OBJECT	The coach selected (*she and him/her and him*) as team representatives.
USE OBJECTIVE CASE	The coach selected **her and him** as team representatives.

In practice, however, you may often find it difficult to decide on the correct pronoun case. The following strategy may help.

Strategy

To choose the correct pronoun form in compound subjects and objects, use the **focus-imagine-choose strategy.**

- **Focus** on the pronoun for which you need to choose the appropriate form.

    UNEDITED   Anne-Marie and **me** will develop videotapes for the sales presentation.
    I or me?

- **Imagine** each possible choice for the pronoun as a singular subject (or object) in a sentence.

    Me will develop videotapes for the sales presentation.
    I will develop videotapes for the sales presentation.

- **Choose** the correct form, and use it in the compound subject (or object). If the correct form is not immediately apparent to you, refer to the chart on page 214. (Choosing the form that "sounds right" can be a misleading strategy with compounds.)

    EDITED   Anne-Marie and **I** will develop videotapes for the sales presentation.

◣◹

15b
case

Writer's Tip

An incorrect pronoun form may pass without much notice in conversation because it "sounds right."

SPOKEN   This is a private agreement between you and **I.**

You need to be alert for problems like this as you edit because readers are likely to notice the faulty choice of pronoun form.

EDITED   This is a private agreement between you and **me.**

As you edit, pay special attention to pronoun forms that sound "wrong" or "unusual." Some of them may actually be correct, as in the following instance.

CORRECT   Responsibility for keeping the coffee room clean is shared between **them** and **us.**

---

2 Choosing pronoun case for subject complements

When you follow a form of the verb *be* (*is, am, are, was, were*) with a pronoun renaming the subject, you create a **subject complement** (see 14b-2). Because you are renaming or restating the subject, choose the subjective form of the pronoun.

CORRECT   The last pharmacy graduates to get jobs at Upstate Medical Center were Rebecca Soares and **I.**

In conversation, even educated speakers occasionally use the objective case in complements.

CONVERSATION   The new traffic reporter is **him.**

In writing, however, you should aim for correctness. If correcting the problem leads to a stilted or unnatural statement, rewrite the entire sentence.

STILTED   The new traffic reporter is **he.**

REWRITTEN   **He** is the new traffic reporter.

3 Choosing *we* or *us* with a noun

When you pair *we, us,* or other pronouns with nouns, make sure the case of the pronoun—*we, they* (subjective) or *us, them* (objective)—matches the role played by the noun (subject or object).

CORRECT   **We taxpayers** ought to demand that the city fill the potholes on Pine Avenue.

CORRECT   The award went to the coach, but it really belonged to **us team members** who worked so hard during the season.

CORRECT   If a customer returns to our store because of the quality of the service, the credit belongs to **you salespeople.**

▶◀

Strategy

Check for a correct match of pronoun and noun by imagining a sentence in alternative versions without the noun.

SENTENCE   The teaching evaluation should be conducted by (*us? we?*) students, not by the faculty or administration.

VERSION 1 (INCORRECT)   The teaching evaluation should be conducted by **we.** . . .

VERSION 2 (CORRECT)   The teaching evaluation should be conducted by **us.** . . .

EDITED   The teaching evaluation should be conducted by **us** students, not by the faculty or administration.

Us is the object of a preposition and takes the objective form (see 15a-2).

▶◀

15b case

4 Choosing pronoun form in an appositive

When you put a pronoun in an appositive phrase (see 14c-3), it renames a preceding noun or pronoun; consequently, it must match the case of the word being renamed.

CORRECT   As an investment, the two sisters, **she** and her twin, bought a small chain of dry cleaners.

Strategy

As you edit, look for pronouns that act as appositives in renaming a noun or another pronoun. Check for the correct pronoun form by imagining alternative versions in which you leave out the noun (or pronoun) that was renamed in the original sentence.

SENTENCE   The two children's book illustrators on the panel, (*she? her?*) and (*I? me?*), discussed all the questions asked by the audience.

VERSION 1 (INCORRECT)   **Her and me** discussed all the questions asked by the audience.

VERSION 2 (CORRECT)   **She and I** discussed all the questions asked by the audience.

EDITED   The two children's book illustrators on the panel, **she and I,** discussed all the questions asked by the audience.
The pronouns rename the subject, so the subjective forms are correct.

15b
case

5 Choosing pronoun case following comparisons with *than* or *as*

When you end a comparison with a pronoun, make sure the case you choose accurately signals the information left out. A pronoun in the subjective case acts as the subject of the implied statement; a pronoun in the objective case acts as the object.

SUBJECTIVE   I rely more on computers for help with the problems than **he** [does].

OBJECTIVE   I gave her sister more help than [I gave] **her.**

You can leave out part of a sentence containing a comparison with *than* or *as* so long as your readers are able to fill in the missing part easily and accurately.

CLEAR   I have better grades in chemistry than she [*does*].

Even a sentence whose meaning is precise—in a grammatical sense, at least—may be unclear if readers are likely to miss the grammatical signals. If there is any chance of confusion, rewrite the sentence.

POTENTIALLY AMBIGUOUS   I like working with Aisha better than she.
READER'S RESPONSE: Does this mean you prefer to work with Aisha? Or that you like to work with Aisha better than someone else does?

REWRITTEN   She doesn't like working with Aisha as much as I do.

6 Using possessive case with gerunds

A **gerund** is the *-ing* form of a verb used as a noun (see 14a-4). Choose the possessive case when you put a noun or pronoun before a gerund in order to modify it.

CORRECT   **My** skidding across the wet floor frightened me.

CORRECT   **Roseanna's** skidding across the wet floor frightened me.

15b
case

Why is using the possessive case important? Versions of a sentence with and without the possessive may differ considerably in meaning.

WITH POSSESSIVE We were surprised by the principal's golfing.
He was golfing, and we were surprised that he had taken up the sport (or that he was so good at it).

WITHOUT POSSESSIVE We were surprised by the principal golfing.
We were golfing, and he came up to us unexpectedly.

Admittedly, placing a possessive before a gerund can make some sentences hard to read. When this is the case, rewrite the sentence.

INCORRECT   The new store manager was surprised by virtually **everybody** in town showing up for the sale.
READER'S RESPONSE: Does this writer mean that *virtually everybody* managed to surprise the new manager? Wasn't it the number of people who showed up that was so surprising?

AWKWARD   The new store manager was surprised by virtually **everybody's** in town showing up for the sale.

REWRITTEN   The new store manager was surprised **that virtually everybody in town showed up for the sale.**

7 Using myself and other reflexive pronouns cautiously

People sometimes use *myself, yourself,* and other **reflexive pronouns** (see 14a-2) inappropriately as sentence subjects or objects, perhaps because they are not sure which pronoun form is correct and assume that *myself* and the other *-self* pronouns will stretch to fit all cases.

INCORRECT   The Nucor project led to some major disagreements between Stan and myself.

CORRECT   The Nucor project led to some major disagreements between Stan and **me.**

> *Me* is the object of a preposition, so the objective case is correct; see 15a-2.

You can use *myself, itself, themselves,* and other reflexive pronouns to refer correctly to the subject or object of a sentence.

I made the check out to **myself.**

You can also use them as **intensive pronouns** to add emphasis.

The building's design **itself,** and not poor construction, is responsible for the leaky roof.

Writer's Alert

Forms such as *hisself, themself, theirselves,* and *themselfs* occur frequently in various spoken dialects of English. In writing, however, use *himself* and *themselves,* the correct forms in standard written English.

15b
case

Exercise 2

A. Correct any errors in pronoun case in the following sentences.

EXAMPLE
Denise and ~~her~~ *she* joined the Disney film group in our class.

1. The rest of us team members decided we should use recent animated movies as the subject of our project.
2. Because their parents own a video store, her brother and her brought in tapes of the movies we planned to study.
3. Bill and I decided to take notes on *Aladdin*; Pat and her chose to study *Beauty and the Beast.*
4. I thought the notes we took were more detailed and better than they.
5. Writing the final paper led to some disagreements between the other members and myself.

B. Working with a group, create a brief story invoving three or four characters. Use at least five of the troublesome pronoun case patterns discussed in 15b, avoiding problems in their use.

15c   Using *who* and *whom*

Many writers and speakers find it hard to choose between *who* and *whom*. They will be inclined to forgive, and even ignore, an occasional misuse of *who, whom, whoever,* and *whomever*. Nonetheless, the places where you are most likely to have trouble with these pronoun forms, in relative clauses and at the beginning of questions, are also places where the pronouns can affect the meaning of a sentence substantially. To guide readers to your meaning, therefore, you need to be precise in your use of *who* and *whom*.

1 Choosing between *who* and *whom* in relative clauses

You probably often use the pronouns *who* and *whom, whoever* and *whomever* to begin the subordinate clauses known as **relative clauses** or **adjective clauses** (see 14a-2). Choose *who* and *whoever* when you use the pronouns as subjects; choose *whom* and *whomever* when you use them as objects (see 15a-1 and 15a-2).

SUBJECT   The artist **who creates a painting or sculpture** ought to benefit from its sale.

OBJECT   Give this delicate assignment to **whomever you trust.**

Deciding between *who* and *whom* can be difficult. You need to choose the appropriate form according to the role the pronoun plays *within the relative clause*. You need to ignore the role the clause plays *within the sentence*.

INCORRECT   The fine must be paid by **whomever** holds the deed to the property.
Although the whole relative clause is the object of the preposition *by*, within the clause the pronoun acts as a subject, not an object.

EDITED   The fine must be paid by **whoever** holds the deed to the property.

2 Choosing between *who* and *whom* in questions

You should use *who* at the beginning of a question when the pronoun is the subject of the sentence. You should use *whom* when the pronoun is an object. (See 15a-1 and 15a-2.)

SUBJECT   **Who** is most likely to get the reader's sympathy at this point in the novel, Huck or Jim?

OBJECT   **Whom** can Cordelia trust for counsel at the conclusion of the scene?

	SUBJECTIVE	OBJECTIVE	POSSESSIVE
Case of *Who* and *Whoever*			
First, second, and third person	who whoever	whom whomever	whose whosever

Exercise 3

A. Correct any errors in pronoun case in the following sentences.

EXAMPLE   *Whoever*

Whomever᠕has taken an IQ test probably remembers the score.

1. In the past, psychologists assumed that whomever scored well on IQ tests was likely to succeed at school and work.
2. Recent studies of IQ tests have produced evidence of them being unable to predict success.
3. A test of constructive thinking skill may tell more about your or mine ability to meet challenges.
4. Reporting on research conducted by he and two of his colleagues, Robert Sternberg points out that "the ability to sell" is an important part of practical intelligence.
5. Other psychologists claim that personal qualities like self-confidence and optimism may by theirselves have as much to do with our mental abilities as IQ does.

B. Working with fellow writers, identify the pronouns in the following passage, and correct any mistakes in case. Keep a record of those identifications and corrections you found most difficult, and be ready to try to explain why you found them difficult.

For we humans, yawning is a familiar activity. You and me probably yawn when we stretch, though not always. Boredom is also a likely cause for us yawning. People often think that no one yawns as much as them, but this is seldom true. We all yawn frequently during a day. We may even start yawning ourselves when we notice someone else whom is yawning.

C. Make a list of the trouble spots discussed in 15b and 15c, and use it as a checklist for editing a paper of your own to eliminate problems with pronoun case.

15c
case

CHAPTER 16

Verbs

Perhaps no other aspect of your speech reveals as much about your education, dialect region, or social class as your verb forms.

We went **a-fishin'** and **a-huntin'** way down into the holler.
My daddy **be pushin'** me to do good in school.
Jimmy **should'a went** with them.
I keep telling him the lawn **needs mowed.**
The kids **done gone and ruint** the whole dinner.

In casual speech, these different verb forms are likely to be acceptable to some listeners, though not to all, of course. If you use such nonstandard verb forms in your writing, however, most readers will be distracted and may assume that you are uneducated. Until you gain complete control of the rules and nuances of the English verb system, you'll need to identify verb problems in your own writing and edit them before you turn in your final drafts.

16a Using simple present and past tense correctly

When you use a simple verb in a sentence, you will put that verb into the present or past tense depending on when the action of the verb occurred. **Present tense** indicates that the action is occurring now; **past tense** indicates it has already occurred. The present tense form of a verb is also called the **base form.** The vast majority of verbs form their past tense with the addition of *-ed* to the base or present tense form, an addition that can be pronounced as *-t, -d,* or *-ed,* depending on the particular verb.

Present tense (base form)	Past tense	Pronunciation
bake	baked	bake + **t**
call	called	call + **d**
defend	defended	defend + **-ed**

**16a
verb**

1 Using present tense correctly

Most of the time, present tense verb forms will give you no trouble. You need no special endings to mark the present tense of verbs *except* in the third person singular form (when you use the pronouns *he, she,* or *it* or a singular noun).

Occasionally, however, you may need to check that your verbs agree in **number** and **person** with their subjects (see 17a and 17b). Be sure that your verbs take singular or plural forms to agree with the number (singular or plural) of their subjects.

PLURAL SUBJECT/PLURAL VERB

Most of the people at the retirement community **eat** three meals a day.

SINGULAR SUBJECT/SINGULAR VERB

Because of his recent operation, **Mr. Richardson eats** five small snacks a day.

ESL Advice: The Third Person *-s* or *-es* Ending

ESL

**16a
verb**

The present tense verbs in English are easy to write, but you must remember to add an *-s* or *-es* to verbs that are third person singular.

Subject	Verb	Subject	Verb + *-s*
I you (sing., pl.) we they	} write	he she it (an animal, a thing, a concept)	} writes

Check the following points to make sure that your present tense verbs are correct when you edit your writing.

• Check the subject and the verb in a simple sentence.

   NOT APPROPRIATE The hummingbird gather nectar from flowers.
                                  subject   verb

   CORRECT   The **hummingbird gathers** nectar from flowers.

• Check whether the subject and the verb are separated by phrases.

   NOT APPROPRIATE The hummingbird of those regions gather nectar.
                                  subject   verb

   CORRECT   The **hummingbird** of those regions **gathers** nectar.
                        Hummingbird, not *regions,* is the subject.

- Check for compound verbs (more than one verb) in a simple sentence.

	subject	verb		verb

NOT APPROPRIATE The hummingbird visit our garden, gather nectar, and

verb
leave quietly.

CORRECT The **hummingbird visits** our garden, **gathers** nectar, and **leaves** quietly.

- Check for agreement between the subject and the verb in a complex sentence (see 14d-1).

adverb clause
NOT APPROPRIATE When the **snow fall,** we enjoy the scenery.

subject verb
CORRECT When the **snow falls,** we enjoy the scenery.

adjective clause
NOT APPROPRIATE The young **man** that I work with **live** in town.

subject   verb
CORRECT The young **man** that I work with **lives** in town.

Writer's Alert

Sometimes you need to be careful to match the -*s* and -*es* endings of verbs in the main clause and in the adjective clause.

adjective clause
The young **man** that **works** with me **lives** in town.

subject   verb   verb

- Check for correct use of the auxiliary *do, don't, does,* and *doesn't.*

NOT APPROPRIATE That restaurant do give special discount dinners.

CORRECT That restaurant **does** give special discount dinners.

- Check for correct use of modal auxiliaries.

NOT APPROPRIATE The president might gives a speech this evening.

subject   modal
CORRECT The president **might give** a speech this evening.

Writer's Tip

A few irregular verbs are still undergoing change, so their usage is less certain. Should you say *sneaked* or *snuck* for the past tense of *sneak? Weaved* or *wove? Strived* or *strove? Creeped* or *crept?* Dictionaries and editors don't always agree on the preferred forms, so you may have to choose a form your audience is likely to prefer. In all cases, however, check your dictionary first to see if there is a clearly preferred form and to make sure the form you are using is acceptable and not simply an error. *Webster's New Collegiate Dictionary,* for example, prefers *sneaked* but accepts *snuck,* prefers *wove* but accepts *weaved,* prefers *strove* but accepts *strived,* and recognizes *crept* but not *creeped.*

2 Using past tense correctly

When you form the past tense of regular verbs in writing, you will usually add *-ed* to the infinitive of the verb. Ordinarily, you won't make errors marking the past tense in this way. Occasionally, however, you may not "hear" the *-ed,* particularly when the verb is followed by a word beginning in *-d* or *-t.* In writing, make sure that every regular verb in the past tense ends in *-ed.*

**16a
verb**

DRAFT   Harold **bake** Donna a huge cake.

EDITED   Harold **baked** Donna a huge cake.

DRAFT   Joey **use** to spend his summers selling hot dogs in Central Park.

EDITED   Joey **used** to spend his summers selling hot dogs in Central Park.

About sixty or seventy common verbs are irregular—exceptions to the "add *-ed*" rule for the past tense. Most **irregular verbs** change an internal vowel in the simple past tense, such as *run* (present) and *ran* (past). A few don't change written form but are pronounced differently.

Present tense form	Past tense form
catch	caught
dive	dove
eat	ate
fight	fought
read (rhymes with *seed*)	read (rhymes with *bed*)
run	ran

Because the forms of each irregular verb must be learned independently, you may occasionally use a past tense form that is not acceptable in standard written English. Keep track of any verbs that are troublesome for you, and scan your drafts for them when you edit.

DRAFT   The movie was disappointing because the characters **sweared** at each other constantly.

EDITED   The movie was disappointing because the characters **swore** at each other constantly.

ESL Advice: Simple Present and Simple Past

These are the two tenses that add no helping verbs to form the verb. No other verb forms can stand alone!

SIMPLE PRESENT   They **live** in the dormitory this semester.

SIMPLE PAST   They **lived** in an apartment last semester.

ESL

16a verb

NOT APPROPRIATE   The student **studying** in the library yesterday.
The writer uses the present participle without any helping verb. In English this is not possible.

CORRECT   The student **was studying** in the library yesterday.
Now the verb form is a completed verb phrase with a helping verb and a verb form.

(For more about helping verbs, see ESL Advice: Helping Verbs.)

Did You Know?

The reason English contains irregular verbs can be traced historically to a time when the past tense and past participle forms of verbs were created mainly by internal sound changes. Most verbs, called *strong verbs*, once followed a special system of sound changes, and a smaller number (called *weak verbs*) added -ed. Over time, most strong verbs became weak verbs. Today, only about seventy strong verbs remain. A few have alternative forms, such as *dive/dived* versus *dive/dove* and *weave/weaved* versus *weave/wove*. All newly invented verbs now take the -ed ending (witness the recent *fax/faxed*).

Albert C. Baugh and Thomas Cable, *A History of the English Language* (London: Routledge, 1978).

16b Using complex tenses, helping verbs, and mood

To create complex tenses, you need to provide the main verb in a sentence with a **helping** or **auxiliary verb** (such as *is* or *has*) and change the form of the main verb. When linked to main verbs (see 14a-3), helping verbs can specify a range of time relationships. Consider the following sentences.

> After **having eaten** up all the cake, little Jennifer **would have begun** to feel guilty **had it not been** for her father's unexpected treat—a box of delicious parfaits for the family.

> Assuming he **would be going** on the trip, Terry **had started** packing when to his surprise the whole apartment **began** to tremble from a small earthquake that **will be remembered** as the July Surprise.

The complex verb forms in these sentences convey important aspects of past, present, or future time. But how can you be sure you are using the correct verb forms when creating such sentences?

1 Recognizing problems with participles

The **participle** is the form a verb takes when it's linked to a helping verb. Verbs can take two participial forms, the **past participle** and the **present participle.** When writers have problems with complex tenses, they typically use the wrong participle.

The present participle is formed by adding *-ing* to the base form of the verb (the form with no endings or markers).

Helping verb	Participle (main verb)
He was	loading the truck.
He will be	loading the truck.
He had been	loading the truck.

Chan is **greeting** the jugglers at the airport as we speak.

The past participle form of most verbs is just like the simple past tense.

Helping verb	Past participle (main verb)
Mike has	rented the truck.
Mike had	rented the truck.

Chan has **greeted** the jugglers every year for the past five years.

Other participial forms are irregular, involving an internal vowel change or an *-en* ending.

INCORRECT   Louise lost the pie-eating contest because she **had drank** three glasses of lemonade just before it began.

EDITED   Louise lost the pie-eating contest because she **had drunk** three glasses of lemonade just before it began.

INCORRECT   By the end of the trial, the lawyers **had went** too far in their defense of the rapist.

EDITED   By the end of the trial, the lawyers **had gone** too far in their defense of the rapist.

The following list of the principal parts of some common irregular verbs should help you identify and use the correct participle.

Common Irregular Verbs		
PRESENT	**PAST**	**PAST PARTICIPLE**
arise	arose	arisen
be	was/were	been
bear	bore	borne
begin	began	begun
bite	bit	bitten/bit
blow	blew	blown
break	broke	broken
bring	brought	brought
buy	bought	bought
catch	caught	caught
choose	chose	chosen
come	came	come
creep	crept	crept
dive	dived/dove	dived
do	did	done
draw	drew	drawn
dream	dreamed/dreamt	dreamt
drink	drank	drunk
drive	drove	driven
eat	ate	eaten
fall	fell	fallen
fight	fought	fought

PRESENT	PAST	PAST PARTICIPLE
fly	flew	flown
forget	forgot	forgotten
forgive	forgave	forgiven
freeze	froze	frozen
get	got	got/gotten
give	gave	given
go	went	gone
grow	grew	grown
hang	hung	hung
hide	hid	hidden
know	knew	known
lay	laid	laid
lead	led	led
lie	lay	lain
light	lit	lit
lose	lost	lost
prove	proved	proved/proven
ride	rode	ridden
ring	rang	rung
rise	rose	risen
run	ran	run
see	saw	seen
seek	sought	sought
set	set	set
shake	shook	shaken
sing	sang	sung
sink	sank	sunk
sit	sat	sat
speak	spoke	spoken
spring	sprang	sprung
steal	stole	stolen
sting	stung	stung
strike	struck	struck
swear	swore	sworn
swim	swam	swum
swing	swung	swung
take	took	taken
tear	tore	torn
throw	threw	thrown
wake	woke/waked	woken/waked/woke
wear	wore	worn

**16b
verb**

ESL Advice: Verb Forms

To use verb forms correctly, you need to consider four things: verb form, subject-verb agreement, verb tense, and verb voice. (See 14a-3.) In English, verbs can have the following forms.

Principle Parts of Verbs in English

BASE FORM	PAST	PRESENT PARTICIPLE	PAST PARTICIPLE
REGULAR VERBS			
hope	hoped	hoping	hoped
live	lived	living	lived
want	wanted	wanting	wanted
IRREGULAR VERBS			
come	came	coming	come
eat	ate	eating	eaten
run	ran	running	run

ESL

16b verb

Most verbs are formed by combining one or more helping verbs with a main verb (see 14a-3). The main verb plus any helping verb is called a **verb phrase.**

> verb phrase
>
> **ONE HELPING VERB**   I **was walking** to school during the snowstorm.

> verb phrase
>
> **TWO HELPING VERBS**   I **have been walking** to school for many years.

Exercise 1

A. In each of the following sentences, a correct or incorrect irregular verb form appears in parentheses. Edit each sentence to make it correct, or indicate that it's already correct. If necessary, consult the list in 16b-1 or look in a dictionary for the principal parts of a particular verb.

                     had fallen

EXAMPLE The rain (~~had falled~~)ₐall night.

1. Jeremy (*had chose*) to work along the levee as part of the volunteer corps.
2. The floodwater (*had rised*) rapidly during the night.
3. The work team (*had heaved*) sandbags on top of the levee for almost twenty-four hours.

4. Jim O'Connor and Rebecca Gomez (*had hung*) plastic sheeting up to plug a leak.
5. By eight o'clock in the morning, people (*had woke*) up to find that the river (*had fell*) by six inches and the town was safe.

B. Review the list of irregular verbs in 16b-1. Compose five sentences in which you correctly or incorrectly use the past or past participle form of an irregular verb. In a small group, exchange lists and edit your sentences. Discuss the changes you made or did not make.

C. Review your paper in progress for any cases of irregular past tense verbs or past participles. Circle the cases you are not sure about, and then check these against 16b-1 or, if necessary, a good dictionary.

ESL Advice: Helping Verbs

Helping verbs can be used alone or in combination.

ESL

16b verb

Forms of Helping Verbs That Work Alone

BE	MODALS
am, is, are	will, would
was, were	can, could
am being, is being, are being	should
was being, were being	ought to
	might, may
	must
	have to, has to, had to
HAVE	**DO**
have, has	do, does
had	did

Forms of Helping Verbs That Work Together

have	+ be	have been, has been, had been
all modals	**+ be**	will be
	+ have	will have
	+ have + be	will have been

In order to know which helping verb to use, you need to know which tense to use.

Verb Forms and Helping Verbs for Commonly Used Verb Tenses

The past, present, and future progressive use *be*.

PAST
subject + *was/were* + present participle
I **was** working in my studio yesterday.

PRESENT
subject + *am/is/are* + present participle
I **am** working in my studio right now.

FUTURE
subject + *will* (modal) + *be* + present participle
I **will be** working in my studio tomorrow.

The past, present, and future perfect use *have*.

PAST
subject + *had* + past participle
I **had** tried to call you all day.

PRESENT
subject + *have/has* + past participle
I **have** tried to call you all day.

FUTURE
subject + *will* (modal) + *have* + past participle
I **will have** called you by midnight.

ESL

16b verb

2 Using progressive and perfect tenses correctly

The three tenses usually called the **present, past,** and **future progressive** allow you to show an action in progress at some point in time. When you attach a helping verb to a main verb in the **progressive tense,** the main verb must take the *-ing* ending. In the future tense, the progressive must also include the verbal element *be*.

PRESENT PROGRESSIVE   The carousel **is turning** too quickly.

PAST PROGRESSIVE   The horses **were bobbing** up and down crazily.

FUTURE PROGRESSIVE   The children **will be laughing** from the thrill.

Note that irregular main verbs are not affected in any unique way by the progressive tense; all consist of the base form plus *-ing*.

The park ranger **is catching** the injured raccoon.
The campers **will be hanging** their food from a tree at night.

Most errors in progressive tense will occur when you either use the wrong form of the helping verb or, as is common in some dialects, omit part of the auxiliary verb.

DRAFT   The amusement park always **opening** five minutes late.

EDITED   The amusement park **is** always **opening** five minutes late.

DRAFT   The kids **was running** for the front seat of the roller coaster.

EDITED   The kids **were running** for the front seat of the roller coaster.

Three special verb tenses, the **perfect tenses**, are used to show the order in which events take place. The **past perfect tense** allows you to indicate that something had already happened before something else happened. The form consists of *had* plus the past participle (see 16a-1 for participle forms).

The fires **had burned** for an hour before the brigade arrived.

Carmen **had drunk** three beers and wisely gave her car keys to the designated driver.

Errors commonly occur when a writer chooses the past perfect tense but doesn't construct it with the correct form of the past participle, substituting a simple past tense form instead.

16b
verb

DRAFT   Pierre **had rode** for six years before he got injured in a rodeo.

EDITED   Pierre **had ridden** for six years before he got injured in a rodeo.

The **present perfect tense** works much like the past perfect, but the action is something that has recurred or that the writer is insisting has already occurred.

Never **have I seen** such a commotion at an elegant party.
But officer, **I have reported** the burglary already.

The present perfect also presents something begun in the past and continuing into the present.

I **have lived** in St. Louis for three weeks.

The **future perfect tense** shows that something will have happened by the time something else will be happening. This form consists of the helping verb *will* plus *have* plus the past participle of the main verb.

Nancy **will have finished** by the time the dentist is ready.
Otto **will have eaten** all the fries before his brother gets home.

ESL Advice: Simple Present and Present Progressive Tenses

In English, both the simple present and the present progressive tenses can describe activities that happen in the present.

Simple present

Use the simple present tense to describe activities that are factual or habitual. These activities occur in the present, but they are not necessarily activities in progress.

subject + verb (with -s if third person singular)

SHOWS FACT The planets **revolve** around the sun.

SHOWS HABIT The bus usually **arrives** late.

Some Common Time Expressions for Present Tense Habitual Activities		
all the time	every month	often
always	every semester	rarely
every class	every week	sometimes
every day	every year	usually
every holiday	most of the time	
every hour	never	

Present progressive

Use the present progressive tense to describe activities that are in progress.

subject + *am/is/are* + present participle
Rachael   **is**   **writing** a book.

In this sentence, it is clear that Rachael is in the process of writing a book.

Some Common Present Progressive Time Expressions to Show Activities in Progress		
at the moment	this evening	this semester
right now	this month	this year
this afternoon	this morning	today

Many present progressive time expressions can be added to the sentence to show more precisely the time of the writing.

> Rachael **is writing** a book **this semester.**
> Now readers know that the activity is in progress over the semester.

Choosing between simple present and present progressive

When you choose between the simple present and present progressive tenses, think about which time expression best describes the activity.

NOT APPROPRIATE All people are communicating in some language.
Is it happening only at the moment (present progressive) or all the time (simple present)?

CORRECT All people communicate in some language.
This is a fact, and the correct tense must be simple present tense.

NOT APPROPRIATE The students are always speaking their own languages in class.
Do the students speak their own languages all the time as a habit (simple present), or is it happening at the moment or one time only (present progressive)?

CORRECT The students speak their own languages in class.
This is a habitual activity that occurs all the time, and the correct tense is simple present.

ESL

16b
verb

Verbs That Are Troublesome in Progressive Tenses		
SENSES	**EXAMPLE**	**OTHER USAGES AND MEANINGS**
see	I **see** the beauty.	Also: I **am seeing** that dentist. (meeting with, visiting, dating)
hear	I **hear** the birds.	Also: I **have been hearing** about the problem for a while. (receiving information)
smell	The flowers **smell** strong.	Also: I **am smelling** the flowers. (action in progress)
taste	The food **tastes** good.	Also: The cook **is tasting** the soup. (action in progress)

(cont.)

Verbs That Are Troublesome in Progressive Tenses *(cont.)*

	EXAMPLE	OTHER USAGES AND MEANINGS
POSSESSION		
have	We **have** many friends.	Also: We **are having** a lot of fun. (experiencing)
own	They **own** many dogs.	
possess	She **possesses** much knowledge.	
belong	The book **belongs** to me.	
STATES OF MIND		
be	I **am** tired.	
know	I **know** the city well.	
believe	She **believes** in God.	
think	I **think** it is true. (know, believe)	Also: I **am thinking** about vacation. (having thoughts about)
recognize	His dog always **recognizes** him. (know)	
understand	The professor **understands** the equation.	
mean	I **don't mean** to pry. (don't want)	Also: I **have been meaning** to visit you. (planning, intending)
WISH OR ATTITUDE		
want	We **want** peace.	
desire	He **desires** his freedom.	
need	We **need** rain.	
love	Children **love** snow.	Also: I **have been loving** this book. (enjoying)
hate	Cats **hate** getting wet.	
like	He **likes** skiing.	
dislike	He **dislikes** skiing.	
seem	She **seems** gentle.	
appear	He **appears** tired. (seems to be)	Also: He **is appearing** at the theater. (acting, performing)
look	He **looks** tired. (seems to be)	Also: We **are looking** at photographs. (action of using eyes)

ESL

16b
verb

Tenses of Regular and Irregular Verbs in the Active Voice

PRESENT, PAST, AND FUTURE

PRESENT

I examine/begin	we examine/begin
you examine/begin	you examine/begin
he/she/it examines/begins	they examine/begin

PAST

I examined/began	we examined/began
you examined/began	you examined/began
he/she/it examined/began	they examined/began

FUTURE

I will examine/begin	we will examine/begin
you will examine/begin	you will examine/begin
he/she/it will examine/begin	they will examine/begin

PRESENT, PAST, AND FUTURE PERFECT

PRESENT PERFECT

I have examined/begun	we have examined/begun
you have examined/begun	you have examined/begun
he/she/it has examined/begun	they have examined/begun

PAST PERFECT

I had examined/begun	we had examined/begun
you had examined/begun	you had examined/begun
he/she/it had examined/begun	they had examined/begun

FUTURE PERFECT

I will have examined/begun	we will have examined/begun
you will have examined/begun	you will have examined/begun
he/she/it will have examined/begun	they will have examined/begun

PRESENT, PAST, AND FUTURE PROGRESSIVE

PRESENT PROGRESSIVE

I am examining/beginning	we are examining/beginning
you are examining/beginning	you are examining/beginning
he/she/it is examining/beginning	they are examining/beginning

PAST PROGRESSIVE

I was examining/beginning	we were examining/beginning
you were examining/beginning	you were examining/beginning
he/she/it was examining/beginning	they were examining/beginning

16b
verb

(cont.)

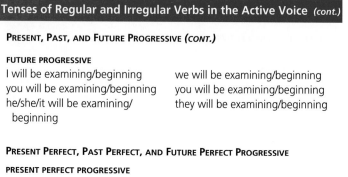

Tenses of Regular and Irregular Verbs in the Active Voice *(cont.)*

PRESENT, PAST, AND FUTURE PROGRESSIVE *(CONT.)*

FUTURE PROGRESSIVE

I will be examining/beginning
you will be examining/beginning
he/she/it will be examining/
  beginning

we will be examining/beginning
you will be examining/beginning
they will be examining/beginning

PRESENT PERFECT, PAST PERFECT, AND FUTURE PERFECT PROGRESSIVE

PRESENT PERFECT PROGRESSIVE

I have been examining/
  beginning
you have been examining/
  beginning
he/she/it has been examining/
  beginning

we have been examining/
  beginning
you have been examining/
  beginning
they have been examining/
  beginning

PAST PERFECT PROGRESSIVE

I had been examining/
  beginning
you had been examining/
  beginning
he/she/it had been examining/
  beginning

we had been examining/
  beginning
you had been examining/
  beginning
they had been examining/
  beginning

FUTURE PERFECT PROGRESSIVE

I will have been examining/
  beginning
you will have been examining/
  beginning
he/she/it will have been
  examining/beginning

we will have been examining/
  beginning
you will have been examining/
  beginning
they will have been examining/
  beginning

3 Using the subjunctive mood correctly

Sentences can be classified according to **mood,** a term that highlights the speaker's or writer's attitude as reflected in the statement. Most of your sentences will be in the **indicative mood** (characterizing statements intended as truthful or factual) or the **imperative mood** (characterizing statements like "Stop!" or "Watch out!," which function as commands). Most of the information in this chapter focuses on verbs in the indicative mood.

Because it is not used heavily in ordinary speech, you may have trouble with the **subjunctive mood** in your writing. The subjunctive mood is used to express uncertainty—a supposition, prediction, or possibility.

Were the contest to start today, our entry would not be ready.

The subjunctive mood has faded from most casual speech and even some writing, but it is still used on occasion, particularly in formal writing. Teachers or highly educated readers may expect you to use the subjunctive.

Whenever you create sentences that express desires or wishes, both positive and negative, the subjunctive may be required.

DRAFT	Jacqueline wished the news **was** not true.
EDITED (SUBJUNCTIVE)	Jacqueline wished the news **were** not true.

Many **conditional statements,** expressing the improbable or hypothetical and often beginning with *if,* require the subjunctive.

DRAFT	If Sandy **was** a person who always wore a helmet, his family would be much less worried about his riding motorcycles.
EDITED (SUBJUNCTIVE)	If Sandy **were** a person who always wore a helmet, his family would be much less worried about his riding motorcycles.

16b verb

Writer's Alert

When you write conditional sentences using the past perfect tense, be careful not to add the auxiliary *would* to the *had + verb* structure in the conditional clause. This serious error is common, in part because the clause after the conditional often does correctly contain that structure.

DRAFT	If Sandy **would have worn** his helmet on the night of the party, he **would have hurt** himself less seriously.
EDITED	If Sandy **had worn** his helmet on the night of the party, he **would have hurt** himself less seriously.

Finally, some clauses with *that* require a subjunctive verb when they follow certain verbs that make demands or requests. The common error here is to use the incorrect form of the main verb, which should be the same as for the past participle (see 16a-2).

DRAFT The judge asked that the eyewitnesses **be swore** in before testifying.

EDITED The judge asked that the eyewitnesses **be sworn** in before testifying.

How can you decide which form of the verb is the subjunctive? Simply use the present tense form of the verb, even in the third person singular where the verb usually varies in form. Subjunctive forms of the verb *appear* are *I appear, you appear, he/she/it appear* (not appears), *we appear,* and *they appear*. For the verb *is*, however, the subjunctive forms are *be* in the present and *were* in the past.

Exercise 2

A. Rewrite each of the following sentences in the tense or mood indicated in brackets by substituting appropriate main verb forms and any necessary helping verbs for the verb in parentheses.

EXAMPLE

has been failing

The airplane assembly plant ^ (~~*fail*~~) for several years. [present perfect progressive]

1. First, the recession (*hurt*) the market for small airplanes. [past perfect]
2. Then a new management team announced, "We (*close*) the plant unless productivity increases." [future]
3. At the same time, the company (*lose*) a product liability lawsuit. [past progressive]
4. This week, the company president (*announce*), "Unless we get some new orders in a few days, we (*declare*) bankruptcy." [simple past; future progressive]
5. If the plant (*be*) closed, three hundred workers would lose their jobs. [past subjunctive]

B. Write five sentences of your own, three using different complex tenses and two employing the subjunctive mood. Exchange sentences with a fellow writer and check that your partner has used the tenses and the subjunctive mood correctly.

ESL Advice: Conditionals

As a writer, you may at times want to express three types of ideas that are dependent on a condition or are imagined. These ideas may be (1) *true* in the present, true in the future, or possibly true in the future; (2) *untrue* or contrary to fact in the present; or (3) *untrue* or contrary to fact in the past.

Type I: True in the Present

IF CLAUSE   RESULT CLAUSE

- Generally true as a habit or as a fact

  if + subject + present tense verb   subject + present tense verb
  If I drive to school every day,   I get to class on time.

- True in the future as a one-time event

  if + subject + present tense verb   subject + future tense verb
  If I drive to school today,   I will get to class on time.

- Possibly true in the future as a one-time event

  if + subject + present tense verb   subject + modal + base form verb
  If I drive to school today,   I ⎰ may   get to class on time.
                                              ⎱ might
                                                could
                                                should

Type II: Untrue in the Present

IF CLAUSE   RESULT CLAUSE

if + subject + past tense verb   subject + ⎰ *would* + simple form of verb
                                                    ⎱ *could*
                                                      might

If I drove to school,   I ⎰ would   arrive on time.
                                              ⎱ could
                                                might

Writer's Alert

With the Type II conditional, when you use the verb *be*
in the *if* clause, the form is always *were*.

  I, you, he/she/it, we, they + *were*

NOT APPROPRIATE If he **was** president, he would reform tax laws.

CORRECT   If he **were** president, he would reform tax laws.

Type III: Untrue in the Past	
IF CLAUSE	**RESULT CLAUSE**
if + subject + past perfect tense	subject + $\begin{cases} would + have + \text{past participle} \\ could \\ might \end{cases}$
If I had driven to school,	I would not have been late.

Let's look at these examples to understand the meaning of conditionals.

Type I

CONDITION   If I **study** hard, I always **get** good grades.
This is true habitual behavior.

CONDITION   If I **study** hard for tomorrow's test, I **will get** a good grade.
This is true as a prediction of the future.

CONDITION   If I **study** hard for tomorrow's test, I **might get** a good grade.
This is possibly true as a prediction of the future.

Type II

SITUATION   I **don't have** enough money to go to Canada for vacation, so I **won't go.**
This is a true situation in the present.

CONDITION   If I **had** enough money to go to Canada for vacation, I **would definitely go.**
This is an imagined condition in the present.

Type III

SITUATION   I **did not have** enough money last month to go to Canada, so I **didn't go** there.
This is a true situation in the past.

CONDITION   If I **had had** enough money last month to go to Canada, I **would have gone** there.
This is an imagined condition in the past.

Expressing a continuous action with conditionals

If he **were living** in Hong Kong, he **would be spending** time with his family.
This is an untrue condition in the present because he is not living in Hong Kong.

If he **had been living** in Hong Kong last year, he **would have been spending** more time with his family.

This is an untrue condition in the past.

Writer's Alert

Sometimes you may want to express ideas about events that happen at different times, and you can shift from one tense to another to do this.

SITUATION
past
I **did not expect** to meet a lot of people from
present
my country in the United States, so I **am** surprised.

CONDITION
past
If I **had expected** to meet a lot of people from my
present
country in the United States, **I would not be surprised.**

ESL

16c
verb

16c Keeping tense sequence clear

In conversation, we often shift from verb tense to verb tense indiscriminately, sometimes moving from past to present and back again with little warning or planning. In writing, however, such tense shifts can be annoying to readers who expect consistency. Thus you need to maintain a clear **tense sequence** in your writing, making plain the time relationships of events and ideas. In the following passage, the shift from past to present is logical and clear.

LOGICAL
In the 1950s, great ocean liners still **offered** an attractive way to travel. Nowadays, people **prefer** jet travel because it is so much faster.

When changes in tense do not reflect clear relationships in time or do so inconsistently, your readers may become confused.

INCONSISTENT
The author **begins** by giving a factual account of the storm. He **said** that if people had heeded the warnings, many lives would have been saved.

EDITED
The author **begins** by giving a factual account of the storm. He **says** that if people had heeded the warnings, many lives would have been saved.

You can shift tenses inside a sentence without creating confusion as long as you make the tense sequence logical.

> past   present
LOGICAL   Although my mother and father both **loved** cats, I **dislike** them.

> present   past
LOGICAL   People **forget** that four serious candidates **ran** in the 1948 presidential election.

> future   present
LOGICAL   I **will accept** your report even if it **is** a bit late.

> past
LOGICAL   The accountant **destroyed** evidence of the embezzlement
> past perfect
because the police **had forgotten** to warn him of the importance of the records.

> past perfect
LOGICAL   None of the expedition's crew **had recognized** that food
> present
stored in cans sealed with lead solder **is** poisonous.

Putting *is poisonous* in the present tense is appropriate because the phrase is a generally true (or widely applicable) statement.

16c
verb

Writer's Tip

Use the present tense to discuss events, ideas, and statements in a piece of literature, a film, an essay, a painting, or a similar creative production.

INCORRECT   In P. G. Wodehouse's *The Mating Season,* the main character **described** an unpleasant relative as a person "who chews broken bottles and kills rats with her teeth."

CORRECT   In P. G. Wodehouse's *The Mating Season,* the main character **describes** an unpleasant relative as a person "who chews broken bottles and kills rats with her teeth."

Exercise 3

A. Decide whether the complex verb forms highlighted in the following sentences are correct. Edit those that are not; explain why you left any as they appear.

EXAMPLE

The team leader **is planning** to ask for reports just after the production meeting ~~will begin.~~ *begins*

1. Kamal **is finished** testing the circuit board by the time the production meeting **had started.**
2. The team members **will ask** Kamal if he **was planning** to test the remainder of the circuit boards.
3. As I prepare this report on the project, Michelle **is assembling** the prototype using the circuit boards.
4. The other people **will assemble** the extra machines as soon as the delivery van **arrived.**
5. If our customers **will be able** to recognize the advantages of our product, they **would order** more of the machines.

B. Compose five sentences with correct and incorrect subjunctive mood and/or tense shifts. Edit each other's sentences in a small group; then discuss the changes you made.

C. Read your paper in progress, paying special attention to consistency of tense. Look for any shifts in tense from sentence to sentence or paragraph to paragraph, and then analyze those shifts to see if they are logical or in error.

16d Using active and passive voice

16d
verb

Verbs in the **active voice** appear in sentences in which the doer of an action is the subject of the sentence.

	Agent (subject)	Action (verb)	Goal (object)
ACTIVE	The car	hit	the lamppost.
ACTIVE	Everyone	likes	a comedian.

To rewrite an active sentence in the **passive voice,** add a form of *be* as a helping verb, and use the participle form of the verb. Place the subject (or doer) into the object position after the word *by.* (A prepositional phrase states the doer and is optional.)

	Goal (subject)	Action (verb)	[Agent] [prepositional phrase]
PASSIVE	The lamppost	**was hit**	[by the car].
PASSIVE	A comedian	**is liked**	[by everyone].

The active voice and passive voice versions of a sentence create different kinds of emphasis because they use different words as sentence subjects. In addition, a passive sentence that eliminates any mention of the doer can mask responsibility for an action.

ACTIVE VOICE	The city council banned smoking in restaurants.
PASSIVE VOICE	Smoking in restaurants was banned by the city council.
AGENT ELIMINATED	Smoking in restaurants was banned.

(For a discussion of use and misuse of the passive voice, see 11c.)

ESL Advice: The Passive Voice

In English you can choose to use either active or passive voice for stylistic reasons (see 16d). All verbs in English may be written in the passive voice *except* the progressive forms of the present perfect, past perfect, future, and future perfect.

In all the sentences in the following chart, the agent of the action is not the subject, *food,* but rather *chef.*

Verb Forms in the Passive Voice

TENSES	SUBJECT + *BE* FORM + PAST PARTICIPLE
PRESENT	The food **is prepared** by the chef.
PRESENT PROGRESSIVE	The food **is being prepared** by the chef.
PAST	The food **was prepared** by the chef.
PAST PROGRESSIVE	The food **was being prepared** by the chef.
PRESENT PERFECT	The food **has been prepared** by the chef.
PAST PERFECT	The food **had been prepared** by the chef.
FUTURE	The food **is going to be prepared** by the chef. The food **will be prepared** by the chef.
FUTURE PERFECT	The food **will have been prepared** by the chef.

Writer's Alert

Be sure to edit your passive verbs to check for correct forms. Each passive verb must have a form of *be* and a past participle. With regular verbs, the past participle will have the *-ed* ending. Sometimes it is difficult to hear these *-ed* endings in spoken English, so be careful to include them in your writing.

NOT APPROPRIATE	The young man was **call** by the draft board.
CORRECT	The young man was **called** by the draft board.

Exercise 4

A. Edit the following passage by rewriting unnecessary uses of the passive voice into the active voice. In rewriting passive voice sentences that do not indicate an agent (doer), fill in the names of the person(s) or thing(s) you consider responsible for the action.

Having cash registers full of change was found to increase the like-lihood of a late-night robbery. In one example, a store clerk was held up at gunpoint. It was decided by management that requiring full payment for gasoline in advance of a purchase would minimize the risk of further holdups. This course of action had been voted on by the board of directors prior to implementation. The decision was posted at each location. Following implementation, it was discovered that holdups were not minimized unless large signs indicating the clerk's lack of available cash were placed in plain view. Once this was done, fewer holdups were experienced, and the turnover of late-night per-sonnel was decreased.

B. Compare your rewritten version of the passage in Exercise 4A with those produced by other students. Be sure you explain why you have decided to let any sentences remain in the passive voice. Working with several other students, produce one version of the passage reflect-ing group agreement on the best way to rewrite the sentences.

C. Read a draft of your current paper and circle every passive sen-tence. Write an active version of each, and decide which of the ver-sions best suits your purposes in writing. (See 11c.)

ESL

**16e
verb**

16e Editing troublesome verbs (*lie, lay, sit, set*)

Even for experienced writers, a few verbs can be tricky. For example, you may confuse the past or past participle forms of different verbs that "share" one or more forms. Until you can remember their correct forms, you should identify these verbs when you edit your drafts and then check them by reviewing this section. Here are the verbs most often confused (which, incidentally, also have the longest dictionary entries of any verbs in English).

Verb	Present	Past	Participle
lie (oneself)	lie	lay	lain
lay (an object)	lay	laid	laid
sit (oneself)	sit	sat	sat
set (an object)	set	set	set

1 *Lie* and *lay*

When you use the verb *lie* to mean "place one's body in a horizontal position," as in "lie down," you may confuse it with the verb *lay,* which means to put something (but not one's body) down, as in "Lay the book on the table." *Lie* is an intransitive verb, meaning that it can't be used with a **direct object** (see 14b), whereas *lay* must be used with a direct object.

DRAFT   I **laid** down yesterday afternoon for a nap. I **have laid** down at around 2 p.m. each day for over a year now.

EDITED   I **lay** down yesterday afternoon for a nap. I **have lain** down at around 2 p.m. each day for over a year now.

DRAFT   Dr. Parsons **lay** the cadaver on the table and began the autopsy.

EDITED   Dr. Parsons **laid** the cadaver on the table and began the autopsy.

A third verb, *lie,* meaning "to tell an untruth," is a regular verb whose past tense ends in *-ed* ("I *lied* to my sister"). Don't confuse it with the form for the other verb *lie.*

2 *Sit* and *set*

The verb *sit* means to place oneself on or in something, such as a chair. *Set,* however, means to place an object, such as a book, on a surface. Like choosing between *lie* and *lay,* you figure out which form to use by asking yourself whether there is a direct object in your sentence. *Sit* can't be used with a direct object, but *set* must be used with a direct object.

DRAFT   First Erica and Steve **sat** the popcorn down on the seat next to them. Then they **set** down and endured the first hour of the boring movie.

EDITED   First Erica and Steve **set** the popcorn down on the seat next to them. Then they **sat** down and endured the first hour of the boring movie.

16e verb

> ### Writer's Tip
>
> Some problems with irregular verbs come from spelling, not grammar. Don't spell *laid* ("The chicken *laid* three eggs") incorrectly as *layed*. Also watch out for spelling the past tense of *lead* the same way as the present; *lead*, which rhymes with *bed*, is a heavy metal, not the past tense of *lead,* which rhymes with *seed.*
>
> **DRAFT**   The scoutmaster **lead** us up the mountain.
>
> **EDITED**   The scoutmaster **led** us up the mountain.

Exercise 5

A. For each sentence, circle the appropriate verb form from the two within parentheses.

EXAMPLE

A fire last Saturday (*lead,* (*led*)) to Sandy's first big assignment as a reporter.

16e
verb

1. Sandy (*laid/lay*) the article for the newspaper on her editor's desk.
2. To get information for the article, she (*sat/set*) in the waiting room of the fire commissioner's office for three days.
3. During the interview she (*layed/lay/laid*) on his desk a copy of the report criticizing the fire department's performance during the Brocklin Warehouse fire.
4. The commissioner looked the report over and then (*sat/set*) it next to the other report, which praised the department's performance.
5. After she had (*lead/led*) the three-hour discussion with the commissioner, Sandy was convinced that the department had done an adequate job at the fire.

B. Write four or five sentences in which you use *incorrect* forms of *sit, set, lie,* and *lay.* Exchange your sentences in a small group, edit them, and then discuss your changes.

EXAMPLE

Mrs. Jones sat the tuna salad dangerously close to Puff, her Siamese cat.

CHAPTER 17

Agreement
(Subject and Verb, Pronoun and Antecedent)

What is wrong with the following sentence?

Barbara Walters and Diane Sawyer is known for skill at interviewing.

You probably read the opening of the sentence assuming it would be about *two* people—Barbara Walters and Diane Sawyer—but when you encountered the verb *is* you probably started wondering if the sentence was actually about *one* person because the verb is *singular* in form. The sentence sends mixed signals, unlike the version below.

CORRECT   Barbara Walters and Diane Sawyer **are** known for skill at interviewing.

Readers expect you to make subjects and verbs work together grammatically—by showing **agreement** in number and person. They also expect you to make a pronoun agree with its **antecedent,** the word to which it refers. Lack of **pronoun-antecedent agreement** can cause inconsistency or confusion, thus undermining the effectiveness of a statement.

INCONSISTENT   Business memos should address the needs, motivations, and values of its audience.

CLEAR   **A business memo** should address the needs, motivations, and values of **its audience.**

CLEAR   **Business memos** should address the needs, motivations, and values of **their audiences.**

17a   Creating subject-verb agreement

You need to make sure that subjects and verbs agree in **number** (singular or plural) and **person** (first, second, and third person) so that your sentences can convey consistent, clear meaning to readers.

SINGULAR   The **worker** <u>tears</u> down the platform.

PLURAL   The **workers** <u>tear</u> down the platform.

FIRST PERSON   **I** <u>operate</u> the air compressor.

We <u>operate</u> the air compressor.

SECOND PERSON   **You** <u>operate</u> the air compressor.

THIRD PERSON   **He** (**she, it**) <u>operates</u> the air compressor.

They <u>operate</u> the air compressor.

▶◀

Strategy

To edit your writing for **subject-verb agreement**, look for a subject, identify its number (singular/plural) and person (first, second, or third), and then make sure the verb agrees with it in grammatical form.

▶◀

17a
agr

Agreement: Number, Person, and Gender

Number shows whether words are singular or plural in meaning.

SINGULAR WORDS
1. Nouns naming individual people, animals, ideas, and things
2. Personal pronouns referring to individuals: *I, you, he, she, it*
3. Indefinite pronouns (*each, someone*) or relative pronouns (*who, which, that*) referring to singular nouns or pronouns
4. Verbs in their singular forms (I *am*, she *is*; I *analyze*, she *analyzes*)

PLURAL WORDS
1. Nouns naming more than one person, animal, idea, or thing
2. Personal pronouns referring to more than one individual: *we, you, they*
3. Indefinite pronouns (*all, none*) or relative pronouns (*who, which, that*) referring to plural nouns or pronouns
4. Verbs in their plural forms (we *are*, they *are*; we *analyze*, they *analyze*)

(cont.)

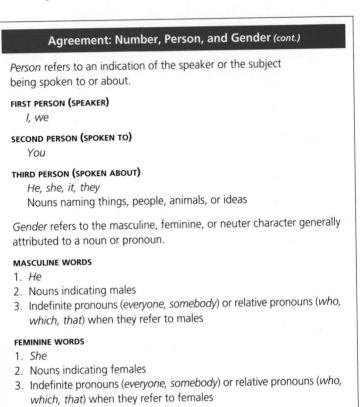

Agreement: Number, Person, and Gender *(cont.)*

Person refers to an indication of the speaker or the subject being spoken to or about.

FIRST PERSON (SPEAKER)
I, we

SECOND PERSON (SPOKEN TO)
You

THIRD PERSON (SPOKEN ABOUT)
He, she, it, they
Nouns naming things, people, animals, or ideas

Gender refers to the masculine, feminine, or neuter character generally attributed to a noun or pronoun.

MASCULINE WORDS
1. *He*
2. Nouns indicating males
3. Indefinite pronouns (*everyone, somebody*) or relative pronouns (*who, which, that*) when they refer to males

FEMININE WORDS
1. *She*
2. Nouns indicating females
3. Indefinite pronouns (*everyone, somebody*) or relative pronouns (*who, which, that*) when they refer to females

NEUTER WORDS
1. *It*
2. Nouns indicating places, things, and ideas
3. Indefinite pronouns (*everything, something*) or relative pronouns (*which, that*) when they refer to places, things, and ideas

---

In many cases, you will find errors in subject-verb agreement easy to spot and correct.

INCORRECT   The basements is wet.

CORRECT   The **basements** are wet.

CORRECT   The **basement** is wet.

At other times, however, you may need to pay careful attention to number and person in your subjects and verbs, even consulting the chart on agreement of number, person, and gender. This is most likely to be the case with the troublesome sentence constructions discussed in 17b.

Exercise 1

A. Fill in the blanks in the following sentences with verbs that agree in number and person with their antecedents.

EXAMPLE

Every day I _walk_ past the Valois Cafeteria.

1. The retired men in the neighborhood _____ lunch at the cafeteria.
2. The cafeteria's motto, "See What You Eat," _____ on the sign above the entrance.
3. The restaurant _____ run down.
4. Nonetheless, it _____ a clean and safe place.
5. A sociologist has studied the ways people of different races and cultures _____ with each other at the cafeteria.

B. Copy a paragraph from one of your papers or a book, but replace the verbs with blanks (as in Exercise 1A). Exchange paragraphs with a partner and fill in the blanks in that paragraph. Work together to check your answers.

C. If instructors in any classes have noted errors in subject-verb agreement on your papers, fix the agreement problems. (You may need to refer to 17b as you edit.)

ESL

17a
agr

ESL Advice: Subject-Verb Agreement

Watch out for the following troublesome verbs that change form according to person or tense. Be sure to select the correct verb form so that your subject and verb agree.

- *Be* verbs (present and past)

I **am/was**

You (sing., pl.)
We   **are/were**
They

He
She   **is/was**
It

- Helping verb *be* in the present progressive and past progressive tenses

Present progressive

I **am** talking.
You
We   **are** talking.
They
He, She, It **is** talking.

Past progressive

I
He, She, It   **was** talking.

We
You   **were** talking.
They

- *Have* verbs (present)

I
You
We   } **have** a new home.
They

He, She, It **has** a new home.

- Helping verb *have* in the present perfect and present perfect progressive tenses

Present perfect

I
You   } **have** been here
We   } for many years.
They

He, She, It **has** been here
for many years.

Present perfect progressive

I
You   } **have** been living
We   } here for a long time.
They

He, She, It **has** been living here for
a long time.

- *Do* or *does* to show emphasis

I, You, We, They   **do** enjoy hiking!
He, She, It   **does** enjoy hiking!

- *Doesn't* or *Don't* to show the negative

I, You, We, They   **don't** exercise enough.
He, She, It   **doesn't** exercise enough.

- Present tense for all other verbs in the third person singular. You must add -*s* to the verb.

I, You, We, They   **walk** every day.
He, She, It   **walks** every day.

Writer's Alert

In English there are many nouns, called **mass** or **noncount nouns,** which use the singular form (see 14a-1). Look out for these nouns as the subjects of your sentences, and make sure the verbs are singular.

Her **clothing** was made by hand.
Rush-hour **traffic** is always heavy.
Important **information** is found in the telephone book.
Last night's **homework** was challenging.

17b Editing for subject-verb agreement: Troublesome constructions

The usually simple process of checking for agreement between subjects and verbs can become quite complicated with sentence constructions that involve plural and compound subjects, widely separated subjects or verbs, or subjects like *all* or *who*.

1 Choosing verb forms with plural and compound subjects

Be alert for subjects that are plural in form (*shoes, filters, children, mathematics, we, they*) and for compound subjects (*cheese and yogurt, neither Charlene nor I*). Both often need a plural verb—but not always.

Plural Subjects. Plural subjects generally need plural verbs, just as singular subjects generally need singular verbs.

Singular	Plural
The shoe **fits.**	The shoes **fit.**
The child **swims** in the pond.	The children **swim** in the pond.
I **am** the group leader.	We **are** the group leaders.

17b agr

Strategy

To identify plural subjects, look for *-s* or *-es* endings. Remember that most singular nouns become plural with the addition of these endings. In contrast, present tense verbs become *singular* with the addition of *-s* or *-es*.

SINGULAR   The dam prevent**s** flooding.

PLURAL   The dam**s** prevent flooding.

> EXCEPTIONS
> * Nouns with irregular plurals, such as *person/people, child/children,* or *louse/lice,* and nouns with the same form for singular and plural, such as *moose/moose*
> * Verbs with irregular forms, including *be* and *have* (see 16a-2)

In a verb phrase (see 14a-3), the helping verb sometimes changes form for singular and plural, but the main verb remains the same.

HELPING VERB CHANGES FORM

SINGULAR   The **room** <u>does</u> seem brighter.

PLURAL   The **rooms** <u>do</u> seem brighter.

HELPING VERB DOES NOT CHANGE

SINGULAR   The **room** <u>might</u> seem brighter.

PLURAL   The **rooms** <u>might</u> seem brighter.

Subjects Joined by *And.* By joining two or more subjects with *and* or *both
. . . and*, you create a **compound subject.** Because *and* makes the subject
plural even if one or all of the individual parts are singular, you generally need
to choose a plural verb.

> **Jim and the rest of the Boy Scouts** <u>were</u> responsible for the res-
> cue.

> **Heather, Luis, and I** <u>contribute</u> to the Cerebral Palsy Association
> each year.

However, if the parts of a compound subject designate a single person, thing,
or idea or if the parts should be taken as a unit, you need to choose a singular verb.

UNIT (SINGULAR)   **Ham and eggs** <u>is</u> still my favorite breakfast.

SEPARATE
ELEMENTS   **Ham and eggs** <u>are</u> the main ingredients in my favorite casse
(PLURAL)   role.

ONE PERSON   **My fellow art teacher and friend** also <u>has</u> paintings in
                  the show.

TWO PEOPLE   **My fellow art teacher and my friend** also <u>have</u> paintings
                  in the show.

Subjects Within Phrases. When you use a phrase like *as well as, in addition to, together with,* and *along with* in a sentence, you may be tempted to
treat a noun that follows it as the sentence's subject and make the verb agree
with that noun rather than with the real subject.

MISTAKEN   A regular tune-up, with frequent oil **changes,** <u>prolong</u> the
                  life of your car.

To identify the real subject, imagine the sentence without the intervening
phrase: "A regular tune-up . . . prolongs the life of your car."

EDITED   A regular **tune-up,** along with frequent oil changes, <u>prolongs</u>
                  the life of your car.

**17b
agr**

Because phrases like *as well as* can be easily mistaken for *and,* you may unintentionally treat a singular subject as a compound (plural) subject.

MISTAKEN   The university's **provost,** as well as the deans, have issued new guidelines emphasizing teaching.

EDITED   The university's **provost,** as well as the deans, has issued new guidelines emphasizing teaching.

If you mean *and,* use the word itself.

REWRITTEN   The university's provost **and** the deans have issued new promotion guidelines emphasizing teaching.

Writer's Alert

Depending on where you place the words *each* or *every,* you can give a compound subject a singular or plural meaning.

EACH BEFORE COMPOUND SUBJECT
compound subject   singular verb
Each child and adult **watches** one clutch of eggs for signs of hatching.

EACH AFTER COMPOUND SUBJECT
compound subject   plural verb
The children and adults **each watch** one clutch of eggs for signs of hatching.

ESL

**17b
agr**

ESL Advice: Quantifiers

A **quantifier** is a word that indicates the amount or quantity of a subject—a word like *each, one,* or *many.*

Expressions followed by a plural noun and a singular verb

Each of
Each one of
Every one of   plural noun + singular verb
One of   the ESL **students lives** on campus.
None of

Expressions followed by a plural noun and a plural verb

Several of
Many of $\quad\Big\}\quad$ plural noun + plural verb
Both of $\qquad$ the **students live** off campus.

Expressions followed by either a singular or a plural verb

In the following cases, the noun after the expression determines the verb form. If the noun is noncount or collective, it takes a singular verb. If the noun is plural, it takes a plural verb.

Some of
Most of $\quad\Big\}\quad$ noncount noun + singular verb
All of $\qquad$ the **produce is** fresh.
A lot of

Some of
Most of $\quad\Big\}\quad$ plural noun + plural verb
All of $\qquad$ the **vegetables are** fresh.
A lot of

ESL

17b agr

Much and *most* with noncount and plural nouns

Look at the following examples, and be sure to watch for these errors in your writing.

$\qquad\qquad$ quantifier + noncount noun
NOT APPROPRIATE Much ~~of~~ traffic occurs during rush hour.

CORRECT $\qquad$ **Much traffic** occurs during rush hour.

$\qquad\qquad$ quantifier + plural noun
NOT APPROPRIATE Most ~~of~~ Americans live in the cities or suburbs.

CORRECT $\qquad$ **Most Americans** live in the cities or suburbs.

Subjects Joined by *Or* or *Nor*. The words *or* and *nor* allow you to link the parts of the subject while at the same time creating a sense of separation or choice between them.

When you have joined parts of a subject with *or* or *nor* (*either . . . or, neither . . . nor*), make the verb agree with the closer part.

BOTH SINGULAR The **mayor** or **the deputy mayor** holds a press conference each week.

BOTH PLURAL	**Heads of departments** or **building supervisors** prepare monthly efficiency reports.
SINGULAR + PLURAL	**The city auditor** or **the staff accountants** review each efficiency report.
PLURAL + SINGULAR	**Incomplete records** or **dishonest reporting** weakens the review process.

In general, putting the plural element closer to the verb makes a sentence less awkward.

AWKWARD	Either members of the city council or the **mayor** drafts amendments to the city charter.
BETTER	Either the mayor or **members** of the city council draft amendments to the city charter.

When the parts of a subject differ in person and therefore need different verb forms (for example, *I have, he has*), you should make the verb agree with the closer part of the subject. If this strategy makes a sentence awkward, rewrite the sentence.

ESL

**17b
agr**

INCORRECT	Either the other new residents or **I** are going to file a complaint over the way our children were treated.
AWKWARD	Either the other new residents or **I** am going to file a complaint over the way our children were treated.
REWRITTEN	Either the other new **residents** are going to file a complaint over the way our children were treated or **I** am.

ESL Advice: Paired Conjunctions

Paired conjunctions like *both . . . and, either . . . or, neither . . . nor,* and *not only . . . but also* pose some problems for subject-verb agreement.

Both . . . and always needs a plural verb, whether the elements being joined by the conjunction are singular or plural.

both . . .   and   +   plural verb
Both the president **and** her advisor **are** in Tokyo this week.

both . . .   and   +   plural verb
Both the president **and** her advisors **are** in Tokyo this week.

Either . . . or, neither . . . nor, and *not only . . . but also* may take either a singular or a plural verb. The subject closer to the verb determines the form of the verb.

singular subject   + singular verb
Either the president or her **advisor**
Neither the president nor her **advisor**   } **is** in Tokyo.
Not only the president but also her **advisor**

plural subject   + plural verb
Either the president or her **advisors**
Neither the president nor her **advisors**   } **are** in Tokyo.
Not only the president but also her **advisors**

Collective Nouns as Subjects. A **collective noun** is singular in form yet identifies a group of individuals (*audience, mob, crew, troop, brood, tribe,* or *herd*). When you use a collective noun to refer to a group that acts as a single unit, choose a singular verb.

The **staff** is hardworking and well trained.
The **number** of novelists writing mysteries is surprisingly large.

When you focus on group members and their individual actions, choose a plural verb.

The **staff** have earned many sales awards this year.
A surprisingly large **number** of novelists write mysteries.

If using a plural verb makes a sentence sound awkward, rewrite the sentence using a plural subject.

AWKWARD   The congregation react to Reverend Cullen's sermons in different ways, ranging from boredom to enlightenment.

REWRITTEN   **Members** of the congregation react to Reverend Cullen's sermons in different ways, ranging from boredom to enlightenment.

Nouns with Plural Forms and Singular Meanings. Some nouns, such as *politics, statistics, linguistics, news, physics, mumps,* and *athletics,* have the -*s* endings of plural nouns but are generally singular in meaning. Choose singular verbs to go with them.

Mathematics is an increasingly popular field of study for undergraduates.

The **news** about the job market for the coming year is surprisingly good.

A measurement or number ending in *-s* may still be singular if it names a quantity or unit as a whole.

Four years is the amount of time Dr. Santiago spent studying the effects of stress on lawyers.

One-third of the price of books consists of production and transportation costs.

Yet when figures or measurements refer to individual elements, treat them as plural.

One-third of the job trainees leave the program in the first five weeks.
They (plural) leave individually.

The **economics** of the arrangement are suspect.
Economics refers to the many different financial relationships and procedures involved.

17b
agr

Did You Know?

In 1867, William Bingham wrote, "The verb agrees with its subject in number and person: as, *I write; thou writest; he writes.*" The rule still applies, but *thou* is no longer a familiar part of the language.

Bingham taught school in North Carolina, so in giving the following example of agreement with a collective noun he might have been reflecting on the experience of the Civil War: "The army *destroys* everything in the line of *its* march."

William Bingham, *A Grammar of the English Language* (Philadelphia: Butler, 1867) 98.

Exercise 2

A. In each of the following sentences, choose the word inside the parentheses that creates subject-verb agreement.

EXAMPLE

The mayor, as well as members of the city council, (has/have) been searching for better ways to fund the zoo.

1. Several large lizards and an eight-foot python (*makes/make*) up the main attractions in the reptile building of the tiny zoo.
2. The displays as well as the building itself (*appears/appear*) well designed and well maintained.
3. The animals each (*displays/display*) good health and normal behavior.
4. Neither the zoo's overseers nor its director (*is/are*) satisfied with the reptile building and the number of animals on display.
5. Of the zoo's visitors, three-quarters (*says/say*) that the collection should be enlarged.
6. This year the Cajun and Bluegrass Festival (*features/feature*) several new bands.
7. The group *Beausoleil* (*appears/appear*) twice on the program.
8. The Cajun food, along with more familiar snacks, (*does/do*) draw many people to the refreshment tent.
9. The festival staff (*wears/wear*) buttons saying "Ask me for help."
10. Both the dancing lessons and the crafts display (*occupies/occupy*) the same tent.

17b
agr

B. Make up five sentences like those in Exercise 2A on any topic of your choice. Give them to a partner to complete, and work on those your partner has created.

C. Working with a paper in progress of your own, circle all plural, compound, and collective subjects. Then edit to make sure these subjects agree with their verbs.

2 Choosing verb forms with unusual sentence structures

When you separate subjects and verbs with other words, invert word order, or use linking verbs (*is, seems, feels*), you need to pay special attention to subject-verb agreement.

Subject and Verb Separated by Other Words.   Words coming between a subject and a verb can cause an agreement error if you mistake them for the subject. This is especially true when the intervening words are nouns. You may be tempted to make the verb agree with the nearest noun rather than the actual subject.

FAULTY
AGREEMENT
The new brand, with its startling variety of textures, colors, and flavors, are especially popular with teenagers.

The words *textures, colors,* and *flavors* are not the subject of the sentence.

EDITED   The new **brand,** ⌐with its startling variety of textures, colors, and flavors, is especially popular with teenagers.

ESL Advice: Separated Subjects and Verbs

When phrases or clauses come between the subject and the verb of the sentence, you need to check for agreement carefully.

PHRASES

NOT APPROPRIATE A person with sensitive eyes have to wear sunglasses.

CORRECT   A **person** with sensitive eyes **has** to wear sunglasses.

CLAUSES

NOT APPROPRIATE A person whose eyes are sensitive have to wear sunglasses.

CORRECT   A **person** whose eyes are sensitive **has** to wear sunglasses.

Writer's Alert

When the subject is the same in both the main clause and the dependent clause, the verbs must agree.

NOT APPROPRIATE A person who want to protect her eyes wears sunglasses.

                 same subject

CORRECT   A **person** who **wants** to protect her eyes **wears** sunglasses.

Inverted Word Order. The verb should agree with the subject even when you alter typical word order in a sentence to create emphasis or ask a question.

                        verb   subject

QUESTION   Are **popular comedy and action films** merely a form of escape?

                                verb   subject

EMPHASIS   Following landslide victories comes **overconfidence** for many politicians.

In editing, pay attention to expletive constructions such as *there are* and *it is* (see 11b). They invert (reverse) the usual subject-verb sentence order, allowing you to present the subject *after* the verb. As a result, you need to make the verb agree with the subject that follows it.

verb   subject

SINGULAR   There **is opportunity** for people starting new service industries in this city.

verb   subject

PLURAL   There **are** many new **opportunities** for service industries in this city.

You may use *there is* if the first part of a compound subject is singular.

There is **a guard and an alarm system** protecting the warehouse.

Linking Verbs. Examine sentences built around a linking verb such as *is, appears,* and *feels* (see 14a-3) to make sure the verb agrees with the subject. Do not mistakenly make it agree with the complement, that is, the noun or pronoun renaming the subject (see 14b-2).

17b
agr

subject   verb   complement

INCORRECT   The chief **obstacle** to change are the **mayor and her political allies.**

CORRECT   The chief **obstacle** to change is the mayor and her political allies.

3 Using special subjects (*all, everybody, none; who, which, that*)

Indefinite Pronouns (*All, Everybody, None*) as Subjects. Indefinite pronouns do not refer to specific ideas, people, or things. Most have clearly singular meanings and require singular verbs.

Someone is ringing the doorbell.
Everybody has the duty to vote.

A few indefinite pronouns, such as *all, any, most, none,* and *some,* can be either singular or plural, according to their meaning.

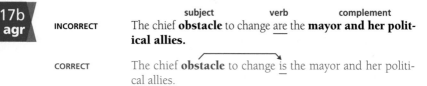

Strategy

Choose a singular or plural verb for words like *all, any,* and *none* on the basis of the noun or pronouns to which they refer. Consider whether the pronouns refer to something that *cannot be counted* (singular) or two or more elements of something that *can be counted* (plural).

Some Indefinite Pronouns		
all	enough	no one
another	every	nothing
any	everybody	one
anybody	everyone	some
anyone	everything	somebody
anything	many	someone
each	neither	something
either	nobody	

SINGULAR   **All** of the food is for the camping trip next week.

all = singular noun

food = food in general (not countable)

PLURAL   **All** of the food supplies are for the camping trip next week.

all = plural noun

supplies = many different kinds of supplies (countable), such as flour, meat, and dried fruit

ESL

17b

agr

ESL Advice: *Other, Others,* and *Another* as Pronouns or Adjectives

When *others, the others,* and *the other* are used as pronouns in a sentence, they require particular grammatical patterns.

Pronouns
***OTHERS* + PLURAL VERB** Adds points about a topic; there may be more points. I enjoy Paris for many reasons. Some reasons are the beautiful architecture and gardens; **others are** the wonderful people, culture, and language. ***THE OTHERS* (SINGULAR) + PLURAL VERB; *THE OTHER* (SINGULAR) + SINGULAR VERB** Adds the last point or points about the topic; there are no more. There are fourteen people on the tour. Half the people want to visit museums; **the others want** to go hiking. I have two travel books. One is about New Zealand, and **the other is** about Australia.

Another, other, and *the other* are sometimes used as adjectives in a sentence, and they require particular grammatical patterns.

Adjectives

***ANOTHER* + SINGULAR NOUN**
Adds an idea about the topic; there may be more ideas.

***OTHER* + PLURAL NOUN**
Adds more ideas about the topic; there may be more ideas.

> There are some reasons to visit California. One reason is to see the beautiful landscape. **Another reason** is to meet interesting people.

> **Other reasons** to visit California are the weather, the ocean, and the mountains.

***THE OTHER* + SINGULAR OR PLURAL NOUN**
Adds the final point or points to be discussed.

> There are two very important sights to see in Paris. One is the Louvre Museum, and **the other one** is the Cathedral of Notre Dame.

> There are many sights to see in Paris. One sight is the Louvre Museum. **The other sights** are the Eiffel Tower, the Champs-Élysées, the Cathedral of Notre Dame, and the Arc de Triomphe.

Who, Which, and That as Subjects.   The **relative pronouns** *who, which,* and *that* (see 14a-2) do not have singular and plural forms, yet the words to which they refer, their antecedents, generally have separate singular and plural forms. Choose a singular or plural verb for *who, which,* or *that* according to the number of the antecedent.

SINGULAR   He likes **a film** that <u>focuses</u> on relationships between characters.

PLURAL   I prefer **films** that <u>combine</u> action and romance.

Titles and Names as Subjects.   When you need to use the title of a work or the name of a company as a sentence subject, choose a singular verb even if the name or title is plural.

> New West Consultants **pays** staff high wages and **has** an excellent benefits package.
> Think to yourself: The **company** <u>pays</u> . . .

The White Roses **is** second on the paperback best-seller list this month.
Think to yourself: The **book** is . . .

"Tall ships" **is** the name given to the largest sailing ships.

Writer's Alert

Watch for the phrases *one of the* and *the only one of the.* They can create agreement problems when they come before a relative pronoun (*who, which,* or *that*).

Dr. Gotari is **one** of those professors who help students succeed.
Who refers to the plural *professors;* consequently the verb, *help,* is plural. There are other professors like Dr. Gotari.

Dr. Gotari is **the only one** of the professors who helps students succeed.
Who refers to the singular *Dr. Gotari;* consequently, the verb, *helps,* is singular. Dr. Gotari is the only supportive instructor.

Remember that adding the -s to the verb makes it singular, not plural.

17b
agr

Exercise 3

A. For each of the following sentences, give the correct present tense form of the infinitive verb indicated in parentheses.

EXAMPLE
None of the department heads (*to have*) the same administrative style. *has*

1. Frieda O'Connor is one of those managers who (*to lead*) by example.
2. All the other department heads (*to respect*) her leadership ability.
3. She knows each of the employees who (*to work*) in her department
4. Each year, Alberti and Campos Design Associates (*to give*) a plaque and a bonus to the employee who receives the highest rating in a company-wide survey.
5. The award, both the plaque and the money, (*to be*) given to Frieda almost every other year.

B. Working with another student, correct the errors that have been introduced into the following passage from Thomas R. McDonough's "Is Anyone Out There?" Not all the sentences contain an error, and some may have more than one. If correcting an error results in an awkward sentence, rewrite it, but do not rewrite simply to avoid having to deal with an agreement problem. When you are finished, compare your corrections with those of another pair of students, and explain the differences.

Each of the scientists involved in the search are pretty sure something is out there. A lot of numbers, some high and some low, is thrown around to express the probability of intelligent life somewhere else in the universe. Here is some figures that are middle-of-the-road. There is an estimated four hundred billion stars in the Milky Way. Planets may be fairly common, so you can figure one out of every ten of these stars have planets, which equals forty billion stars with planets. If every such star has ten planets, that is four hundred billion planets. But how many of these places seems suitable for life? Neither too hot nor too cold is the conditions needed for life forms similar to our own. An atmosphere along with some water are also necessary. In our solar system only Earth qualifies, though Mars and Venus each comes close. Let us be conservative and estimate that only one of each solar system's planets fit the pattern. That's still forty billion habitable planets.

17c
agr

C. Edit a draft paper of your own for subject-verb agreement. Make note of any recurrent kinds of agreement problems so you can pay attention to them on future papers.

17c Editing for pronoun-antecedent agreement

A pronoun refers to an **antecedent.** The antecedent can be either a noun or another pronoun.

antecedent   pronoun

Campers should treat **their** tents and sleeping bags with a mildew-preventing spray.

pronoun   antecedent

Its preference for damp fabric makes **mildew** a major problem for campers.

By choosing forms of nouns and pronouns that agree in *gender, person,* and *number,* you help readers understand how the ideas in your sentence relate. **Number** refers to the forms a noun or pronoun may take to indicate singular or plural. **Person** refers to word forms indicating the speaker or the subject spoken to or about.

First person	=	*I, we*
Second person	=	*you*
Third person	=	*he, she, it,* and nouns naming things, people, and ideas

Gender refers to masculine, feminine, or neuter qualities generally associated with a noun or pronoun. (See detailed chart on pp. 255–256.)

1 Using antecedents joined by *and*

When you join two or more antecedents with *and* (Luis *and* Jennifer, for example), make sure you refer to them with a plural pronoun (such as *they*). The pronoun should be plural even if one or more of the antecedents are singular.

> **Luis and Jennifer** said that the tests they ran on the groundwater were successful.

> **The other students and I** admit that the tests we tried did not work very well.

This rule has two exceptions.

- A compound antecedent can refer to a single person, thing, or idea. When it does, use a singular pronoun.

  My colleague and co-author is someone very skilled at analyzing soil samples.

- You can place *each* and *every* before a compound antecedent to single out the individual members of the compound. When you do, use a singular pronoun.

  Each of the soil and water samples is brought to the lab in **its** own sterile container.

  Every soil and water sample brought to the lab undergoes at least three tests.

2 Using antecedents joined by *or* or *nor*

When you join the parts of an antecedent with *or* or *nor* (or *either . . . or, neither . . . nor*), make sure the pronoun agrees with the part that is closer to it.

> **Neither** the project manager **nor** the engineers submitted their accident reports on time.

17c
agr

If one part of a subject is singular and the other part plural, consider putting the plural element second or rewriting to avoid an awkward or confusing sentence.

CONFUSING   Either Jim and Alan or **Richard** will include the sales projections in his report.

    READER'S RESPONSE: Does this mean that Jim and Alan may be putting things in Richard's report? Or does it mean that there will be two reports, Richard's plus Jim and Alan's, one of which will contain the projections?

EDITED   Either Richard or **Jim** and **Alan** will include the sales projections in their report.

REWRITTEN   Either Richard will include the sales projections in his report, or Jim and Alan will include the projections in theirs.

17c
agr

3 Using indefinite pronouns (*everyone, any, something*) as antecedents

Many indefinite pronouns are singular. When you use them as antecedents, make sure the pronouns that refer to them are singular. (See pp. 178–179 for a list of common indefinite pronouns.)

> **Somebody** on the team left her racket on the court.
> **Each** of the young men has his own sleeping bag.

Sometimes you may use an indefinite pronoun to mean *many* or *all*. When you do, it's safer to provide a plural antecedent.

INFORMAL   Everyone in the class handed in their project reports.

EDITED   **The students** in the class handed in their project reports.

To avoid sexist language (see 30a), use *both* a plural pronoun and a plural antecedent.

SEXIST   Everybody should include charts and slides in his sales talk.

INFORMAL SPOKEN   **Everybody** should include charts and slides in their sales **talks.**

WRITTEN   **All presenters** should include charts and slides in their sales **talks.**

ESL Advice: Demonstrative Adjectives

Besides subjects and verbs, other elements in a sentence must agree. **Demonstrative adjectives** or **pronouns** (*this, that, these,* and *those*) must be either singular or plural, depending on the noun being modified. (See also 14a-2.)

MIXED	This crystals of water make snowflakes.
BOTH PLURAL	**These crystals** of water make snowflakes.
MIXED	Those snowflake crystal is made of frozen water.
BOTH SINGULAR	**That snowflake crystal** is made of frozen water.

4 Using collective nouns as antecedents

A collective noun such as *team, group, clan, audience, army,* or *tribe* can act as a singular or plural antecedent, depending on whether it refers to the group as a whole or to the members acting separately.

SINGULAR	The **subcommittee** submitted its revised version of the report.
PLURAL	The **subcommittee** brought their different suggestions for a revised report to the meeting for discussion.

ESL

**17c
agr**

Exercise 4

A. Correct any errors in pronoun-antecedent agreement in the following sentences. You may need to change other parts of a sentence besides the pronoun or the antecedent. Each sentence can be corrected in more than one way.

EXAMPLE *People   like*
A person who likes camping should no longer feel they are unusual.

1. In any circle of friends, several are likely to say that he or she enjoys camping.
2. Everyone who goes camping needs to pay attention to their equipment.
3. All hikers should select good shoes and socks to protect your feet.
4. A camper or a hiker needs to choose their clothing carefully, paying attention to comfort, durability, and protection as well as style.
5. Both regular campers and occasional campers should be willing to

put his or her money into well-designed tents, sleeping bags, and cooking equipment.

6. Each store or chain of stores in the retail camping industry meets the needs of their customers in a different way.

7. A store catering to campers and the hiker usually offers him or her a wide choice of equipment at different prices.

8. Eddie Bauer or L. L. Bean provides mail-order service to his customers.

9. A camping supplies and athletic equipment store may provide a narrower range of choices to their customers because of the need to stock sporting goods as well as camping equipment.

10. Nonetheless, any of these businesses should be able to provide you and their other customers with good, safe camping equipment.

B. Working with a group of students, compare your corrections for the sentences in Exercise 4A. Make note of any differences, and decide which version (if any) is preferable and why.

C. Look over some of the papers that have been returned to you by instructors in any class. Highlight any pronoun-antecedent agreement problems marked by instructors, and carefully read the papers to locate any others. See whether there is a pattern of agreement errors in your writing, and state briefly what the pattern is.

CHAPTER

18

Adjectives and Adverbs

If you use adjectives and adverbs improperly, your readers will be likely to notice the errors.

DRAFT	The new medication acts **quick.**
EDITED	The new medication acts **quickly.**
DRAFT	They **hadn't never** implemented the cost-saving program.
EDITED	They **had never** implemented the cost-saving program.

Admittedly, not all kinds of misuse are likely to irritate or confuse your readers. Some readers, for example, may not notice any difference in meaning between the following sentences.

The fumes from the mixture smelled **bad.**
The fumes from the mixture smelled **badly.**

Others, however, will recognize that the shift from *bad* to *badly* makes the second sentence say the fumes themselves have a sense of smell, but one that isn't working very well.

18a Recognizing what adjectives and adverbs do

Adjectives and adverbs modify other words. You use them to add to, qualify, focus, limit, or extend the meaning of words they modify.

red car	Adjective adds to meaning of the noun *car.*
cut **carefully**	Adverb qualifies the meaning of the verb *cut.*
very small crowd	Adjective *small* focuses the meaning of the noun *crowd;* adverb *very* limits the meaning of *small.*

Features of Adjectives and Adverbs

ADJECTIVES

Modify nouns and pronouns.

Answer the questions "How many?," "What kind?," "Which one (or ones)?," and "What size, color, or shape?"

Consist of words like *blue, complicated, good,* and *frightening* as well as words created by adding endings like *-able, -ical, -less, -ful,* and *-ous* to nouns or verbs (such as *controllable, sociological, nervous, seamless, careful*).

ADVERBS

Modify verbs, adjectives, and other adverbs.

Modify phrases (*almost* beyond the building), clauses (*soon after* I added the last ingredients), and sentences (*Remarkably,* the mechanism was not damaged).

Answer the questions "When?," "Where?," "How?," "How often?," "Which direction?," and "What degree?"

Consist mostly of words ending in *-ly,* like *quickly, carefully,* and *smoothly,* as well as some common adverbs that do not end in *-ly,* such as *fast, very, well, quite,* and *late.*

ESL

**18a
modif**

The table above summarizes the features of adjectives and adverbs. (See 14a-5 and 14a-6 for further discussion.)

Because the *-ly* ending does not appear on all adverbs, and because some familiar adjectives do end in *-ly* (such as *friendly, lonely*), you may sometimes have to determine whether a word is an adjective or adverb by looking at how it is used in sentences or by looking it up in a dictionary.

ESL Advice: Adjectives in a Series

When you use two or more adjectives in a series, you need to place them in the correct order before the main noun. The following chart explains the categories and the order of adjectives in English

DETERMINER	QUALITY	PHYSICAL DESCRIPTION		NATIONALITY	MATERIAL	QUALIFYING NOUN	MAIN NOUN
that	expensive	smooth	black	German	fiberglass	racing	car
our	friendly	big	old	English		toy	spaniel
four	little	round	white		plastic	Ping-Pong	balls
several	beautiful	young	red	Japanese		maple	trees

18b Avoiding confusion between adjectives and adverbs

Much of the time you will have little trouble deciding whether to use an adjective or an adverb. Nonetheless, some pairs of words, such as *real/really* or *good/well,* and some common sentence structures may need special attention as you edit.

1 Watch out for adjectives used mistakenly to modify verbs, adjectives, and adverbs

Remember that you need to use adverbs—not adjectives—to modify verbs, adjectives, or other adverbs.

INCORRECT   Write **careful** so that anyone reading the directions will be able to understand them easily.

EDITED   Write **carefully** so that anyone reading the directions will be able to understand them easily.

INCORRECT   Because of the heat, the rubber insulation underwent **remarkable** quick deterioration.

EDITED   Because of the heat, the rubber insulation underwent **remarkably** quick deterioration.

18b
modif

Did You Know?

Dictionary entries tell whether a word is an adjective, an adverb, or both. They also indicate the comparative and superlative forms of many adjectives and adverbs. In their introductory chapters, most dictionaries also briefly explain the forms that adjectives and adverbs take and discuss their roles in sentences.

---

2 Use adjectives following *is, seems,* and other linking verbs

You use a linking verb (such as *is, smells, appears,* or *becomes*—see 14a-3) to tie together a subject and a **complement** (see 14b-2). A complement can be a noun, a pronoun, or an adjective—but never an adverb.

Subject	Linking verb	Complement (adjective)
The room	smelled	musty.
The procedure	proved	unreliable.

Verbs such as *look, feel, turn,* and *prove* can cause you problems because they can function both as linking verbs (indicating states of being) and as action verbs. When your sentence presents a state of being, use an adjective; when it presents an action, use an adverb.

ADJECTIVE (STATE OF BEING)	The metal cover over the motor **turned hot.**
ADVERB (ACTION)	The large wheel **turned quickly.**
ADJECTIVE	The movement grew **rapid.**
	The motion became quick.
ADVERB	The movement grew **rapidly.**
	The group got bigger, and its ideas spread quickly.

Writer's Alert

Pay special attention to *real/really, sure/surely, bad/badly,* and *good/well* as you edit. Some common uses of these words, especially *sure* for *surely,* may be acceptable in informal speech or writing but not in academic papers.

Real/Really; Sure/Surely

Real and *sure* are adjectives that often turn up in place of the adverbs *really* and *surely.*

- Use *really* to modify an adjective like *fast, accurate,* or *hot.*

INCORRECT	The electronic timer is **real** accurate.
EDITED	The electronic timer is **really** accurate.

- Use *surely* as an adverb to modify adjectives like *misleading, outdated,* or *courageous.*

INCORRECT	This drawing of the mechanism is **sure** misleading.
EDITED	This drawing of the mechanism is **surely** misleading.

Bad/Badly; Good/Well

The words in these pairs are often switched during informal speaking, sometimes without ill effect: I feel *bad* (or *badly*) about that. The project is going *good* (or *well*). Your readers, however, are likely to notice the error and be distracted by it.

- Use *bad* (adjective) with linking verbs.

INCORRECT	I feel **badly** that our group isn't working well together.

EDITED	I feel **bad** that our group isn't working well together.
	Someone who *feels badly* has a poor sense of touch.

- Use *badly* (adverb) with action verbs.

INCORRECT	The expensive new breathing apparatus works **bad.**
EDITED	The expensive new breathing apparatus works **badly.**

- Use *good* (adjective) with linking verbs.

INCORRECT	The oil and garlic dressing tastes **well.**
EDITED	The oil and garlic dressing tastes **good.**

- Use *well* (adverb) with action verbs unless it refers to health.

INCORRECT	The new pump works **good.**
EDITED	The new pump works **well.**
EDITED	After using the new medication pump for a week, the patient began feeling **well** again.

**18b
modif**

3 Use adjectives to complete direct objects

You can complete (or complement) the meaning of a direct object by following it with an adjective.

The review panel considered the researcher **objective.**
Objective completes *researcher* by indicating the person's qualities.

(See 14b-2 on complements.)
You can place an adverb after the direct object, but it will modify the sentence's verb.

The review panel considered the researcher **objectively.**
Objectively describes their manner in evaluating the researcher.

An adjective that completes a direct object must appear just after or before the object; in contrast, an adverb that modifies the verb can usually appear at other places in a sentence.

COMPLETES OBJECT The agency judged her artwork **competent.**
(ADJECTIVE)

MODIFIES VERB **(ADVERB)**	The agency judged her artwork **competently.**
MODIFIES VERB **(ADVERB)**	The agency **competently** judged her artwork.

....

Exercise 1

A. Rewrite the following sentences to eliminate any problems in adjective or adverb use.

EXAMPLE

          bad
I thought the band sounded ~~badly,~~ though many of my friends enjoyed the music.

1. Many scholars have begun studying some real surprising subjects such as rock music.
2. At first, they had trouble persuading many people to take their work serious.
3. Now they produce careful researched studies of musicians like the Beatles as well as biographies of influential figures like Sid Vicious and Johnny Rotten.
4. Remember, just because a piece of rock music sounds well does not mean that it is worth careful study.
5. At a time when the careers of many rock musicians are going bad, rock is doing quite good on campus.

B. Working in a group, decide which advice in sections 18a and 18b applies to the particular problem in adjective or adverb use illustrated by each of the following sentences. Make a note of each relevant section of the discussion, and rewrite the sentence to eliminate the problem.

EXAMPLE

             surprisingly
Some dead rock musicians have ~~surprising~~ large and active fan clubs.
Relevant section: 18a–1

1. Over the past year, the number of books devoted to rock groups or rock stars has grown remarkable.
2. The writer Greil Marcus has produced several high-regarded books that praise Elvis Presley as an artist and person.
3. The title of one of Marcus's books, *Dead Elvis: A Chronicle of a Cultural Obsession,* may suggest that he views Elvis "sightings" and memorabilia as humorously.
4. Some of the events he describes are undoubted weird.
5. Nonetheless, he feels surely that Elvis and his music really deserve respect.

C. Edit your own paper in progress, paying special attention to pairs of easily confused adjectives/adverbs: *real/really, sure/surely, bad/badly,* and *good/well.* Circle any of these adjectives appearing in your paper, and check that you have used each of them correctly.

18c Using comparatives and superlatives

You can use most adjectives and adverbs in three forms: positive, comparative, and superlative.

Positive	Comparative	Superlative
clean	cleaner	cleanest
shiny	shinier	shiniest
imaginatively	more imaginatively	most imaginatively
carefully	more carefully	most carefully

Use the **positive form** when you have no comparison in mind.

> This is a **quick** route.
> Rainha drove **quickly** through the circuit.

Use the **comparative form** when you are comparing two things.

> This is a **quicker** route.
> Rainha drove **more quickly** through the circuit.

Use the **superlative form** when you are comparing three or more things.

> This is the **quickest** route.
> Rainha drove **most quickly** through the circuit.

In conversation we sometimes ignore the system of positive, comparative, and superlative forms. Someone says "She is my oldest daughter," even though he has only two daughters, yet listeners grasp the intended meaning. In writing, you need to be more precise, especially if you are presenting facts and figures.

INACCURATE   The survey covered four age groups: 20–29, 30–44, 45–59, and 60+. The people in the older group smoked the least.

READER'S RESPONSE: Is the sentence supposed to mean that the people in the older *groups* smoked the least or that the people in the *oldest* group smoked the least?

PRECISE   The survey covered four age groups: 20–29, 30–44, 45–59, and 60+. The people in the **oldest group** smoked the least.

Writer's Alert

Some adjectives and adverbs cannot logically take comparative or superlative form. These include *unique, impossible, pregnant, infinite, dead, gone, perfectly,* and *entirely.* If you give such words comparative or superlative form, careful readers will notice the lack of logic.

ILLOGICAL   The large painting on the far wall is **most unique.** It is the only self-portrait Gottlieb created.

READER'S RESPONSE: *Unique* means "one of a kind." How can a thing be *more* or *most* if it is the only one?

LOGICAL   The large painting on the far wall is **unique.** It is the only self-portrait Gottlieb created.

You can create the comparative and superlative forms of adjectives and adverbs in a number of different ways, as the following chart indicates.

18c
modif

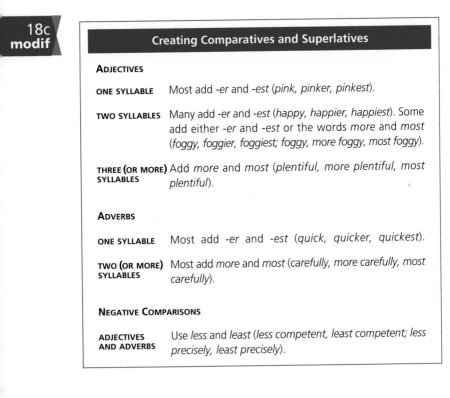

Creating Comparatives and Superlatives

ADJECTIVES

ONE SYLLABLE   Most add *-er* and *-est* (*pink, pinker, pinkest*).

TWO SYLLABLES   Many add *-er* and *-est* (*happy, happier, happiest*). Some add either *-er* and *-est* or the words *more* and *most* (*foggy, foggier, foggiest; foggy, more foggy, most foggy*).

THREE (OR MORE) SYLLABLES   Add *more* and *most* (*plentiful, more plentiful, most plentiful*).

ADVERBS

ONE SYLLABLE   Most add *-er* and *-est* (*quick, quicker, quickest*).

TWO (OR MORE) SYLLABLES   Most add *more* and *most* (*carefully, more carefully, most carefully*).

NEGATIVE COMPARISONS

ADJECTIVES AND ADVERBS   Use *less* and *least* (*less competent, least competent; less precisely, least precisely*).

Writer's Alert

Your readers will not accept a double comparative (combining the *-er* form and *more*) or a double superlative (combining the *-est* form and *most*). Avoid using either.

INCORRECT	As the temperature dropped, the weather got **more foggier.**
EDITED	As the temperature dropped, the weather got **foggier.**
INCORRECT	Jorge is the **most agilest** athlete on the team.
EDITED	Jorge is the **most agile** athlete on the team.

Some familiar modifiers change in irregular ways to indicate comparative and superlative forms.

Irregular Comparatives and Superlatives

POSITIVE	COMPARATIVE	SUPERLATIVE
ADJECTIVES		
bad	worse	worst
good	better	best
ill (harsh, unlucky)	worse	worst
a little	less	least
many	more	most
much	more	most
some	more	most
well (healthy)	better	best
ADVERBS		
badly	worse	worst
ill (badly)	worse	worst
well (satisfactorily)	better	best

18d
modif

18d Avoiding double negatives

Negative words include *no, none, not, never, neither, hardly, scarcely, barely,* and words like *haven't* and *don't* (formed with *n't,* the abbreviation for *not*). In general, negative words do not become more forceful when more than one appears in a sentence. Instead of enhancing a statement, a **double negative** often undermines it. Readers may view the negatives as canceling each other out.

DOUBLE NEGATIVE   The state hasn't done nothing about the dangerous exit ramp
                  on the interstate.

          READER'S RESPONSE: If the state hasn't done nothing, maybe it *has*
          done *something.*

EDITED   The state hasn't done anything about the dangerous exit
                  ramp on the interstate.

18e   Using noun modifiers

By using nouns to modify other nouns, you can save space. Many familiar and useful terms do this.

role model	child care
parent substitute	relief pitcher
pocket calendar	muscle pains
rain repellent	party platform

Too many nouns in a row, generally three or more, or too many clusters of long nouns can make reading difficult. (See also 11a-4.)

Strategy

Avoid problems with noun modifiers by taking one of the following steps.

• Use the possessive forms of nouns.

AWKWARD   We need to refer to the **hospital noise reduction plan**
          as we design the new building.

EDITED   We need to refer to the **hospital's noise reduction plan**
          as we design the new building.

• Use a prepositional phrase rather than a noun.

AWKWARD   The company has developed an **employee health care
          financing policy.**

EDITED   The company has developed a **policy for financing the
          health care of employees.**

• Rewrite to break up a cluster of noun modifiers.

  AWKWARD   I have developed a **personal stress management program.**

  EDITED   I have developed my own way of managing stress.

Exercise 2

A. Revise the following sentences to eliminate any incorrect use of adjectives, adverbs, or noun modifiers.

EXAMPLE

I think the real difference between Necco Wafers and Skittles is that Necco Wafers last longest. *longer*
                                                ^

1. Of the three candy bars, Snickers, Three Musketeers, and Baby Ruth, which is older?
2. Which of the two kinds of gummy bears is more sweeter?
3. Most candy companies have consumer preference research programs.
4. Trying to create a candy bar that pleases everyone's taste is a most impossible task.
5. Some people can't hardly bear the taste of sour-flavored candy.

18e modif

B. Working in a group, create two different correct versions of each of the following sentences. Then decide as a group which version of each sentence you prefer and why.

1. Candy taste preference surveys are expensive.
2. They are not unlikely to be a waste of money.
3. One survey showed that consumers find a blend of hazelnuts and raspberries a most tastier combination.
4. The bar showed no profit production capability, however.
5. By adding marshmallows to the blend, the company eventually turned the bar into a most complete marketing success.

C. Edit a draft paper of your own by underlining each comparative or superlative, any double negatives, and all noun modifiers. Then edit them for both correctness and effectiveness in conveying your meaning.

EDITING FOR SENTENCE PROBLEMS

Sentence Fragments

A **sentence fragment** is part of a sentence treated as a complete sentence, with a capital letter at the beginning and a period at the end. A fragment may lack an important sentence element such as a subject or a verb, thus confusing readers by leaving out crucial information.

SUBJECT MISSING Began pumping water out of the basement.
READER'S RESPONSE: Who was pumping, or what was doing the pumping?

EDITED **The fire truck** began pumping water out of the basement.

VERB MISSING The insurance company responsible for the costs.
READER'S RESPONSE: What did the company do?

EDITED The insurance company **became** responsible for the costs.

Fragments may be phrases or clauses mistakenly asked to stand on their own as sentences. Such fragments make readers do the writer's job, forcing them mentally to reattach a word group to a nearby sentence.

FRAGMENT They were able to get the pump started again. **By replacing the gas filter.**
The second statement is a modifying phrase detached from the preceding sentence.

EDITED They were able to get the pump started again **by replacing the gas filter.**

In the following passage, for example, a reader has to do extra work by either supplying a subject for the second statement or mentally combining it with the preceding sentence.

FRAGMENT Recent immigrants from Asia and Latin America now fill many seats in elementary schools and high schools. **And**

have inspired many changes in curriculum and teaching methods.

SUBJECT SUPPLIED   Recent immigrants from Asia and Latin America now fill many seats in elementary schools and high schools. **They** have inspired many changes in curriculum and teaching methods.

WORD GROUPS COMBINED   Recent immigrants from Asia and Latin America now fill many seats in elementary schools and high schools and have inspired many changes in curriculum and teaching methods.

Fragments that confuse readers or make them do extra, unnecessary work are serious errors. On occasion, an **intentional fragment** that causes little difficulty may effectively create emphasis or a change of pace, especially in imaginative or emphatic writing (see 19d). For the most part, however, academic, business, and professional readers will judge a piece of writing (and its writer) harshly when they encounter a fragment.

19a   Recognizing sentence fragments

Sentence fragments occur in all shapes and sizes. Some are easy to identify, others less so. To edit effectively, however, you need to be able to identify word groups lacking a subject or a verb and to recognize clauses detached from sentences to which they belong.

1 Look for a subject and a verb

A **complete sentence** must contain both a subject and a complete verb, expressed or implied. If a word group punctuated as a sentence lacks either, it is a fragment (see 14b).

Strategy 1

A good way to identify subjects and verbs is to ask *Who* (or *what*) *does?* or *Who* (or *what*) *is?*

- If a word group does not answer "Who?" or "What?" then it lacks a subject and is a sentence fragment.

FRAGMENT   Yet also needs to establish a family counseling program.

READER'S RESPONSE: This doesn't say *who* (or *what*) needs to establish the program.

EDITED   Yet **Community Health Clinic** also needs to establish a family counseling program.

- If a word group does not answer "Does?" or "Is?" then it lacks a verb and is a sentence fragment.

FRAGMENT   The new policy to determine scholarship size on the basis of grades rather than on the basis of need.

READER'S RESPONSE: This doesn't indicate anything about what the new policy *does* or *is*.

EDITED   The new policy **determines** scholarships on the basis of grades rather than on the basis of need.

In trying to identify the "Who" in a passage, remember that in commands, the subject *you* is understood and does not have to appear in the sentence.

**IMPERATIVE
SENTENCE**   [**You**] Use the spectrometer to test for the unknown chemical ingredient.

Some familiar sentence patterns also use a clearly implied verb.

VERB IMPLIED   John went to Stanford, Regina [**went**] to UCLA.

Strategy 2

Another way to identify a missing subject or verb is to create a question. See if you can turn a word group into a question that can be answered *yes* or *no*. If it can be, it is a sentence.

WORD GROUP   They bought a van to carry the new equipment.

QUESTION   Did they buy a van to carry the new equipment?

CONCLUSION   The word group is a sentence.

To decide whether a subject or a verb is missing, see if you need to add or alter an element to create a question.

Here are two examples of Strategy 2 at work.

WORD GROUP   Bought the building to use as a warehouse.

QUESTION   Did _____ buy the building to use as a warehouse?

CONCLUSION   The question does not have a subject, so the word group is a fragment lacking a subject.

EDITED   **Johnson Manufacturing** bought the building to use as a warehouse.

WORD GROUP	The company providing repairs for our computers.
QUESTION	Does the company **providing** repairs for our computers? Caution: Do not begin the question with *is/are* or *has/have*. In doing so you may unintentionally provide a verb for the word group you are testing.
CONCLUSION	The word *providing* cannot act as the verb in its present form. The word group is a fragment lacking a verb.
EDITED	The company **is** providing repairs for our computers.

··· ►◄ ···

Writer's Alert

In checking for fragments, be careful not to mistake a verbal for a verb. A **verbal** is part of a verb acting as a noun or modifier. Verbals include participles (*testing, tested*), infinitives (*to test*), and gerunds (*testing*). (See 14c-2.) A verbal alone can never act as the verb in a sentence. When combined with a helping verb (such as *is, has, can,* or *should*—see 14a-3), a verbal can be part of a complete verb (*was testing, should test*).

FRAGMENT	The laboratory **testing** the samples for traces of platinum.
COMPLETE SENTENCE	The laboratory **was testing** the samples for traces of platinum.

19a
frag

Did You Know?

In a survey conducted by the authors of this book, college instructors listed sentence fragments as the sentence-level error they considered the most serious. The people surveyed included teachers of chemistry, business, nursing, mathematics, literature, and psychology as well as composition. According to their answers, these instructors almost always notice sentence fragments and believe these errors confuse and irritate readers. You may be used to seeing sentence fragments in advertising and sometimes in magazine or newspaper articles. Nonetheless, sentence fragments can easily undermine whatever confidence academic and professional readers have in your authority and skill as a writer.

Chris M. Anson and Robert A. Schwegler, "A Survey of Attitudes Toward Error Among Instructors at Four Colleges," unpublished ms.

Exercise 1

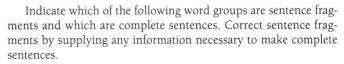

Indicate which of the following word groups are sentence fragments and which are complete sentences. Correct sentence fragments by supplying any information necessary to make complete sentences.

EXAMPLE

Our job *is* to find a new head for nursing services.

1. Several people applying for the job.
2. The job description in the newspaper asks for someone who is a good administrator and also an innovator.
3. Is able to convince fellow workers to develop their own innovative staffing plan and present it to the hospital administration.
4. Julie Kim, the prior head of nursing services responsible for so much turmoil during her time in the job and also so many important changes in the way nurses interact with patients and physicians.
5. A study suggesting that nursing administrators develop in-service programs to create improved morale among the professional staff and also better patient care.

19a
frag

2 Look for subordinating words

A word group containing both a subject and a complete verb may still be a sentence fragment if it is controlled by a subordinating word (such as *although, because, that,* or *since*) that turns it into a modifier. Placed at the beginning of a clause, subordinators tell readers to regard the word group as part of a larger statement, as a subordinate (dependent) clause needing to be attached to a main clause that it qualifies or modifies.

MAIN CLAUSE
Potential homebuyers have learned about the low crime rate and the excellent school system.

MODIFYING CLAUSE
Because potential homebuyers have learned about the low crime rate and the excellent school system.
This clause cannot act as a complete sentence.

MODIFYING CLAUSE + MAIN CLAUSE
Because potential homebuyers have learned about the low crime rate and the excellent school system, demand for housing in the area has risen considerably in the past few years.

Strategy

To identify subordinate clause fragments, look for a word group beginning with a subordinating conjunction such as *after, although, if, because, unless,* or *since* (see 26b-2) or with a relative pronoun (*that, what, which,* or *who*). Then check whether this word group is attached to a main clause. If it is not, then it is a fragment.

This Strategy can help you identify subordinate clause fragments like those that follow. Like many subordinate clause fragments, these come right next to the main clause they modify.

FRAGMENT	Most residents love the friendly, unspoiled nature of the town. **Which has led to rapid population growth and a rise in property values.**
EDITED	Most residents love the friendly, unspoiled nature of the town, which has led to rapid population growth and a rise in property values.
FRAGMENT	Many experts think that the SAT and the ACT are somewhat biased. **Although they also consider most criticism of the tests overblown.**
EDITED	Many experts think that the SAT and the ACT are somewhat biased, although they also consider most criticism of the tests overblown.
EDITED	Many experts think that the SAT and the ACT are somewhat biased yet also consider most criticism of the tests overblown.

19a
frag

Exercise 2

A. Indicate which of the following word groups are sentence fragments and which are complete sentences. Correct all the sentence fragments by supplying any information necessary to make complete sentences or attaching a fragment to an adjacent main clause.

EXAMPLE

Although many people think that afternoon sleepiness is caused by a heavy lunch, Researchers say this is not true.

1. People such as interns and truck drivers often feel drowsy. Even though they are aware of a need to stay awake and alert.
2. Having an afternoon nap can greatly increase your alertness. Whether or not you got enough sleep the night before.

3. Almost accidentally, researchers started becoming aware of the importance of naps while they were mapping the cycles of drowsiness and alertness that we each go through during an entire day.
4. Almost everyone experiences sleepiness and a decline in mental alertness during the afternoon. Because our internal clocks tell us it is time to nap and get out of the sun's strongest rays.
5. Despite a widespread belief that siestas and naps are cultural customs. They actually have a biological base.

B. Working with a group, look through one or more popular magazines, focusing on either the advertising or the articles. Identify ten sentence fragments and list them. Indicate which fragments lack a subject or a verb (or both), and indicate which fragments are modifying clauses that contain a subject and verb but are controlled by a subordinating word.

C. Edit a paper of your own, looking for sentence fragments. Make a list of any you find, and then see if they follow any pattern(s) that you can spot in future writing.

19b   Editing sentence fragments

You can correct sentence fragments in four different ways. As you edit, choose the Strategy that best suits the particular kind of fragment, your purpose for writing, the meaning you wish to emphasize, and the stylistic effect you wish to create.

Strategy 1

Supply the missing sentence element.

FRAGMENT (LACKS VERB)   Several arguments favor allowing adopted children to contact their natural parents. **Among the most important the need to find out about any hereditary diseases.**

EDITED   Several arguments favor allowing adopted children to contact their natural parents. Among the most important **is** the need to find out about any hereditary diseases.

Strategy 2

Attach the fragment to a nearby main clause. Rewrite the passage if necessary.

FRAGMENT (SUBORDINATE CLAUSE)   Modern trauma centers are equipped to give prompt care to heart attack victims. **Because rapid treatment can minimize damage to heart muscles.**

EDITED   Modern trauma centers are equipped to give prompt care
                to heart attack victims because rapid treatment can mini-
                mize damage to heart muscles.

>◄►◄

Strategy 3

Drop a subordinating word so the subordinate clause can act as a
complete sentence (main clause).

FRAGMENT   **Although** several people argued strenuously against the
                motion. It passed by a considerable majority nonetheless.

EDITED   Several people argued strenuously against the motion. It
                passed by a considerable majority nonetheless.

>◄►◄

Strategy 4

Rewrite a passage to eliminate the fragment.

FRAGMENT   Some sports attract large numbers of participants in their
                fifties, sixties, and even seventies. **For example, tennis and
                bowling.**

REWRITTEN   Some sports, **such as tennis and bowling,** attract large
                numbers of participants in their fifties, sixties, and even sev-
                enties.

**19b
frag**

>◄►◄

Exercise 3

A. Correct each of the fragments in the following passages in two
different ways.

EXAMPLE
Some innovative rock groups have been touring this year. Drawing
large crowds.

*Some innovative rock groups have been touring this year. They
have been drawing large crowds.*

*Some innovative rock groups have been touring this year,
drawing large crowds.*

1. Realizing that musical tastes are probably changing. Many record
   companies have decided to explore new and newly rediscovered
   kinds of music.
2. Some formerly popular musical artists no longer have recording contracts. Their sales of tapes and CDs having dropped dras-
   tically.
3. In recent campus concerts, jazz artists have attracted large and

enthusiastic audiences. Because of their innovative melodies and sounds.

4. The rhythm section of one group consists of a single unusual instrument. An electronic instrument making sounds like a drum but looking like a guitar.

5. Undecided about whether to sign new groups to long-term contracts. Some companies agree to produce and sell a single CD with an option for future recordings.

 B. Instead of doing Exercise 3A on your own, work with another person and create *three* correct versions of each passage, rewriting extensively if necessary. Note the ways each of you prefer to correct fragments, especially any differences between your choices.

 C. Work on the list of fragments you identified in a paper in progress (Exercise 2C), and correct each of the fragments using the four Strategies discussed in 19b.

19c Editing troublesome constructions

Some familiar sentence structures are often mistakenly punctuated as sentences, forming unacceptable sentence fragments.

1 Watch out for disconnected word groups

As you edit, watch for two kinds of word groups that are often incorrectly treated as complete sentences: (1) word groups beginning with phrases like *for example,* and (2) split predicates (parts of a compound predicate).

***For Example* Fragments.** Word groups beginning with phrases like *for example, such as,* or *for instance* are sometimes disconnected from sentences and made to stand on their own, thus creating sentence fragments. You can identify such fragments by looking for one of these phrases at the beginning of a word group and then checking whether the word group either is attached to a main clause or contains all the elements needed to act as a complete sentence.

To correct *for example* fragments, decide whether the examples are simply brief illustrations that ought to be attached to the statement they illustrate or whether they deserve emphasis in sentences of their own.

> **FRAGMENT**
> We are trying to hire a new staff member who has skills that none of us possess. **For example, knowledge of computer-aided design.**

EDITED (SEPARATE SENTENCE)

We are trying to hire a new staff member who has skills that none of us possess. For example, **we need** someone with knowledge of computer-aided design.

FRAGMENT

Very few people are aware of the familiar species that are suffering from pollution or mismanagement. **Such as the striped bass or the snook.**

EDITED (ATTACHED TO MAIN CLAUSE)

Very few people are aware of the familiar species, **such as the striped bass or the snook,** that are suffering from pollution or mismanagement.

Split Predicate. A **compound predicate** contains two or more complete verbs (for example, "I *unfastened* the seat and *removed* it"), and writers sometimes split off the second (or last) element as a separate sentence. Perhaps they create fragments of this kind because they unconsciously assume that the subject in the first part of the predicate is also somehow present in the second part. To recognize a split predicate fragment, look for a word group whose verb comes near the beginning (generally following a conjunction like *and* or *but*) and whose subject is nearby—but in another sentence.

19c
frag

FRAGMENT

Beethoven's work as a composer began in a style similar to that of Mozart. **But soon took on its own unique style.**

To correct fragments like this, either supply the missing subject or reattach the elements of the compound predicate.

CORRECTED (SUBJECT ADDED)

Beethoven's work as a composer began in a style similar to that of Mozart. But **his work** soon took on its own unique style.

CORRECTED (REATTACHED)

Beethoven's work as a composer began in a style similar to that of Mozart **but** soon took on its own unique style.

2 Pay attention to verbal phrases

Because verbals are similar in form to verbs (for example, *swimming*—verbal; *is swimming*—verb), writers may easily mistake a verbal plus its objects and modifiers (a verbal phrase) for a complete sentence. To identify verbal phrase fragments as you edit, you need to be aware of the difference between verbs and verbals. (Sections 14a-4 and 14c-4 offer helpful advice.)

To correct a fragment consisting of a verbal phrase, consider attaching it to a nearby main clause, or turn the verbal into a verb and rewrite the passage.

FRAGMENT (PARTICIPIAL PHRASE)
Frustrated by the meager offerings in journalism. She decided to transfer to another university.

EDITED (ATTACHED TO MAIN CLAUSE)
Frustrated by the meager offerings in journalism, she decided to transfer to another university.

FRAGMENT (INFINITIVE PHRASE)
Divorcing parents should seek advice from a counselor. **To help lessen emotional problems for their children.**

EDITED (ATTACHED TO MAIN CLAUSE)
Divorcing parents should seek advice from a counselor to help lessen emotional problems for their children.

FRAGMENT (GERUND PHRASE)
Introducing competing varieties of crabs into the same tank. He did this in order to study aggression.

EDITED (REWRITTEN)
He **introduced** competing varieties of crabs into the tank in order to study aggression.

19c
frag

Exercise 4

A. Correct each of the fragments in the following passages in two different ways.

EXAMPLE
Living and working in another country creates many challenges for families. For example, arranging for children's schooling.

Living and working in another country creates many challenges for families. Arranging for children's schooling is one such challenge.

1. The armed forces run elementary and secondary schools around the world. To provide education for dependents.
2. Japanese executives working in North America worry about educating their children in the Japanese language. And worry about whether they will fit into Japanese culture when they are adults.
3. Americans and Canadians working outside of North America often look for schools conducted in English. To make sure their children will be prepared to attend college when the families return home.

4. The modern world makes many demands on parents. Who must spend considerable time and energy educating their children.
5. Whoever grows up with knowledge of two different cultures. I think that person will have some distinct advantages.

B. Working with a group, identify the fragments in the following word groups. Then combine the word groups to form a paragraph made up of complete sentences. Feel free to alter the wording or to add information necessary to make the paragraph interesting and clear.

1. One store chain asks people to provide an address when cashing a check. And uses the information to create a mailing list for its advertising flyers.
2. As a result, people who buy two pairs of pants and a few blouses are going to be receiving something in the mail each week for the next few months. For instance, a colorful flyer about home furnishings or automobile accessories.
3. Some people resent this marketing strategy. And complain to the post office or the company itself.
4. Lots of people consider advertising brochures fun to read. And a way to make shopping easier.
5. I think they are just one of many small irritations we encounter every day. Such as free samples of useless products and computerized telephone calls.

C. Identify and correct any sentence fragments in a draft paper of your own. Pay particular attention to those fragments caused by the troublesome constructions discussed in 19c-1 and 19c-2.

> 19d
> **frag**

19d   Using partial sentences

In magazine articles, in reports, in advertising, and even in essays generally regarded as models of good writing, you are likely to encounter sentence fragments used properly and effectively. Fragments of this kind can be called **partial sentences.** Here is a concise definition of a partial sentence offered by a student.

> A partial sentence is an effective sentence fragment used for emphasis, often to call attention to a particular idea. It isn't a whole sentence and doesn't need to be.

Used sparingly, partial sentences can call attention to details, provide special emphasis for ideas, or heighten contrasts. They can help you recreate a scene piece by piece, just as a painter creates a scene with multiple brushstrokes and images. They can create emphasis or a change of pace, as in the following passage.

> Our house stood apart. A gaudy yellow in a row of white bungalows. We were the people with the noisy dog.   — RICHARD RODRIGUEZ, "Aria"
> By highlighting the house's color in a fragment, Rodriguez calls special attention to it, just as the yellow paint made the house stand out in the neighborhood.

Some other appropriate uses of partial sentences include questions and answers ("Where should I put the printout?" "On my desk."); exclamations ("Wish I had time to run this experiment again!"); and transitional phrases ("Next, the results."). With the exception of transitional phrases, these uses of fragments are most common in speech and informal writing.

Even when a writing situation is one in which readers are likely to consider a sentence fragment acceptable, you need to pay attention to several important guidelines.

1. Have a clear purpose in mind, such as building a description, highlighting parallel ideas, or providing strong emphasis and contrast.
2. Make sure that your readers will recognize the purpose and not mistake the fragment for an unintentionally detached modifier or incomplete phrase.
3. Take care that your readers will be able to supply the missing elements or will be able to perceive connections between word groups without confusion.

19d
frag

Exercise 5

If you have not already completed Exercise 2C, do so now, making a copy of each of the fragments you locate. Working with a group, share your different sets of fragments. Identify those fragments you consider effective partial sentences. Explain how each effective fragment fits the criteria outlined in 19d, and tell what purpose each one fulfills.

Comma Splices
and Fused Sentences

You can easily confuse and annoy readers if you inappropriately join two or more sentences using either a comma only (comma splice) or no punctuation at all (fused sentence). Because a comma splice does not clearly specify the relationship between main clauses, readers may have to look over a sentence several times to be sure of its meaning.

COMMA SPLICE CBS was founded in 1928 by William S. Paley, his uncle and his father sold him a struggling radio network they had bought to advertise their La Palina cigars.

  READER'S RESPONSE: At first I thought CBS had three founders: Paley, his uncle, and his father. Then I realized that the sentence probably means Paley founded CBS after buying the radio network from his relatives.

EDITED CBS was founded in 1928 by William S. Paley**;** his uncle and his father sold him a struggling radio network they had bought to advertise their La Palina cigars.

Even after a close examination, readers may find it difficult to understand a fused sentence, two sentences joined with no punctuation at all.

FUSED SENTENCE The city had only one swimming pool without an admission fee the pool was poorly maintained.

  READER'S RESPONSE: I can't decide if the *single* swimming pool in the town is poorly maintained or if the only swimming pool that does not charge a fee is in bad shape.

EDITED The city had only one swimming pool**,** **but** without an admission fee, the pool was poorly maintained.

Always avoid fused sentences in your writing. They are especially misleading because they do not provide readers with an indication of the boundary between the main clauses in the sentence.

Use the strategies outlined in this chapter to recognize comma splices and fused sentences and to edit them by linking main clauses appropriately.

20a   Recognizing comma splices and fused sentences

A **comma splice** is the linking of two sentences (independent or main clauses—see 14c) by a comma alone.

COMMA SPLICE
: Eight inches of rain fell in twenty-four hours, all the creeks swelled rapidly.

  READER'S RESPONSE: I had to read this sentence twice because at first glance I couldn't tell where one part ended and the next began.

EDITED
: Eight inches of rain fell in twenty-four hours, **and** all the creeks swelled rapidly.

EDITED
: Eight inches of rain fell in twenty-four hours; all the creeks swelled rapidly.

In a **fused sentence** (or **run-on sentence**), neither a punctuation mark nor a connecting word shows where one main (independent) clause ends and the next begins.

20a cs/fs

FUSED SENTENCE
: That night the river overflowed its banks and spread over the lowlands thousands of people were left homeless by the time the waters receded.

  READER'S RESPONSE: When I first read that the river "spread over the lowlands thousands of people," I immediately imagined a mass of people being pushed over the land.

EDITED
: That night the river overflowed its banks and spread over the lowlands. **Thousands** of people were left homeless by the time the waters receded.

EDITED
: That night the river overflowed its banks and spread over the lowlands; **as a result,** thousands of people were left homeless by the time the waters receded.

To identify comma splices and fused sentences, be alert for situations in which they often occur.

1 Identify comma splices

As you edit, look for sentences containing word groups that could stand on their own as sentences. Make sure that the word groups are joined by more than a comma alone, perhaps by a comma with a coordinating conjunction or by a semicolon.

COMMA SPLICE In a typical Navajo family, the husband serves as a trustee, the mother and her children are the real owners of the family's property.

EDITED In a typical Navajo family, the husband serves as a trustee **, but** the mother and her children are the real owners of the family's property.

EDITED In a typical Navajo family, the husband serves as a trustee **;** the mother and her children are the real owners of the family's property.

Strategy

Pay attention to writing likely to contain comma splices. When you are drafting quickly, adding idea to idea and clause to clause, you may sometimes use commas to string word groups together, creating comma splices. Writing of this sort often occurs when you are working under pressure or rushing to record ideas and details. As you edit, pay special attention to sentence boundaries.

20a
cs/fs

2 Identify fused sentences

Look carefully at long sentences. Fused sentences can be any length, but as you edit, pay special attention to long sentences without internal punctuation. Check to see if they contain freestanding (main) clauses joined without punctuation.

Strategy

As you edit, ask, "How many statements are there in this sentence?" A fused sentence is not a single unit but two (or more) units whose relationship is not clearly signaled to readers. If a sentence appears to contain more than one statement, check for appropriate punctuation and connecting words. For example, the following sentence makes two statements: one about the troubles encountered by the scientists and one about the nature of the skeleton. These two statements come in main clauses whose relationship is not appropriately signaled to readers.

FUSED SENTENCE   The scientists had trouble identifying the fossil skeleton it resembled both that of a bird and that of a lizard.

EDITED   The scientists had trouble identifying the fossil skeleton **because** it resembled both that of a bird and that of a lizard.

Did You Know?

Preferences in punctuation and in sentence style can change over time. Today, when you join two main clauses with a coordinating conjunction (*and, but, or, for, nor, yet,* or *so*), you must also punctuate with a comma. Over a hundred years ago, however, in *A Common-School Grammar of the English Language,* Simon Kerl recommended joining short main clauses with a coordinating conjunction but adding a semicolon for a longer clause. In *A New English Grammar for Schools* (1900), Thomas W. Harvey repeated this advice: "A clause, introduced by *for, but, and,* or an equivalent connective, is often set off by a semicolon" (294). Harvey also offered an example of a correctly punctuated sentence that highlights, by contrast, our modern taste for short, direct sentences: "The person he chanced to see, was, to appearance, an old, sordid, blind man; but upon his following him from place to place, he at last found, by his own confession, that he was Plutus, the god of riches, and that he was just come out of the house of a miser" (244).

Thomas W. Harvey, *A New English Grammar for Schools* (New York: American Book, 1900), and Simon Kerl, *A Common-School Grammar of the English Language* (New York: Ivison, 1871).

**20a
cs/fs**

3 Watch for sentence patterns that may lead to comma splices and fused sentences

You join sentences (main clauses) because they are related, and in joining them you emphasize the relationship. A number of relationships, however, seem to lead to more than their fair share of comma splices.

Strategy

As you edit, look for sentences (main clauses) related in the following ways. Make sure they are not linked by a comma alone, and make sure they are joined with either the correct punctuation or a connecting word.

Sentences with the same subject
One sentence illustrated by another
Balanced sentences with contrasting ideas
Sentences with related ideas

If you have particular trouble with comma splices or fused sentences in your writing, use this list as an editing checklist. Add to it any sentence patterns or relationships that are problems for you. (See 20b for ways to correct comma splices and fused sentences.)

- Sentences (main clauses) with the same subject

    COMMA SPLICE   The ice cream cake had begun to melt, it was dripping onto Grandmother's lace tablecloth.

    EDITED   The ice cream cake had begun to melt, **and** it was dripping onto Grandmother's lace tablecloth.

    FUSED SENTENCE   The small commuter plane held only twelve people it bumped and swayed throughout the flight.

    EDITED   The small commuter plane held only twelve people, **and** it bumped and swayed throughout the flight.

- One sentence (main clause) illustrated by another

    COMMA SPLICE   Children with Down syndrome feel the same emotions as the rest of us, they get sad, puzzled, and silly.

    EDITED   Children with Down syndrome feel the same emotions as the rest of us; they get sad, puzzled, and silly.

    FUSED SENTENCE   Contemporary American literature no longer means Hemingway and Faulkner it means Louise Erdrich, Raymond Carver, and Adrienne Rich.

    EDITED   Contemporary American literature no longer means Hemingway and Faulkner; it means Louise Erdrich, Raymond Carver, and Adrienne Rich.

- Balanced sentences (main clauses) with contrasting ideas

    COMMA SPLICE   The students got good scores on the reading test, none did well on the advanced math test.

    EDITED   The students got good scores on the reading test; **however,** none did well on the advanced math test.

**20a
cs/fs**

FUSED SENTENCE   The engineering and social work programs get the most public attention the medical technology and marketing programs get the largest enrollments.

EDITED   The engineering and social work programs get the most public attention, **but** the medical technology and marketing programs get the largest enrollments.

- Sentences (main clauses) with related ideas

COMMA SPLICE   She had already founded a successful company, she saw no reason to get an advanced degree.

EDITED   She had already founded a successful company; **therefore,** she saw no reason to get an advanced degree.

FUSED SENTENCE   Health costs are rising rapidly solutions to the problem are not clear.

EDITED   Health costs are rising rapidly; **moreover,** solutions to the problem are not clear.

**20a
cs/fs**

Writer's Alert

Writers developing the useful habit of joining clauses with conjunctive adverbs (such as *however, nonetheless, therefore, consequently, moreover,* and *thus*) often forget that the technique also requires a semicolon between the clauses (see also 32a).

COMMA SPLICE   The health risks of video display terminals have not been proved, nonetheless, computer users should not sit too close to their screens.

EDITED   The health risks of video display terminals have not been proved; nonetheless, computer users should not sit too close to their screens.

Exercise 1

A. First, use the strategies discussed in 20a to identify the comma splices in the following passage.

The subarctic region provides little variety in food, therefore, Eskimo diet includes large quantities of meat such as seal and caribou. The cold weather and the available materials determine dressing habits, a loose shirt with a hood, trousers, stockings, and mittens (often made of caribou skin and fur) are a common outfit for men, women, and children alike. Social affairs are important in Eskimo communities, favorite gatherings include carnivals, Christmas parties, and feasts of game brought in by hunters. Children in Eskimo communities begin school at the age of five or six, most quit by the time they are twelve in order to go to work. Boys usually go hunting with their fathers, girls learn to sew and cook.

Next, draw a double vertical line between each of the main clauses making up the following fused sentences.

EXAMPLE

Casinos used to operate legally in only a few states‖they are now springing up all over the country as states make casino gambling legitimate.

1. The gaming industry is one of the fastest-growing industries in some areas it is a major employer.
2. Legalized gambling takes many forms bingo, lotteries, casinos, and video games are run under government supervision in many states.
3. State lotteries are popular they may also encourage people to gamble unwisely.
4. The economic and law enforcement objections to legalized gambling get the most public attention the moral and psychological objections may deserve the most attention.
5. Legalized gambling now goes beyond people in casinos betting on roulette or sports events it includes people playing bingo at a charity event or playing video poker in a family restaurant.

> 20b
> cs/fs

B. Working in a group, decide which, if any, of the sentences in the first section of Exercise 1A follow sentence patterns likely to lead to comma splices or fused sentences, and identify the patterns.

C. Review a paper in progress of your own. Identify and underline any comma splices and fused sentences.

20b   Editing comma splices and fused sentences

You can correct comma splices and fused sentences in many ways. Each Strategy that follows offers a different means for creating emphasis and highlighting relationships. Often, you will bring your ideas in a draft into sharper perspective through careful editing of these errors.

Strategies for Revising Comma Splices and Fused Sentences

1. Create two separate sentences.
2. Join main clauses with a comma plus a coordinating conjunction (*and, but, or, for, nor, so,* or *yet*).
3. Join main clauses with a semicolon.
4. Join main clauses with a semicolon plus a conjunctive adverb or transitional expression (*however, moreover, for example, in contrast,* and similar words or phrases).
5. Subordinate one of the clauses.
6. Join main clauses with a colon.

ORIGINAL   Ultimate Frisbee combines elements of football, basketball, baseball, and soccer it also has a few quirks that make it unique. The sport calls for a total of fourteen people (or twelve people and two dogs) divided into two teams (with one dog each), they throw a disk (called a Frisbee) up and down a football field. The object is to catch the disk in the other team's end zone and thereby score.

20b
cs/fs

EDITED   Ultimate Frisbee combines elements of football, basketball, baseball, and soccer **;** it also has a few quirks that make it unique. The sport calls for a total of fourteen people (or twelve people and two dogs) divided into two teams (with one dog each)**.** **They** throw a disk (called a Frisbee) up and down a football field. The object is to catch the disk in the other team's end zone and thereby score.

Strategy 1

Create two separate sentences. When the ideas in two main clauses are loosely related, you can generally express them best in separate sentences.

COMMA SPLICE   Costa Rica's political life has been relatively free of damaging conflict, the same cannot be said of its neighbors. El Salvador and Nicaragua, in particular, have long histories of civil unrest.

EDITED   Costa Rica's political life has been relatively free of damaging conflict**.** **The** same cannot be said of its neighbors. El Salvador and Nicaragua, in particular, have long histories of civil unrest.

FUSED SENTENCE   Football does not cause the most injuries among student athletes gymnastics is the most dangerous sport.

EDITED	Football does not cause the most injuries among student athletes. **Gymnastics** is the most dangerous sport.

Strategy 2

Join main clauses with a comma plus a coordinating conjunction (*and, but, or, for, nor, so,* or *yet*). When main clauses convey ideas or information of approximately equal importance, consider linking the clauses with a comma plus a coordinating conjunction that indicates their relationship.

COMMA SPLICE	The more experienced teams use complicated strategies for offense and defense, the inexperienced teams concentrate on the basics.
EDITED	The more experienced teams use complicated strategies for offense and defense **, but** the inexperienced teams concentrate on the basics.
FUSED SENTENCE	Schizophrenia is a mental illness its causes may be physical.
EDITED	Schizophrenia is a mental illness **, yet** its causes may be physical.

20b
cs/fs

Writer's Alert

Three or more closely related clauses can be punctuated as a series in order to emphasize their relationship. Be sure to include the coordinating conjunction before the last item.

We collected the specimens, we cleaned them with a mild detergent **, and** we measured them.

Strategy 3

Join main clauses with a semicolon. You can use a semicolon to emphasize the similar importance of two main clauses.

COMMA SPLICE	During flight an airplane tends to drift up or down, left or right due to air turbulence. An autopilot is a device that detects and corrects drift, the system senses changes in the aircraft's motion and reacts accordingly.

EDITED During flight an airplane tends to drift up or down, left or right due to air turbulence. An autopilot is a device that detects and corrects drift; the system senses changes in the aircraft's motion and reacts accordingly.

FUSED SENTENCE Most colleges offer alternatives to spending four years on the same campus study abroad, exchange programs with other schools, and cooperative programs are common.

EDITED Most colleges offer alternatives to spending four years on the same campus; study abroad, exchange programs with other schools, and cooperative programs are common.

Strategy 4

Join main clauses with a semicolon plus a conjunctive adverb *or* with a semicolon plus a transitional expression. *However, nonetheless, therefore, consequently, moreover, thus,* and other conjunctive adverbs specify relationships between clauses. You can use transitional expressions such as *for example, in contrast,* and *in addition* for similar purposes.

20b
cs/fs

COMMA SPLICE To draw the human body, you must understand it, art schools sometimes ask students to dissect cadavers.

EDITED To draw the human body, you must understand it; **therefore,** art schools sometimes ask students to dissect cadavers.

FUSED SENTENCE Commercially raised animals such as chickens or beef cattle can reach marketable size within a matter of months or a year the American lobster must grow for an average of six to eight years before it reaches the proper size.

EDITED Commercially raised animals such as chickens or beef cattle can reach marketable size within a matter of months or a year; **in contrast,** the American lobster must grow for an average of six to eight years before it reaches the proper size.

Strategy 5

Subordinate one of the clauses. Subordinators such as *although, while, when, because, since,* and *unless* and relative pronouns such as *who, which,* or *that* enable you to specify a wide range of relationships between clauses (see 26b).

COMMA SPLICE Automobiles are becoming increasingly complex, experienced mechanics have to spend up to several weeks a year in training programs.

EDITED **Because** automobiles are becoming increasingly complex, experienced mechanics have to spend up to several weeks a year in training programs.

FUSED SENTENCE Margaret Atwood is best known for her novels her essays and poems are also worth reading.

EDITED **Although** Margaret Atwood is best known for her novels, her essays and poems are also worth reading.

Writer's Alert

Conjunctive adverbs (such as *however, nonetheless,* and *thus*) and transitional expression (like *for example* and *on the other hand*) can appear not only at the beginning of a second main clause but also within it. Wherever the adverb or expression appears, it must be set off by a comma or commas, and the clauses themselves must be joined by a semicolon.

AT BEGINNING OF CLAUSE The Great Lakes once supported a thriving fishing industry**;** **however,** in recent years pollution has reduced the catch greatly.

IN MIDDLE OF CLAUSE The Great Lakes once supported a thriving fishing industry**;** in recent years**,** **however,** pollution has reduced the catch greatly.

AT END OF CLAUSE The Great Lakes once supported a thriving fishing industry**;** in recent years pollution has reduced the catch greatly**,** **however.**

20b
cs/fs

Strategy 6

Join main clauses with a colon. When a clause summarizes, illustrates, or restates a preceding clause, you can join the two with a colon (see 32b).

COMMA SPLICE The water damage under the loose roof shingles brought one conclusion to my mind, I should have hired a professional.

EDITED The water damage under the loose roof shingles brought one conclusion to my mind**:** I should have hired a professional.

FUSED SENTENCE   Foreign study calls for extensive language preparation vaccinations and a passport are not enough.

EDITED   Foreign study calls for extensive language preparation: vaccinations and a passport are not enough.

Exercise 2

A. Identify and edit in *two* ways the following comma splices and fused sentences. Use the methods of revision indicated in brackets after each sentence.

EXAMPLE

Children often fight among themselves, these conflicts pose many challenges for parents. [comma plus coordinating conjunction; semicolon]

Children often fight among themselves, and these conflicts pose many challenges for parents.

Children often fight among themselves; these conflicts pose many challenges for parents.

20b
cs/fs

1. Some parents refuse to become involved in their children's squabbles, they fear the children will resent the interference. [subordination; semicolon]
2. Siblings have special reasons to fight competing for space and playthings or for attention from a parent can turn playmates into rivals. [colon; semicolon plus transitional phrase]
3. Sibling fights offer an opportunity for children to become sensitive to the feelings of others, the arguments pose dangers as well. [comma plus coordinating conjunction; semicolon plus conjunctive adverb]
4. Bickering is common and normal excessive fighting can be a sign of more serious trouble. [semicolon plus conjunctive adverb; separate sentences]
5. By adolescence, most children have worked out compatible relationships with their siblings, they may still occasionally argue. [subordination; comma plus coordinating conjunction]

B. Working with a group, edit each of the following sentences in two ways, using Strategies discussed in 20b. You may need to make changes in wording or punctuation.

1. One group claims that cattle raising is hard on the environment another group argues that raising wheat and other cereal grains causes water pollution and destroys topsoil.

2. In Central Florida, cattle waste has polluted Lake Okeechobee runoff from fertilizer has greatly increased the growth of algae in the lake.
3. The waters off Long Island's south shore are also polluted the main culprit is lawn fertilizer.
4. In my state, pesticides from potato farming have polluted the groundwater pig and chicken farming have caused problems.
5. Our large population makes a massive farming industry necessary we are going to have to deal with the problems caused by large-scale farming and livestock raising.

C. Edit any comma splices or fused sentences you identified in a draft paper as part of Exercise 1C.

20b
cs/fs

CHAPTER

21

Pronoun Reference

You can often make a sentence less repetitive and easier to understand by having pronouns take the place of nouns (or even other pronouns). For the substitution to work effectively, your readers must recognize the word to which a pronoun refers, known as its **antecedent** (or headword). In the passage below, for example, *they* and *their* clearly refer to *kangaroos.*

CLEAR REFERENCE **Kangaroos** normally walk on four feet unless **they** wish to move quickly, at which time **they** make large leaps using only **their** hind legs.

When **pronoun reference**—the connection between a pronoun and its antecedent—is not clear, however, readers may be confused.

AMBIGUOUS REFERENCE Much of my supposedly glamorous life with the circus consisted of hosing the elephants down after leading **them** from **their** cages.
READER'S RESPONSE: What got hosed down? The elephants? The cages? Both?

In contrast, by creating clear pronoun reference you help tie ideas and sentences together, clarifying their relationships and guiding your readers.

EDITED Much of my supposedly glamorous life with the circus **consisted** of hosing the elephants down after leading **them** from **their** cages.

21a Making pronoun reference clear

Make sure each pronoun in your writing refers *clearly* to a *single* antecedent. The antecedent can be one word.

Freud claimed that slips of the tongue reveal subconscious thoughts and desires. **He** offered no real evidence to support the claim, however.

Or it can be a **compound antecedent,** a group of words acting as a unit.

> **Calvin Klein, Liz Claiborne**, and **Donna Karan** started out as clothing designers. **They** now head major corporations bearing their names.

Watch out for pronouns that can easily refer to more than one possible antecedent (ambiguous reference) or that are widely separated from their antecedents (remote reference). Both of these can confuse your readers.

1 Watch for pronouns with several possible antecedents

Look for sentences containing two or more words to which a pronoun might possibly refer. If readers cannot easily identify the appropriate antecedent, you need to correct the **ambiguous reference.**

AMBIGUOUS REFERENCE Detaching the measuring probe from the glass cylinder is a delicate job because **it** breaks easily.

READER'S RESPONSE: Which is especially fragile, the probe or the cylinder?

21a
pr ref

You can correct this problem in two ways: (1) replace the troublesome pronoun with a noun, or (2) reword the sentence.

REPLACED WITH A NOUN Detaching the measuring probe from the glass cylinder is a delicate job because **the probe** breaks easily.

REWORDED Because the measuring probe breaks easily, detaching it from the glass cylinder is a delicate job.

In addition, watch for pronouns that can refer to each of two or more subjects in earlier sentences.

AMBIGUOUS REFERENCE Robespierre and Danton disagreed over the path the French Revolution should take. **He** was convinced that the Revolution was endangered by its internal enemies; **his opponent** believed the Revolution had been won.

EDITED Robespierre and Danton disagreed over the path the French Revolution should take. **Robespierre** was convinced that the Revolution was endangered by its internal enemies; **Danton** believed the Revolution had been won.

You can use more than one pronoun in a sentence if readers can readily identify the antecedent for each.

CLEAR REFERENCE   The Reign of Terror began with **Robespierre** leading the **Jacobins** as **they** guillotined over two thousand supposed opponents of the revolution and ended with **his** being led to the guillotine **himself.**

Writer's Tip

You may sometimes create confusion with **indirect quotations** using *said* or *told* to report in a general way what someone has said.

UNCLEAR REFERENCE   When the project was finally completed, Jennifer's supervisor said **she** needed a few days off because **she** had been working so hard.
READER'S RESPONSE: Who needs the time off, Jennifer or her supervisor?

To correct this problem, report the person's words exactly **(direct quotation).**

REWRITTEN WITH DIRECT QUOTATION   When the project was finally completed, Jennifer's supervisor said, "**You** need a few days off because **you** have been working so hard."

Or rewrite the indirect quotation, using one or more nouns rather than pronouns.

REWRITTEN WITH NOUN   When the project was finally completed, her supervisor said that **Jennifer** needed a few days off because **she** had been working so hard.

---

2 Pay attention to pronouns widely separated from their antecedents

When you place a pronoun at a distance from its antecedent (**remote reference**), your readers may have a hard time recognizing the connection between the two. This problem can occur even though no other possible referent comes between them. In editing, therefore, you need to look for pronouns preceded by detailed information that draws the reader's attention away from the antecedent.

REMOTE REFERENCE James Van Allen designed an instrument that the first American space satellite used to detect what are now known to be two doughnut-shaped rings of high-energy particles extending from between several hundred to fifty thousand kilometers above the earth. The belts were eventually named for **him.**

To correct the problem, either bring the pronoun closer to its antecedent, or drop the pronoun and repeat the noun or pronoun to which it refers.

EDITED James Van Allen designed an instrument that the first American space satellite used to detect what are now known to be two doughnut-shaped rings of high-energy particles extending from between several hundred to fifty thousand kilometers above the earth. They were eventually named **the Van Allen belts after the man instrumental in their discovery.**

Keeping pronouns and antecedents close together is especially important for the relative pronouns *who, which,* and *that.* Avoid confusion by placing the relative pronoun right after its antecedent.

**21a
pr ref**

CONFUSING As I lay on the carpet in my old bedroom, I noticed two stale pieces of the bubble gum under **the dresser that I loved to chew as a boy.**

EDITED As I lay on the carpet in my old bedroom, I noticed under the dresser two stale pieces of **the bubble gum that I loved to chew as a boy.**

Exercise 1

A. Rewrite each of the following sentences to create clear pronoun reference.

EXAMPLE
Someone needs to pick up the weekend shipment ~~at the airport~~ that
                                                    at the airport
may arrive ⌃ late Saturday night.

1. Both Carlo and Andy agree that he will be responsible for getting the cartons of replacement parts from the air terminal.
2. The accountant has told his client that he will be answerable for any problems with billing.
3. Airfreight offers weekend shipment and is cheaper, which means that work doesn't have to stop on Monday morning while workers wait for delivery of the replacement parts.

4. The van used to pick up shipments is the old one the company's owner purchased right after her divorce which is covered with rust spots.

5. The sales projections used to order supplies are often inaccurate because the sales manager calculates them using a formula on a spreadsheet that is overly optimistic.

B. Working with a group of fellow students, compare the choices each of you made in editing the sentences in Exercise 1A.

C. Review a draft paper of your own, and underline any pronouns with more than one possible antecedent and any pronouns widely separated from their antecedents. Then edit the passages to create clear reference.

3 Create clear reference chains

You can connect sentences by creating a chain of pronouns whose antecedent is stated in the opening sentence. Such a **reference chain** guides your readers through the passage and reminds them of the topic you are addressing. In this way, some of the pronouns can be relatively remote from their antecedent, even three or four sentences away, for example, but the reference will still be clear.

Strategy

To create effective reference chains, take the following steps.

- State the antecedent clearly in the opening sentence.
- Make sure no other possible antecedents interrupt the links in the chain.
- Make sure you do not interrupt the chain and then try to pick it up again after several sentences.
- Call attention to the links by giving the pronouns prominent positions (usually at the beginning of sentences); vary their positions only slightly.

UNCLEAR

Sand paintings were a remarkable form of Pueblo art from the Southwest and Southern California. An artist would sprinkle dried sand of different colors, ground flower petals, corn pollen, and similar materials onto the floor to create **them**. The sun, moon, and stars as well as animals and objects linked to the spirits were represented in the figures **they** contained. **Their** purpose was to encourage the spirits to send good fortune to humans.

Because the pronouns *them* and *they* are buried at the ends of sentences in the middle of the paragraph, readers can easily lose sight of the paragraph's topic, sand paintings.

EDITED TO CREATE A REFERENCE CHAIN

Sand paintings were a remarkable form of Pueblo art from the Southwest and Southern California. To create **them,** an artist would sprinkle dried sand of different colors, ground flower petals, corn pollen, and similar materials onto the floor. **They** contained figures representing the sun, moon, and stars as well as animals and objects linked to the spirits. **Their** purpose was to encourage the spirits to send good fortune to humans.

Did You Know?

According to research conducted by the authors, college instructors view problems with pronoun reference as among the most irritating and potentially confusing errors they encounter in student writing. The instructors believe that problems with pronoun reference are likely to arise more frequently as the content and ideas in an essay become more complex. They also think that appropriate and careful use of pronoun reference is a key tool for writers who wish to guide and focus the attention of readers.

Chris M. Anson and Robert A, Schwegler, "A Survey of Attitudes Toward Error Among Instructors at Four Colleges," unpublished ms.

21a
pr ref

Exercise 2

A. Revise the following sentences so that they form a reference chain giving appropriate emphasis to the information provided in the passage. You will need to give some ideas and details more emphasis than others.

When it comes to reading material, Americans have some clear favorites. In terms of circulation, the top five newspapers in the country are the *Wall Street Journal, USA Today,* the *New York Daily News,* the *Los Angeles Times,* and the *New York Times.* Sales of softbound books far outnumber sales of hardbound books. Our favorite subject areas for books are medicine, history, fiction, sociology and economics, religion, and technology. The top three magazines in terms of revenue are *Time, Sports Illustrated,* and *People.* More people subscribe to *Modern Maturity* and the *AARP Bulletin* than to any other magazines, including *Reader's Digest,* which is number three on the subscription list. *1,001 Home Ideas* and *The Elks Magazine* have larger paid circulations than *Vogue, Rolling Stone,* and *Mademoiselle.*

 B. Working with a group of writers, share your versions of the passage in Exercise 2A. Choose two versions that give the information different emphasis. Identify the ways each writer has created a reference chain, and indicate which ideas and details have been highlighted and which have been moved to the background.

 C. Choose two sections from a paper you are preparing, and make each one clearer by editing to create a reference chain.

21b Making reference specific

21b
pr ref

If readers say they "get lost" reading your work or "can't quite figure out what you are saying," part of the problem may be vague pronoun reference. **Specific pronoun reference** points out for readers the precise relationships between statements. **Vague pronoun reference,** however, makes pronouns refer to antecedents that are implied rather than stated. It does not clearly indicate the part of a preceding statement, if any, to which a pronoun refers.

You need to be alert, therefore, to contexts in which you are most likely to create vague pronoun reference: (1) with certain troublesome words like *it, which, this,* and *that;* and (2) with antecedents that are implied rather than stated.

1 Use *it, which, this, that,* and *you* with care

Some very useful pronouns are also easy to misuse. For example, writers often use *it, which, this,* or *that* to refer broadly to a preceding passage but end up giving readers only a vague idea of the antecedent. Or writers may ask a word like *it* to refer to several different antecedents within a short passage.

Overly Broad Reference. You are most likely to misuse words like *it, which, this,* or *that* when you want to refer to the entire idea of a preceding sentence, sentence part, or group of sentences. When you use the pronouns effectively to refer to an entire idea, you create **broad prounoun reference.** In the following pair of sentences, the writer uses *this* and *that* clearly and appropriately for just such a purpose.

Every few million years an extremely large asteroid collides with the earth. **This** has not happened in historic times, so we have no experience of the consequences of **that** event.

— Robert Jastrow, *Journey to the Stars*

Used carefully, broad reference can help you sum up ideas in order to comment on them, as in the preceding example. On the other hand, you can easily confuse readers if you fail to make clear the *specific* antecedent of *it, which, that,* or *this.* Consider the following example.

VAGUE REFERENCE Redfish have been heavily harvested for years, but in the last decade they have been subjected to oil pollution and to the destruction of their mangrove swamp habitat by waterfront building. **That** has led to a recent and rapid decline in the redfish population.

READER'S RESPONSE: Does *that* refer to the destruction of habitat, to oil pollution, to overfishing, or to some combination?

To edit for vague or overly broad reference, look for words like *it, which, this,* and *that,* and then see if you have provided a specific word or group of words to which the pronoun clearly refers. If not, correct the problem using one of the following Strategies.

21b
pr ref

Strategy 1

Specify. Right after *this, that,* or another troublesome word, add a word or phrase that specifies (or explains) the pronoun's referent.

EDITED (SPECIFIES) Redfish have been heavily harvested for years, but in the last decade they have been subjected to oil pollution and to the destruction of their mangrove swamp habitat by waterfront building. That **combination** has led to a recent and rapid decline in the redfish population.

EDITED (EXPLAINS) Redfish have been heavily harvested for years, but in the last decade they have been subjected to oil pollution and to the destruction of their mangrove swamp habitat by waterfront building. That **increasingly serious set of challenges** has led to a recent and rapid decline in the redfish population.

Strategy 2

Replace. Drop the pronoun, and use a noun or noun phrase in its place.

VAGUE One test conducted by the Mars lander discovered some evidence of life on Mars, but the other uncovered no evidence whatsoever. **This** led many scientists to conclude that there is no life on the planet.

REPLACED One test conducted by the Mars lander discovered some evidence of life on Mars, but the other uncovered no evidence whatsoever. **The reliability of the second test** led many scientists to conclude that there is no life on the planet.

Strategy 3

Reword. Rewrite the sentence or sentences so that the pronoun is no longer needed.

REWORDED One test conducted by the Mars lander discovered some evidence of life on Mars, but the second and more reliable test uncovered no evidence whatsoever, leading many scientists to conclude that there is no life on the planet.

It **Used in More Than One Sense.** You can employ *it* in many ways.

PERSONAL PRONOUN
I threw the blender out after **it** broke for the third time.

WAY OF POSTPONING SUBJECT
It is the lack of sunshine in winter that often causes depression.

IDIOMATIC EXPRESSION
It is raining.

By using *it* in more than one sense in a single sentence or a short passage, however, you risk confusing readers.

CONFUSING When I was young, I always found **it** surprising that my father would come home from a hard day at his job and go out to the garden to work in **it,** even when **it** was raining.

EDITED When I was young, I was always surprised when my father came home from a hard day at his job and went out to work in the garden, even when **it** was raining.

2 Be alert for antecedents that are implied rather than stated

In the following sentence, the writer has an antecedent in mind but fails to communicate it to readers.

IMPLIED   In the West, **they** often prefer Japanese cars; in the center of the country, **they** drive mostly Detroit-made autos; and in the Northeast and Southeast, **they** often choose European models.

Most readers would guess that *they* refers to people in general, because that is the antecedent words like *drive* and *cars* suggest. But *they* might also mean rich people, people under forty, or some other group. By stating the antecedent directly the writer could have eliminated both guessing and possible misunderstanding.

STATED   In the West, **people under forty** prefer Japanese cars; in the center of the country, they drive mostly Detroit-made autos; and in the Northeast and Southeast, they often choose European models.

As you edit, check that you have provided readers with a *stated* antecedent rather than an *implied* one. Watch out, as well, for the following troublesome words and contexts that may lead to implied or missing antecedents.

They or **It** Without an Antecedent.   In most writing, especially academic writing, you need to make sure readers can identify an antecedent in your text so your statements are precise and clear. If you *imply* an antecedent but do not actually *state* it, your writing becomes vague and often confusing.

21b
pr ref

IMPLIED   In February, a deep frost damaged most of the citrus groves in the state, but **it** has not yet been determined.
READER'S RESPONSE: I can't be sure what *it* is.

STATED   In February, a deep frost damaged most of the citrus groves in the state, but **the extent of the loss** has not yet been determined.

You Without an Antecedent.   When you intend to address the reader directly, *you* is acceptable in most writing. It means "you, the reader." In effect, *you* makes the reader the antecedent, that is, the person to whom the pronoun refers. (See also 23a.)

ACCEPTABLE   In implementing the recommendations of this report, **you** may find that staff members resist some of the suggestions for long-term patient care. The following statistics should help **you** convince them that the new procedures will be useful.

When *you* refers indefinitely to experiences, situations, and people in general, it is not appropriate and often leads to wordy and misleading sentences.

MISLEADING   In Brazil, you pay less for an alcohol-powered car than for a gasoline-powered one.

READER'S RESPONSE: Who is *you*? After all, I'm not likely to be buying a car in Brazil.

EDITED   In Brazil, alcohol-powered cars cost less than gasoline-powered ones.

EDITED   In Brazil, consumers pay less for an alcohol-powered car than for a gasoline-powered one.

Possessive Noun or Modifier as Antecedent. In academic writing, using a possessive noun as an antecedent will seem like an error to most readers, even though the pattern appears often in informal writing.

INAPPROPRIATE   In William Faulkner's *The Sound and the Fury,* he presents the first part of the story from the point of view of a mentally retarded person.

EDITED   In *The Sound and the Fury,* William Faulkner presents the first part of the story from the point of view of a mentally retarded person.

21b
pr ref

Because a modifier may *suggest* an antecedent, you may sometimes mistakenly use an adjective as the referent for a pronoun. In doing so, you confuse readers by forcing them to guess at your intentions. To avoid this problem, supply a specific antecedent.

CONFUSING   Whether or not a product is successfully marketed may depend on how many demographic studies were conducted. As a result, people trained in **it** often get good jobs in major corporations.

Demographic is an adjective. It is not the name of a field of study, as the writer seems to assume.

EDITED   Whether or not a product is successfully marketed may depend on how many demographic studies were conducted. As a result, people trained in **demography** often get good jobs in major corporations.

Noun Implied by Another Word. If you make a pronoun refer to a noun that is not in a sentence but is merely implied by some other word, your sentence is likely to be clumsy or hard to understand. Make sure a pronoun refers to a noun or phrase that is actually stated, not implied.

CLUMSY   Growing up in the Southwest, Alice dreamed of studying oceanography, though she had never seen **one.**

EDITED   Growing up in the Southwest, Alice dreamed of studying oceanography, though she had never seen **an ocean.**

UNCLEAR   Rosalind Franklin participated in the discovery of DNA's molecular structure, though she is seldom given credit for **it.**

EDITED   Rosalind Franklin participated in the discovery of DNA's molecular structure, though she is seldom given credit for **her contribution.**

Writer's Alert

When you use a possessive noun, you must pair it with a possessive pronoun, for example, *Kristen's . . . hers.*

UNCLEAR   The **company's** success with a well-known jazz fusion artist led **it** to contracts with other musicians.

EDITED   The **company's** success with a well-known jazz fusion artist led to **its** contracts with other musicians.

Another way you can correct the problem is to rewrite the sentence to eliminate the possessive noun.

EDITED   Success with a well-known jazz fusion artist led the company to contracts with other musicians.

21b
pr ref

Exercise 3

A. Edit the following sentences to eliminate vague pronoun reference and provide specific antecedents.

EXAMPLE   *The committee's report*
~~In the committee's report it~~ points out that students generally benefit from participating in a music program.

           (or In its report, the committee points out . . .)

1. Many people study a musical instrument in high school though few students intend to become one.
2. At most secondary schools they offer a variety of music programs.
3. Last February, the town began investigating the quality of its high school band program, but it has not yet been completed.
4. In many regional high schools in the West, the band's large size mirrors the role it plays in the school's social life.

5. In the Northwest you quickly get used to marching and playing in the rain.

B. Compare your revised versions of the sentences in Exercise 3A with those of other writers. As a group, choose the best version of each sentence, and state the reasons for your choice.

C. Read a draft paper of your own carefully to identify any problems with vague or missing antecedents, and edit the paper to correct the problems.

21c Matching *who, which,* and *that* to antecedents

Who refers to people and may refer to animals with names.

Branford and Wynton Marsalis, **who** are brothers, rank among the top contemporary jazz musicians.

Which refers to animals and things (including ideas).

Quantum theory, **which** includes the work of Einstein, Planck, Bohr, and others, was the chief contribution of early twentieth-century physics.

Writer's Alert

Many readers will expect you to use *which* with **nonrestrictive clauses** and either *that* or *which* with **restrictive clauses** (see 31c for a discussion of restrictive and nonrestrictive modifiers). Though other readers may pay little attention to the distinction between *that* and *which,* you should generally maintain the distinction in formal writing.

RESTRICTIVE (ESSENTIAL, LIMITS MEANING)
Drugs **that** limit tissue rejection are necessary for the survival of transplant recipients.

NONRESTRICTIVE (NONESSENTIAL)
The license, **which** will cost you twenty dollars, permits you to fish anywhere in the state for seven days.

That refers to animals, to things, and to anonymous people or people viewed collectively.

> Rheumatoid arthritis is a disease **that** affects the entire body, though it appears mainly in the form of joint inflammation.

> The patients **that** this hospital serves can make use of the institution's Part-Time Patient program for extended physical and occupational therapy.

Exercise 4

A. Revise the following sentences to correct inappropriate pronoun references. Indicate which sentences, if any, contain appropriate pronoun reference.

EXAMPLE
                                      who
Many scholars ~~which~~ ‸are interested in Buddhism have begun to study Tibetan religious practices.

1. The gathering was addressed by the Dalai Lama, a man which is one of the spiritual leaders of Tibetan Buddhism.
2. Tibetan Buddhism is characterized by large monastic organizations who practice yoga and other spiritual and intellectual rituals.
3. It is also true that this form of Buddhism retains features that it inherited from the folk religions of Tibet.
4. Up until the recent Chinese invasion, that occurred in 1959, Tibetan life was dominated by religious practices.
5. Although Lamaism has its greatest influence in Tibet and in countries who are nearby, such as Nepal and Mongolia, it is beginning to spread its influence in the West, including North America.

**21c
pr ref**

B. At a library, find a magazine with somewhat complicated, information-filled articles. Choose an article that interests you, and identify several paragraphs where the author uses a variety of the pronoun reference patterns discussed in this chapter. Make enough copies of these paragraphs to share with a group of fellow students. As a group, identify each of the pronoun reference strategies and try to decide why the author used each one.

C. Edit a current draft of your own, looking for confusing, vague, or incorrect pronoun reference. Start a list of pronoun reference problems you encounter, and add to the list as you edit future papers. If you discover a clear pattern to reference problems in your writing, reread the appropriate sections of this chapter, and concentrate on reducing the number of errors in your work.

Misplaced, Dangling, and Disruptive Modifiers

The following sentences leave readers with some unanswered questions.

MISPLACED MODIFIER   When I was at the store last week, I only looked at the cassette tape player.

READER'S RESPONSE: *Only* is confusing. Do you mean you just looked and didn't try the cassette player out? You didn't have time to look at other equipment, such as the CD player? You were the only person who looked at the cassette player?

DANGLING MODIFIER   Rushing to get to the post office before it closed, my shoe hit the edge of a sidewalk grate, and the sole tore off.

READER'S RESPONSE: Was the shoe really rushing to the post office?

Because a **modifier** qualifies, adds to, or limits the meaning of another word or word group, the relationship between a modifier and the word it modifies (its **headword**) needs to be clear to readers. The misplaced modifier in the first sentence (*only*) and the dangling modifier in the second (*Rushing to get to the post office . . .*) cause confusion because they are not clearly related to the words they ought to modify.

EDITED   When I was at the store last week, I looked only **at the cassette player.**

EDITED   Rushing to get to the post office before it closed, **I** hit my shoe on the edge of a sidewalk grate and tore the sole off.

A misplaced modifier is one that is not placed closely enough to its intended headword and appears to modify something else. A dangling modifier is one that appears in a sentence that contains no headword or phrase to which the modifier can be reasonably linked.

A third problem you may encounter is a disruptive modifier that separates closely connected elements such as a subject and a verb, making the sentence difficult to read and understand.

DISRUPTIVE MODIFIER	The chief accountant, **even though her assistant first uncovered evidence that the company president had been embezzling funds,** assumed the responsibility of reporting the crime to the police.
EDITED	**Even though her assistant first uncovered evidence that the company president had been embezzling funds,** the chief accountant assumed the responsibility of reporting the crime to the police.

22a Recognizing and editing misplaced modifiers

If you do not make the relationship between a modifier and its headword clear and specific, you may mislead or confuse readers. To recognize a **misplaced modifier,** look for a word that fails to modify its intended headword and instead appears to modify some other word or phrase in the sentence. Sometimes a misplaced modifier even modifies *both* the word before it and the word after.

**22a
mm/dm**

Strategy

To correct a misplaced modifier, either move it closer to its headword or rewrite the sentence so the connection between modifier and headword is clear.

MISPLACED MODIFIER	After you have finished talking about the assignment, write the directions for the students on the overhead projector. READER'S RESPONSE: Are the students on the overhead projector?
MOVED NEXT TO HEADWORD	After you have finished talking about the assignment, write the directions **on the overhead projector** for the students.
MISPLACED MODIFIER	People who abuse alcohol frequently have other problems. READER'S RESPONSE: Does *frequently* refer to the rate of alcohol abuse or the likelihood of problems?
REWRITTEN	People who abuse alcohol tend to have other problems as well.

1 Pay attention to a modifier's location

You can choose to word a sentence in many different ways to create emphasis and rhythm. With so many choices, don't be surprised if you position a modifier inappropriately on the first try. As you edit, therefore, check that modifiers are placed closely enough to their intended headwords that the relationship is clear. For example, the following draft sentence does not accurately convey its author's meaning.

DRAFT Following a divorce, toddlers demand to be fed often instead of feeding themselves.

While editing, the writer noticed that her sentence could be read as a statement that *all* toddlers regress after a divorce by demanding to be fed *often*. She moved the modifier *often* to make the sentence state clearly that demanding to be fed is a common though not universal response.

EDITED Following a divorce, toddlers **often** demand to be fed instead of feeding themselves.

22a
mm/dm

When you are drafting, you may occasionally add new ideas and details to the end of a sentence next to a word that seems to be a headword but is not the word you actually intend to modify.

MISPLACED MODIFIER The wife believes she sees a living figure behind the wallpaper in the story by Charlotte Perkins Gilman, which contributes to her sense of entrapment.
READER'S RESPONSE: This sounds as if the story itself causes a feeling of entrapment.

EDITED (MODIFIER MOVED) The wife **in the story by Charlotte Perkins Gilman** believes she sees a living figure behind the wallpaper, which contributes to her sense of entrapment.

EDITED (MODIFIER MOVED) **In the story by Charlotte Perkins Gilman,** the wife believes she sees a living figure behind the wallpaper, which contributes to her sense of entrapment.

You may sometimes draft sentences that present prepositional phrases or participial phrases (see 14c-1 and 14c-4) in confusing order.

CONFUSING It was not a good idea to serve food to the guests standing around the room on flimsy paper plates.
READER'S RESPONSE: Surely the guests were not standing on their plates!

| EDITED
(MODIFIER
MOVED) | It was not a good idea to serve food **on flimsy paper plates** to the guests standing around the room. |

Exercise 1

Identify and correct the misplaced modifiers (words or phrases) in the following sentences. You may decide to move the modifier or to rewrite the entire sentence.

EXAMPLE *in pet store windows*
Puppies͵spend a lot of time staring at people͵in pet store windows.

1. They decided to buy the beagle puppy confused by the many exotic breeds of dogs.
2. This dog would replace the one killed by a truck running across a busy highway.
3. They forgot to buy a dog bed distracted by the crowd of people in the store.
4. Hurriedly, John sighed and began tearing up newspapers in order to begin house-training the puppy.
5. The parents could hear the children playing outside with the dog yelling and laughing.

22a
mm/dm

2 Pay attention to limiting modifiers

You can alter the meaning of a sentence considerably by moving around words like *only, almost, hardly, just, scarcely, merely, simply, exactly,* and *even* (these are called **limiting modifiers**).

During this recession, **only** charities for disabled children are maintaining their normal levels of support.
They are the sole charities that have been able to maintain normal levels.

During this recession, charities for disabled **only** children are maintaining their normal levels of support.
The charities are for disabled children from families with one child.

During this recession, charities for disabled children are **only** maintaining their normal levels of support.
They are not increasing the levels of support.

Be ready to move a limiting modifier or rewrite a sentence to achieve the meaning you intend. Remember, a limiting modifier generally applies to the word that immediately follows, though not always.

22a
mm/dm

Did You Know?

In some languages, words change form to indicate their role in a sentence. In Latin or German, for example, the relationship between a modifier and the word being modified is generally clear from the form or ending of the words. In English, however, modifiers tend to change location, not form, to show which words they describe. As a result, a modifier's position in a sentence can make a big difference in the sentence's meaning. Checking on the position of modifiers as you edit is a challenging job even for professionals, such as magazine editors, as J. N. Hook points out.

Should you write "Smith only wanted one" or "Smith wanted only one"? A study by Bryant reported in 1962 that 86 percent of magazines placed *only* as in the second sentence. Logic supports that placement: it was *only one* that Smith wanted. Bryant added that in spoken English, sentences like the first predominated. Her findings, although dated, still appear valid.

J. N. Hook, *The Appropriate Word* (Reading, MA: Addison, 1990) 180.

3 Be alert for squinting modifiers

Readers become understandably confused when they encounter a modifier that appears to modify *both* the word or phrase that comes before it and the one that comes after. As you edit, look for **squinting modifiers** that present two possible meanings to readers, and rewrite to avoid possible confusion. To edit squinting modifiers, ask yourself which word or phrase you intend to modify, then move the modifier into a position that repairs the ambiguity.

SQUINTING MODIFIER	People who enjoy listening to Aaron Copland's music **often** claim that he was the finest American composer of the twentieth century.
	READER'S RESPONSE: Does this mean that they *listen often* to the music or that they *often claim* something about Copland?
EDITED	People who enjoy **listening often** to Aaron Copland's music also tend to claim that he was the finest American composer of the twentieth century.
EDITED	People who enjoy listening to Aaron Copland's music **will often** claim that he was the finest American composer of the twentieth century.

Exercise 2

A. Each of the following sentences contains either ambiguity caused by a squinting modifier or a limiting modifier that can be moved to different positions. Indicate the type of problem in each sentence.

EXAMPLE

A good car costs a lot of money often. *(limiting modifier)*

1. Five years ago, many people were interested only in buying fancy cars.
2. Today, anyone hardly has the money to buy a basic automobile, let alone a luxury car.
3. People who have big families frequently drive passenger vans.
4. Paying attention simply to a vehicle's initial price and likely trade-in value is not enough.
5. Anyone who buys cars infrequently may get a lemon.

B. Working with a group of other writers, edit the sentences in Exercise 2A by rewriting each in two different ways.

C. Edit a paper in progress of your own by circling limiting modifiers (see the list in 22a-2) and checking that their placement accurately reflects your intended meaning.

22a
mm/dm

4 Pay attention to dependent clauses

You should generally place a modifying clause beginning with *who, which,* or *that* right after its intended headword. (See relative clauses, 14a-2.) If you do not, the clause may modify the wrong word, creating unintended meanings.

MISPLACED MODIFIER
The environmental engineers discovered another tank behind the building that was leaking toxic wastes.

READER'S RESPONSE: I know a building can leak, but I'll bet the writer meant to identify the tank as the culprit.

EDITED
Behind the building, the environmental engineers discovered another tank that was leaking toxic wastes.

Modifying clauses that begin with other subordinators, such as *when, although, because, since,* and *while* (see 14a-8), allow you more flexibility in placement. Nonetheless, you still need to make sure the relationship between modifier and headword is clear.

MISPLACED MODIFIER	The company has decided to switch from the old health plan to one offered by a competing insurance company because premiums are rising rapidly.
EDITED	**Because premiums are rising rapidly,** the company has decided to switch from the old health plan to one offered by a competing insurance company.

Exercise 3

A. Revise the following sentences to eliminate any misplaced modifiers.

EXAMPLE

Sliding into second base, ~~my leg~~ broke.   *I*   *my leg*

1. The coach tossed out the practice balls to the players, wet and soft from yesterday's rain.
2. They worked on hitting and catching for fifteen minutes before the first game which was the only practice time they had.
3. The coach who was known as a strict disciplinarian of the championship Little League team invented a rigorous new set of conditioning exercises.
4. A proposal to follow the infield fly rule was defeated by the coach's committee which no one understood.
5. The coach is unable to present the award given in memory of Father Baker because he is sick.

B. Compare your edited versions of the sentences in Exercise 3A with those of other students. As a group, decide which versions you prefer and why you prefer them.

C. Underline any modifying clauses in a draft paper of your own, and check that they are placed closely enough to the words they modify. Edit any that create confusion or unintended meanings.

22b   Recognizing and editing dangling modifiers

If you begin a sentence with a modifying word or phrase that does not mention the person, idea, or thing being modified, readers will assume that the modifier refers to the subject of the main clause immediately following. When it does not do so—at least in a reasonable way—the modifier is a **dangling modifier.**

DANGLING MODIFIER	**Leaking in several places,** the scouts abandoned their tents for the dry cabin.
	READER'S RESPONSE: Surely the tents were leaking, not the scouts themselves.

EDITED   **Their tents** leaking in several places, the scouts decided to spend the night in the dry cabin.

EDITED   The scouts decided to spend the night in the dry cabin **because their tents were leaking in several places.**

Because they are often vague, illogical, or unintentionally humorous, dangling modifiers can needlessly distract readers. A sentence with a dangling modifier can also leave out important information.

DANGLING MODIFIER   Looking for a way to reduce the complaints from non-smokers, a new ventilation fan was installed.

READER'S RESPONSE: This sentence doesn't tell *who* is looking to reduce complaints, though the opening makes me expect such information.

EDITED   Looking for a way to reduce the complaints from non-smokers, **the company installed** a new ventilation fan.

Strategy

22b
mm/dm

To correct a dangling modifer, take *one* of the following steps.

1. Add a subject to the modifier.

   DANGLING   While shopping for a birthday gift for my brother, the stuffed alligator caught my eye.

   EDITED   While **I was** shopping for a birthday gift for my brother, the stuffed alligator caught my eye.

2. Or change the subject of the main clause.

   DANGLING   Trying to decide what to have for lunch, the hot dogs smelled delicious.

   EDITED   Trying to decide what to have for lunch, **I noticed** the hot dogs smelled delicious.

3. Or rewrite the entire sentence.

   DANGLING   Having debated changes in the regulations for several months without reaching a decision, the present standards were allowed to continue.

   EDITED   The commission debated changes in the regulations for several months without reaching a decision, then decided to allow the present standards to continue.

In checking your writing for dangling modifiers, remember that a modifier at the beginning of a sentence may also dangle when the word to which it should refer appears later in the sentence in some role other than the subject.

DANGLING MODIFIER

Jumping into the water to save the drowning swimmer, the crowd cheered the lifeguard.

EDITED (HEADWORD BECOMES SUBJECT)

Jumping into the water to save the drowning swimmer, **the lifeguard** was cheered by the crowd.

Remember, too, that a modifier in the body of a sentence dangles when the sentence contains no word or phrase to which it can reasonably refer.

DANGLING MODIFIER

The emergency repairs were completed by noon, having become aware of the problem only at ten o'clock.

READER'S RESPONSE: Who became aware of the problem?

EDITED (PHRASE ADDED)

The emergency repairs were completed by noon, **the telephone company** having become aware of the problem only at ten o'clock.

....

Exercise 4

A. Rewrite each of the following sentences in the *two* ways indicated in brackets in order to eliminate dangling modifiers.

EXAMPLE
Unable to meet with an advisor, ~~Marion's research was poorly designed~~.   *Marion designed her research poorly*.
[add subject to main clause; rewrite]
Because Marion was unable to meet with an advisor, she designed her research poorly.

1. Because of a failure to gather enough data, her study was incomplete. [rewrite; add subject to modifier]
2. Lacking the money to pay skilled interviewers, minimally trained volunteers were relied upon. [add subject to main clause; rewrite]
3. Many subjects were not asked appropriate questions because of poor training. [add subject to modifier; add subject to main clause]
4. Anxious and tired, the two-day attempt to write the research report was unsuccessful. [add subject to modifier; add subject to main clause]
5. After spending over twenty hours writing at the computer, the report was still not satisfactory. [rewrite; add subject to modifier]

B. Compare your edited versions of the sentences in Exercise 4A with those of another student, and decide which versions are the most successful and why.

C. Edit a paper in progress of your own by circling any dangling modifiers and correcting them.

22c Recognizing and editing disruptive modifiers

Readers generally expect subjects and verbs to stand close to each other in sentences. The same is true for verbs and their objects or complements. However, you can add variety and suspense to your sentences by using a brief interruption that provides relevant information.

CLEAR — The researcher, **unfamiliar with chimpanzees,** was surprised when they purposely undermined the experiment he was trying to conduct.

Longer interruptions and those with less relevant information can be **disruptive modifiers.**

DISRUPTIVE — The researcher, **because he had not worked with chimpanzees before and was therefore unaware of their intelligence,** was surprised when they purposely undermined the experiment he was trying to conduct.

Disruptive modifiers make a sentence difficult to understand when they come between subjects and verbs, verbs and objects, and verbs and complements. Disruptive modifiers also cause problems when they split infinitives or verb phrases.

1 Pay attention to separated subjects and verbs

Some modifiers placed between subject and verb are disruptive; others are not. How can you recognize the difference? Modifiers that provide information related to both the subject and the verb are disruptive when they appear between these elements. Modifiers that provide information related to the subject alone are generally not disruptive even when they come between subject and verb.

subject   modifier

DISRUPTIVE — Work on the building, **due to problems with the construc-**

verb

tion permits, was completed three months late.

	subject		modifier		verb

NOT DISRUPTIVE   The electronics store **that opened last month** has drawn crowds of customers.

Move a potentially disruptive modifier out of its position between subject and verb so that it no longer disrupts the flow of the sentence and makes it hard to understand.

DISRUPTIVE MODIFIER   Contractors, **because house building is a boom-or-bust business,** should be ready to do home repairs when housing starts are down.

EDITED (MODIFIER MOVED)   **Because house building is a boom-or-bust business,** contractors should be ready to do home repairs when housing starts are down.

In contrast, modifiers that are adjective phrases or relative clauses (see 14a-2 and 14c-5) simply add information to a subject, expanding the sentence without disruption, the way single-word adjectives work.

ADJECTIVES   **long and bitter** negotiations

ADJECTIVE CLAUSE   negotiations **that are long and bitter**

CLEAR   Negotiations **that are long and bitter** may lead to unsatisfactory contracts.

22c mm/dm

2 Pay attention to separations between verbs and objects or complements

Readers expect an object or complement to come right after the verb. If you split these elements with an adverb phrase or clause, you may create a sentence that seems clumsy or difficult, even if most readers are able to understand it.

CLUMSY   Joanne began collecting, **with special attention to survey results,** data for her study of dating preferences.

EDITED   **With special attention to survey results,** Joanne began collecting data for her study of dating preferences.

3 Be alert for split infinitives or verb phrases

If you split the parts of an infinitive (*to* plus a verb, as in *to run* or *to enjoy*), you may make it hard for readers to understand the relationship between the parts.

UNCLEAR   The office designer tried **to** respectively **address** each of the workers' concerns.

EDITED   The office designer tried **to address** each of the workers' concerns **respectively.**

Even when such a **split infinitive** is easy to understand, you might consider revising it because some readers find split infinitives irritating.

IRRITATING   When the lead Canada goose changes direction in flight, all the rest of the geese move **to** <u>very rapidly</u> **align** themselves with it.

EDITED   When the lead Canada goose changes direction in flight, all the rest of the geese move <u>very rapidly</u> **to align** themselves with it.

At times, however, you may discover that a split infinitive is the clearest and most concise way of phrasing a statement.

Our goal is to more than halve our manufacturing errors.

The alternatives are more wordy and complicated—for example, "Our goal is a rate of manufacturing error less than half the present rate."

You usually cause no difficulty for readers if you separate the parts of a verb phrase (helping verb plus main verb, as in *had been digging*) by adding one or more adverbs.

22c
mm/dm

CLEAR   The archaeologists had been **carefully** digging at the site for three years.

Longer word groups within a verb phrase may be disruptive, however.

DISRUPTED   The archaeologists <u>had been,</u> **because of initial discoveries made during construction of a new house,** <u>digging</u> at the site for three years.

CLEAR   **Because of initial discoveries made during the construction of a new house,** archaeologists <u>had been digging</u> at the site for three years.

....

Exercise 5

A. Rewrite each of the following sentences to eliminate disruptive modifiers and to make the sentence easier to read and understand.

EXAMPLE
~~The architect,~~ ᵦbecause she was unfamiliar with eighteenth-century
                    the architect
interior design and furnishings,ₐhad to do some research before completing the project.

1. The overall design of a building and its interior decoration ought to thoughtfully and harmoniously work together.
2. Furniture design has at least for the past several centuries been greatly influenced by a handful of designers, including Hepplewhite, Chippendale, Sheraton, and, most recently, Eames.
3. Design in Colonial America, because of economic limitations and social customs, was generally simple and practical.
4. Americans had, by the early 1800s in what is now known as the Federalist period, developed more refined and expensive tastes.
5. Today, magazines like *Architectural Digest* and *House Beautiful* illustrate the tendency for styles in interior design to rapidly change and to add considerably to the cost of a home.

 B. Working with a group of fellow writers, compare your revisions of the sentences in Exercise 5A. Decide which versions you prefer and why.

 C. Edit a paper in progress of your own by underlining any disruptive modifiers and then rewriting the sentences containing them.

22d   Using absolute phrases effectively

An **absolute phrase** consists of a noun or pronoun, a participle, and modifiers (for example, *the water level rising* and *her view of market conditions changing almost daily*). An absolute phrase qualifies or limits an entire sentence rather than a specific word or group of words. (See 14c-2.)

> **The water level rising,** people in the valley feared that the dam was about to burst.
> The absolute phrase sets the scene for the rest of the sentence.

> The stockbroker began pelting her clients with urgent and sometimes contradictory advice, **her view of market conditions changing almost daily.**
> The absolute phrase provides a context for the behavior described in the first part of the sentence.

Because absolute phrases do not modify a particular word, you may be tempted to avoid using them for fear of creating dangling modifiers. An absolute phrase provides its own noun or pronoun subject, however, so it does not dangle. Absolute phrases are expressions that can add variety and flair to your writing.

CHAPTER

23

Shifts

In most kinds of writing, you are likely to ask readers to shift their attention many times. For example, you might ask them to focus first on events occurring in the past, then on those occurring in the present or likely to occur in the future. Or you might ask readers to consider your point of view ("I argue that this solution is unworkable") and then ask them to reject the perspective offered by others ("They made their proposal without considering the practical consequences").

As long as shifts such as these are consistent and are signaled clearly, your readers should have little trouble following them. You can mislead readers, however, if you are inconsistent or confusing when you signal **shifts** in pronoun form, verb form, or direct and indirect quotation. You may even cause readers to doubt your authority and ability as a writer.

23a Keeping person and number consistent

In grammatical terms, **person** refers to the ways you can use pronouns and nouns to shape the relationship involving you, your readers, and your subject.

- **First person (*I, we*).** Use *I* to refer to yourself as the writer or the person whose experiences and perceptions are the subject of an essay. *We* is appropriate when more than one person is author or subject. You may use *we* to refer to both yourself and your readers when you are discussing shared experiences or understandings. This use of *we* is appropriate in some academic fields, such as the study of literature ("At this point in reading the novel, we begin realizing that Amelia is not the self-sacrificing person she seemed to be in the opening chapters"). It is not appropriate in other fields, such as chemistry or engineering.

- **Second person (*you*).** Use *you* to refer directly to the reader ("you, the reader"). In most kinds of formal writing, including academic and professional writing, readers will consider *you* inappropriate unless it is called for by the situation, as in a set of instructions.

- **Third person (*he, she, it, they; one, someone, each,* and other indefinite pronouns).** Use third person pronouns for the ideas, things, and people you are writing about. *People* and *person* are third person nouns, as are names of groups of things, ideas, and people (for example, *students, teachers, doctors*).

1 Pay attention to shifts in person

Watch out for unwarranted shifts in person in your writing. In particular, look for inconsistencies created by illogical shifts between first and second person or between second and third person.

<table>
<tr><td>INCONSISTENT</td><td>**I** am thinking of taking out a two-year certificate of deposit because **you** can get a high interest rate on it.

READER'S RESPONSE: I don't think the writer means that *she* bought the certificate of deposit because *someone else* can get a good interest rate.</td></tr>
<tr><td>EDITED</td><td>**I** am thinking of taking out a two-year certificate of deposit because **I** can get a high interest rate on it.</td></tr>
<tr><td>INCONSISTENT</td><td>If a **person** is looking for a higher interest rate on certificates of deposit, **you** might consider the securities offered by stockbrokers.</td></tr>
<tr><td>EDITED</td><td>If **you** are looking for a higher interest rate on certificates of deposit, **you** might consider the securities offered by stockbrokers.</td></tr>
</table>

23a
shift

2 Pay attention to shifts in number

To keep your sentences logical and consistent, check that pronouns and their antecedents agree in number (see 17c). Writers often make shifts in number when using nouns that identify groups or members of a group, such as *business executives* or *a student.*

<table>
<tr><td>SHIFTED</td><td>When **a business executive** is looking for a new job, **they** often consult a placement service.

READER'S RESPONSE: I think this writer had business executives in mind as a group and referred to them as *they,* even though the sentence mentions only one *business executive.*</td></tr>
</table>

EDITED   When **business executives are** looking for **new jobs, they** often consult a placement service.

Words like *person* and *people* often cause difficulty. Remember that *person* is singular and *people* is plural.

SHIFTED   If **a person has** some money to invest, **they** should seek advice from a financial consultant.

EDITED   If **a person has** some money to invest, **he or she** should seek advice from a financial consultant.
READER'S RESPONSE: I know *he or she* is correct, but it seems more complicated than it needs to be.

EDITED   If **people have** some money to invest, **they** should seek advice from a financial consultant.

Exercise 1

A. Rewrite the following sentences to make them consistent in person and number.

EXAMPLE   *People have*
~~Each person has~~ ᴧtheir favorite fast-food restaurants.

1. A would-be restaurant owner often fails to carefully consider the competition they will face from other restaurants of all kinds, both fancy and informal.
2. Good franchise chains survey competition, tell potential owners how much money they will need to open the business, and help you with the many problems a restaurant owner faces.
3. Admittedly, running a doughnut shop or a pizza place gives one less prestige than you get from owning a gourmet restaurant.
4. I would still rather run a successful business than one where you lose money.
5. Not all franchise arrangements are good ones, so people should do some research before he or she decides to open a franchised restaurant.

B. Working with a group of fellow students, write a brief paragraph on a topic of general interest. Choose a topic about which the group members have some knowledge, for example, finding a good summer job, developing effective study habits, or buying good clothing cheaply. Then rewrite the paragraph so it contains several nouns and pronouns that do not agree in person and number. Give a copy of the faulty paragraph to another group as a "quiz." Correct the paragraph they have created, in turn, for you.

**23a
shift**

23b   Keeping tense and mood consistent

The **tense** of a verb indicates time as past, present, or future. The **mood** of a verb indicates the writer's aim or attitude (see 16b and 16c).

1 Pay attention to shifts in tense

When you change verb tense within a sentence or group of sentences, you signal a change in time and the relationship of events in time. (See 16a and 16b.)

> Until synthetic fabrics like nylon, rayon, and Dacron **were invented** in the 1930s and 1940s, clothes **had been made** primarily of natural fabrics. Blends of synthetics with linen, cotton, or wool now **dominate** the clothing industry and **will** probably **be** the most popular textiles in the coming decade.

Watch out for unnecessary, illogical shifts that can mislead your readers and that contradict your meaning.

23b shift

ILLOGICAL SHIFT   Scientists digging in Montana **discovered** nests and clutches of eggs that **indicate** how some dinosaurs **take care** of their young.

Indicate (present tense) is appropriate because the scientists and others interpret the evidence in the present. *Take care* (present tense) is inappropriate because the actions of the dinosaurs clearly occurred in the past.

LOGICAL   Scientists digging in Montana **discovered** nests and clutches of eggs that **indicate** how some dinosaurs **took care** of their young.

In particular, if you begin by narrating events in the past tense, avoid shifting suddenly to the present tense under the mistaken assumption that this will make the events seem more vivid.

TENSE SHIFT   We had been digging at the Dry Gulch site for several weeks without finding any further evidence of dinosaur bones when suddenly Tonia **starts yelling,** "Eggs! I think I've found fossil eggs!"

EDITED   We had been digging at the Dry Gulch site for several weeks without finding any further evidence of dinosaur bones when suddenly Tonia **started yelling,** "Eggs! I think I've found fossil eggs!"

2 Watch out for tense shifts in indirect quotation

In an **indirect quotation** you *report* what someone has said. You don't quote word for word as you do in **direct quotation.** Use the past tense for indirect quotations.

DIRECT	In 1980, a report from the state Department of Commerce said, "The region will lose one-third of its manufacturing jobs over the next ten years."
INDIRECT (TENSE INCONSISTENT)	In 1980, a report from the state Department of Commerce says that the region **will** lose one of every three factory jobs over the next ten years.
INDIRECT (EDITED)	In 1980, a report from the state Department of Commerce said that the region **would** lose one of every three factory jobs over the next ten years.

In contrast, use the present tense when you summarize or comment on events and information from a written work or from another source, such as a film or television show.

INCONSISTENT	At the beginning of the novel, Ishmael **arrives** at New Bedford with the intention of shipping out on a whaler, which he soon **did.**
CONSISTENT	At the beginning of the novel, Ishmael **arrives** at New Bedford with the intention of shipping out on a whaler, which he soon **does.**

23b shift

Did You Know?

Watching for inappropriate shifts is one job done by the copy editor who reads and corrects an author's manuscript, preparing it for publication. According to Elsie Myers Stainton, one of the dangers a copy editor should look for is "mixing tenses." She says the work of any author, living or dead, may be discussed as

living, existing in the present. . . . The choice of tense usually depends upon a nearby verb: "Whitman *was* just a clerk in the Attorney General's office, but he *said,* 'I celebrate myself.'" If excerpts are quoted from the poet's work as though from the living present, the present tense can be used: "Whitman *says:* 'Sing on, there in the swamp!/O singer bashful and tender!'" (54).

Elsie Myers Stainton, *The Fine Art of Copyediting* (New York: Columbia UP, 1991).

3 Be alert for shifts in mood

The term *mood* refers to the forms a verb takes according to your purpose in a sentence: to make a command or a request (**imperative mood**), to present a statement or question (**indicative mood**), or to offer a conditional or hypothetical statement (**subjunctive mood**). (See 16b-3.)

If you shift mood inappropriately, your sentences will be inconsistent and difficult for readers to follow.

INCONSISTENT   It is essential that our small company **cut** costs and **increases** revenue.

        Sentence shifts from subjunctive to indicative.

EDITED   It is essential that our small company **cut** costs and **increase** revenue.

Watch especially for shifts from the imperative to the indicative when you give directions. If you use the imperative consistently, your directions will be less wordy and easier to understand.

INCONSISTENT   To reduce costs for office supplies, **order** reusable ribbons for printers, and **you should** encourage employees to use electronic mail in place of paper memos.

CONSISTENT   To reduce costs for office supplies, **order** reusable ribbons for printers, and **encourage** employees to use electronic mail in place of paper memos.

**23b
shift**

Exercise 2

A. Rewrite the following sentences to make them consistent in tense and mood.

EXAMPLE

                                       couldn't
I went to the video store last week, and after half an hour I still ∧can't
                    wanted
figure out which movies I∧want.

1. The video store manager said that if I bought two tapes I will get a third one free, and then he tells me about several of his favorite tapes.
2. In the movie *Sacrifice for Glory,* set in World War II, a British Mosquito bomber crashes in the jungle, and only the copilot managed to survive the long walk through the tropical heat back to civilization.
3. The hot sun beat on the shoulders of the copilot as he wades through the waist-deep, crocodile-infested swamp.

4. At the beginning of *Ghostbusters,* the three main characters have jobs as researchers, but later on they founded a company ridding people and places of ghosts.

5. In *Ghoulish Lunch,* the main character was reaching into the refrigerator around the guacamole dip for the last piece of apple pie when suddenly a cockroach crawls out from under the crust.

B. In a newspaper or magazine, locate a brief review of a movie, performance, book, or recording. Make sure the review contains numerous shifts in tense and mood. Make a copy of the review to share with a group of fellow students. After looking over all the reviews brought in by the group, choose one with particularly complex shifts. As a group, identify each shift and describe its nature. Continue working through as many reviews as you can.

C. If inappropriate tense shifts are frequently a problem in your writing, underline the verbs in a draft paper, then check whether any changes in tense are appropriate.

23c Keeping voice consistent

When a verb is in the **active voice,** the agent or doer of the action functions as the sentence's subject; when a verb is in the **passive voice,** the goal of the action functions as the sentence's subject. (See 16d.)

ACTIVE
         subject   verb   object
        The lava flow **destroyed** twelve houses.
         agent   action   goal

PASSIVE
         subject   verb
        Twelve houses **were destroyed** [by the lava flow].
         goal   action   [agent]

In general, stick to either active or passive voice within a sentence, and be alert for unwarranted shifts as you edit. In shifting between active and passive, you risk blurring a sentence's focus and confusing readers.

                                           active
INCONSISTENT   Among the active volcanoes, Kilauea **erupts** most frequently,
                           passive
        and over 170 houses **have been destroyed** since 1983.

READER'S RESPONSE: The first part of the sentence focuses on Kilauea, but the volcano is not mentioned in the second part. Did Kilauea alone destroy the houses, or were some of the other volcanoes mentioned at the start also responsible?

EDITED   Among the active volcanoes, Kilauea has erupted most frequently in recent years, and **it has destroyed** over 170
houses since 1983.

Occasionally, you may need to shift between active and passive voice
to highlight a sentence's subject or emphasize your meaning.

                active   active

UNEMPHATIC   Volcanic activity **built** Hawaii, and the island still **has** active
volcanoes.

      The sentence seems to shift subjects from *volcanic activity* in the first part
to *the island* in the second part.

               passive

EDITED   Hawaii **was built** by volcanic activity, and the island still
        active
has active volcanoes.

      The shift between passive and active voice keeps Hawaii as the sen-
tence's focus.

Writer's Tip

    When you write instructions, watch out for shifts between
active and passive voice that make sentences hard to follow.

CONFUSING   **You can purchase** the necessary hiking clothes
from any good outdoor equipment store, and picks,
specimen bags, and other useful rock-collecting
equipment **may be obtained** through a mail-order
geological supply company.

EDITED   **You can purchase** the necessary hiking clothes
from any good outdoor equipment store, and **you
can obtain** picks, specimen bags, and other useful rock-collecting equipment through a mail-order
geological supply company.

Exercise 3

A. Rewrite the following sentences to make them consistent in voice.

EXAMPLE
                             and   *much*
We enjoyed the expedition, ~~and much was~~ learned about fossils.

1. In the morning we dug in the base of the ravine, and during the
afternoon the walls were explored.
2. The team found fossils of trilobites, and other fossils were also
found at the site.

3. Team members learned many things about the science of pale-ontology, and much was learned about the geological history of our area as well.

4. A chart helped in identifying fossilized animals, and we also learned useful identifying strategies from the lecture given by Bill Gonzales, the team leader.

5. After you fill out the application for next month's dig, the form should be given to Bill or sent to his office.

B. Working in a group, use the sentences in Exercise 3A as the basis for a brief narrative telling the story of the "dig." Add sentences to fill in the information needed to make the story believable and interesting. Make your narrative consistent in voice.

C. Review a draft paper of your own, and place a check mark at the beginning of every sentence that contains a shift between active and passive voice. Then return to these sentences and edit the paper by eliminating any unwarranted shifts in voice.

23d Avoiding shifts between direct and indirect quotation

**23d
shift**

In direct quotation you present a speaker's or writer's ideas and feelings in that person's exact words, setting the material off by using quotation marks. Through indirect quotation you report the substance of what the speaker or writer said, but you put it into your own words and do not use quotation marks.

DIRECT   According to the writer Adam Frank, stars "form deep within clouds of interstellar gas and dust so dense and opaque that no visible light can escape."

INDIRECT   The writer Adam Frank points out that stars develop inside thick gas and dust clouds which trap all perceivable light.

Try to avoid mixing direct and indirect quotation within sentences, and edit any mixed sentences in order to make them less confusing and easier to read.

MIXED   Writing about the Teenage Mutant Ninja Turtles, Phil Patton names cartoonists Peter Laird and Kevin Eastman as their creators and says, "They were born quietly in 1983, in the kitchen of a New England farmhouse."

EDITED   Writing about the Teenage Mutant Ninja Turtles, Phil Patton says, "Cartoonists named Peter Laird and Kevin Eastman dreamed up the characters," who "were born quietly in 1983, in the kitchen of a New England farmhouse."

Be especially alert for sentences that mix indirect and direct quotations without using quotation marks to indicate the difference.

CONFUSING
Before we set out on our glacier hike, the guide told us to stay in line, and you should obey all orders immediately.

EDITED TO INDIRECT QUOTATION
Before we set out on our glacier hike, the guide told us to stay in line and to follow every order right away.

EDITED TO DIRECT QUOTATION
Before we set out on our glacier hike, the guide told us, "You should stay in line and obey all orders immediately."

....

Exercise 4

**23d
shift**

A. Rewrite each of the following sentences twice. First use direct quotation consistently, and then use indirect quotation consistently. (Feel free to invent direct quotations in order to complete the exercise. Be sure to change direct quotations into your own words when you present them as indirect quotations.)

EXAMPLE
The article began by saying, "People often fear bees," and that this fear is a result of ignorance.

The article began by saying, "People often fear bees, and this fear comes from ignorance."

The article began by saying that the widespread fear of bees is caused by ignorance.

1. I once heard a beekeeper claim that unless beekeeping becomes more popular as a hobby, "I believe that agriculture in this country may suffer."
2. At a meeting last night, the county agriculture commissioner argued that increased beekeeping would aid agriculture in our area and "We should be willing to provide beekeepers with financial support for their efforts."
3. Having eaten honey every day for sixty years, my grandfather says, "I may not look as good as I did when I was younger," but that he feels just as good.
4. My grandfather also says that he has stayed mentally alert because "I manage a large beekeeping and honey business."

5. My neighbor told me, if you are too busy to sell your honey at a roadside stand I should see if the supermarket in town would sell it for me.

 B. Share your edited sentences from Exercise 4A with a group of your fellow students. Decide which versions of each sentence are best and why.

 C. Review a draft paper of your own to identify any unwarranted shifts between direct and indirect quotation, and correct any such errors.

**23d
shift**

Mixed and Incomplete Sentences

When someone you are talking with switches topics abruptly, you can ask for an explanation. When you are reading, however, you can't ask the author to explain a confusing shift of topic that comes in the middle of a sentence, as in the following.

SHIFTED TOPIC   One **skill** I envy is **a person** who can study despite noise and other distractions.

Clearly, a *skill* is not a *person*.

EDITED   One **skill** I envy is **the ability** to study despite noise and other distractions.

Just as confusing are sentences that begin with one grammatical pattern, then shift to another.

SHIFTED
STRUCTURE   Because the new television show did poorly in the ratings **explains why** programming executives decided to move it to a slot between two hit shows.

EDITED   Because the new television show did poorly in the ratings **programming executives** decided to move it to a slot between two hit shows.

Sentences with mismatched topics or with shifted grammatical structures (both referred to as mixed sentences) confuse readers by undermining sentence patterns they rely on. Incomplete sentences do much the same. An **incomplete sentence** either lacks grammatical completeness, in which case it is a fragment (see Chapter 19), or omits wording necessary to make a logically complete and consistent statement. For example, if you start by saying, "X is larger," you should be ready to complete the comparison: "X is larger *than* Y."

INCOMPLETE   When they are first introduced, high-definition televisions are likely to cost three times as much.

           READER'S RESPONSE: Are the new TVs likely to cost more when they are first introduced than they will cost later? Or are they likely to cost more than TVs being sold now?

EDITED   When they are first introduced, high-definition televisions are likely to cost three times as much **as the most expensive TV sets currently available.**

Spotting mixed and incomplete sentences in your writing may require extra effort. Because you know what your sentences are supposed to mean, you may mentally supply missing elements or compensate for shifts as you read your own work and thus mistakenly treat your sentences as correct.

24a   Editing mixed sentences

24a
mixed

Mixed sentences shift topics or grammatical structures without warning and for no clear reason. They throw readers off the track and make illogical statements. To recognize and edit mixed sentences, you need to keep certain basic sentence patterns in mind and watch for a number of troublesome phrases.

1 Recognizing topic shifts

In most sentences, the subject announces a topic, and the predicate comments on or renames the topic.

             subject   predicate
The Old PC Network publishes a newsletter about outdated computers.
             topic   comment

           subject   predicate
The Kaypro 64 is an out-of-date (but useful) computer.
      topic   topic renamed

You create confusion if you mistakenly make each part of a sentence address a *different* subject. In a sentence with a **topic shift** (**faulty predication**), the second part of a sentence comments on or names a topic different from the one announced at the beginning of the sentence. As a result, readers are likely to have trouble deciding on the true focus of the sentence.

SHIFTED TOPIC   The **presence** of ozone in smog is the **chemical** that causes eye irritation.
Presence is not a chemical, though that is what the sentence says.

EDITED   The **ozone** in smog is the **chemical** that causes eye irritation.

Strategy

To identify shifted topics, try asking the question "Who does what?" or "What is it?" If the answer is illogical, the sentence needs editing.

SHIFTED TOPIC   In this factory, **flaws** in the product noticed by any worker **can stop** the assembly line with the flip of a switch.
QUESTION: Who does what? Certainly flaws can't stop the line or flip a switch.

EDITED   In this factory, **any worker** who notices flaws in the product **can stop** the assembly line with the flip of a switch.

SHIFTED   An **actuary** is the **process** of determining insurance risks and premiums.
QUESTION: What is it? An actuary is a person, not a process.

REVISED   An **actuary** is a **person** who determines insurance risks and premiums.

**24a
mixed**

2 Editing topic shifts

In general, you can eliminate problems with mixed sentences by making sure the topic in both parts of a sentence, subject and predicate, is the same. Most mixed sentences follow one of a small number of common patterns, and for these sentences the following tips on editing may prove helpful.

Rename the Subject. In building a sentence around the verb *be* (*is, are, was, were*), you may use the sentence predicate to rename the subject. When you do, make sure the topics on each side of the verb are roughly equivalent, as in the following sentence.

Jane Goodall is a **scientist** whose work has added to our understanding of chimpanzee behavior.

If the topics are not equivalent, edit the sentence by making sure the second part of the sentence renames the topic that appears in the first part.

SHIFTED TOPIC   **Irradiation** is **food** that is preserved by the use of radiation.

EDITED   **Irradiation** is a **process** that can be used to preserve food.

Cut *Is When* or *Is Where*. In building a definition around the verb *is*, you need to balance the topics on each side of the verb.

noun (noun phrase,   noun (noun phrase,
pronoun)   verb   pronoun)

In field events, a **hammer**   **is**   a **steel ball** (like the one used in shot put events) attached to a chain.

Is when and *is where* make this kind of balance impossible. Cut them and rewrite to balance the topics.

NOT BALANCED   **Blocking** is **when** a television network schedules a less popular program between two popular ones.

EDITED   **Blocking** is the **practice** of scheduling a less popular television program between two popular ones.

24a
mixed

Did You Know?

Few things are as distressing to readers as a sentence that starts out in one direction, then abruptly shifts to another. In her classic study *Errors and Expectations,* Mina Shaughnessy devoted a long discussion to the ways writers and readers can be derailed within sentences containing mixed structures. The mixed and incomplete patterns described in this chapter provide a small (but useful) start at an understanding of sentence strategies to avoid or correct in your writing. Because the number of potential mixed and incomplete structures is so great, perhaps the best overall advice we can give you is to reread your work carefully (aloud, if possible), trying to view it as a reader or listener might.

Mina Shaughnessy, *Errors and Expectations* (New York: Oxford UP, 1977).

Omit *The Reason . . . Is Because*. In informal conversation, the phrase *the reason . . . is because* causes little confusion. In writing, however, readers will recognize that it creates an illogical statement. A phrase opening with *because* is a modifying phrase that cannot logically rename the subject (topic) of the first part of a sentence. Its job is to modify, not rename.

NOT LOGICAL   One **reason** for research into alternative fuels **is because** of the need to reduce air pollution.

EDITED   One **reason** for research into alternative fuels is **the need** to reduce air pollution.

Strategy

To edit sentences containing *the reason . . . is because,* either rewrite the entire sentence or use one of these patterns.

- Drop *the reason . . . is.*

    INCORRECT   The **reason** he took up figure skating **is because** he wanted something to do during the long winter.

    EDITED   He took up figure skating **because** he wanted something to do during the long winter.

- Change *because* to *that.*

    EDITED   The **reason** he took up figure skating **is that** he wanted something to do during the long winter.

24a
mixed

Edit for Intervening Words. Watch out for words or phrases coming between the subject and the verb. Writers sometimes mistake these intervening words for the actual sentence topic.

SHIFTED TOPIC   Programming **decisions** by television executives generally keep in mind the need to gain audience share.
    READER'S RESPONSE: I know that network executives can keep an audience in mind, but according to this sentence it is programming decisions that are thinking about the viewers.

EDITED   **Television executives** making programming decisions generally **keep** in mind the need to gain audience share.

EDITED   When **they are making** programming decisions, **television executives** generally **keep** in mind the need to gain audience share.

Exercise 1

A. Rewrite the following sentences to eliminate topic shifts.

EXAMPLE

Hides ~~that are~~ treated with tanning chemicals turn ~~them~~ into leather.

1. Tanning is when animal hide is made supple and resistant to decay.
2. The first step is when the hides are thoroughly scraped and cleaned.
3. The use of diluted acid is the substance that pickles the hides to prepare them for tanning.
4. The reason leather is supple is because it is lubricated with oil after pickling, then dried and impregnated with resins.
5. The final steps are when the leather is dyed and given a shiny surface through compression.

B. Compare your edited sentences for Exercise 1A with those produced by other writers. Decide which versions you prefer and why you prefer them.

3 Recognizing mixed grammatical patterns

Occasionally, you may begin a sentence with one grammatical pattern in mind only to shift to another partway through. The resulting sentence confuses readers.

MIXED

Because of the rebellious atmosphere generated by protests against the Vietnam war helps explain the often outrageous fashions of the time.

READER'S RESPONSE: When I encounter a word like *because,* I expect it to modify or qualify a main clause. But this sentence doesn't contain a main clause for it to modify. Besides, the sentence says the same thing twice: *because* and *helps explain.*

EDITED (MAIN CLAUSE ADDED)

Because of the rebellious atmosphere generated by protests against the Vietnam war, **fashions of the time became outrageous.**

EDITED (REWRITTEN)

The rebellious **atmosphere** generated by protests against the Vietnam war **helps explain** the often outrageous fashions of the time.

Mixed grammatical constructions can take so many forms that you may find them difficult to recognize and edit. The three suggestions in this Strategy may be useful, however.

24a
mixed

Strategy

- Pay attention to the *meaning* of sentences, checking that all the elements, especially subjects and predicates, stand in clear and reasonable relationships to each other. Read aloud sentences that seem potentially confusing.

- Ask, "What is the topic of this sentence, and how does the rest of the sentence comment on or rename the topic?"
- Check that the sentence clearly indicates who does what to whom.

MIXED   By wearing bell-bottom pants, love beads, long hair, and tie-dyed T-shirts was how many young people expressed their opposition to mainstream values.
This sentence ought to be edited to make clear who did what to whom.

EDITED   By wearing bell-bottom pants, love beads, long hair, and tie-dyed T-shirts, many young people expressed their opposition to mainstream values.

4 Editing mixed grammatical patterns

Because sentences can mix grammatical patterns in many different ways, you may have to study a mixed sentence carefully in order to decide how to edit it. Nonetheless, the next four Strategies for editing the following kinds of mixed sentences are relatively easy to use.

**24a
mixed**

Rewrite Sentences That Begin Twice. When writers try to give more emphasis to a topic than is allowed by a sentence's structure, they often mistakenly start the sentence over again, treating the sentence's object as a second subject.

Strategy 1

Rewrite the sentence, moving most or all of the information in one of the two main clauses to a modifying phrase or clause.

MIXED   **The new procedures for testing cosmetics, we** designed them to avoid cruelty to laboratory animals.
READER'S RESPONSE: It seems like the writer starts this sentence twice.

EDITED   **We** designed **the new procedures for testing cosmetics** to avoid cruelty to laboratory animals.

EDITED   **The new procedures for testing cosmetics** were designed to avoid cruelty to laboratory animals.

Edit Whole Sentences Used as Subjects. Another way writers mistakenly give emphasis to a topic is to put it in a complete sentence (main clause) used incorrectly as the subject of another sentence.

Strategy 2

Rewrite the sentence so that most or all of the information in one of the two main clauses appears instead in a modifying phrase or clause.

MIXED

In 1872, Claude Monet exhibited the painting *Impression, Sunrise* was the source of the term *Impressionism*.

EDITED (PHRASE CREATED)

The source of the term *Impressionism* was the painting *Impression, Sunrise*, **exhibited by Claude Monet in 1872.**

EDITED (CLAUSE CREATED)

In 1872, Claude Monet exhibited the painting *Impression, Sunrise*, **which was the source of the term *Impressionism*.**

Rewrite Adverb Phrases or Clauses Used as Subjects. When readers encounter a phrase like "By designing the questionnaire carefully" at the beginning of a sentence, they expect it to be followed by the sentence's subject. They do not expect it to act as the subject.

Strategy 3

Either add a new subject, or alter the form of the phrase so that it can act as a subject.

	adverb phrase
MIXED	**By designing the questionnaire carefully** made Valerie's psychology study a success.
EDITED	By designing the questionnaire carefully, **Valerie made** her psychology study a success.
EDITED	The **careful design** of the questionnaire **made** Valerie's psychology study a success.

Similarly, readers expect a clause introduced by a subordinating conjunction such as *when, because, if, while, as,* or *despite* (adverb clauses) to be followed by a main clause, not to act as a sentence subject.

Strategy 4

Either add a subject, or rewrite the sentence by dropping the subordinating word and turning the introductory clause into a subject.

MIXED   subordinate clause
Even if an audition gets off to a bad start does not mean giving up hope of getting the part.

EDITED (SUBJECT ADDED)
Even if an audition gets off to a bad start, **you** should not give up hope of getting the part.

EDITED (SUBORDINATING WORD DROPPED)
An audition that gets off to a bad start does not mean you should give up hope of getting the part.

◄►

Exercise 2

A. Rewrite the following sentences to eliminate shifts in grammatical pattern.

EXAMPLE
                                                            ~~S~~
~~Many people used to die from infectious diseases was why~~ ~~s~~cientists
worked hard to develop vaccination~~s~~, *because many people used*
                    to die from infectious diseases.

1. By observing that farm workers who had had cowpox were resistant to smallpox led Jenner to develop an inoculation for smallpox in the 1790s.
2. Paying attention to Jenner's methods was why Pasteur was able to develop vaccines for chicken pox, rabies, and human anthrax.
3. Vaccinations produce antibodies are the sources of immunity.
4. Because they are not effective against all infections means that vaccinations are not a perfect solution for diseases.
5. Making sure your vaccinations are up to date, you need to do this during your regular medical checkup.

B. In a group, compare your edited sentences for Exercise 2A with those produced by other writers. Identify those edited versions you consider correct, consistent, and clear.

C. Make a checklist of the kinds of topic shifts and mixed grammatical patterns discussed in 24a-1 through 24a-4. Then edit a paper in progress, using the list to help you spot problems.

24b   Editing incomplete sentences

Incomplete sentences fail to complete an expected logical pattern, such as a comparison, or they leave out words necessary to the meaning or logic of a statement. They make readers do extra, unnecessary work. (Sentences missing a *grammatical* element are fragments; see Chapter 19.)

1 Avoiding incomplete and illogical comparisons

When readers encounter a written comparison, they expect to learn something about the relationship of the things being compared, as in the following sentence.

> The long-term costs for inexpensive, moderately reliable computers are greater than those for expensive, highly reliable computers.

If you create comparisons that are incomplete or illogical, you disappoint your readers' expectations and make them work harder to understand your writing.

Supply the Elements Missing from an Incomplete Comparison. You create an **incomplete comparison** when you omit one of the items being compared.

INCOMPLETE   The sound quality of the new digital audiotapes is much better.
    READER'S RESPONSE: The tapes are better than what? Than they used to be? Than the old analog tapes? Than CDs?

EDITED   The sound quality of the new digital audiotapes is much better than **that of the older analog tapes.**

You also create an incomplete comparison when you omit a word or words necessary to complete a comparison or make it clear.

AMBIGUOUS   The most experienced members of the maintenance staff respect the new supervisor more than their fellow workers.
    READER'S RESPONSE: Do the experienced staff members respect the supervisor more than they respect their fellow workers, or do they respect the supervisor more than their fellow workers do?

CLEAR   The most experienced members of the maintenance staff respect the new supervisor more **than do** their fellow workers.

CLEAR   The most experienced members of the maintenance staff respect the new supervisor more highly **than they respect** their fellow workers.

To edit either kind of incomplete comparison, you must provide the missing element. However, you can omit part of the wording of a comparison

**24b
inc**

when the meaning is clear without it and when the meaning can be easily inferred by readers.

> **CLEAR**   Most customers like dealing with a bank teller better than [dealing with] a machine.
>
> The second *dealing with* can be left out because the sentence has only one possible meaning.

Correct Illogical Comparisons. An **illogical comparison** seems to be comparing things that cannot be reasonably compared.

To make seemingly illogical comparisons reasonable, consider either filling in the missing words or using the possessive.

> **ILLOGICAL**
>
> Even a small hamburger's fat content is higher than a skinless chicken breast.
>
> **READER'S RESPONSE:** The writer probably wants to compare the fat content of two foods, but the sentence actually compares one *kind* of food (chicken breast) to the *fat content* of the other.

> **EDITED (WORDS PROVIDED)**
>
> The fat content of even a small hamburger is higher than **that of** a skinless chicken breast.

> **EDITED (POSSESSIVE USED)**
>
> Even a small **hamburger's** fat content is higher than a skinless chicken **breast's.**

Make Comparisons Within and Between Groups Logical. When you are comparing items belonging to the *same group,* you need to distinguish each item (for example, field hockey) from other members of the class to which it belongs (all *other* team sports). Otherwise, the comparison will be illogical.

In making such distinctions, the word *other* serves to keep the two things separate by marking off the group as a whole from one of its members.

> Field hockey has a higher percentage of women players than does any **other** team sport.

Therefore, if you leave out the word *other* when comparing members of a group or class, your comparison will be illogical.

> **ILLOGICAL**   At times, more cargo was loaded onto ships docked at New Orleans than at **any** city in North America.
>
> **READER'S RESPONSE:** Do you mean that New Orleans is not in North America?

EDITED	At times, more cargo was loaded onto ships docked at New Orleans than at any **other** city in North America.

For *different groups,* however, a comparison using the word *other* is inappropriate and illogical.

ILLOGICAL	Though he wrote in the last century, Dickens painted as vivid a picture of oppressive government and society as **any other** author writing today.
	READER'S RESPONSE: Do you mean that Dickens is still writing even though he is dead?
EDITED	Though he wrote in the last century, Dickens painted as vivid a picture of the ways government and society can oppress people as **any** author writing today.

2 Recognizing appropriate and inappropriate omissions

Leaving out repeated words or phrases can make a compound construction easier to read.

24b
inc

LEFT IN	Some presidents spend much time mastering the facts before making a major decision; others spend little **time mastering the facts before making a major decision.**
OMITTED BUT CLEAR	Some presidents spend much time mastering the facts before making a major decision; **others spend little.**

As long as they do not undermine meaning or confuse readers, **elliptical constructions** of this sort can make writing concise and effective. For example, you can frequently eliminate the word *that* from sentences where it introduces a noun clause after a verb: "Artists know [that] there is a difference between oil and acrylic paints." On some occasions, however, an omission can create confusion, so reread your sentences carefully to determine whether their intended meanings are clear.

Careless omissions of articles, prepositions, pronouns, and parts of verbs may occur when you are hurried or are focusing on the information and ideas rather than on the details of your writing. Careful editing (including reading passages aloud) is normally the best way to identify such omissions.

INCOMPLETE	A corporation issues common stock a way raising money. People buy stock because it can be easily converted cash and because the shares can gain in value if the company is doing well.

REVISED   A corporation issues common stock **as** a way **of** raising
                 money. People buy stock because it can be easily converted
                 into cash and because the shares can gain in value if the
                 company is doing well.

Exercise 3

A. Rewrite the following sentences to eliminate any incomplete or illogical constructions.

EXAMPLE
                                                    other
Both Shannon and Bill like tennis more than any͜ game.

1. His tennis serve has more speed and accuracy than Bill.
2. He also has better sense of where an opponent is going hit ball.
3. Bill's commitment to tennis is greater than his family.
4. He has more fun playing tennis.
5. Like many exercise-addicted people, Bill would be exercising than eating, and he would rather be playing tennis than doing anything else.

24b
inc

B. In a small group, compare the effectiveness of your edited sentences in Exercise 3A with those of your fellow writers. Make sure the members of your group agree on what is incomplete or illogical in the original version of each sentence.

C. Edit a draft of a paper in progress of your own in order to identify and correct any mixed or incomplete sentences. Begin by reading the paper through and underlining any sentences that shift topics, mix grammatical patterns inappropriately, or lack necessary elements or information. Next, correct any of the underlined problems, using the Strategies described in this chapter.

Parallelism

Parallelism is the expression of similar or related ideas in similar grammatical form, as in the following sentence.

I furnished my first
  apartment with **purchases | from department stores,
            items | from the want ads,**
  and **gifts | from my relatives.**

Parallelism enables you to present ideas concisely while highlighting their relationships.

Parallelism can also offer pleasure and surprise. You can use it to create intriguing sentence rhythms while highlighting unexpected images and contrasts.

> According to **how** and **when** you said it, zydeco meant either **the kind of music itself,** or **the kind of two-step touch-dancing that you did at parties to the music.** In theory, this meant that you could **zydeco** to **zydeco** at the **zydeco.**
> — SUSAN ORLEAN, *Saturday Night*

> At this writing, **with** television in **more** American homes than indoor plumbing, **with more than half** of American households **possessed** of two or more TV sets, **with more than** 60 percent **possessed** of a VCR and 25 percent **possessed** of two or more VCRs, **with** the average set in use roughly seven hours a day, it is hard to recall that **for decades, for better or worse,** movies were the centerpiece of America's popular culture.   — TODD GITLIN, "Down the Tubes"

25a Building parallelism

Readers generally find a sentence with parallel elements easy to read and understand. They also appreciate the touch of style parallelism can bring even to everyday sentences. Once you begin a parallel pattern, however, you need to complete it. Incomplete or **faulty parallelism** (with mixed structures) disappoints readers' expectations and may make sentences confusing and hard to read.

MIXED
: Consider swimming if you are looking for exercise that **aids** cardiovascular fitness, **develops** overall muscle strength, and **probably will not cause** injuries.

PARALLEL
: Consider swimming if you are looking for exercise that **aids** cardiovascular fitness, **develops** overall muscle strength, and **causes** few injuries.

In deciding which elements to make parallel and where to place them, you should consider each sentence's message as well as the emphasis you wish to create within an entire passage. In the following selection, for example, the poet Nikki Giovanni uses parallel structures to point out similarities between people who often see themselves as different.

25a
//

> The true joy, perhaps, of being a Black American is that we really have no home. **Europeans bought** us; but the **Africans sold.** If we are to be human we must forgive **both . . . or neither.** It has become acceptable, in the last decade or so, for intellectuals to concede Black Americans **did not come here** out of our own volition; yet, I submit that just as **slavery took away our choice, so also did** the overcrowded, disease-ridden cities of Europe; **so also did** religious persecution; **so also did** the abject and all but unspeakable Inquisition of the Spanish; **so also did** starvation in Italy; **so also did** the black, rotten potatoes lying in the fields of Ireland. **No one came** to the New World in a cruise ship. **They all came** because they had to.   — NIKKI GIOVANNI, "Pioneers: A View of Home"

Giovanni uses parallelism in ways that highlight and persuade. Her conclusion that African Americans and European Americans share an essentially similar immigrant experience comes up against an obvious objection: African Americans first came to the United States as slaves, and many people hold the ancestors of European Americans responsible for the slave trade. In the second sentence, therefore, Giovanni uses parallel forms ("Europeans bought," "Africans sold") to show that both Europeans and Africans shared responsibility for the slave trade. In the body of the paragraph, she points out that although African Americans came against their will ("did not come here out of our volition," "slavery took away our choice"), so did the various groups of European American immigrants, a point she makes by parallel phrases beginning "so also did." The final set of statements in parallel form ("No one came" and "They all came") re-emphasizes the main point: African Americans and European Americans have much in common.

25b Editing for parallelism within the sentence

Whether you create parallelism with words, phrases, or clauses, you need to make sure all the elements employ the same grammatical forms. Your readers will also expect this consistency when you use common writing strategies such as series, paired elements (*either . . . or, neither . . . nor*), and lists.

1 Use parallelism in a series

When you place items in a series, make sure they are parallel in grammatical form. Using mixed grammatical categories can make a series clumsy and distracting.

WORDS — MIXED	To get along with their parents, teenagers need to be patient, tactful, and **to display tolerance.**
WORDS — PARALLEL	To get along with their parents, teenagers need to be patient, tactful, and **tolerant.**
PHRASES — MIXED	The singer Jim Morrison is remembered for his innovative style, his flamboyant performances, and for behavior that was self-destructive.
PHRASES — PARALLEL	The singer Jim Morrison is remembered for his innovative style, his flamboyant performances, and **his self-destructive behavior.**
CLAUSES — MIXED	In assembling the research team, we looked for engineers whose work was innovative, with broad interests, and who had boundless energy.
CLAUSES — PARALLEL	In assembling the research team, we looked for engineers whose work was innovative, **whose interests were broad, and whose energy was boundless.**

25b
//

You don't have to create word-for-word parallels. Sentence elements that differ somewhat in length and wording can still be parallel as long as they have the same structure. In creating sentences with this kind of parallelism, you need to pay attention both to the overall structural similarity and to the meaning you are trying to convey.

Writer's Tip

In creating parallelism, make sure you repeat all words necessary to the meaning of a sentence, including all the words called for by grammatical structures or idiomatic expressions. You need not repeat a lead-in word, however, if it is the same for all elements in a series.

> Mosquitoes can breed in puddles, ~~in~~ ponds, and ~~in~~ swimming pools.

If the lead-in words differ, you must include them.

> You need to **chop** the cilantro, **grind** the coconut, and **grate** the nutmeg.

As you edit, read each series with the structure of the full sentence in mind so you can decide what words are necessary to the meaning.

INCOMPLETE   The main character from the novel *Tarzan of the Apes* has appeared on television, films, and comic books.
READER'S RESPONSE: Do you really mean to say he appeared *on* films and *on* comic books?

EDITED   The main character from the novel *Tarzan of the Apes* has appeared *on* television, *in* films, and *in* comic books.

25b
‖

An effective manager must be **ready to set** goals, **willing to encourage** criticism and advice from employees, and **able to lead** by example.
The three phrases are generally parallel in structure even though they differ in length. The verb *must be* sets up the parallelism because it applies to all three phrases: *must be ready, must be willing,* and *must be able.*

The final position in a series often receives the greatest emphasis from writers and the most attention from readers. Use this knowledge to create sentences with a strong cumulative effect, directing attention to the final element.

When VG Industries moved, the town was left with abandoned buildings, unused rail lines, and **thousands of unemployed workers.**

If you fail to make the last element in a series parallel, you undermine a potentially strong climax.

WEAK   To complete their training for the marathon, runners need stamina, courage, and, most of all, to want very much to succeed.

EFFECTIVE   To complete their training for the marathon, runners need stamina, courage, and, most of all, **ambition.**

··

Exercise 1

A. Underline the parallel structures in each of the following sentences.

1. We've told you about the bombs, the fires, the smashed houses, and the courage of the people.
   — Edward R. Murrow, "From London, September 22, 1940"
2. She looked at a man because she liked the way the hair was tucked behind his ears, or she liked the question-mark line of a long torso curving at the shoulder and straight at the hip.
   — Maxine Hong Kingston, "No Name Woman"
3. But far below, in the warren of passages on the starboard side forward, in the forward holds and boiler rooms, men could see that the *Titanic's* hurt was mortal.
   — Hanson W. Baldwin, "R.M.S. *Titanic*"
4. In that context three groups of wounded soldiers are identified: those whose survival depends on their receiving immediate treatment; those who need medical attention but will survive even if they do not get it immediately; and those who are hurt so badly they would not survive even with medical attention.
   — Ruth Macklin, *Mortal Choices*
5. For in each American marriage there is a special code, developed from the individual pasts of the two partners, put together out of the accidents of honeymoon and parents-in-law, finally beaten into a language that each understands imperfectly.
   — Margaret Mead, *Male and Female*

B. Working in a group, rewrite the following sentences to correct faulty parallelism and create appropriate emphasis. Include all necessary words. If a sentence can be rewritten in several ways, choose the version the group considers most effective.

1. What kind of job would be appropriate for a person who enjoys sailboarding, skiing, and to skydive?

2. The college's career counselor suggested that Rosalie write out her personal goals, read some materials on choosing a profession, or that she might take a career interest test.
3. Optimism, stamina, and being a good thinker are three traits of a good sales representative.
4. If you wish to choose a career at which you can succeed, you might start by making a list of the things you like to do, anything you are very good at, and also jobs or experiences you always try to avoid.
5. You can locate possible jobs in newspaper ads, friends, and employment agencies.

C. Read a draft paper of your own and underline all the series of words, phrases, or clauses. Next, edit them to add parallelism or make the parallel elements more consistent.

2 Use parallelism for paired sentence elements

When you use paired sentence elements to emphasize similarities and heighten contrasts, you should present them in parallel form.

Paired Elements Joined with Coordinating Conjunctions. Use parallel grammatical structures when you connect sentence elements with a coordinating conjunction (*and, but, or, for, nor, so,* or *yet*). The parallelism will direct your readers' attention to the relationship of the elements and make the sentence easier to read.

LACKS PARALLELISM
A well-trained scientist learns to keep a detailed lab notebook and make the entries accurately.

PARALLEL WORDS
A well-trained scientist learns to keep a **detailed and accurate** lab notebook.

LACKS PARALLELISM
First-year chemistry courses are supposed to teach students how to take notes on an experiment and the ways of writing a lab report.

PARALLEL PHRASES
First-year chemistry courses are supposed to teach students **how to take notes on an experiment** and **how to write a lab report.**

LACKS PARALLELISM
Because she is interested in science and organizing complex information intrigues her, Lynn has decided to become a technical writer.

PARALLEL CLAUSES
Because she is interested in science and intrigued by organizing complex information, Lynn has decided to become a technical writer.

Paired Elements Joined with Correlative Conjunctions. When you wish to call special attention to a relationship or a contrast, you may wish to use pairs of connectors such as *both . . . and, not only . . . but also, either . . . or, neither . . . nor,* and *whether . . . or* (known as **correlative conjunctions**). You need to use parallel form for the elements you are joining.

Our dilemma is clear: **either** we must reduce manufacturing costs **or** we must file for bankruptcy.

Correlative conjunctions are also effective strategies for organizing sentences with long phrases or clauses.

ORIGINAL
People in this country claim to marry "for love," yet their pairings follow clear social patterns. They choose partners from the same social class and economic level. Most marriages bring together people with similar educational and cultural backgrounds. Similarities in race and ethnic background are important as well.

25b
//

EDITED (CORRELATIVE CONJUNCTIONS ADDED)
People in this country claim to marry "for love," yet their pairings follow clear social patterns. They choose partners **not only with the same class and economic background but also with the same educational, cultural, racial, and ethnic background.**

The items you link with a correlative conjunction should be clearly related in meaning and similar in grammatical form. If you fail to match the elements that follow the first and second connectors, you may create a sentence that is hard to follow or unclear in meaning.

AMBIGUOUS
Léon Blum's election represented a significant change in French politics and society because he was not only the first Socialist premier but also the first Jew.

PRECISE (PARALLELISM ADDED)
Léon Blum's election represented a significant change in French politics and society because he was not only the first Socialist premier but also **the first Jewish premier.**

Comparison and Contrast.   Putting items to be compared or contrasted into parallel form helps you call attention to them.

DRAFT   This new ingredient will reduce the calories in our frozen yogurt, and the yogurt will have more taste.

EDITED   This new ingredient in our frozen yogurt will **reduce the calories** and **improve the taste.**

As you edit, you may wish to create sentences built around pairs of parallel phrases and clauses (known as **balanced sentences**). This strategy is particularly useful if you wish to emphasize a sense of balance between opposing ideas. (The use of parallel structure to develop contrast is called **antithesis.**)

> If women are not always perfectly satisfied by their friendships with women, neither are all men perfectly happy with their friendships with men.   — DEBORAH TANNEN, *You Just Don't Understand*

> The only thing history teaches us, a wise man once said, is that history doesn't teach us anything.   — MICHAEL LEWIS, *Liar's Poker*

25b
//

Writer's Alert

When you use two parallel clauses beginning with *who(m),* *which,* or *that,* check that both clauses begin with the same relative pronoun. If they do not, the clauses will lack parallelism because they will not have the same grammatical form.

LACKS PARALLELISM   The sailor embarking on hazardous voyages and who wore one earring of his lover's matched pair believed he would always be reunited with her.

PARALLEL   The sailor **who** embarked on hazardous voyages and **who** wore one earring of his lover's matched pair believed he would always be reunited with her.

Because nouns and adjectives are different parts of speech (see 14a-1 and 14a-5), the two cannot be parallel in grammatical form or perform the same function within a sentence.

                                                                  adjective
LACKS PARALLELISM   Sociologists view marriage as both a **social** and a
                        noun
                        system of economics.

PARALLEL   Sociologists view marriage as both a **social** and an **economic** system.

Exercise 2

A. Rewrite the following sentences to eliminate faulty parallelism.

EXAMPLE

In choosing a career, you should plan carefully and ~~also~~ some research ~~, is needed.~~

^{do} inserted above "and"; "also" crossed out

1. Anthony could not decide whether he wanted to be a lawyer or if investment banking was a more promising career.
2. His friends thought Anthony's career plans were not suited to his abilities and his interests didn't fit the plans either.
3. After thinking about his goals, Anthony realized that the two things he wanted most from a career were stability and an income that was reasonable.
4. The counselor suggested that he might consider either working for the federal government or a job with a large, stable corporation.
5. Anthony had been reading about corporations in financial trouble and which had been laying off employees, so he decided to look carefully at government jobs.

B. Working with a group of fellow students, gather a number of pamphlets offering advice. Campus offices, libraries, clinics, banks, and similar places usually provide pamphlets on all kinds of subjects, from health care and home safety to job hunting. Choose one of the pamphlets, identify those places where parallelism is used effectively with paired sentence elements, and edit to correct any faulty parallelism. Enhance the parallelism when appropriate in order to highlight ideas and their relationships.

C. Review a paper in progress of your own. Read the paper once to identify all paired sentence elements, both those that are already parallel and those that need to be edited to add parallelism, and underline all of them. Read the paper again to identify any places where the paper might be improved by adding paired sentence elements, including those using correlative conjunctions, and underline these places twice. Finally, edit the underlined sections, adding parallelism to create clarity and emphasis.

25c
//

25c Editing for parallelism beyond the sentence

As you write or edit, you can use parallelism beyond the sentence level to organize clusters of sentences and even paragraphs. By introducing parallelism into a draft essay, you can often clarify complicated information for readers or highlight the overall pattern of an argument or explanation.

1 Use parallelism in sentence clusters

By adding parallelism to groups of sentences, you call attention to **sentence clusters,** groups of sentences that develop related ideas or information. You can use parallel elements to link related items, guide readers through the steps in an explanation or argument, and highlight patterns like cause-effect and comparison (see 10b on patterns of development).

One way you can draw readers' attention to a sentence cluster is through using parallel sentence openers. For example, in editing a draft of the following passage, the writer added parallel sentence openings to link the examples, thereby emphasizing the general applicability of the experience she is discussing.

> Each of us likely belongs to several organizations whose values are in conflict. **You may belong to** a religious organization that **endorses restraint in** alcohol use or **in** relations between the sexes while at the same time **you belong to** a social group whose activities

---

Did You Know?

Many well-known writers make frequent and skillful use of parallelism. Here is E. B. White.

> The yellow squash illuminates the aging vine, the black-billed cuckoo taps out his hollow message in code (a series of three dots), and zinnias stand as firm and quiet as old valorous deeds. This is the day the farmer picks up the first pullet egg, a brown and perfect jewel in the grass; the day a car stops and a man gets out and tacks up a poster advertising the country fair. You couldn't get us to swap this one day for any six other days.

And here is Annie Dillard.

> Back in New Orleans where he was headed they would play the old stuff, the hot, rough stuff—bastardized for tourists maybe, but still the big and muddy source of it all. Back in New Orleans where he was headed the music would smell like the river itself, maybe, like a thicker, older version of the Allegheny River at
>
> Pittsburgh, where he heard the music beat in the roar of his boat's inboard motor; like a thicker, older version of the wide Ohio River at Louisville, Kentucky, where at his family's summer house he'd spend his boyhood summers mucking about in boats.

E. B. White, "Late August," in *Writings from* The New Yorker: *1927–1976*, ed. Rebecca M. Dale (New York: HarperCollins, 1990) 74, and Annie Dillard, *An American Childhood* (New York: HarperCollins, 1987) 6.

seem to endorse a contrasting set of values. **You may belong to** a sports team **that endorses** conflict and winning and a club **that promotes** understanding among people and conflict resolution. **You may belong to** a political club whose platform contradicts the policies of your professional organization.

The loose parallelism within the sentences also helps reinforce the writer's opening point about conflicting values.

2 Use parallel paragraphs

Paragraphs that are parallel in structure and wording can help you reinforce the overall pattern of a report or essay and alert readers to your line of argument or explanation. The parallel element can be as simple and unobtrusive as a brief opening phrase for each paragraph.

> **One reason for acting** on this recommendation now is that the flooding gets worse every spring.

> **A second reason for action** is that the city currently has a budget surplus that could be spent on drainage improvement.

> **A third, and most important, reason for taking immediate steps** is that the health and safety of city residents is endangered by the floods.

25c
//

You can also employ parallel elements to create patterns of repetition that clarify a complicated explanation or that convey patterns of thought such as cause-effect analysis, comparison-contrast, or classification (see 10b).

Exercise 3

A. Underline all examples of parallelism in the following passage.

Large computers have some essential attributes of an intelligent brain: they have large memories, and they have gates whose connections can be modified by experience. However, the thinking of these computers tends to be narrow. The richness of human thought depends to a considerable degree on the enormous number of wires, or nerve fibers, coming into each gate in the human brain. A gate in a computer has two, or three, or at most four wires entering on one side, and one wire coming out the other side. In the human brain, a gate may have as many as 100,000 wires entering it. Each wire comes from another gate or nerve cell. This means that every gate in the human brain is connected to as many as 100,000 other gates in other parts of the brain. During the process of thinking innumerable gates open and close throughout the brain. When one of these gates "decides" to open, the decision is the result of a complicated assessment involving inputs from thousands of other gates. This circumstance explains much of the difference between human thinking and computer thinking. — Robert Jastrow, "Brains and Computers"

B. Working in a group, decide what each example of parallelism in Exercise 1A contributes to the effectiveness of an individual sentence or the entire passage. Note any differences of opinion, and discuss whether these difference reveal alternative ways of viewing the meaning or purpose of the passage.

25d Maintaining parallelism in lists

Listing can summarize key points, instructions, or stages in a process. To avoid confusing readers, edit lists to make sure the elements are as nearly parallel as possible.

UNEDITED (CONFUSING)

The early 1960s were characterized by the following social phenomena.

1. A growing civil rights movement
2. Kennedy pursued a strongly anticommunist foreign policy.
3. An emphasis on youth in culture and politics
4. Taste in music and the visual arts was changing.
5. Government support for scientific research increased greatly.

EDITED (CLEAR)

The early 1960s were characterized by the following social phenomena.

1. **A growing** civil rights movement
2. **A strongly** anticommunist foreign policy (encouraged by President Kennedy)
3. **A youthful** emphasis in culture and politics
4. **A changing** taste in music and the visual arts
5. **A marked** increase in government support for scientific research

If you present every item on a list in a different grammatical form, readers must shift expectations often and will find it difficult to concentrate on the differences and similarities between the items. Parallelism makes it easy for readers to pay attention to the ideas and information in the list, and it encourages readers to compare the items covered in the list.

Exercise 4

A. Arrange the following materials into a list whose elements maintain parallel form.

The awards for arts and entertainment for 1985 offer an interesting picture of American culture in the middle of the decade.

Academy Award: *Out of Africa* (Best Picture); William Hurt, *Kiss of the Spider Woman* (Best Actor); Geraldine Page, *The Trip to Bountiful* (Best Actress); Don Ameche, *Cocoon* (Best Supporting Actor); Anjelica Huston, *Prizzi's Honor* (Best Supporting Actress).

The Emmy Awards went to *The Golden Girls* (Outstanding Comedy Series), *Cagney & Lacey* (Outstanding Drama Series), William Daniels and Sharon Gless (Outstanding Lead Actor/Actress in a Drama Series), and Michael J. Fox and Betty White (Outstanding Lead Actor/Actress in a Comedy Series).

Tony Awards for Broadway Theater. Best Play: *As Is* by William Hoffman. Best Musical: *Big River* by Roger Miller.

MTV Video Music Awards. Best Video: Don Henley, "The Boys of Summer." Best Male Video: Bruce Springsteen, "I'm on Fire." Best Female Video: Tina Turner, "What's Love Got to Do with It." Best Group Video: USA for Africa, "We Are the World."

25d
//

B. Compare your list for Exercise 4A with the lists of several other students. Note any differences in the ways your lists are organized.

C. Look over an essay you have finished drafting, and identify any places where you might use parallelism to highlight paragraph clusters or use parallel passages to emphasize the pattern of argument or explanation. If you use any lists, also check their elements for parallel form. Edit your draft appropriately.

Coordination and Subordination

Suppose you were asked to edit a report containing the following passage. Reading it for the first time, you notice that the sentences are short and choppy and that they fail to emphasize connections among the ideas.

California's farmers ship fresh lettuce, avocados, and other produce to supermarkets. They never send fresh olives. Fresh olives contain a substance that makes them bitter. They are very unpleasant tasting. Farmers soak fresh olives in a solution that removes oleuropein, the bitter-tasting substance. They make sure just enough is left behind to produce the tangy "olive" taste.

How could you edit the passage to make the sentences read more smoothly and to help readers see relationships among the statements? You could *coordinate* the sentences by linking them with a comma and a coordinating conjunction (*and, but, or, for, nor, so,* and *yet*), with a semicolon plus a conjunctive adverb (like *however*), or with either a semicolon or a colon. Using **coordinates,** you indicate how the sentences are related and you give equal emphasis to each of the linked statements.

COORDINATED

California's farmers ship fresh lettuce, avocados, and other produce to supermarkets**,** **but** they never send fresh olives. Fresh olives contain a substance that makes them bitter**,** **so** they are very unpleasant tasting. Farmers soak fresh olives in a solution that removes oleuropein, the bitter-tasting substance**;** **however,** they make sure just enough is left behind to produce the tangy "olive" taste.

You could also make some of the sentences modify others by using **subordination.** By beginning some of the sentences with subordinating words (such as *because, although,* and *since*) and attaching these sentences to others, you specify the relationships between ideas and indicate their relative weight.

SUBORDINATED

California's farmers ship fresh lettuce, avocados, and other produce to supermarkets, **though** they never send fresh olives. **Because** fresh olives contain a substance that makes them bitter, they are very unpleasant tasting. **When** farmers soak fresh olives in a solution that removes oleuropein, the bitter-tasting substance, they make sure just enough is left behind to produce the tangy "olive" taste.

26a Using coordination

When you want to link words, clauses, or phrases and emphasize their equal weight, use coordination.

WORDS	trims **and** shapes
PHRASES	in the shallow water, near the islands, **or** in the middle of the main channel
MAIN CLAUSES	The winter freeze prevents boats from sailing, **but** the residents are still able to fish through holes in the ice.

When you coordinate main (independent) clauses (see 14c), you create a single sentence, known as a **compound sentence,** that gives equal prominence to the ideas in each clause.

Winds of almost one hundred miles per hour surge through the surrounding river valleys, **and** these winds create violent storms on the lake during spring and summer.

Effective coordination enables you to specify and highlight relationships between ideas.

RELATIONSHIPS NOT SPECIFIED	Cats have no fear of water. They do not like getting their fur wet and matted. Cats like to feel clean and well groomed.
CLEAR RELATIONSHIPS	Cats have no fear of water, **but** they do not like getting their fur wet and matted, **for** they like to feel clean and well groomed.
CHOPPY	Cats are able to swim. A hungry cat will gladly jump into water to catch a fish. House cats are usually well fed. They are not willing to get soaked for an extra bite to eat.

26a
coord

SMOOTHER   Cats are able to swim, **and** a hungry cat will gladly jump into water to catch a fish. House cats are usually well fed; **therefore,** they are not willing to get soaked for an extra bite to eat.

Editing for Coordination

WORDS AND PHRASES

1. **Use *and, but, or,* or *nor* (coordinating conjunctions).**

   cut **and** hemmed   smooth **or** textured   intrigued **yet** suspicious

2. **Use pairs like *either . . . or, neither . . . nor,* and *not only . . . but also.***

   either music therapy **or** pet therapy

   not only a nursing care plan **but also** a psychological treatment program

MAIN (INDEPENDENT) CLAUSES

1. **Use *and, but, or, for, nor, so,* or *yet* (coordinating conjunctions) preceded by a comma.**

   The psychology students observed the responses of supermarket shoppers to long lines **, and** they interviewed a number of people waiting in line.

   Most people in the study were irritated by the lines at the checkout counter **, yet** a considerable minority found the wait enjoyable.

2. **Use a semicolon (see 32a).**

   The wait provoked physical reactions in some people **;** they fidgeted, grimaced, and stared at the ceiling.

3. **Use conjunctive adverbs like *however, moreover, nonetheless, thus,* and *consequently* (see 14a-6) preceded by a semicolon.**

   Store managers can take simple steps to speed up checkout lines **;** **however,** they seldom pay much attention to the problem.

4. **Use a colon (see 32b).**

   Tabloids and magazines in racks by the checkout counters serve a good purpose **:** they give customers something to read while waiting.

Writer's Tip

Do you sometimes want to emphasize the *contrast* between two main clauses? Do you occasionally want to get readers themselves to think about the relationship between the ideas and information in the clauses? Consider using a semi-colon to create these effects.

> People gain weight during the winter holidays **;** they try to lose it before the summer holidays.

When you use a second clause to illustrate, sum up, or comment on the preceding clause and you want to give this relationship particularly forceful emphasis, you might join the clauses with a colon.

> For three weeks we used a new program of radio and television ads to invite customers to our once-a-year sale **:** they came in droves.

Both a colon and a semicolon alone create an abrupt stop between clauses, unlike other connectives such as *and* and *moreover*. This stop generally encourages readers to single out each clause for attention.

26a
coord

Exercise 1

A. Combine each of the following pairs of sentences into a single sentence using coordination. Make sure you use each of the strategies listed in the preceding table for joining main clauses, and do not use any particular conjunction (such as *and* or *however*) more than once. Rewrite the sentences if necessary to avoid awkwardness or confusion.

EXAMPLE

Winter weather makes outdoor exercise difficult, Winter has its own ,so forms of exercise.

1. Ice skating can be enjoyable. It is also physically demanding.
2. Recreational skaters need to be in good shape physically. They should exercise to increase their fitness.
3. Skaters who are not in good shape get tired quickly. These skaters are also more likely to pull a muscle or fall.
4. To get in shape for skating, try a program of regular exercise for at least several weeks. Pay special attention to exercises focusing on knees and ankles.
5. Other areas to exercise are hip and leg muscles. Exercises aimed at each muscle group are best.

B. Working with a group of fellow writers, prepare a brief paragraph (five to seven sentences) offering advice on some subject: fitness, cooking, appliance repair, gardening, or the like. Make sure all but one or two of the sentences are compound sentences containing at least two main clauses. Connect the clauses using a variety of strategies for coordination, making sure they are appropriate for your subject and purpose.

1 Edit for excessive coordination

If you use words like *and, so,* or *but* simply to string together loosely related sentences, you risk boring readers with excessive coordination. This problem often arises during drafting when you jot down ideas quickly. Later on, while editing, you need to complete the job of specifying their relationships.

DRAFT   Ripe fruit spoils quickly, **and** the fresh grapefruit for sale in supermarkets is picked before it matures to avoid spoilage, **and** it can taste bitter, **but** the grapefruit in cans is picked later, **and** it tastes sweeter.

EDITED   Ripe fruit spoils quickly. The fresh grapefruit for sale in supermarkets is picked before it matures, **so** it can taste bitter. The grapefruit in cans is picked later; **consequently,** it tastes sweeter.

Even if you have specified relationships through coordination, you need to edit carefully. Too much coordination and too many conjunctions can create sentences that are "stringy" or hard to follow.

STRINGY   The toy was designed in Japan, **but** its parts are made in Brazil, **and** it is assembled in St. Louis, **so** what is the country of origin for tax purposes?

EDITED   The toy was designed in Japan, its parts are made in Brazil, **and** it is assembled in St. Louis. What is the country of origin for tax purposes?

Writer's Tip

You can punctuate three or more coordinated main clauses as a series, placing a coordinating conjunction only before the last clause. (See 25b-1 on using a series to create emphasis.)

The lawyers drew up the contract, the accountants checked it for accuracy, **and** we signed it in good faith.

---

2 Edit for illogical coordination

Check that clauses you have linked (or plan to link) by coordination are related closely enough to deserve equal emphasis within a single sentence. To correct illogical coordination, try adding information to a sentence or changing its emphasis.

ILLOGICAL   Antarctica is a remote continent with an unusually harsh climate, and scientists are now studying its unique animal life in detail.

READER'S RESPONSE: What do the remoteness and the climate have to do with either the scientists or the animals?

EDITED   Antarctica's remoteness and harsh climate **have made exploration difficult,** and scientists are **only now beginning detailed study** of its unique animal life.

EDITED   Antarctica is a remote continent with an unusually harsh climate; **therefore,** much of its animal life is unique.

Don't coordinate clauses unless they belong together logically.

ILLOGICAL   Miles Davis was an innovative musician, and record companies often made sure his album covers featured him in a dramatic pose.

READER'S RESPONSE: I can't see any relationship between the qualities of Davis's music and the choice of album covers.

EDITED   Miles Davis was an innovative musician, and the title of his album *Birth of the Cool* reflects his progressive approach.

EDITED   Miles Davis attracted many listeners because of his "star quality"; therefore, record companies often made sure his album covers featured him in a dramatic pose.

26a
coord

Writer's Tip

And connects ideas that are similar or closely related, emphasizing their likeness. *But* and *yet* emphasize contrasts and unlikeness. If you fall into a habit of using only *and,* you may miss appropriate occasions for *but* and *yet,* creating inappropriate connections in the process.

Make sure you link clauses in ways that indicate their relationships precisely and clearly.

VAGUE   Penguins swim in frigid water **and** stand on ice, **and** their feet never seem to freeze.

EDITED TO SHOW   Penguins swim in frigid water and stand on ice**,** **yet** their feet
CONTRAST   never seem to freeze.

Exercise 2

A. Revise the following passage to eliminate excessive or illogical
coordination. Combine short sentences with coordination when appropriate to clarify relationships and eliminate choppiness.

Working for someone else can be unrewarding, and this is also
true of working for a large corporation, so many people in their early
thirties decide to open businesses of their own, but they often do not
have very original ideas, so they open restaurants or small retail stores,
for these are the small businesses they are most familiar with, yet they
are also the ones that are most likely to fail, and they face the most competition. Franchises are small businesses, and they often provide help
to people getting into business on their own for the first time. Fast-
food restaurants are often franchises, and they are quite expensive to
start up, or they face a lot of competition. What many potential small-
business owners fail to investigate are the many less familiar kinds of
franchise operations. Enterprising people can own the local office of
an armored car service, or they can run a regional unit of a nation-
wide cleaning service for commercial buildings, and they can open
hardware stores with the name of a national chain over the front door.
Electronics stores, fabric stores, and real estate offices can be locally
owned yet parts of a national chain, so people who want to be their
own bosses have many opportunities.

B. Work with a group of fellow writers to produce two versions of the
passage in Exercise 2A, each with a different emphasis.

C. Review a paper in progress of your own, circling all the coordinating conjunctions it contains. Count to see how often you use each
of the coordinating conjunctions (*and, but, or, for, nor, so,* and *yet*).
Edit your paper to use coordinating conjunctions more effectively
and to introduce greater variety (if appropriate) into your choice of conjunctions.

26b Using subordination

In sentences containing subordination, one clause modifies another
and in so doing helps readers perceive links between ideas or information.

26b
sub

1 Edit and punctuate for subordination

To create a sentence using subordination, you present a central idea in a main (or independent) clause and add a **subordinate clause** that modifies, qualifies, or comments on the ideas or information in the main clause. You signal the relationship to readers by beginning the subordinate clause with a subordinating word like *because, while, although, who, which,* or *that* (see list on p. 389) and by attaching the subordinate clause to the main clause. (A sentence with a main clause and one or more subordinate clauses is a **complex sentence.**)

In using subordination, you create a sentence with unequal elements: one presenting the central idea (main clause), and one (or more) acting as a modifier (subordinate clause).

MAIN CLAUSES | I use a personal computer to keep track of my finances. I know how much rent I pay each year for my apartment.

SUBORDINATED | **Because** I use a personal computer to keep track of my finances, I know how much rent I pay each year for my apartment.

READER'S RESPONSE: Now I know how the ideas relate—one is a cause and the other an effect.

MAIN CLAUSES | Most first-time homebuyers are people in their late twenties or early thirties. They have tired of paying rent.

SUBORDINATED | Most first-time homebuyers are people in their late twenties or early thirties who have tired of paying rent.

READER'S RESPONSE: The second clause adds information to the statement presented in the first and ties the ideas together.

SUBORDINATED | Sales of single-family homes are up, **although** sales of the more expensive homes are still depressed.

READER'S RESPONSE: The second clause not only qualifies the meaning of the opening statement—it also takes the sentence in a new direction.

SUBORDINATED | I am saving money **so that** I can make a down payment **as soon as** I find an affordable house.

READER'S RESPONSE: I like the way the subordinate clauses add more and more focus to the opening statement.

2 Indicate relationships through subordination

As you write and edit, you can use subordination to precisely describe the relationships among ideas or information. Subordination enables you to put some information in the foreground (in a main clause) and other information in the background (in a subordinate clause). Thus, you can help readers distinguish primary statements from secondary statements,

Creating and Punctuating Subordination

SUBORDINATING CONJUNCTIONS
You can use a subordinating conjunction such as *although, because,* or *since* (see list on p. 389) to create a subordinate clause at the beginning or end of a sentence. (See 14c-5 on adverb clauses.)

PUNCTUATION WITH SUBORDINATING CONJUNCTIONS
Use a comma *after* an introductory clause that begins with a subordinating conjunction.

At the end of a sentence, do not use commas if the clause is *essential* to the meaning of the main clause (restrictive); use commas if the clause is *not essential* (nonrestrictive). (See 21c.)

BEGINNING   **Once she understood the problem,** she had no trouble solving it.

END   Radar tracking of flights began **after several commercial airliners collided in midair.**
Essential

END   The present air traffic control system works reasonably well, **although accidents still occur.**
Nonessential

RELATIVE PRONOUNS
You can use a relative pronoun (*who, which, that*) to create a relative clause (also called an adjective clause) at the end or in the middle of a sentence. (See 14c-5 on adjective clauses.)

PUNCTUATION WITH RELATIVE PRONOUNS
When the modifying clause contains information that is *not essential* to the meaning of the main clause, the modifying clause is nonrestrictive and you should set it off with commas. When the information is *essential,* the modifying clause is restrictive and you should not set it off with commas. (See 21c.)

RESTRICTIVE   The anthropologists discovered the site of a building **that early settlers used as a meetinghouse.**

NON-RESTRICTIVE   At one end of the site they found remains of a smaller building, **which may have been a storage shed.**

RESTRICTIVE   The people **who organized the project** work for the Public Archaeology Lab.

NON-RESTRICTIVE   A graduate student, **who was leading a dig nearby,** first discovered signs of the meetinghouse.

**26b
sub**

Expressing Relationships Through Subordination

TIME	before, while, until, since, once, whenever, whereupon, after
CAUSE	because, since
RESULT	in order that, so that, that, so
CONCESSION OR CONTRAST	although, though, even though, as if, while
PLACE	where, wherever
CONDITION	if, whether, provided, unless, rather than
COMPARISON	as
IDENTIFICATION	that, which, who

---

new information and ideas from old, and important information from background.

SECONDARY/
PRIMARY

> **Although** energy costs are declining, costs for raw materials have more than doubled in the past six months.
>
> READER'S RESPONSE: *Although* shows the declining energy costs to be less important than the rising costs of raw materials.

OLD/NEW

> **Though** most biographies of Charles Dickens have spent considerable time examining his experiences as a child, his latest biographer pays little attention to these important events.

IMPORTANT/
BACKGROUND

> Raymond Carver, **who** died in 1990, created a stir with his "minimalist" short stories.

26b
sub

You can also vary the meaning of a sentence considerably, depending on the subordinating conjunction you choose.

> **As soon as** the copier is repaired, we can print the newsletter.

> **Whenever** the copier is repaired, we can print the newsletter.

> **If** the copier is repaired, we can print the newsletter.

In addition, subordination can help you turn short, choppy sentences into smooth, graceful ones.

CHOPPY

> For each moon, the Seneca have a name. They draw the name from the season. The sixth moon is called the Strawberry Moon. Strawberries ripen in June.

EDITED   For each moon, the Seneca have a name **which** they draw
from the season. **Because** strawberries ripen in June, the
sixth moon is called the Strawberry Moon.

Exercise 3

A. Use subordination to combine each of the following pairs of sentences. Choose appropriate subordinating conjunctions, and create emphasis consistent with each sentence's meaning. Rewrite the clauses if necessary to produce effective sentences.

EXAMPLE
Newspapers often contain reports of car accidents. ~~The accidents~~ *that* were preventable.

1. Comedian Sam Kinison died in a car crash. A pickup truck swerved across the road and hit his car.
2. Kinison was not wearing a seat belt. A seat belt might have saved his life.
3. Driving quickly off the road to the right is one thing you can do. This will help you avoid collisions.
4. Drive a large car. Big, heavy cars and passenger vans are much safer in crashes.
5. Buying a car with air bags and antilock brakes is an excellent way to reduce your chances of getting injured or dying. These cars cost more money.

B. Working with a group of fellow students, conduct some research to determine which subordinating words are widely used. Each person should locate a five- to seven-paragraph segment of a magazine article and make a list of all the subordinating words in it, tallying the number of times each word appears. (The list on p. 389 and a dictionary can help you decide whether a word is a subordinator.) Pool your lists, and determine how often the various words appear in the articles you sampled.

26b
sub

3 Edit for illogical subordination

Sometimes the subordinating word you choose may fail to specify a relationship clearly or correctly.

Strategy

To identify illogical subordination, state a sentence's meaning to yourself with slightly different wording. You may discover that the original sentence does not convey your intended meaning or that the subordinating word you have chosen can convey several conflicting meanings. In either case, edit the sentence by choosing a more appropriate subordinator. The list on page 389 provides alternatives.

UNCLEAR EMPHASIS	Since she taught junior high school, Jean developed keen insight into the behavior of twelve- and thirteen-year-olds.
	READER'S RESPONSE: I'm not sure whether *since* here means she developed insights *because* she was a teacher or *after* she quit teaching.
EDITED	**Because** she taught junior high school, Jean developed keen insight into the behavior of twelve- and thirteen-year-olds.

Watch out, too, for subordination that confuses readers by putting key ideas in a subordinate clause and secondary ideas in a main clause. To correct this problem, make sure the main clause presents the sentence's most important statement.

FAULTY	His training and equipment were inferior, although Jim was still able to set a school record throwing the discus.
	READER'S RESPONSE: Isn't Jim's achievement the key point?
EDITED	**Although** his training and equipment were inferior, Jim was still able to set a school record throwing the discus.

26b
sub

Did You Know?

The conjunctions *because* and *for* offer you two different ways to arrange sentences dealing with causes and effects. *Because* creates subordination; *for* creates coordination. Here is what one authority on style and usage has to say about these words and ways to use them.

BECAUSE/FOR
Often interchangeable. *Because* clearly indicates cause or reason: "They stayed at home because it was snowing." *For* (after a comma) normally joins two independent statements and may suggest cause, reason, or evidence. Cause or reason: "They stayed at home, for it was snowing." Evidence: "They may have decided to drive into town, for faint tire tracks remain in their driveway."

J. N. Hook, *The Appropriate Word* (Reading, MA: Addison, 1990) 34.

4 Edit for troublesome subordinators

Certain subordinators can be ambiguous, confusing, or simply incorrect and therefore irritating to your readers. These subordinators come in two groups: (1) *as* and *while,* and (2) *and which, but that,* and *and who.* Be alert for these words as you edit, and use the following discussions to help you make the correct choice.

As, While. You can use *as* correctly to create a comparison, or you can use it to indicate simultaneous events.

COMPARISON   Our team spent **as much** time on the accounting problems **as** the other, less successful teams did.

TIME   They began interviewing students **as** the semester was coming to an end.

However, if you use *as* to point out a cause-effect relationship, you will probably confuse some readers. Other readers may consider this use of *as* unacceptable in standard written English.

AMBIGUOUS   **As** the level of achievement in the morning and afternoon classes differed, the researchers looked for possible explanations.
READER'S RESPONSE: Does *as* mean "while" or "because"?

EDITED   **Because** the level of achievement in the morning and afternoon classes differed, the researchers looked for possible explanations.

Do not use *as* in place of *whether* or *that.* This substitution is always incorrect in writing and formal speaking.

INCORRECT   They were not sure **as** the differences in achievement were significant.

EDITED   They were not sure **whether** the differences in achievement were significant.

EDITED   They were not sure **that** the differences in achievement were significant.

While can indicate events occurring at the same time. *While* can also signal a concession.

SIMULTANEOUS   I can get some work done at home **while** the children are at
EVENTS   school.

CONCESSION   **While** she thinks the presentation was a success, I am not so sure.

Nonetheless, *while* may be ambiguous in some sentences, and you may need to replace it with another, clearer subordinator.

UNCLEAR   **While** they interviewed the students, the researchers did not come to any conclusions.
READER'S RESPONSE: Does *while* mean "although" or "when"?

EDITED   **When** they interviewed the students, the researchers did not come to any conclusions.

EDITED   **Although** they interviewed the students, the researchers did not come to any conclusions.

In addition, *while* is never an acceptable replacement for *but* or *and*.

INCORRECT   One researcher claimed that teachers in the morning classes were more effective than those in the afternoon, **while** the other researcher disagreed.

CORRECT   One researcher claimed that teachers in the morning classes were more effective than those in the afternoon, **but** the other researcher disagreed.

And Which, But That, And Who.   When you place *and* or *but* at the head of a clause along with *which, that,* or *who,* you add an unnecessary word and confuse readers by obscuring the relationship signaled by the subordinating word.

CONFUSING   The research was funded by the Champlin Foundation, **and which** also published the results.

EDITED   The research was funded by the Champlin Foundation, **which** also published the results.

5 Edit for excessive subordination

When you use too much subordination in a sentence, you create a pattern of relationships so intricate that it overloads readers. To clear up such confusion, separate your ideas into several sentences, and rewrite them so that readers can grasp your meaning more easily.

CONFUSING   The election for mayor will be interesting this year **because** the incumbent has decided to run as an independent **while** his former challenger for the Democratic nomination has

26b
sub

decided to accept the party's endorsement **even though** the Republican nominee is her former campaign manager **who** switched parties last week.

EDITED   The election for mayor will be interesting this year. The incumbent has decided to run as an independent. His former challenger for the Democratic nomination has decided to accept the party's endorsement **even though** she will have to run against her former campaign manager. He switched parties last week to become the Republican nominee.

Exercise 4

A. Revise the following sentences to eliminate illogical, incorrect, or excessive subordination. Combine short sentences through subordination when appropriate to clarify relationships and eliminate choppiness.

EXAMPLE

Because
~~Since~~ my doctor said I need more exercise, I have been looking for a sport I might enjoy.

1. As I am not particularly good at athletics, I want a sport that is not too demanding. I would also like a sport that is fun.
2. I enjoy volleyball, although it is a serious, highly competitive sport demanding considerable quickness and coordination. Volleyball is not the answer.
3. Since I have played tennis, I have thought about trying out for the tennis team. I have also thought about talking this idea over with the tennis coach.
4. Some of my friends think I should give the tennis team a try while others think the idea is laughable.
5. What I really want to find is a brand-new sports program, and which will give me the training I need, because I don't have the experience necessary to succeed in established sports, although I am willing to work as hard as I need to in order to bring my skills up to a competitive level.

B. Working in a group, share your revisions of the sentences in Exercise 4A. Decide which versions of the sentences are the best, and be ready to explain and defend your choices.

C. Review a draft of a paper you are working on, circling all subordinating conjunctions and underlining all relative pronouns. Next, make a list of all the different subordinating words you have used. Edit

26b
sub

the paper, choosing subordinators that indicate relationships clearly and eliminating illogical, incorrect, or excessive subordination.

ESL Advice: Grammatical Structures for Coordination and Subordination

It is good composition style to use the four varying sentence types in your writing: the simple sentence, the compound sentence, the complex sentence, and the compound-complex sentence (see 14d).

Using coordination to form a compound sentence

When you combine two simple sentences to make a compound sentence, you can use a coordinating conjunction, a conjunctive adverb, or a semicolon.

Coordinators		
COORDINATING CONJUNCTION	CONJUNCTIVE ADVERB	MEANING
, and	; in addition, ; furthermore,	add an idea
, but	; in contrast,	opposite idea
, yet	; however, ; nonetheless,	
, so	; therefore, ; thus, ; consequently,	result
, for		because
, or	; otherwise,	choice
, nor		also not

These are just some of the conjunctive adverbs you can choose in your writing (see 14a-6).

ESL

26b
sub

	main clause + main clause
COMPOUND SENTENCE	The helicopter is a versatile aircraft **, and** it can be used for many kinds of jobs.
COMPOUND SENTENCE	The helicopter is a versatile aircraft **; therefore,** it can be used for many kinds of jobs.

main clause   +   main clause

COMPOUND SENTENCE The helicopter is a versatile aircraft; it can be used for many kinds of jobs.

Using subordination to form a complex sentence

When you combine a simple sentence with a dependent clause to form a complex sentence, you use a subordinating conjunction.

Subordinating Conjunctions		
after	once	whether
although	provided that	which
as soon as	rather than	while
because	so/so that	who/whoever
before	though	whom/whomever
even though	until	whose
how/however	when/whenever	
if	where/wherever	

ESL

**26b
sub**

main
clause

        subordinate clause

COMPLEX SENTENCE **After** the invention of the helicopter in the 1930s, this air-craft became very useful in rescue missions.

subordinate
clause

        main clause

COMPLEX SENTENCE Many rescue missions have been successful **because** heli-copters take off and land vertically.

Using coordination and subordination to form a compound-complex sentence

When you combine two main clauses and a dependent clause, you use both coordination and subordination.

        subordinate clause

**COMPOUND-
COMPLEX
SENTENCE** **Because** the helicopter can fly in any direction and hover in

        main clause   main clause

midair, it can maneuver in many places, **and** it can be use-ful for all kinds of jobs.

Writer's Alert

It is necessary to use coordinators or subordinators when you write different sentence types, but you must be careful not to mix the two grammatical structures.

MIXED · · · · · · **Although** frogs can live both on land and in water, **but** they need to breathe oxygen.

This sentence has both a subordinator, *although,* and a coordinator, *but.* You must use one pattern, but not both.

CORRECT
COORDINATION

main clause
Frogs can live both on land and in water, **but**
main clause
they need to breathe oxygen.

CORRECT
SUBORDINATION

subordinate clause
Although frogs can live both on land and in
main clause
water, they need to breathe oxygen.

ESL

26b
sub

EDITING FOR
WORD CHOICE

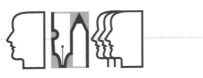

CHAPTER

27

....

Choosing Appropriate Words

....

When you search for appropriate words, you will want first to ask yourself whether you have used the correct word to express your intended meaning. Consider the following sentence.

Dr. Parsippani [*caused to die*] Mr. Rollet.

In this sentence, several words meaning "cause to die" could fill the slot, including *killed, slaughtered, assassinated, exterminated,* and *murdered.* Choosing the best word means first avoiding words that are incorrect or inaccurate. *Assassinate* would be ruled out unless Mr. Rollet were an important political figure; *slaughtered* is usually reserved for deaths involving brutal, deliberately inflicted bodily injury; *murdered* indicates foul play; *exterminated* applies, at least for humans, to cases of genocide. If you meant none of these more specific meanings, *killed* might be the simplest and most precise word to use.

Choosing the right words also means choosing words appropriate to your intended purpose, audience, and context. In a formal paper, writing "This guy's theories, well, I think they're just plain garbage" represents an inappropriate choice of words and phrases, or **diction.** A word like *guy* does, in fact, refer to a person (usually male), so technically it's not *incorrect.* But as slang, it would violate any reader's expectations if it were used in the context of a formal academic paper, and it is therefore *inappropriate.*

27a Thinking about word choice

Whenever you choose specific words while you write, you base your decisions partly on your writing situation, which includes your purpose, audience, context, and persona (the image of yourself that you project in your writing). Considering each of these can help you choose appropriate words as you draft and revise.

1 Adjust your diction to your readers' needs

The characteristics of your readers should play a major role in your choice of words (see Chapter 6). Whenever you write for teachers or students in college, you should maintain a fairly high level of formality in your diction (the exceptions being deliberately informal notes, responses, journal entries, or quoted speech). Avoid **colloquialisms.**

TOO INFORMAL   The stock market crash didn't seem to **faze** many of the investors with **megabucks stashed** in property assets.

READER'S RESPONSE: This seems really colloquial; I'm not sure I trust the writer's authority.

EDITED   The stock market crash did not profoundly affect investors with extensive property assets.

Writer's Tip

Because much college writing assumes an academic, sophisticated diction, it is easy to forget that not all readers are experts who will recognize complex vocabulary. College student Steven Hoecht discovered this as he edited his write-up of an activity he used in his volunteer work at a nearby elementary school.

TOO TECHNICAL   In order to create effective leaf silhouettes, it is necessary first to procure several preferably truncated and partially dehydrated leaves.

EDITED   To start making your leaf rubbing, first gather a few large, partly dried leaves.

**27a
words**

---

2 Adjust your diction to your purpose

Your *purpose* for writing plays an important role in determining your diction (see Chapter 5). In much academic writing, your main purpose will be to inform your readers, providing them with a balanced, detailed assessment of a topic. Using inflammatory, highly emotional, unreasoned, or outrageous language will only subvert your own purposes.

BIASED   Most proponents of rock-music censorship grew up listening to pablum and thinking even wimpy bands like the Beach Boys were a bunch of perverts.

READER'S RESPONSE: I thought this was a paper weighing the sides of the rock-music censorship debate. This seems too biased and emotional.

EDITED   Proponents of rock-music censorship may unfairly stereo-
                  type all of rock-and-roll culture as degenerate or evil.

3 Adjust your diction to your persona

Writing can portray you in many different roles. Through your choice
of words, you can sound like a mean-spirited, unyielding demagogue or a
reasonable, open-minded arbiter of conflicting opinion. Your **persona** as a
writer refers to the public role or character you assume. Thinking carefully
about how *you*, as a writer, portray yourself can help you to choose appropriate words.

For example, your persona in a clinical experiment will be objective
and detached; using too many personal references may call into question
the accuracy of the experiment. But using such clinical diction in a classified ad selling puppies may convey too cold and unfeeling a persona for the
occasion.

TOO CLINICAL   [*in a classified ad selling unpedigreed puppies*] Three domes-
                  tic canines, *Canis familiaris,* type Shetland sheepdog, @29
                  centimeters, 0.522 kilograms; age: 8 weeks; normal soma-
                  totype; iris: brown; coloring: burnt umber with variegated
                  blond diameters; behaviorally modified for urination and
                  defecation; inoculated. $25 per canine.
                  READER'S RESPONSE: The writer seems uncaring, treating puppies like
                  laboratory specimens.

EDITED   Three healthy shelty puppies 8 weeks old, brown with light
                  spots, housebroken, all shots. $25 each.

ROBOT-LIKE   The river having been reached, it was decided to portage to
                  the campsite. A camp was set, and dinner was prepared and
                  eaten. The sunset was observed at the lake. Then eight hours
                  of sleep ensued.
                  READER'S RESPONSE: This narrative lacks vitality. The characters seem
                  like robots.

EDITED   When we reached the river, we decided to portage to the
                  campsite. There, we set camp, cooked dinner, enjoyed the
                  sunset at the lake, and slept for eight hours.

4 Use specialized diction appropriately

If you're writing in a certain field or discipline, you need to adjust
your diction to your context. For example, in a history course, readers of
your papers will expect certain terms and language that might not be appropriate in a physics course.

Many specialized terms eventually find their way into general usage,

27a
words

two examples being *ego* from Freudian psychology and *modem* (*modulator-demodulator*) from computer science. When you write for general audiences, your readers will find highly specialized language inappropriate. "No shop talk allowed at this party" is a lighthearted way to stop guests from using the language of their specialized careers, boring or confusing their listeners. If you use diction too general for readers in a specialized field, however, your writing may seem naive *in that context*. Revise your drafts to include specific terms used in the field (if you actually understand those terms, and if they improve accuracy and economy).

TOO GENERAL [*in an analysis of a painting for an art history course*] Tiepolo's *Apotheosis of the Pisani Family* (1761) is a lively painting with lots of action going on in it, with nice colors, and typical of the period when it was painted.
READER'S RESPONSE: The diction seems too general for a specialized analysis in my field of art history.

EDITED Tiepolo's *Apotheosis of the Pisani Family* (1761) shows affinities with typical rococo frescoes of the period, including bright colors with characters in various highlighted actions set against dark border accents.

27a
words

When you learn new words in one field, you may inadvertently use those words in another field in which they are inappropriate.

TOO COMPLEX [*in an economics paper on the influence of sexuality in the marketplace*] Ego gratification, originating in the neo-erotic domains of the pleasure principle, remains one of the chief factors influencing the attractiveness of sexuality in marketing.
READER'S RESPONSE: I'm an economics major, not a Freudian psychoanalyst. Talk in my language, please.

EDITED Freudian theory can help us to explain why sexuality sells in the American marketplace. According to Freud, humans are biologically caught in a kind of sexual rhythm. This rhythm causes us to seek certain kinds of gratification not always explicitly sexual.

Exercise 1

A. Assume that the following paragraph is part of a brochure on dental hygiene found in a dentist's office. Examine the passage, and circle words and phrases you find inappropriate. Write a paragraph explaining the problems in diction that you identified in the passage. Consider its intended audience, purpose, context, and persona.

Brushing and flossing of human dentin has been shown to be instrumental in the systematic reduction of invasive caries. When brushing, it is advisable to rotate the cusp of the preventive maintenance tool at alternating angles during upward and downward motion. When flossing, it is advisable to insert and retract the flossing material several times between the dentitial spaces.

 B. In a group, compare your responses to Exercise 1A. Which choices of diction did everyone find inappropriate? As a group, try editing the passage.

C. Read through your current draft, looking for diction that is inappropriate to your purpose, audience, and persona. Be on the lookout for diction that is too specialized or too general for the level of your intended reader.

Did You Know?

The insurance industry has been attacked for writing policies that the average citizen can hardly read. Policy writers were caught up in the special legal terminology of their profession and forgot their audience. Recently, the industry has tried hard to correct this problem, and now many policies are written in plain, readable English. This projects a warmer, more positive image of the industry as well.

27b Using precise diction

Because you may write most fluently when you're not weighing every word you put on the page, you'll find it helpful to work with diction during the editing process. Think of this as adjusting your prose to match your intended meaning.

1 Choose specific words

Try whenever possible to edit for more specific, accurate words.

TOO VAGUE   [*in a do-it-yourself brochure describing bathroom remodeling*]
Note: Do not put any new flooring over old uneven floor or with evidence of wood rot. Remove damaged area before flooring.
READER'S RESPONSE: The language is vague and imprecise. What does "damaged area" mean?

EDITED Note: Do not **install** any new flooring over **existing** floors that are **weak or uneven or show signs of wood rot.** Remove any damaged **flooring material or tiles** before **installing new flooring.**

2 Choose words with appropriate connotations

English is full of **synonyms**, words that are identical or nearly identical in meaning. When you make a choice between two words, you will often consider the words' **connotations**—"shades" of meaning, or associations that words acquire over time. For example, if someone *retreated* from a gathering, they literally left; but the word suggests that the person felt attacked, bewildered, or overcome. When editing, look for any inappropriate connotations in your choice of words.

IMPRECISE When I **came to** on Saturday morning, Billy had already left for Chicago.

READER'S RESPONSE: Was the writer knocked out? Or did he or she just wake up?

EDITED When I **awoke** on Saturday morning, Billy had already left for Chicago.

27b
words

3 Edit for stuffy language

English is filled with Latin words that entered the language centuries ago, creating an abstract, educated way of speaking and writing that may be alluring because it sounds sophisticated. Heavily Latinized language, however, can make your writing seem unnecessarily wordy and complicated (see Chapter 29). Notice how direct the following words are compared with their more abstract synonyms.

Plain word	Latin-based
bathroom	lavatory
bickering	disputatious
die	expire
drunk	intoxicated
graveyard	cemetery
split	bifurcate
stingy	penurious
think	cogitate

In general, use simple, direct diction unless the context of your writing calls for specialized language or unless a more abstract term better reflects your intended meaning than its concrete counterpart.

LATINATE   The reflections upon premarital cohabitation promulgated
by the Supreme Court eventuated in the orientation of the
population in the direction of moral relaxation on this issue.
READER'S RESPONSE: The diction seems stuffy. Say it more plainly,
please.

EDITED   The Supreme Court's views about living together before
marriage led to greater public acceptance of this practice.

4 Edit for archaic words and neologisms

The English language constantly changes. Some words are doomed
to disuse and eventual death. Other, new words enter the vocabulary by the
hundreds. Still others shift their meanings, as in the case of *gay*, which used
to mean "carefree" but now almost exclusively means "homosexual."

Most **archaic words**—words that are rarely used any more but are
still found in older literature—will be labeled as such in the dictionary. In
general, you should avoid archaic words unless you're using them for a special reason. **Neologisms**—words coined very recently—may not be in the
dictionary at all. You may have a harder time recognizing neologisms because
they tend to be used in casual speech. Whenever you suspect that a term is
too new to be acceptable in writing, identify it as a neologism and define it,
or else avoid it altogether.

27b
words

ARCHAIC/   Good reviews of our previous play had been scarce (**save**
NEOLOGIC   in *Fanfare*), and this time around we had to **forfend** the
trashing of the critics again.
READER'S RESPONSE: *Save* and *forfend* seem old-fashioned, and
what's *trashing*?

EDITED   Good reviews of our previous play had been scarce (**except**
in *Fanfare*), and this time around we had to **defend ourselves against** the critics' **attacks** again.

5 Edit for idiomatic and trite expressions

Idioms are words and phrases whose meanings have changed, usually to something quite different from their literal definitions. These terms
often have "forgotten histories." Here are some common idioms.

Idiom	Meaning
bust a gut	work extremely hard
get in the fast lane	be ambitious, rise up; lead a fast-paced, self-destructive life-style
get some z's	sleep, take a nap
lose your marbles	go insane

meet your maker	die
pack it in	quit, resign
stack the deck	cheat
take a spin	go for a ride
toss cookies	vomit
wipe the slate clean	start over

In most academic writing, idioms are too informal or have become trite from overuse. Replace them with precise words.

IDIOMATIC The winning team was **placed high upon a pedestal**, while the losers, **wallowing in a slough of despond**, reminded themselves of what a **dog-eat-dog** world it is in sports.

EDITED The winning team was idolized and cheered by the fans, while the losers, despondent and humorless, consoled themselves over their defeat.

Exercise 2

A. Read the following paragraph and identify as many cases as you can of inappropriate diction. Look for imprecise, misused, stuffy, or trite words, checking in a dictionary if you need to. Then edit the passage by replacing the misused words or expressions with more appropriate ones.

27b
words

The inaugural time I witnessed someone parachuting from a plane was when I was in college. The parachuting establishment was located in the desert of Arizona. First we apprised ourselves on the diminutive single-prop plane and shackled ourselves into the seats. Three employees of a local business were the jumpers. We circled around until we reached the pinnacle for jumping, about 6,000 feet up. The first customer was about to detort but became lugubrious with fear and couldn't jump. The second man faced us with his back to the open side of the plane and a verecund expression on his face, then fell back deliberately and dejected himself from the craft, spinning downward toward the verdurous desert.

B. In a small group, compare your edited versions of the passage in Exercise 2A. Discuss all your choices, and then try to reach consensus on the best substitutions.

C. Edit your current draft for cases of vague diction, inappropriate connotations, stuffy language, archaic or neologistic words, and idiomatic or trite expressions.

> ## Did You Know?
>
> Some idiomatic expressions have interesting histories. For example, the phrase *kick the bucket* (meaning "to die") is thought to come from a crude method of suicide in which the victim stood on a bucket, put a noose around his or her neck, and then kicked away the bucket. However, the term may have come from medieval slaughterhouses. Immediately after being slaughtered and hung on the "buckets" (or beams), the livestock would inevitably "kick the buckets" as they died. The phrase *rule of thumb* also has a disputed history, possibly coming from brewers' practice of gauging the temperature of a brew by dipping a thumb into the vat. However, others believe the word comes from centuries-old English common law and refers to the maximum size (the diameter of a human thumb) of the instrument with which women were permitted to be beaten. Some people now avoid the term because of its possibly sexist history.
>
> Ebenezer Cobham Brewer, *Brewer's Dictionary of Phrase and Fable,* rev. ed. (New York: HarperCollins, 1963), and William Morris and Mary Morris, *Morris' Dictionary of Word and Phrase Origins* (New York: HarperCollins, 1962).

27c
words

27c Using strategies for editing diction

Having a wide-ranging vocabulary—not just *knowing* lots of words, but knowing how to use them thoughtfully—is clearly helpful for editing your diction. But even the most experienced writers will tell you that when it comes to choosing words, they are always searching for just the right flavor, testing one idea and then another, even asking other people's opinions by thrusting unfinished work at them and saying, "Read this, and tell me what you think." Use the following strategies when you think common sense isn't enough.

1 Use the dictionary

As suggested in Chapter 28, the dictionary will be your most important tool when you work on diction. Dictionaries give you precise definitions as well as usage notes.

Strategy

When editing your work, circle any words that you have learned fairly recently or have not used often; then look them up to be sure you've used them correctly.

IMPRECISE	Employees should know that their contracts may be terminated if they deliberately **abrogate** their usual work hours.
	READER'S RESPONSE: The term *abrogate* means to abolish or nullify, usually by some formal means. Do you really mean this?
EDITED	Employees should know that their contracts may be terminated if they **miss work.**

━━►◄━━

2 Use a thesaurus

A thesaurus provides good lists of synonyms when you're editing diction and want to replace an existing word that you question for some reason. But be careful. Be sure you are familiar with a synonym and its connotations before simply substituting it.

Writer's Tip

Some writers begin using a thesaurus and then become so addicted to it that their prose begins to suffer from "thesaurus-ese," a disease that leads to the proclivity for excessively prolix and convoluted linguistic verbiage that can stray several standard deviations from definitional accuracy. In plainer English, such writers may reject good, common words, choosing instead to pepper their prose with sophisticated-sounding synonyms, often without knowing whether they're using them correctly. When possible, stick to words that are part of your vocabulary. Jot down alternatives that are unfamiliar, and learn to use them in your speech before you use them more formally in your writing.

**27c
words**

━━►◄━━

Strategy

When using a thesaurus, ask yourself whether your new word choice captures your meaning more accurately, gives more flavor, or avoids redundancy better than your original choice. When in doubt, stick with words you know. (See Chapter 28.)

ORIGINAL	She was **angered** to the point of frustration and could no longer hold her dissatisfaction inside.
	WRITER'S RESPONSE: I'm not satisfied with *anger*. My thesaurus suggests the alternatives *vexed, irritated, exasperated, infuriated, inflamed, miffed,* and *enraged*.

IMPRECISE   She was **enraged** to the point of frustration.

> **WRITER'S RESPONSE:** The word is too strong and does not convey the woman's true feelings.

EDITED   She was **irritated** to the point of frustration.

---

3 Use the slash/option technique

Sometimes you already have several alternatives in mind for a particular word while you're writing. Stopping to weigh the alternatives may break your train of thought.

Strategy

Write down the alternative words and separate them with slashes. Later, as you revise and edit, you can choose which word most accurately fits your intended meaning.

DRAFT   Steve and Esme stopped their chess matches only long enough to enjoy John's delicious **culinations/cuisine/ cooking/delectables/repasts/meals.**

EDITED   Steve and Esme stopped their chess matches only long enough to enjoy John's delicious **meals**.

---

4 Fight insecurity with simplicity

Vagueness, words with wrong connotations, overused expressions—you can slice all these from your prose if you develop a keen eye for style and clarity in your writing. But the problem of overblown, deliberately complex diction, diction intended to puff up your writing with "sophisticated" language, often has its roots in insecurity. When writers worry about their intellectual status, they often toss away good, direct vocabulary in favor of gobbledygook. Professionals in advanced fields have earned the right to use words with *specialized* meanings. They sound sophisticated because, in their fields, they *are*. But using overly complex prose out of a fear of sounding naive only makes you sound more naive than ever.

Whenever you have the slightest urge to puff up your prose with jargon or needlessly complicated diction, *stop*. Ask yourself what kind of salesperson in an audio store you would be more likely to trust—one who talks to you in simple, honest language about the pros and cons of various CD players, or one who uses dozens of alien-sounding words for acoustic features and for complex mechanisms inside the machines. Then return to your draft. Be direct; choose concrete, visually appealing words when you can.

Exercise 3

A. Locate a short passage in a newspaper or magazine article. Rewrite the passage, substituting words that are inappropriate or inaccurate.

B. Make several copies of your original passage and the changed version in Exercise 3A. In a group, work on each other's passages to "repair" the damage. When you finish, compare your edited versions with the original passages. How close did you come to the originals? What differences can you see between your "repaired" versions and the originals?

C. In the paper you are currently working on, circle any words that strike you as inexact or make you feel uncertain. Then list alternative words that might replace your questionable ones and improve the paper.

27c
words

CHAPTER

28

Using Dictionaries
and Building Vocabulary

In cultures that have no writing, all the words in the language must be passed orally from generation to generation. The entire "dictionary" exists in the memories of the speakers. In societies with advanced literacy, such as ours, no one could hope to know all the words in the language. Most educated Americans use a working vocabulary of about 25,000 words. That's less than 4 percent of the total vocabulary of the English language, which exceeds 1 million words. Under these circumstances, it's easy to see why the dictionary is such an important tool for any writer or reader. But there are many kinds of dictionaries, for many purposes. What are your special needs as a writer?

28a **Choosing dictionaries to serve your needs**

As you work with your writing, you will need different kinds of dictionaries for different purposes, even beyond the typical need to check on the correct spelling, pronunciation, and definition of a word. Here are some common questions writers ask about dictionaries and their use.

What's the best kind of all-purpose dictionary I can get?

Desk dictionaries are suitable for most routine academic and professional tasks. Although they don't pretend to give an exhaustive list of English vocabulary, they are still quite substantial reference works. Desk dictionaries are often called *college dictionaries* because they represent the standard of vocabulary used by educated people. Less bulky and less expensive than full-length dictionaries, they are widely used in most homes and workplaces.

What if I don't want to lug around a huge book when I'm working on my writing away from home?

Most people use a **pocket dictionary** for quick checks on spelling or syllable division. Pocket dictionaries are **abridged dictionaries,** mean-

28a
dctnry

ing that they contain far fewer words and much less information than standard dictionaries. They are inexpensive and convenient, but you'll still want to use a more substantial dictionary for checking definitions and etymologies (the origins of words).

What's a good place to get really full information on a word? What's the most authoritative source?

If your desk dictionary doesn't answer your questions or contain the word you're looking up, you can consult much more comprehensive **unabridged dictionaries,** which are found in most libraries and schools. These dictionaries contain many more words than desk and pocket dictionaries. They usually provide detailed information about words in common use, and they include specialized words from various fields, archaic words, words "borrowed" into English from other languages, and so on. Unabridged dictionaries often provide glosses on usage as well as complete etymological information.

The *Oxford English Dictionary* (OED for short) is the most comprehensive dictionary ever compiled in English. It takes up many volumes, but a compact version is available in two massive books of 4,116 pages accompanied by a magnifying glass for reading the very small print. There is also a new "shortened" edition of two (legible) volumes. For every word listed, the OED quotes the earliest known use of the word in a written document and explains or illustrates many uses that followed. Because they provide such complete etymological and other information, dictionaries like the OED are considered research tools.

**28a
dctnry**

Sometimes I feel that I use the same words over and over. Is there a book that can help me to find alternatives?

A **thesaurus** is a dictionary of **synonyms** and **antonyms**—words related or opposite in meaning to each other. A thesaurus is useful when you want to find an alternative to a word you've already considered, or perhaps to remember a word that has temporarily slipped your mind. Under the word *funny,* for example, *Webster's Collegiate Thesaurus* lists the synonyms *laughable, comic, comical, droll, farcical, gelastic, ludicrous, ridiculous,* and *risible.* Obviously, not every synonym listed means exactly what the word *funny* does; your choice of word will depend on your context. The thesaurus lists the related words *antic, bizarre, fantastic,* and *grotesque.* It gives as an idiom *too funny for words,* and it provides the contrasting words *doleful, dolorous, lugubrious, melancholy,* and *plaintive,* along with the single antonym *unfunny.*

What if I just want to check on correct spelling?

Spelling dictionaries are dictionaries without definitions. They provide spellings and information on word division (**syllabification**). Spelling dictionaries range from lists of the one hundred most commonly misspelled words (these brief lists are often preferred by secretaries because they're so easy to use) to much more substantial works with thousands of words. If you own a good desk dictionary, you probably won't need a spelling dictionary unless you're a frequent misspeller or do a good deal of your writing away from your desk.

Occasionally when I'm writing poetry I need to find rhymes for words. Is there a reference that can help me?

If you want to rhyme a word, you can consult a **rhyming dictionary.** Most rhyming dictionaries are organized into clusters of rhymed words accessible through an index.

I've often needed to know the complete history of a specific word. What reference should I use?

Most good dictionaries include etymological information, and research dictionaries, especially the OED, will give you very complete accounts. **Etymological dictionaries,** however, specialize in the history of words **(etymology)** and will often give fuller histories of some words. A few, such as John Ciardi's *A Browser's Dictionary,* make enjoyable reading.

I've noticed that some words just aren't in the standard dictionary. How can I find their proper spellings and meanings?

Most formal dictionaries don't include every word that might be heard in casual conversation, much less the sort of jargon found among drug users, avid sports fans, surfers, and the like. Dictionaries of colloquialisms, slang, idioms, and informal usage fill the gaps. They're often revised to keep up with new expressions, such as *za, undertoad,* or *mommy track.*

In some of my classes, I hear words that I can't find in the dictionary, probably because they're specialized. Where can I look them up to make sure I understand them and can use them correctly?

Many disciplines use and require complex vocabularies that sound like a foreign language to the average person. To ensure the precise use of specialized terms, these disciplines have their own academic and professional dictionaries. It's a good idea to ask a librarian or teacher to help you locate such dictionaries for your field of study. As you gain expertise in your chosen field, you may want to add such resources to your personal reference library.

Exercise 1

A. Conduct a brief "anatomy exam" of your own dictionary by answering the following questions.

1. What kind of information does your dictionary give for words?
2. How complete are the entries?
3. How have the definitions been determined?
4. How many separate entries does the dictionary include? (A good reference dictionary should contain at least 150,000 words.)

5. Are variant uses, definitions, and spellings given?
6. Does the dictionary contain acronyms (such as SIDS, ARC, NATO, FDA)?
7. Does it contain abbreviations?
8. Does it include often-used foreign words such as *tête-à-tête, pied-à-terre, calzone, karate,* and *kibosh?*
9. Does the dictionary show when to *italicize* words such as *cogito ergo sum* or *mea culpa?*
10. What is contained in the introduction or preface? Is there an appendix? Are there any special features?

B. Compare your notes from Exercise 1A (and your dictionaries) with those of other students.

Did You Know?

Most people think of dictionaries as timeless authorities on matters of spelling, word division, and definition. But dictionaries constantly change. As you're reading this, experts called *lexicographers* are working to keep abreast of important changes in the word stock of American English. One of their jobs is to decide whether certain new words should be put into the dictionary. James Lowe, an editor of *Webster's Ninth New Collegiate Dictionary,* said that most of the new material in that edition consisted of "high-tech" terminology (such as *camcorder, CD, colorize, hard disk, icon, laser printer, LAN,* and *uplink*), but other new terms included *cash cow, Cornhusker* (a native of Nebraska), and *liposuction.* Special reference works like the *Barnhart Dictionary of New English* compile new words not yet found in conventional dictionaries. That one, in particular, includes some 12,000 entries, such as the acronyms ARC (AIDS-related complex) and CRT (cathode ray tube); abbreviations such as *veejay;* and terms such as *sick-building syndrome, sequencing,* and *wilding.*

"'Ninja' Nixed from Dictionary," *Minneapolis Star Tribune* 21 May 1991, and *Third Barnhart Dictionary of New English* (New York: Wilson, 1990).

**28b
dctnry**

28b Using a dictionary

In one sense, you already know how to use a dictionary. You've done this hundreds of times: flipped the book open, found the word, checked the spelling or the definition, and slapped the book shut again. But have you really *used* the dictionary to its fullest potential? If anything in an entry has seemed like so much gobbledygook to you, you may have skipped over some useful information.

The annotated illustration of the word *college* (Figure 28-1) appears in *Webster's Third New International Dictionary of the English Language* (Unabridged). As you read the annotations, note what sorts of important information are provided in the entry.

This brief example shows that deciphering the more technical and abbreviated language of dictionary entries is not difficult if you use the explanations and keys found in the front. And once you start looking *carefully* at dictionary entries, you'll find yourself thinking more critically and deeply

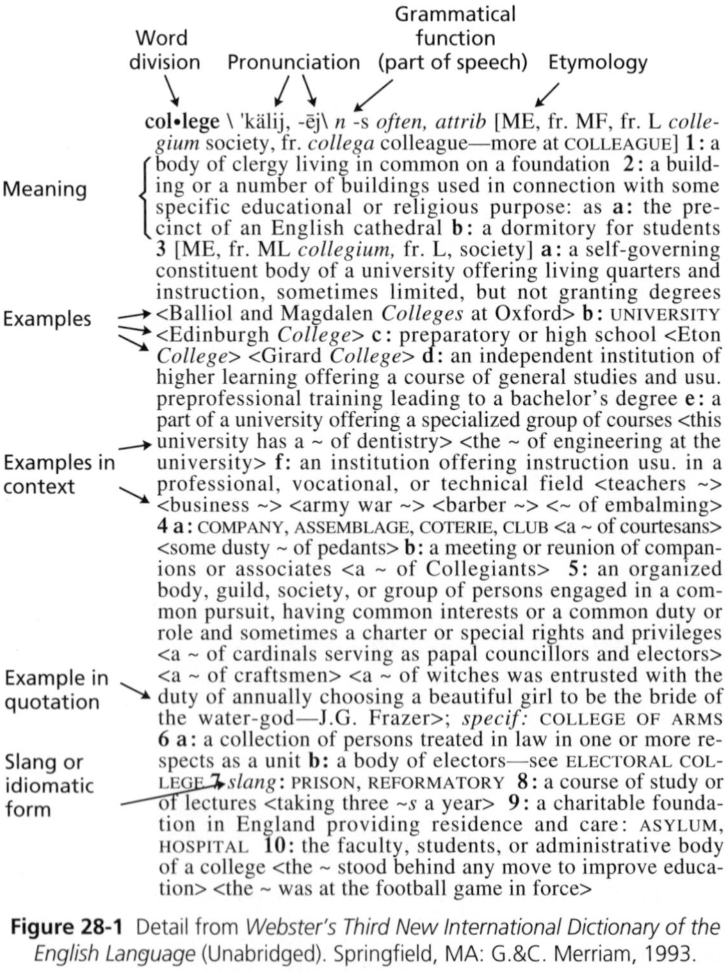

28b
dctnry

Word division   Pronunciation   Grammatical function (part of speech)   Etymology

col•lege \ 'kälij, -ēj\ *n* -s *often, attrib* [ME, fr. MF, fr. L *collegium* society, fr. *collega* colleague—more at COLLEAGUE] **1 :** a body of clergy living in common on a foundation **2 :** a building or a number of buildings used in connection with some specific educational or religious purpose: as **a :** the precinct of an English cathedral **b :** a dormitory for students **3** [ME, fr. ML *collegium,* fr. L, society] **a :** a self-governing constituent body of a university offering living quarters and instruction, sometimes limited, but not granting degrees <Balliol and Magdalen *Colleges* at Oxford> **b :** UNIVERSITY <Edinburgh *College*> **c :** preparatory or high school <Eton *College*> <Girard *College*> **d :** an independent institution of higher learning offering a course of general studies and usu. preprofessional training leading to a bachelor's degree **e :** a part of a university offering a specialized group of courses <this university has a ~ of dentistry> <the ~ of engineering at the university> **f :** an institution offering instruction usu. in a professional, vocational, or technical field <teachers ~> <business ~> <army war ~> <barber ~> <~ of embalming> **4 a :** COMPANY, ASSEMBLAGE, COTERIE, CLUB <a ~ of courtesans> <some dusty ~ of pedants> **b :** a meeting or reunion of companions or associates <a ~ of Collegiants> **5 :** an organized body, guild, society, or group of persons engaged in a common pursuit, having common interests or a common duty or role and sometimes a charter or special rights and privileges <a ~ of cardinals serving as papal councillors and electors> <a ~ of craftsmen> <a ~ of witches was entrusted with the duty of annually choosing a beautiful girl to be the bride of the water-god—J.G. Frazer>; *specif :* COLLEGE OF ARMS **6 a :** a collection of persons treated in law in one or more respects as a unit **b :** a body of electors—see ELECTORAL COLLEGE **7** *slang :* PRISON, REFORMATORY **8 :** a course of study or of lectures <taking three ~s a year> **9 :** a charitable foundation in England providing residence and care : ASYLUM, HOSPITAL **10 :** the faculty, students, or administrative body of a college <the ~ stood behind any move to improve education> <the ~ was at the football game in force>

Meaning

Examples

Examples in context

Example in quotation

Slang or idiomatic form

Figure 28-1 Detail from *Webster's Third New International Dictionary of the English Language* (Unabridged). Springfield, MA: G.&C. Merriam, 1993.

about the word stock of your language, especially as you choose appropriate words for your papers.

Exercise 2

A. Using a good college-level dictionary, look up one or more of the following words:

caduceus   hoist   surprise   denizen   picnic

Using the annotation of *college* in Figure 28-1 as a guide, list the types of information your dictionary provides for each word—part of speech, etymology, definitions, hyphenation for word division, and so on. Be sure to look at every piece of information given for each word. What did you learn about each of the words that you looked up for this exercise?

B. Compare your answers to Exercise 2A with those of other students in a small group. Look for differences in the kinds of information your dictionaries provide for these words and in the ease with which you can access that information.

28c
dctnry

Did You Know?

One of the first English dictionaries was Robert Cawdrey's *A Table Alphabetical,* published in 1602, which contained about 2,500 words. By the end of the seventeenth century, dictionaries routinely included as many as 25,000 words, and they have been growing ever since.

Paul Roberts, *Understanding English* (New York: HarperCollins, 1958).

28c Using dictionaries in the age of technology

You probably already know how helpful computer technology is to college-level research and writing. A single CD-ROM disk (similar to a disk used in a CD player) can contain an entire encyclopedia. With the touch of a few keys, you can retrieve the information on a personal computer.

Several dictionaries and dictionary-like programs are currently available for microcomputers. Those used most often are actually simple spelling checkers that scan your document for any words that don't fit the spellings in the computer's memory. Most spelling checkers are little more than matching programs; they don't contain definitions or guides to usage. A few newer programs, however, do. Software versions of major dictionaries contain definitions, notes on correct usage, hyphenation information, and spelling correctors. Some have accompanying thesauruses capable of producing a million responses for as many as forty thousand entries. These programs can provide acronyms, synonyms, antonyms, contrasted words, compared words, and related words. A few programs boast average access times of less than one second and can insert a replacement word directly into a document.

Computerized dictionaries have several advantages over typical printed dictionaries. For one thing, they are far less bulky. They can be upgraded more easily and more quickly than a book can be edited, updated, and republished. You can usually also personalize a computer dictionary, unlike a standard shelf dictionary, adding your own special words to the dictionary's memory (good mainly for spelling checks).

Computerized dictionaries also have their limitations. It's difficult to browse through them. They may cost three or four times more than a good college dictionary. If you like to write in different locations, you won't be able to use your dictionary without a computer (and power to drive it). Computerized dictionaries, unlike a good sturdy book, can easily be damaged or can simply go bad. Still, many avid computer users find them a valuable resource in lieu of or in addition to standard desk dictionaries.

28d
vocab

Did You Know?

The word stock of English has increased dramatically over the past several centuries. The vocabulary of English (spoken and written) contains an estimated 3 million words. The King James Bible, famous for its elegant prose, contains only about 7,000 different words. Taken together, all the works of William Shakespeare contain less than three times that number (around 18,000 words). Yet a single issue of the *New York Sunday Times* contains, on average, about 25,000 different words.

Bill Bryson, *The Mother Tongue* (New York: Morrow, 1990), and Joseph T. Shipley, *In Praise of English* (New York: Times Books, 1977).

28d Building vocabulary

A rich, varied vocabulary is the mark of an educated person—and is absolutely essential to effective writing and easier reading. To understand the importance of a good vocabulary, try reading the following sentences, which contain some words that may be unfamiliar to you.

The mouse debouched valiantly from the hole.
The senate engaged in an internecine feud over the bill.
Harold died by defenestration.
It wasn't so much a tome as a missal.

The point should be clear: the better your vocabulary, the more able you are as a writer, reader, speaker, and listener.

1 Vocabulary and the writing process

Without many options for word choice, you essentially put a stranglehold on your prose, limiting its variety, its accuracy, and its metaphoric potential. Consider the six versions of one line written by Johanna Vaughan in her paper about food-shelf programs.

> Without the help of local and state government, the food-shelf program in Seattle will become **ineffective.**

> Without the help of local and state government, the food-shelf program in Seattle will become **obsolete.**

> Without the **beneficence** of local and state government, the food-shelf program in Seattle will **die.**

> Without the beneficence of local government, the food-shelf program in Seattle will die **of starvation.**

> Without the **financial nurturing** of local government, Seattle's food-shelf program will die of **nutritional neglect.**

> Without the financial **sustenance** of local government, Seattle's food-shelf program will **slowly** die of starvation.

28d
vocab

Many of Vaughan's changes depend on more than the substitution of individual words, but it's hard to overlook the role her vocabulary plays in her writing process. She can revise more effectively *because she has more options*—she can experiment with words like *sustenance, beneficence,* and *obsolete.*

Although it can become tedious to keep moving between your emerging sentences and that 1,500-page dictionary on your desk, there is something to be said for some modest vocabulary development during the process of completing each of your writing assignments. Especially while revising, take time to consider alternatives to some of your words, perhaps circling those that seem repetitive or bland, then listing alternatives or using a dictionary or thesaurus (as long as you're confident that you know the exact meaning of the replacements).

2 Vocabulary and the reading process

Every time you pick up a book or newspaper, you're exposed to new words. If you're like most people, you probably pass over them, as long as you're not hopelessly confused without knowing their meaning. In many cases, the mere exposure to these words, in their contexts, helps you to acquire them as part of your vocabulary. But a few techniques can help.

Strategy

Each day, select one word from something you've read, look up its definition, and check its etymology. Then, without sounding too unnatural, try incorporating the word into your speech at least three times during the day. If that's not possible, just make up sentences on your own, and say them silently to yourself. You'll find that the word stays with you, and you'll begin using it more regularly.

Keep an ongoing list of unfamiliar words, look them up, and review them periodically, crossing them out when they've become part of your vocabulary. Your journal is an excellent place to do this (see Chapter 2). This method works much more effectively than the one recommended by some self-improvement books, which advise you to cram dozens of words into your brain each day in the hope that you'll actually remember them later and be able to use them accurately. The words on your list should come directly from material you're reading and studying, from the daily newspaper to the most complex textbook chapters.

Every time you look up a word for its meaning, check its etymology. Most English words have Anglo-Saxon, Latin, Greek, or French origins. When you look up a word's roots, you will develop your vocabulary. Over time, you will become able to make educated guesses at the meanings of new words on the basis of their parts.

28d vocab

Learning about a word's origins is a particularly interesting and useful way to expand your vocbulary. The word *elevate,* for example, comes to us from Latin *elevatus,* "lightened" or "lifted up." The parts of the word include a prefix, *e-*; the form *lev(is),* which means "light" (as in "not heavy"); and the suffix *-ate.* The root word *lev(is)* is found in several related words. If you didn't know the meaning of the word *levitate,* your knowledge of the etymology of *elevate* might help you, and the context of the word might do the rest to define it for you.

Many word origins will also surprise you and reveal the linguistic diversity of English, which has absorbed words from dozens of other languages. The word *cookie,* for example, comes from the Dutch spoken by early settlers of Manhattan. The word *alcohol* is from Arabic. The word *typhoon* hails originally from the Chinese *tai fung,* "great wind." *Chicago* was an Algonquian word meaning "place of the wild onion" or "foul-smelling place." The *tomatoes* you eat have their word origins in Nahuatl, an indigenous language spoken in Mexico and Central America. *Hibachi* is Japanese. *Goober* is African. *Cockroach* is Spanish. *Sauna* is Finnish.

Exercise 3

A. To practice studying the etymologies of words, look up the following interesting ones in a good, full-length (unabridged) dictionary. The best source will be the OED in your college library. Look for anything unusual or interesting about the history of these words.

EXAMPLE: *KANGAROO*

The OED says that the word probably comes from an indigenous aboriginal language of Australia and meant "I don't know" or "I don't understand," the response given to visitors who asked the aborigines the name of the animal.

barbecue	guillotine	mesmerize	sadist
blimp	juke (box)	muscle	sandwich
blurb	ketchup	OK or okay	serendipity
dollar	laser	robot	voodoo

B. In a group, compare your etymologies for the words in Exercise 3A. What surprised you about the origins of these words?

**28d
vocab**

Did You Know?

The development of your vocabulary began in your infancy and exploded by the time you were between two and three years old. If you were a typical preschooler, you learned around ten to fifteen new words *each day,* or approximately 14,000 new words between the ages of two and six. Your vocabulary development slowed as you became older and already had a large fund of words at your disposal, but the college years are also increasing your store of words. Every course you take exposes you to dozens and sometimes hundreds of new terms. In many ways, getting a degree in a certain area or major means being able to use the specialized language of your discipline—including its vocabulary.

Mildred C. Templin, *Certain Language Skills in Children* (Minneapolis: U of Minnesota P, 1964).

Wordiness

As a writer, you can state similar thoughts in different ways to achieve different effects on your readers. For example, you can create a short, direct sentence.

Incentive pay improves work quality.

You can then add words to anticipate readers' reactions and guide the effect of the sentence.

Incentive pay **often encourages** work **of higher** quality.

Or you can bury the message with unnecessary language that clogs the meaning and frustrates or bewilders your reader.

There is evidence that the use of pay **as an** incentive **can be a contributing or causative factor** in the improvement **of the** quality **of** work.

Wordy writing includes words not necessary to the meaning or desired effect of a passage. Of course, even the best writing often starts out wordy. While drafting, you may pay more attention to exploring ideas and conveying information than to writing concisely. Most rough drafts contain sentences that need pruning.

Avoiding **wordiness** does not always mean using the fewest words possible. It means including all the words appropriate for your meaning, purpose, and audience, but no more. Defining every medical term in an article on a rare skin disorder might seem wordy to specialists in the field but appropriate for general readers. Other aspects of wordiness are more universal, such as redundancy or overblown vocabulary. To make sure your final drafts are concise, you need to learn how to edit for wordiness, a process that involves cutting unnecessary words and phrases, substituting better words, and rewriting entire sentences.

29a Editing for common types of wordiness

Redundancy can creep into your writing when you use everyday phrases and patterns of expression. Their familiarity disguises their wordiness.

1 Eliminate empty words and phrases

Cut Empty Phrases. **Empty phrases** like *at this point in time, totally overcome, due to the fact that,* or *each and every* add length but little meaning to your writing. Cut them.

WORDY	**At this particular juncture,** the fire damage **makes it incumbent** upon us to decide whether **or not** to rebuild the old plant. READER'S RESPONSE: What exactly is a "particular juncture"? What does "incumbent upon" mean? Doesn't deciding "whether" imply "or not"?
CUT	The fire damage **now** forces us to decide whether to rebuild the old plant.

29a wordy

Reduce Redundant Pairs. English is rich in pairs of synonyms and near-synonyms. Because they say the same thing twice, **redundant pairs** are always candidates for editing.

above and beyond	free and clear	questions and problems
aid and abet	full and complete	ready and willing
any and all	kith and kin	various and sundry
around and about	one and only	way, shape, or form
each and every	part and parcel	

WORDY	To encourage innovation, the manager spoke with **each and every individual** team assigned to the project. Team One made a complex task manageable by dividing it into **bits and pieces.**
CUT	To encourage innovation, the manager spoke with **each** team assigned to the project. Team One made a complex task manageable by dividing it into **pieces.**
REPHRASED	To encourage innovation, the manager spoke with **each** team assigned to the project. Team One made a complex task manageable by **splitting it up.**

Shorten Wordy Phrases. You can shrink many familiar phrases to just one or two words. The shorter versions are easier to read, and they convey your message more effectively.

WORDY   Carbon 14 can be used to date a site only **in the event that** organic material has survived. **In a situation in which** rocks need dating, potassium-argon testing is appropriate.

CUT   Carbon 14 can be used to date a site only **if** organic material has survived. **When** rocks need dating, potassium-argon testing is appropriate.

Wordy phrases are so familiar that they may be hard to recognize. Use the following list as a guide until you develop the habit of turning phrases into words.

29a
wordy

Common Wordy Phrases	
PHRASE	**REPLACEMENT**
as a result of	because, since
being that	
due to the fact that	
for the reason that	
on account of	
on the grounds that	
has the capability of	can
is able to	
possesses the ability to	
at the present moment	now
at this juncture	
at this point in time	
within the current time frame	
a considerable proportion of	many, most
a large number of	
the greater number of	
the substantial majority of	
a case in point is	for example
an example of this would be	
in regard to	
in the case of	
with attention to	
it is evident that	clearly, obviously
it should be obvious that	
concerning the matter of	about

PHRASE	REPLACEMENT
circumstances dictate that	should, must
it is imperative that	
it is incumbent upon	
it is of great importance that	
there is a need for	
at a time which	when
during an occasion when	
in a situation in which	
on the occasion of	
despite the conditions that	although
even taking into consideration the fact that	
even though	
regardless of the fact that	
at all times	always

Cut Intensifying Phrases. **Intensifying phrases** meant to add force (*for all intents and purposes, in my opinion,* and *all things considered*) carry little meaning. Your reader will find your sentences more effective and forceful without them.

**29a
wordy**

WORDY   **As a matter of fact,** most archaeological discoveries can
            be dated accurately.

CUT   Most archaeological discoveries can be dated accurately.

Shorten or Rewrite Redundant Phrases. **Redundant phrases** say the same thing twice, adding unnecessary words to your writing. Sometimes an adjective simply repeats the meaning of the noun it modifies; *true facts, free gifts,* or *final outcomes* are redundant because by definition facts are true, gifts are free, and outcomes are final.

added bonus	baby puppies	each individual
end result	fresh news	future plan
necessary requirements	past history	terrible tragedy
unintentional mistake	cheap bargain	unexpected surprise

Similar repetition occurs in redundant verb phrases (*completely finished, totally overcome,* and *revert back*).

Some redundancies occur when you use a specific word that implies a more general term you've used with it. *Blue,* for example, clearly implies the category *color,* so it is redundant to state both (*blue in color*).

aggressive ~~by nature~~	circle ~~around~~
consensus ~~of opinion~~	curved ~~in form~~
expensive ~~in cost~~	first ~~in order~~
handsome ~~in appearance~~	~~in a~~ clumsy ~~manner~~
~~in a~~ grumpy ~~mood~~	old ~~in age~~
plans ~~for the future~~	small ~~in size~~

WORDY Because it was sophisticated **in nature** and tolerant **in style,** Kublai Khan's administration aided the development of China in the late 1200s.

CUT Because it was **sophisticated and tolerant,** Kublai Khan's administration aided the development of China in the late 1200s.

REWRITTEN Kublai Khan's **adept and tolerant administration** aided the development of China in the late 1200s.

Edit or Rewrite to Cut All-purpose Words. They sound serious and important, yet **all-purpose words** like *factor, aspect, situation, type, field, range, thing, kind, nature, character,* and *angle* are often fillers. By eliminating the fillers and rewriting, you can make sentences easier to understand.

**29a
wordy**

WORDY Viewed **from a** sociological **perspective,** the president's popularity **factor** might be **a type of** result of the changing **nature of** our attitude toward authority.

EDITED Viewed sociologically, the president's popularity might be a result of our changing attitude toward authority.

All-purpose modifiers include *very, totally, major, central, secondary, unlikely, peripheral, great, really, surprisingly, definitely, absolutely, marginal, quite, superlative,* and similar terms. They are appropriate when used precisely and sparingly but can easily become clutter.

WORDY In the short story, Young Goodman Brown is so **totally** overwhelmed by **his own** guilt that he becomes **extremely** suspicious of the people around him and **absolutely** destroys his relationships. [*30 words*]

EDITED In the short story, Young Goodman Brown is so overwhelmed by guilt that he becomes suspicious of the people around him and destroys his relationships. [*25 words*]

REWRITTEN In the short story, Young Goodman Brown's **overwhelming** guilt makes him suspicious **of everyone** and destroys his relationships. [*18 words*]

Exercise 1

A. Edit the following sentences to make them more concise. Use one of the three editing options for wordiness: cut unnecessary words, substitute better words, or rewrite the sentence entirely. Keep track of your changes.

EXAMPLE

~~In spite of the fact that~~ *Although* most ~~ordinary~~ middle-aged people ~~say they generally~~ feel ~~physically~~ healthy,~~and in good shape,~~ ~~severe physical~~ catastrophes such as ~~debilitating~~ strokes ~~and/~~or heart attacks can strike ~~suddenly~~ at any time.

1. As a matter of fact, my uncle had just come back from playing nine holes of golf when he suffered the terrible tragedy of his heart attack.
2. We all thought my aunt was absolutely in the very best of health, but she also died extremely suddenly.
3. For me, the end result of these experiences has been regular visits to the doctor to check on my health.
4. On account of my last visit to the doctor, I have started exercising on a regular basis.
5. A regular exercise program helps me to a better kind of feeling about myself.

29a
wordy

B. In a small group, compare your revised versions of the sentences in Exercise 1A. Create a "best" version of each sentence by pooling the changes in your group. Try to base your decisions on which version gets the writer's point across most concisely.

C. Work through a near-final draft of your current paper, looking for wordiness. Cut unnecessary words, substitute better words, or rewrite entire sentences.

Did You Know?

Legal writing is full of redundancies, perhaps because the law is written to exclude as much uncertainty as possible. Because many legal expressions have a long history, they tend to change slowly. However, recent movements in the law have begun to eliminate such wordy expressions as *cease and desist, null and void,* and *give and bequeath.*

2 Edit wordy and repetitive sentences

Some sentence patterns encourage wordiness, which will annoy your readers. You should always treat them as likely candidates for cutting and rewriting.

Rewrite Sentences with Expletive Constructions. Beginning a sentence with a construction like *There is, There are,* or *It is* allows you to hold off announcing the subject—a strategy sometimes useful for creating emphasis or surprise. You should use this technique sparingly, however (see 11b). Using strong verbs in the place of expletive constructions can yield shorter, more forceful sentences.

OVERUSED **It was** between 1346 and 1350 **that** the bubonic plague struck swiftly and horribly. **There were** over 20 million deaths from the plague—one-fourth of Europe's population. **It is** not surprising that records from the period are confusing and incomplete.

REWRITTEN Between 1346 and 1350, one-fourth of Europe's population—about 20 million people—died swiftly and horribly from the bubonic plague. Not surprisingly, records from the period are confusing and incomplete.

29a wordy

Substitute Active for Passive Constructions. Sentences in the active voice often strike readers as livelier and more direct than their passive counterparts. (See 16d.) This impression may come from the presence of a strong verb closer to the beginning of the sentence, tied to the subject or doer of the action. Favor the active voice in your writing unless you have good reason to use the passive.

PASSIVE Even more unanswered questions **are posed** by Mercury, the smallest planet. Pictures of Mercury **were taken** from within 300 kilometers.

ACTIVE Mercury, the smallest planet, **poses** even more unanswered questions. *Mariner X* **took** pictures of Mercury from within 300 kilometers.

Substitute Verbs for Nominalizations. A **nominalization** is a verb transformed into a noun or an adjective.

Verb	Nominalization
analyze	analysis
combine	combination
fail	failure

move	movement
propose	proposition
recognize	recognition
vary	variable

Some professions and disciplines heavily nominalize their prose. However, you can resist this tendency and create shorter, livelier sentences if you turn nominalizations into verbs.

NOMINALIZED The committee held **a discussion of** the new regulations for airplane safety. **A limitation on** flammable seat materials now is necessary.

EDITED The committee **discussed** the new regulations for airplane safety. Airlines now **must limit** flammable seat materials.

Turn Clauses into Phrases and Phrases into Words. You can often shorten clauses and phrases or reduce them to single words. Look for clauses beginning with *which, who,* or *that* and phrases beginning with *of.*

CLAUSES The Comstock Lode, **which was a vein of high-quality silver ore**, was named after Henry T. P. Comstock, **who staked one of the first claims.**

29a
wordy

CUT TO PHRASES The Comstock Lode, **a vein of high-quality silver ore**, was named after Henry T. P. Comstock, **one of the first claimants**.

CLAUSES An airplane **which is on fire** often produces fumes **that are toxic**.

CUT TO WORDS A **burning** airplane often produces **toxic** fumes.

PHRASES Bridge joints **covered with paint** cannot flex to relieve pressure or to avoid **fatiguing of the metal**.

CUT TO WORDS **Painted** bridge joints cannot flex to relieve pressure and avoid **metal fatigue.**

Eliminate Unnecessary Repetition. When you are writing quickly, you may become repetitive. Such careless repetition, which will tire and annoy your readers, can occur even when you are actually varying your wording of ideas. As you revise and edit, look for ideas *already stated or implied* elsewhere in your sentence or paragraph.

WORDY GPS is a **navigation** system that helps sailors and pilots **navigate.** By getting inforamtion **about their position** from

orbiting satellites, travelers can pinpoint their **global** posi-ton **on a chart.**

EDITED | GPS is a system that helps sailors and pilots navigate. By getting information from satellites, travelers can pinpoint their position.

Good writing may repeat information in order to help readers keep track of an explanation or argument. On the other hand, excessive repetition makes a passage dull and difficult to read.

REPETITIVE | **Our proposal** outlines a **three-step** program for **converting the building** into a **research center** for the study of literature, film, and culture. Each of the **three steps** discussed in **our proposal** should be complete in six months. We expect that **the building** will be **converted** to its new use as a **research center** eighteen months from the time work is begun.

CUT | Our proposal outlines a **three-step** program for **converting the building** into a center for the study of literature, film, and culture. Each **step** should be completed in six months. We expect that **the building** will be **converted** to its new use eighteen months from the time work is begun.

REWRITTEN | We propose **three steps** for **converting the building** into a center for the study of literature, film, and culture. At six months per **step,** the project should be completed in eighteen months.

**29a
wordy**

Exercise 2

Rewrite the following sentences to make them less wordy.

EXAMPLE ~~It was an~~ My interest in ancient cultures ~~that first sparked my interest in an~~ anthropology course ~~taught by~~ (Professor Donaldson's) attracted me to

1. There is much information and detail in this informative course about the civilizations of the pre-Columbian Americas.
2. Anthropologists have spent a great deal of time studying and investigating Machu Picchu, which was the center point of an advanced culture high in the Andes Mountains.
3. There are many excavations in the area that have received support from American universities.
4. It seems to be true that the ruins are a breathtaking sight.

5. Proposals for further exploration are now being made to funding organizations by several groups of anthropologists.

29b Editing for clichés, generalizations, and overblown language

Many writers in college choose language that is either overused (clichéd) or too stuffy or complicated (see 27b). They may do this because they're unfamiliar with a specialized topic or think they must sound "smart" to their reader, a teacher with considerable knowledge. But most teachers are more irritated than impressed by such language.

1 Omit clichés and vague generalizations

Much wordiness stems from a lack of the tough, careful attention to language characteristic of the best writing. **Clichés** and **vague generalizations** are like the sayings in fortune cookies, empty of meaning until the reader plugs in some concrete association. But it's a serious mistake to assume that your reader will do your work for you.

CLICHÉD
: In **today's modern world,** college graduates **stumble across a startling discovery** before they **strike out on their own.** The best jobs are not necessarily the ones that give you a **shot at big money** but the ones that **turn you on** personally.

EDITED
: Almost before they have received their diplomas, today's college graduates begin to rethink the idea of employment. The glamour of high-salary positions soon wears thin, replaced by hopes of happiness, job security, and friendly colleagues.

A passage with vague generalizations may be short but still wordy because it offers relatively little information. To revise, *add specific details* or *combine sentences* to eliminate repetition and highlight relationships.

WORDY
: Glaciers were of central importance in the shaping of the North American landscape. They were responsible for many familiar geological features. Among the many remnants of glacial activity are deeply carved valleys and immense piles of sand and rock.

COMBINED
: Glaciers carved deep valleys and left behind immense piles of sand and rock, shaping much of the North American landscape in the process.

29b
wordy

DETAILS ADDED   Glaciers carved deep valleys and left behind immense piles of sand and rock, shaping much of the North American landscape in the process. Cape Cod and Long Island are piles of gravel deposited by glaciers. The Mississippi River and the Great Lakes were left behind when the ice melted.

2 Edit overblown language

Overblown language consists of words too formal or technical for the writer's purpose and audience. Students often use formal language and technical terms in an attempt to impress their instructors and sound authoritative. Rein in your formal diction and technical words, using them only when you are sure of their meaning and when they contribute directly to your point.

OVERBLOWN   Under the **present conditions of** our society, marriage **practices** generally **demonstrate a high degree of** homogeneity.

APPROPRIATE   In our culture, people tend to marry others who are like themselves.

29b
wordy

3 Eliminate excessive writer's commentary

In certain contexts, talking directly to readers can be an acceptable strategy. If you use such **writer's commentary,** do so cautiously. You can use phrases like *as previously stated* or *I intend to demonstrate* to remind your readers of a point you made earlier or to set the stage for what's to come, but such phrases can become superfluous if you use them too often.

IRRITATING   **As I have already shown,** considerable research suggests that placebos (pills with no physical effect) can sometimes lead to improvements or a cure. However, **my paper documents the tendency of** experts in medical ethics to question the ethics of placebo use, calling it a form of lying. **I intend to show** that the effects of placebos **(mentioned above)** overcome any moral concerns **such as the one I have just described.**

EDITED   Considerable research has shown that placebos (pills with no physical effect) can sometimes lead to improvements or a cure. Experts in medical ethics, however, question the ethics of placebo use, calling it a form of lying. **This paper** will argue that the effects of placebos overcome any such moral concerns.

TOO OVERT   **The thesis of my paper is that** American culture associates the pursuit of knowledge with social ineptitude and the denial of emotion. **I have chosen to focus on** Mr. Spock from the *Star Trek* series as an exemplar of this unfortunate public attitude toward education.

EDITED   American culture associates the pursuit of knowledge with social ineptitude and the denial of emotion. This unfortunate public attitude toward education is well represented in the character of Spock, the brilliant but only half-human Vulcan in the *Star Trek* series.

Exercise 3

A. Rewrite the following passage to eliminate overblown language, unnecessary commentary, vague generalizations, and clichés. As you revise, make the passage more concise.

The social psychologist and student of human behavior Peter Marsh several years ago published a tome entitled *Tribes* in which he set forth the challenging, and for many readers, downright revolutionary, conception that the denizens of our modern world perpetuate the primitive form of social organization known as a tribe. According to Marsh in his book, as a reaction against the tendency of our modern society to break up the social networks characteristic of the more rural life-styles of earlier decades and centuries, many people form formal and informal groups based on their preferences in food, clothing, recreation, and work. Some of these groupings are of remarkably short duration, consisting of what we might call fads. Let me point out that, in my opinion, Marsh is trying to be critical of many of these groups, particularly those that seek to raise the social status of members by excluding nonmembers from certain privileges. Yet I think that a careful reading of Marsh's book would also indicate that he is favorably predisposed toward the tendency of modern people to form tribes.

29b
wordy

B. In a small group, compare your revisions of the passage in Exercise 3A. What specific changes did you and your peers make that were especially effective?

C. Using the suggestions in this chapter, work through a draft of your current paper, looking for wordiness. Try eliminating at least five words per page without loss of meaning.

30

Avoiding Sexist and Discriminatory Language

Prodded by the women's movement, writers and editors have begun to eliminate sexist language from published work. But what is **sexist language?** People disagree about some common terms. For example, *seminal* is widely used to mean "highly original and influencing future events or developments"—but the literal meaning of the word is "pertaining to, containing, or consisting of semen." As such, it represents a potentially sexist usage: why should originality and creativity be associated with maleness? Some people think the term should be dropped in favor of words like *important* or *influential;* others argue that it's perfectly acceptable to use the common English word *seminal* to describe an important and influential work.

No matter how you feel about the issue of gender, as a writer you *must* be concerned with the reactions of your readers to the way you represent men and women and members of minority groups. You don't want to alienate your readers, to prejudice people against your ideas, or to perpetuate unhealthy attitudes.

30a Recognizing and editing sexist language

As you edit your writing, try to read what you've written from the perspective of a person of the opposite gender or another culture. If you're male, for example, ask yourself whether women might object to anything you've said. If you're white, think about your paper from the perspective of an African American or a member of another minority group. Be especially sensitive when you're characterizing such groups, discussing occupational roles, or referring to all human beings.

1 Avoid demeaning characterizations of women

Your readers are likely to object to language that demeans women or plays into negative stereotypes of women's behaviors, roles, and attributes.

DEMEANING   Pasquale's defense attorney called on **three blonde babes** to testify that they had seen him in a bar on the night Smith was shot.

EDITED   Pasquale's defense attorney called on **three women** to testify that they had seen him in a bar on the night Smith was shot.

DEMEANING   Two undergraduates and **a co-ed** were jointly awarded the prize for the most unusual recipe.
READER'S RESPONSE: I'm angered by the implication that women aren't real students.

EDITED   **Three undergraduates** were jointly awarded the prize for the most unusual recipe.

DEMEANING   Driving **like a typical woman,** Susan backed her car into the shopping cart.
READER'S RESPONSE: This unfairly stereotypes women as incompetent.

EDITED   Susan **inadvertently** backed her car into the shopping cart.

30a
discrm

2 Avoid gender-stereotyping roles and occupations

Our use of language has not entirely kept pace with social changes in men's and women's roles, especially in the area of occupation. Be on the lookout for unfair or inaccurate stereotyping.

STEREOTYPED   The most important thing **a mother can do** to facilitate language growth in **her** child is to read aloud to **him** as much as possible.
READER'S RESPONSE: I'm the father of a little girl. I object to the implication that only mothers can care for their children or that all these children are boys.

EDITED   The most important thing **parents can do** to facilitate language growth in **their children** is to read aloud to **them** as much as possible.

STEREOTYPED   Setting industry standards, the OnCall Remote Beeper is **smaller than most doctors' wallets and easier to answer than a phone call from their wives.**
READER'S RESPONSE: I'm a woman and a doctor. I'm insulted by the assumption that all doctors are male and the negative reference to "wives."

EDITED   Setting industry standards, the OnCall Remote Beeper **will appeal to doctors because of its small size and ease of operation.**

3 Beware of male terms used generically

The most common form of sexist language uses *mankind* or *men* for humankind; *he, his,* or *him* for all people; and a host of words that imply male roles for occupations (*fireman, policeman,* and the like). Most cases are easily edited: *police officer* for *policeman, garbage collector* for *garbageman.* Editing out the generic *he,* however, may prove more difficult. When possible, try first to make the construction plural. For example, you can substitute *their* for *his* or for the clumsy *his or her.*

SEXIST   Every child should bring **his** lunch money to school with **him** each day.

AWKWARD   Every child should bring **his or her** lunch money to school with **him or her** each day.

BETTER   All children should bring **their** lunch money to school with **them** each day.

SEXIST   The Alejandro Restaurant serves **man-sized** portions of paella.

EDITED   The Alejandro Restaurant serves **heaping** portions of paella.

Writer's Alert

Some nonsexist style manuals suggest avoiding the use of generic *he* by making a pronoun plural even if it does not agree in number with the subject (see 17c). Some readers, however, object more strenuously to the error in agreement than to the sexist language. The solution is to avoid both problems whenever possible.

ORIGINAL   **Everyone** has at one time or another squandered **his** money at a gambling casino.

PROBLEMATIC   **Everyone** has at one time or another squandered **their** money at a gambling casino.

BETTER   **Most people have** at one time or another squandered **their** money at a gambling casino.

              Everyone has at one time or another squandered money at a gambling casino.

Exercise 1

A. The following list of words and proposed replacements ranges from the obviously sexist (and therefore inflexible and in need of revision) to the highly debatable and even absurd. For each word, decide whether you would accept the alternative term, and explain why. (Tip: Consult a dictionary when in doubt.)

1. *Persondible* for *mandible*
2. *People-eating tiger* for *man-eating tiger*
3. *Personic depressive* for *manic depressive*
4. *Face-to-face talk* for *man-to-man talk*
5. *Sanitation employee* for *garbageman*
6. *Actor* for both *actor* and *actress*
7. "*Our parent, who art in heaven . . .*" for "*Our Father, who art in heaven. . .*"
8. *Chair* or *chairperson* for *chairman*
9. *Waitperson* or *waitron* for *waiter* and *waitress*
10. *Flight attendant* for *steward* and *stewardess*

B. Compare your responses to Exercise 1A with those of your fellow writers. (And, while you're at it, add *fellow* to your list in Exercise 1A.)

30a
discrm

Did You Know?

In 1990, staff administrators for the city of Sacramento decided to eliminate the term *manhole cover* from city documents, suggesting *maintenance access cover* as a suitable substitute. The access holes are used by both male and female maintenance workers, and it is misleading and inappropriate to characterize them in male terms. Such a change is not all that different from the now widespread use of *flight attendant* for *stewardess, police officer* for *policeman*, or *letter carrier* or *postal worker* for *mailman*.

Anne Rudin (former Sacramento mayor), telephone interview, 17 September 1993.

---

4 Avoid implying sexist views

Whenever you revise your prose, read it once through paying special attention to the ways you characterize men and women and their roles and relationships. Avoid making any offhand remarks that could be interpreted as sexist.

SEXIST   **Being a girl,** Sondra was chosen to be at the top of the cheerleading pyramid.
READER'S RESPONSE: I'm not comfortable with what's being implied about girls' abilities here.

EDITED   **Being the lightest person on the team,** Sondra was chosen to be at the top of the cheerleading pyramid.

SEXIST   **Naturally,** Mike wrestled with the flat tire while Natasha **tried to seduce someone into pulling over and helping.**
READER'S RESPONSE: This stereotypes men as inherently strong and capable and women as sex objects.

EDITED   Mike **struggled to change the tire** while Natasha **tried to flag down a car for help.**

5 Avoid making unwarranted claims

Much sexism finds its energy in misunderstandings about the biological and intellectual nature of men and women. Men are assumed to be stronger, more agile, and more aggressive. Women are assumed to be weaker, worse at math and science but better at language (especially stereotypically "effeminate" forms such as poetry), and less able to manage and negotiate. Many of these assumptions either are unsubstantiated or have come about as self-fulfilling prophecies. In your writing, avoid reinforcing such unfair and incorrect notions.

STEREOTYPED   The anti-abortion protest became more heated when several people appealed to the **instinctive nurturing emotion of the women** in the crowd.
READER'S RESPONSE: Aren't men nurturers too?

EDITED   The anti-abortion protest became more heated when several people appealed to the **feelings of nurture among the parents** in the crowd.

STEREOTYPED   **Behaving like a wimp,** Roger chose to stay home and read instead of playing football with his friends.
READER'S RESPONSE: This attaches negative stereotypes to men who engage in intellectual activities.

REVISED   Roger chose to stay home and read instead of playing football with his friends.

Exercise 2

A. Examine the following paragraph. Then revise its sexist language. Add to the original if you wish.

Preschool programs for children in poor families have always been underfunded and at best only a stopgap measure for more permanent educational reform. This was the message delivered by the man-and-wife team, Dr. and Mrs. Herbert Kline, Ph.D.s, at the Eleventh Regional Conference on Preschool Education. About seven hundred elementary school teachers came to the conference to hear the Klines debunk some old wives' tales about education. The Klines also focused on what the future holds for those interested in becoming public school teachers, including the need to balance work with attending to one's husband and family. Every teacher of young children, Mrs. Herbert Kline pointed out, must not only practice her craft well but also keep abreast of new theory and research which she can then integrate into her classroom in a way rewarding to her and to her students.

 B. In a small group, compare your responses to Exercise 2A. What strategies did you use to revise the sexist language?

Did You Know?

Sensitivity to sexist language has to some extent already changed the way we write. A study examined how frequently masculine forms such as *man* and *he* appeared in print between 1971 and 1979. At the start of that period, the masculine forms were used twelve times in every 5,000 words, but by the end of the period the proportion had dropped to around four forms per 5,000 words. The steepest decline took place in women's magazines, followed by science magazines and newspapers. Congressional records came in last.

David Crystal, *The English Language* (New York: Penguin, 1988) 257.

30b Avoiding discriminatory language

Members of minority groups often suffer from discriminatory practices, especially those that are manifested in language. Most readers won't tolerate racism, and as soon as they encounter **discriminatory language,** they'll stop reading or throw the material away.

1 Avoid derogatory terms

You may be used to hearing certain derogatory terms and epithets in others' speech. Now is the time to make sure that they don't appear in your writing so as not to anger and alienate your readers.

RACIST | The economic problems in the border states are compounded by an increase in the number of **wetbacks** from Mexico, some of whom are illegally trying to rip off jobs from good, taxpaying citizens.
READER'S RESPONSE: I object to characterizing a group of people this way. This derogatory name is offensive.

EDITED | The economic problems in the border states are compounded by an increased number of illegal immigrants from Mexico, some of whom are able to get jobs in this country.

HOMOPHOBIC | The talk show included a panel of **dykes** and **faggots** who spoke about what it's like to be a **pervert.**
READER'S RESPONSE: Using emotionally loaded names for people doesn't encourage reasonable discussion. You'll have to be more objective than this if you want me to pay attention to your ideas.

EDITED | The talk show included a panel of lesbian and gay guests who shared their thoughts about homosexuality.

DEROGATORY | In a typically **white-male** fashion, the principal argued against the schoolteachers' referendum.
READER'S RESPONSE: The fact that white men are in the majority doesn't give you permission to stereotype all white males negatively.

30b
discrm

EDITED | The principal argued against the schoolteachers' referendum.

DISCRIMINATORY | The Johnsons managed to **jew down** the sellers to $196,000.
READER'S RESPONSE: What made you think that you could say this without offending people? It's anti-Semitic! Casual stereotyping is just as offensive as deliberate insults.

EDITED | The Johnsons managed to negotiate a purchase price of $196,000.

2 Revise unfair stereotypes

Some racial and cultural stereotypes are so ingrained in our society that you may not notice them at first. Try to maintain a critical consciousness about these stereotypes, and then edit sentences or words that run the risk of unfairly stereotyping various groups. Don't rely on your intentions here; think first about how your reader *might* construe your words.

RACIST/ELITIST | The Wellingtons described how they **shopped around** in South Carolina for the perfect **mammy** to be a live-in **servant** for their son Bartholomew.
READER'S RESPONSE: I object to the off-hand acceptance of a term like "mammy" and to the condescending attitude about someone who will join the family.

EDITED   The Wellingtons described how they **met** a perfect **live-in nanny** in South Carolina, who **agreed** to care for their son Bartholomew.

DEMEANING   My paper focuses on the **weird** courtship rituals of a **barbaric** Aboriginal tribe living in southwestern Australia.
READER'S RESPONSE: Your paper already sounds biased. How can you fairly inform me about this topic if you don't speak respectfully about this tribe yourself?

EDITED   My paper focuses on the unusual courtship rituals of an Aboriginal tribe living in southwestern Australia.

Writer's Tip

In attempts to create an ideally just world, some social critics have proposed new names and terms for various groups, such as the homeless, the physically and mentally disabled, and even the short or the fat. The terms *vagabond, bum,* and *tramp,* for example, are no longer acceptable; *homeless* is now generally preferred. More questionable, however, are the terms *differently abled* for *disabled, vertically challenged* for *short,* and *prewoman* for *girl.* Debates about such proposed substitutions don't seem likely to subside in the near future. Again, the advice on this matter is to test your choices on your readers and keep up with changes in the language.

**30b
discrm**

3 Choose appropriate group names and terms

Just as the issue of sexism in language continues to evolve, the representation of various groups, especially minorities, cannot be seen as "finally" corrected. Making informed decisions about how to identify different groups may require some thought or consultation. The term *American Indian* is still widely accepted, but a preferred form, *Native American,* has entered the vocabulary. Some Native American groups prefer their tribal names (*Hopi, Navajo, Havasupai*). In the 1960s, the word *Negro* gradually gave way to *black,* but not without considerable overlap in usage and much debate in both the black and white communities, including whether the terms should be capitalized. The term *colored* has been out of use for some time, but *people of color* is now preferred for members of any "nonwhite" minority group. (Many people also object to the term *nonwhite.*) *African American* itself has been gaining popularity in place of *black,* though even African Americans do not agree on which is preferred. Terms for people of Hispanic descent can also be confusing, from *Chicano* (and its feminine form, *Chicana*) for Mexicans to *Latino* and *Latina* for people from South and Central America more generally.

How, then, should you decide what terms to use to describe members of various groups?

1. Whenever possible, use the term preferred *by the group itself.*
2. When there is disagreement within the group itself about the preferred name or term, choose the *most widely accepted term* or the one favored by a majority of the group's members.

Exercise 3

A. The chief editor of a large city newspaper received several complaint letters from readers about a sportswriter's use of the word *niggardly* to characterize the owner of a major football team who was reluctant to pay the salary asked by a new superstar player. In a column, the chief editor explained that the word *niggardly* means "stingy" or "cheap" (from Old Norse) and has absolutely no etymological connection with any racial terms. Yet some readers were offended. And, he argued, as long as they were simply *reminded* of a more offensive word, he had a duty to avoid it. He subsequently asked all reporters and editors to use alternative words. In your judgment, did the chief editor do the right thing? What issues are at stake here? Write a position statement.

B. Share your position statement from Exercise 3A with your classmates.

C. Read a draft of your current paper to find any sexist or discriminatory language. Edit or rewrite those sentences that contain offensive or potentially offensive terms or expressions.

30b
discrm

EDITING FOR PUNCTUATION

31

Commas

Of all the punctuation marks in written English, the comma is probably the one you find easiest to misuse. At some places in a sentence, commas are mandatory; at others, they are optional. Moreover, unneeded or inappropriate commas can confuse your readers or disrupt a sentence's meaning. Consider the following sentence.

31a

> During interviews avoid dominating the discussion because doing so especially with reticent subjects can affect whatever they say cut off the free flow of their ideas and contaminate your data.

Clearly, it's difficult to read this sentence with the commas missing. But where should you use them? In the following version, the correctly used commas make the sentence easier to read and understand.

> During interviews, avoid dominating the discussion because doing so, especially with reticent subjects, can affect whatever they say, cut off the free flow of their ideas, and contaminate your data.

31a Using commas to help join sentences

Whenever you wish to use *and, but, or, for, nor, so,* or *yet* (coordinating conjunctions) to link two word groups that can stand alone as sentences (main clauses—see 14c), you need to use a comma *before the conjunction.*

The air was cold **, and** he could see his breath.

He heard the dog barking on the other side of the field **, so** he decided to investigate.

The ground was rough **, yet** the dog still ran quickly through the grass.

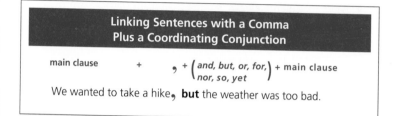

Remember to join main clauses with a comma *plus* a coordinating conjunction, not with a comma alone. If you join the clauses with only a comma, you create a **comma splice,** a serious sentence error that can distract or irritate readers (see 20a).

COMMA SPLICE   The heavy rains loosened the soil by the highway, the mud slide tore the guardrail away.

EDITED   The heavy rains loosened the soil by the highway, **and** the mud slide tore the guardrail away.

EDITED   The heavy rains loosened the soil by the highway, **so** the mud slide tore the guardrail away.

31a

If the main clauses you plan to join are quite short, you can sometimes omit the comma.

The temperature dropped **and** the snow began falling.

A comma is appropriate even with short clauses, however.

Writer's Alert

When you use a comma plus a coordinating conjunction to join main clauses, make sure you do not distract readers by adding commas at the following inappropriate places.

- *After* a coordinating conjunction linking main clauses rather than *before* the conjunction

  INCORRECT   I coated the table with varnish **and,** I sanded it again.

  EDITED   I coated the table with varnish, **and** I sanded it again.

- Between sentence elements other than main clauses—words, phrases, or clauses—that are linked by a coordinating conjunction

INCORRECT	We sanded, and stained the old oak table.
	The comma splits parts of a compound verb that belong together. (See 14b-1 and 14b-2.)
EDITED	We sanded and stained the old oak table.
INCORRECT	I bought a wood stain that was inexpensive, and that cleaned up easily.
	The comma comes between subordinate clauses, not main clauses. (See 14c.)
EDITED	I bought a wood stain that was inexpensive and that cleaned up easily.

Exercise 1

A. Combine each of the following sentence pairs into a single sentence, using commas and coordinating conjunctions.

EXAMPLE

Shopping by mail can be convenient. ~~It~~ sometimes helps save money.   *⌃ and it*

1. Jim wanted to buy paper for his copier. He went to all the office supply stores in town.
2. The stores had plenty of paper. It cost more than Jim was willing to pay.
3. Jim then heard about a mail-order office supply company. He called the company for a catalog.
4. The catalog contained more than fifty different kinds of reasonably priced copier paper. The paper was available in packs of one thousand sheets. For an even greater discount, the paper came in bulk orders of five thousand sheets.
5. He ordered five thousand sheets of medium-quality paper. It lasted for the next three months.

B. Compare your versions of the sentences in Exercise 1A with those produced by a group of classmates. Decide which versions are the most effective and why.

31b Using commas to set off introductory phrases

A comma can help your readers sort sentence parts that might otherwise run together and create confusion. The simplest sentences, consisting of a noun phrase and a verb phrase, need no comma.

noun phrase   verb phrase
Jessica mowed the lawn.

When you add another layer to this basic sentence—a word or a word group—you may need to signal the addition with a comma.

> **Tirelessly,** Jessica mowed the lawn.
> **On Saturday,** Jessica mowed the lawn.
> **After running five miles,** Jessica mowed the lawn.
> **In spite of the throbbing pain in her ankle,** Jessica mowed the lawn.

Strategy

Place a comma after an introductory sentence element when the comma makes the sentence easier to read and understand.

The following sentence needs a comma to avoid confusing readers.

CONFUSING   Forgetting to remove the hose Jessica mowed the lawn.

EDITED   Forgetting to remove the hose, Jessica mowed the lawn.
The comma lets readers know where the introductory word group ends and the main sentence begins.

In contrast, the following sentences are easy to understand without a comma.

CLEAR   By noon Jessica will be finished mowing the lawn.

CLEAR   Suddenly it started raining and Jessica quit mowing.

In general, you need to put a comma at the end of a long introductory element to let readers know where the main sentence begins.

CONFUSING   When Ruane came home and saw the chopped pieces of hose she was furious at Jessica.

CLEAR   When Ruane came home and saw the chopped pieces of hose, **she** was furious at Jessica.

You should also use a comma with a short introductory element that might otherwise briefly confuse readers.

CONFUSING   By six boats began showing up.

EDITED   By six, boats began showing up.

31b

CONFUSING   Adamant that man kept shouting at the bank teller.

EDITED   Adamant, that man kept shouting at the bank teller.

You can insert a comma to tell readers which of two possible meanings you intend.

Curious, George went deeper into the cave.

Curious George went deeper into the cave.
Curious George is a character in a series of children's books.

Well, over there was where I saw him, officer.

Well over there was where I saw him, officer.
Well over there is a location.

Writer's Alert

Sometimes the comma after an introductory word or word group is required; sometimes it is optional. When you are uncertain, stay on the safe side: use a comma.

31b

1 Use a comma after an introductory clause beginning with *because, although, if,* and similar words

When you open a sentence with a subordinate clause (see 26b-1) that begins with a subordinating conjunction such as *since, although, because,* or *when* (see 26b-2 for a detailed list), place a comma after the clause to mark the beginning of the main sentence.

Although I am healthy, I see a physician for a regular checkup.

When I need to see my doctor because I feel ill, I can usually schedule an appointment within a day.

2 Use a comma after an introductory phrase

Phrases lack one or more elements necessary to form a complete sentence, such as a subject, a predicate, or both (see 14b). When you start a sentence with a phrase, you generally add a comma to signal the boundary between the phrase and the main sentence.

During the past decade, Dr. Bandola has worked for an HMO.

Growing tired of the HMO's management, she decided last year to open her own medical practice.

Worried about the costs of a new office, she consulted a real estate broker specializing in medical and dental offices.

To furnish her waiting room, she went to a discount office furniture company.

Her office now furnished, she is ready to begin seeing patients.

Did You Know?

Writers sometimes claim that commas (and other punctuation) ought to appear where someone reading a text aloud would be likely to take a breath. They often use this argument to excuse their highly personal or inconsistent punctuation. As William Bridgwater points out, however, if you try to follow the punctuation marks when you read aloud, you may find yourself "panting like a dog on a hot day." Bridgwater admits that "in English punctuation there are fashions, just as there are in dress and in popular use of phrases," yet he observes that many punctuation practices are "fairly stable" while others, such as the use of commas with nonrestrictive modifiers, "are almost universally accepted by English-speaking readers." His job as a copy editor is to recognize the conventions and "promote punctuation that will aid the reader today."

William Bridgwater, "Copyediting," in *Editors on Editing,* ed. Gerald Gross (New York: HarperCollins 1985) 79–81.

31b

3 Use a comma after introductory words like *however* or transitional phrases like *for example*

Words like *however, nonetheless,* and *moreover* are **conjunctive adverbs** (see 14a-6). *For example, in addition, in contrast,* and similar word groups are **transitional expressions.** Set off both of these elements with a comma when they begin a sentence.

Nonetheless, I do not think we should ban all use of chemical pesticides in the region.

In contrast, a group of organic farmers has been urging us to rely on natural methods of pest control.

You may occasionally wish to open a sentence with an interjection, such as *yes, no, well,* or *oh.* When you do, follow it with a comma unless an exclamation mark is more appropriate as a way to express strong emotion.

> **Yes,** I cleaned the beakers and the test tubes.
>
> **No!** I do not want to attend any more meetings on the problem.

Exercise 2

A. Edit the following sentences by placing commas after introductory elements where necessary.

EXAMPLE

In the past, mailboxes usually had simple designs.

1. In contrast mailboxes today come in many surprising designs.
2. Occasionally people in the suburbs choose an unusual mailbox, but residents of small towns generally display the most imagination.
3. On a recent trip through rural Iowa I noticed mailboxes in the shape of log cabins, igloos, Eiffel Towers, cows, cats, and even parrots.
4. One morning I drove down a block on which each mailbox took the shape of a different kind of fish, including bass, trout, bluegill, shark, pike, and salmon.
5. Whenever you start thinking that people in big cities or suburbs are more creative than people in small towns remember the mailboxes.

31b

B. Working in a group, combine each of the following pairs of sentences by making one an introductory element for the other. Insert commas when appropriate.

EXAMPLE

Because
~~T~~he morning was gray and foggy. ~~M~~any people woke up late.

1. People felt sleepy. They still had to go to their offices and plants for a full day's work.
2. People were trying to get to work on time. They jammed the highways and commuter trains.
3. Avi felt rested and alert. The gloomy weather did not bother him.
4. Avi worked hard throughout the afternoon. The other people in Avi's office were exhausted by two o'clock in the afternoon.
5. Avi still felt awake at seven o'clock in the evening. He went to see a movie.

C. Underline all the introductory sentence elements you use in a paper you are preparing. Then edit the paper by adding any necessary commas after the introductory elements and deleting unnecessary commas.

31c Using commas to set off nonrestrictive modifiers

Restrictive and nonrestrictive modifiers are common midsentence elements. You use a **restrictive modifier** to present information that is essential to the meaning of a passage. You use a **nonrestrictive modifier** to add information that is interesting or useful but that is not essential to the meaning (see 21c).

Strategy

When the information in a modifier is essential to the meaning of a passage, present it without commas so that readers will regard it as a necessary, integral part of the sentence (that is, restrictive clauses need no commas).

RESTRICTIVE   The charts **drawn by hand** were hard to read.

> **READER'S RESPONSE:** This sentence implies that the other charts, presumably those that were computer-generated, were easier to read than the handwritten ones.

When the information in a modifier adds to a passage but is not essential to its meaning, set it off with commas so that readers will regard it as providing helpful but not necessary detail (that is, nonrestrictive modifiers require commas).

NONRESTRICTIVE   The charts**,** **drawn by hand,** were hard to read.

> **READER'S RESPONSE:** This sentence says that all the charts were hard to read. It adds the detail that the charts were hand-drawn but doesn't indicate that this was necessarily related to the problem with legibility.

Because of the difference between restrictive and nonrestrictive modifiers, you can change the meaning of a sentence considerably by deciding whether or not to set off a modifier with commas.

1 Identify nonrestrictive modifiers

As you edit, you need to identify nonrestrictive modifiers and set them off with commas. You also need to be able to identify restrictive modifiers, which require no commas to set them off.

Strategy

To identify a nonrestrictive modifier, try eliminating the modifier from a sentence. If you can do so without altering the sentence's essential meaning, then the modifier is nonrestrictive and you should use commas with it. Remember, eliminating a nonrestrictive modifier may make a sentence less informative but will not change its basic meaning.

UNEDITED SENTENCE	Their band **which performs primarily in small venues like clubs** has gotten many fine reviews for its music.
WITHOUT MODIFIER	Their band has gotten many fine reviews for its music. The meaning is retained, though the sentence does not offer as much interesting information. The modifier is nonrestrictive.
EDITED	Their band, **which performs primarily in small venues like clubs,** has gotten many fine reviews for its music.

If eliminating a modifier changes a sentence's meaning, the modifier is restrictive. Do not set it off with commas.

31c

UNEDITED SENTENCE	Executives, **who do not know how to cope with stress,** are prone to stress-related illness.
WITHOUT MODIFIER	Executives are prone to stress-related illness. The intended meaning of the original sentence is that *some* executives are susceptible to stress-related problems; in contrast, the shortened sentence says they *all* are. The modifier is restrictive.
EDITED	Executives **who do not know how to cope with stress** are prone to stress-related illness.

2 Place commas before, after, or around nonrestrictive modifiers

If a nonrestrictive modifier appears in the middle of a sentence, enclose it with commas. Place a comma after one coming at the beginning of a sentence and before one coming at the end.

main clause begins,   nonrestrictive modifier,   main clause ends
The public hearing, scheduled for 7 p.m., will gather responses to cable TV rates.

nonrestrictive modifier,   main clause
Because their costs are rising, the cable companies have requested a rate hike.

main clause,   nonrestrictive modifier
Many residents oppose the hike, which is larger than last year's.

3 Pay special attention to modifying clauses, phrases, and appositives

In identifying nonrestrictive (and restrictive) modifiers as you edit, keep in mind that they can be clauses, phrases, or words (see 21c).

Modifying Clauses Beginning with *Who* and *Which*. Pay special attention to clauses beginning with *who, which, that, whom, whose, when,* or *where* (see 14c-5), and decide whether or not they should be set off with commas. These common modifying elements can appear in the middle or at the end of a sentence.

NONRESTRICTIVE   Preventive dentistry**,** **which is receiving greater emphasis,** may actually reduce the number of times each of us has to visit a dentist's office.

NONRESTRICTIVE   At the heart of preventive dentistry are toothbrushing, flossing, and rinsing**, which are all easily done.**

RESTRICTIVE   Dentists **who make a special effort to encourage good oral hygiene** often provide helpful pamphlets and samples of toothbrushes and floss.

Modifying Phrases. Be alert as well for phrases (word groups lacking a subject, a predicate, or both) that are nonrestrictive and should be marked with commas. These modifying elements can appear at the beginning, middle, or end of sentences.

NONRESTRICTIVE   **Occupying the daily headline of the local newspaper for the last two weeks,** our city's budget crisis now threatens to spread to the state budget.

NONRESTRICTIVE   The governor has called for a conference of the people most directly involved in trying to solve the budget problem**, including the mayor, state legislators, and the city's budget director.**

RESTRICTIVE   City services **popular with voters** are seldom cut from the budget.

Appositives. An **appositive** is a noun or pronoun that renames or stands for a preceding noun. Since most appositives are nonrestrictive, you generally need to set off appositives with a comma. Be on the lookout for an occasional restrictive appositive, however, and do not use commas with it.

NONRESTRICTIVE   Amy Nguyen**,** **a poet from Vietnam,** recently published her second collection of verse.

31c

NONRESTRICTIVE   The athletic performance drink, **a concoction of elec-trolytes, vitamins, minerals, and fructose,** contributed to Jose's endurance in the marathon.

NONRESTRICTIVE   Stump grinding, **a method for removing old tree roots with a special machine,** is much easier than digging the roots out with a shovel.

RESTRICTIVE   The well-known executive **Louis Gerstner** went from heading RJR Nabisco to the top job at IBM.

RESTRICTIVE   The terms ***cognitive* and *neural pathways*** are familiar to anyone involved in brain research.

Exercise 3

A. Edit the following sentences to set off all nonrestrictive modifiers with commas and to eliminate any commas that unnecessarily set off restrictive modifiers.

EXAMPLE
My mother, who is ninety, lives in the retirement residence/called South Bay Manor.

1. Fifty years ago, a residence that served retired people, was called an old folks' home.
2. These homes which provided few services for residents were apartment buildings with dining rooms.
3. A retirement residence today offers many things to do including recreational activities, fitness programs, trips, classes, and social events.
4. The image of infirm people, sitting in rocking chairs, has been replaced by one of senior citizens, who are vigorous and involved.
5. Retirement residences often known as retirement communities are small towns, where people go to lead active lives.

B. Have each member of a small group bring in a paragraph from a magazine article, both in original form and rewritten to eliminate the commas setting off all nonrestrictive modifiers. As a group, first attempt to restore the commas to the rewritten versions; then check the originals to see if you agree with their punctuation.

C. Edit a draft paper of your own by first underlining all restrictive and nonrestrictive modifiers and then adding or eliminating commas as appropriate. You may wish to focus your editing on modifiers that give you particular trouble, such as clauses beginning with *who, which, that, when,* or *where.*

31c

31d Using commas to set off parenthetical expressions

Remember that the basic structure of a sentence can be interrupted with all sorts of words and word groups that add information or modify its various elements, including conjunctive adverbs (like *however* or *nonetheless*), transitional words (like *in contrast*), and parenthetical remarks.

Use commas to set off conjunctive adverbs like *however* and *moreover* (see 14a-6, 20b) when they appear in the middle of a sentence or at the beginning or end. Do the same with transitional expressions like *on the other hand* or *for example* and with parenthetical remarks like *in fact* or *more importantly* (sometimes called **interrupters**).

TRANSITIONAL EXPRESSION	The hailstorm last week, **on the other hand,** caused severe damage.
INTERRUPTER	**In fact,** the hailstorm was so powerful that it broke a dozen priceless stained glass windows on the west side of the church.
CONJUNCTIVE ADVERB	We should not be surprised, **therefore,** if someone takes up a collection for the windows' repair.

31d

You should also use commas to set off tag questions, statements of contrast, and words indicating direct address.

TAG QUESTIONS	We should be ready to contribute to the cause even if we don't attend the church, **shouldn't we?**
STATEMENT OF CONTRAST	The windows' beauty touched all of us in the community, **not just the church members.**
DIRECT ADDRESS	Please remember, **friends of beauty,** that your contribution will help restore the windows to their former magnificence.

Exercise 4

Edit the following sentences to add or eliminate commas as appropriate.

EXAMPLE

Scheduling may be‸in fact‸the toughest job any manager faces.

1. Project schedules need to be arranged so that the job gets done on time of course.
2. Moreover meetings need to be set up so they do not interrupt people's work, unnecessarily.

3. Most staff members are cooperative however, and may even offer suggestions for scheduling.
4. Management training programs should, I think offer instruction in scheduling techniques.
5. Remember your staff's time is too valuable to be wasted.

31e Using commas in a series

Whenever you list items in a series and give each roughly equal status, you should always separate the items with commas. In one sense, commas take the place of a repeated *and,* which appears only before the last item in the series.

HARD TO READ   Harvey's favorite novels are *Moby Dick* **and** *The Awakening* **and** *Jane Eyre* **and** *Things Fall Apart.*

EDITED   Harvey's favorite novels are *Moby Dick*, *The Awakening*, *Jane Eyre*, **and** *Things Fall Apart.*

Note how difficult the following sentence is to read when the series lacks commas.

HARD TO READ   Tiffany's favorite novels, however, are *War and Peace Of Time and the River Heart of Darkness* and *The Color Purple.*

EDITED   Tiffany's favorite novels, however, are *War and Peace*, *Of Time and the River*, *Heart of Darkness*, and *The Color Purple.*

Placing a comma before the *and* to introduce the last item in a series helps avoid confusion. Many readers prefer this practice, especially in academic and professional writing.

CONFUSING   The ingredients for the casserole are peas, potatoes, ham, caramelized sugar and bread crumbs.

> **READER'S RESPONSE:** Does *caramelized sugar and bread crumbs* refer to some special mixture, or are they two separate ingredients?

EDITED   The ingredients for the casserole are peas, potatoes, ham, caramelized sugar, and bread crumbs.

A numbered or lettered list that is part of a sentence should be punctuated as a series.

To make sure your analysis is complete, you should (1) check the bottom of the container for residue, (2) measure the salinity of the water, (3) weigh any organic waste in the filter, and (4) determine the amount of dissolved oxygen in the water.

Writer's Tip

When the items in a list are long and complex or contain commas, separate the items with semicolons rather than commas (see 32a).

CONFUSING The company is marketing a line of jigsaw puzzles of cities, like San Antonio, Texas, states, like Michigan and Montana, and countries, like Mexico, Japan, and France.

EDITED The company is marketing a line of jigsaw puzzles of cities, like San Antonio, Texas; states, like Michigan and Montana; and countries, like Mexico, Japan, and France.

31f Separating coordinate adjectives with a comma

In a pair of **coordinate adjectives,** each adjective modifies a noun on its own. Therefore, separate coordinate adjectives with commas to indicate that they apply to the noun (or pronoun) in an equal manner.

COORDINATE (EQUAL) These drawings describe a **quick, simple** solution to the drainage problem.

With **noncoordinate adjectives,** one modifies the other, and it, in turn, modifies the noun (or pronoun). Do not separate adjectives of this kind with a comma.

NONCOORDINATE (UNEQUAL) We can use **flexible plastic** pipe to carry water away from the building.

In place of a comma, you can connect coordinate adjectives with *and* or *but.*

COORDINATE These drawings describe a **quick and simple** solution to the drainage problem.

Strategy

To identify coordinate adjectives, ask one of the following questions. If the answer is *yes,* the adjectives are coordinate and should be separated with a comma.

- Can you place *and* or *but* between the adjectives?

  COORDINATE   Through irrigation, the region's farmers have turned dry, infertile [*dry and infertile?—yes*] land into orchards.

  EDITED   Through irrigation, the region's farmers have turned dry, infertile land into orchards.

  NOT COORDINATE   Five percent of the budget goes to new telecommunications [*new and telecommunications?—no*] equipment.

- Does the sense of the passage change if you invert the adjectives?

  COORDINATE   We wanted to move from our small cramped [*cramped small?—no change*] apartment.

  EDITED   We wanted to move from our small, cramped apartment.

  NOT COORDINATE   We considered buying a red brick [*brick red?—changes*] house.

  Since *brick red* is a color, the house could be made of wood.

Exercise 5

A. Edit the following sentences so that any series and any coordinate adjectives are correctly punctuated. Let any correct sentence stand.

EXAMPLE
McDonald's, Burger King, and Wendy's are worldwide symbols of American culture.

1. McDonald's and the others offer quick appetizing meals and clean pleasant surroundings.
2. In the late 1940s, the McDonald brothers opened a restaurant serving a limited inexpensive menu, including fifteen-cent hamburgers french fries and shakes.
3. The brothers did not want to expand their modestly successful restaurant into a chain.
4. Ray Kroc, a manufacturer of milkshake machines, recognized the potential of the brothers' innovations joined their business to help it expand and, frustrated by their lack of ambition, eventually bought them out.
5. Kroc continued to develop innovative imaginative ways to serve customers, and these fast efficient practices have come to characterize today's fast-food restaurants.

B. Working with a partner, exchange your current papers. Edit your partner's draft so that all series and coordinate adjectives are correctly punctuated.

31g Using commas with dates, numbers, addresses, place names, people's titles, and letters

You should separate the elements in dates, place names, long numbers, and addresses according to conventional practice. Separate the elements whether or not they appear in sentences.

1 Dates

Put a comma between the date and the year and between the day of the week and the date.

> The first computer in this office arrived on August 17, 1983.
> The workshop will begin on Wednesday, September 11.

In the middle of a sentence, follow the year with a comma when you are giving the full date.

> On February 4, 1923, the woman destined to be my mother was born in the middle of a snowstorm.

31g
⌇

Do not use commas when the date contains only a month and year or a month and a day.

> A test version of the software will be available in January 1997. The regular version will be shipped to stores on June 1.

Likewise, do not use commas with dates stating a season and a year.

> The fall 1996 issue of the magazine arrived late.

You do not need to use commas when you present the elements of a date in inverted order: 5 July 1973.

2 Numbers

In order to help your readers understand long numbers, use commas to create groups of three, beginning from the right. In numbers with four digits, you may choose whether or not to use the comma, but keep your practice consistent within an essay or report.

> During the livestock census on the ranch, we counted **1, 746** sheep, **835** beef cattle, and **3, 589** chickens.

The combined income for people in our rural town is \$8,543,234.

The best personal copier available costs \$1,525 at Electronics World.

Omit commas in addresses or page numbers of four numbers or more.

18520 South Kedzie Drive   page 2054

3 Addresses and place names

Separate names of cities and states with commas.

Kansas City, Missouri, is a larger town than Kansas City, Kansas.

For addresses appearing within a sentence, place a comma between all elements *except* the state and ZIP code.

You can order the zucchini and carrot seeds from Fredelle and Family, Seed Brokers, Box 389, Holland, Michigan 30127.

31g

Do not place a comma after the ZIP code unless the punctuation of some other sentence element requires one.

NO COMMA   Send the bill to Mr. Robert Mfume at 82 Nassau Avenue, Kenmore, New York 11327-8501 for a full refund.

COMMA NEEDED   The pamphlet can be obtained from Bradley Hospital, Veterans Memorial Parkway, East Providence, Rhode Island 02915, a children's psychiatric center.

4 People's names and titles

Place a comma before a title that comes after a person's name.

The report on possible lung damage among plant employees was prepared by **Luis Aguayo, M.D.**

If the name and title come at the beginning of a sentence or in the middle, use a comma after the title as well.

We hired **Crystal Bronkowski, A.I.A.,** to design the new building.

When you give a person's surname (last name) first, separate it from the first name with a comma: **Shamoon, Linda K.**

5 Openings and closings of letters

Use a comma after the opening of personal or informal letters.

Dear Tiffany**,**   Dear Fellow Volleyball Players**,**

Use a colon after the introduction in business and formal letters.

Dear Specialty Metals Customers**:**   To Whom It May Concern**:**

Use a comma after a letter's closing, just before the signature.

Sincerely**,**   Best wishes**,**   With affection**,**   Regards**,**

Exercise 6

A. Edit the following sentences by adding or eliminating commas as appropriate.

EXAMPLE

My mother remembers assembling her first jigsaw puzzle in autumn**⁄** 1953, several months before my birth on January 22**⁁**1954.

31g

1. Puzzles have fascinated me for the last thirty years, and last year I spent exactly $1479.83 on them.
2. For my birthday this year, one cousin gave me a map of Chicago Illinois in the form of a jigsaw puzzle, and another cousin gave me a puzzle of a seventeenth-century print from the Beinecke Library at Yale University New Haven Connecticut.
3. I have ordered a puzzle map of Atlanta Georgia from Buffalo Games, Inc. P.O. Box 85 601 Amherst Street Buffalo New York 14207 and a puzzle of Edward Hopper's painting, *Nighthawks* from Galison Books 36 West 44th Street New York New York 10036 .
4. From January through June 1994, I assembled one puzzle a week, with the puzzles ranging from 500 to 1250 pieces each for a total of somewhere between 10500 pieces and 26250 pieces.
5. I am planning to have a business card made up with both my official and unofficial titles, Jessica Montoya Ph.D. Puzzle Assembler.

B. Working in a group, share copies of magazine or newspaper articles that contain numbers, addresses, people's names and titles, or openings and closings of letters. Check the articles to see whether they follow the same conventions for comma use as those described in 31g. If not, or if the author uses commas inconsistently, edit each article so that it agrees with the recommendations for comma use covered in 31g.

31h Using commas with quotations

When you introduce or conclude a quotation by indicating its source or explaining the context, you should remind readers of the difference between your explanation and the quotation itself by using commas to separate them.

> At the grand opening, he said **,** "This facility is dedicated to the physical and mental health of the citizens of Oakdale."

> "Some books are meant to be chewed **,**" said Francis Bacon **,** "and others to be digested."
> Because the explanatory words interrupt the quotation, the first part ends with a comma.

> "The fire doors need to be replaced before the school can be reopened **,**" the commissioner wrote.

When a quotation ends with a question mark or an exclamation point, you should keep this punctuation even if you provide an explanation after the quotation.

> "We can't afford the $30,000 to replace the doors right away **!**" the school board president responded angrily.

> "Why can't you understand the paramount importance of fire safety **?**" the commissioner retorted.

If your explanation ends with *that* just before the quotation, do not include a comma.

> Lorene Cary begins her story by saying that "they had just come home from Woolworth's, where they both worked at the cheap-and-greasy fountain on Friday nights and Saturdays in a town they and their friends called 'Tacky' Darby."

When you quote a person's words indirectly (rather than word for word in quotation marks), do not use a comma after *that*.

FAULTY	He testified that **,** he did not damage the machinery as a protest during the strike.
EDITED	He testified that he did not damage the machinery as a protest during the strike.

Exercise 7

A. Edit the following passages by adding, deleting, or moving commas so that quotations are appropriately punctuated.

"Ice cream is virtually the only food we eat frozen, which means that its flavor, which we define as a composite of taste and smell, is only fully released upon melting" explains Arun Kilara, a 43-year-old professor of food science at Penn State and one of the world's acknowledged authorities on ice cream.

Not surprisingly, few true ice cream connoisseurs are fond of the industry's use of fat substitutes, such as the complex protein found in NutraSweet's Simplesse. "The search for the perfect fat substitute" Kilara says "is like a contemporary version of alchemy—lots of useful discoveries, but they'll never turn lead into gold." While some protein-based fat substitutes approximate fat's texture, or "mouth feel" he explains, they cannot dissolve flavor compounds in the same way.

"The smaller the ice crystals, the smoother the ice cream" says Kilara. "You get the smallest crystals when the drop in temperature is the most rapid and when agitation is most vigorous."

"There's one basic truth about ice cream—its quality begins deteriorating from the moment it is made" Kilara concludes. "Over the product's lifetime, ice cream's air escapes, its fat clumps, its ice melts, and its water freezes." —LAWRENCE E. JOSEPH, "The Scoop on Ice Cream"

31i

B. Working in a group, write a paragraph that presents information drawn from a newspaper or magazine article. Include several quotations from the article in your paragraph. Indicate the source or context for the quotations, and use commas appropriately to introduce or conclude the quoted material.

C. Edit a draft paper of your own for proper comma use at the beginning and end of quoted material.

31i Using commas to make your meaning clear

Even if no rule specifies a comma, you may still include one in a sentence if it is necessary to make your meaning clear to readers, to remind them of deleted words, or to add emphasis.

CONFUSING	When food is scarce, animals that can expand their grazing territory at the expense of other species.
EDITED	When food is scarce, animals that can, expand their grazing territory at the expense of other species.
HARD TO READ	Anyone who can afford to buy this high-speed file management program should.

EDITED   Anyone who can afford to buy this high-speed file management program, should.

The comma reminds readers that *should* means "should do so."

UNEMPHATIC   Stocks go up and down.

EMPHATIC   Stocks go up, and down.

The comma emphasizes the contrast.

31j Avoiding commas that do not belong

When they are not sure precisely where to put commas, some writers insert them at every possible point. The result is confusing and irritating to readers. Try to avoid scattering commas throughout your writing with no clear purpose in mind. If you are not sure whether to add a comma, leave it out until you have checked to make sure one is required. In addition, avoid using commas in the situations discussed below.

1 Do not insert a comma after words like *although* and *because* when introducing a clause

Certain conjunctions and other words may mislead you into thinking you need a comma. Among the most common words of this type are subordinating conjunctions like *although, when,* and *since* (see 26b-2 for a detailed list). They introduce an entire subordinate clause and should not be set off with commas. One reason writers set off subordinating conjunctions with commas is that they mistake the words for conjunctive adverbs (like *however*) and transitional expressions (such as *for example*), which should be set off with commas (see 20b).

INCORRECT   **Although,** Jim had just started to learn how to ski, we took him to the most expert slope on his first trip up the mountain.

EDITED   **Although** Jim had just started to learn how to ski, we took him to the most expert slope on his first trip up the mountain.

2 Do not insert a comma between a subject and a predicate

Unless subjects and predicates are separated by a modifying clause, don't insert a comma between them.

INCORRECT	Cézanne's painting *Rocks at L'Estaque*, hangs in the Museu de Arte in São Paulo, Brazil.
EDITED	Cézanne's painting *Rocks at L'Estaque* hangs in the Museu de Arte in São Paulo, Brazil.

3 Do not overuse commas

Today readers generally prefer a style in which commas are not used heavily. Too many commas, even when they are correctly used, can lead to a style that is choppy and hard to read. Whenever possible, avoid sentence structures that call for a large number of commas. If necessary, edit and rewrite to eliminate excessive comma use.

TOO MANY COMMAS	Samantha, always one, like her mother, to speak her mind, loudly protested the use of force, as she called it, by two store detectives, who had been observing her while she, looking for bargains, absentmindedly slipped a pair of gloves into her jacket pocket.
EDITED	Always one to speak her mind, like her mother, Samantha loudly protested what she considered the use of force by two store detectives who saw her absentmindedly slip a pair of gloves into her jacket pocket while she was looking for bargains.

31j
no ⌇

In the first passage, none of the commas are incorrect, but the comma is clearly overused. In the second passage, careful editing turns a nine-comma sentence into one with two commas.

Exercise 8

A. Edit each of the following sentences in two ways: (1) by removing any unnecessary commas, and (2) by rewriting to create sentence structures that contain fewer commas, all of which are necesssary.

EXAMPLE
When/they realized they had no job prospects, the five friends/ formed/a company, which they called Home Restorers, Inc.
When they realized they had no job prospects, the five friends formed Home Restorers, Inc.

1. Because, she likes the outdoors, Sandy, a devoted gardener, takes care of landscaping, grass cutting, and outdoor cleanup.
2. Strong, tireless Jun, does roofing, paving, and similar work.
3. Interior design was, Padmaja's major, so she, everyone agrees, is the person best qualified to do interior decorating.

4. Having painted, her parents' house one summer, Rachael was, chosen, by her partners, as the company's painting supervisor.

5. Desperate, for a place in the company, Joel decided that, marketing, because it would draw on his undergraduate work in sociology, was the best thing for him to do.

B. Exchange draft papers with another writer, and edit each other's work to eliminate unnecessary commas. When you encounter a sentence that might be rewritten to reduce the number of commas, underline it. When your partner returns your paper, check over the editorial changes and consider rewriting any underlined sentences.

31j
no ⌃

Semicolons and Colons

Semicolons and colons help you connect words, word groups, or sentences in useful and varied ways. Compare the following brief passages.

> On April 12, 1861, at 4:30 a.m., one of Beauregard's batteries fired upon Fort **Sumter . The** Civil War had begun.

> On April 12, 1861, at 4:30 a.m., one of Beauregard's batteries fired upon Fort **Sumter ; the** Civil War had begun.

> On April 12, 1861, at 4:30 a.m., one of Beauregard's batteries fired upon Fort **Sumter : the** Civil War had begun.

The first version consists of two sentences; the second and third join the sentences with a semicolon and a colon, respectively. All three examples are correct, yet each encourages readers to take a different perspective. Note, for example, that in the first version there is no *necessary* connection between the two sentences. Readers may choose whether to view the sentences as a simple statement of facts or as the presentation of a dramatic moment. In the second version, however, the semicolon connects the two statements and encourages readers to link the firing of a gun battery to the beginning of the Civil War. In the third sentence, the colon provides even more direction to readers. It encourages them to view the guns' firing as a dramatic and significant moment: the beginning of the Civil War.

32a Using semicolons

A semicolon joins two main clauses that could act as complete sentences on their own. The semicolon indicates that the clauses are linked logically; at the same time, it creates a brief reading pause between them.

1 Try joining main clauses with a semicolon

You can use a semicolon to join two complete sentences (main clauses—see 14c) into a single unit. Think of a semicolon as an alternative to using a period and starting a new sentence.

TWO SENTENCES	The demand for paper products is at an all-time high. Business and industry alone consume millions of tons of paper each year.
ONE SENTENCE	The demand for paper products is at an all-time high; business and industry alone consume millions of tons of paper each year.

You signal the relationship between main clauses by joining them with a semicolon, though you do not specify the logical link as you might by joining clauses with a conjunction such as *and, but,* or *yet* (see 26a). A semicolon can highlight the close relationship of ideas or dramatically emphasize a contrast between clauses.

> The city council wants more parks, an expanded recreation program, and a civic center; the mayor wants to cut expenses and limit services.

When you join main clauses with a semicolon, make sure readers will be able to recognize the logical relationship without having to puzzle over the sentence.

32a
;

Strategy

Remember that a semicolon joins main clauses that can stand on their own as sentences. If you can't convert the clauses on either side of a semicolon into complete sentences, the semicolon has probably been misused.

INCORRECT	The demand for recycled paper has also increased greatly; with manufacturers rushing to develop reliable supplies of scrap paper.
TEST	The demand for recycled paper has also increased greatly. The first clause is a complete sentence. With manufacturers rushing to develop reliable supplies of scrap paper. The second part is a sentence fragment.
CORRECT	The demand for recycled paper has also increased greatly; manufacturers are rushing to develop reliable supplies of scrap paper.

Did You Know?

Historically, the semicolon was often used to mark an abbreviation, indicating that something had been eliminated or cut off. The word *Esquire,* for example, was often abbreviated with a semicolon (*Esq;*), as were *Mr;* and *Mrs;*. This usage fell out of favor in the United States in the nineteenth century. Many Europeans still use the semicolon to indicate abbreviation, and some use it occasionally in formal citations where Americans would use a comma (*Dear Sir:* can become, for example, *Monsieur;* in French).

2 Use a semicolon with transition words

When you use a semicolon alone to link main clauses, you ask your readers to recognize the logical link between the clauses. When you use a transition word like *however* or a transitional expression like *on the other hand*, you create a different effect. The transition specifies the relationship of the clauses, so the effect on readers is something like the following.

Assertion → semicolon → transition → assertion
          (pause)   *(consider relationship)*

I like apples **;** **however ,** I hate pears.
assertion pause contrast   assertion

To specify the transition between clauses, you can choose a **conjunctive adverb** such as *however, moreover, thus,* or *therefore* (see p. 390 for a detailed list) or a **transitional expression** like *for example, in contrast,* or *on the other hand.* The linking word or phrase can appear between clauses (just after the semicolon), within one of the clauses, or at the end of a clause. If such a transition comes between clauses, right after a semicolon, it must be followed by a comma; if it comes within a clause, it must be preceded and followed by commas; if it comes at the end of a clause, it must be preceded by a comma.

BETWEEN CLAUSES Joe returned from the Arctic **;** **however ,** Alan was never found.

WITHIN A CLAUSE Joe returned from the Arctic **;** Alan **,** **however ,** was never found.

AT END OF CLAUSE Joe returned from the Arctic **;** Alan was never found **,** **however.**

32a
;

Writer's Tip

Consider joining a series of short to medium-length sentences with semicolons when (1) the sentences are logically linked, (2) the unlinked sentences seem choppy or disconnected, and (3) commas separate the elements enough to encourage readers to consider each one fully.

CHOPPY	The shelty took first prize. The German shepherd took second. The poodle walked away in third place.
BETTER	The shelty took first prize, the German shepherd took second, **and** the poodle walked away in third place.
MOST EFFECTIVE	The shelty took first prize; the German shepherd took second; and the poodle walked away in third place.

32a
;

3 Use a semicolon with deleted structures

There are exceptions to the rule that semicolons must join main clauses. In some cases, elements within a second clause can be deleted if they "match" elements in the first clause. The two clauses can be joined with a semicolon even though the second could not stand on its own as a sentence.

ELEMENTS INCLUDED	In winter, **the hotel guests enjoy** the log fire in the dining room; in summer, **the hotel guests enjoy** the patio overlooking the river.
ELEMENTS DELETED	In winter, **the hotel guests enjoy** the log fire in the dining room; in summer, the patio overlooking the river.

4 Use a semicolon with a complex series

Most of the time, you can use commas to highlight and separate elements in a series, with no risk of confusion (see 31e). When some of the items themselves contain commas, however, readers may have a hard time deciding which commas mark the parts of the series and which belong within the items, as in the following example.

CONFUSING	For the project, I interviewed Debbie Rios, my roommate, Rhonda Marron, my former employer, and my calculus instructor. READER'S RESPONSE: How many people were interviewed? Three, four, or five?

To avoid confusion, put semicolons between elements in a series when one or more of the elements contain commas or some other internal punctuation, such as a dash, parentheses, or a colon.

EDITED   For the project, I interviewed Debbie Rios, my roommate; Rhonda Marron, my former employer; and my calculus instructor.

Exercise 1

A. The following passage contains some semicolons used correctly and some used incorrectly. It also contains some sentences that might be more effective if joined with semicolons and others that would be better as separate sentences. Rewrite the passage, adding or eliminating semicolons and making any other changes necessary to create a more effective piece of writing.

The Grateful Dead came back into my life recently; largely because of my children's interest. My daughter has been *associated* with the group; I find it difficult to apply the common description of a fan as a Deadhead; since she was fifteen. Her school band; the Cosmic Country Sound, was patterned after the Grateful Dead; she was its lead singer and tambourine player.

I had no idea that my son, four years younger; had any interest in the group. His room is decorated with posters of Boris Becker and Albert Einstein. But then a year ago he let his hair grow into a mane; started wearing beaded necklaces and rope wristlets, and, sure enough; turned up one day at my study door to announce, "Dad; there's this concert I'd like to go to...."

Both of my children have urged me to go to a Grateful Dead concert. I hadn't taken them up on the offer until this summer; when by chance I met someone way up in the band's hierarchy who gave me not only some tickets to a concert at the Meadowlands in New Jersey; but also a backstage pass. I told my son. His eyes widened at the news. He invited three of his friends. His sister; with a job on the West Coast, was devastated that she couldn't be on hand.

— Adapted from GEORGE PLIMPTON, "Bonding with the Grateful Dead"

32a
;

B. The passage in Exercise 1A can be rewritten in many ways, depending on the focus and stylistic effect a writer wishes to create. Share your version of the passage with a group of fellow students. Each group member should be ready to explain the reasons for his or her choices when they differ from those of other writers in the group. As a group, rewrite the passage, and share that version with the class.

C. Circle the semicolons in a paper you are currently working on. Check to see whether each one is used effectively and correctly. If you've used few or no semicolons, check for short sentences, and decide whether semicolons could link them effectively. Check also for sentences with lists or with many commas, and decide whether editing to use semicolons would make these sentences more forceful.

32b Using colons

You can use a colon to introduce or "set up" an example, illustration, or list. By calling attention to what follows, a colon seems to say "Here is . . ." or "Pay attention to this." In most cases, the words coming *before* a colon form a complete sentence while those coming after take the form of a dependent clause, a phrase, or even a single word.

WORDS   Bring these things with you: paintbrushes, a drop cloth, and gloves.

WORDS, PHRASES, Each year the river claims something that optimistic humans
AND CLAUSES   have built on its banks: part of a yard, a toolshed, a drive-
                        way edged with bushes, or a house that people admired for
                        its dramatic view from the bluff.

Sometimes, however, you may wish to use a colon to join two sentences, the first providing a relatively broad statement and the second offering a sharper focus, a summary, or a change in direction.

After searching through the house most of the day, she finally admitted the obvious: her grandmother's ring was lost.

1 Use a colon to introduce lists and examples

You can use colons to introduce quotations, examples, concluding generalizations, and items in a series. Commonly, a colon comes after the first part of a sentence, which offers a statement or generalization that the remainder of the sentence illustrates, explains, or makes concrete and particular.

Mulholland believed that the growing city at the edge of the desert would have to tap another source of water: the Owens Valley, several hundred miles away.

She has only one remaining vice: coffee.

By asking readers to pause partway through a sentence, a colon calls special attention to the second half of the statement and avoids the run-together effect that a comma may create.

RUN TOGETHER   After saving for eleven years, the Cranes finally had enough money to get what they wanted, a ranch in Wyoming where they could live out their own version of self-reliance.

EDITED   After saving for eleven years, the Cranes finally had enough money to get what they wanted: a ranch in Wyoming where they could live out their own version of self-reliance.

A colon can also introduce a more formal series or list.

Though baseball doesn't reign in England, the British enjoy a wide variety of sports: soccer, golf, rugby, cricket, tennis, croquet, polo, and billiards, to name just a few.

The prosecutor introduced into evidence the following exhibits: a nine-inch knife, a piece of clothing belonging to the victim, and a bloodstained rag from the suspect's car.

Writer's Tip

When a complete sentence follows a colon, you can choose to begin it with either a capital or lowercase letter. Stick to one style or the other throughout an essay.

CORRECT
The airline lost the bag containing my insulated jacket, pants, and boots: **our** long-awaited winter hike in the Rockies was ruined.

ALSO CORRECT
The airline lost the bag containing my insulated jacket, pants, and boots: **Our** long-awaited winter hike in the Rockies was ruined.

When the word group following a colon is not a sentence, begin it with a lowercase letter.

LOWERCASE
The symptoms are as follows: **sore** throat, joint pain, fever, and headache.

32b
:

2 Use a colon to introduce quotations

You can also use a colon as a convenient way to introduce quotations, either short ones that you integrate into your own words or longer ones that you set off from the body of your text (see Chapter 34). The word group before the colon must be a complete sentence; if it is not, use a comma instead.

Ms. Johnson responded to criticism of the sales campaign **:** "For a program launched in the middle of a recession, sales were actually quite strong."

3 Use a colon to separate titles and subtitles

Colons separate the main titles of books, movies, and the like from their subtitles.

Computers for the Absolute Novice **:** *An Introduction*

Freddie's Dead **:** *The Final Nightmare*

Date Rape **:** A Major Problem on Today's Campuses
The title of your own paper should not be italicized.

Colons are also used in separating hours from minutes (10:32); in certain chapter and verse notations, such as those in the Bible (John 8:21–23); and in some reference styles, such as that of the Modern Language Association (MLA) (see 46b).

4 Use a colon to join sentences

A colon is one of the strategies you can use to join complete sentences (main clauses). (See 20b.) It works most effectively when the second sentence sharply focuses, sums up, or illustrates the first.

Hearing a sound like both rushing water and cloth being ripped, she knew it was too late to abandon her house in the canyon **:** The mud slide had begun.

In the middle of a week filled with heavy rain and mud slides, Joel thought of the bushes and grasses now sprouting **:** Next summer the hillside might be on fire.

5 Avoid overuse and misuse of colons

Because colons add emphasis to examples and assertions, you may be tempted to use them often. Don't. Vary your style. Remember that anything is weakened by overuse.

COLON OVERUSED Suzanne had an obsession for books **:** there were bookshelves in her kitchen, her bathrooms, and even her closets. She read voraciously **:** in the morning, at lunch, after dinner, and late at night. Her house soon turned into a lending library **:** friends and relatives borrowed books by the dozen. And she liked everything: classics, mysteries, pulp romances, autobiographies.

EDITED   Suzanne had an obsession for books. There were book-shelves in her kitchen, her bathrooms, and even her clos-ets. She read voraciously **whenever she could, from morning to** late at night. Her house soon turned into a lend-ing library, friends and relatives borrow**ing** books by the dozen. And she liked everything: classics, mysteries, pulp romances, autobiographies.

You can use a colon to introduce a list at the end of a complete sentence. When you introduce a list with a word group other than a complete sentence, however, do not use a colon.

INCORRECT   Her three favorite activities were: jogging, volunteering at the local homeless shelter, and cooking.

EDITED   Her three favorite activities **were jogging,** volunteering at the local homeless shelter, and cooking.

EDITED   **She had three favorite activities:** jogging, volunteering at the local homeless shelter, and cooking.

INCORRECT   The room had: a fireplace, oak floors, and an oak buffet.

EDITED   The room **had a** fireplace, oak floors, and an oak buffet.

32b
:

Exercise 2

A. Edit the following sentences by deleting misused or overused colons, adding colons where needed, or retaining any colons that are appropriate. You may need to rewrite some sentences to correct overuse or misuse of colons.

EXAMPLE
For the Hirsches, retirement meant a trip to France.

1. They prepared for the trip by: first looking for inexpensive hotels in Paris.
2. The Residence Rivoli seemed like a good value clean, centrally located: private bath.
3. Mr. Hirsch, however, wanted to splurge: He argued that an upper-bracket hotel would be so much more enjoyable: a shining mar-ble bath, plush dining room, and elegant meals. There would be parking as well: essential for anyone with a car.
4. But Mrs. Hirsch wasn't impressed: the expensive hotels would be

comfortable, but she wanted atmosphere: and small, charming hotels would have that in abundance.

5. Finally, they reached a compromise; they would: stay in a chateau near the Loire, which would be cheaper than a fancy Paris hotel but afford plenty of atmosphere. Then they could: drive into Paris; enjoy the sights; and have a peaceful night: all without driving more than an hour or so each way.

B.   Share your edited versions of the sentences in Exercise 2A with a group of classmates. For each sentence, choose one version the group considers both correct and effective. Then share your chosen sentences with the other groups in order to see how often you have made similar and different choices.

C.   Look through a paper you are currently preparing, and circle any colons. Then decide whether or not you have used them correctly and effectively. Read the paper again, and underline any passage that might be more effective if rewritten using a colon. Look especially for lists and quotations. Then edit the paper to add colons.

CHAPTER

33

Apostrophes

Like the dot above the *i,* the apostrophe may seem trivial. But without the help of apostrophes, your readers would stumble over your sentences and might have to go back to the beginning to figure out what you're saying. Misplaced apostrophes are also distracting.

MISUSED OR LEFT OUT James horse cant canter, but two months rest and his leg's will heal, and then well see him in race's at Blueberry Down's again.

No doubt you had difficulty reading this sentence. You weren't sure which words were possessives, which were contractions, and which were plurals; the omitted and misplaced apostrophes misled you into putting some words into the wrong categories. Try reading it again.

CORRECTED **James's** horse **can't** canter, but two **months'** rest and his **legs** will heal, and then **we'll** see him in **races** at Blueberry **Downs** again.

At first, you may need to work consciously with apostrophes in your writing, hunting for misused or omitted cases. Eventually, the correct use of apostrophes will become second nature in your writing.

33a Using apostrophes to mark possession

A noun that expresses ownership is said to be a **possessive noun.** In writing, you must mark possessive nouns to distinguish them from plurals. In the phrase *the cats meow,* for example, a reader will assume that *cats* is plural and will expect certain kinds of structures to follow it, such as *all night* or *in the house.*

APOSTROPHE MISSING	The **cats** meow is becoming fainter.
CORRECTED	The **cat's** meow is becoming fainter.

Without a way of distinguishing between the plural and the possessive in writing, readers would be misled and frustrated by many such constructions.

1 Add an apostrophe plus -s to mark possession in singular nouns

In general, when you write a singular possessive noun, you will follow it with an apostrophe plus -s.

> Bill's coat
> the dog's collar
> Connecticut's taxes

When a noun ends with -s, though, showing possession may be tricky. Writers follow two different conventions in such circumstances (and editors will usually adopt one of these and stick to it).

33a

1. Add an apostrophe and another -s, just as you would do with any other noun. This is the more common and preferred method.

> Chris's car
> Elliott Ness's next move

2. Alternatively, simply add an apostrophe to the final -s.

> Chris' car
> Elliott Ness' next move

For nouns ending in -s, choose one of these conventions and stick to it throughout an essay.

INCONSISTENT	After driving closer to the **lioness'** cub, we discovered that **Hess's** camera had no film.
EDITED	After driving closer to the **lioness's** cub, we discovered that **Hess's** camera had no film.

Writer's Tip

To avoid the awkward sound of possessive nouns ending in -s ("the bass's solo part," "the hiss's sound from the cat"), try revising the construction ("the part of the solo bass," "the sound of the cat hissing").

Occasionally, adding a possessive -s to a word already

ending in that sound will seem awkward to say ("Hodges-es"). In such cases it may be preferable to indicate the typical pronunciation (with only one -s sound) by using only the apostrophe (Hodges**'**).

Writer's Alert

Be careful with personal pronouns. You may be tempted to add an apostrophe plus -s to these, but they're already possessive.

INCORRECT   If the car was **your's,** why did you tell Jose that it was Lida's and then take **her's** and dent **it's** fender?

EDITED   If the car was **yours,** why did you tell Jose that it was Lida's and then take **hers** and dent **its** fender?

Be especially wary of confusing *it's* and *its*. Practice expanding the contraction *it's* (*it + is*) whenever you use it in writing, and you'll locate any slips more easily.

DRAFT   **Its** not the muffler shop employees who were responsible for the fraud, but **its** managers.

EXPANDED   **It is** not the muffler shop employees who were responsible for the fraud, but ~~it is~~ managers.

EDITED   **It's** not the muffler shop employees who were responsible for the fraud, but **its** managers.

33a
v

---

2 Add an apostrophe to mark possession in plural nouns

Most English nouns end in -s or -es in the plural. When you want to make a plural noun possessive, simply add an apostrophe after the -s.

PLURAL POSSESSIVE   The **Solomons'** house had its lead paint removed.

PLURAL POSSESSIVE   The **roses'** petals had begun to wither.

Some irregular nouns form their plurals differently (*mice, children, fish*). In these cases, the word will be plural without ending in -s or -es. Mark possession by adding an apostrophe + -s unless the word does not change in the plural (*deer/deer, fish/fish*). For these cases, add an -s plus apostrophe.

IRREGULAR PLURAL	The new auto plant threatened the **oxen.**
PLURAL POSSESSIVE	The new auto plant threatened the **oxen's** habitat.

Writer's Alert

Even though third person singular verbs end in *-s*, remember that these are not possessive nouns, so they don't require an apostrophe.

INCORRECT	The *Enterprise* **speed's** out of the galaxy with the Klingons in hot pursuit.
EDITED	The *Enterprise* **speeds** out of the galaxy with the Klingons in hot pursuit.

---

3 Add an apostrophe plus *-s* or an apostrophe to only the last word in a noun phrase

33a

Hyphenated and **multiple-word nouns** are becoming increasingly common in English. As a general rule, treat the entire noun phrase as a single unit, marking possession on the last word.

HYPHENATED NOUN	My **father-in-law's** library is extensive.
MULTIPLE-WORD NOUN	The **union leaders'** negotiations fell through at the last minute.

When you use a compound noun phrase (two or more nouns connected by *and* or *or*) as a possessive, you'll need to decide whether these nouns function as separate items or as a single unit.

SEPARATE ITEMS	**Billy's and Harold's** lawyers were ruthless. READER'S RESPONSE: Billy must have one lawyer and Harold another, since the possessive is marked on both.
SINGLE UNIT	**Billy and Harold's** lawyers were ruthless. READER'S RESPONSE: Billy and Harold must have shared the same team of lawyers, since the entire noun phrase is marked as possessive.

Exercise 1

A. Edit the possessive forms in the following sentences so that each uses possessive apostrophes correctly. You may also have to add or move apostrophes, but do not change any correct forms. Some of the possessive forms may be correct.

EXAMPLE

France˙ longest river, the Loire, has its source in Vivarais and winds its way some 600 miles to the Atlantic.

1. The rivers name is especially associated with the many chateaux that line its bank's.
2. Serious sightseers visits to the Loire Valley should include tours of several of this regions beautiful castles.
3. The Loires reputation is also founded on its renowned cuisine and its sophisticated wines.
4. Barton and Jone's wine import businesses have flourished in the United States ever since Jones came up with the companys award-winning advertising campaign.
5. Several other companies have found an eager market for Frances excellent wine's.

 B. In a small group, compare your corrections to Exercise 1A, and discuss any especially difficult cases.

Did You Know?

The apostrophe has an interesting history. Its early use to show contractions grew into its present use to mark possession. Centuries ago, possession was often marked in writing by the addition of *-es,* as in *the foxes lair.* Then the apostrophe was substituted for the *-e* (*fox's*) and was widely used to "contract" plural nouns. (*Folioes* became *folio's* and then *folios.*) Eventually the apostrophe was no longer used to replace *-e* in plural nouns, but it was extended to all possessives (even those that hadn't had an *-e* to begin with, such as *man's* or *children's*).

The Oxford English Dictionary, compact ed. (New York: Oxford UP, 1971)

33b
ᵛ

33b Using apostrophes to mark contractions and omissions

You can use the apostrophe to indicate the omission of one or more letters when two words are brought together to form a **contraction.** Contractions generally suggest an informal style to which some college teachers may object. When in doubt, always err on the side of formality.

For those times when you do want to use contractions, follow a simple rule: learn exactly where the apostrophe goes. Most contractions are so common that you've already memorized them. But you still may inadvertently omit apostrophes from even simple words. For example, perhaps you've written *your* (a possessive pronoun) when you really meant *you're* (*you are*).

1 Use an apostrophe to contract a verb form

You can contract pronouns and verbs into a single unit by "splicing" them, eliminating the first part of the verb and substituting an apostrophe. Use the following chart to check your work.

it's	=	it	+	is
who's	=	who	+	is
they're	=	they	+	are
can't	=	can	+	not
you'll	=	you	+	will
you're	=	you	+	are

You can also splice nouns followed by *is*. Such forms are informal and should be avoided in most academic writing.

INFORMAL   **Shoshana's** going to the ballet, but her **seat's** in the very last row of the theater, and **she's** concerned that **she'll** miss the action.

33b
v

MORE FORMAL   **Shoshana is** going to the ballet, but her **seat is** in the very last row of the theater, and **she is** concerned that **she will** miss the action.

Writer's Tip

Edit your papers *very* carefully for contractions before turning them in. Take note of these often-confused forms.

they're	=	they + are
there	=	an adverb
you're	=	you + are
your	=	a possessive pronoun
who's	=	who + is
whose	=	a possessive pronoun
it's	=	it + is
its	=	a possessive pronoun

---

2 Use an apostrophe to mark plural numbers or letters

When you want to make individual letters and numbers plural, add an apostrophe + -*s*.

LETTERS   Mind your **p'**s and **q'**s.
                 The **x'**s mark the spots.

NUMBERS   I'll take two size **5'**s and two size **7'**s.

Writer's Tip

Occasionally the apostrophe is omitted from the plural form of numbers, letters, and abbreviations, especially if it runs the risk of making the word look like a possessive. "I took all my freshman courses from **TAs**" might be just as acceptable as "**TA'**s" because the abbreviation is capitalized. Again, when you decide on a certain form, be consistent.

---

3 Use an apostrophe to abbreviate a year

You can abbreviate years by omitting the first two numbers of the century as long as the century is understood by your reader. Such contractions represent informal usage.

INFORMAL   Sam has a **'75** Johnson class M sixteen-foot sailboat for sale.

UNCLEAR   Victorian details on houses in our neighborhood remained popular throughout the **'70s.**
                 READER'S RESPONSE: Does this mean the 1870s (in the Victorian period)? I'm confused.

EDITED   Victorian details on houses in our neighborhood remained popular throughout the **1970s.**

4 Use an apostrophe to show colloquial pronunciation

When quoting people, you can use apostrophes to indicate certain omissions and other features of colloquial speech and dialects.

DIALECT   I'm **a-goin'** down to the dock today for some **o'** them shrimp **an'** oysters.

Exercise 2

A. The following paragraph contains sentences with some contracted words that require apostrophes and some "look-alikes" that do not. All these words appear in italics. Insert apostrophes where they belong.

Many medical scholars believe that the age of molecular biology *didnt* really begin until April 1953 when Watson and Crick's article on the double helix appeared in a scientific journal. These researchers *werent* sure at that time how influential their ideas would become. *Its* generally thought, for example, that if several important researchers *hadnt* immediately seen the underlying brilliance of the double helix, the whole idea *wouldnt* have gained such a quick following. "*Your* basic educator," Professor Ewell Samuels asserts, "*couldnt* have seen beyond what was already a given in biology. *Its* when *youre* presented with many scholars *whose* ideas agree that things really begin to happen. *Whos* going to argue with a whole field jumping on the bandwagon of a new theory?"

B. In a small group, compare your corrections to the passage in Exercise 2A. After reaching agreement on which cases are actual errors, try to decide as a group which contractions in the passage, if any, are too informal. Would you use no contractions in this passage? Some?

C. Circle every apostrophe in your paper in progress. Then correct any misused apostrophes, or check on those you're not sure about.

33b
v

Quotation Marks

You learn about some of the many uses for quotation marks almost as soon as you begin to read.

> The three soldiers went on to the house of Albert and Louise. **"**Could you spare a bit of food? And have you some corner where we could sleep for the night?**"**
> **"**Oh no,**"** said Albert. **"**We gave all we could spare to soldiers who came before you.**"**
> **"**Our beds are full,**"** said Louise.
>
> — MARCIA BROWN, *Stone Soup*

And when you start reading about pets, you encounter some other uses.

> Whereas no reptile alive today can be considered aerial, we do come close with the Asian genus of **"**flying dragons,**"** *Draco.*
>
> — ROBERT G. SPRACKLAND, JR., *All About Lizards*

You use quotation marks in still other ways when you incorporate other people's words and ideas in your writing.

> As Ruth Macklin points out in *Mortal Choices,* however, **"**many state laws now permit involuntary hospitalizaton of mental patients only if they are judged dangerous to themselves or others.**"**

Quotation marks have many important roles, so keeping track of the various conventions for their use is both difficult and necessary.

34a Marking quotations

Use quotation marks whenever you quote someone else's words. Quotation marks tell readers which words are someone else's (and which words are yours). Quoted material can make your writing lively and interesting while providing explanation and support for your ideas.

To use quotation marks effectively and correctly, you need to know whether you are quoting words directly or indirectly, on their own or within another quotation.

1 Direct quotations

Whenever you quote someone directly, use double quotation marks (" ") both before and after the quotation unless the quotation is long or needs special emphasis (see 34b). Make sure that the words within the quotation marks are the exact spoken or written words of your source.

> **DIRECT QUOTATION (SPOKEN)**
> "The loon can stay beneath the water for several minutes," the park ranger told us as we walked along the shore.

> **DIRECT QUOTATION (WRITTEN)**
> Samuel Gross has written that "every generation looks with scorn upon its offspring's own developing culture."

As you edit, check that you have placed quotation marks around all directly quoted material.

> **QUOTATION NOT FULLY MARKED**
> "Had it not been for the flight navigator," the pilot said, we wouldn't have been able to make the emergency landing.
> **READER'S RESPONSE:** The second part of the sentence doesn't have any quotation marks, so at first I didn't notice that it was also something the pilot said.

> **EDITED**
> "Had it not been for the flight navigator," the pilot said, "we wouldn't have been able to make the emergency landing."

Make sure you use quotation marks within a sentence to separate quoted material from the words you use to introduce or comment on it. This is an especially important practice when your words interrupt a quotation.

> **QUOTATION MARKS MISSING**
> "I'm grateful, too, commented one passenger dryly, though I would have gladly missed the whole experience."
> **READER'S RESPONSE:** "Commented one passenger dryly" seems like part of the quotation.

> **EDITED**
> "I'm grateful, too," commented one passenger dryly, "though I would have gladly missed the whole experience."

2 Indirect quotations

Whenever you **paraphrase** or **summarize** someone else's speaking or writing, do not use quotation marks. Reserve the marks for cases when you quote someone's words exactly.

INDIRECT QUOTE (PARAPHRASE)

The pilot told us that if it hadn't been for the flight navigator, the plane would not have made a safe landing.

INDIRECT QUOTE (SUMMARY)

Samuel Preston believes that after just one generation, the social consequences of a major war have almost completely vanished.

3 Quotations inside quotations

Whenever the quotation you are presenting contains another quotation, use single quotation marks (' ') for the inside quotation and double quotation marks (" ") for the one enclosing it.

> Goddio became interested in searching for the sunken ship *San Diego* after reading an account by De Morga who "wrote of a struggle 'obstinately and bitterly waged on both sides so that it lasted more than six hours,' until the pounding of the battle caused his ship to 'bust assunder at the bows.'"

Note how the comma is placed inside the single quotation marks and the period is inside both the single and double quotation marks. (See 31h.)

34b   Using block quotations

When you quote more than four typed lines of prose, you should use a **block quotation** rather than quotation marks. To create a block quotation, begin on a new line after the sentence preceding the quotation, indent ten spaces (or one inch on a word processor), and present the quotation double-spaced without quotation marks. Do not indent the opening line if you are quoting only one paragraph or part of a paragraph.

> According to Postman, we can no longer ignore the profound effects of technology on all aspects of American life.
>
> > To be unaware that a technology comes equipped with a program for social change, to maintain that technology is neutral, to make the assumption that technology is always a friend to culture is, at this late hour, stupidity plain and simple.

In a longer quotation, indent three spaces (or one-fourth inch) for the first line of each full paragraph. In addition, include any quotation marks that appear within the original, but do not add any at the beginning or end of the block quotation.

Clifford Geertz's discussion of cockfights on the island of Bali illustrates the personal, almost informal tone of much contemporary anthropology.

> My wife and I were still very much in the gust-of-wind stage, a most frustrating, and even, as you soon begin to doubt whether you are really real after all, unnerving one, when, ten days or so after our arrival, a large cockfight was held in the public square to raise money for a new school.
>
> Now, a few special occasions aside, cockfights are illegal in Bali under the Republic (as, for not altogether unrelated reasons, they were under the Dutch), largely as a result of the pretensions to puritanism radical nationalism tends to bring with it. The elite, which is not itself so very puritan, worries about the poor, ignorant peasant gambling all his money away, about what foreigners will think, about the waste of time better devoted to building up the country. It sees cockfighting as "primitive," "backward," "unprogressive," and generally unbecoming an ambitious nation. And, as with those other embarrassments—opium smoking, begging, or uncovered breasts—it seeks, rather unsystematically, to put a stop to it.
>
> — CLIFFORD GEERTZ, "Deep Play: Notes on the Balinese Cock-Fight"

(See 46c-1 for a discussion of parenthetical documentation with block quotations; see 32b-2 for the use of colons to introduce block quotations.)

When you are quoting more than three lines of verse, present them in a block quotation, beginning on the next line after an introductory sentence and indented ten spaces from the left margin. If the verse contains any quotation marks, include them, but do not add any of your own at the beginning and end of the quotation.

> Donald Hall also uses lines of uneven length and varying rhythm in his poem "The Black-Faced Sheep."
> If one of you found a gap in a stone wall,
> the rest of you—rams, ewes, bucks, wethers, lambs;
> mothers and daughters, old grandfather-father,
> cousins and aunts, small bleating sons—
> followed onward, stupid
> as sheep, wherever
> your leader's sheep-brain wandered to.
>
> My grandfather spent all day searching the valley
> and edges of Ragged Mountain,
> calling "Ke-*day!*" as if he brought you salt,
> "Ke-*day!* Ke-*day!*"

34c Writing dialogue

When writing dialogue, use the conventions for direct quotations (see 34a). Whenever a new person speaks, indent as if you're beginning a new paragraph, and begin with new quotation marks.

> Finally the old man woke.
> "Don't sit up," the boy said. "Drink this." He poured some coffee in a glass.
> The old man took it and drank it.
> "They beat me, Manolin," he said. "They truly beat me."
> "*He* didn't beat you. Not the fish."
> "No. Truly. It was afterwards."
>
> —ERNEST HEMINGWAY, *The Old Man and the Sea*

When a character in a written dialogue speaks for more than one paragraph with no interruption, begin each new paragraph with quotation marks, but don't end with them. End only the *last* paragraph with quotation marks.

CORRECT

> "And then that imbecile crowd down on the deck started their little fun, and I could see nothing more for smoke.
> "The brown current ran swiftly out of the heart of darkness, bearing us down towards the sea with twice the speed of our upward progress...."
>
> —JOSEPH CONRAD, *Heart of Darkness*

34c
" "

Did You Know?

The most common way to quote someone's words directly is by enclosing the words with quotation marks. Writers in the past and some contemporary writers striving for special effects have used other devices, including colons or semicolons, to mark the start of quoted speech. For example, the King James version of the Bible uses no quotation marks, even though dozens of people are quoted throughout its pages. Instead, each quotation is introduced with a comma and starts with a capital letter:

> Then cried a wise woman out of the city, Hear, hear; say, I pray you, unto Jo'ab, Come near hither, that I may speak with thee.
>
> —2 Samuel 20:16

Other devices, including colons and semicolons, can be used for introducing quoted speech. These devices are rare, but you may encounter them in your reading.

34d Labeling titles of short works

You should use quotation marks to enclose titles of short works, such as articles, essays, stories, songs, and short poems; parts of a larger work or series, such as chapters in a book, episodes in a television series, or sections of a musical work; and unpublished works, such as doctoral dissertations or speeches.

Quotation Marks with Titles

ARTICLES AND STORIES

"TV Gets Blame for Poor Reading"	newspaper article
"Feminism's Identity Crisis"	magazine article
"The Idea of the Family in the Middle East"	chapter in book
"Baba Yaga and the Brave Youth"	story
"The Rise of Germism"	essay

POEMS AND SONGS

"A Woman Cutting Celery"	short poem
"Evening" (from *Pippa Passes*)	section of a long poem
"Riders on the Storm"	song

EPISODES AND PARTS OF LONGER WORKS

"Billy's Back"	episode of a TV series
"All We Like Sheep" (from Handel's *Messiah*)	section of a long musical work

UNPUBLISHED WORKS

"Renaissance Men—and Women"	unpublished lecture
"Sources of the Ballads in Bishop Percy's Folio Manuscript"	unpublished dissertation

---

Writer's Tip

Remember, *never* put the title of your own paper in quotation marks. This is a common mistake that irritates many teachers. If your title contains quoted material, place that material in quotation marks, not the entire title.

INCORRECT	"The Theme of the Life Voyage in Crane's ' Open Boat' "
EDITED	The Theme of the Life Voyage in Crane's "Open Boat"

34e Indicating special meanings of words and phrases

You can use quotation marks to set off words and phrases you are using in a special sense or to indicate terms that are part of a technical vocabulary or that are unusual in some way. In using quotation marks to call attention to words and phrases, remember an important principle: Go lightly to avoid distracting readers with too many highlighted words.

Most disciplines use a host of specialized words that readers *within* the discipline readily recognize. If you are writing for a general audience, however, consider calling attention to specialized terms and phrases by setting them off with quotation marks. Quotation marks can also help you highlight a term you are defining. (Italics can be used for this purpose as well; see 38a-4.)

> The phenomenon that draws each person into the crowd's irrational and often destructive and confrontational behavior is known among social psychologists as "crowd contagion."

> The "FSBO" (sometimes actually pronounced as "fizbo") is generally used in the real estate industry to refer to a home that is "for sale by owner."

When deciding whether to use quotation marks to set off specialized terms, ask yourself whether the term is likely to be known to your intended readers. Ask also whether the term is unusual enough to require highlighting or will seem clear to readers. In the following sentence, for example, a well-known writer includes quotation marks that most readers will probably consider unnecessary.

UNNECESSARY

The number of these folds varies from individual to individual and each adult has a characteristic "frown pattern" of one, two, three or four lines.   —DESMOND MORRIS, *Body Watching*

READER'S RESPONSE: I have no trouble figuring out what a frown pattern is, so for me the quotation marks make the sentence appear cluttered.

Exercise 1

A. Add quotation marks to the following passage as appropriate.

The shame of illiteracy—or so Robert Cullany puts it—affects millions of adults in the United States alone, but the problem is not nearly as prevalent as innumeracy, Cullany's term that means being unable to use numbers. Cullany writes, illiteracy and innumeracy are a national blight on our intellectual landscape, and cannot be tolerated. He also points out that they cripple our productivity, lead to familial dysfunction (poor family structures), and deny people the ability to become what Cullany calls self-learners. The ALVC, or Adult Literacy Volunteer Corps, is made up of dedicated people who believe they can help this so-called mind plague.

 B. Working in a small group, share your edited versions of the passage in Exercise 1A. Which quotation marks did you all agree on? Which ones did members of your group miss or disagree on?

Writer's Tip

Clichés and idioms, perhaps because they seem informal or slang-like, often fool writers into placing them in quotation marks. Doing so, however, only calls more attention to their presence, further weakening the prose. Instead of placing such expressions in quotation marks, simply replace them with stronger words and phrases.

DRAFT   After pulling an "all-nighter," Joe said, in the "clear light of day," that he felt like he'd just "kicked the bucket" and "cashed in his chips."

EDITED   After cramming all night for his test, Joe spent the next day complaining that he was exhausted and ached all over.

34f
" "

34f Indicating irony, sarcasm, and authorial distance

You can—*sparingly*—use quotation marks to indicate irony or sarcasm or to show a reader that you don't "lay claim" to a specific term or expression.

To the people who oppose animal rights, the suffering of helpless animals is somehow justified by the "great medical advances" that are encouraged by what they view as "legitimate research" on animals.

This strategy is easy to misuse or overuse, and careful word choice is generally a more effective way of conveying disapproval (see 27a-1 and 27a-2).

Exercise 2

A. Edit the following passage by adding or deleting quotation marks as appropriate. Leave in place any quotation marks that are correctly used.

On April 12, 1633, Galileo was interrogated by the Inquisitor for the Holy Roman and Universal Inquisition. The focus was Galileo's book, the *"Dialogue on the Great World Systems,"* in which he posited the theory of a "spinning" earth that "circulated" around the sun. The theory itself was "bad" enough given the Pope's "beliefs," but one of the "characters" in the book's "dialogue" was cast as a "simpleton," and the Pope thought that perhaps it referred to him because he didn't go along with Galileo's "theory." At one point, the Inquisitor asked Galileo, "Did you obtain permission to write the book? To which Galileo replied, I did not seek permission to write this book because I consider that I did not disobey the instruction I had been given. "Did you disclose the Sacred Congregation's demands when you printed the book?" asked the Inquisitor. "I said nothing, Galileo replied, when I sought permission to publish, not having in the book either held or defended opinion. In the end, "Galileo" had to retract his "book," and was also shown instruments of torture "as if" they were going to be used—a "scare tactic," to be sure.

—Adapted from Jacob Bronowski, *The Ascent of Man*

B. Working in a small group, share your edited versions of the passage in Exercise 2A. Discuss each of the changes, and note any that gave you trouble. Indicate whether all group members agreed about each change.

C. Mark all quoted matter in a draft paper of your own. Check for correct use of quotation and punctuation marks, especially commas and periods (see Chapter 31). If your paper includes prose quotations of more than four lines or verse quotations of more than three lines, check whether you used block quotation form correctly and included quotation marks (if any) from the source.

34f
66 99

CHAPTER

35

Periods, Question Marks, and Exclamation Points

When you speak, you mark boundaries between sentences with changes in pitch or with pauses of various lengths. When you write, however, you must mark these divisions with visual symbols because your reader can't "hear" a rising pitch in a word or a pause between sentences. When you want to mark the end of a sentence, you will use one of three symbols: a period, a question mark, or an exclamation point.

35a Using periods

Use a period when you want to mark the end of a sentence. A sentence is like a train, sometimes moving directly from one location to another, sometimes taking a few structural diversions before completing its journey. For each sentence, a period marks the end of the line. The period can also be used in abbreviations.

1 End a sentence with a period

No matter how long or complicated, all sentences that are *statements* must end with periods. However, sometimes a sentence will contain embedded clauses that appear to be something other than statements. Use a period to end a sentence when the main, or "outer," sentence is a statement.

INCORRECT Ten-year-old Naomi affectionately kissed her little brother on the forehead but wondered whether he really knew that she was sorry for startling him**?**

READER'S RESPONSE: The sentence as a whole is a statement; the question in the second half is being reported in the sentence, but the sentence doesn't ask the question.

EDITED   Ten-year-old Naomi affectionately kissed her little brother
                on the forehead but wondered whether he really knew that
                she was sorry for startling him.

2 Use periods in abbreviations

Periods are also used to punctuate abbreviations and to mark decimal points in numbers.

Most abbreviations require periods to let the reader know that something has been eliminated from the word or term.

Dr.	Mrs.	Ms.	Ph.D.
pp.	ave.	in.	abbr. (for *abbreviation*)
a.m. (or A.M.)			B.C. (or B.C.E.)

Many common abbreviations, including *a.m.* and *p.m.,* come from Latin,
and, for brevity, have been "permanently" shortened (it would seem odd to
spell out *a.m.* and *p.m.* as *ante meridiem* and *post meridiem*).

Some abbreviations, especially acronyms (see 41a), may not require
periods at all. When the entire term is capitalized, periods are generally not
used (NASA, NATO, SALT talks, GOP). (See Chapter 41.) Use of periods
in abbreviations varies considerably. When in doubt, use the preferred choice
in a dictionary.

When an abbreviation that requires a period occurs at the *end* of a
sentence, that period will also end the sentence.

CORRECT   Before he became a freelance writer, Richard Rodriguez
                earned a Ph.D.

If the abbreviated word occurs in the *middle* of a sentence, the period may
be followed by another punctuation mark, such as a comma, dash, colon,
or semicolon.

INCORRECT   Officials from the paper industry testified until **10 p.m,**
                well before the meeting adjourned.

EDITED   Officials from the paper industry testified until **10 p.m.,**
                well before the meeting adjourned.

35a

Exercise 1

Edit the following sentences so that periods are used correctly, adding
or omitting punctuation as appropriate.

EXAMPLE

Every two years the French department at St. Joseph's College organizes a group trip to a foreign country.

1. On our trip to France, we visited the medieval city of Carcassonne
2. As we approached the inner city, which was surrounded by high walls and a real moat, we wondered whether we were still in the twentieth century?
3. "Have we fallen into a time warp or something" Trish said?
4. As we climbed up to the ramparts at 10 p.m, we decided that the experience was almost as good as watching a N.A.S.A. space shuttle launch.
5. Mr Siefert, the hotel manager, told us that the Bastille Day fireworks would begin at 9:30 p.m..

Did You Know?

The use of periods in pronounceable acronyms often follows a pattern of change. The common word *laser* was originally an acronym meaning "*l*ight *a*mplification by *s*timulated *e*mission of *r*adiation." The abbreviation process began with periods separating the capital letters designating each word: *L.A.S.E.R.* Soon the periods disappeared, yielding *LASER*. Then the capital letters disappeared, though in some contexts the first letter may still have been capitalized. Finally, the term became a common, lowercase, pronounceable word, which has even been clipped into the verb *to lase*. Similar processes appear to have happened for other pronounceable acronyms, including *scuba* (*s*elf-*c*ontained *u*nderwater *b*reathing *a*pparatus), *TV*, and *telex*. Keep your eye on ones in transition, like *AIDS, fax,* and *DJ* (now commonly spelled out as *deejay*).

Chris M. Anson, ms., U of Minnesota.

35b
?

35b   Using question marks

A question mark indicates that something has been asked, either directly or hypothetically.

1 End a direct question with a question mark

Always end a direct question with a question mark.

DIRECT   When is the train leaving**?**

DIRECT   Considering all the attention given in the media to the issue of homestead tax breaks, why aren't more homeowners filing for the exclusion**?**

When a sentence (like the preceding example) has more than one clause, the main clause will usually determine the proper punctuation. Occasionally you may embed a direct question within an outer statement, generally using parentheses to set off the embedded question.

EMBEDDED   The telephone repair technician arrived only after the electricians had removed the power lines (did they pose a danger**?**) and disconnected the service box.

Writer's Tip

End **indirect questions** with a period. These are sentences whose main clause is a statement and whose embedded clause asks a question.

INDIRECT   Phil wondered whether to support the department's proposal to create a new program**.**

INDIRECT   Jose asked if he could help out on the bid for the highway project**.**

When you present the exact words, your quotation is *direct* rather than *indirect*, and you need to include the question mark.

QUOTED   It was Laitan who said, "Why is the temperature in the solution rising so quickly**?**"

35b
?

2 Watch for other uses of question marks

Question marks may appear in writing for more specialized reasons. In various kinds of informational writing, for example, a question mark may signal a date or other fact that is uncertain or that has been questioned.

David Robert Styles, 1632**?**–1676
Meadville, pop. 196**?**

Occasionally writers will call attention to or mock other people's statements by including a parenthetical question mark. Sometimes this may come from a genuine lack of information; more often it's a device for sarcasm.

PARENTHETICAL   The veterinarian informed us that our Siamese cat had contracted a rare (**?**) ailment.

SARCASTIC   We dispute R & D's finding that the lubricant burns off (**?**) under high heat.

Such a use of question marks is usually colloquial or informal; in general, try to find other ways to convey the same message in academic writing.

Unless you're writing very informally (in a note to a friend, for example), avoid using more than one question mark for emphasis or combining question marks and exclamation points.

INAPPROPRIATE   Can you believe they arrested him for parking in front of the building **?!** How can they do that **?????**

EDITED   Can you believe they arrested him for parking in front of the building **?** How can they do that **?**

Exercise 2

A. Edit the following passage by removing any inappropriate question marks or adding any that are required.

Are you bat-phobic. Although bats have been hated and feared for centuries, most species are harmless to humans and beneficial to the environment. In his article "Are We Batty Over Bats," Harlan Sneed wonders whether our destruction of bats is really justified? Should we be smoke-bombing caves that are breeding places for thousands of bats, just because we are afraid of them. Sneed also gives examples of cultures that are contributing to the extinction of bats not through fear but through excessive trapping—for food; they are a delicacy (!?) in some parts of the world. Sneed ends his article with a reminder: "Environmental protection is as much a matter of the way we think as the way we act. Maybe you have never *acted* against your environment but are you entirely inculpable in your thoughts and attitudes."

B. In a small group, compare your edited versions of the passage in Exercise 2A. Create one collaboratively edited version.

35c Using exclamation points

When you use an exclamation point, you make your statement emphatic, alerting your reader to its importance. You can also use exclamation points to indicate commands or, in quotations, words that are shouted.

1 End an emphatic statement with an exclamation point

Exclamation points are often used to end emphatic statements such as commands or warnings.

EMPHATIC   Keep all the camp children away from the precipice **!**

Writer's Tip

Avoid overusing exclamation points to do the work that should be assigned to strong, carefully chosen words. Treat the exclamation point like a rare and powerful spice: If you don't saturate your text with exclamation points, they will carry much more flavor when you do decide to use them. When you want to make your prose more dramatic, try some revision and add vivid details.

OVERUSED   I couldn't believe it! Andrea and I were face to face with a small black bear! We were terrified! I screamed! Andrea jumped back into the tent and buried herself under her sleeping bag! That left me holding an entire bag of delicious corn chips right under the hungry creature's nose!

REVISED   Suddenly, I began to realize we were not alone. Out of the shadows, just three feet from the front of our tent, appeared the black nose and sharp, glinting teeth of a small black bear.

Also avoid using more than one exclamation point at the end of any sentence. A single exclamation point is worth exactly as much as a hundred.

INCORRECT   The bear was grunting right outside our tent!!!!!

EDITED   The bear was grunting right outside our tent!

35c
!

2 Watch for other uses of exclamation points

Like question marks, exclamation points can be used parenthetically or marginally in casual writing to express dismay, outrage, shock, or strong interest. In more formal contexts, look for other ways to emphasize the word or idea in question.

INAPPROPRIATE   Emergency rescue workers spent several hours (!) trying to reach the stranded toddler.

EDITED   Emergency rescue workers spent several **agonizing** hours trying to reach the stranded toddler.

When you quote people's words directly, you can use exclamation points to indicate emphatic statements or commands.

QUOTED   Halfway to the airport, Sybil suddenly shouted, "Oh, no**!** We forgot the plane tickets**!**"

Use exclamation points sparingly and realistically in quotations and dialogue. Few people continue to speak emphatically for very long.

Remember that when you use an exclamation point, you are punctuating the end of your sentence. Don't add another mark, such as a comma, when you use an emphatic sentence within an outer sentence.

INCORRECT   "Stop**!** **,**" yelled Steve.

EDITED   "Stop**!**" yelled Steve.

Exercise 3

A. Edit the following passage by removing or adding exclamation points to make them correct and stylistically acceptable.

Seventy-five miles (!) from anywhere, Frank's old Buick decided to sputter and stall out on the edge of Route 61. Meanwhile, the temperature had fallen to 16 below!!!! To make matters worse, the wind had whipped up to 30 miles per hour! That's an incredible wind chill of around 75 below zero!!!!! "Hey," yelled Bill, "don't anyone leave this car. If we stay put, maybe the highway patrol will spot us." "Who are you kidding!!??," shouted Frank. "It's 3 a.m.!"

B. In a small group, compare your edited versions of the passage in Exercise 3A. Discuss any differences, and create one collaboratively edited version.

C. Scan your paper in progress for end punctuation, looking especially for cases of overused exclamation points and for periods or question marks used incorrectly within embedded sentences.

35c
!

Special Punctuation Marks

Most punctuation symbols—dashes, commas, semicolons, colons, slashes, ellipses, quotation marks, and the like—make up a kind of toolbox for writing. You can use the tools in various ways to change the style and sense of your prose and its effects on your readers. Five "special" punctuation marks—parentheses, brackets, dashes, ellipses, and slashes—can be useful strategies for guiding readers through complex sentences and for providing emphasis appropriate to your purpose for writing.

36a Using parentheses

Parentheses *enclose* a word, sentence, or clause: you can't use just one. Whatever you write between two parentheses takes on the quality of an aside—something in a "softer" voice than the rest of a sentence. Or it becomes information and ideas presented in the background rather than the foreground.

1 Use parentheses to set off words or sentences

With parentheses, you can set off a word, a group of words, or an entire sentence from the rest of your text. By using parentheses to place some information in the background, you can direct your readers' attention to the main assertions and details in a passage without having to omit worthwhile (though potentially distracting) secondary material.

INFORMATION SET OFF WITHIN A SENTENCE
Although most of the team always eats a hearty and varied breakfast (if also a little high in fats and cholesterol), Jim feels he performs much better with less food in his stomach. Invariably, this means only one thing: a bowl of Cheerios (without milk).

INFORMATION SET OFF IN A SEPARATE SENTENCE

Consuelo had tried for two years to get a hearing about her immigration status. (Her employer, during this time, had been unsympathetic to her pleas.) Then, in June, she finally received a letter.

Use parentheses sparingly and carefully. Too many parenthetical statements can clutter your sentences, distracting readers and obscuring your main assertions.

DISTRACTING   Handico, Inc., decided (early in 1993) to use their waste milling chips (which had been warehoused in Detroit) to manufacture pencils (described as "environmentally friendly") to donate to public schools (which gave the company a tax credit).

CLEAR   Early in 1993, Handico, Inc., decided to use their waste milling chips (warehoused in Detroit) to manufacture "environmentally friendly" pencils. These they donated to public schools, resulting in a tax credit for the company.

36a ( )

2 Watch for special uses of parentheses

You can use parentheses to present information that is not part of the structure of a sentence. You can also use parentheses in numbered lists.

NUMBERS AND LISTS   Harry's Bookstore has a fax number (349-0934) for (1) ordering books, (2) inquiring about the availability of specific items, or (3) requesting publication information.

3 Punctuate parenthetical statements correctly

Don't use a comma *before* a parenthetical statement placed in the middle of a sentence. *After* the closing parenthesis, use whatever punctuation would normally occur at this point in the sentence if the parenthetical statement were not there.

WITHOUT PARENTHESES   If you sign up for Telepick by August 15, you are eligible for one hour of free long-distance calls.

WITH PARENTHESES   If you sign up for Telepick by August 15 (and list up to four commonly called numbers), you are eligible for one hour of free long-distance calls.

When a parenthetical statement *inside a sentence* comes at the end of the sentence, always place the sentence's end punctuation *after* the closing parenthesis.

INCORRECT	People on your Telepick list can also call you at the same discounted rate (as long as they, too, use Coombs Communication as their long-distance carrier.)
CORRECT	People on your Telepick list can also call you at the same discounted rate (as long as they, too, use Coombs Communication as their long-distance carrier).

When parentheses enclose an entire freestanding sentence, however, place the end punctuation *inside* the closing parenthesis.

CORRECT	You can sign up for Telepick's "Free Hour" program until August 10. (This offer does not include international calls.)

36b Using brackets

Use brackets to indicate that you have added words of your own to a quotation or to act as parentheses within parentheses.

1 Use brackets for interpolations

Sometimes you need to introduce your own words into a quotation to help clarify a word or a statement for readers or to provide important background information. To indicate that the words are your own, and not those of the writer or speaker being quoted, enclose the **interpolation** in brackets.

INTERPOLATION	My friends Paula and Kent decided to have their wedding on a sailboat off Key West. When I asked them if the ceremony would take place at a specific place offshore, Kent said, "It's a surprise even to us. Captain Sims [the boat's owner] has chosen a special place within two hours of Key West."

2 Use brackets within parentheses

When you need to include a parenthetical statement *within* a parenthetical statement, use parentheses first, and then use brackets for the inner statement. Try to limit your use of brackets because they can make your writing seem unnecessarily complex.

You can contact Rick Daggett (Municipal Lumber Council [Violations Division], Stinson County Municipal Center) to report violations of the rules governing logging of old-growth trees.

36c   Using dashes

You can use dashes, like parentheses, to set off material within a sentence. Dashes call more attention to a word or group of words than parentheses do; use them to create emphasis or indicate a change in tone. Dashes differ in function from hyphens, which are used to connect words or to separate words into parts (see Chapter 39). On typewriters and computers, dashes appear as two unspaced hyphens, with no space before, between, or after them: --. In professional typesetting, the dash is represented by a single line:—.

1 Use dashes for emphasis

Use dashes in pairs to highlight a word or group of words in the middle of a sentence.

> MATERIAL SET OFF IN THE MIDDLE
> After picking out two pet mice——**one brown with white spots and one white with a brown forehead**——the little boy realized he had only enough money to buy one of them.

When the word or words you want to emphasize appear at the *end* of a sentence, however, use one dash to introduce the material. Conclude with the appropriate end punctuation for the sentence.

> MATERIAL SET OFF AT THE END
> Heartbroken at the thought that someone might buy the mouse, the boy offered his six quarters as a deposit——**along with his Mickey Mouse watch and his school notebook.**

You can use dashes to create contrasts in tone or structure within a sentence. When you use dashes, you don't need to make the material within them part of the grammatical structure of the sentence or make it consistent in tone with the rest of the sentence. Inside the following sentence, for example, the dashes enclose another complete sentence.

> FULL SENTENCE SET OFF
> The mice——**by this time they were fully domesticated**——frolicked in the cedar chips.

Remember that dashes call attention to the material within them. In contrast, enclosing material in commas provides no real emphasis, and using parentheses de-emphasizes the enclosed material.

STRONG EMPHASIS
When the boy——**clutching three weeks' allowance**——returned to the store, it had already closed.

NO SPECIAL EMPHASIS
When the boy, **clutching three weeks' allowance,** returned to the store, it had already closed.

LOSS OF EMPHASIS
When the boy **(clutching three weeks' allowance)** returned to the store, it had already closed.

2 Use dashes to set off introductory and concluding ideas

You can use dashes to set off an idea or a series of items. This is a dramatic way of opening a sentence or calling attention to the assertion it makes.

ITEMS SET OFF IN OPENING
Extended TV hours, better meals, and more physical exercise—— these were the inmates' three major demands for prison reform.

You can also use dashes instead of a nonemphatic colon to list a series of items at the *end* of an assertion.

ITEMS SET OFF AT THE END
Charles had learned several ways to forestall the effects of long flights **——drinking lots of water, avoiding alcohol, and moving around the cabin as much as possible during the flight.**

3 Avoid overuse of dashes

Dashes can become addictive, resulting in sentences and paragraphs that seem to be clusters of fragmented statements.

OVERUSED   There had been some interest——chiefly by Stockton——in an automated navigation system——a way to track cars by telecommunication and let drivers know if they are going in the right direction——or give them directions.

> **READER'S RESPONSE:** This sentence highlights so many points with dashes that it is hard to tell what the writer considers the most important point.

MORE EFFECTIVE   There had been some interest, chiefly by Stockton, in an automated navigation system——a way to track cars by telecommunication and let drivers know if they are going in the right direction or give them directions.

36c

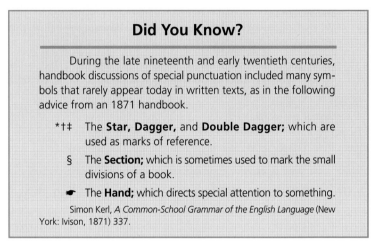

Did You Know?

During the late nineteenth and early twentieth centuries, handbook discussions of special punctuation included many symbols that rarely appear today in written texts, as in the following advice from an 1871 handbook.

*†‡   The **Star, Dagger,** and **Double Dagger;** which are used as marks of reference.

§   The **Section;** which is sometimes used to mark the small divisions of a book.

☞   The **Hand;** which directs special attention to something.

Simon Kerl, *A Common-School Grammar of the English Language* (New York: Ivison, 1871) 337.

36c

Writer's Tip

If you find yourself using too many dashes in your writing, look over a draft and circle the dashes that seem really important—those that help emphasize the key point in an entire section of an essay, for example. Then either replace the other dashes with commas, colons, or parentheses or create emphasis through word choice and sentence structure. (See Chapter 12 for advice on creating emphasis within sentences.)

Exercise 1

A. Some dashes and parentheses have been added to the following paragraph. Edit the paragraph to make it more effective, deciding which of these punctuation marks should stay and which should be replaced. Change sentence structure and strategy if necessary.

The next morning—their donkeys carried them—to the site of the excavation. Carter and his assistant—A. R. Callender—had already begun clearing the stairway (again). As more of the doorway was exposed, the seals (of Tutankhamun) could be seen—in addition to those of the royal necropolis. When all sixteen steps had been cleared (and the entire doorway could be seen), Carter got a jolt—holes had been cut into the (upper) part of the door. The damage had been repaired—and bore the seals of the necropolis, but the question remained—had this tomb, too, been pillaged?

— METROPOLITAN MUSEUM OF ART, *The Treasures of Tutankhamun*, p. 13

B. Compare your edited version of the passage in Exercise 1A with those created by some of your fellow students. Remember that there will be no single—or "most correct"—answer. Compare the relative strengths and weaknesses of each version.

36d   Using ellipses

The **ellipsis** (from Greek *elleipsis,* "an omission") is a series of three or four *spaced* periods telling your reader that something has been left out. You will use ellipses chiefly for two purposes: to omit parts of a quotation and to suggest gaps in a sentence, either in dialogue or in quoted speech.

1   Place and space ellipses correctly

Correct placement and spacing of ellipses can be tricky. The following guidelines should cover most cases.

- Use three spaced periods • • • for ellipses within a single sentence.
- Use a period before an ellipsis that falls at the end of a sentence • • • •
- Leave a space before the first period • • • and after the last period of all ellipses.
- When another punctuation mark occurs before omitted words, you can eliminate it if it is not necessary to the grammar of the sentence, but you must retain it if it is necessary to the grammar.

EXAMPLE   The newspapers reported that "Officer Hatt testified solemnly , • • • often staring at his hands and slowly shaking his head."

36d
• • •

2   Use ellipses in quotations with omitted words

Ellipses are especially useful when you want to quote some (but not all) words in a passage. You may wish to omit the material because it doesn't offer relevant ideas or information, because it makes the quotation too long for your purposes, or because you want to "skip" from one part of a long quotation to the next without including everything between. The following examples from a student's paper on sailing show his original draft, from which he wanted to cut the boldfaced sentence in the block quotation, and his edited draft, in which he has used ellipses to do so.

ORIGINAL   Drummond, in his *Complete Guide to Sailing,* blames the instability of the sandbagger on its sail-to-hull ratio:

Extremely fast, sandbaggers were very wide and shallow. They carried an enormous amount of sail area on an expanded rig. **As a result, when they were raced, they carried twenty-five or more bags of sand in the cockpit as ballast. When a boat came about, a crew of husky men quickly shifted the bags of sand to the windward side.** The boats ran from eighteen to twenty-eight feet in length, and carried a bowsprit almost as long as the hull and a main boom that extended ten feet or more beyond the stern.

EDITED   Drummond, in his *Complete Guide to Sailing,* blames the instability of the sandbagger on its sail-to-hull ratio:

Extremely fast, sandbaggers were very wide and shallow. They carried an enormous amount of sail area on an expanded rig. . . . The boats ran from eighteen to twenty-eight feet in length, and carried a bowsprit almost as long as the hull and a main boom that extended ten feet or more beyond the stern.

You can also eliminate *parts* of a sentence. When you do so, maintain normal sentence structure and grammatical form; don't just rip out words at random. The following example from a student's interview paper shows the original quotation from his notes; the way he incorporated this into his rough draft (with ellipses); and his corrected, edited version.

36d
. . .

ORIGINAL QUOTATION   "We've always played well against Duke. Year before last, we creamed them. Last year their defense fouled us up, but we still won. This year we've got a deep bench. I bet we'll take them to the cleaners, for sure."

INCORRECT DRAFT   When I pressed him to predict the team's performance, Coach Harms paused for a minute, then said with determination, "We've always played well against Duke. Year before last, we creamed them. Last year . . . but we still won . . . we'll take them to the cleaners. . . . "

EDITED   When I pressed him to predict his team's performance, Coach Harms paused for a minute, then said with determination, "We've always played well against Duke. Year before last, we creamed them. Last year . . . we still won. This year . . . we'll take them to the cleaners. . . . "

3 Use ellipses for other gaps

Occasionally you may want to indicate a pause or a gap in your own writing, not just in quoted material. In fiction and personal narrative, for example, ellipses are often used to show suspense, hesitation, or uncertainty or to suggest continuing action.

FOR SUSPENSE   When we returned to our campsite, we were stunned. The
tent was in a shambles. Our food was strewn everywhere.
Our water jug was fifty yards away. Muddy claw marks were
everywhere. • • •

36e Using slashes

You will use slashes mainly to indicate alternative forms of words.
You can also use slashes in a more specialized way to quote lines of poetry
when those lines are not already set off from your text.

1 Use slashes with alternative words

When used to indicate alternative words, the slash translates as "or"
or "and." It is a shorthand often used in technical documents and manuals.

Be certain that the **on/off** switch is in the vertical position.
The **conservative/liberal** distinction does not apply here.
There is no exemption from the Composition **101/102** sequence.

Slashes show up most often in combinations such as *he/she, him/her,* or
and/or. Many good alternatives for the *he/she* combinations are available.
(See 30a.)

Use the slash in moderation. Some fields or professions require the use
of *or* in place of the slash.

The choice of **conservative or liberal** does not apply here.

2 Use slashes when quoting lines of poetry

When you quote lines of poetry *within* your text rather than setting the
material off in a block quotation (see 45c-3), separate the lines of verse with
a slash. Type a space before and after the slash.

The speaker in Sir Philip Sidney's sonnet addresses the moon by saying, "With how sad steps, O Moon, thou climb'st the skies, / How
silently, and with how wan a face."

Exercise 2

A. Find or create a short paragraph that uses as many of the punctuation marks described in this chapter as possible: parentheses, brackets, dashes, ellipses, and slashes. Choose one example of each case,
and explain what purpose it serves in the paragraph.

B. Write or type out another version of the paragraph in Exercise 2A, stripped of its special punctuation. Make two copies to exchange with classmates. Ask the members of your group to edit the two copies, which lack parentheses, brackets, dashes, ellipses, and slashes. They should insert these punctuation marks wherever they think the marks are appropriate. Then compare your original and the versions punctuated by your classmates. Decide which marks of punctuation you consider effective and ineffective, and give reasons for your judgments.

 C. Choose one of the special punctuation marks described in this chapter. Circle every use of the mark in a draft of your paper in progress. Then assess the effectiveness of this punctuation mark. Have you overused it? Are there places where an alternative punctuation mark or a change in sentence structure would be more effective? Edit accordingly.

36e
/

PROOFREADING
FOR MECHANICS
AND SPELLING

Capitalization

Capital letters call attention to themselves and to words containing them. Your readers expect capitalization to signal the start of sentences or to identify specific people, places, and things. Capitalization that follows convention not only makes reading easier but also reflects a general sense that certain people and things deserve the kind of recognition that capital letters can provide. In the passage that follows, notice how hard it is to pay attention to specific details when some capitals are removed.

37a
cap

> Then, as i cross the state line, i remember a florence, alabama, composer named william christopher handy. After moving to memphis and writing songs about boss crump, beale street, st. james infirmary, and st. louis, he became known as "the father of the blues." Maybe i should turn north. — HUGH MERRILL, *The Blues Route*

The general rules for capitalization are easy to remember.

* Use a capital letter at the beginning of a sentence.
* Capitalize proper nouns, proper adjectives, and most words in titles of works.

Specific conventions are often harder to keep in mind, and you may need to consult this chapter for answers to questions: Should I capitalize a sentence after a colon? What about the beginning of a sentence within parentheses? When should I use *president* and *President*? How can I recognize when a noun is "proper" and requires capitalization?

37a Using a capital at the beginning of a sentence

Sentences begin with capital letters. This convention applies to regular sentences and sentence fragments used appropriately as partial sentences. (See 19d on partial sentences.)

Two national parks, Yellowstone and Grand Teton, are in Wyoming.
Are camping spots in the parks hard to get in the summer?
Make your reservations early!
No camping without a reservation.

1 Capitalize the opening word in a quoted sentence

When you quote someone else's words or sentences, you will ask, "When should I capitalize within the quotation?" The answer generally depends on the relationship between the main (outer) sentence and the material you are quoting within it.

Capitalize the first word in the quotation when it is a complete sentence or when it begins your own sentence.

COMPLETE SENTENCE QUOTED	Speaking of *Blind Man with a Pistol,* James Lundquist says, "**T**he novel begins with an opening chapter that, without exaggeration, is one of the strangest in American literature."

If you interrupt a quotation with your own words, do not capitalize after the interruption.

QUOTATION INTERRUPTED	"**T**he novel," claims James Lundquist, "**b**egins with an opening chapter that, without exaggeration, is one of the strangest in American literature."

Also drop the capitalization if you integrate the quotation into the structure of your own sentence.

INTEGRATED QUOTATION	On the other hand, James Lundquist claims that "**t**he novel begins with an opening chapter that, without exaggeration, is one of the strangest in American literature."

If you are quoting only part of someone else's sentence, capitalize the quoted material when you use it to open your sentence but not when you place it in the middle or at the end. (Indicate any changes in capitalization in brackets.)

OPENING QUOTATION	"[**O**]ne of the strangest in American literature" is how Lundquist describes the first chapter.
	The first word is not capitalized in the source, so the writer indicates the change in brackets.
CONCLUDING QUOTATION	James Lundquist overstates his case when he argues that the first chapter remains "**o**ne of the strangest in American literature."

37a
cap

2 Capitalize a freestanding sentence in parentheses

Capitalize the first word of any sentence that stands on its own within parentheses.

FREESTANDING   By this time, the Union forces were split up into nineteen
SENTENCE   sections. (**G**rant was determined to unite them.)

However, when you place a sentence within parentheses (or dashes) inside another sentence, do not begin the enclosed sentence with a capital.

ONE SENTENCE   Saskatchewan's economy depends heavily on farming (**o**ver
INSIDE ANOTHER half of Canada's wheat crop comes from the province),
                though oil production and mining have also become impor-
                tant in recent decades.

3 Capitalize the first word of a line of poetry

Lines of poetry generally begin with a capital letter, regardless of where the initial word appears in the "sentence."

Long since, we pulled brown oak-leaves to the ground
In a winter of dry trees; we heard the cock
Shout its unplaceable cry, the axe's sound
Delay a moment after the axe's stroke.
— LOUISE BOGAN, "Old Countryside"

For special effect, however, poets sometimes ignore this and other conventions of capitalization.

new **h**ampshire explodes into radio primary,
newspaper headlines & beer—
well-weathered tag-lines from lips of schoolchildren.

we triumph by not being clear.
— T. R. MAYERS, "(snap)shots"

When you are quoting poetry, follow the author's practice.

4 Decide whether to capitalize following a colon

If a complete sentence follows a colon, you can choose to capitalize it or put it in lowercase (see 32b on colon use). Since either choice is correct, you might make your decision on the basis of style or emphasis. But be consistent.

37a
cap

CORRECT	The province of New Brunswick is bilingual both by law and in practice: **O**ne-third of the population is French-speaking and the remainder English-speaking.
ALSO CORRECT	The province of New Brunswick is bilingual both by law and in practice: **o**ne-third of the population is French-speaking and the remainder English-speaking.

If the word group following the colon is not a sentence, however, then you do not need a capital letter.

> Foremost among the educational issues in New Brunswick is another problem related to language: **b**ilingualism in the schools.

5 Decide whether to capitalize elements in a series or list

You can treat questions in a series or elements in a list in a variety of ways.

Questions in a Series. You can choose whether to use capital letters to highlight the opening of each question in a series.

37a
cap

CORRECT	Should we spend our limited campaign funds on television ads? **O**n billboards? **O**n smaller signs and posters? **O**n flyers?
ALSO CORRECT	Should we spend our limited campaign funds on television ads? **o**n billboards? **o**n smaller signs and posters? **o**n flyers?

Stick to one style throughout an essay.

Run-In Lists. Several conventions exist for **run-in lists** (lists whose items aren't placed on separate lines). If the items in your list are full sentences, you may decide to capitalize the first letter of each element, joining the items with semicolons.

CAPITALIZED	In estimating the project's costs, remember the following: (1) **L**ab facilities must be rented; (2) **L**ight, heat, and other utilities need to be charged to the project's account; and (3) **M**easuring equipment should be leased.

Don't capitalize when the elements are words or partial sentences.

NOT CAPITALIZED	In estimating the project's costs, remember that you need to pay for the following: (1) **l**ab facilities; (2) **u**tilities; and (3) **m**easuring equipment.

Vertical Lists. You may choose whether to capitalize the elements in a **vertical list** when they are either words or partial sentences. You must use capitalization with complete sentences, unless they appear in an outline without periods (see 4b on outlining).

CORRECT   When you estimate the project's costs, remember the
              following:
              1. **L**ab facilities
              2. **U**tilities
              3. **M**easuring equipment

ALSO CORRECT When you estimate the project's costs, remember the
              following:
              1. **l**ab facilities
              2. **u**tilities
              3. **m**easuring equipment

Use the same pattern of capitalization in all the lists in a paper, and make sure the items in each list are parallel in form (see 25d).

Did You Know?

In other languages, capitalization conventions can be quite different from those for English. In German, for example, nouns and pronouns are capitalized: Ich werde Sie ihrer Blumen zurückgeben (I will give you your flowers back). In Spanish, pronouns and the names of days and months are not capitalized: Almuerzo con ella los lunes (I lunch with her on Mondays).

37b Using capitals for proper nouns and adjectives

To capitalize a word is to highlight its importance. Readers pay special attention to words naming specific people, places, and things (proper nouns) and to adjectives created from the nouns (proper adjectives). When readers come across the title of a work, they are also aided if you identify this title with capitals.

1 Capitalize proper nouns and adjectives

You should capitalize the names of specific people, places, and things (**proper nouns**) as well as adjectives derived from them (**proper adjectives**).

Proper nouns	Proper adjectives
Brazil	Brazilian music
Dickens	Dickensian portrait
Venice	Venetian architecture

Writer's Tip

An article (*a, an,* or *the*) preceding a proper noun or adjective should not be capitalized unless it begins a title or starts a sentence.

All other nouns and adjectives are **common nouns** and **common adjectives.** Do not capitalize them except in special contexts, such as at the beginning of a sentence, in titles of works, or as parts of proper nouns.

Common noun (lowercase)	Part of proper noun (capitalized)
lake	Lake Jackson
river	Danube River
park	Prospect Park
computer company	Mesa Computer Company

37b
cap

The following categories should help you recognize words that need to be capitalized.

Capitalized	Lowercase
Individuals	
Michael Jordan	his boyfriend
Georgia O'Keefe	my teacher's father
Relatives	
Aunt Rosa; Uncle Jack	an uncle; my cousin
Mother; Dad	your mother; her dad
Groups of people and languages	
Caucasian	Negro
Japanese	African American
Hopi	Russian
Time periods and seasons	
Thursday; October	spring, summer, fall, winter
Easter; Ramadan;	holiday
Yom Kippur; Labor Day	

Capitalized	Lowercase
Religions and related subjects	
Judaism, Jews	
Christianity, Christians	
Catholic	catholic (meaning "universal")
Protestant	
Hinduism	
Buddhist practices	
Talmud; Bible	talmudic; biblical
God; Jesus Christ	a god, goddess; godly
Organizations, institutions, and members	
Chicago Bulls	the team
Democratic Party, Democrat	democratic
Heritage Foundation; Conservative Party; Tory	conservative
Girl Scout; Boy Scouts of America	the scout
Metropolitan Opera; Cincinnati Symphony	the opera, the string quartet
Rolling Stones	a band
Florida State Police	the police, the state police
Coast Guard; Virginia Board of Ethics	the sailors; the board
House of Commons; U.S. Senate	a member of parliament; a senator
Air Line Pilots Association	the union, union member
Places, their residents, and geographic regions	
Malaysia, Malaysian	the country, the citizen
Cape Verde Islands, Cape Verdean	the state, the resident
Tibet, Sino-Tibetan	
Berlin, Berliner	the city, the resident
Erie County; Nassau Avenue	the county; the street
South China Sea; Volga River	the sea; the river
Amazon Basin; Mars	the region; the planet
the Southwest, the East; East Coast	southwest, east southwestern, eastern (directions)
Buildings and monuments	
Taj Mahal; Peace Bridge	Jim's garden; our backyard
Tower of London; Busch Stadium	the tower; a stadium
Space Needle; Getty Museum	a landmark; a museum
Piazza Navona; Grant's Tomb	the piazza; her tomb

37b
cap

Writer's Tip

Sometimes a time period such as a week or season refers to a specific event. In such cases the time period is capitalized because it is part of the name of the event.

PART OF THE EVENT'S NAME
At Bardstown College, **F**all **O**rientation runs from September 3–5.

NOT PART OF THE NAME
The **f**all **o**rientation at Bardstown College runs from September 3–5.

Capitalized	Lowercase
Historical periods, events, and movements	
Thirty Years' War; Dorr's Rebellion	the war; the rebellion
Algerian Revolution; Ming Dynasty	the revolution; a dynasty
Romantic period; Impressionism	the period or style
First Great Awakening; Postmodernism	the movement; a trend
Jazz Age; Renaissance	a cultural epoch
Academic institutions and courses	
Auburn University; Utica College	a university
English Department	an English department
Department of Chemistry	chemistry department
Sociology 203; English 101	sociology or English course

**37b
cap**

Writer's Tip

Some names include both a proper noun and a common noun. Both parts are capitalized because together they form a proper name.

  proper   common
Sandberg **U**niversity

Once you have given the full name, you may wish to abbreviate future references by using the common name. You can capitalize the common name so your readers can distinguish this reference from a more generic use of the common name.

Sandberg University has developed a strong academic support system for student athletes. The **U**niversity reports that the system has helped many athletes earn degrees in four years, a goal to which many universities aspire.

Capitalized	Lowercase
Vehicles	
Boeing 767; Pontiac Bonneville SSE	a passenger plane; my car
J Boat; Space Shuttle	a sailboat; the reentry vehicle
Company names and trade names	
Siemens; Monsanto Chemical	the company, the chemical company
GTE, Fuji Heavy Industries, Xerox	a manufacturer; an employer
Luvs; New Balance; Kleenex, Toblerone; Patagonia	diapers; shoes; tissues, chocolate bar; outdoor equipment
Scientific, technical, and medical terms	
Big Dipper; Earth (planet)	earth (ground)
Marxism	marxian theory
Heisenberg's uncertainty principle	
Alzheimer's disease; Down syndrome	tuberculosis
organ of Corti	pancreas
Pistacia vera; Gazella dorcas	pistachio tree; gazelle

37b
cap

2 Use capitals in titles of works

In titles, you should capitalize the first word, the last word, and all words in between *except* articles (*a, an,* and *the*), prepositions under five letters (such as *in, of,* and *to*), and conjunctions under five letters (such as *and* or *but*). These rules apply to titles of long works, short works, and parts of works as well as titles for your own papers. If a colon divides the title, capitalize the first word after the colon.

> *The Mill on the Floss*
> "Factory of the Future: A Survey"
> *Thelma and Louise*
> *Briefing for a Descent into Hell*
> "Politics and the English Language"
> *Fragile Glory: A Portrait of France and the French*
> "Just Like Romeo and Juliet"
> "The Civil Rights Movement: What Good Was It?"
> Developing a Growth Plan for a Small Retail Business (your own title)

(For the rules governing the use of italics and quotation marks in titles, see 38a and 34d.)

3 Capitalize the pronoun *I* and the interjection *O*

Whenever **I** try to argue with my parents, they make me feel as if **I'm** still a child.

Trust in him, **O** people, and pour out your heart.

Although *oh* would seem to be capitalized by analogy with *O,* convention requires that *oh* remain in lowercase unless it begins a sentence or is capitalized in material you are quoting.

"**O**h dear, no," said the housekeeper.

— WILKIE COLLINS, *The Woman in White*

Exercise

A. Add capitalization wherever necessary in the following sentences. Replace any unnecessary capitals with lowercase letters. Circle the cases that seem the toughest to figure out.

EXAMPLE

Over the next ten years, *I*ndia will become an increasingly important

trading partner for *N*orth *A*merica.

1. Located on a subcontinent in the southern part of asia, the republic of india has a territory of about 1.2 million Square Miles.
2. India's population of almost 800 Million falls into two main groups, dravidians and indo-aryans, which in turn are made up of many other cultural groups.
3. Dravidians live mainly in the south, an area that is dominated geographically by the deccan plateau.
4. The religion of the Majority is hinduism, though other religious groups such as sikhs and muslims are important.
5. Recently, religious conflicts have broken out in the provinces of kashmir and uttar pradesh.
6. Indian History is long and complicated, but in Modern Times it has been dominated by the british rule over the Country and by attempts to escape that rule and found a democratic State.
7. British Rule over most of the country began after the sepoy rebellion of 1857–58.
8. It ended after world war II with the independence movement led by mahatma gandhi.
9. The move toward industrialization has been the main goal of indian leaders since Independence, though this movement has at times been complicated by the problem of overpopulation and by conflicts stemming from the hindu social (or caste) system.

37b
cap

10. The dominant political Party since Independence has been the congress Party, with leaders such as jawaharlal nehru, indira gandhi, and rajiv gandhi.

B. In a small group, compare your list of difficult cases from Exercise A. What did you do to figure out your answer to each difficult case? Compare your answers.

C. Edit a draft paper of your own for capitalization. Read through the paper to identify all proper nouns, and make sure they are capitalized. Check all titles of works cited for appropriate capitalization, and check your own title as well. Make sure you have properly capitalized quotations. Look for consistency of capitalization in lists.

37b
cap

Italics (Underlining)

Type that slants to the right—***italic type***—gives special emphasis to words and ideas. In handwritten or typed texts, <u>underlining</u> is the equivalent of italic type: <u>The Color Purple</u> = *The Color Purple.*

Convention requires you to use underlining (or italics) to give distinctive treatment to titles of full-length works such as books and films, foreign words, names of vehicles, and words named as words. (Titles of shorter works, such as stories and articles, or parts of works, such as chapters, require quotation marks rather than italics. See 34d and 38a-1.)

If you write your papers out in longhand or use a conventional typewriter, you will <u>underline</u> all such words and phrases. A computer word processing program may give you the option of *italics,* though some readers, including college instructors, may prefer you to underline.

TYPEWRITTEN   Alice Walker's novel <u>The Color Purple</u> has been both praised and <u>criticized</u> since it appeared in 1982.

COMPUTER PRINTOUT   Alice Walker's novel *The Color Purple* has been both praised and criticized since it appeared in 1982.

You can also occasionally use underlining or italics to add emphasis to your writing and clarify your meaning.

> Not only was he one of the captains of the Permian team, not only was he number one in his class, but now he was thinking of applying to Harvard.
> *Harvard?*
> Never in a thousand years could Tony Chavez have imagined it turning out this way. Never in a million.
>
> —H. G. Bissinger, *Friday Night Lights*

38a Following conventions for underlining (using italics)

Knowing when to use underlining (italics) can sometimes be difficult. As you proofread, therefore, you may need to consult the lists and discussions that follow in order to answer your questions. For example, should Stephen Crane's novel be written as *Maggie: A Girl of the Streets* or as "Maggie: A Girl of the Streets" (in quotation marks)? Should the borrowed French word "quiche," meaning a dinner pie with a filling, be written *quiche* (italicized or underlined) or quiche (in plain type)? Should the name of the famous Star Trek vessel be written as *The Enterprise*, the *Enterprise,* "The Enterprise," or The Enterprise?

1 Underline titles of long or complete works

Underline (italicize) titles of most long works, such as books, magazines, and films, and of complete works such as paintings and sculptures. For parts of works, however, and for short works such as stories, reports, magazine or newspaper articles, and episodes in a television series, use quotation marks rather than underlining. Some titles, such as those of sacred books (like the New Testament, Pentateuch, or Koran), require neither underlining nor quotation marks. (See the following list.)

Underline or Italicize	Use Quotation Marks
Books and pamphlets	
Generations: The History of America's Future, 1584 to 2069 (nonfiction book)	"Boomers" (book chapter)
Maggie: A Girl of the Streets (novel)	"Preface" (chapter in novel)
Beetroot (collection of stories)	"The Purloined Letter" (story)
The White Album (collection of essays)	"Once More to the Lake" (essay)
Tracing Your Family's History (pamphlet)	"List Your Relatives" (section of pamphlet)
Poems	
Paradise Lost (long poem)	"Richard Cory" (short poem)
The One Day (long poem)	"Whoso list to hunt" (first line of poem, used as title)
Plays	
King Lear	
'night Mother	
Fences	

Underline or Italicize	**Use Quotation Marks**

Movies and television programs

Murphy Brown (TV show) — "Is She or Isn't She?" (episode in TV series)

Ghostbusters (film)
20/20 (TV news show) — "Daycare Dilemmas" (report on news program)

Paintings and sculpture

Nude Descending a Staircase (painting)
Winged Victory (sculpture)

Musical works

Nixon in China (opera) — "Luck Be a Lady" (song in a musical)

Nutcracker Suite (work for orchestra) — "Waltz of the Flowers" (section of longer work)

Invisible Touch (album) — "Big Money" (song on album)
Camille Saint-Saëns's *Organ Symphony* — Saint-Saëns, Symphony no. 3 in C Minor, op. 78

Magazines and newspapers

Discover (magazine) — "What Can Baby Learn?" (article in magazine)

Review of Contemporary Fiction (scholarly journal) — "From Krazy Kat to Hoodoo: Aesthetic Discourse in the Fiction of Ishmael Reed" (scholarly article)

the *New York Times* — "Asbestos Found in Schools" (newspaper article)

No Underlining, Italics, or Quotation Marks

Sacred books
Bible, Koran, Talmud

Public, legal, or well-known documents
United States Constitution
Last Will and Testament

Title of your own paper
The Attitudes of College Students Toward Intramural Sports
    (paper for sociology class)
The Role of Verbal Abuse in *The Color Purple*
    (title of work being discussed is italicized)

EXCEPTION   If your paper has been published and you are citing it, enclose the title in quotation marks

Writer's Alert

A reader needs to know whether certain end punctuation (such as a question mark) is part of a title or part of your own sentence in which the title appears. Underline any punctuation *only* when it's part of the title.

INCORRECT	What did he think of <u>Thelma and Louise?</u>
CORRECT	What did he think of <u>Thelma and Louise</u>?
CORRECT	The book <u>What's Up, Doc?</u> provides an intriguing history of cartoons.

The comma and question mark are part of the title, so they need to be underlined.

2 Underline names of specific vehicles

Underline (italicize) the names of specific ships, airplanes, trains, and spacecraft, but not the names of *types* of vehicles. Note that USS and SS are not underlined.

Specific vehicles	Types of vehicles
Voyager VI	Boeing 767
Orient Express	Chris Craft
USS *Corpus Christi*	Arctic Cat snowmobile
SS *Norway*	Chevrolet Lumina
Memphis Belle	Honda 750
Enterprise	Boston Whaler

3 Underline foreign words and phrases

Foreign words and phrases pass through stages of familiarity as they are first adopted and then become more and more common. When a word or phrase has not moved into common use and still seems very foreign, highlight it with underlining or italics. Extremely common words and phrases have lost their foreignness—for example, quiche, junta, taco, and kvetch. You need not underline such words. When you can't decide whether to treat a word or phrase as part of the language, look it up in a dictionary.

FOREIGN	The code of <u>omertà</u> supported a kind of order in the criminal world.
FOREIGN	Many lawyers contribute to their communities by doing <u>pro bono</u> work.
COMMON	I served the vegetables grilled on skewers like shish kebab.

Scientific names for the genus and species of plants and animals also require underlining; the common names do not.

SCIENTIFIC NAME The seaweed <u>Chrodus crispus</u> turns up in processed form in ice cream, in nondairy creamer, and even in hamburgers.

SCIENTIFIC NAME Anthropologists speculate about the social arrangements practiced by early human species such as <u>Homo habilis.</u>

COMMON NAME Tests found algae growing in the Swansons' pool.

4 Underline words, letters, and numbers named as words

When you focus attention on a word, letter, or number by discussing it as itself, you should underline it.

DISCUSSED In several Boston accents, <u>r</u> is pronounced <u>ah</u>, so that the words <u>car</u> and <u>park</u> become <u>cah</u> and <u>pahk.</u>

Also underline a word or phrase you are defining.

DEFINED Electricity can also be generated from a <u>piezoelectric crystal,</u> a piece of quartz or similar material that responds to pressure by producing electric current.

**38a
und/it**

Did You Know?

Most of this book is printed in the familiar vertical letters known as roman type. The slanted letters discussed in this chapter, however, are in *italic* type. Italic type was developed around 1500 from a kind of swift handwriting that scholars and scribes of the period used to write out manuscripts. Italic type first appeared in 1501 in an edition of the Latin poet Virgil published in Venice by the famous Italian printer and print designer Aldus Manutius.

Exercise 1

The following sentences contain words that need to be highlighted by underlining (italics) or by quotation marks. Edit each by supplying any necessary underlining or quotation marks. Star the items that seem the most difficult to decide about.

EXAMPLE

The well-known "<u>Old Farmer's Almanac</u>" contains information about the weather and articles on various topics

1. I first leaned about this famous American almanac from a newspaper article, You Can Look It Up There, that appeared in my local paper, the Record-Advertiser.
2. GQ and Cosmopolitan probably would not print an article like Salt: It's Still Worth Its Salt, which appeared in a recent edition of the almanac.
3. According to this article, the word salary comes from the Latin term for wages paid to some soldiers, salarium argentum, that is, salt money.
4. In an essay on the historic effects of weather, the author points out that freezing temperatures on January 28, 1986, led to the space shuttle Challenger disaster.
5. If you are interested in learning about the ocean, you can find out that high tides occur twice a month at syzygy, the times when the sun and moon are lined up on the same side of the earth or on opposite sides.

38b   Underlining for emphasis

By underlining (italicizing) a word or phrase, you give it special emphasis. You should make use of this strategy on a *very* limited basis, however, since readers become annoyed when you rely too often on underlining to do the work your words should be doing on their own.

EMPHASIZES CONTRAST
A letter of recommendation mixing strong praise with a few reservations seems direct and realistic; a letter filled with <u>faint</u> praise makes the endorsement seem lukewarm.

ADDS FORCE
In releasing themselves from the single ideal of the dependent woman, women have more or less incidentally released a lot of men from the single ideal of the dominant male. The one mistake the feminists have made, I think, is in supposing that <u>all</u> men need this release, or that the world would be a better place if <u>all</u> men achieved it. It would just be duller.   Noel Perrin, "The Androgynous Man"

HIGHLIGHTS IMPORTANT INFORMATION
Whenever you start the generator, <u>make sure there is sufficient oil in the crankcase</u>.

Exercise 2

A. For each of the following sentences, add any underlining required by convention or needed for appropriate emphasis. Circle any words that are underlined but should not be. Star any items that are difficult to decide about.

EXAMPLE

In 1957, Chevrolet produced the Bel Air, a model now considered a classic.

1. As David Halberstam points out in his book The Fifties, automobiles from the period were so hot they were cool.
2. Cars from that period, with enormous tailfins and lots of chrome, are still eye-catchers today.
3. The musical Grease is set in the same era.
4. Television shows from the period included the Ed Sullivan Show and Lassie.
5. Readers could choose from such now-defunct publications as the Herald Tribune newspaper and Look magazine.

B. In a group, compare your corrections to Exercise 2A. Which were the hardest to make, and why?

C. Proofread a paper of your own, adding italics (underlining) wherever needed before you submit the final copy.

38b
und/it

Writer's Alert

Many kinds of informal writing, such as notes, journal entries, and personal letters, rely on underlining to add a certain "oral" emphasis to the prose. Be careful not to rely on underlining for this purpose when writing formal papers and other documents.

INFORMAL	Next time, hand the receipts to me instead of dropping them on my desk.
MORE FORMAL	In the future, give the receipts to me personally instead of placing them on my desk.

Hyphens and Word Division

Hyphens divide words and tie them together as well. At the end of a line, you may need to split a word, completing it on the next line. A hyphen (-) tells readers to treat the divided word as one word, not two.

Hyphens also help to divide words that are hard to read without a break (for example, *anti-intellectual*, not *antiintellectual*), and they link familiar compound words (*three-quarters*, *commander-in-chief*).

39a
-

39a Using hyphens to divide words

To make your readers' job easier, use a hyphen to split a word at the end of a line. Also hyphenate words that may be misleading or hard to read without a visual break. As you proofread, moreover, check that you have divided words whenever necessary and that the hyphens come at appropriate points in words.

1 Divide words at the end of a line

When you don't have enough room at the end of a line to complete a word of *two or more syllables*, type it on the next line unless doing so will create a right margin that is very jagged and distracting. To create a reasonably even margin, split the word *between syllables*, and mark the break with a hyphen at the end of the line.

DISTRACTING   The rate of change in home appliance manufacturing
has accelerated rapidly over the past decade.
Increasingly sophisticated consumers,
international competition, and the need for an
ozone-safe refrigerant to replace CFCs
(chlorofluorocarbons) have provided the impetus.

HYPHENATED   The rate of change in home appliance manufacturing has accelerated rapidly over the past decade. Increasingly sophisticated consumers, international competition, and the need for an ozone-safe refrigerant to replace CFCs (chlorofluorocarbons) have provided the impetus.

A word processing program will automatically move a word to the next line when there is no room for it. This process is called *word wrapping*. In proofreading a word-processed document, you need to be alert for jagged margins created by this process and hyphenate to make margins more regular.

Writer's Alert

A hyphen is a short line used to divide words at syllables or to join parts of compound words and word clusters. Type a hyphen as a *single* line (-) with no space on either side. A dash, in contrast, interrupts sentences (see 36c). Type a dash as *two* lines (--) with no space on either side or in between.

INCORRECT DASH   surprising ingredients - peanut butter, raisins, and whipped cream

CORRECT DASH   surprising ingredients -- peanut butter, raisins, and whipped cream

INCORRECT HYPHEN   one - fourth of the work force

CORRECT HYPHEN   one-fourth of the work force

39a
-

Although it may seem simple, dividing words at the ends of lines can be tricky. The following tips may help you to follow convention.

Divide Words Only Between Syllables.   Readers will have a hard time recognizing words that are split at a place other than a syllable break. For example, the word *adjustable* can be correctly divided in only two places: *ad-just-able.*

CONFUSING   Experts disagree about the wisdom of **adjustable** rate mortgages.

CLEAR   Experts disagree about the wisdom of **adjustable** rate mortgages.

Consult a Dictionary to Determine Where to Divide a Word.   If you rely entirely on your own pronunciation, you may divide some words incorrectly, especially those you encounter in reading but seldom use in conversation. For example, *irrevocable* is divided as *ir-re-vo-ca-ble,* not *ir-rev-oc-able; milieu* is *mi-lieu,* not *mil-ieu.* Your pronunciation of a familiar word may also differ from the standard one given in the dictionary and expected by readers. (For example, you may pronounce the word *nuclear* in two syllables, *nuc-lear,* rather than with the three syllables listed in the dictionary, *nu-cle-ar.*)

Writer's Tip

Some word processing programs will hyphenate words at the ends of lines for you. This feature can be timesaving and helpful, yet the programs often split words incorrectly, especially less common terms. Consequently, the programs allow you to accept or reject proposed word divisions, and effective proofreading includes checking on the accuracy of the hyphenations you are offered.

39a
-

Leave More Than One Letter at the End of a Line and More Than Two at the Beginning.

INCORRECT	Two designers announced they are considering an **a-greement** to produce a line of affordable clothes for professional women.
EDITED	Two designers announced they are considering an **agreement** to produce a line of affordable clothes for professional women.
INCORRECT	The concert ended because a stagehand **disconnect-ed** the power supply for the main amplifiers.
EDITED	The concert ended because a stagehand **discon-nected** the power supply for the main amplifiers.

Divide Compound Words at Natural Breaks.   Generally, divide a compound word at the break between the words making it up. If a compound already includes a hyphen, divide it at that point.

DISTRACTING	If the sports car is the classic European car, the **Volkswa-gen** is the classic California car.
EDITED	If the sports car is the classic European car, the **Volks-wagen** is the classic California car.
DISTRACTING	In his new movie, the actor plays a bumbling, **acci-dent-prone** police detective.

EDITED　　In his new movie, the actor plays a bumbling, **accident‑
prone** police detective.

Don't Divide One-Syllable Words.　Even relatively long words such as
touched, drought, kicked, and *through* have no stopping points in pronunciation and should be left intact. If the undivided word doesn't fit on a line,
you should move it to the next line.

Avoid Confusing Divisions.　When some words are correctly divided,
they form other words with meanings that may be distracting.

DISTRACTING　　The school board is proposing a solution for **sin‑
gle** parents unable to afford child care.

CLEAR　　The school board is proposing a solution for
single parents unable to afford child care.

Don't Split Abbreviations, Numerals, or Contractions.　Abbreviations
and acronymns (NATO, ROTC, NCAA), numerals (528; 100,000), and contractions (didn't, should've) can be sounded out with syllables, but splitting them will distract your readers.

39a

DISTRACTING　　Foreign policy experts disagree about funding the **NA‑
TO** alliance at present levels.

CLEAR　　Foreign policy experts disagree about funding the
NATO alliance at present levels.

....

Exercise 1

A. Look at each hyphen in the following sentences, and decide
whether to retain it, to change within the word, or to eliminate it in
favor of placing the entire word on the next line. Use your dictionary
if you need to, and keep track of the toughest cases.

EXAMPLE
Although receiving a present can be very pleasant, gift-giv—
~~ing~~ *giving* can be equally rewarding.

1. Looking for a job that would be challenging, Jen thought long and hard about taking the position at Hammond's Gift
   Shop.
2. By the next Saturday, however, she was unpacking a truck-
   load of the exquisite vases and figurines that the gift shop sells.
3. Hank wanted only one thing for his birthday: an ornament-
   al Chinese vase that was way beyond Rachel's budget.

4. When he came home one afternoon and saw the vase on the mantle, Hank went right out to get flowers as a way of saying "thank you."

5. The bouquet was lovely, redolent of roses, tulips, and baby's-breath.

 B. In a small group, compare your edited sentences from Exercise 1A. Which were the most difficult, and why?

2 Divide words to prevent misreading

You can use a hyphen to help readers distinguish between words that are spelled the same but have very different meanings.

> Because the contractor was there to **remodel** the studio, Hans asked Victor to **re-model** for the art students the following day.

> For **recreation,** the Prichards staged a hilarious **re-creation** of the argument between Joe and Arnold.

39b
-

You should also hyphenate words that are difficult to read because of repeated letters or odd combinations of letters.

> anti-imperialism (*not* antiimperialism)
> post-traumatic (*not* posttraumatic)
> pot holders or pot-holders (*not* potholders)

39b Using hyphens to join words

Instead of *dividing* whole words, hyphens are often used to *tie together* the elements of compound words and phrases. The conventions for linking compounds, however, tend to be quite mixed; should the mechanical heart regulator be written as *pacemaker, pace maker,* or *pace-maker?*

1 Check hyphens in compound words

A compound word is made from two or more words. Some compounds are hyphenated (*double-decker, time-lapse*), some are treated as one word (*backfire, timekeeper*), and some are treated as separate words (*mail carrier, time bomb*). A dictionary will tell you how to treat a particular compound. Make sure the dictionary is up to date, however, because usage changes. Today's *baby-sitter* can quickly become tomorrow's *babysitter.*

2 Hyphenate familiar compounds correctly

Some familiar compounds generally require hyphens.

Numbers. You should hyphenate all numbers between twenty-one and ninety-nine when they are spelled out.

> forty-one   eighty-six   twenty-five

This rule holds even if the number is part of a larger number.

> fifty-eight thousand   twenty-three million

Use a hyphen to show inclusive numbers.

> pages 163-78   volumes 9-14

Fractions. Hyphenate fractions when you spell them out.

> five-eighths of the liquid in the container
> two-thirds the size of last year's convention

Prefixes and Suffixes. Hyphenate a prefix attached to a capitalized word or a number.

Cro-Magnon	non-Euclidean	post-Victorian	pre-1989
mid-October	pre-Reagan	trans-Canadian	post-1066

Hyphenate a capital letter and a word that together form a compound.

A-frame	I-beam	T-shirt
B-movie	O-ring	X-factor

Some specialized terms, such as those used in music, do not require a hyphen.

> A minor   G sharp   C clef

The prefixes *ex-*, *self-*, and *all-* and the suffixes *-elect* and *-odd* should generally be hyphenated in compounds.

all-encompassing	self-centered	president-elect
ex-partner	self-denial	twenty-odd

39b

Writer's Tip

Writers in academic, technical, and professional fields often present detailed information by using a series of compound modifiers. When you use parallel modifiers, you can save space and reduce repetition by using **suspended hyphens**—hyphens that signal the suspension of an element that readers can find at the end of the series. In strings of three or more modifiers, always leave a space after the hyphen and before the word *and,* but don't leave any space before a comma.

The process is equally effective with **oil- and water-based** compounds.

The testing program calls for **sixth-, eighth-, and tenth-grade students** to submit portfolios of their work.

3 Hyphenate compound modifiers correctly

39b
-

When you ask two or more words to work as a single modifier and you place them *before* a noun, hyphenate them.

BEFORE NOUN   The **second-largest** supplier of crude oil to the United States is Nigeria.

BEFORE NOUN   Ayn Rand's works are among the most popular **twentieth-century** novels.

When the modifiers come *after* a noun, you generally do not need to hyphenate them.

AFTER NOUN   Many of the drugs used to treat cancer are **nausea inducing**.

Remember that modifying compounds can mean something quite different than the sum of their independent meanings. Hyphens help readers to know which meaning to assign the compound.

The director needed three **extra wild** monkeys for the scene.
The director needed three **extra-wild** monkeys for the scene.

The **bird eating** spiders flew away.
The **bird-eating** spiders have enormous fangs.

Do not hyphenate compound modifiers containing -*ly* adverbs or comparative and superlative forms.

The new products were developed by the company's **highly regarded** research team.

Nigeria is the **most populous** country in Africa.

(Compound modifiers differ from coordinate adjectives, which are joined with a comma. See 31f.)

4 Use hyphens to create new compounds

To add vividness and emphasis to your writing, you can occasionally create (or "coin") a new compound word or phrase. Join the elements in such a compound with hyphens to indicate its original, temporary nature.

She entered the program with a **prove-it-to-me** attitude.

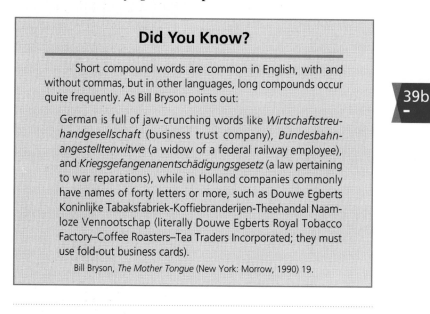

Did You Know?

Short compound words are common in English, with and without commas, but in other languages, long compounds occur quite frequently. As Bill Bryson points out:

German is full of jaw-crunching words like *Wirtschaftstreuhandgesellschaft* (business trust company), *Bundesbahnangestelltenwitwe* (a widow of a federal railway employee), and *Kriegsgefangenanentschädigungsgesetz* (a law pertaining to war reparations), while in Holland companies commonly have names of forty letters or more, such as Douwe Egberts Koninlijke Tabaksfabriek-Koffiebranderijen-Theehandal Naamloze Vennootschap (literally Douwe Egberts Royal Tobacco Factory–Coffee Roasters–Tea Traders Incorporated; they must use fold-out business cards).

Bill Bryson, *The Mother Tongue* (New York: Morrow, 1990) 19.

39b

Exercise 2

A. Insert hyphens in the following sentences wherever appropriate. Consult a dictionary if necessary.

EXAMPLE

The company hired a well‑regarded accounting firm as part of its financial reorganization.

1. Alejo enjoys painstakingly exact work, such as building scale model ships.

2. While working, he likes to listen to Francis Poulenc's jazz influ-enced classical music.
3. One fourth of all his model ships are sold at auction.
4. Tony, his assistant, keeps track of the profits in a pre and post auction sale log.
5. Although his creations are awesome, Alejo harbors many insecu-rities that are mostly selfinflicted.

B. In a small group, compare your edited versions of the sentences in Exercise 2A. Which were the most difficult decisions, and why? Did your dictionaries give all members of the group the same advice?

C. Proofread a draft paper of your own, and underline words that you think need hyphenation. Then go back and decide whether to hyphenate the underlined words. Use this chapter and a dictionary to help you make decisions. As you are preparing the final copy, check for ragged right margins, and hyphenate to make them more pre-sentable.

39b
-

CHAPTER

40

Numbers

You can convey numbers in several ways in your writing—as numerals (37; 18.6), as words (eighty-one; two million), or as a combination of numerals and words (7th, 2nd). Understanding the appropriate ways to present numbers is important because unconventional or inconsistent usage can mislead your readers. This chapter shows you how to present numbers appropriately in general academic writing. For advice about the use of numbers in business, technical, and professional writing, see the reference guides listed in Chapters 46 through 49.

40a Spelling out numbers or using numerals

Whenever you use numbers in your writing, you need to decide whether to spell them out (twenty-five) or use numerals (25). The rules that follow tell you how to use numbers in general writing, including much academic writing. Conventions for the use of numbers may vary according to academic discipline and profession, however, so check with your instructor or with one of the style sheets describing conventions for specific fields (see Chapter 46).

1 Spell out numbers of one or two words

Spell out a number if you can write it in one or two words.

CORRECT   We are ordering **twenty-seven** personal computers.

CORRECT   Folktales have been popular in children's storybooks for the past **two hundred** years.

Treat hyphenated numbers (see 39b-2) as a single word.

CORRECT   This year, our farm produced more than **seventy-eight thousand** eggs.

2 Spell out numbers that begin a sentence

Readers expect every sentence to begin with a capital letter. To avoid unsettling your readers, spell out any number that opens a sentence, even if the number contains more than two words. If the number is long enough to be distracting, rewrite so that it appears elsewhere in the sentence.

INAPPROPRIATE   **428** of the houses in Talcottville are built on leased land.

DISTRACTING   **Four hundred twenty-eight** of the houses in Talcottville are built on leased land.

EASY TO READ   **In Talcottville, 428** houses are built on leased land.

3 Express related numbers in a consistent form

When the numbers in a sentence or passage refer to the same category, treat them consistently by sticking to either words or numerals. If one of the numbers would require numerical form on its own, expressing the rest in numerals will help you keep sentences direct and concise.

INCONSISTENT   Café Luna opened with a menu of **twenty-six** items, which soon expanded to **eighty-five** and then **104** items as word spread about the good food.

CONSISTENT   Café Luna opened with a menu of **26** items, which soon expanded to **85** and then **104** items as word spread about the good food.

Did You Know?

Although numbers might seem unimportant, they may have led to the very birth of writing as a communicative medium. The most ancient written forms (inscribed on stone tablets several thousand years ago) talked of sales, exchanges, cattle, and other possessions—subjects that required a way to represent numbers. Without a way of writing numbers, ancient people would have been unable to record and convey much of the information they considered important.

40b Following special conventions

In using numbers as part of dates, measurements, addresses, and the like, you need to follow some special conventions.

1 Use numerals when appropriate

ADDRESSES AND ROUTES

10 East 53rd Street   Interstate 6   Route 102
2450 Ridge Road, Apartment B3, Alhambra, CA 91801

DATES

September 7, 1976	1998	1880–1910
class of '97 (informal)	the '80s (informal)	1930s
486 B.C. (or B.C.E.)	980 A.D. (or C.E.)	
1955 to 1957	between 1872 and 1876	

PARTS OF A WRITTEN WORK

Chapter 12   page 278
Macbeth 2.4.25–28 (or act II, scene iv, lines 25–28)
Genesis 1:1–6 (reference to the Bible)

MEASUREMENTS USING SYMBOLS OR ABBREVIATIONS

120 MB	55 mph	80 kph
6'4"	47 psi	21 ml

PERCENTAGES, DECIMALS, AND FRACTIONS

7-5/8	27.3	67 percent (or 67%)

TIME OF DAY

10:52	2 p.m.	6:17 a.m.
12 p.m. (noon)	12 a.m. (midnight)	

EXCEPTION   seven o'clock, not 7 o'clock

MONEY (SPECIFIC AMOUNTS)

$7,883 (or $7883) $4.29 $7.2 million (or $7,200,000)

SURVEYS, RATIO, STATISTICS, AND SCORES

7 out of 10   3 to 1   a mean of 23
a standard deviation of 2.5
the Bills defeated the Packers 21 to 17

CLUSTERED NUMBERS

paragraphs 2, 4, 9, and 13–15 (or 13 through 15)
units 23, 145, and 210

40b
num

2 Spell out numbers when appropriate

DATES AND TIMES

the sixties   October seventh   the nineteenth century
four o'clock (or four in the morning)
times rounded to the quarter hour: half past eight, a quarter after one

ROUNDED NUMBERS OR ROUNDED AMOUNTS OF MONEY
about three hundred thousand citizens
close to eleven thousand dollars
sixty cents (and other small dollar or cent amounts)

RANGES OF NUMBERS

LESS THAN 100	Give the second number in full.
	9–13 27–34 58–79 94–95
OVER 100	Give only the last two digits of the second number unless more are needed to prevent confusion. Do not use a comma in four-digit page numbers.
	134–45 95–102 (not 95–02) 370–420
	1534–620 (not 1534–20) 1007–9
YEARS	Supply both years in a range except when they belong to the same century.
	1890–1920 1770–86 476–823 42–38 B.C.

LARGE NUMBERS
For especially large numbers, combine numerals and words.
75 million years   2.3 million new automobiles

40c Avoiding too many numbers

Using too many numbers in a sentence or passage can confuse readers. If numbers come next to each other, first check for any needed hyphens (see 39b).

CONFUSING	For the company picnic we can buy either **forty six packs** of soda pop or **twenty two liter** bottles.
HYPHENS ADDED	For the company picnic we can buy either **forty six-packs** of soda pop or **twenty two-liter** bottles.

When a passage contains so many numbers that readers may have trouble keeping track of the relationships, consider organizing the numbers in a table or chart.

DETAILED DESCRIPTION	The origins of Canada's population include the British Isles (40%), France (27%), other European regions (20%), and Indian (indigenous) or Eskimo (1.5%).

CHARTED NUMBERS

Canadian Population

Origin	Percentage
British Isles	40
France	27
Other European	20
Indian (indigenous) or Eskimo	1.5

This alternative is appropriate only when the numbers identify comparable categories. In other instances, you can avoid confusing readers by rewriting in order to simplify or to separate numbers so they are easier to understand.

Exercise

A. In the following sentences, correct any errors in the use of numbers. Circle any especially difficult items. You may need to rewrite some sentences.

EXAMPLE

When the list of cities for the Rock and Roll Hall of Fame was nar-
                        one
rowed down to *1*, the choice was Cleveland.

1. Of the groups and individuals elected to the Rock and Roll Hall of Fame from 1986 to 1990, 5 were female and 68 were male.
2. The Hall of Fame is increasing its membership goals from nineteen thousand to twenty-one thousand five hundred.
3. 411 of the 2000 questionnaires about favorite rockers were returned by the deadline.
4. This year the Hall of Fame purchased twenty-six articles of clothing, 127 signed memorabilia, and 232 unused concert tickets for the museum.
5. Although subscribers were told the museum would open by 10:30 in the morning on the twelfth, the personnel weren't ready for the large crowd until about 2 o'clock.

**40c
num**

B. In a small group, compare your edited versions of the sentences in Exercise 1A. Which cases gave you the most trouble? How did you resolve them?

C. Proofread a paper you are writing to make sure you have used numbers correctly.

Abbreviations

When they are understood and agreed upon by both a writer and reader, abbreviations act as a kind of shorthand, making a sentence quicker to write and easier to read.

SPELLED OUT   In her course Reporting Economic Issues, new faculty member **Doctor** Marian Hwang will be drawing heavily on her prior employment at both the **Internal Revenue Service** and **the National Broadcasting Company.**

ABBREVIATED   In her course Reporting Economic Issues, new faculty member **Dr.** Marian Hwang will be drawing heavily on her prior employment at both the **IRS** and **NBC.**

Improper or badly placed abbreviations, however, can make a sentence *harder* to read and understand.

CONFUSING   The legal theory known as Law **&** Economics has a strong advocate in **Jg. Rich.** Posner. He is a former **U of C** law **prof.** who now sits on the Seventh **U.S. Cir. Ct. of App.** in Chicago.

   READER'S RESPONSE: Am I supposed to know all these abbreviations? What is "Cir. Ct. of App."? Is "U of C" the University of California? Cincinnati? Chicago?

CLEAR   The legal theory known as Law **and** Economics has a strong advocate in **Judge** Richard Posner. He is a former **University of Chicago** law **professor** who now sits on the Seventh U.S. **Circuit Court of Appeals** in Chicago.

Abbreviations should aid your readers, not distract them. This chapter provides some basic rules for abbreviating words and phrases in your writing.

41a Using familiar abbreviations

Many abbreviations are so widely used that readers have no trouble recognizing them. These abbreviations are acceptable in all kinds of writing as long as you present them in standard form.

1 Abbreviate titles with proper names

When people's titles come right before or after their names, you should use standard abbreviations such as *Dr., Rev., Ms.,* and *Prof.*

BEFORE NAME   **Dr.** Antoinette Plocek; **Mr.** William Choi; **Ms.** Rutkowski; **Mrs.** Stephanie Chenier; **Rev.** Richard Valantasis; **Hon.** Patricia Hacaj; **St.** Rose of Lima.

AFTER NAME   Christine Carruthers, **M.D.;** Cathy Harrington, **D.V.M.;** Angelo Iacono, **Jr.;** James Guptil, **Sr.;** Ralph Romero, **S.J.;** Jane Berger, **M.A.;** Rosemary Anzaldua, **C.P.A.**

When you give a person's entire name, you may abbreviate his or her title, but if you use the title *as part of your reference to the person,* spell out the entire title.

41a
abbrev

INCORRECT   The list included **Prof.** Levesque, **Brig. Gen.** Washington, and **Rep.** Schroeder.

ACCEPTABLE   The list included **Professor** Levesque, **Brigadier General** Washington, and **Representative** Schroeder.

ALTERNATIVE   The list included **Prof. Roland** Levesque, **Brig. Gen. William** Washington, and **Rep. Patricia** Schroeder.

EXCEPTIONS   **Rev.** Mills and **Dr.** Smith were not invited.

Spell out a title when it does not come next to a proper name.

INCORRECT   You should consult the **Dr.** about that knee.

EDITED   You should consult the **doctor** about that knee.

EDITED   You should consult **Dr. Boyajian** about that knee.

Use only one form of a person's title at a time.

INCORRECT   **Dr.** Vonetta McGee, **D.D.S**

CORRECT   **Dr.** Vonetta McGee

CORRECT   Vonetta McGee, **D.D.S.**

Academic titles such as *M.A., Ph.D., B.S., Ed.D.,* and *M.D.* can be used on their own in abbreviated form.

ACCEPTABLE   The university offers an **Ed.D.** specifically designed for schoolteachers who want to become administrators.

2 Abbreviate references to people and organizations

Your readers may be more familiar with some abbreviations (3M, IBM, NATO) than with the names for which they stand (Minnesota Mining and Manufacturing, International Business Machines, North Atlantic Treaty Organization). Such abbreviations are almost always acceptable, as are those that simplify complicated names (AFL-CIO for American Federation of Labor and Congress of Industrial Organizations).

In some abbreviations the letters are pronounced singly (YMCA, USDA). In others, called **acronyms,** the letters form a pronounceable word (AIDS, NATO). Abbreviations and acronyms in which each letter stands for a word are usually written in capitals without periods.

**41a
abbrev**

ORGANIZATIONS	NAACP, AMA, NBA, FDA, NCAA, UNESCO, IBEW
CORPORATIONS	GTE, USX, PBS, GM, CNN, AT&T, PBS, BBC
COUNTRIES	USA (*or* U.S.A.), UK (*or* U.K.)
PEOPLE	JFK, LBJ, FDR, MLK
THINGS OR EVENTS	FM, AM, TB, MRI, AWOL, DWI, TGIF

Writer's Tip

If your reader won't recognize an unfamiliar abbreviation, you can still use it in your document as long as you give the full word or phrase once and show the abbreviation in parentheses. From then on, you can use the abbreviation without confusion.

EXPLAINED   The **American Library Association (ALA)** has taken stands on access to information. The **ALA** opposes book censorship and favors privacy for records of the books borrowed by an individual.

This technique is especially useful in academic or technical writing because it enables you to shorten complicated and often-repeated terms.

3 Abbreviate dates and numbers correctly

Abbreviations of dates and numbers may be used only when they *specify* a number or amount; they are not a substitute for the general term.

Abbreviation	Meaning
A.D. or AD	*anno Domini,* meaning "in the year of Our Lord"
B.C. or BC	*before Christ*
B.C.E. or BCE	*before common era,* used by some writers in place of B.C.
C.E or CE	*Common Era,* used by some writers in place of A.D.
a.m.	*ante meridiem,* meaning "morning"; some writers use A.M.
p.m.	*post meridiem,* meaning "after noon"; some writers use P.M.
no.	number
$	dollars

INCORRECT Because of the lack of capable leadership, the bill providing **$** for inspection of meat-processing plants was not passed until late in the **p.m.,** just before the legislature adjourned.

EDITED Because of the lack of capable leadership, the bill providing **money** for inspection of meat-processing plants was not passed until late in the **evening,** just before the legislature adjourned.

41a
abbrev

You may use either *a.m.* and *p.m.* or *A.M.* and *P.M.* in handwritten or typewritten papers. Book and magazine printers generally set the abbreviations in small capitals (A.M., P.M.). Your word processor may allow you to do this.

Writer's Tip

In a hurried, informal note, you can use abbreviations to avoid spelling out words as long as your reader understands your shortcuts. In formal writing, however, use only familiar, acceptable abbreviations.

INFORMAL If I'm not in the office during the **a.m.,** leave your **ID no.** and have the **$** delivered to **Dr. B.** at the Oak **Blvd.** office.

FORMAL If I'm not in the office during the **morning,** leave your **identification number** and have the **money** delivered to **Dr. Baruti** at the Oak **Boulevard** office.

> ## Did You Know?
>
> Each day we use some common abbreviations without knowing that they were originally longer words or expressions (a famous example being *OK,* which has many proposed origins but most likely comes from an African word pronounced *ah-keh* or *wah-keh*). The term *good-bye,* for example, was abbreviated from the phrase *God be with you,* a kind of blessing and simple statement of departure. The substitution of *good* for *God* may have come about by association with similar phrases like *good day* or *good night.* Today we have gone a step further with the shortened form *bye* or the curious repetition *bye-bye.*

41b Using abbreviations sparingly

You can shorten many words and turn most names into initials, but the resulting sentences are likely to be hard to read and irritating. Their only real use is in shorthand notes to yourself or as a quick drafting technique (see 7b).

UNREADABLE   The descr. in the opening ch. is ~ to that in B̲.̲ H̲o̲u̲s̲e̲ except for the hum. tone and the emph. on a single char.'s pt. of view.

In most formal writing, your readers will expect words in full form except for certain familiar abbreviations (discussed in 41a). In special situations, such as research papers and scientific or technical writing, you can draw on a wider range of appropriate abbreviations to save space, particularly in documenting sources. (See Chapter 46 on abbreviations to use in documentation and in specialized writing.)

1 Avoid inappropriate abbreviations

The following lists should help alert you to inappropriate abbreviations.

DAYS, MONTHS, AND HOLIDAYS

AVOID	Thurs., Thur., Th.	Oct.	Xmas	
USE	Thursday	October	Christmas	

PLACES

AVOID	Wasatch Mts.	Lk. Erie	Phil.	Ont.	Ave.
USE	Wasatch Mountains	Lake Erie	Philadelphia	Ontario	Avenue

EXCEPTION   988 Dunkerhook Road, Paramus, **NJ** 07652
Use accepted postal abbreviations in all addresses with ZIPs.

If an abbreviation is officially part of a company name, you may use it (for example, Newman & Son Mfg. for Newman and Son Manufacturing). Otherwise, spell out the entire name.

Company Names

QUESTIONABLE   The switches were installed by **LaForce Bros. Electrical Conts.**

EDITED   The switches were installed by **LaForce Brothers Electrical Contractors.**

Some contexts require you to use abbreviations in a particular way. The Modern Language Association (MLA) reference style, for example, requires abbreviations of publishing companies; thus, Holt, Rinehart and Winston, Incorporated, becomes just Holt (see 46a). Otherwise, spell out the entire name.

People's Names

AVOID   Wm. and Kath. Newholtz will attend.

EDITED   William and Katherine Newholtz will attend.

41b abbrev

Disciplines and Professions

INCORRECT	econ.	bio.	poli. sci.	phys. ed.	OT
EDITED	economics	biology	political science	physical education	occupational therapy

Abbreviations may be acceptable in particular contexts; for example, reports in medicine or education routinely refer to PT (physical therapy) and OT (occupational therapy).

Parts of Written Works

IN DOCU-MENTATION	ch.	p.	pp.	fig.

Check style guide for academic field or profession (see Chapter 46).

IN WRITTEN TEXT	chapter	page	pages	figure

Use symbols such as @, #, =, ~, and + only in tables or graphs, not in the text of a paper. In general, spell out units of measurement such as *quart* and *mile* when you use them in sentences. You may, however, abbreviate phrases such as *rpm* and *mph,* with or without periods.

Symbols and Units of Measurement

AVOID	pt.	qt.	in.	mi.	kg.
USE	pint	quart	inch	mile	kilogram

CORRECT	Above 5600 **rpm,** viscosity breaks down.
CORRECT	Above 5600 **r.p.m.,** viscosity breaks down.

2 Limit Latin abbreviations

Limit your use of Latin abbreviations such as *et al.* and *e.g.* to documenting sources and making parenthetical comments.

c.f.	compare (*confer*)	i.e.	that is (*id est*)
e.g.	for example (*exempli gratia*)	N.B.	note well (*nota bene*)
et al.	and others (*et alii*)	viz.	namely (*videlicet*)
etc.	and so forth (*et cetera*)		

INCORRECT	Many products, **e.g.,** laptops, have flat-screen displays.
APPROPRIATE IN PARENTHESES	Many products (**e.g.,** laptops) have flat-screen displays.
PREFERABLE	Many products, **such as** laptop computers, have flat-screen displays.

41b
abbrev

Writer's Alert

The abbreviation *et al.* is very often used incorrectly. Meaning "and others," *et al.* comes from the longer Latin phrase *et alii.* No period appears at the end of the word *et,* but a period *always* appears at the end of *al.* because it is an abbreviation. Making the phrase possessive can be awkward; avoid such constructions as "Johnson et al.'s new book." Try "a new book by Johnson et al."

Exercise

A. Revise the following sentences, adding or correcting abbreviations when appropriate and spelling out or rewriting any inappropriate abbreviations. Assume that these sentences are all written in a fairly formal academic context.

EXAMPLE   *New York, Los Angeles,*
People think of ~~NY, LA,~~ and Montreal as international cities, but many small- to medium-sized towns are just as cosmopolitan.

1. At a drugstore in a small Montana town, I talked with a clerk who told me about the Wine Appreciation Guild, Ltd. (155 Conn. St., San Francisco, CA 94107), which publishes nonfiction books on food, wine, etc., e.g., *Wine Technology and Operations* by Yair Margalit, PhD.

2. According to a study by Ernest D. Abrams Consulting, smaller towns like Sioux City, IA, and Vero Bch., Fla., are even more likely to be the homes of inventors and innovators.

3. In one town in upstate NY, an engineer, Chas. D'Angelis, has created a device that measures rpms by counting the # of times a gear with a single tooth interrupts a laser beam.

4. While I was driving through the rural Midwest, I visited Rich. Forer, D.O., who examined my sore back, prescribed an innovative exercise rout. he had developed, and gave me an Rx for a mild painkiller.

5. In a city of twenty thou. people in eastern Tenn. I came across a health coop. that is pioneering a new phys. therapy program.

B. Meet in a small group and compare your editing of the sentences in Exercise A. Which ones seemed the hardest? Why?

C. Proofread a paper you are writing, checking for correct use of abbreviations.

Strategies for Spelling

Consider the fact that the sounds in the word *see* (an *s* and an *e*) can be spelled in at least a dozen different ways, as illustrated in the words *see, senile, sea, scenic, ceiling, cedar, juicy, glossy, sexy, cease, seize,* and *situ.* Or consider the six different pronunciations of the letters *ough* in the words *cough, tough, bough, through, though,* and *thoroughfare.* English spelling is often difficult, and unless you have been gifted with a marvelous visual memory for the way words are spelled, the best you can do is to develop some practical strategies for identifying spelling problems and choosing correct spellings.

42a Spelling as you write

Spelling errors are most likely to occur as you draft. You can deal with them immediately, during drafting, or later, as you edit and proofread. If correct spelling is hard for you, try to keep this difficulty from turning into a fear of misspelling that distracts you from what you are trying to write. Worrying about spelling can draw your attention away from the most important parts of drafting and revising—exploring ideas and expressing them in effective ways. Stopping to check every word you *might* have misspelled is a sure way to disrupt your train of thought.

Giving special attention to spelling is therefore something often best reserved for proofreading. Nonetheless, you can take some positive steps to deal with spelling errors as you write.

1 Recognize possible errors

To recognize possible spelling errors as you draft, consider the following sources of incorrect spelling.

Inattention. You know the correct spelling of a word, but you don't use it. You might make a typing mistake. You might focus so hard on what you want to say or how to say it that you let a misspelling creep in. Usually, you can recognize errors of this sort quickly when you glance back over what you have written.

Guessing. You don't know the correct spelling of a word, so you guess on the basis of reason or of similar-sounding words. You know, for example, that the words *irreconcilable, reasonable, honorable, justifiable,* and *probable* all end with *-able,* so you reason that the word you don't know, *irresistible,* must do the same—and you get it wrong.

"Sounding Out." You don't know the correct spelling of a word, so you "sound it out." Although this strategy works occasionally, it can often lead you astray because of the sound/spelling discrepancies in English. And if you mispronounce a word, your spelling will probably be wrong. Many a motel billboard has mistakenly offered "congradulations" to a graduating class. Perhaps the most common spelling error in the United States is the infamous *alot,* incorrectly spelled as one word because, when spoken, the *a* and the *lot* blend together. Sounding out a word can be helpful during the drafting process, when you need to get the word down on the page and can't, for the moment, look it up. Nonetheless, you can recognize right away that the spelling *might* be wrong.

2 Note possible misspellings as you draft

Instead of interrupting your thoughts to check every possible spelling error while you draft, try the following Strategy.

Strategy

Circle possible misspellings as you write. As you draft, you regularly glance back over a sentence or two in order to review what you have said. When you do this, circle any obvious spelling errors that have slipped into your work as well as any words you think *might* be spelled wrong. You may want to correct some errors right away, but don't allow correcting to distract you from the more important practice of drafting and developing your ideas. Come back to the circled words later, after you have completed drafting, and check them for misspellings.

42b Recognizing and correcting spelling errors

As you edit and proofread, you can use one or more of the following methods to recognize and correct misspellings.

1 Pause to think

While you are editing and proofreading, remind yourself to pay attention to spelling. If you suspect for whatever reason that a word might be misspelled, pause to check the spelling. Think about the sequence of letters, concentrating especially on sequences that are likely to be misspelled. Correct any words whose spelling you know; look up any unfamiliar spellings (see 42b-2). Develop some way to remember the correct spelling for future use. For example, if you often misspell the plural of *quiz*, try to remember that *quizzes* has two *z*'s—perhaps by associating quizzes with boredom (*zzzzzzz*).

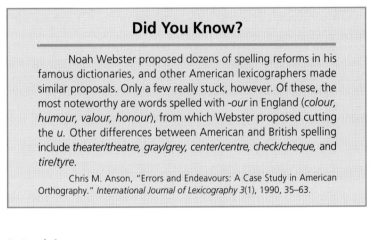

Did You Know?

Noah Webster proposed dozens of spelling reforms in his famous dictionaries, and other American lexicographers made similar proposals. Only a few really stuck, however. Of these, the most noteworthy are words spelled with -*our* in England (*colour, humour, valour, honour*), from which Webster proposed cutting the *u*. Other differences between American and British spelling include *theater/theatre, gray/grey, center/centre, check/cheque,* and *tire/tyre.*

Chris M. Anson, "Errors and Endeavours: A Case Study in American Orthography." *International Journal of Lexicography 3*(1), 1990, 35–63.

2 Look it up

A dictionary will give you the correct spelling of a word, and it may even offer spelling advice. *Merriam-Webster's Collegiate Dictionary* (10th ed.), the *New World Dictionary of the American Language,* the *American Heritage Dictionary of the English Language,* or any other standard dictionary is a good place to start. If you have a general idea of how a word is spelled, especially how it begins, you can usually locate it in a dictionary with a little looking around. If you know how a word sounds but are not sure about the spelling, you can use the lists of correspondences between sound and spelling that some dictionaries offer. If you still can't find your word, you may wish to use a specialized dictionary for people who have considerable trouble with spelling. These dictionaries list words both under the correct spelling (*phantom,* for example) and under likely misspellings (*fantom*).

As shown in the samples from *Merriam-Webster's Collegiate Dictionary* (10th ed.), a dictionary entry will tell you a word's correct spelling and also the spelling of its various forms (Figure 42-1)561. The entry will indicate preferred spellings and alternative forms, and it will contain listings for related

in·fer \in-'fər\ vb **in·ferred; in·fer·ring** [MF or L; MF *inferer,* fr. L *inferre,* lit., to carry or bring into, fr. *in-* + *ferre* to carry — more at BEAR] vt (1528) **1 :** to derive as a conclusion from facts or premises ⟨we see smoke and ~ fire —L. A. White⟩ — compare IMPLY **2 :** GUESS, SURMISE ⟨your letter . . . allows me to ~ that you are as well as ever — O. W. Holmes †1935⟩ **3 a :** to involve as a normal outcome of thought **b :** to point out : INDICATE ⟨this doth ~ the zeal I had to see him —Shak.⟩ **4 :** SUGGEST, HINT ⟨another survey . . . ~s that two= thirds of all present computer installations are not paying for themselves —H. R. Chellman⟩ ~ vi **:** to draw inferences ⟨men . . . have observed, *inferred,* and reasoned . . . to all kinds of results —John Dewey⟩ — **in·fer·able** *also* **in·fer·ri·ble** \in-'fər-ə-bəl\ adj — **in·fer·rer** \-'fər-ər\ n

in·fer·ence \'in-f(ə-)rən(t)s, -fərn(t)s\ n (1594) **1 :** the act or process of inferring: as **a :** the act of passing from one proposition, statement, or judgment considered as true to another whose truth is believed to follow from that of the former **b :** the act of passing from statistical sample data to generalizations (as of the value of population parameters) usu. with calculated degrees of certainty **2 :** something that is inferred; *esp* **:** a proposition arrived at by inference **3 :** the premises and conclusion of a process of inferring

in·fer·en·tial \,in-fə-'ren(t)-shəl\ adj [ML *inferentia,* fr. L *inferent-, inferens,* prp. of *inferre*] (1657) **1 :** relating to, involving, or resembling inference **2 :** deduced or deducible by inference — **in·fer·en·tial·ly** \-'ren(t)-sh(ə-)lē\ adv (1691) **:** by way of inference **:** through inference

Figure 42-1 Detail from *Merriam-Webster's Collegiate Dictionary,* 10th ed. Springfield, MA: Merriam-Webster, 1993.

**42b
spell**

words. It will also provide information about the word's roots and history, and this information may help you remember the spelling.

Exercise 1

A. Assume that you've circled the following words in italics in one of your papers. You're done with your draft, and now you want to double-check your spellings. Look each word up, make any necessary corrections, and then write out one way to remember each correct spelling. Do this whether or not you already know how to spell the word.

EXAMPLE   *pal*
school *principle*
The school principal is not always every kid's "pal."

coal *minor*   *precede* to the gate   *stationery* car
vacume the rug   she was *lieing*   *likelyhood*

B. In a group, share your devices for remembering the spellings in Exercise 1A. Write out those the group thinks are best in order to share them with the rest of the class.

C. Proofread a paper of your own, and circle all the possible misspellings.

3 Be alert for common patterns of misspelling

Many words contain groups of letters that can trip up even the best spellers. Other words have plural or compound forms that may be confusing, and others add suffixes and prefixes that need special attention.

Plurals. For most words, you can form a plural simply by adding -s (*novel, novels; experiment, experiments; contract, contracts*). Watch out for words that end in -o preceded by a consonant; they often add -es for the plural.

ADD -ES	potato, potatoes	tomato, tomatoes
	hero, heroes	zero, zeroes
ADD -S	cello, cellos	memo, memos

When a vowel comes before the -o, add -s.

ADD -S	stereo, stereos	video, videos

For words ending in a consonant plus -y, change y to i and add -es.

etiology, etiologies   gallery, galleries   notary, notaries

EXCEPTION   Add -s for proper nouns (*Kennedy, Kennedys; Tanury, Tanurys*).

For words ending in a vowel plus y, however, keep the y and add -s.

day, days   journey, journeys   pulley, pulleys

For words ending in -f or -fe, you often change f to v and add -s or -es.

hoof, hooves   knife, knives   life, lives   self, selves

Remember, however, that some words simply add -s.

belief, beliefs   roof, roofs   turf, turfs

Words ending with a hiss (-ch, -s, -ss, -sh, -x, or -z) generally add -es.

bench, benches	bus, buses	bush, bushes
buzz, buzzes	fox, foxes	kiss, kisses

A number of one-syllable words ending in -s or -z double the final consonant: *quiz, quizzes.*

Though most plurals follow these simple rules, some do not, and you need to be alert for their irregular forms. Words with foreign roots often follow the patterns of the original language, as is the case with the following words drawn from Latin and Greek.

alumna, alumnae (female)   criterion, criteria
alumnus, alumni (male)   datum, data
bacterium, bacteria   vertebra, vertebrae

Some familiar words form irregular plurals: *foot, feet; woman, women; mouse, mice; man, men.* (If you suspect that a word has an irregular plural, be sure to check a dictionary for its form.)

For compound words, use the plural form of the last word except in those few cases where the first word is clearly the most important.

basketball, basketballs   pegboard, pegboards
meadowland, meadowlands   snowflake, snowflakes

EXCEPTION   sister-in-law, sisters-in-law

Word Beginnings and Endings.   **Prefixes** do not change the spelling of the root word that follows.

precut   post-traumatic   misspell   unendurable

The prefixes *in-* and *im-* have the same meaning, but you should use *im-* before the letters *b, m,* and *p.*

USE *IN-*   incorrect   inadequate   incumbent

USE *IM-*   immobile   impatient   imbalance

Suffixes may change the spelling of the root word that comes before, and they may pose spelling problems in themselves.

Retain the silent *-e* at the end of a word when you add a suffix beginning with a consonant.

KEEP *-E*   fate, fateful   gentle, gentleness

EXCEPTIONS   words like *judgment, argument, truly,* and *ninth*

Drop the silent *-e* when you add a suffix beginning with a vowel.

DROP *-E*   imagine, imaginary   generate, generation
                decrease, decreasing   define, definable

EXCEPTIONS   words like *noticeable* and *changeable*

Four familiar words end in *-ery: stationery* (paper), *cemetery, monastery, millinery.* Most others end in *-ary: stationary* (fixed in place), *secretary, primary, military,* and *culinary.*

Most words with a final "seed" sound end in *-cede: precede, recede,* and *intercede,* for example. Only three are spelled *-ceed: proceed, succeed,* and *exceed.* One is spelled *-sede: supersede.*

42b
spell

The endings *-able* and *-ible* are easy to confuse because they sound alike. Add *-able* to words that can stand on their own and *-ible* to word roots that cannot stand on their own.

USE *-ABLE*   charitable, habitable, advisable, mendable

> Drop the *e* for word roots ending in one *e* (*comparable, detestable*), but keep it for words ending in double *e* (*agreeable*).

USE *-IBLE*   credible, irreducible, frangible

Words Containing *ie* and *ei*. Here is an old rhyme that tells you when to use *ie* and *ei*.

> *I* before *e*
> Except after *c*,
> Or when sounding like *a*
> As in n*ei*ghbor and w*ei*gh.

Most words follow the rule.

USE *IE*   believe, thief, grief, friend, chief, field, niece

USE *EI*   receive, deceit, perceive, ceiling, conceited

There are some exceptions.

EXCEPTIONS   weird, seize, foreign, ancient, height, either, neither, their, leisure, forfeit

4 Watch for commonly misspelled words

Words that sound like each other but are spelled differently (*accept/except, assent/ascent*) are known as **homophones.** Writers often confuse them, creating errors in both spelling and meaning.

INCORRECT   The city will not **except** any late bids for the project.

PROOFREAD   The city will not **accept** any late bids for the project.

The list on pages 559–560 of homophones and other words often confused is designed to help you recognize errors in spelling or meaning as you proofread.

5 Try alternatives to the dictionary

Sometimes when you want to use a particular word, you can't find the correct spelling in a dictionary, no matter how hard you look. Try the alternatives listed in the Strategy on pages 560–61.

Commonly Misspelled or Confused Word Pairs

WORD	MEANING	WORD	MEANING
accept	receive	elicit	draw out, evoke
except	other than	illicit	illegal
affect	to influence; an emotional response	eminent	well known, respected
effect	result	immanent	inherent
all ready	prepared	imminent	about to happen
already	by this time	fair	lovely; light-colored; just
allusion	indirect reference	fare	fee for transportation
illusion	faulty belief or perception	forth	forward
ascent	upward movement	fourth	after *third*
assent	agreement	gorilla	an ape
assure	state positively	guerrilla	kind of soldier or warfare
ensure	make certain	hear	perceive sound
insure	indemnify	here	in this place
bare	naked	heard	past tense of *hear*
bear	carry; an animal	herd	group of animals
board	get on; flat piece of wood	hole	opening
bored	not interested	whole	complete
brake	stop	its	possessive form of *it*
break	shatter, destroy; a gap; a pause	it's	contraction for *it is*
capital	seat of government; monetary resources	later	following in time
capitol	building that houses government	latter	last in a series
cite	quote an authority	lessen	make less
sight	ability to see; a view	lesson	something learned
site	a place	meat	flesh
complement	to complete or supplement	meet	encounter
compliment	to praise	loose	not tight
desert	abandon	lose	misplace
dessert	sweet course at conclusion of meal	no	negative
discreet	tactful, reserved	know	understand or be aware of
discrete	separate or distinct	passed	past tense of *pass*
		past	after; events occurring at a prior time

(cont.)

42b
spell

Commonly Misspelled or Confused Word Pairs *(cont.)*

WORD	MEANING	WORD	MEANING
patience	calm endurance	road	street
patients	people getting medical treatment	rode	past tense of *ride*
		scene	section of a play; setting of an action
peace	calm or absence of war	seen	visible
piece	part of something	stationary	fixed in place or still
plain	clear, unadorned	stationery	paper for writing
plane	woodworking tool; airplane	straight	unbending
		strait	water passageway
persecute	harass	than	compared with
prosecute	take legal action against	then	at that time; next
personal	relating to oneself	their	possessive form of *they*
personnel	employees	there	in that place
precede	come before	they're	contraction for *they are*
proceed	go ahead, continue		
principal	most important; head of a school	to	toward
		too	in addition, also
principle	basic truth, rule of behavior	two	number after *one*
		waist	middle of body
rain	precipitation	waste	leftover or discarded material
reign	to rule; period of ruling		
rein	strap for guiding an animal	which	one of a group
		witch	person with magical powers
raise	lift up or build up		
raze	tear down	who's	contraction for *who is*
right	correct	whose	possessive of *who*
rite	ritual	your	possessive of *you*
write	compose; put words into a text	you're	contraction for *you are*

42b
spell

Strategy

• List as many possible spellings as you can, even if they seem odd. Try looking them all up. Often you will find the right area in the dictionary and will be able to locate the word with a little more searching.
• Try a thesaurus (see 27c) if you know a suitable synonym; the word may be listed there in its correct spelling.

- Ask friends or classmates if they know the spelling, especially for technical terms; then look up the word in the dictionary to be sure you got good information.
- Check the indexes of books that deal with the topic the word relates to.
- Check your textbook, class notes, or handouts to see whether the word appears there.

6 Get help

All writers make some spelling errors that they simply can't fix because they don't know the word is misspelled. If at all possible, ask members of a revision group to identify any spelling errors you haven't caught. But first clean up all the errors you already know, even if you simply circle the words to identify them as misspelled. If someone else finds any more misspellings in your paper, you have the chance not just to fix them before sending the paper on to its reader but also to learn the correct spellings along the way.

42c Using long-term strategies to improve your spelling

42c
spell

Improving your spelling more generally is like improving anything that develops slowly: you need to practice. Here are three useful ways to become a more effective speller.

1 Use memory devices and pronunciation aids

The use of **mnemonics** (memory aids) can greatly improve your spelling by reminding you of odd spelling conventions that don't correspond with pronunciation. In *Beyond the "SP" Label,* Patricia McAlexander, Ann Dobie, and Noel Gregg offer a number of memory aids, including the following.

> *All right* is spelled like *all wrong.*
> *A lot* is like *a little.*
> *Emigrant, immigrant:* An emigrant leaves; an immigrant comes in.
> *Separate: separate* rates two *a*'s; there's a rat in *separate.*

Use these as models to create memory aids of your own.

Some words get misspelled because often they are *not* pronounced fully or correctly. You need to develop an ear for "careful" pronunciations equivalent to spelling. Instead of hearing *new-cue-lar,* a common pronunciation of *nuclear,* hear the word in its carefully pronounced (spelling) form: *new-clee-ar.*

Did You Know?

Experts frequently argue over just how difficult the English spelling system is. In his book *The English Language*, David Crystal tries to show that the system isn't really as bad as we think. He claims that only 400 words have "irregular" or idiosyncratic spellings and cites a study showing that 84 percent follow some sort of general (learnable) pattern, such as *purse, nurse, curse* and *hatch, catch, latch.*

David Crystal, *The English Language* (New York: Viking, 1988) 69.

---

2 Read more and attend to spellings

Nothing boosts literacy (spelling included) so powerfully as reading. The more you read, the more likely you are to see words spelled correctly. When reading, keep a list of words you might use (and might otherwise misspell) someday. Focus consciously on words with difficult spellings (if you've been doing that in this chapter, you may already have learned the spellings of *mnemonic* and *nuclear*).

42c
spell

3 Build your own speller

The most useful spelling aid should look like someone's personal telephone book: filled with names and numbers generally meaningless to other people. If you keep track of words you commonly misspell, perhaps in a little notebook or file, you'll find yourself looking up possible candidates for misspellings much more quickly. As you begin learning and remembering the correct spellings, you can cross some words off your list as you're adding new ones.

....

Exercise 2

A. Without using a dictionary, circle the words that are misspelled in this list.

supercede	conceed	procede
idiosyncracy	concensus	accomodate
dexterous	impressario	irresistable
rhythm	opthalmologist	diptheria
anamoly	afficianado	caesarian
grafitti	judgement	liason

B. Working with a partner or in a small group, compare your answers to Exercise 2A, and *then* resolve any debates with a dictionary.

C. Go back to the possible errors you circled in your own paper in Exercise 1C. Identify any that are actual errors, and correct your paper in progress to eliminate the spelling problems.

42d Spelling and the computer

The personal computer has become for spelling what the hand-held calculator became in the 1970s for routine math. If you use a word processor, you've no doubt discovered the virtues of the spelling checker, a program that searches your document for misspellings and asks you whether they're correct.

1 Understand how spelling checkers work

Most spelling checkers on personal computers work in conjunction with a dictionary that must be present in the computer's memory. Often these computer dictionaries hold several thousand basic words. When you ask the computer to screen your document for any spelling errors, it compares each word in your text with the words in the dictionary. If the word matches a word in the dictionary, the computer assumes the word is correctly spelled, and it moves on to the next word.

When the computer encounters a word that does *not* match any word in its dictionary, it asks you whether the word is misspelled. If it is, you can select an alternative spelling or type in the correction, and the computer then moves on until it finds the next possible error. A typical program also allows you to add words to its often limited dictionary. In this way, you can personalize the dictionary so that an unusual word or technical term won't be flagged every time the computer finds it in your paper.

2 Use a spelling checker cautiously

Using a spelling checker, especially on longer documents, is likely to reveal at least one or two errors. But whatever you do, don't rely *entirely* on a spelling checker to fix your writing.

A spelling checker can't reveal words that are properly spelled but used incorrectly. If it runs across the sentence "The Lakewood High quarterback lead his team to victory in the semifinals," a spelling checker will ignore *lead* because this is a correctly spelled word in the dictionary. But here, *lead* should be *led*.

The computer may flag a word as misspelled and then, on command, offer you other correct spelling options. If you're not careful, you can mistakenly choose the wrong word to be inserted in place of the misspelled one.

4

WRITING STRATEGIES

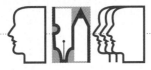

CHAPTER

43

What Is Research?

What is **research?** What is a research paper? Here is one set of answers to these questions given by students.

Choosing a topic that sounds interesting, though you are not sure what it involves or why it is important

Spending hour after hour in the library, poring over books and searching for articles in magazines

Taking countless notes and compiling quotations on 3″ × 5″ cards

Stringing together quotations and facts that, after all the tedious work, no longer hold much interest for you, while hoping your instructor will see how hard you have worked

If this is your view of research and research papers, you may be surprised by the answers that instructors are likely to give.

An exciting quest for new ways to view a subject or new answers to a problem

A way of deepening a writer's understanding and sharing this new understanding with readers

A way to participate in the ongoing, state-of-the art discussion that surrounds a topic and shapes attitudes and events

Research and research papers become exciting and involving activities when you approach them as ways to find answers to questions that matter, as ways to sharpen critical and investigative skills, and as ways to contribute to the ongoing exploration of a subject. Your definition of research will expand beyond books and magazines to include observations, data gathering, and interviews. Your research papers will go beyond facts and ideas from printed sources to incorporate your own insights and data you gathered.

To make research and research papers exciting and involving, you need to do five things.

1. Understand your assignment and audience.
2. Choose an appropriate topic.
3. Plan the time and effort needed for research and writing.
4. Understand your role as a researcher.
5. Define a goal for your writing.

43a Understanding your assignment and audience

Are you setting out for the library because your psychology instructor asked you to analyze the most recent studies on the emotional effects of work-related stress? Are you looking for information to use in a report arguing for company-financed day care? Are you planning to interview friends and family for an essay about the ways different generations view each other? Each of these tasks calls for a different kind of research, different sources of information and ideas, and different purposes and forms for writing. Understanding the demands of your tasks and being ready to shift research strategies should your goals change are two essential elements in the research process.

1 Analyze your assignment

In class and at work, your writing will often begin with an assignment requiring research. If such an assignment comes in written form, analyze it carefully to discover the kind of research required, the sources you need to examine, and the form your writing should take. (See 5a.)

43a
resrch

Strategy

To understand an assignment calling for research, ask the following kinds of questions.

- What is my purpose for writing? Will my paper be informative, analytical, argumentative, or speculative? (See 43h.)
- What key words indicate the goal of the assignment? For example, does it ask me to *analyze, examine, trace, present,* or *enumerate* something?
- What kinds of sources will be appropriate? Will I use books and articles, online databases, interviews, surveys, or field observations?
- Should my writing take a particular form?

- What type of documentation should I use—MLA, APA, CBE, CMS, or some other format? (See Chapters 46–49.)
- What are some possible topics?
- When is the assignment due and how long should my paper be?

Of course, not all writing tasks require research. Yet making research part of your writing process can often enrich your understanding and add depth and insight to the essay or report you are creating. For example, an assignment in a composition course might ask you to explore relationships between the various generations in your family. You could write an essay drawing on your memories alone, but by gathering stories your relatives tell about themselves or about others and by interviewing family members, you can enrich your essay with research that shows how the family passes on values and ways of behaving from generation to generation. (See 43g-2.)

Writer's Alert

The first question many students ask about a research paper assignment is "How long does it have to be?" Students may ask this question so they can plan their time and visualize the kind of paper they need to write. In contrast, instructors often think the question reflects a concern with superficial aspects of the assignment rather than more important questions like "What is the goal of the assignment?" or "What kinds of sources might be appropriate?" A question about length is appropriate, but you should probably ask it *after* you have inquired about matters of purpose, content, and strategy.

Exercise 1

A. Analyze each of the following research paper assignments by asking the kinds of questions outlined in the Strategy on pages 567–568. Write comments and questions in the margins. Underline anything you don't understand. Then write out any questions that you would need to ask your instructor or supervisor in order to complete the assignment successfully.

ASSIGNMENT FROM A JOURNALISM COURSE

Prepare a magazine feature article of between five and ten pages by examining contrasting stands on a specific controversial issue. Then develop your own stand on the issue. Make sure you provide detailed facts, statistics, and quotations to represent the contrasting points of view and to support your own conclusions.

ASSIGNMENT FROM A SOCIOLOGY COURSE

Locate some recent issues of scholarly journals in sociology containing case studies of social or occupational groups. Identify a group and prepare a study of your own. Present your case study in an appropriate format, provide detailed data gathered through your research, and acknowledge other relevant research that bears on your study and supports (or contradicts) your conclusions. Use APA documentation.

ASSIGNMENT FROM AN AMERICAN LITERATURE COURSE

Choose one of the authors represented in our anthology and read a major work (novel, drama, or collection of poems, for example) that is not included in the anthology. Prepare a paper on the major techniques and thematic concerns of the work. Secondary sources are likely to be helpful for your analysis.

ASSIGNMENT AT WORK

Check on the costs, reliability, and speed of the various ways we can ship to our new stores in Oregon from the Des Moines warehouse, and give your recommendations to me in a report next Monday.

B. Exchange your work from Exercise 1A with at least two other students. How do your questions differ? Which questions identify points that need to be clarified? Which ones identify important information that is not presented in the assignment?

C. Analyze the assignment for a research paper you are working on by using questions like those in the Strategy on pages 567–568. Note any questions you have, and be ready to share them with your instructor. In your journal or on your assignment sheet, write out the assignment in your own words.

43a
resrch

2 Consider your audience

You can give direction to your research and writing by defining potential audiences. (See Chapter 6.) One way to discover likely audiences is to use your journal to list possible readers. If your readers are likely to know something about the topic already, you might decide to focus on a specific, less well known aspect of the subject. If your readers are likely to disagree with your perspective, you may need to focus on supporting facts and ideas. And if your topic is new or unusual, you may need to provide readers with a general background that will help them understand the ideas and information you plan to present.

Exercise 2

A. In your journal, jot down the possible specific audiences that would be most interested in your paper. Choose one possible audience, and write a paragraph describing how writing for that audience might narrow or expand your research. List what you will need to include in your paper to meet your audience's expectations.

B. In a group, discuss your first choices for audience in Exercise 2A. Has anyone chosen an audience that is too general or that would expect too much for the scope of your research paper? Help each other define a specific audience and set goals for writing that would best fit that audience.

43b   Choosing an appropriate topic

Although you may think the heart of a research paper is the research itself, the actual information you gather won't mean much unless you're personally interested in the topic you've chosen and unless that topic is well focused and manageable. Many students wait for a topic to "inspire" them, but usually the inspiration doesn't arrive in time, if at all. Try using one or more of the following approaches to avoid this problem.

1 Reread the assignment

When you read over your assignment, does it suggest possible topics or direct you to write about a particular range of subjects? Jot down any topics that come to mind as you read. See what your instructor and your classmates think about these topics. Ask your instructor for suggestions about finding a topic.

43b
resrch

2 List, freewrite, and make connections

Make a list of topics that interest you, no matter how general or trivial they seem. Then choose the topic on the list that strikes you as most interesting. Freewrite on this topic for at least ten minutes, raising questions you might ask and attempt to answer in a paper. (See Chapter 4.)

When you finish listing and freewriting, you should have a range of possible topics and questions, probably pointing in many directions. To start seeing connections among your ideas, arrange your topics and questions into related groups. Ask yourself which group interests you most. From this group, develop one or two **guiding questions** that will give a specific focus for your research and help you choose appropriate sources of information.

3 Read to develop a topic

If you sometimes have trouble thinking of a topic or developing questions to guide your research, don't panic. Some preliminary reading may help you discover a promising subject, interesting ideas, and intriguing questions. You might begin, for example, by reading one or two general articles on a subject that catches your eye. Popular magazines like *Time, Discover, Sports Illustrated, GQ, Glamour, Natural History,* and *The New Republic* can suggest interesting topics for research and writing. So can encyclopedias and books from the nonfiction section of a library. Indexes like the *Readers' Guide to Periodical Literature* use key words to list works. As you skim such works, let the key words suggest topics, and read some of the works listed as a way of focusing your search. (See 44b for more information on encyclopedias and indexes.)

As you look over these various sources for topics, jot down in your journal any subjects that interest you and any guiding questions that spring to mind. If you are working with photocopies, you may wish to make notes in the margins.

43c Developing guiding questions: Research in progress

For his journalism class, Peter Burk needed to prepare a feature article on a controversial issue. He listed the following possible topics: pregnancy, cancer, abortion, and rape and the press. Of these, the issue of rape and the press interested him most.

Peter's freewriting raised a variety of questions about rape and the press.

43c
resrch

> Is the press too sensational when it reports rape cases? Is the press unethical in naming suspects? Should the press be allowed to publish the names of rape victims? Do the defendants in sensational rape cases get fair trials? Does the press influence the justice system? What determines guilt in a rape case? Who are the victims of rape? Why do men rape? Who are the journalists — their race, class, etc. — who report on rape cases? What motivates these journalists? What is the relationship between society and rape as a social issue? What is the boundary between sensationalism and objective reporting?

When he looked for connections among his questions, Peter saw that the questions fell into four groups: questions about the *ethics* of publishing names; questions about the *definitions* of rape, guilt, and objectivity; questions about the *demographics* of victims, suspects, and reporters; and questions about rape as a *social issue*.

The first group of connections interested Peter the most. He chose his guiding question: "Should the press be allowed to publish the names of rape victims?" As he thought more about the topic, he decided on two additional questions to give focus to his writing and guide his research: "Should suspects' names be published?" and "Does the publishing of names have any effect on the outcome of a rape trial?"

Did You Know?

Writing about a topic, especially writing questions about it, may help you integrate new knowledge with what you already know and may help you become more engaged with the topic. Research studies show that certain kinds of writing help students to manipulate, interpret, and transform reading material. Instead of passively waiting for a topic to come to you, read actively and ask questions about interesting or controversial articles or subjects. This may help you develop a focus for your research project.

D. A. Hayes, "The Potential for Directing Study in Combined Reading and Writing Activity," *Journal of Reading Behavior* 19 (1987): 333–52.

Exercise 3

A. In your notebook or on a sheet of paper, list five or more possible research topics that interest you. Choose the most interesting item from this list. In another column, make a list of questions that come to mind about this item.

B. In a group with at least two other students, exchange your lists from Exercise 3A. Read the other students' lists of questions, and add questions of your own to each list. Then work together to arrange each set of questions into related clusters, and decide which of the clusters are likely to make interesting and researchable topics.

43d
resrch

43d Planning your time and effort

Managing all the decisions and activities involved in research is like juggling: you need to plan your moves. To manage time and effort effectively, you need to pay attention to four decision points.

1 Decision point: How much time do I have?

When should my paper be in final form? Do I have to submit any intermediate assignments, such as notes or a draft?

Strategy

Use your deadlines to establish the timeline for your research plan. Then use the next three decision points to help you choose appropriate activities. Include these activities in your research plan.

---

2 Decision point: What is my role as a writer, and what kind of paper am I writing?

Will I be drawing on sources, doing personal learning, or training as a professional? (See 43f and 43g.) Will my paper be informative, analytical, argumentative, or speculative? (See 43h.)

Strategy

Analyze the assignment; choose a topic and focus; develop guiding questions; decide on goals for writing and the kind of paper you will produce; identify your role as a researcher; do preliminary research; record possible topics and ideas; and shape your research plan accordingly.

43d
resrch

3 Decision point: What kind of research must I do?

Will I be doing library research (books, articles, documents, databases), field research (interviews, surveys, observations, experiments), or both?

Strategy

Create a research strategy; identify necessary resources (library research or field research); create a working bibliography or list of informants and observations; examine sources and take notes; and record insights and possible writing strategies in a journal. Put these activities in your research plan.

---

4 Decision point: What plan should my writing follow?

What kinds of detail, ideas, or other features should my paper contain? What special form (if any) must it take?

◄►

Strategy

Develop a tentative plan and thesis; draft the paper, drawing on your notes and sources; get responses from other writers or members of your potential audience; revise and edit your draft; prepare a list of works cited; check citations in your text and their sources; proofread carefully; and submit the final paper. Note these steps in your plan.

◄►

Use your answers to the decision-point questions as a framework for a preliminary **research plan.** Be ready, however, to alter your plan to take account of changes in schedule, shifts in focus or topic, missing (or especially plentiful) resources, and responses from readers.

43e Preparing a research plan: Research in progress

Beth Alstead was assigned a research paper on an important decision she or other students needed to make. Her paper would be due on December 12, so Beth constructed a research plan by working backward from this date to the date of the assignment, October 15.

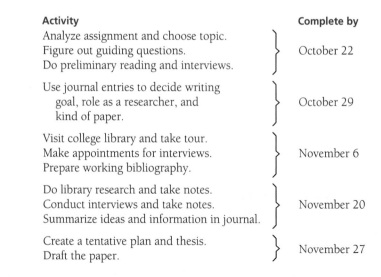

Activity	Complete by
Analyze assignment and choose topic. Figure out guiding questions. Do preliminary reading and interviews.	October 22
Use journal entries to decide writing goal, role as a researcher, and kind of paper.	October 29
Visit college library and take tour. Make appointments for interviews. Prepare working bibliography.	November 6
Do library research and take notes. Conduct interviews and take notes. Summarize ideas and information in journal.	November 20
Create a tentative plan and thesis. Draft the paper.	November 27

43e
resrch

Share draft with classmates.
Begin list of works cited. } December 4

Revise the paper.
Check citations and list of works cited.
Proofread and submit final paper. } December 12

43f Understanding your role as a researcher

Near the beginning of your research and writing process, you need to ask yourself, "What do I want to gain from this research, and what role will I be playing as a researcher?"

You may emphasize gathering information and ideas from sources, then synthesizing them with your insights and analysis in order to create a paper that adds to your readers' understanding and your own. In such a case your role is that of a *writer drawing on sources*.

Your work could also grow out of a writing task that does not necessarily require research and may serve as a way of learning more about yourself and your topic. In such an instance your role is that of a *writer as learner*.

Your research could instead be part of your efforts as a professional or a professional in training. If this is the case, your role is that of a *writer as (professional) researcher*.

43g Developing a role as a researcher: Research in progress

As Beth Alstead, Cesar Vasquez, and Lily Germaine worked on their research projects, each developed a different research role.

**43g
resrch**

1 Beth Alstead, a writer drawing on sources

Beth Alstead chose to major in engineering, in part at the urging of her parents, but she wondered whether she might be happier as an architect than as an engineer. Beth's assignment to prepare a research paper on a decision she or other students might have to make led her to focus on architecture as a possible career.

After library research in order to decide on appropriate questions, Beth interviewed architecture students, their instructors, and a local architect. As her research progressed, Beth was surprised to find that being an architect is not as glamorous as she first thought; however, her research gave her a clear picture of the range of possible architectural careers. In her paper, addressed to an audience of college students, she presented both the positive and negative aspects of the field.

2 Cesar Vasquez, a writer as learner

For his composition course, Cesar Vasquez wrote a paper exploring the relationships between generations in his family. Though his assignment did not require library research, Cesar sought help in exploring the meaning of his grandmother's family stories about her girlhood in Mexico. In a computer-based index (see 44b), he discovered a reference to Vera Rosenbluth's *Keeping Family Stories Alive: A Creative Guide to Taping Your Family Life and Lore,* a book that tells how to collect family stories. Following suggestions in the book, Cesar wrote a questionnaire about the family's history and sent it to relatives in both branches of the family, also asking them to write down any stories they remembered. While waiting for their replies, he taped and transcribed his grandmother's stories. He created an essay that presented his relatives' stories and analyzed what the stories had to say about relationships within a large extended family.

3 Lily Germaine, a professional in training

Lily Germaine planned to be a sociologist and was already thinking about graduate school. She welcomed her sociology class assignment to research and write a case study like the ones that appear in professional journals. Working out in the weight room is popular with many students at Lily's school, and she thought that doing a case study of a bodybuilder might be both fun and challenging. She was particularly interested in finding an answer to the question "Why do people enjoy weight training?" Library research gave Lily a clearer sense of the audience and acceptable format and style for her paper. It helped her map out tentative contents for her paper and create a research plan. Besides library materials, Lily's primary sources of information for her study were her detailed observations of a weight room and her interviews with a bodybuilder.

43h Defining a goal for your writing

Besides fulfilling different personal purposes, research writing comes in various forms that reflect your relationship to your readers. Do you want to inform them about something? Do you want to present a detailed analysis of an idea, issue, or phenomenon? Do you hope to convince your readers, through argument and evidence, to agree with your point of view? Or do you want them to understand your speculations about a topic and raise their own questions?

1 Informative writing

When your research paper is primarily informative, you try to explain a subject in detail, often providing its background or history. Such a paper might present a sequence of events, explore causes or effects, or explain a subject's parts. Your readers will expect objective information from reliable sources, telling the "truth" about the topic.

2 Analytical writing

In an analytical paper, you "take your topic apart," looking carefully at how those parts relate to each other—just as you do when you explicate a poem in a literature class (see Chapter 51) or dissect an animal in a zoology course. Your readers will expect you to *interpret* something, explaining its causes or effects, its role in a problem or solution. You may use some persuasive strategies to convince your readers that your interpretation is valid. Readers will also expect you to mention opposing or supporting points of view and to indicate your sources .

3 Argumentative writing

You may be most familiar with argumentative writing as it appears in editorials, political speeches, and some advertising. When you present a researched argument, your reader will expect you to state your opinions explicitly, to provide detailed support, and to structure your paper logically. A reader may not hold the same opinions as you do but should be willing to entertain sensible alternatives, especially to solve a problem or remedy a condition.

4 Speculative writing

Your purpose in speculative writing is to explore a topic without necessarily taking a stand. Sometimes the subject resists firm conclusions but is still significant and involving. Readers will expect you to discuss several solutions to a problem or to explore its ramifications, all without arguing a firm conclusion. Readers will want the topic "opened up"; they will want you to explore questions they can think about on their own.

**43h
resrch**

Exercise 4

A. Write down your topic and guiding questions for a research paper you are preparing, and then create a detailed research plan using the four sets of decision-point questions as a framework.

B. Share your topic, goals, and research plan with a group of fellow students working on their own research projects. Working together, indicate whether you think each group member's topic is interesting and researchable, and tell whether you find the goals realistic. Examine each research plan in detail to see whether it is workable. Whenever appropriate, suggest changes in the timeline or in the specific activities. After the group meeting, write a brief analysis of your role as a researcher and a statement of your goal(s) for writing.

CHAPTER

44

Locating Sources and Reading Critically

When you start research for a paper or report, you may worry about finding enough information. This problem does occur occasionally, yet the opposite is more likely to be true. If you follow a careful and thorough search strategy, you will probably end up with many potential sources, so that you can choose those that are most useful and readily available.

44a Designing a search strategy

To locate good sources and to use them effectively, you need a search strategy. A **search strategy** helps you identify the kind of research appropriate for your project (library, electronic, or field research) as well as the different sources you might consult (general or specialized, primary or secondary). A search strategy also identifies the research tasks you need to perform, such as focusing on a topic or surveying current ideas, interpretations, and information. Each search strategy you design should be different, reflecting your particular subject, your goals for writing, your audience, and the resources available to you.

**44a
source**

1 Remember the different kinds of research

Library research focuses primarily on materials such as books, articles, pamphlets, microfilm, databases, recordings, artworks, and reproductions. Depending on the resources of your library, these materials may be available in various forms, including print media, film, CD-ROMs, computer files, or recordings. This kind of research generally takes place in a library or a similar resource center, though it can certainly occur at home or anywhere you choose to examine library materials. Access to this kind of information depends on your skill with indexing and reference systems and your ability to read critically.

> **Writer's Tip**
>
> To decide whether you should do library research, electronic research, field research, or some combination, ask yourself the following questions.
>
> 1. Has your topic been frequently discussed in books, articles, and newspapers? If so, you need to do library research so that your writing can build on what others have said, and you may find similar material in electronic sources.
> 2. Is your subject a text (book, poem, document), an object (painting, sculpture), or an event (play, musical performance, film) that you need to locate in a library or museum or theater? Is your subject a historical event that you can study only through written documents, films, or pictures? If so, you will need to do library research to learn about your subject, its background, and what others have to say about it, and you may be able to locate information and discussions in electronic sources.
> 3. Is your subject an event, a situation, a set of attitudes, or a pattern of behavior that has not been widely studied and that you can investigate directly? If so, you need to do field research, using observation, interviews, questionnaires, or surveys to gather data and evidence.
> 4. Is your subject one of current interest to researchers and others who frequently use e-mail and other electronic means of exchanging ideas? If so, you need to consult e-mail lists and other electronic sources.

44a
source

Electronic research generally takes place through networks linking computers, computer users, and computer files, both locally and worldwide. The rapidly growing body of resources includes e-mail (electronic mail), mailing lists, electronic references, document and media databases, and interactive programs as well as search programs for locating specific resources. Access to this kind of information depends on the computer resources available to you, either personally or through a library, university, or other institution. It also depends on your skill with computers and computer networks or the help available to you.

Field research focuses primarily on events and oral texts that the researcher gathers through observations, interviews, surveys, experiments, note-taking, and recording. The research takes place wherever the subjects are, generally in settings other than a library or resource center. Access to this kind of information depends on your skill at interviewing, administering surveys, and observing as well as your ability to interpret the data you gather.

These kinds of research often overlap, of course. Libraries can provide access to electronic documents or reports of field research, for example, and computer networks can provide copies of research articles, photographs, and other documents. Many research projects likewise require you to do more than one kind of research, so you need to be aware of the opportunities each offers.

2 Note the different kinds of sources

Whether they are primary or secondary, source materials can be used to explore general information on a topic or locate more specialized information. Some of the sources you encounter in your research will be primary sources.

Primary sources consist of information and ideas in their original (or close-to-original) form: historical documents, works of literature, e-mail resources, letters, tapes of interviews, survey data, videotapes, raw statistics, and other kinds of basic information that contain little or no interpretation by the observer or gatherer. When you collect primary sources, you are bringing together the materials you will examine or interpret.

Other sources you use will be **secondary sources.** They consist of works that analyze, summarize, sort, interpret, or explain the information in primary sources. When you gather information and ideas from secondary sources, you are really finding out what other writers have said about your area of research.

3 Identify your research tasks and appropriate resources

In conducting your research, you will usually begin exploratively, and then, after identifying issues and narrowing your focus, you will locate more specific sources relevant to your topic. Although these important tasks overlap considerably, they involve certain kinds of resources.

44a
source

Explore Possible Topics. Usually you will begin your research by skimming general, informative sources to locate broad background information on a subject or to highlight contemporary issues, questions, controversies, and topics of interest. Such **preliminary** or **exploratory sources** include encyclopedias, magazine articles, ready references, electronic exchanges on bulletin boards or mail lists devoted to a particular subject, and general indexes or databases. These sources can help you focus on a topic, arrive at guiding questions, or identify key words to use in searching through indexes and databases.

Identify Current Issues. Books, articles in less specialized magazines and academic journals, indexes to professional publications, and topics in databases or electronic information sources can provide background and information to help you begin analyzing specific problems, controversies, and ideas. These **general sources** can also point the way to the more specialized research that you will need to do if you want to offer your readers fresh, detailed information and close examination of a topic.

Locate Relevant Research. As you identify more specific areas or questions from your exploratory research, you will begin to focus on certain areas or domains, often defined by specific key words or subject headings. To begin your research journey, you will need to consult **bibliographic sources** to find out what specific resources are available to you. Such sources include bibliographies of all kinds, electronic databases, indexes, abstracts, catalogs, and computer-generated reference lists. These bibliographic resources give you a road map for your research, and they are essential if you want to reach specific destinations in your search for information.

Gather Detailed Information. Research reports, scholarly articles, interviews with experts, surveys, field notes, technical documents, theoretical books, specialized databases, e-mail discussions of current research, and scientific reference works offer specific information, concepts, and perspectives on your guiding question. These **specialized sources,** identified through your bibliographic search, can provide both substance and support for the explanations, interpretations, and arguments you advance in your paper.

Exercise 1

A. To begin developing a search strategy for your research paper, write out your ideas about the directions your research is likely to take. Ask yourself whether you are likely to do library, electronic, or field research or some combination, and consider whether you are likely to consult primary sources, secondary sources, or both. Make notes about the kinds of resources you think you might consult first and the kinds you might consult later on.

44a
source

B. Share with a group the ideas you developed in Exercise 1A about possible search strategies. Help each person in the group create and write out a working search strategy. Try to suggest possible sources or alternative directions for research.

C. Write out a working search strategy for a research paper you are writing. (This may be the same strategy that you develop in Exercise 1B.) Revise this strategy during the course of your research to reflect what you have learned from the process and any new directions you choose to pursue.

44b   Locating library resources

Your topic, your guiding questions, or your search strategy will probably lead you to examine books, articles, microfilms, indexes, CD-ROM databases, or the many other documentary sources provided by libraries. You need to be familiar with the categories in which these resources are commonly arranged, the names of some of the most useful ones, and the ways you can best consult them. While no two libraries are the same, almost all provide general references, specialized indexes and databases, a library catalog, and government documents or other specialized collections. Most also provide these resources in various forms: in print, on microfilm, on CD-ROMs, or on computer networks.

Be aware that new CD-ROMs and other electronic materials are becoming available almost daily. Many of these are specialized and can provide a wealth of information from a single source, as the following titles suggest: *Beetle Larvae of the World; Motif Index to Folk Literature; Bugs on Disk; Bibliography of New Zealand;* and *CD-ROM Atlas of the Deepwater Ports of the U.S.* Because such resources are too specific and too exhaustive to include in a book like this one, your best course is to check any catalogs or indexes of CD-ROM and electronic sources in your library or consult a reference librarian to see what may be available. Many computer stores and mail-order houses sell general CD-ROM and computer-disk resources, such as encyclopedias, dictionaries, atlases, histories, and information on the natural sciences.

1 Turn to general sources for an overview

Use general sources to gain a broad overview of a subject area, including a sense of its relationships to other subjects. Such an overview can lead to topics, issues, controversies, events, and ideas you may wish to investigate further. You can also use general sources to identify names and key words useful for tracing a topic through more specialized sources, including indexes and electronic databases (see 44b-2). In addition, some general works include bibliographies of sources that you can consult. Try to use the most recent edition of a reference work so you get the most up-to-date information and bibliographic entries.

General Encyclopedias. For preliminary research and background information, consider turning to a general encyclopedia. An encyclopedia article will suggest how broad a subject area is and identify specific ideas, people, or topics you may wish to examine in your research. Most encyclopedia articles also provide a bibliography to help you locate additional information.

**44b
source**

Collier's Encyclopedia, 24 vols.
Encyclopedia Americana, 30 vols. plus yearbooks
Grolier Multimedia Encyclopedia (CD-ROM)
Microsoft Encarta (CD-ROM; contains 24-volume *Funk and Wagnalls New Encyclopedia*)
The New Encyclopaedia Brittannica, 32 vols.
World Book Encyclopedia, 22 vols. plus yearbook (elementary but useful)

For information about both general and specialized encyclopedias, see Kenneth Kister's *Best Encyclopedias: A Guide to General and Specialized Encyclopedias.*

Ready References. Ready references include one-volume encyclopedias with brief subject entries summarizing key ideas and information; almanacs with useful facts and statistics on places, people, and events; and yearbooks with events and data for a particular year.

Editorials on File
The New Columbia Encyclopedia
Information Please Almanac
World Almanac and Book of Facts
Canadian Almanac and Directory
Facts on File Yearbook
Statesman's Year-Book
Statistical Abstract of the United States

General Dictionaries. General dictionaries are useful if you want to research the definitions or etymologies of particular words or key terms or to find brief nuggets of information on concepts, famous people, objects, natural phenomena, countries, important historical events, and the like. For information on choosing and using general dictionaries, see Chapter 28.

44b
source

The American Heritage Dictionary of the English Language
The American Heritage Talking Dictionary (CD-ROM)
The Concise Oxford Dictionary of Current English
The Oxford Dictionary of the English Language
The Oxford Dictionary of the English Language on Compact Disk
The Random House Dictionary of the English Language
Webster's New World Dictionary of the American Language
Merriam-Webster's Collegiate Dictionary, 10th edition

Specialized Encyclopedias and Dictionaries. Specialized encyclopedias and dictionaries focus on a particular academic discipline or professional area. You can use them to help narrow your search for information, to gather background details, to distinguish major issues and research trends, and to identify key words useful for locating further resources in specialized indexes (see 44b-2).

Economics and Business
Encyclopedia of Advertising
Encyclopedia of American Economic History
Encyclopedia of Banking and Finance
Encyclopedia of Management
Handbook of Modern Marketing
McGraw-Hill Dictionary of Modern Economics
Occupational Outlook Handbook

History
An Encyclopedia of World History
Cambridge Ancient History
Cambridge History of China
Concise Dictionary of American History
Dictionary of American History
Encyclopedia of Latin-American History
Guide to Historical Literature
New Cambridge Modern History
Reference Encyclopedia of the American Indian
Total History (Bureau of Electronic publishing; CD-ROM)

Literature, Film, Television, Music, and Art
The Cambridge Guide to English Literature
Dance Encyclopedia
Encyclopedia of Pop, Rock, and Soul
Encyclopedia of World Architecture
Encyclopedia of World Art
Encyclopedia of World Literature in the 20th Century
International Encyclopedia of Film
International Television Almanac
McGraw-Hill Encyclopedia of World Drama
The New Grove Dictionary of American Music
The New Grove Dictionary of Music and Musicians
Oxford Companion to American Literature

Religion and Philosophy
Dictionary of the History of Ideas
Eastern Definitions: A Short Encyclopedia of Religions of the Orient
Encyclopedia of Philosophy
Encyclopedia of Religion
Encyclopedia of Bioethics
Interpreter's Dictionary of the Bible

New Standard Jewish Encyclopedia
Oxford Dictionary of the Christian Church
Religion Bookshelf CD (CD-ROM)
Thompson Chain HyperBible (CD-ROM)

Social Sciences

Encyclopedia of American Political History
Dictionary of Anthropology
Encyclopedia of Crime and Justice
Encyclopedia of Educational Research
Encyclopedia of Psychology
Funk and Wagnalls Standard Dictionary of Folklore, Mythology, and Legend
The Guide to American Law
International Encyclopedia of the Social Sciences
The Literature of Geography
Literature of Political Science
New Dictionary of the Social Sciences

Science and Technology

Encyclopedia of the Biological Sciences
Encyclopedia of Chemistry
Encyclopedia of Computer Science and Technology
Encyclopedia of Oceanography
Encyclopaedic Dictionary of Physics
Grzimek's Animal Life Encyclopedia
Health and Medical Horizons
Introduction to the History of Science
McGraw-Hill Encyclopedia of Science and Technology
Van Nostrand's Scientific Encyclopedia
Voyager II (CD-ROM containing 19-million-star Hubble Telescope Guide Star Catalog)

Bibliographies.   Turn to bibliographies for lists of resources in specific subject areas.

Bibliographic Index: A Cumulative Bibliography of Bibliographies
Books in Print
Film Research: A Critical Bibliography with Annotations and Essays
Foreign Affairs Bibliography
International Bibliography of the Social Sciences
MLA International Bibliography of Books and Articles on the Modern Languages and Literatures
Paperbound Books in Print
References Sources in English and American Literature: An Annotated Bibliography
United States History: A Selective Guide to Information Sources (CD-ROM)

Did You Know?

Each year *Books in Print* and its companion volume, *Paperback Books in Print,* list by title and author hundreds of thousands of books currently available from publishers. The 1993–94 edition of *Books in Print,* for example, contains 136,000 new entries added to 370,000 retained from the previous year's edition.

Books in Print (New Providence: Bowker, 1993).

Biographical Sources.   You can use these resources for details about people's lives and times as well as for references to other sources of information about them.

> *Current Biography*
> *International Who's Who*
> *Dictionary of American Biography*
> *Webster's Biographical Dictionary*
> *Who Was Who in America*
> *Who's Who in America*

Maps and Atlases.   An **atlas** is a book containing a number of maps as well as information about the distances between places. A **gazetteer** is a dictionary of place names that tells where cities and geographical features are located.

> *A Geological Map of the Sea Floor* (CD-ROM)
> *National Atlas of the United States*
> *National Geographic Atlas of the World*
> *The New International Atlas*
> *Street Atlas USA* (CD-ROM)
> *Times Atlas of the World: Comprehensive Edition*
> *Webster's New Geographical Dictionary*

44b
source

2 Use printed and electronic indexes, databases, and catalogs

For many research projects, the most interesting, up-to-date, and informative resources appear as research articles in academic journals, reports in professional publications, and magazine or newspaper articles. You can use **printed** and **electronic indexes** to locate articles by different authors in these **periodicals** (recurring publications, including magazines, scholarly journals, and newspapers). Books on specific topics are listed in these indexes as well as in the library's **card catalog,** which in an increasing number of libraries is available as an **online catalog** in electronic form. Electronic resources known as **databases** have been growing in size and variety in recent years; they offer extensive resources, including bibliographies, statistics, graphics, articles, and even books.

While some indexes, catalogs, and databases are arranged primarily by authors and titles, others include subject indexes or systems of cross-referencing based on **key words** or subject names. Knowing how to search by key words or subject is an increasingly important skill for researchers.

Using Printed Indexes. Indexes come in a wide variety, covering both general and specialized sources. They may include listings for articles in magazines, scholarly journals, newspapers, and similar periodical publications. For many people, the most familiar printed index is the *Readers' Guide to Periodical Literature.* It lists articles from approximately two hundred general interest magazines. The *Readers' Guide* appears in monthly paperbound issues that are combined at year-end into a single hardbound volume. You generally need to examine the hardbound volumes for recent years along with the current paperbound issues to make sure your search has been reasonably thorough.

The *Readers' Guide* lists articles by title, author, and subject. To locate a particular topic (rather than, say, the work of a particular writer), you will probably look under a topic heading. (If you do not find an entry, try alternative wording or a related subject.) Once you have located your topic, you will find entries for articles given in abbreviated form; look up the abbreviations at the beginning of the *Guide.* Right under the topic heading, below the direction *See also,* you will find any related topic headings. Pay attention to these cross-references; they often lead to interesting and worthwhile sources.

Here are some of the resources that one student, Lily Germaine, discovered when she looked under *bodybuilding* in a recent volume of the *Readers' Guide.*

44b
source

> **BODYBUILDING**
> *See also*
> Gold's Gym (Firm)
> Metamorphosis [excerpt from Muscle] S. W. Fussell. il pors
> *Men's Health* 6:74-7+ Ap '91
> The world of Atlas [C. Atlas] P. Bushyeager. il pors *Men's Health* 6:56-61 S/O '91
> **Competitions**
> The black bodybuilder who beat Arnold Schwarzenegger's record [Mr. Olympia L. Haney] M. R. Barber. il pors *Ebony* 46:60+ Mr '91
> Movie muscle [former Ms. Olympia champion C. Everson] D. Grogan. il pors *People Weekly* 36:71-2 S 9 '91
> **Photographs and Photography**
> Body building. J. Meehan. il *Petersen's Photographic Magazine* 20:20-3+ O '91
> Pro profiles [M. Neveux] J. Meehan. il *Petersen's Photographic Magazine* 20:58 N '91
> **Psychological aspects**
> Pumped up and strung out [addiction to anabolic steroids by bodybuilders] B. Bower. il *Science News* 140:30-1 Jl 13 '91

Under *exercise* in a later volume of the *Reader's Guide,* she found the following cross-references.

EXERCISE
      See also
  Aerobics
  Arm exercises
  Back exercises
  Bodybuilding
  Boxercise
  Cross training
  Exercising equipment
  Gymnastics
  Health clubs
  Interval training
  Knee exercises
  Leg exercises
  Pilates method
  Postpartum exercises
  Pregnancy exercises
  Rope jumping
  Running
  Sports
  Strength training
  Stress reducing exercises
  Stretching exercises
  T'ai chi ch'üan
  Videotapes—Exercise
  Walking
  Water exercises
  Weight lifting
  Winter sports
  Yoga

Though a general index like the *Readers' Guide* or the *New York Times Index* (see the following list) can suggest some useful sources, your research project will probably require more detailed information and authoritative research. For information about scholarly and technical articles and papers, you can turn to one of the academic and professional indexes in your field.

44b
source

General Indexes
Editorials on File
Reader's Guide to Periodical Literature
For periodicals from the nineteenth century, see *Poole's Index to Periodical Literature*

Newspaper Indexes
New York Times Index
Wall Street Journal Index
Washington Post Index

Specialized Indexes

Humanities
America: History and Life
Art Index

Humanities Index
Music Index
Philosopher's Index

Social sciences, business, and law
Business Periodicals Index
Education Index
ERIC Current Index to Journals in Education (Educational Resources Information Center)
Index to Legal Periodicals

Science and technology
Engineering Index
General Science Index
Index Medicus and *Cumulated Index Medicus*

Lily did not find the heading *bodybuilding* in the *Social Sciences Index*, but she discovered some possibly useful entries under the heading *exercise*.

Exercise
>*See also*
>Aerobic exercises
>Physical education
>Physical fitness
>T'ai chi ch'üan
>Yoga

Body shape satisfaction in female exercisers and nonexercisers. P. S. Imm and J. A. Pruitt. *Women Health* 17 no 4:87-96 '91

A 'water walkers' exercise program for the elderly. C. A. Heyneman and D. E. Premo. *Public Health Rep* 07:213-17 Mr/Ap '92

Accidents and injuries

Incidence of injury during moderate- and high-intensity walking training in the elderly. J. F. Carroll and others. *J Gerontology* 47:M61-6 My '92

Physiological effects

The association of physical activity with mortality among older adults in the Longitudinal study of aging (1984-1988). W. Rakowski and V. Mor. *J Gerontology* 47:M122-9 Jl '92

The cardiac-locomotor coupling phenomenon: the contribution of Coleman. R. L. Kirby. bibl *Percept Mot Skills* 74:498-90 Ap '92

A comparison of the ventilatory responses to exercise of elderly and younger humans. A. K. McConnell and C. T. M. Davies. bibl *J Gerontology* 47:B137-41 Jl '92

Exercise training improves fat distribution patterns in 60- to 70-year-old men and women. W. M. Kohrt and others. *J Gerontology* 47:M99-105 Jl '92

Psychological aspects

Manifest reasons for jogging and for not jogging. W. F. Vitulli and A. N. DePace, III. *Percept Mot Skills* 75:111-14 Ag '92

Relation of anxiety about social physique to location of participation in physical activity. K. S. Spink. *Percept Mot Skills* 74:1075-8 Je '92 pt2

44b
source

Writer's Tip

Most libraries have reading rooms or current periodical collections where the most recent issues of periodicals are shelved. For earlier issues, you need to consult the library's catalog or list of periodicals for the call numbers of bound copies kept on shelves or for **microfilm** and **microfiche** copies. To save space, many libraries have started buying back issues of newspapers, magazines, and journals on microform, so make sure you check your library's **microform collection** before you decide that a particular issue of a periodical is not available. If your library does not subscribe to a periodical you want or if a particular issue is missing, you may be able to get a copy of an article through an interlibrary loan service.

Using Electronic Indexes. Most libraries now have computerized electronic indexes that allow you to search rapidly and widely for resources, periodicals, printed books, and documents available in microform. By using the cross-referencing capabilities of these indexes, you can quickly locate resources within your subject area as well as those in related subject areas. When you type a writer's name, a title, or a subject, you get a list of entries and suggested cross-references. Most indexes also allow you to browse by typing in one or more key words related to your topic, and some provide abstracts or full texts of selected items.

Using electronic indexes is relatively easy, as Lily Germaine discovered when she typed the key word *bodybuilding* into the InfoTrac Academic Index in her library's computer.

44b
source

Musclebound: in fashion.

The New Yorker, Jan 11, 1993 v68 n47 p30(8).

Author: Holly Brubach

Abstract: Body building for men and women has become fashionable and exercise is part of everyday life in New York, NY. Topics discussed include combination gym and night clubs, fashions for muscular bodies and the sex appeal of muscular women.

Subjects: Physical fitness centers – Public opinion
Bodybuilding – Public opinion
Fashion – Social aspects
Physical fitness – Social aspects
New York, New York – Popular culture

Locations: New York, New York

AN: 13550961

One of the advantages of such electronic indexes is that they not only provide an article's title, its author's name, and its place of publication—they also frequently include a brief summary of its content (as in the preceding example) so that you can decide whether you need to consult the entire article as part of your research.

Writer's Tip

Always search for information with a pen and paper at hand, even if you are using electronic indexes or databases. Write everything down for your records unless the index allows you to print out copies of all the references you have located.

If you use an electronic index that allows full-text retrieval, you can type in a command and get the entire article or document on your screen. You can then print a paper copy or save the article on a computer disk.

The following electronic indexes are often useful for researchers.

Info Trac	Index of nearly two thousand periodicals, mostly general audience and trade magazines. (This is a good place to start, but it covers only the last several years and is not specialized enough for extensive research.)
Academic Index	Index of journals and magazines, some full-text, since 1985
Agricola	Database providing information on agricultural publications
America: History and Life	Index to books and articles on U.S. events, issues, and history
Anthropological Literature	Index to anthropology resources since 1984
Applied Science and Technology Index	Index to many fields in the applied sciences since 1983
ArticleFirst	Index to over 12,000 journals and magazines since 1990
Arts and Humanities Citation Index	Index to publications in the arts and humanities since 1980
Art Index	Index to topics in art and aesthetics since 1984

44b
source

Avery Index to Architectural Periodicals	Index to periodicals covering architecture since 1977
Biological and Agricultural Index	Index to publications on biology, agriculture, and related topics since 1983
BIZZ (Business Index)	Index to business periodicals, some full-text, since 1982
CIRR (Corporate and Industry Research Reports)	Index to company and industry reports since 1979
Compendex	Index to engineering resources since 1992
Current Contents	Index to contents and abstracts of current scholarly journals
EconLit	Index to journals and books in business and economics
ERIC (Educational Resources Information Center)	Index to journals in education and database listing unpublished papers since 1966
Geobase	Index to resources in geology, geography, and ecology since 1980
Government Documents Catalog Service (GDCS)/GPO Index	Index to U.S. government documents since 1976
Government Periodicals Index	Index to 175 federal government journals since 1993
Hispanic American Periodicals Index	Guide to periodicals since 1970
History of Science and Technology	Index to resources on science history since 1976, adding technology in 1987
IIN (Inside Information)	Indexes contents information for 10,000 current journals
Index to United Nations Documents and Publications	Index to UN publications since 1990
INSPEC	Index on physics, electronics, and computing since 1987
Legi-Slate	Index of federal legislation and regulations, including congressional votes

44b
source

Medline	Index to health sciences journals since 1966
MLA International Bibliography	Index to articles and books on language and literature since 1963
NTIS (National Technical Information System)	Index to technical documents from U.S. Departments of Defense and Energy, NASA, and other federal agencies
OCLC/World Catalog	Index to books and magazines in U.S. libraries, including 30 million records dating from the eleventh century
PAIS (Public Affairs Information Services) Decade	Index to statistical reports and government documents on general issues, current ten years
PsycLIT	Index to publications in psychology and related fields since 1974
Social Sciences Index	Index to wide range of social sciences since 1983
Sociofile	Index to works in sociology and related fields

Using Abstracts. Brief summaries of articles, called **abstracts,** can give you an initial overview of research and can help you decide whether to examine a particular source in detail. Many academic and professional fields produce printed collections of abstracts; electronic databases often provide abstracts as well.

44b
source

Collections of Abstracts
Abstracts of English Studies
America: History and Life
Biological Abstracts
Chemical Abstracts
Dissertation Abstracts International
Historical Abstracts
Language and Language Behavior Abstracts
Microcomputer Abstracts
Newspaper Abstracts
Psychological Abstracts (PsycINFO)
Sociological Abstracts (SocioAbs)

Using Electronic Databases. Databases are files of information stored in electronic form—on computer disks, on CD-ROMs, or on mainframe com-

---

Writer's Tip

Today, the word *database* usually implies the word *electronic*. However, many databases are compilations of information published in print form. When you search for databases in your library's catalog, be careful to note the medium of the database—book or periodical, computer disk, CD-ROM, microfilm or microfiche, or online source. To find electronic databases in your subject area, you might consult one of the updated catalogs of electronic databases, such as the *Gale Directory of Databases,* which is published semiannually, or the *Federal Data Base Finder: A Directory of Free and Fee-Based Data Bases and Files Available from the Federal Government.* In addition to consulting any self-help materials published by your library, you may wish to look for useful general guides to database searching, such as Robert Berkman's *Find It Online!*

---

puter systems accessible from a computer terminal in a library or from a home computer linked by a telephone modem. Databases can supply information on publications, events, and speeches and can include abstracts, information resources, or statistics. Depending on the capabilities of the systems that store and retrieve the databases, they can also be presented in multimedia with graphics and sound.

Electronic databases are especially powerful tools for research because, unlike printed materials, they can be updated constantly. Databases provide both specialized and general information. TIGER/Line, for example, is a database that provides a coast-to-coast digital map useful to people in many fields, while the International Coal Statistics database offers specialized information relevant to the coal industry.

As you conduct your research, be aware that some databases may be accessible over electronic mail pathways, either nationally or worldwide, while other databases are stored in the computer system you access at your school or another institution. You may need to learn a specific set of commands in order to access local databases. However, most systems that retrieve information from databases include onscreen instructions to guide you through their sometimes complicated procedures.

Selected Electronic Databases

Compact Disclosure   Statistics database providing financial information on public companies

Company Profiles   Database giving profiles and other information on 140,000 private and public companies

Computer Select	Database providing bibliographic information, abstracts, and extensive information on computers and the computer industry
Database of African-American Poetry	Database providing information on African-American poetry from 1760 to 1900
EPA's Pesticide Fact Sheet	Database giving facts, policies, and other information from the Environmental Protection Agency on pesticides
U.S. Census Online	Database giving all U.S. Census statistics

Strategy

Determining the correct key word, concept, or topic name is essential for identifying references to your subject in indexes, databases, catalogs, and similar sources. Make a list of different words or concepts that could be used to identify your subject in whole or in part. Don't stop with the most obvious or the one you have become accustomed to using when you think about the topic. Think of synonyms or alternative terms. Think about the ways other people speak or write about the subject. Skim something you have read on the topic in order to discover possible terms.

Then use your list as a set of possible key words to look up in a reference book or to type in when an electronic index or database asks you to identify the subject you wish to search.

Indexes and databases may provide cross-references, identifying them with phrases like *see also* or *related topics*. Add them to your list.

44b
source

Using the Library Catalog. After searching for sources in general reference texts, specialized texts, and print or electronic indexes, you should have a list of places to look for information and ideas on your topic. Next you will need to discover which of these promising resources your library has on hand or can obtain through an interlibrary loan (see 44b-3). To identify your library's resources, go to the library's catalog, which will also help you identify books and other resources not mentioned in the reference works you consulted.

Your library's catalog is in either printed form (a **card catalog**) or electronic form (an **online catalog**). Card catalogs and online catalogs are similarly organized. You can find a work by searching under the author's name, under the title of the work, under the title of a periodical or series containing the work, or under the subject area. Suppose, for example, you were preparing a paper on illusions, escapes, and other professional magic tricks. In your reading, you would undoubtedly come across the name of

Harry Houdini, perhaps the most famous illusionist and escape artist of all time and the inventor of many acts still performed by modern magicians. You would also probably come across a recently published book on Houdini, *The Life and Many Deaths of Harry Houdini.* You could locate this book in several ways in an online catalog—by subject, title, or author. If you knew neither the title nor the author of the book, the best strategy would be to search by subject. The general key word *magic* would bring up hundreds of entries—too many for you to scan quickly. A better choice would be the more specific key word *Houdini.* Below is a typical online list of books found under that key word.

Search Request: S=HOUDINI   U-CAT--University Library
Search Results: 12 Entries Found   Subject Index

HOUDINI HARRY 1874-1926
1 GREAT HOUDINI MAGICIAN EXTRAORDINARY<1950> (UL)
2 HOUDINI A MIND IN CHAINS A PSYCHOANALYTIC PO <1976> (UL)
3 HOUDINI A PICTORIAL LIFE <1976> (UL)
4 HOUDINI AND CONAN DOYLE THE STORY OF A STRAN <1932> (UL)
5 HOUDINI HIS LIFE AND ART <1976> (UL)
6 HOUDINI HIS LIFE STORY <1928> (UL)
7 HOUDINI THE MAN WHO WALKED THROUGH WALLS <1959> (UL)
8 HOUDINI THE UNTOLD STORY <1969> (UL)
9 HOUDINIS SPIRIT EXPOSES FROM HOUDINIS OWN MA <1928> (UL)
10 LIFE AND MANY DEATHS OF HARRY HOUDINI <1994> (UL)
11 SIXTY YEARS OF PSYCHICAL RESEARCH HOUDIN AN <1950> (UL)
   HOUDINI HARRY 1874-1926--JUVENILE LITERATURE
12 ESCAPE KING THE STORY OF HARRY HOUDINI <1975> (UL)

Names and dates of books {

STart over   Type number to display record   <F8> FORward page
HELp
OTHer options

44b
source

Choosing the title of the book by entering its corresponding number (10) in the list, you could then bring up the following "brief" form of catalog entry on the computer screen.

Search Request: S=HOUDINI   U-CAT--University Library
BOOK-Record 10 of 12 Entries Found   Brief View

Author's name Author: Brandon, Ruth.

Title of book Title: The life and many deaths of Harry Houdini/Ruth Brandon.

Edition Edition: 1st ed.

Publisher and date Published: New York: Random House, 1993<i.e. c1994>

Library branch LOCATION: CALL NUMBER: STATUS:
        MAIN LIB.   GV1545 .H8 B73 1994   Not checked out   *Availability*
           Call number to locate in stacks ↑

Asking the computer to provide a "long view," or more detailed entry, yields additional information about the book.

Search Request: S=HOUDINI   U-CAT--University Library
BOOK-Record 10 of 12 Entries Found   Long View

Author: Brandon, Ruth.

Title: The life and many deaths of Harry Houdini/Ruth Brandon.

Edition: 1st ed.

Published: New York: Random House, 1993<i.e. c1994>

Description: x, 355 p.:ill.;24 cm.   *Number of pages, whether illustrated, size*

Subjects, Library of Congress (Use s =):   *Library of Congress headings*
     Houdini, Harry, 1874–1926.
     Magicians--United States--Biography.

Notes: Copyright date from bookjacket.
         Includes bibliographical references and index.   *Additional notes on contents*

ISBN: 0679424377   *Book number (useful for locating or purchasing)*

LOCATION: CALL NUMBER: STATUS:
MAIN LIB.   GV1545 .H8 B73 1994   Not checked out

Notice that this more detailed entry provides the Library of Congress headings, or key words, under which this entry is cataloged. If you were to use the subheading *magicians—United States—biography,* you would find additional books about magicians, including the useful *Encyclopedia of Magic and Magicians,* which could then offer you more information about your subject beyond the realm of Houdini. Moving between general and specific entries in this way can be a powerful way to search for materials about your guiding question.

Writer's Tip

Once you've found the location of a reference in the card catalog or the online catalog, be sure to write the call numbers next to the title on your own list. If you forget to do this, you'll have to return to the catalog later to find the number again. If you are using an online catalog connected to a local printer, you can print out the entire entry, which will save you time and give you accurate bibliographic information directly from the source.

3 Use government documents and other resources

Most libraries have a wide variety of other resources that you can inquire about and use. Congressional reports, documents issued by federal agencies, and pamphlets or regulations issued by state and local governments are just a few of the resources generally known as **government documents.** These rich sources of information, both general and technical, are sometimes housed in separate collections in a library and are increasingly available electronically. They may also have their own catalog, such as the *Monthly Catalog of U.S. Government Publications,* to aid your search.

Library **special collections** may include rare books, manuscripts, and documents, including materials of local historical interest. A **vertical file** contains clippings, pamphlets, and other useful materials. **Audiovisual collections** contain videotapes, films, audio recordings, and other similar resources. A **microform collection** generally contains books, periodicals, newspapers, and unpublished documents in a variety of forms, especially microfilm and microfiche. Ask a reference librarian about any such collections and data files, about catalogs listing their contents, and about any rules governing the use of materials.

If the library you are using does not have sources that seem important for your work, check as soon as possible with the library's reference or circulation services for loan arrangements. Almost all libraries can arrange for **interlibrary loans** within a few days. Many have overnight arrangements with local libraries and college or university reference libraries. Some library online catalogs even list the holdings of regional libraries and allow you to arrange for a loan at the catalog terminal.

4 Use other electronic resources

44b
source

In addition to electronic databases, indexes, abstracts, and catalogs, other rapidly developing electronic resources may be useful to your research. Most of these can be accessed from a home computer using a telephone and a modem. As you conduct your research, it's a good idea to explore such online resources; you may find information that is not available in other forms. Because the variety of electronic resources is growing rapidly, be sure to ask a reference librarian what's available.

Using E-mail. Electronic mail (**e-mail**) allows you to send and receive messages, information, and other text along electronic pathways connected via computer systems. To use e-mail, you usually need an account so that you can gain access to the host system through which the information is channeled. To learn more about setting up an account, you should contact the appropriate office at your college or university.

Once you have set up an account, you can begin sending and receiving messages. You can contact someone directly by sending a message to his or her e-mail address, or you can contact many people using chat lines, congresses, conferences, and other information exchanges.

> **Writer's Tip**
>
> Because the process of research often means working alone in a library—a context where silence is demanded—it can be difficult to benefit from social and academic exchange as you put together a paper. Now that electronic resources are readily available, your projects can encompass a wider social dimension. You can link up with your classmates via e-mail; you can chat online with experts and other people interested in your topic; and you can even send drafts of your papers or published materials to other people via computer for their feedback and reactions. These new resources can turn a research paper into an exciting experience filled with dialogue and discussion.

Using Mail Lists, E-journals, and E-newsletters. Mail lists are lists of people and organizations who share a common interest or context. When you send a message to a mail list, everyone on the list will receive that message. Mail lists are used often in academic work because they allow the exchange of information quickly and efficiently.

You can enhance your own research by using established mail lists to contact experts or other people who share an interest in your topic. Many colleges and universities have clubs and academic organizations whose members are on a mail list. You can use the list to ask questions about your topic and gather information and advice quickly and efficiently. Before e-mail, your alternative would have been to send letters or to contact each person in the organization individually.

Academic discussion lists and chat lines are designed for interactive exchange of information and opinions. Thousands of such networks have been established around the world, linking people together in academic and social discussions which were impossible before the advent of computer technology. Searching in your online catalog under key words like *electronic conferences* will often lead you to catalogs of such lists.

A number of national organizations have established **e-journals** that are distributed electronically. When you sign up for the e-journal, articles or information will be sent to your e-mail address. Some journals require membership in a corresponding organization or carry a fee; others are free. **E-newsletters** are like e-journals but often contain information about upcoming events such as conferences and may be somewhat less formal.

Using the World Wide Web. Online research became much easier when browsers such as *Netscape* were developed. Now even word processing programs incorporate Web access features. Using a browser, you can search the World Wide Web for sites that list information on your topic—for example, U.S. history. Your search will obtain URL (universal resource locator)

44b
source

addresses such as http://lcweb2.loc.gov/cwphome.html, which connects you to a Library of Congress resource with Civil War photographs, bibliographies, information about Civil War photographer Mathew Brady, and other material you can obtain online. A Web search can link you to computer sites around the world.

Exploring Fee-Based Online Services. Using a home computer and a modem, you can connect with various online services, such as America Online or CompuServe, that may offer you useful sources of information for a paper or project. Typically, these commercial systems provide access to a range of services—chat lines, *Time* magazine, online encyclopedias that are constantly updated, news, weather reports, travel information and reservation services, stock quotes, sports information and statistics, personal finance services, and information on entertainment, goods and services, or computing. Be aware that in addition to an access fee, you may need to pay for long-distance telephone charges when you use a commercial online service.

Exercise 2

A. To familiarize yourself with the resources of your library, take tours or library introduction sessions offered by the staff or locate the following resources on your own (using any maps the library provides): general and specialized encyclopedias, bibliographies, print indexes, electronic indexes and databases, the library catalog, government documents, and the periodical collection.

B. Each person in a work group should look up entries for a particular topic in one or more of the kinds of resources listed in Exercise 2A, then report back to the group. You may all research a topic someone in the group is working on, or each of you may look up the topic you are researching for a paper of your own.

44C   Using indexes and catalogs: Research in progress

When Candace Shilting began searching for sources to answer her guiding question ("Should English be the official language of the United States?"), she started with InfoTrac, an electronic index. The only subject she could think of was quite general: *English language*. After typing these key words into the computer, she was dismayed to learn that *English language* had nearly 600 entries. But she also noticed that InfoTrac included a list of subheadings. Two seemed promising: *English language in the United States* and *Education, bilingual.* The first heading gave her a list of 12 articles, several with titles that seemed to address her guiding question. One of the titles included the word *bilingualism,* so she typed this into the index as a subheading and got 36 more entries, including 12 that seemed likely to be useful.

1 Turn to a specialized index

After doing some preliminary reading in the sources she had identified, Shilting continued her search with a more specialized index, the *MLA International Bibliography,* an electronic index published by the Modern Language Association. Using the heading *bilingualism* she got 1,558 entries, and using *English language* she got 24,785. She then decided to combine her key words into *bilingualism and United States* and received a much more manageable 174 entries. By this time, however, Shilting was aware that the phrases *official language, English only,* and *English language amendment* were central to her research topic, so she amended her string of key words to read *English and (official language),* a strategy that yielded 38 citations, including the title of a book directly linked to her research topic: *The English-Only Question: An Official Language for Americans?*

2 Use the library catalogs

Next Shilting went to her library's online catalog to see if she could locate a copy of this book. She typed the book's title into her library's online catalog, and the following entry appeared on the screen.

```
Call Number -- P119.32 U6 B37 1990
Author -------- Baron, Dennis E.
Title -------- The English-only question: an official language for....
Item Number -- 1001101758
Copy Number -- 1              Historical Data....
Units -------- 2              Last Checked in on 10FEB
Location ------ Newman        Entry date into system: 22OCT90
Loan Period --- 0090          Circulation count to date: 9
Status: CHECKED OUT ON 10FEB 16:38 DUE: 10MAR
```

44c
source

From this entry, Shilting learned that one of the university's two copies of the book was available at the library's Newman branch.

3 Check the card catalog

The online system at Shilting's library also gave her several related titles when she typed *English only controversy.* All these titles were recent, however, because in her school's library system, older works are listed in the card catalog. After reviewing the subject headings she had consulted in her original database search, Shilting tried several terms as subject headings to search in the card catalog. Looking under *bilingualism,* she discovered a number of cards, including the following.

Bilingual education in a binational school.

LC   Mackey, William Francis
3719   Bilingual education in a binational school; a study
M32   of equal language maintenance through free alternation.
       Foreword by Joshua A. Fishman. Rowley, Mass., New-
       bury House [1972]

       xviii, 183 p. illus. 23 cm. (Studies in bilingual education)
       Bibliography: p. [173]-176.

              1. Education, Bilingual. I. Title

       LC 3719.M32   371.97   72-86255
       ISBN 0-912066-17-2   MARC
       Library of Congress

---

4 Search for articles

Having located some good books on the subject of English language legislation, Shilting next decided to try a computer search for journal articles on the topic. Using a terminal in the computer lab, she connected with the library computer services. Opening the menu for *indexes,* she found 5 electronic index categories. The first, *multidisciplinary databases,* offered her the broadest range; it listed 7 specific indexes. Shilting chose Academic Index, which indexes journals and magazines published since 1985, some in full text. Using the key words *English only,* she obtained a list of 62 documents. The first screen of the list appears below.

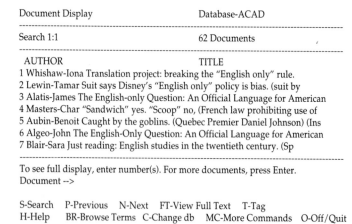

```
Document Display                    Database-ACAD
------------------------------------------------------------------
Search 1:1                          62 Documents
------------------------------------------------------------------
   AUTHOR                          TITLE
1 Whishaw-Iona Translation project: breaking the "English only" rule.
2 Lewin-Tamar Suit says Disney's "English only" policy is bias. (suit by
3 Alatis-James The English-only Question: An Official Language for American
4 Masters-Char "Sandwich" yes. "Scoop" no, (French law prohibiting use of
5 Aubin-Benoit Caught by the goblins. (Quebec Premier Daniel Johnson) (Ins
6 Algeo-John The English-Only Question: An Official Language for American
7 Blair-Sara Just reading: English studies in the twentieth century. (Sp
------------------------------------------------------------------
To see full display, enter number(s). For more documents, press Enter.
Document -->

S-Search   P-Previous   N-Next   FT-View Full Text   T-Tag
H-Help     BR-Browse Terms   C-Change db   MC-More Commands   O-Off/Quit
```

So many of the articles seemed potentially useful that Shilting decided to spend some time browsing through the list. But the second item especially caught her eye, so she opened it first.

```
Document Display          Screen 1 of 2        Database-ACAD
----------------------------------------------------------------------
Search 1:1                              62 Documents
----------------------------------------------------------------------
  Document:2
Accession No.: 15802341. 9411.
    Database: NOOZ.
    Author: Lewin-Tamar.
    Source: The-New-York-Times. volume 144, Oct 13, 1994, Thu edition,
        pA14(N) pA23(L), col 4. (941013).
  Coden/ISSN:ISSN:0362-4331.
    Year: 1994.
    Title: Suit says Disney's "English only" policy is bias. (suit by
        Teamsters union against Walt Disney World Dolphin Hotel, Orlando,
        Florida) (National Pages).
  SIC Code: 7011 Hotels and motels.
Descriptors: International-Brotherhood-of-Teamsters: Cases.
  ----------------------------------------------------------------------
To skip to a screen, enter a screen number, or press Enter for next screen.
Screen -->
S-Search    RD-Resume Display    FT-View Full Text    K-Keyword Paragraph
H-Help    BR-Browse Terms    C-Change db    MC-More Commands    O-Off
```

Because the full text of the article wasn't available electronically, Shilting wrote down the reference information so she could locate it later in the newspaper archives of the library. Her topic was yielding so much information that she could begin considering a narrower focus, perhaps on lawsuits resulting from English-only legislation.

Scanning the other index options, she soon discovered Newspaper Abstracts, an electronic index abstracting the contents of 25 national newspapers, including the *New York Times*. To see whether it was worth her time to read the article on the Disney World lawsuit, she accessed this index and soon located the abstract of the article.

44c
source

```
--------------------------------Full Record Display----------------------------------
DATABASE: NewsAbs           LIMITED TO:
SEARCH: su:english only

Record 16 of 213 --------------------------------------------------------------------
NEWSABS NO: 03196855
AUTHOR: Lewin, Tamar
TITLE: Suit accuses hotel at Disney World of "English only" policies
SOURCE: New York Times
SEC,PG:COL: A, 23:1
DATE: Oct 13, 1994
    ABSTRACT: The teamsters union filed civil-rights charges against a Walt Disney
        World Hotel on Oct 12, 1994, contending that its "English only" policies
        discriminated against the hotel's Haitian and Hispanic housekeeping and
        laundry workers. The class-action complaint said the Dolphin Hotel
        recruited Haitian and Hispanic workers who speak no English for the jobs
```

that require little customer contact, but issued its job manual, safety warnings and work orders only in English. The complaint also charges that workers were harassed for speaking their native language.
ARTICLE TYPE: News
ARTICLE LENG: Medium (6-18 col inches)
DESCRIPTORS: Employment discrimination; Foreign labor; Class action lawsuits; English language
COMPANIES: Walt Disney World; Dolphin Hotel; Teamsters Union
AVAILABILITY: UMIACH; 60001.01
JOURNAL CODE: NY
JOURNAL ISSN: 0362-4331

ACTIONS: Help Search And Limit Print Forward Back BYE Reset

5 Move online

After having some trouble locating additional articles on lawsuits resulting from English-only legislation, Shilting decided that she wanted to find out what other people knew about this angle of her topic. Using her library's online resources, she located a list of several hundred academic groups that carry on discussions electronically. Of the several dozen such online discussion groups listed under the heading *languages and linguistics,* one, Multi-L, claimed to "provide for the exchange of information, news, and opinions about all aspects of minority language education" and was sponsored by the International Association of Applied Linguistics. At the end of the entry was the name of the list server that would give her access to this group's discussions.

Shilting wrote a brief message explaining who she was and asking for help.

> Friends: I am an undergraduate writing a paper on the legal implications of the English-only movement. I am interested in lawsuits that have resulted from English-only legislation in the states where it has been passed. Do you know of any books or articles that discuss such suits? Your quick response would help me greatly on my project. Thanks in advance for your help!

44d
source

Within a day of sending this question to the list server for Multi-L, she had received five messages from people around the United States, each with useful suggestions about what to read. One person sent her a long note about an anti–English-only group in California that publishes a newsletter. Further responses provided her with reading suggestions, opinions, and news about English-language legislation. After a week of electronic searches and library research, Candace had gathered enough information on her narrowed guiding question to begin her paper.

44d Maintaining a working bibliography

As you consult online and print indexes, specialized bibliographies and encyclopedias, library catalogs, and similar reference materials, keep track of the possible resources you discover. One good way to do this is to construct a **working bibliography** listing articles, books, documents, films, and other resources likely to provide useful ideas and information on your topic. If you construct your working bibliography in a flexible form, you can add further items as you examine sources listed in your bibliography. Likewise, you can eliminate items if your research leads you to shift the focus of your topic or if some sources are not likely to be relevant.

1 Decide what to include in a working bibliography

In looking up your topic in indexes, bibliographies, catalogs, and other resources, you will probably discover more books, articles, and other materials than you can possibly consult or use for your writing. Consequently, you need to decide what to put in your working bibliography and what to leave out.

Include

- **More sources than you expect to use for your final paper.** Some will be unavailable at your library; others may be less useful than you anticipate.
- **Items whose titles or lengths suggest they will be relevant.** A descriptive title can sometimes be a good guide, and a long article may contain more useful information than a short one.
- **Sources that are recent enough to provide up-to-date information.** Older sources may be useful, too, but be selective.
- **A variety of sources.** Choose some that are broad surveys and others that focus on specific aspects of your topic.

Exclude

- **Resources that may be difficult to obtain.** Check your library's periodical directory and other listings to eliminate items not readily available. If a hard-to-get source is particularly valuable, arrange to obtain it through interlibrary loan.

44d source

- **Sources whose relationship to your topic is questionable.** Some may be only loosely related to your topic; others may clearly be too general or too specific and technical.

Writer's Tip

Many bibliographies include annotations that summarize the content of a book or article. These annotations can help you decide whether to include an item in a working bibliography. Computerized indexes may also provide brief summaries (called abstracts) of selected items.

2 Make complete and accurate entries

Entries in a working bibliography should contain the following information to locate the source. If you make sure the bibliographical information for the entries is complete and accurate, you can also use your working bibliography to compile the list of works consulted for your final paper or report (see 46e).

Books
Call number and library collection or location
Author(s), editor(s), translator(s)
Title and subtitle
City of publication, name of publisher, and date of publication

Articles
Author(s)
Title and subtitle of article
Periodical name
Volume and issue number (if the periodical uses them)
Date
Page number(s)

Electronic Information
Name of source
Date of receipt of information
Name of sender, if the information is sent by e-mail
Availability information such as vendor, service, and access route
Original publication information for materials also in print form

(See the sample bibliography entries that follow. For detailed information on bibliographic form, see Chapters 46 through 49.)

3 Choose a format to record entries

You can create a working bibliography in several different formats: on 3″×5″ cards, in a notebook or on sheets of paper, or in a computerized card file or database. Each format has advantages.

3″×5″ Cards. If you write out each bibliography entry on a 3″×5″ card, you can easily arrange the cards in alphabetical order for eventual use in your list of references. You can also arrange them in categories appropriate for your topic or research plan. Adding, eliminating, or rearranging items is relatively simple with cards.

When Lily Germaine was doing research on bodybuilding and weight training, she created the following card.

Laurence Shames
"Betrayed by My Body"
Men's Health
vol. 7
January/February 1992
pp. 24-5

Notebook or Computer Printouts. Keeping a working bibliography in a notebook is convenient, especially if the notebook also has pockets for the printouts that many electronic indexes produce for you (see 44b-2). Rearranging, adding, eliminating, and alphabetizing items is much less convenient in a notebook, of course, though you can organize them with marginal comments or highlighter.

Here are several notebook entries for a working bibliography that Lisa Yap assembled on the different ways that men and women argue.

Douglas W. Maynard
"How Children Start Arguments"
Language in Society 14 (1985): 1-29

Ann R. Eisenberg and Catherine Garvey
"Children's Use of Verbal Strategies in Resolving Conflicts"
Discourse Processes 4 (1981): 149-70

Deborah Tannen
You Just Don't Understand: Men and Women in Conversation
New York: Morrow, 1990

44d
source

Electronic Card Files and Databases. Electronic card file systems and database programs have most of the advantages of 3″ × 5″ cards and often resemble onscreen collections of cards. The electronic systems have some other advantages as well. By specifying subtopics or categories on each card, you can enable a computer to sort and reorganize entries and to retrieve material on a particular subtopic. You can also easily transfer the contents of the entries to a word processing program when you wish to create a list of works cited or a list of works consulted for your paper. Lisa Yap used a notebook at the library to list items for her working bibliography, then transferred the entries to her computer's card file when she was back in her dorm room. Here is one of the records she created.

P95.45
C65
1990

Allen D. Grimshaw, editor

Conflict Talk: Sociolinguistic Investigations of Arguments in Conversations

Cambridge: Cambridge UP, 1990

Exercise 3

A. Using one of the formats described in 44d-3, prepare a working bibliography for a research paper you are writing. Choose a format appropriate for your habits as a reader, writer, and researcher.

B. Share your working bibliography with a group of fellow writers. Tell the group members what resources you have consulted, and ask whether they can suggest any other directions for your research.

44e Reading sources critically and taking notes

After creating a working bibliography and locating some promising sources, you are ready to start the process of reading and note-taking.

> ### Writer's Tip
>
> Learn to be selective. Read through your working bibliography and mark those works that seem accessible, most relevant to your topic, or most likely to answer your guiding questions. Start with just a few; after you locate and read (or skim) them, you will understand your topic more fully and can decide which other sources on your list are most worth examining.

Your reading and note-taking should focus on ideas, information, and quotations that help you develop your own insights, that help you explain or argue, and that help you represent a point of view, either your own or someone else's. If you want to write a strong research paper, you need to read your sources critically, summarizing ideas and information and recording details and quotations with an eye to using the material in your paper, either directly or as a springboard for your own thinking.

Reading critically involves *understanding* what you've collected, *synthesizing* the ideas of two or more sources, *interpreting* texts, and *evaluating* writers' styles and rhetorical stances. Note-taking means either directly recording the words and details from a text (*quoting*) or putting them into your own language (*paraphrasing*).

To read critically and take effective notes, you need to view the parts of your sources—ideas, evidence, arguments, examples, vocabulary, metaphors—in terms of the overall discussion to which they contribute. Thus, prereading for the general gist of an article or book chapter and then rereading for the particulars is an essential research strategy (see Chapter 3 for a discussion of these approaches).

1 Take notes

Many writers prefer to take notes on index cards, generally either 4″×6″ or 5″×7″ cards. This method has some advantages. Cards are easily portable and convenient for brief note-taking. If you write the topic of each card clearly at the top and restrict each card to one kind of note-taking (quotation, summary of facts and ideas, paraphrase), you can arrange and rearrange cards in related groups as you plan a paper and then draw on them easily in sequence as you write. Make sure that you indicate the source on each card and write down the page number(s) to which your notes refer. Simeon Parks created the following note card for a paper on two-career families.

> *Effective responses to problems*
>
> Apostal and Helland, pp. 122–3
>
>   The partners in a two-career family are generally committed to balancing work and family, yet they often need to learn ways to negotiate work and domestic roles in order to avoid stress. Many come from traditional families and lack models for negotiation. As a result, two-career families frequently have trouble balancing responsibilities.

**44e
source**

If you use a research journal (usually a notebook) instead of cards, you will have space not only to record information but also to reflect on new knowledge and assemble the parts of your paper (see Chapter 2 for advice on using a journal).

Make sure each entry indicates the source and page numbers to which the notes refer. Identify all quoted material clearly by using quotation marks and recording the source page(s). Use an entry's heading or make marginal comments to indicate the aspect of your topic covered in the notes. These annotations will help you organize your notes later for use as you write. Here's what Simeon Parks might record in a research journal.

Effective responses to problems
Apostal and Helland

> "Dual career partners may hold fast to an ideology of equality, but may often lack the skills or knowledge to negotiate role behaviors in such a way that would maintain a balance between home and career responsibilities." (p. 123)

Really good statement of the problem—use this to sum up my discussion of the stresses facing two-career families.

I wonder if readers would be interested in the solutions to the problem? This passage seems to suggest that other researchers have written about possible solutions. Check the rest of the article, especially the references.

If your research journal is a notebook with pockets or a folder, you can also use it to store photocopies of sources that you make in order to record detailed information or passages you wish to quote. Write the source and topic at the top of the photocopy (if the source title is printed on the page, circle it). Here's how Simeon Parks might annotate a photocopy.

Effective responses to problems

"Commitment to and Role Changes in Dual Career Families."
Journal of Career Development 20 (Winter 1993): 121-9.

Robert A. Apostal and Carol Helland   **123**

these families is needed. The literature also indicates that a genera-ion of Americans has embraced the ideology of the dual career family without the benefit of role models and normative guidelines to dictate role behaviors. Dual career partners may hold fast to an ideology of equality, but may often lack the skills or knowledge to negotiate role behaviors in such a way that would maintain a balance between home and career responsibilities. Studies are needed to examine role change in dual career families to identify just what type of roles must be most frequently negotiated.

   Thus, the present study was designed to assess level of commit-ment, identify types and numbers of role changes, and examine the relationship between commitment and role change in a sample of partners from dual career families. In this study a role change oc-curred when the partners increased or decreased a role activity during the marriage.

44e
source

Writer's Tip

If you're working with original sources (actual books and journals, not photocopies), be extremely careful when you write quotations in your notebook. You should be *absolutely certain* that you've copied them word for word and that you've recorded the exact page number(s) where each quotation appears. Remember that after you've closed the book or journal and left the library, if there was something you didn't write down, you must find it again in your source—and you can end up wasting time. If you're using photocopies of original sources that you can take away with you, you can circle quotations for use later in your paper. Keep a log in your notebook of what material you want to use; otherwise you'll be searching through pages of material trying to find "lost" quotations and references.

2 Prepare to read critically

To use sources successfully, think critically about them before you begin reading. Then concentrate on their meaning and their relationship to your guiding questions as you read. Write down questions and comments both before and during your reading.

Strategy

After reading the title and first paragraph of a source, jot down any questions or statements that come to mind. Reflect on what the title and opening tell you about the content of the work, its audience, and the relationship of the writer to that audience. Indicate what you think you will learn from the work and what role you think the information in the source might play in your paper.

44e
source

Exercise 4

A. Choose an article you think may be useful for a research paper you are working on. Read the opening paragraph, and write down any questions and comments that come to mind. In addition, speculate on the ways the article might be useful for your paper.

B. Working with a partner, swap your articles and responses from Exercise 4A, and let your partner know how similar or different your responses are to the opening of his or her article.

44f Paraphrasing and summarizing: Research in progress

From her list of possible sources on the reasons for weight training's popularity, Lily Germaine chose two that seemed to promise different perspectives and information. She thought that "Hulk Triumphant," from *Esquire,* would view bodybuilding favorably and that "Muscleheads: Bodybuilding's Bottom Line," from *The New Republic,* would be critical of it.

1 Record your questions and comments

After reading the opening paragraph of "Hulk Triumphant," Lily wrote the following preliminary questions and comments in her research journal.

> *Photo—called a "portrait"—of an old Charles Atlas sitting at home; photo looks sad, but also kind of flattering. Will this article give some sort of history of bodybuilding, with Atlas as its founder? The article is short, with two huge "artsy" pictures of Atlas and Arnold Schwarzenegger. The pictures seem to say that the two men are heroes of bodybuilding and that "bodybuilding is good"—nothing too critical here.*

As Lily expected, the article didn't say much directly about the sources of weight training's popularity. Nonetheless, her previewing of the article suggested why bodybuilders are sometimes viewed as popular and heroic: big muscles are "the ornaments of fitness" and are indicative of a "new patriotism" linked to "Rambo and Springsteen." Lily quoted each phrase in her notebook, noting its page number. Next to the quotations she wrote, "How are Rambo and Springsteen patriotic symbols? Would college-age people using weight training in their exercise routines (including many women) agree with this? If so, why? The writer seems to want to make bodybuilding more important by making it symbolic."

The other article Lily read began this way.

MUSCLEHEADS: BODYBUILDING'S BOTTOM LINE

"I'm lucky to have clearly delineated ab plates sliced down the middle with a sharply curved rectus" is how bodybuilding champion Rich Gaspari modestly put it while pondering his career. "One writer described my abdominals as looking like 'giant raviolis,' which pleased my mom, Gilda, no end." Bodybuilders are the first to point out that theirs isn't just another sport. It's an entire subculture.

Here are her journal notes on this article's opening.

> *"Muscleheads"—I get the sense that the writer is making fun of bodybuilders, or else playing on the stereotype of*

bodybuilders as stupid and narcissistic. Starting the article with that quotation from Gaspari adds to this idea. Why? Because of the words "modestly" and "pondering" and "career." These three words seem to be used ironically, first of all because he is not very modest in describing his body; second because "pondering" indicates wisdom, which is seldom linked to pride in one's body; and third because most people (non-bodybuilders, anyway) think of bodybuilding as a sport rather than a career. "Bodybuilders are the first to point out" is a very subtle put-down. I expected "are <u>not</u> the first," emphasizing the <u>immodesty</u> of bodybuilders.

Having spotted the ironic tone, Lily read the rest of the article with a double focus, paying attention to the author's opinion (revealed through the tone) but also noting specific facts about bodybuilding, such as the sales figures of four top "muscle magazines." She also focused on a third aspect of the article, the reasons it gave for bodybuilding's popularity: that "lifting weights is like sex"; that the male bodybuilder's goal is to "get a new identity," to "impress" or "threaten" women, and to "achieve a mental transcendence." Lily copied these reasons into her notebook word for word (along with the page numbers where she found them) and then annotated them with her questions and comments.

Lily's writing after reading each essay's opening paragraph enabled her to focus on her own ideas and plans, pay attention to what the author was saying, and avoid bogging down in details. As a result, while she was reading "Hulk Triumphant" and "Muscleheads," Lily looked ahead to her interviews of bodybuilders on campus and decided to concentrate on asking about reasons for bodybuilding.

2 Paraphrase your sources

Writing your own questions and comments before and while you read helps you understand sources and identify roles they can play in your final paper. A paraphrase helps you relate ideas and information from the sources more directly to your own thinking about a subject. In a **paraphrase,** you restate an author's ideas in your own words, retaining the content and sense of the original but providing your own expression.

A good paraphrase doesn't add to or detract from the original. Though paraphrasing is most obviously useful as a way to understand a difficult work, it can also help you to understand the bias of a seemingly objective work and to notice facts and points of emphasis you did not perceive clearly on a first or even a second reading.

**44f
source**

Strategy

To paraphrase part of a source, put the information in your own words, retaining the content and ideas of the original. You may wish to retain some of the wording of the original because it is particularly effective. If you do, enclose it in quotation marks, and note in parentheses the page(s) on which the wording appears.

Paraphrasing can be especially useful when a source makes information or ideas seem more complex than they really are. In such a case you can incorporate a paraphrase rather than a quotation from the original into your final paper (as long as you indicate clearly the source of the material you are paraphrasing). For example, Lily found a study of bodybuilders titled "Effect of Weight Training on Self-Concept: A Profile of Those Influenced Most" in the academic journal *Research Quarterly for Exercise and Sport*. Although it was a little dated, she thought the article, especially its opening paragraph, might be useful for her paper, but she realized that the technical language of the original was complex and might confuse her readers. She decided to paraphrase the opening paragraph.

ORIGINAL

There appears to be minimal contention to the assertion that exercise is a relevant component of psychological health. Folkins and Sime (1981) suggest in their recent and extensive literature review and evaluation that fitness training seems to help people cope with physical and psychological stresses and tends to promote well-being. In their summary of the influence of exercise on various affects, particularly anxiety, they indicate that "almost all outcomes have been positive" (p. 378). Conversely, they infer that there is no evidence to support the claim that global changes in personality follow from fitness training, although some isolated traits seem to be more sensitive to exercise than others. The reviewers conclude that the research "with the highest payoff has been that which focuses on self-concept variables" (p. 380), where the majority of inquiries have revealed significant and favorable changes as a result of systematic exercise. A similar review by Browman (1981) supports these findings.

LILY'S PARAPHRASE IN HER RESEARCH JOURNAL

No one argues against the idea that exercise is an important part of mental health. That exercise is important is supported by two researchers who summarized other studies done on this topic. They found that fitness training—that is, working out in the gym or with a specific program—helps us deal with both physical and mental stress and generally makes us feel good. In particular, they found that anxiety is lessened by exercise. They didn't find that personality was changed by exercise, although some traits might be affected (which indicates that they cannot positively say whether personality is affected.) The two researchers say that the studies with the clearest results *are those about "self-concept variables" (the positive or negative images one has of oneself?) because exercise has been shown to have obvious and positive effects on this "self-concept." Another study says the same thing.*

Lily's paraphrase displays two important qualities: it retains the ideas, information, and general order of the original without interpreting it; and the paraphrase substitutes Lily's words and phrases for those of the original, allowing her to think about the ideas in her own terms. The original passage, with its academic language and sentence structure, makes the content seem more complex than it really is. Lily's "translation" of the passage into her own language lets her see that the content is actually quite simple.

Exercise 5

A. Choose an article that interests you in a magazine such as *Natural History* or *Scientific American*. Paraphrase the first paragraph or two, or any passage of about 250 words. Do as Lily Germaine has done, and try to "translate" the passage sentence by sentence. Use the simplest words and most concise phrasing that you can.

B. In a group, paraphrase the same passage and then compare paraphrases. Discuss which paraphrases are the most accurate and thorough, yet the most concise.

C. If you already have a topic for a research paper, choose an article from your working bibliography, one in an academic journal or a magazine written for a highly educated audience. Paraphrase one or two introductory paragraphs.

44f
source

3 Summarize your sources

Like a paraphrase, a **summary** presents the essential information in a text without interpreting it. But it is shorter than the original, *compressing* the information and presenting only the key ideas and support.

Strategy

Present the content of a passage in a sentence or two of your own words. Your summary may take one of two forms. In an **objective summary,** you focus on the content of a passage and avoid speculating on the author's line of reasoning. In an **evaluative summary,** you add your own opinions, evaluating or commenting on the original passage or text.

Summarize complex sources in large sections. Begin by looking for any natural divisions of your source, such as headings or other organiza-

OBJECTIVE SUMMARY
Effects of Exercise   Tucker, "Effect of Weight
                        Training"

Most researchers agree that exercise contributes to
mental health, though it probably has little overall
effect on personality. (p. 389)

EVALUATIVE SUMMARY
Effects of Exercise   Tucker, "Effect of Weight
                        Training"

Researchers generally agree that exercise has positive
effects on mental health but little to do with overall personality, yet in noting the observation that
"some isolated traits seem to be more sensitive to
exercise than others," the author seems to suggest
that the exceptions are worth examining. (p. 389)

tional features. Then write an objective or evaluative summary of each section so you can more easily see the entire argument. Then you can choose
parts to discuss or refer to in your paper.

44f
Source

In her research journal, Lily wrote the following summary; the first
part of the summary is objective, the second part evaluative.

Tucker, Larry A. "Effect of Weight Training on Self-
Concept: A Profile of Those Influenced Most." Research
Quarterly for Exercise and Sport, Introduction,
pp. 389-91.

Objective   According to Tucker, many studies have been done to
Summary   determine whether exercise programs influence the self-concept
                 of those in the programs. There is no debate over the
                 definition of self-concept: it is the interrelationship of
                 "beliefs, attitudes, and perceptions of one's own abilities,
                 traits, values, physical characteristics, and the like" (389).

However, Tucker questions the assumption that any and all exercise programs tend to result in the same kind of improved self-concept. Tucker cites "contradictory findings," which he says may be due to inconsistencies in methodologies, in definitions of terms, or in the type of exercise studied. Most studies have been on aerobic exercise; Tucker believes that weight training would make a better topic of study. The effects can be more objectively recorded since, as he asserts, "almost anyone can achieve success while training with weights" (390), and it is easier to establish a reliable control group. The focus of his study is a four-month weight-training program for college males. He measures "extroversion, neuroticism, body cathexis, somatotype, and muscular strength" and compares these to improved self-concept.

Evaluative
Summary
Tucker uses the word "although" at least four times when summarizing other studies, and he tends to use phrases such as "only a few studies have shown...." He's being nice on the surface but is setting his readers up to find fault with the other studies. That basic fault is their lack of objective methodology, which he seems to plan on rectifying by using mathematical measurements and rigid definitions of terms. A glance through the rest of the article reveals lots of equations and two tables of statistics. He seems to think he can be completely objective in determining such a slippery thing as "self-concept." I really have to question this assumption.

When she wrote her paper on weight training, Lily was able to use her questions and comments (see 44f-1), her paraphrase (see 44f-2), and her summaries (see 44f-3). From her questions and comments she developed an opening that highlighted different ways of viewing bodybuilders: as people who have achieved something admirable or who exercise for selfish reasons. She drew on her paraphrase as a way of presenting research that emphasizes the positive mental effects of weight training, and she drew on her summaries to support her belief that some of the positive claims for weight training may be overstated. In short, each form of critical reading and note-taking was a valuable resource as she wrote her paper.

**44f
source**

Exercise 6

A. Read the entire article that you found for Exercise 5A, and write an objective summary of it. Try to limit your summary to one paragraph. Then, add to this an evaluative summary that presents your ideas about the author's conclusions.

B. In a group, compare your summaries from Exercise 6A. If all members of the group worked on the same article, discuss which summaries most clearly describe the content of the article. Which specific words and phrases make those summaries most successful? If everyone summarized different articles, discuss how well you can understand the content and the writer's evaluation in each summary. Which words and phrases in the summaries seem unclear or too technical?

C. Summarize at least one of the articles in your working bibliography for your own paper. Make sure you include an evaluative summary for possible use when you write your draft.

44g Investigating field resources

Original documents, interviews, surveys, questionnaires, and personal observations are called **field resources** because they're firsthand sources: they enable you to collect information and ideas directly rather than through reading a book or article that is the work of another writer. Two important advantages to field resources are that the material in your paper is the product of your own work, not borrowed from someone else's research, and that the information and ideas in your paper are more likely to be fresh and original. Field research also involves interpretation. "Read" the data you collect as critically as you read secondary sources.

> **Writer's Tip**
>   Don't launch into field research without doing some background reading and developing a plan. Begin your research in the library, especially if the subject is unfamiliar.

The most common form of primary research is the interview, but your topic may lend itself to other ways of gathering firsthand information, such as a survey or poll, a questionnaire, or observation. Some documents, such as the U.S. Census and other statistical reports, present raw data with little interpretation. Working with them can be considered field research as well.

1 Conduct interviews

As you gather information in the library and think about ways to investigate a topic, consider people to interview—campus experts; members of associations, trade groups, or public service agencies; and the like.

▶━◀

Strategy

List possible interviewees. Begin by writing down specific questions you would like answered; then list people who might be able to answer them. Consider whether you will need to do a thorough, lengthy interview or just collect short answers to a few questions.

▶━◀

Writer's Tip

Before conducting any field research, you should describe your plans to your instructor. You may need to clear your research with a campus committee that oversees research on human subjects; your instructor can tell you who to contact.

In addition, whenever you call someone for an interview or for information for your paper, always state your name, where you are calling from, and the purpose of the call. Briefly describe your research, and provide enough background that the person will not be anxious, defensive, or puzzled by your call.

Good interviews feel like good conversations—lively, interesting, and spontaneous—but spontaneity follows careful preparation. Know what you want to find out, and carefully draft a list of questions.

▶━◀

Strategy

Write out questions you want to ask your interviewee. If possible, rehearse these questions with friends to discover which questions are confusing or unproductive. Arrange your questions logically. Avoid questions that can be answered with *yes* or *no,* unless you plan to follow up such questions.

44g
source

▶━◀

Your list of questions should serve as a guide, but don't be shackled by it. Interesting topics you hadn't considered may arise during your interview; follow the trail of new information as long as it serves your purposes. You can always focus the interview by asking the next question on your list. Try also to include a personal element, perhaps by asking for anecdotes or experiences that illuminate the topic.

Writer's Tip

Consider tape-recording your interview instead of writing everything down. This will let you focus on the content of the interview, and you'll take away much more "text" for use later in your paper. But be sensitive to your context and the topic of your paper in deciding whether you want to bring along a tape recorder, and *always* ask your interviewee's permission to use it. Check your tape recorder before the interview, and bring along extra tapes and batteries.

After an interview, send a thank-you note to the interviewee. This is not just for politeness—you may need a follow-up interview to clarify something said. Here is a model.

271 First Street
Yourtown, CT 06510
January 5, 1996

Recipient's Name
Address
City, State 01234

Dear _____,

Thank you for speaking with me yesterday. I appreciated the time you took from your busy schedule.

You provided me with valuable information and clarified several questions I had about _____. If you would like a copy of my finished paper, let me know. I would be happy to send you one.

Sincerely,

Your Name

44g
source

2 Administer surveys and polls

Unlike interviews, surveys and polls collect short answers, often in *yes/no* form. They provide statistics you can present in charts and tables, measure against other research findings, or use to support your opinions.

►◄

Strategy

First, consider the people that you will survey or poll. Do you want to poll on the basis of gender, age, or occupation? For example, if you were comparing the opinions of college students and parents about the drinking age, you would want to get a large enough sample from each age group to enable you to generalize about the differences between them. Second, always draft, test, and revise your questions to make them as effective as possible. And third, think carefully about where you will conduct your survey or poll. A popular campus hangout will yield different results than a faculty lounge.

3 Use questionnaires

Unlike simple polls, questionnaires allow you to gather in-depth information, sometimes from a large number of people. Because they're usually mailed, most questionnaires don't require the "live" contact time of interviews, but they demand no less care in preparation. Even the smallest mistakes in wording can confuse respondents and ruin a project.

Strategy

Begin by considering the form of your questionnaire. Will you ask respondents to write out explanations, check boxes, or circle answer choices? Will you use a multiple-choice format or a rating scale? Next, draft a list of questions that will yield the information you want. Scrutinize your wording very carefully to ensure your readers won't be confused. Test your draft on at least two or three people. Ask them to describe any points at which they were confused or needed more information. Give a draft to your instructor for his or her advice. Finally, revise the questionnaire and prepare it for distribution. Try to fit your questions on one page (front and back) if possible, but leave enough space for longhand comments if you will have time to analyze them.

44g
source

> ### Writer's Tip
>
> When you are mailing or distributing your questionnaire, include a brief explanation of your project at the top of the form, as well as any guarantees of confidentiality. If you expect each respondent to mail the questionnaire back to you, include a stamped, self-addressed envelope. You might also offer to send respondents the results when your research is complete.

4 Conduct observations

Perhaps your research project calls for in-depth observation and interpretation of a situation. If so, you can turn to either personal experience or structured observation. For example, as part of his research on recycling, Shane Hand accompanied a recycling team and drew on this experience to make practical suggestions to his readers about recycling. In writing about the juvenile justice system, Patrick Luce supported his conclusions with details from the case of a young cousin falsely accused of vandalism.

In a **structured observation,** you carefully and objectively look at a situation, object, or phenomenon in order to understand its parts, its function, or its behavior. For example, for research on the ways preschoolers use language during play, you could arrange and plan in detail a series of structured observations during specific hours at a day-care center.

Strategy

The care with which you plan an observation session determines the validity and usefulness of your data.

1. Choose the site for your observation. If necessary, get permission to conduct the observation.
2. Decide how and where you will situate yourself. Will you move around? Do you want to remain inconspicuous? If not, how will you characterize your role to any people whom you observe?
3. Decide what sorts of information you want to gather and why. How will you use this information in the paper?
4. Choose your means of recording information. Will you use a tape recorder? A notepad? A video camera?
5. Make a list of problems that could impede your observation. Develop strategies for dealing with these, should they arise.

44h Conducting field research: Research in progress

The next sections show how students have used interviews, surveys, questionnaires, and observations to collect firsthand information.

1 An interview on the juvenile justice system

When Patrick Luce decided to write a paper analyzing the juvenile justice system in his county, he realized that he would have to get some expert opinions before he could say that the system needed reforming. A telephone call to the criminal court provided him with a few names, including that of the director of special services for the juvenile court, with whom Patrick immediately made an appointment for a personal interview.

Before his interview, Patrick drafted a list of questions. He practiced them with his roommate and then revised them. His list began with general background questions that helped him understand the court system and fill in gaps in his library research.

- What generally happens to juvenile criminals in Fairfax County's criminal court?
- How are juveniles treated differently from adult criminals before and after arrest? Before and after a trial? When they are in jail or prison?
- Is the current system working? If not, what most needs to be reformed?
- Do you think the current system is too lenient? If so, in what ways?
- Should penalties be tougher, or should juvenile cases be tried more strictly, or both? Why? How could cases be tried more strictly? Should they be handled more formally? With juries? Made public?

2 A survey on recycling

To back up the library's heavily statistical sources on recycling, Shane Hand decided to get a large number of responses from the "average consumer." Instead of using a small sample from a particular age group, he chose to conduct a poll at various places around campus and the town, as well as in his hometown. He asked people if they would be willing to answer a few brief *yes/no* questions on recycling. As they answered, he put a mark on a tally sheet keyed to eleven questions, including these:

Do you ...

Use coffee mugs instead of polystyrene cups?	Yes	No
Reuse plastic wrap, foil, and plastic bags?	Yes	No
Recycle newspapers and/or magazines?	Yes	No

Are you willing to ...

Take your own bags to the store?	Yes	No
Shop at a store that's harder to get to, but carries biodegradable products?	Yes	No

44h source

Shane collected responses from about three hundred people. He put the results into a table, which he included in his paper and discussed in detail. (His paper with the complete survey form appears in Chapter 46.)

3 A questionnaire on stereotypes

Elizabeth Bowden was writing a humorous paper titled "What Do Men Want?" She wanted to test the stereotype that men want to date one kind of woman (the "bimbo" type) and to marry another (the "nice" type). Though she wanted to take a lighthearted approach to the paper, she still wanted to present interesting information to her readers. To get the information she needed, she administered a three-part questionnaire to twenty-five men in her dorm and classes. Each part of the questionnaire was identical, with only the introductory prompt and the verb tense changed. The prompts were (1) How would you describe the perfect woman you would want to date, with no strings attached and with the knowledge you could do whatever you wanted to do? (2) How would you describe the woman you are dating now? and (3) How would you describe the woman you want to marry? She intentionally used subjective language in her questionnaire.

Circle one answer for each question.
1. What color is her hair?
   a. brown   b. blond   c. red   d. black
2. What is her height?
   a. short   b. average   c. tall
3. What is her build?
   a. slim   b. medium   c. heavy
4. What kind of look does she have?
   a. exotic   b. nice   c. plain/homey   d. pretty   e. gorgeous
5. What kind of clothes does she wear?
   a. jeans and T-shirt   b. sweater and slacks   c. tight minidress
6. What would you and she do on a date?
   a. watch movies   b. have dinner   c. play sports   d. go to bed
   e. sit and talk
7. What kind of job would she have?
   a. teacher   b. flight attendant   c. businesswoman   d. scientist
8. What kind of attitude would she have?
   a. town sweetheart   b. fun-loving   c. serious   d. "bad girl"
9. Would you want her to . . .
   a. be totally devoted to you and not worry about her friends
   b. be with you a lot but still spend time with her friends
   c. be with you very little and spend a lot of time with her friends
10. What would her intelligence level be compared to yours?
    a. not as smart as you   b. as smart as you   c. smarter than you
11. Now in your own words describe this woman: _____
    _____

**44h
source**

4 An observation at a gym

Through her classmates, Lily Germaine first found several college students who weight-trained regularly. From these she selected three to interview, asking them to tell her why they weight-train, to describe themselves before and after they began training, and to comment generally on weight training. After these interviews, she asked one man to be her main subject for the paper. He agreed and introduced her to the manager of the gym where he worked out, who gave her permission to conduct her observation.

Lily feared that her presence might make the people working out act differently—becoming self-conscious or showing off—so she conducted her observation as unobtrusively as possible. The objective information she wanted to record was how long people worked out at the gym, what equipment they used most frequently, what weights or machines they used, and what they wore (to assess the role of fashion). To prepare, she drew up a rough chart with spaces to describe her subjects, the equipment they used, minutes on each machine, clothing worn, and other data. Mainly, though, she wanted to observe interactions between the people working out (particularly what they said to each other), whether or how they looked at themselves in the mirrors, and what other behaviors they engaged in. This was more subjective information—dependent upon what she noticed and recorded.

Lily's objective information was fairly easy to record from an unobtrusive corner of the room. But for the more subjective, impressionistic information, she needed to get close enough to hear what people said. Since she wanted to make her presence as inconspicuous as possible, she decided to split her visit into two parts. During the first half hour, she filled out her chart, recording any other objective information she could gather along the way. During the next hour, she positioned herself in three different spots in the room, closer to the weight machines but behind them.

Exercise 7

A. With a general topic in mind, choose one method of gathering information through primary research (use a survey, interview, or questionnaire—not observation). Draft five to ten questions you would ask about that topic, and try to render these in a form appropriate for your primary research. Before you write, determine who would be the best person or persons to interview, poll, and so on.

B. Working in a small group or with a classmate, exchange drafts of your questions from Exercise 7A. Ask your partner to play the role of your intended interviewee or respondent. Are any questions confusing? Do any of them elicit only vague or cursory answers? If you have chosen interviewing as your primary research method, try role-playing the situation. Ask other members of the group to observe you and the respondent, and ask them to comment on the way you ask questions, how you interact with the respondent, and the like.

**44h
source**

C. Plan the type of primary research that would be most effective for your actual research project. Consider what experiences of your own you can incorporate into the project. Write a draft of the questions or observation materials you need. Rehearse your questions with classmates or a roommate before revising them.

CHAPTER

45

Turning Research Into Writing

How do you know when to begin *writing* your research paper? Actually, there's no set time; if you've been writing down your questions and responses as part of a critical reading and research process, you have already begun drafting. Think of researching and writing not as separate, sequential steps but as interrelated activities. As you write, you'll move back and forth between your journal or your notes and your draft, perhaps making additional trips to the library to double-check your references or to find another source to back up a claim, creating your paper piece by piece rather than in one sitting.

45a Using critical reading to synthesize, interpret, and evaluate

Critical reading and note-taking strategies like paraphrasing and sum-marizing can help you understand your research sources, and they can also suggest directions for your research and your writing. Other critical reading strategies—synthesizing, interpreting, and evaluating—can help you decide how and when to incorporate your research into a paper. If you make these more advanced critical reading strategies part of your research process, ide-ally in a research journal, you'll find that you can develop many of your informal ideas and speculations into sections of your final paper.

The benefits of synthesizing, interpreting, and evaluating are that they enable you to work out your thinking informally and flexibly, without being constrained by a preset outline. They also help you analyze sources in sophis-ticated ways that can add depth and variety to the insights you offer. Using such strategies will help you avoid writing one of those unenlightened, dry papers that merely report information and other people's ideas.

1 Synthesize your sources

To understand any subject in depth, you must bring together facts and ideas from many sources and explore potential connections among them. A **synthesis** combines concepts and details from a variety of sources to form a unified discussion of a topic.

In synthesizing several sources, be alert to agreements and disagreements. For example, if all but one of the sources agree, your synthesis should summarize and explain the similarities but also try to account for the source that disagrees. You might try to explain the cause of the disagreement: Could it be the method used in the study, the author's political stance, or the time and place it was written? You might also record your responses as a reader: With which side do you agree? Is there anything in your own background that makes you especially receptive to one point of view?

To synthesize effectively, follow these guidelines.

1. Be true to the ideas and information presented by your sources.
2. Suggest relationships among concepts and facts that go beyond the relationships discussed in your sources.
3. Summarize the relations in a thesis statement (see 5c) or a statement of the central idea of the synthesis.
4. Be selective; present material from the sources that relates directly to the central idea of your synthesis.
5. Be balanced; instead of leaving out facts and opinions that contradict the central idea advanced in your synthesis, acknowledge that they represent alternative perspectives.
6. Base your synthesis on your own thinking as well as the material presented in your sources.

Strategy

Look back over your sources and notes, especially your summaries of long passages or entire sources. Synthesize (sum up) the main ideas, positions, or facts of your sources. To do this, imagine that you're an expert on the topic and that you're trying to give someone a quick state-of-the-art overview based on your sources. The result should be a preliminary synthesis of what you've gathered from your sources.

45a
read

2 Interpret your sources

In an **interpretation,** you build on synthesis by explicitly including your opinions about what you read, adding your understanding to that of the authors and giving priority to your own ideas and points of view. Interpreting involves coming to broad conclusions about what a writer has to say—*generalizing*—and going beyond this to connect an author's ideas to your own—*extending.*

When you generalize, you state key ideas, both those the author states explicitly and those you infer from the text. To extend means to place the text within some larger context and to draw from your own knowledge to discuss the significance of that text in that context.

To create a successful interpretation, note these guidelines.

1. Present material from your sources accurately, selecting those materials most relevant to the point you want to make but not suppressing points that contradict your ideas.
2. Present your point of view and provide supporting evidence.
3. Add interpretations and conclusions not present in the sources or present in a different form.

Strategy

Begin writing your interpretation by stating the point of view of the source as accurately as possible. Then add your own ideas, perhaps comparing the perspective of the chosen source to the views of other sources. How do you respond to the source? What is the main point of your source?

3 Evaluate your sources

Evaluation is closely linked to interpretation. Not everything you read is equally valuable, accurate, or persuasive. Part of your task as a researcher is to evaluate what a source says or presents, whether the source comes from library research or field research. You have to decide what material to cite as an authority and what to reject or refute.

You can't evaluate a text or information gathered from field research unless you already know something about the subject, but this doesn't mean you have to know everything. The strength of your assertions will depend on the extent to which you are knowledgeable, and you should already have enough information from your research to make reasonable judgments. When you evaluate your sources, keep the following guidelines in mind.

45a
read

1. Support your judgments with examples from the texts or data you are evaluating.
2. Explain your judgments of one text or body of data by comparing it to other texts or data.
3. Base your evaluation on your own ideas.

Strategy

Use the following guidelines to write an evaluation.

- Ask how accurate your source is, especially if it presents facts as truth. Look for obvious errors, but also look for points that seem detailed and well documented.

- Find and test the generalizations in the source. Does the writer support them, and if so, with what? Do they go beyond the facts in the text? Are they consistent with what you know about the subject?
- Think about the main ideas presented in the source, and review your synthesis of it. Are the ideas generally consistent with those in your other sources? If different, do they seem original and insightful or misleading and eccentric?

4 Use your guiding questions to synthesize, interpret, and evaluate

When you use synthesizing, interpreting, and evaluating as critical reading and writing strategies, always keep in mind how your writing relates to your research project. The questions you have developed to guide your research (see 43b and 43c) can also help you employ these strategies.

Strategy

Consider how the works you are using answer the questions guiding your research or how they support or undermine the main idea you are planning to develop. What alternative answers or contrasting main ideas might someone advance? Try asking, "What if we look at it another way, such as . . . ?" Imagine situations not mentioned in your sources, and test the ideas in your sources against these hypothetical situations. Finally, add something to the conclusions offered in your sources—try to think of a practical application, a different problem, an alternative solution. Doing this will strengthen your own ideas, resulting in a more sophisticated paper.

45b
read

45b Doing critical reading and thinking: Research in progress

1 A synthesis of articles

In her journal, Lily Germaine wrote a synthesis of the articles she read on weight training and her interviews with people who engaged in this kind of exercise regularly. As she wrote, she found it was difficult to reconcile the different perspectives represented in her research. Here is a selection from her synthesis of the ideas represented in her various sources.

The reason my respondents most frequently mentioned for weight training was "fitness" but not with the ultimate goal of attracting other people. Rather, they linked "fitness" to a sense of well-being and to both physical and mental health. Another important reason discussed by the men interviewed was "male bonding," a sense of comradeship with other men engaged in weight training. The third-ranked reason was "exhilaration," described as a kind of "high." Fourth was "looking good" (four respondents), both to "impress women" and "get guys' attention." This reason included "making other men envious" and "standing out in a crowd of women."

These responses corresponded to my secondary research, in particular the study by Tucker, which establishes that weight training does have a positive effect on the self-image of college men and women. However, his definition of this term is broad enough to encompass all of the above reasons. Other studies, notably the ones by Johnson and by Strickland, narrow the definition somewhat to exclude the reasons "exhilaration" and "male bonding." They all say, in effect, "Weight training has only beneficial results, particularly in psychological well-being." They all imply the argument "Colleges should encourage more people to weight-train."

2 An interpretation of a text

In preparing to write a paper on ocean dumping, Robert Weinman prepared the following interpretation. Note how he starts his interpretation with the ideas explicitly stated in a text and then adds his own thoughts.

> Johannsen's discussion of the major warm and cold thermal currents in the Atlantic notes the different materials, natural and artificial, distributed throughout the ocean by the currents. He claims this distribution process is one of the major ways that pollutants move throughout the region. Yet we might also view the currents as a mechanism by which the ocean protects itself from rapid changes, including an increase in pollutants.

45b
read

The framework of ideas in Robert's interpretation is based on Johannsen's work, yet the application is entirely Robert's. Although Robert is influenced by Johannsen, he doesn't *borrow* but instead *develops*. He has gone beyond paraphrasing, summarizing, and synthesizing, though these were certainly part of his reading. Instead, he takes Johannsen's ideas a step further, though without altering their original presentation.

3 An evaluation of sources

Naomi Williams had gathered a number of articles for her paper on art censorship. In them, she found not only conflicting arguments but what seemed to her to be conflicting facts as well. She decided to write evaluations in order to isolate ideas and information that struck her as suspicious. In the following excerpt, note how she picks out several suspicious facts from one article and compares them to the findings of other sources.

In Richardson's article reporting interviews with people who attended controversial art exhibits, he seems to have asked misleading questions. He also twists the words of those who fail to give him the "right" answers; anyone who (probably) disagreed with him is quoted in phrases, with crucial verbs or nouns missing. He also adds an arsenal of statistics—for instance, that 63 percent of Americans are against the depiction of sexuality in art. Oddly, he doesn't identify his sources but quotes facts and opinions to support his own very suspect generalization that controversial artists are responsible for the moral decay of our society.

Although this is an especially weak source, some of the opinions of the people he interviewed are consistent with other articles. However, none of these articles seems credible individually. My own poll of over 150 people in a busy downtown area suggests that most Americans have moderate views on the issue, for instance, 30 percent instead of Richardson's 63 percent.

Exercise 1

A. Choose one or more sources from your research, and try out one of the approaches to critical reading mentioned in 45a. Write in your research journal or in your regular notebook. Use the guidelines that precede each Strategy in 45a as a checklist for your own writing.

B. In a group, share your writing for Exercise 1A. Discuss what additions or revisions could be made to each person's writing.

45c
draft

C. In your journal or notebook, write about how the work you did for Exercise 1A relates to your research project as a whole. What information could come before or after this writing? Is it part of the core of the paper, or something you can use as a supporting paragraph?

45c Drafting your research paper

When you have gathered enough material to begin seriously assembling a draft of your research paper, you can piece together some of your preliminary and less formally written material, then add significant new material to make a more complete and coherent text. Instead of trying to draft your paper by launching right into the first word of the first line, start by thinking strategically about the nature and shape of your task.

1 Consider audience, purpose, and persona

The shape of your paper will be strongly influenced by the nature of your audience, your purpose (which may govern the form of your paper), and your persona (the role or stance you take in the paper).

Audience. Although you'll write most academic papers for teachers and fellow students, you may want to invoke a specific **audience** for your research paper (see Chapter 6). It is important to get beyond the "general reader" audience, even if your paper would appeal to a varied group of people, because papers addressed to general readers often are too broad and vague. Instead, imagine an ideal reader to help you focus on what your purpose should be and which information you should include.

▶◀

Strategy

Write informally about your imagined reader. What single, specific type of individual or group would most benefit from or be interested in reading about your topic? What are the ideal reader's age, gender, position, and concerns? You might even want to try writing a brief description of that person or group. (For further advice on audience analysis, see Chapter 6.)

▶◀

Purpose. In choosing a purpose for your paper, you may want to refer to Chapter 43, which describes four kinds of research writing. For instance, if you're writing about reforms in the drinking age, your research may suggest an argumentative approach. If your ideal reader is your representative in Congress, you may decide to write your paper in the form of a letter to him or her (with your general audience being anyone else who is interested in this topic—perhaps primarily other college students). Your purpose, then, is already suggested for you: to convince your representative to reform the law (in accord with your own proposals, of course). The purpose of Lily Germaine's paper on weight training, discussed in Chapters 43 through 45, is analytical. Though she does provide some historical information, she mainly tries to explain why weight training is popular—that is, to inform and enlighten her readers. Shane Hand's paper on waste disposal, presented in full in Chapter 46, is basically informative, though it has an argumentative edge.

45c draft

▶◀

Strategy

If your assignment doesn't specify a purpose, ask yourself what you want your paper to *do*. Then ask what form it might take, given this purpose. What do you want your audience to learn, to do, or to feel? Does your research suggest an argument? Does it suggest a history, case study, or narrative?

▶◀

Persona. The term **persona** refers to the way you represent yourself in your writing—the role you play (see 27a-3). In a research paper, you can remove yourself almost entirely from the text, hiding behind the scenes as your reader focuses on information you present. Or you can be at the center of the paper, perhaps by describing your own role in your study of a group or subculture. Although you may play a detached, clinical role, many kinds of descriptive research now assume that the researcher should be acknowledged as "part of" what is being studied.

Strategy

Write informally about how you want to represent yourself in your paper. Will you use the pronoun *I* when you describe your work? Do you want to express your opinion or stay out of the paper altogether? Do you want to seem impassioned or detached, opinionated or objective?

Lily Germaine's research on weight training (discussed in 44h-4) offered her several options for her persona. If she simply reported the results of her library research on weight training and self-concept, she could remain detached and objective, synthesizing what she had found. However, after observing at the gym, she felt strongly that she, like many others, had fallen prey to stereotypes about weight training. She decided to include these feelings in her paper, representing a general attitude toward her topic.

Exercise 2

A. Determine your audience, purpose (and form), and persona. If you don't have these specifically in mind, make a list of potential forms for your paper, linking each form with a suitable audience and purpose.

45c
draft

B. In a group, discuss your possible or chosen audience-purpose-persona relationships from Exercise 2A. With one of these relationships in mind, have other students take on the role of the audience and tell you their expectations as that group of readers. Discuss what you would need to include in your paper to satisfy that audience.

C. Make some final decisions about your audience, purpose, and persona. List the information you will need to include in the paper, and list the probable concerns of your audience.

2 Create a purpose structure

Having decided on a topic, done your research, and considered your audience, purpose, and persona, you have some idea of the things you want your paper to do. At this point, you should be able to create a purpose structure for your paper. This planning technique is especially valuable for long papers that have multiple purposes and present detailed information.

A **purpose structure** is a series of statements that briefly describe what you intend to do in each section of a paper (see also 5b-1). It is a tentative blueprint that helps you bring together the work you have done and begin to visualize the finished product. A purpose structure can suggest a working thesis (see 45c-3), help you create an outline (see 45c-4), or alert you to areas where you need to do further research.

Suppose, for example, that you had been doing research on controversies over who owns the design patterns for different kinds of computer software. You might create the following purpose structure.

BEGINNING   Explain the importance of copyrights, patents, and intellectual property rights, especially for computer software.

MIDDLE   Discuss questions of intellectual property rights as they evolved in three legal controversies: Apple's Macintosh user interface versus Microsoft's Windows, Lotus 1-2-3 versus similar spreadsheets, and Compton's patented design of CD-ROM reference works versus designs of other CD-ROM publishers.

ENDING   Describe recently proposed solutions to the problem of establishing ownership of software designs.

3 Develop a thesis

A successful research paper is not a simple listing of the ideas and information you have gathered on a topic. Above all, it conveys your perspective, interpretation, or opinion regarding the subject, supported and developed through use of the material you have gathered in your research.

To make sure your planning reflects a clear focus and to keep your perspective in mind as you draft and revise, develop a thesis statement in a sentence or two. Your initial thesis should be a **tentative** (or **draft**) **thesis statement** that you are willing to modify as your insight develops and deepens in the course of drafting and revising.

If you were working on a paper about intellectual property rights for computer software, you might arrive at the following tentative statement.

DRAFT THESIS   Determining ownership of the design features in computer software is difficult and has led to many controversies.

This tentative thesis would help you focus on your subject and begin planning your paper, but it doesn't provide a clear opinion or perspective around which to build your paper. You would need to think about your topic a bit more and perhaps even do more research. You might decide that your paper should both provide your perspective on the problem and suggest possible solutions. You could put this new insight into a **working thesis** to guide your planning and drafting.

WORKING THESIS   The lack of effective ways of determining ownership of design features in computer software has led to many controversies between software companies, yet these controversies can be avoided in the future with laws that clearly define *intellectual property* as the term applies to software.

In your final paper, you might modify this thesis, breaking it into several sentences so it is easier to read. In addition, you might use the thesis as an organizing strategy, repeating parts of it in modified form at key points in the paper to remind readers of your perspective.

4 Plan your paper

As you conduct your research and as you synthesize, interpret, and evaluate your sources, you should always keep in mind the overall questions guiding your research and remember your purpose for writing. In a sense, you begin planning your paper from the start of your research. But when you've done most of the necessary research, you need to shift to a more text-centered way of thinking. Your aim should be to work out a specific plan for the organization and contents of your paper.

Many useful planning strategies are provided in detail in Chapter 4. Those strategies can be recast or supplemented for use with research papers, which are generally longer and more complex than other kinds of writing.

45c
draft

Did You Know?

College students who planned their papers with a partner and took turns asking questions about each other's plans ended up paying considerable attention to their purposes for writing.

Linda Flower and L. Higgins, *Collaboration and the Construction of Meaning,* Technical Report no. 56 (Berkeley: Center for the Study of Writing, University of California, 1991).

Outlining. The traditional method of planning is outlining (see also 4b-6). With a long research paper, however, it's often best not to try to make a detailed, exact outline before writing a draft. You could become frustrated trying to fit into an outline all the bits of information you've gathered— information that may not prove useful as you develop your reasoning in a draft. A **working outline** that shows the general sequence of information, along with the relationships (transitions) between segments of information, will probably be more useful.

▶━◀

Strategy

In an informal outline, quickly block out the main parts of your paper. Write detailed transitions between the parts. Focus on the largest units of your paper first, and then work on smaller organizational chunks such as sections and paragraphs. This will give you a clear sense of how the parts fit together and how the paper will progress.

▶━◀

Many students wait until they've finished a full first draft before outlining. They feel more comfortable writing informally without being restricted by an outline. This method works best if you have a lot of information that is fairly well sorted out in your mind and also have a clear sense of audience and purpose. Outlining after you draft is useful because the outline reveals the pattern in what you have written. You can easily see what's missing, what parts can be expanded, and what needs to be rearranged. You can also write transitions at that point, as student writer David Kokoc did in the following excerpt from his working outline.

> I. The drug war: Who's fighting whom?
>   A. Overview of the "war on drugs": the players in the game (generals, soldiers, victims, enemies, etc.); "battle" statistics.
>
> *Transition*   Something short and sweet, like "The government can pat itself on the back when it wins major battles in the war, such as the ..."
>
>   B. Story of one victory: the drug warehouse raid in Miami.
>
> *Transition*   Begin by pointing out the obvious benefits of raids, but, also turn this around by questioning such raids when they are applied broadly: "Such victories, however, are few, extremely costly (put cost of the raid in parens?), and they are not effective, since the enemy remains in power and in control. Take, for example, the case of ..."
>
>   C. Story of another "victory": the raid of a local small-time marijuana grower.
>
> *Transition*   Raise questions about the effectiveness of such raids, and quote from interviews to make specific points.

Grouping Information. Like outlining, other techniques for grouping your information (see 4b-1 and 4b-2) are useful if you have many bits of information but not a particularly clear idea of how they relate to each other.

45c
draft

Try moving your information around physically until you find groupings and relationships that seem right.

Strategy

Write down or describe separate pieces of information (such as major points from your sources, informal paraphrases or summaries, or thoughts and ideas you want to include) on pieces of paper. If you took notes on $3'' \times 5''$ cards, you may be able to use these. Now arrange the pages or cards in relation to one another. As you begin to see patterns emerge, you may think of additional information that fits into one grouping or another.

Cutting and Pasting. If you've been using a research journal extensively to record and reflect on research, you may already have written much of a draft paper, in segments, and you may not need to spend time creating an outline, map, or tree.

Strategy

If you have written on both sides of your journal pages or don't want to cut up the original, make a photocopy of the relevant pages. Now cut out the separate entries. Arrange the entries to reflect a cohesive relationship, and think of or draft transitions. Depending on how extensive your journal entries are, you may end up with a rough draft by the time you finish cutting and pasting.

**45c
draft**

Writer's Tip: Using a Computer

Cutting and pasting can be done easily using a word processing program. Choose relevant passages from your journal or research notes; copy them into the computer's working memory; then paste them into a new file wherever they seem to fit. Print out the results from time to time so you can more clearly see the overall organizational patterns emerging.

Focusing on the Introduction and Conclusion. Instead of starting with one of the planning methods discussed above, sometimes you might want to write the introduction and the conclusion for a paper first. In creating these two elements, you'll have to consider your ideal readers, both their familiarity with your topic and their level of interest, and you'll have to be able to predict your paper's design and goals.

Strategy

In writing the introduction, ask yourself, "How can I engage the reader from the start? How can I make that reader want to read on?" Think of interesting ways to begin the paper—even formal academic papers don't have to have dull openings. Write one or two (or more) different opening paragraphs, experimenting with style and content.

In writing the conclusion, ask yourself, "How can I give a sense of closure to the paper without closing down the topic? How can I make my readers want to keep thinking about the topic?" Think of endings that don't merely summarize the paper, that don't hide behind a quotation, and that avoid sentimental or patriotic clichés. Try several versions.

Exercise 3

A. In a group, choose one of the planning methods (outlining, grouping, cutting and pasting, or introducing and concluding), and collaboratively apply it to one person's project. If the group chooses to write an introduction and conclusion, everyone should prepare a separate one-paragraph introduction and a brief (one- or two-sentence) conclusion. Compare all the versions.

B. Apply one or more of the planning methods described in this chapter or in Chapter 4 to your own paper in progress.

45c draft

5 Integrate your sources

The big question for most students writing research papers is "How many quotes do I need?" But remember: a research paper is *based* on sources but is not merely a *collection* of those sources. The essential voice in a research paper is your own. The sources you use should support your ideas, not the other way around. So unless your teacher wants a specific number of quotations, ask yourself, "How many quotes does *my* paper need?"

If you're taking a controversial stance, you may need more references than you would need for a speculative paper. Whatever the number of references, however, avoid stringing quotations together or using a lot of long quotations set off in blocks (which may look suspiciously like padding). Too many quotations, especially in block form, can distract your reader by detracting from the flow of *your* prose. Use some of the following ideas for incorporating your research material into your own writing. (For more information about what to document and how to use different kinds of citations, see the beginning of Chapter 46.)

Choosing What to Cite. By the time you're ready to draft major portions of your paper, you will probably have collected many sources, each containing hundreds of possible phrases, sentences, or paragraphs to quote. You need some principle to guide your choice of what to include.

▶◀

Strategy

Check your paraphrases, other research notes, and sources for significant notes you made while reading. These usually mark points you thought were informative, controversial, or notable in some way. Then decide whether any of these "hot spots" identify material important enough to be incorporated into your paper. Remember, when you're working from sources to function, you're deciding whether the structure of your paper has a place for your reference material. Another equally valid way of working is to begin with function (the point or idea you're trying to develop) and then to scan your references for facts, illustrations, or supporting details.

▶◀

Using Embedded Quotations. To embed a quotation means that you use it within a sentence of your own. This technique helps you maintain the flow of your own prose so your paper reads smoothly. You can also embed quotations when you want to use the exact language of the source—for instance, when the source defines a term in a special way or uses an unusual word or descriptive phrase. Don't embed a quotation if it is long (more than a line or two) or if it can more smoothly be paraphrased or summarized.

45c draft

UNNECESSARY | In 1968, when Bob Dylan was 26, a critic wrote, "A few songs are weak" (Saal 93).
READER'S RESPONSE: What's so special about Saal's language here that it needs to be quoted directly?

AMBIGUOUS | Some critics found weaknesses in Dylan's album (Saal 93).
READER'S RESPONSE: Did Saal find Dylan's album weak or just say that some critics did?

REVISED | Some critics, such as Saal (93), found a few weaknesses in Bob Dylan's 1968 album.

Using Block Quotations. A **block quotation** is a longer passage from a source, set off from your own prose because of length. Use a block quotation when you want to analyze or supply a close reading of a passage, when

> ### Writer's Tip
>
> Avoid "setting up" direct quotations with a lot of short phrases or parenthetical details.
>
> **AWKWARD** In one article I read (1974), the author, who had just seen Dylan perform, said, "Dylan's earliest songs were not only still alive but resonant with new meanings" (Willis 110).
>
> **REVISED** One critic, seeing Dylan perform in 1974, said his early songs "were not only still alive but resonant with new meanings" (Willis 110).

a source presents an extended but vital definition, or when you want to illustrate a writer's style. Block quotations are frequently used in literary papers for these reasons. Remember, however, that readers expect you to *do* something with block quotations, not just to insert them and leave it up to the reader to figure out why you have included them. (For the proper format of block quotations, see 34b.)

UNNECESSARY QUOTATION   Adrienne Rich continues in *On Lies, Secrets, and Silence* with the role of women in American society and culture.

> Women's culture, on the other hand, is active: women have been the truly active people in all cultures, without whom human society would long ago have perished, though our activity has most often been on behalf of men and children. (12)

Women have been crucial to the successes of many cultures, and Rich expresses the need for a universal appreciation of all different types of women and the roles they play.
READER'S RESPONSE: The quotation could easily be summarized without losing its meaning.

REVISED   In *On Lies, Secrets, and Silence,* Adrienne Rich points out that women have been crucial to the successes of many cultures; she expresses the need for a universal appreciation of all different types of women and the roles they play. (12)

Using Paraphrases and Summaries. To make your writing smoother and more sophisticated, be selective in your use of quotations. Usually, you can summarize or paraphrase (see 44f) rather than quoting sources directly. You can also combine several sources in a summary (see 44f-3).

45c draft

45d Avoiding plagiarism

When you include quotations, paraphrases, and summaries in your writing, you *must* acknowledge their sources. If you do not, you are claiming, in effect, that someone else's work is your own. (Failure to cite a source is **plagiarism,** which can lead to serious punitive actions by your school.)

Whenever you quote someone's exact words, be sure you enclose the words in quotation marks and cite their source. Make sure that paraphrases and summaries are in your own words, and be sure to cite the source of the ideas and information that you are summarizing or paraphrasing.

Learning to paraphrase and summarize effectively without inappropriately borrowing the language of your source takes practice. You may need to write several versions of a paraphrase to find effective wording of your own. The following paraphrase is too close to the original to be presented without quotation marks and would be considered plagiarized.

ORIGINAL PASSAGE

Malnutrition was a widespread and increasingly severe problem throughout the least developed parts of the world in the 1970s, and would continue to be serious, occasionally reaching famine conditions, as the millennium approached. Among the cells of the human body most dependent upon a steady source of nutrients are those of the immune system, most of which live, even under ideal conditions, for only days at a time. As nutritional input declines, these vital cells literally run out of fuel, fail to perform their crucial disease-fighting tasks, or, in worst cases, die off. The body may also lack nutritional resources to make replacement cells, and eventually the immune deficiency can become so acute that virtually any pathogenic microbe can cause lethal disease. (From Laurie Garrett, *The Coming Plague,* New York: Penguin, 1994, p. 199.)

PLAGIARIZED VERSION

In her book about newly emerging global diseases, Garrett points out that malnutrition can give microbes an advantage as they spread through the population. Malnutrition continues to be a **severe problem throughout the least developed parts of the world.** The human immune system contains cells that are **dependent upon a steady source of nutrients.** These cells may **live, even under ideal conditions, for only days at a time.** As the amount of **nutritional input declines,** the immune cells stop fighting diseases **or, in worst cases, die off.** Worse, if the body lacks enough nutrition to replace dead cells, **virtually any** microorganism **can cause lethal disease.** Under such conditions, it is not hard to imagine powerful new bacteria sweeping through a population of malnourished people.

45d
draft

As you can see, the writer of the plagiarized version made only minor changes in some phrases and "lifted" other phrases verbatim. The writer identifies the source but copies the source's language, staying very close to the structure of the original sentences. Furthermore, by substituting the more general word "microorganism" for Garrett's "pathogenic microbe," the writer creates the false assertion that *any* microorganism can kill a person whose immune system is compromised by malnutrition.

Understandably, you may find it difficult to reword complex or unfamiliar material, especially if you haven't given yourself time to think about the meanings and implications of what you have read. The wording of expertly written sources can easily take over your own language. This is where using a journal to paraphrase sources comes in handy. The writer of the plagiarized paragraph could have paraphrased the passage as follows.

APPROPRIATE PARAPHRASE

In her book about newly emerging global diseases, Garrett points out that malnutrition can give microbes an advantage as they spread through the population. The human body contains immune cells that help to fight off various diseases. When the body is deprived of nutrients, these immune cells will weaken, creating an environment in which an invading microbe can thrive. In serious cases of malnutrition, the cells may die, and the body may not be able to replace them. When the case becomes serious enough, Garrett claims, almost any disease-causing microbe can result in death. Under such conditions, it is not hard to imagine powerful new deadly bacteria sweeping through a population of malnourished people (Garrett 199).

Because this writer's paper focused on the general threat of global disease, he also could have simply summarized the passage.

APPROPRIATE SUMMARY

It has been suggested that widespread malnutrition can so weaken people's immune systems that diseases they would otherwise fight off will thrive, killing their hosts (Garrett 199).

Did You Know?

Definitions of plagiarism vary widely. In a federal appeals case in which a university professor had been accused of plagiarism, the court upheld the university's right to choose its own definition of plagiarism.

Rebecca Moore Howard, *Standing in the Shadow of Giants: Plagiarism and Authorship in Composition Pedagogy* (Norwood: Ablex, 1996).

Exercise 4

A. Choose a passage from one of your secondary sources, and write a summary and a paraphrase of it. Then embed a quote from the source into a sentence of your own.

B. With a group or partner, discuss your writing for Exercise 4A. Does any of it seem plagiarized? If so, help each other to rewrite. Also, discuss how to improve the passages. How can they be made to read more smoothly? How can they be made more concise?

C. Select the sources you definitely want to cite in your paper, and decide whether each would most smoothly fit into your paper as a paraphrase, summary, or quotation. Prepare paraphrases, summaries, embedded quotations, or block quotations for these references.

45e Revising, editing, and proofreading

After drafting a research paper come three distinct activities requiring quite different mental attitudes: revising, editing, and proofreading.

1 Revise your draft

Revision is an especially important part of writing a research paper. This is the stage when you rethink what you have written, when your audience's needs and your purpose for writing come to the forefront. If possible, put a draft aside for a night, a few days, a week—whatever time you can afford—so that you can see it more objectively and decide whether you need to change the order of material, to add or delete sections, or even to change your opinions, interpretation, or argumentative stance.

Along with setting the draft aside, ask other readers to respond to it. A research and writing group can be an invaluable resource for possible revisions. Group members will know your assignment, audience, and purpose as well as your struggles with the project. If you have not been working regularly with a group, assembling one for the revision stage can still be useful. When you work with people unfamiliar with your project, fill them in on the assignment, your audience, and your purpose. At the top of your draft, write specific questions or concerns for your readers, such as these.

Do you like my opening? Is it interesting? How could I improve it?

Please help me with transitions between paragraphs 3 and 4 and between 8 and 9. Are the connections clear for each pair?

What do you think I'm saying on page 3, paragraph 1? Please summarize the paragraph in the margin. Is this part ambiguous?

If your readers also record responses and questions in the margins, they will help you understand how other readers are likely to react to the various sections of your paper. (For further advice on revising, see Chapter 8.)

2 Edit your draft

When you have finished arranging the material in your paper and are satisfied that you have included all needed information and cited all appropriate sources, you are ready to begin editing. This is when you fine-tune your paper: you reword phrases, alter sentence structure, adjust the rhythm and flow of your language, and correct errors in grammar, sentence structure, and word usage. (See Chapter 13 for advice.)

You can also edit effectively with the help of others. Reading your draft aloud gives your listeners a chance to raise questions and note possible rough spots. Or you can have another person read the paper while you listen and note possible changes on your own copy. Reading aloud exposes awkward sentence patterns, such as too many short sentences in a row, long sentences with subjects and verbs widely separated, sentence fragments, faulty pronoun references, and too many repeated words or phrases. Thus, even if you do not have the help of others, try reading aloud to yourself. (For detailed advice on editing, see Chapters 14 through 36.)

3 Proofread your final paper

When you proofread, look over your paper carefully for errors in spelling, usage, punctuation, and grammar. Double-check your source citations and documentation form (see Chapters 46 through 49). Make sure that any quotations are accurate; check page numbers and authors' names. Try exchanging papers with another writer and proofreading as an outsider. (For more advice on proofreading, see Chapters 13 and 37 through 42.)

45e
revise

Documenting Sources: MLA

As you read the following paragraph from a research paper, note how the writer uses **in-text citations** to provide support for his conclusions and give credit to others for the words, ideas, and facts he is drawing from their work. Note, too, that he uses two simple citation strategies: naming the source in the course of the discussion or giving the source's name (and sometimes a page number) within parentheses.

> Students in high school and college often resort to cheating to get high grades. In a recent survey of almost nine thousand high school and college students, 61 percent of the high schoolers and 32 percent of the college students admitted to cheating on an exam at least once in the previous year (Schroeder 74). Some research points out that cheating is frequently related to low self-esteem (Kibler and Kibler). Christina Hoff Sommers argues, however, that the lack of concern with personal morality in contemporary education may have a good deal to do with the problem. Both explanations may be needed to analyze the complex motivations for cheating, which are frequently similar to those one student expressed recently to a reporter for the *Campus Echo*: "I sometimes cheat on a test because I think that doing really well in a course is beyond my ability and because I don't think cheating is terribly wrong if you are looking out for yourself and your own survival" (Capelli 5). — Timothy Dunbar, College Student

If you or any other reader wanted to learn more about the sources Timothy Dunbar cites or if you wanted to consult the originals, you could turn to the list of **works cited** at the end of his paper and locate the source using the information provided in the text, generally the author's last name.

```
                    Works Cited
Capelli, Chris. "Anything for a Better Grade."
      Campus Echo 23 Nov. 1993: 1+.
Kibler, William L., and Pamela Vannoy Kibler.
      "When Students Resort to Cheating."
      Chronicle of Higher Education 14 July 1993:
      B1-2.
Schroeder, Ken. "Give and Take: Part II."
      Education Digest 58.6 (1993): 73-74.
Sommers, Christina Hoff. "Teaching the Virtues."
      Public Interest 111 (1993): 3-13.
```

The in-text references and the list of works cited are parts of a process known as **documentation.** Documentation lets readers know that you are drawing words, concepts, or information from someone else's work. The documentation in Timothy Dunbar's paper follows the style suggested by the Modern Language Association. This style is one of four widely used styles of documentation.

Modern Language Association (MLA) style is generally used in English, foreign languages, and some other fields in the humanities and the arts. (See the following discussion in this chapter.)

American Psychological Association (APA) style is generally used in the social sciences. (See Chapter 47.)

Council of Biology Editors (CBE) style is generally used in the natural sciences. (See Chapter 48.)

Chicago Manual of Style (CMS) style is generally used in history and other fields in both the humanities and the sciences. (See Chapter 49.)

46a Understanding what to document, what not to document

In general, you need to document the words, ideas, and information you draw from another person's work. As you decide what to document and what not to document, bear in mind the two most important reasons for documenting sources: (1) to add support to your conclusions and credibility to your explanations by showing they are based on careful research, and (2) to acknowledge another person's hard work.

You need not document all ideas and information, however. Concepts and information that are common knowledge, such as facts or ideas that appear in several different sources you consult or that are likely to be familiar to people reading your paper, need no documentation. "Widely known" is a relative concept, however. If you are writing to a general audience, your readers may expect you to cite sources for your discussion of subatomic particles. If you are a physicist or are writing for a physics professor, however, you can probably assume that such matters are common knowledge.

You Must Document

Word-for-word (direct) quotations taken from someone else's writing, speaking, or electronic communication

Paraphrases or summaries of someone else's work, whether or not the work was published or was presented in a more informal setting such as an interview or e-mail

Ideas, opinions, and interpretations that other people have developed and presented, even if those concepts or theories are based on common knowledge

Facts or data that someone else has gathered or identified if the information has not become widely known enough to be considered common knowledge

Information that is not widely accepted or that is disputed

Illustrations, charts, graphs, photographs, recordings, original software, performances, interviews, and the like

But Do Not Document

Ideas, opinions, and interpretations that are your own

Widely known ideas and information—the sort that you can locate in common reference works or that people writing or speaking on a subject usually present as common knowledge

Commonly used quotations ("To be, or not to be")

**46b
doc**

46b Using in-text citations

The **MLA documentation style** is easy to use. It consists of an in-text citation (generally in parentheses) and a list of works cited (presented at the end of the text).

IN-TEXT CITATION

Although the average Haitian peasant calls himself a Catholic and
views himself as such, he generally continues to call on his African
ancestors' gods, or *loa,* for spiritual and emotional support. As one
peasant put it, "One must be Catholic to serve the loa" (Metraux 59).

— FREDZA LÉGER, College Student

ENTRY IN THE LIST OF WORKS CITED

Metraux, Alfred. Haiti: Black Peasants and
   Their Religion. London: Harrap, 1960.

For detailed treatment of the MLA documentation system, see the
MLA Handbook for Writers of Research Papers (4th ed., New York: MLA, 1995)
and *MLA Style Manual and Guide to Scholarly Publishing.* (New York: MLA,
1998).

An MLA in-text citation identifies the source, generally by giving the
author's name, and in doing so helps readers locate the source in the list of
works cited at the end of the paper. In addition, many in-text citations provide a page number or other specific reference to indicate exactly where in
the source readers can find the information being cited. Such information
can be cited in parentheses or in the text itself.

1. Use Parenthetical Citations

You can choose to provide the author's name (or other information
needed to identify the source in the list of works cited) within parentheses.
For quotations and other specific information, however, you need to do
more than provide the author's name. You also need to indicate the location in the source by providing a page number within parentheses. (For
advice on where to place parenthetical references within a passage, see p. 651.)

AUTHOR'S NAME IN PARENTHESES

Comparing the writing styles of individual authors in classic Chinese
literature is difficult because ancient China had "no concept of single authorship" (Liu 30).

Both the author's name and the page number are given in parentheses.

2. Include Citations in Your Discussion

You also can include the author's name, and sometimes other information as well, within your discussion.

AUTHOR'S NAME AS PART OF THE DISCUSSION

James Liu reminds us that it is difficult to compare the writing styles
of individual authors in classic Chinese literature because ancient
China had "no concept of single authorship" (30).

Only the page number is given in parentheses because the author has already been
mentioned in the discussion.

Writer's Tip

Punctuation and abbreviations are kept to a minimum when you use in-text parenthetical citations following the MLA documentation style. You do not place a comma between an author's name and a page number in a parenthetical reference, for example, nor do you use *p.* or *pp.* to indicate page(s), as in (Jenkins 134). (For advice on punctuating sentences containing parenthetical references, see p. 651.)

46c   Citing different kinds of references

Reference documentation comes in three kinds: general, specific, and informational. A **general reference** refers to the main ideas in a source or to information presented throughout the work, not in a single place. It may also refer to a book, article, or some other source as a whole. A **specific reference** documents words, ideas, or facts appearing in a particular place in a source, on a specific page, for example, or in a chart or drawing. An **informational reference** provides background information or discussion useful to some readers but too cumbersome or distracting to include in the text itself.

1. Cite Specific References to Pinpoint Information

When you use a quotation or specific information from a source, let your readers know the precise location of the original material by providing a page number or similar location within parentheses.

SPECIFIC REFERENCE

PARENTHETICAL   People have trouble recognizing the sound patterns dolphins use to communicate. Dolphins can perceive clicking sounds "made up of 700 units of sound per second," yet "in the human ear the sounds would fuse together in our minds at 20–30 clicks per second" (Bright 52).
The page number cites the specific location of the quotation.

AUTHOR NAMED IN DISCUSSION   According to Michael Bright, dolphins recognize patterns consisting of seven hundred clicks each second, yet such patterns begin to blur for people at around twenty or thirty clicks each second (52).
The page number cites the specific source of the paraphrase and facts.

2. Cite General References to Identify Main Ideas

When you are referring to the main ideas in a source or to ideas and information appearing throughout the source rather than in specific locations, you need not provide page numbers.

**46c
doc**

GENERAL REFERENCE

PARENTHETICAL Many species of animals have developed complex systems of communication (Bright).

> The statement summarizes one of the work's main points, so the reference cites the work as a whole, not a specific page or group of pages.

AUTHOR NAMED IN DISCUSSION According to Michael Bright, many species of animals have developed complex systems of communication.

Strategy

Use questions like these to help decide whether to make in-text citations general or specific and whether to make them parenthetical or part of the discussion.

- Am I trying to weave broad concepts into my own explanation or argument (general), or am I looking for precise ideas and details to support my conclusions (specific)?
- Will this part of my paper be clearer and more effective if I draw on the author's own words (specific), or if I merely point out that the author's text as a whole presents the concepts I am discussing (general)?
- Do I wish to highlight the source by naming the author (part of discussion), or to emphasize the information itself (parenthetical)?
- Will this passage be more concise, emphatic, or effective if I put the author's name in parentheses, or if I work it into the discussion?
- Do I wish to refer to more than one source without distracting readers (parenthetical), or do the several sources I am citing need individual attention (part of discussion)?

3. Consider Using Informative Footnotes and Endnotes

At times you may wish to comment on the usefulness or reliability of a source, provide some additional background details, or discuss a specific point at length, but you may recognize that to do so would disrupt the flow of the discussion and would be useful for only a few of your readers. At such points, the MLA documentation system suggests placing a number (raised slightly above the line of text) at a suitable point in your discussion. Then you can provide the note itself, labeled with a corresponding number, before the list of works cited on a page titled "Notes." (When a note comes at the end of a paper rather than at the bottom of a page, it is called an endnote rather than a footnote.)

> 1 Anyone still inclined to question the
> intricacy of video games and the conceptual

challenges they pose might consider investigating the numerous publications devoted to strategies for games like <u>Sonic the Hedgehog</u>, <u>Warrior of Rome</u>, and <u>Inspector X</u>.

Placement and Punctuation of Parenthetical Citations

In general, put parenthetical citations close to the quotation, information, paraphrase, or summary you are documenting. Place the parenthetical citation either at the end of a sentence (before the final punctuation) or at a natural pause in the sentence.

Wayland Hand reports on a folk belief that going to sleep on a rug made of bearskin can relieve backache (183).

If the citation applies to only part of the sentence, put it after the borrowed material at the point least likely to disrupt the sentence.

The folk belief that "sleeping on a bear rug will cure backache" (Hand 183) is yet another example of a kind of magic in which external objects produce results inside the body.

When you place an in-text parenthetical citation at the end of a long quotation set off as a block (see 34b), leave a space after the ending punctuation, then add the citation.

Many athletes are superstitious, especially baseball players, but perhaps the most suspicious of all are pitchers.

On the days they are scheduled to appear, many pitchers avoid activities that they believe sap their strength and therefore detract from their effectiveness, or that they otherwise generally link with poor performance. Many pitchers avoid eating certain foods on their pitching days. Some pitchers refuse to walk anywhere on the day of the game in the belief that every little exertion subtracts from their playing strength. One pitcher would never put on his cap until the game started and would not wear it at all on the days he did not pitch. (Gmelch 280)

If the material you are quoting contains quotation marks, use double quotation marks to enclose the quotation as a whole and single quotation marks to enclose the interior quotation.

According to Dubisch, "Being a 'health food person' involves more than simply changing one's diet or utilizing an alternative medical system" (61).

46c
doc

Did You Know?

Electronic information sources multiply rapidly every month and sometimes every day. They pose significant challenges for style guides and for writers preparing documentation. (Microform sources were a similar challenge twenty years ago.) Internet and CD-ROM sources have come on the scene within the last few years. Now the World Wide Web offers information at various electronic addresses. The next new source may be even more valuable and will certainly deserve accurate documentation.

46d Creating MLA in-text citations

In-text citations following MLA documentation style may take slightly differing forms depending on the number of authors, the number of volumes in a work, and the number of works being cited. (For advice on placing in-text citations within a passage and providing appropriate punctuation, see p. 651.)

Guide to MLA Formats for In-Text Citations

1. **Work with One Author**
2. **Work with Two or Three Authors**
3. **Work with More than Three Authors**
4. **Work with a Corporate or Group Author**
5. **Work with No Author Given**
6. **More than One Work by the Same Author**
7. **Authors with the Same Last Name**
8. **Work Cited in Another Source**
9. **Multivolume Work**
10. **Literary Work**
11. **Two or More Sources in a Citation**

46d
MLA

1. Work with One Author

For one author, provide the author's last name in a parenthetical citation. If you choose instead to make the author's name part of the discussion, use either the author's full name or last name alone. Then give only specific page references in parentheses.

PARENTHETICAL During World War II, government posters often portrayed homemakers "as vital defenders of the nation's homes" (Honey 135).

AUTHOR NAMED According to Maureen Honey, government posters during
IN DISCUSSION World War II often portrayed homemakers "as vital defenders of the nation's homes" (135).

2. Work with Two or Three Authors

For two authors, connect the names with *and* either in the text or in
a parenthetical citation. For three authors, use commas after the first two
names plus *and* before the third name. No comma is needed between the last
author's name and the page number.

PARENTHETICAL A century ago, whale oil was used not only for lighting but
also for making soap, wool cloth, paint, rope, and leather;
the bone was used not just for corsets but for making umbrellas, furniture, springs, fishing rods, and luggage (Norman
and Fraser 209).

If the book had three authors, the citation would read (Norman, Fraser,
and Jenko 209).

AUTHOR NAMED As Norman and Fraser point out, a century ago, whale oil was
IN TEXT used not only for lighting but also for making soap, wool
cloth, paint, rope, and leather; the bone was used not just
for corsets but for making umbrellas, furniture, springs, fishing rods, and luggage (209).

3. Work with More than Three Authors

With more than three authors, supply the first author's name and
then the phrase *et al.* (meaning "and others"). Do not place commas between
the author's name, *et al.*, or the page number in a parenthetical citation.

PARENTHETICAL Much of the writing that schoolchildren are required to do
takes the form of tests or teacher-designed exercises (Britton
et al. 24).

AUTHOR NAMED Britton and his colleagues point out that much of the wri-
IN TEXT ting schoolchildren are required to do takes the form of tests
or teacher-designed exercises (24).

If you give all the authors' names rather than "et al." in the entry in the
works cited list, you must also give all the names in the in-text citation (see
p. 660).

4. Work with a Corporate or Group Author

If an organization or government agency is named as the author of a
work, use its name (shortened, if cumbersome) to refer to the work. If the
name is long, consider placing it in your text to avoid an intrusive parenthetical citation.

46d
MLA

INTRUSIVE CITATION

Even in 1969, critics of the government's anti-communist policies were challenging the government's decision to divert money earmarked for education, health, and other "more fruitful programs" into "so-called national security" (American Friends Service Committee 118).

This form is correct, but the parenthetical reference is long and perhaps intrusive.

SOURCE NAMED IN TEXT

Even in 1969, the American Friends Service Committee criticized the government's decision to divert money earmarked for education, health, and other "more fruitful programs" into "so-called national security" (118).

Naming the organization responsible for the work in the discussion itself avoids the long parenthetical reference.

UNINTRUSIVE CITATION

Even in 1969, critics of the government's anti-communist policies were challenging the government's decision to divert money earmarked for education, health, and other "more fruitful programs" into "so-called national security" (American Friends 118).

The shortened name of the organization makes the parenthetical reference unintrusive.

5. Work with No Author Given

When your source does not indicate an author, use an abbreviated title in place of the author's name in a parenthetical citation. Begin the abbreviated title with the word used to alphabetize the work in the list of works cited.

On January 1, 1993, the former state of Czechoslovakia split into two new states, the Czech Republic and the Slovak Republic (*Baedeker's* 67).

The shortened title refers to *Baedeker's Czech/Slovak Republics,* a book for which no author is given.

6. More than One Work by the Same Author

When the list of works cited includes more than one work by the same author, add a shortened version of the title in the parenthetical citation. Use a comma between the author's name and the shortened title. You may use the entire title if it is brief.

The members of some Protestant groups in the Appalachian region view the "handling of serpents" during worship "as a supreme act of faith" (Daugherty, "Serpent-Handling" 232).

"Serpent-Handling" is a shortened version of "Serpent-Handling as Sacrament."

7. Authors with the Same Last Name

When the authors of two or more sources have the same last name, cite these sources by giving the first initial (or the full first name, if necessary) in order to identify the specific author.

> Although a number of Hebrew texts mention rebellious demons under the leadership of "Satanail" or "Satan" (D. Russell 110), the story of Satan and the rebellious angels gets its fullest development in Greek sources (J. Russell 192).

8. Work Cited in Another Source

When your source provides you with a quotation (or paraphrase) taken from yet another source, you need to include the phrase *qtd. in* (for "quoted in") to indicate accurately the source of the material.

> The play combines parts of two others, Shakespeare's *Hamlet* and Samuel Beckett's *Waiting for Godot,* in a manner Harold Bloom describes as a "kind of interlacing between an old play and a new one" (qtd. in Meyer 106).
>
> Meyer is the source of the quotation from Harold Bloom.

When referring to an indirect source, you should generally include in your discussion the name of the person from whom the quotation is taken. If the same information were presented in a parenthetical citation—(Bloom, qtd. in Meyer 106)—some readers might mistakenly look for Bloom rather than Meyer in the list of works cited.

9. Multivolume Work

If the work you are citing has several volumes, give the volume number followed by a colon and a space before you give the page number: (Franklin 6: 434). If you are referring to the volume as a whole, use a comma after the author's name and add *vol.* before the volume number, as in (Franklin, vol. 6).

> In the classic Chinese novel *The Story of the Stone*, the character Xi-chun outwardly accepts her fate but secretly wishes for a different life: "If only I had been born into a different family! If only I were free to become a nun!" (Cao 4: 177).
>
> The author's name is Cao, the volume number is 4, and the page number is 177.

10. Literary Work

When you refer to a literary work, consider including information that will help readers find the passage you are citing in any of the different

46d
MLA

editions of the work. Begin by giving the page number of the particular edition noted in your list of works cited followed by a semicolon; then add the appropriate chapter, part, or section numbers.

> In *Huckleberry Finn,* Mark Twain ridicules the exaggerated histrionics of provincial actors through his portrayal of the King and the Duke as they rehearse Hamlet's famous soliloquy: "So [the duke] went to marching up and down, thinking, and frowning horrible every now and then; then he would hoist up his eyebrows; next he would squeeze his hand on his forehead and stagger back and kind of moan; next he would sigh, and next he'd let on to drop a tear" (178; ch. 21).

Note that there is a semicolon after the page number, followed by *ch.* (for "chapter"). If you also include a part, use *pt.* followed by a comma and the chapter, as in (386; pt. 3, ch. 2). For a play, note the act, scene, and line numbers, if needed, as in (*Ham.* 1.2.76). If you are quoting the Bible, MLA style uses a period instead of a colon between the chapter and verse numbers (Mark 2.3–4).

11. Two or More Sources in a Citation

When you wish to use one parenthetical citation to refer to more than one source, separate the sources with a semicolon.

> Differences in the ways people speak, especially differences in the ways men and women use language, can often be traced to who has power and who does not (Tannen 83–86; Tavris 297–301).

46e   Creating an MLA list of works cited

In a list titled "Works Cited" and placed right after the last page of your paper, provide detailed information about the sources you have cited in your paper. If your assignment requires you to indicate all the works you consulted even if you did not cite them all in your paper, you may provide a list titled "Works Consulted." A list of works consulted shows the breadth of your research and includes all those works that would be placed in a list of works cited. (See the sample MLA research paper at the end of this chapter.)

When you prepare your list of works cited, alphabetize the entries according to the author's last name. Use last name and first name for authors with the same last name. If some of your sources do not identify an author, use the first word in the title (other than *a, an,* or *the*) for alphabetizing.

Guide to MLA Formats for a List of Works Cited

1. ENTRIES FOR BOOKS AND WORKS TREATED AS BOOKS

BOOKS
1. Book with One Author
2. Book with Two or Three Authors
3. Book with Four or More Authors
4. Book with a Corporate or Group Author
5. Book with No Author Given
6. More than One Book by the Same Author
7. Book with One Editor
8. Book with Two or More Editors
9. Book with an Author and an Editor
10. Book with a Translator
11. Book in an Edition Other than the First
12. Book Reprinted
13. One or More Volumes of a Multivolume Work
14. Book in a Series
15. Book Published Before 1900
16. Book with a Publisher's Imprint
17. Anthology or Collection of Articles
18. Book with a Title Within Its Title

WORKS TREATED AS BOOKS
19. Pamphlet
20. Published Dissertation
21. Unpublished Dissertation
22. Conference Proceedings

2. ENTRIES FOR ARTICLES AND SELECTIONS FROM BOOKS

ARTICLES
23. Article from a Journal Paginated by Volume
24. Article from a Journal Paginated by Issue
25. Article from a Weekly or Biweekly Periodical
26. Article from a Monthly or Bimonthly Periodical
27. Article from a Monthly or Weekly Periodical with No Author Given
28. Article from a Daily Newspaper
29. Editorial
30. Letter to the Editor
31. Published Interview
32. Review with a Title
33. Review Without a Title
34. Article from an Encyclopedia or Reference Volume, with Author
35. Article from an Encyclopedia or Reference Volume, with No Author Given
36. Article from an Annual Reference Series, with Author

SELECTIONS
37. Selection from an Anthology or Collection
38. Anthology Selection Reprinted from Another Source
39. More than One Selection from an Anthology or Collection (Cross-reference)

**46e
MLA**

(cont.)

Guide to MLA Formats for a List of Works Cited *(cont.)*

40. Preface, Foreword, Introduction, or Afterword
41. Letter Published in a Collection
42. Dissertation Abstract

3. ENTRIES FOR OTHER PRINTED AND FIELD RESOURCES
43. Government Publication
44. Map or Chart
45. Cartoon
46. Advertisement
47. Unpublished Interview
48. Unpublished Letter
49. Surveys and Questionnaires
50. Observations

51. Performance
52. Lecture

4. ENTRIES FOR MEDIA AND ELECTRONIC RESOURCES
53. Film or Videotape
54. Television or Radio Program
55. Recording
56. Artwork
57. Database Scholarly Project, or Information Service
58. Online Book
59. Online Article
60. Online or CD-ROM Abstract
61. Personal or Professional Site
62. E-mail and Online Postings

---

1 Entries for books and works treated as books

MODEL FORMAT FOR BOOKS AND WORKS TREATED AS BOOKS

period + space   period + space   colon + space

Author(s). <u>Title of Work</u>. Place of Publication:

Publisher, Year Published.

indent five spaces   comma + space   period

46e
MLA

- **Author(s).** Give the author's last name first, followed by the first name (spelled out unless the author uses initials) and any middle name or initial. Use a period at the end of the name. Do not include titles like M.D. or SJ, but include other parts of a name, like *III* or *Jr.,* placing them at the end of the name preceded by a comma: Louis Valantasio, Jr. If the book has more than one author, give the other names in regular order, separated by commas, unless there are more than three authors. (See Entries 1, 2, and 3 on pages 659–660 for the correct forms for authors' names.)
- **Title of Work.** Next give the title of the work, including any sub-title. (Use a colon to introduce a subtitle except when the primary

title ends with a question mark, dash, or exclamation point.) Underline the title with the main words capitalized and end with a period unless the title ends with some other mark of punctuation. Do not underline the period.

- **Publication Information.** Following the title, provide publication information, beginning with the city where the work was published, followed by a colon and a single space. If a city is in another country and is likely to be unfamiliar or confusing to your readers, add the country's name, abbreviated as in Dover, Eng. If more than one place of publication appears in the work, use the first one in your citation. Then give the publisher's name followed by a comma and the date of publication followed by a period. Use the minimal information needed to identify the publisher—*Publisher, Inc.,* and *Co.* are not necessary. (For example, use just McGraw, not McGraw-Hill, Inc.) University presses are abbreviated by substituting *U* and *P* for the words *University* and *Press* where they appear in the publisher's name (for example, U of Chicago P). If any of the basic publication information is not provided in the work, use *n.p.* (no place or no publisher) or *n.d.* (no date).
- **Spacing.** Double-space all entries, and indent five spaces for the second and any additional lines in each entry. Leave spaces between each of the major elements in an entry (author's name, title of work, and publication information).

Books

1. Book with One Author

Sunstein, Cass R. <u>Feminism and Political</u>
<u>Theory</u>. Chicago: U of Chicago P, 1990.

2. Book with Two or Three Authors

Give the first author's name, starting with the last name, followed by the other names in the sequence in which they appear on the title page. Give the other names in regular order, first name and then last name. Use commas to separate the names, and conclude with a period. Introduce the second of two names or the third name with *and,* for example, Russell, Christina G., and Robert L. McDonald, *or* Slotnick, Marvin M., Kente Obote, and Patricia Jones Robinson.

Howe, Henry F., and Lynn C. Westley. <u>Ecological</u>
<u>Relationships of Plants and Animals</u>. New
York: Oxford UP, 1988.

3. Book with Four or More Authors

Use the first author's name and then the phrase *et al.*, which means "and others."

> Bellah, Robert N., et al. <u>Habits of the Heart:</u>
>
>   <u>Individualism and Commitment in American</u>
>
>   <u>Life</u>. Berkeley: U of California P, 1985.

You may choose to give all the names rather than use the phrase *et al.* If you do, you must give them all in any parenthetical references as well (see p. 653).

> Bellah, Robert N., Richard Madsen, William M.
>
>   Sullivan, Ann Swidler, and Steven M.
>
>   Tipton. <u>Habits of the Heart: Individualism</u>
>
>   <u>and Commitment in American Life</u>. Berkeley:
>
>   U of California P, 1985.

4. Book with a Corporate or Group Author

Treat the corporation, organization, or government agency as the author, and list the entry alphabetically by the first main word of the organization's name. If the organization is also the publisher, include the name again as publisher, abbreviated if appropriate.

> American Friends Service Committee. <u>Anatomy of</u>
>
>   <u>AntiCommunism: A Report Prepared for the</u>
>
>   <u>Peace Education Division of the American</u>
>
>   <u>Friends Service Committee</u>. New York: Hill,
>
>   1969.
>
> American Library Association. <u>500 Books for the</u>
>
>   <u>Senior High School Library</u>. Chicago:
>
>   American Library Association, 1930.

5. Book with No Author Given

List the work alphabetically according to the first main word of its title.

> <u>Guide for Authors</u>. Oxford: Blackwell, 1985.

6. More than One Book by the Same Author

When you include multiple works by an author, list them alphabetically by the first main word of the title. For the first source, include the author's full name. For any additional sources, use three hyphens in place of the author's name, followed by a period and a space. Use this format only if the author or authors are *exactly* the same for each source. For instance, do not use the hyphens if the author wrote the first book by herself but was one of several authors of the second book; in such a case, include the names of all the authors in full.

> Tannen, Deborah. <u>Conversational Style:</u>
>
>   <u>Analyzing Talk Among Friends</u>. Norwood:
>
>   Ablex, 1984.
>
> ---. <u>That's Not What I Meant! How Conversational</u>
>
>   <u>Style Makes or Breaks Your Relations with</u>
>
>   <u>Others</u>. New York: Morrow, 1986.

Use a comma rather than a period after the hyphens, followed by *ed.*, *trans.*, or the like, when the person's role is other than that of author.

7. Book with One Editor

If the book is a collection of materials and has an editor rather than an author, begin your entry with the editor's name. Follow the editor's name with a comma and the abbreviation *ed.*

> Davis, Marianna W., ed. <u>Contributions of Black</u>
>
>   <u>Women to America</u>. Columbia: Kenday, 1982.

8. Book with Two or More Editors

If a book has two or more editors, use the format for multiple authors (see Entries 2 and 3 earlier in this list), and include the abbreviation *eds.*

> Achebe, Chinua, and C. L. Innes, eds. <u>African</u>
>
>   <u>Short Stories</u>. London: Heinemann, 1985.

9. Book with an Author and an Editor

> Weber, Max. <u>The Theory of Social and Economic</u>
>
>   <u>Organization</u>. Ed. Talcott Parsons. Trans.
>
>   A. M. Henderson and Talcott Parsons. New
>
>   York: Free, 1964.

46e
MLA

10. Book with a Translator

Refer to the book by its author, not its translator, even though the English words are the translator's. Abbreviate the translator's title as *Trans.* You do not have to use *by.*

> Rheims, Maurice. <u>The Flowering of Art Nouveau</u>.
>
>   Trans. Patrick Evans. New York: Abrams,
>
>   1966.

If you are using the citation to refer specifically to the work of the translator, give that person's name first, adding a comma and *trans.* Then supply the title, and use *By* to introduce the author's name.

> Evans, Patrick, trans. <u>The Flowering of Art</u>
>
>   <u>Nouveau</u>. By Maurice Rheims. New York:
>
>   Abrams, 1966.

For a work with both an editor and a translator, give the names in the order they appear on the title page, preceding each with the appropriate abbreviation.

11. Book in an Edition Other than the First

Follow the title with a period; then give the edition number or description (*Rev. ed.* or *1996 ed.*, for example).

> Zinsser, William. <u>On Writing Well</u>. 3rd ed. New
>
>   York: Harper, 1985.

**46e
MLA**

12. Book Reprinted

Supply the original publication date after the title; you do not need to include the original publisher or place of publication, though you may choose to do so if the information is pertinent. Follow the original date with the publication information from the work you are using, including its publication date.

> Ondaatje, Michael. <u>The Collected Works of Billy</u>
>
>   <u>the Kid</u>. 1970. Harmondsworth, Eng.:
>
>   Penguin, 1984.

13. One or More Volumes of a Multivolume Work

Indicate the total number of volumes after the title or after the editor's or translator's name. (Use your parenthetical in-text citation to specify the volume and page where you found particular information.)

```
Tsao, Hsueh-chin. The Story of the Stone.

    Trans. David Hawkes. 5 vols.

    Harmondsworth, Eng.: Penguin, 1973-86.
```

If you are citing a particular volume instead of the whole work, supply only its number and publication information. When citing this volume in your text in a parenthetical entry, you need not specify the volume number because the list of works cited will refer only to the particular volume. (If you wish, you may indicate the total number of volumes at the end of the entry.)

```
Tsao, Hsueh-chin. The Story of the Stone.

    Trans. David Hawkes. Vol. 1.

    Harmondsworth, Eng.: Penguin, 1973. 5

    vols.
```

14. Book in a Series

Supply the series name and any item number after the title of the specific work. Use abbreviation for familiar words in the name of the series (such as *ser.* for *series*).

```
Hess, Gary R. Vietnam and the United States:

    Origins and Legacy of War. International

    History Ser. 7. Boston: Twayne, 1990.
```

15. Book Published Before 1900

The publisher is not needed in citations for books published before 1900, although you may include the information if it is relevant to your paper. Use a comma rather than a colon after the place of publication.

46e
MLA

```
Darwin, Charles. Descent of Man and Selection

    in Relation to Sex. New York, 1896.
```

16. Book with a Publisher's Imprint

Some books are issued with special imprint names. Put the imprint name first, supply a hyphen, and then add the main publisher's name.

```
Weyler, Rex. Song of the Whale. Garden City:

    Anchor-Doubleday, 1986.
```

The special imprint is Anchor Books.

17. Anthology or Collection of Articles

To refer to an anthology or a collection of scholarly articles as a whole, supply the editor's name first, followed by *ed.*, and then the title of the collection.

> Zipes, Jack, ed. Don't Bet on the Prince:
>
> Contemporary Feminist Fairy Tales in North
>
> America and England. New York: Methuen,
>
> 1986.

To cite a selection within an anthology or collection, use the forms outlined in Entries 37 to 39 (pages 669–670).

18. Book with a Title Within Its Title

When a book title contains the title of another work, do not underline the second work. If the title of the second work would normally be enclosed in quotation marks, however, underline the entire title and include the quotation marks in your entry (see Entries 37 to 39).

> MacPherson, Pat. Reflecting on Jane Eyre.
>
> London: Routledge, 1989.
>
> Golden, Catherine, ed. The Captive Imagination:
>
> A Casebook on "The Yellow Wallpaper." New
>
> York: Feminist, 1992.

Works Treated as Books

19. Pamphlet

Use the same form for a pamphlet as for a book. If you don't know the author, publisher, or date, include as much information as you can find. If no author is identified, put the title first and alphabetize by the first main word of the title.

> Ellis, Alec. Books in Victorian Elementary
>
> Schools. London: Library Assn., 1971.

20. Published Dissertation

Treat a published doctoral dissertation as a book, underlining the title, but include the abbreviation *Diss.*, the school for which the dissertation was written, and the year the degree was received. (See Entry 42 for a dissertation abstract.)

```
Said, Edward W. Joseph Conrad and the Fiction
     of Autobiography. Diss. Harvard U, 1964.
     Cambridge: Harvard UP, 1966.
```

21. Unpublished Dissertation

Use quotation marks rather than underlining for the titles of unpublished dissertations; include the abbreviation *Diss.*, the school for which the dissertation was written, and the date of the degree. (See Entry 42 for a dissertation abstract.)

```
Anku, William Oscar. "Procedures in African
     Drumming: A Study of Akan/Ewe Traditions
     and African Drumming in Pittsburgh." Diss.
     U of Pittsburgh, 1988.
```

22. Conference Proceedings

Alphabetize the citation by title unless an editor is named. Follow this with details about the conference, including its name and the date it was held.

```
Environmental Impacts and Solutions. Proc. of
     the International Conference on
     Residential Solid Fuels, 3-7 June 1981.
     Beaverton: Oregon Graduate Center, 1982.
```

46e
MLA

2 Entries for articles and selections from books

MODEL FORMAT FOR ARTICLES AND SELECTIONS

```
        period + space          period space          space
             ↓                    ↓ ↓                   ↓
Author(s). "Title of Article." Title of Journal
        Volume Number (Year Published): Page numbers.
     ↑                    ↑                   ↑              ↑
indent five spaces      space          colon + space     period
```

- **Author(s).** Begin with the author's name, followed by a period. Give the last name first, followed by the first name and any initial. If the piece has more than one author, give subsequent names in regular order separated by commas with *and* preceding the final name.

- **Title of Article.** Give the article's full title in quotation marks, concluding with a period, unless the title ends with a question mark or exclamation point.
- **Title of Journal, Periodical, or Book.** Give the publication's title, underlined, but not including an opening *The, A,* or *An.* Do not end the title with a period.
- **Publication Information.** Next supply the volume number (and sometimes the issue number), the year of publication (in parentheses), and the page numbers for the full article or selection. The volume number is always found on the publication's cover or title page; even if it is in Roman numerals, use Arabic numerals for your entry. For a scholarly journal, you don't need to include the month. Introduce the page numbers with a colon.
- **Spacing.** Double-space all entries, and indent five spaces for the second and any additional lines in each entry. Leave a space between each of the major elements in an entry (author's name, article or selection title, and journal title along with publication information). Leave a space between the colon and the page number and also between the journal title, the volume number, and the date of publication.

Articles

23. Article from a Journal Paginated by Volume

A volume is generally made up of several issues of a journal. If the journal is paginated by volume, the whole volume is numbered in one sequence from page 1 on; each issue begins where the preceding left off—at page 254, for example—rather than at page 1.

```
Tobacyk, Jerome. "Superstitions and Beliefs

     About the Prediction of Future Events."

     Psychological Reports 68 (1991): 511-12.
```

24. Article from a Journal Paginated by Issue

In a journal paginated by issue, each issue begins with page 1. You need to include the issue number in the entry as well as the volume so that readers know where to look for the source. Include the volume number first, followed by a period and the issue number.

```
Decker-Collins, Norma. "Freewriting, Personal

     Writing, and the At-Risk Reader." Journal

     of Reading 33.8 (1990): 654-55.
```
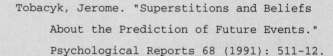
The volume number is 33; the issue number is 8.

25. Article from a Weekly or Biweekly Periodical

Treat popular magazines differently from academic journals. Instead of the volume and issue numbers, for weekly or biweekly magazines, provide the date. Put the day first, then the month (abbreviated except for May, June, and July), and then the year followed by a colon. Give inclusive page numbers. If the articles pages are not consecutive, give the first page with a plus sign (for example, 23+).

```
Gorman, Christine. "Invincible AIDS." Time 3

     Aug. 1992: 30-34.
```

26. Article from a Monthly or Bimonthly Periodical

Treat these references as you would weekly magazines (see Entry 25), but without listing the day.

```
Harris, Daniel. "Blonde Ambitions: The Rise of

     Madonna Studies." Harper's Magazine Aug.

     1992: 30-33.
```

27. Article from a Monthly or Weekly Periodical with No Author Given

When the author is not named in your source, begin with the title (ignoring *A, An,* and *The* when alphabetizing).

```
"Horseplay." New Yorker 5 Apr. 1993: 36-38.
```

28. Article from a Daily Newspaper

Treat a newspaper as a weekly magazine (see Entry 25), but include the section number with the page number. Omit *The, A,* or *An* at the beginning of a newspaper's name. For a local newspaper, give the city's name in brackets after the title unless the city is named in the title. (For pages that are not consecutive, see Entry 25.)

```
Roth, Terence. "Stumbling Blocs? It's Too Soon

     to Tell Whether Regional Trade Groups Will

     Help--or Hinder--GATT." Wall Street

     Journal 24 Sept. 1992: R23.
```
The section is *R;* the page number is 23.

29. Editorial

Supply the title first for an unsigned editorial and the author's name first for a signed editorial. Use the word *Editorial* to identify this kind of source.

```
"Academics and Athletics." Editorial. Providence

     Journal-Bulletin 15 July 1995: A8.
```

```
Bethel, Martha A. "Terror in Montana."

     Editorial. New York Times 20 July 1995:

     A23.
```

30. Letter to the Editor
Use the word *Letter* to identify this type of source.

```
Varley, Colin. Letter. Archaeology May-June

     1993: 10.
```

31. Published Interview
The person interviewed, not the interviewer, should be considered the author because interviews are transcriptions of the person's actual words. For untitled interviews, include the word *Interview* (without underlining or quotation marks) in place of a title. (See Entry 47 for unpublished interviews.)

```
Tan, Amy. "Joy, Luck, and Literature." By Anita

     Merina. NEA Today 10 (1991): 9.
```

32. Review with a Title
When a review has a title, give it after the name of the reviewer. Cite an unsigned review by its title.

```
Honig, Alice Sterling. "Helping Children

     Problem-Solve." Rev. of I Can Problem

     Solve: An Interpersonal Cognitive

     Problem-solving Program, by Myrna Shure.

     Day Care and Early Education 21.1 (1993):

     34-35.
```

46e
MLA

33. Review without a Title
Begin the entry with the name of the reviewer. Follow the name with the abbreviated phrase *Rev. of* ("Review of") before giving the title of the work reviewed followed by a comma, the word *by,* and the author of the work. The periodical information should follow the appropriate format for its type. To cite a review of a performance, follow the title with a comma and provide information about the production, such as the director, the group responsible for the presentation, or the theater.

```
Stuttaford, Genevieve. Rev. of Imaginary

     Homelands, by Salman Rushdie. Publishers

     Weekly 1 Mar. 1991: 61.
```

34. Article from an Encyclopedia or Reference Volume, with Author

Give the author's name before the title. Many reference works use initials after an entry to identify the author and then list all the authors' full names at the beginning or end of the work. (See also Entry 35.)

```
Hansen, Klaus J. "Mormonism." The Encyclopedia
     of Religion. Ed. Mircea Eliade. 20 vols.
     New York: Macmillan, 1987.
```

35. Article from an Encyclopedia or Reference Volume, with No Author Given

Begin with the title of the article and then the name of the reference work. You do not need to include the publisher or place of publication for a common reference work or series. If the work arranges entries in alphabetical order, do not provide a volume number; give the volume number if the reader needs it to determine which volume contains the selection being cited. For well-known reference works and those with frequent new editions, the edition number (when available) and the date are sufficient. For reference works that are not well known or that have appeared in only one edition, give the full publication information. (See the examples below and those for Entry 34.)

```
"The History of Western Theatre." The New
     Encyclopaedia Britannica: Macropedia. 15th
     ed. 1987. Vol. 28.
"Sir Philip Sidney." Literature Criticism from
     1400 to 1800. Vol. 19.
```

36. Article from an Annual Reference Series, with Author

You do not need to include the publisher or the volume number when a common reference series has only one volume per year, includes the year in the title, and arranges articles in alphabetical order.

```
Caldwell, Joseph. "Shiva Naipaul." Dictionary
     of Literary Biography Yearbook: 1985.
```

Selections

37. Selection from an Anthology or Collection

List the author of the selection you are citing. Put the title of the selection in quotation marks, but underline titles of novels, plays, and other works first published on their own. Next provide the underlined title of the book in which it appears. Make sure you include the selection's page numbers at the end of the citation. Give a translator's name after the selection's title.

> Atwood, Margaret. "Bluebeard's Egg."
>
>   "Bluebeard's Egg" and Other Stories. New
>
>   York: Fawcett-Random, 1987. 131-64.

38. Anthology Selection Reprinted from Another Source

Begin with information on the original source using the appropriate form, such as that for a work included in an anthology (see Entry 37) or for an article in a journal. Then give information about the source you are using prefaced by *Rpt. in* ("reprinted in"), including the publication information for the reprinted source.

> Atwood, Margaret. "Bluebeard's Egg."
>
>   "Bluebeard's Egg" and Other Stories. New
>
>   York: Fawcett-Random, 1987. 131-64. Rpt.
>
>   in Don't Bet on the Prince: Contemporary
>
>   Feminist Fairy Tales in North America and
>
>   England. Ed. Jack Zipes. New York:
>
>   Methuen, 1986. 160-82.

39. More than One Selection from an Anthology or Collection (Cross-reference)

When you cite two or more works from an anthology or collection, include an entry for the collection itself and provide cross-references for individual selections.

> Howard, Jean E., and Marion F. O'Connor, eds.
>
>   Shakespeare Reproduced: The Text in
>
>   History and Ideology. New York: Methuen,
>
>   1987.

Entry for collection.

> Erickson, Peter. "The Order of the Garter, the
>
>   Cult of Elizabeth, and Class-Gender
>
>   Tension in The Merry Wives of Windsor."
>
>   Howard and O'Connor 116-42.

Individual selection.

> Goldberg, Jonathan. "Speculation: Macbeth and
>
>   Source." Howard and O'Connor 242-64.

Individual selection.

40. Preface, Foreword, Introduction, or Afterword

Indicate whether the section is a preface, foreword, introduction, or afterword immediately following the name of its author. Then give the title of the work, the word *By* plus the name of its author, and publication information. Conclude with the page numbers for the section.

```
Boring, Edwin G. Introduction. ESP: A

    Scientific Evaluation. By C. E. M. Hansel.

    New York: Scribner's, 1966. iii-xi.
```

41. Letter Published in a Collection

Treat the letter writer as the author. Include the date of the letter or the collection number of the letter if the information is available. Letter collections usually have an editor, so make sure you include the editor's name. (For unpublished letters, see Entry 48.)

```
Brevoort, Henry. "To Washington Irving." 9 July

    1828. Letter 124 of Letters of Henry

    Brevoort to Washington Irving. Ed. George

    S. Hellman. New York: Putnam, 1918.
```

42. Dissertation Abstract

To cite an abstract of a dissertation appearing in *Dissertation Abstracts International (DAI)* or *Dissertation Abstracts (DA),* give the author's name, the title in quotation marks, the abbreviation *Diss.* (for dissertation), the name of the institution, and the date of the degree. Follow this with the publication information for the volume of abstracts. (See Entries 20 and 21 for published and unpublished dissertations.)

```
Hawkins, Joanne Berning. "Horror Cinema and the

    Avant-Garde." Diss. U. of California,

    Berkeley, 1993. DAI 55 (1995): 1712A.
```
A is the series of volumes for humanities and social sciences.

3 Entries for other printed and field resources

Use the following formats for sources other than books or articles.

43. Government Publication

Begin the citation with the government or agency names. Start with "United States" if the document is a congressional document or a report from a federal agency. Occasionally you may cite a report written by an independent agency and submitted to the government, in which case you include the independent agency as author. Include any other information necessary for a reader to find the document easily. If it is a congressional document, write *Cong.* to indicate that it is from the Congress, identify the branch (Senate or House), and give the number and session (for example, 101st Cong., 1st sess.). Include the title of the specific document and the title of the book in which it is printed. Use the abbreviation *GPO* for the federal Government Printing Office.

> United States. National Research Council.
>
>> Committee on Global Change. Research
>>
>> Strategies for the U.S. Global Change
>>
>> Research Program. Washington: National
>>
>> Academy, 1990.
>
> United States. Cong. Senate. Committee on
>
>> Environmental and Public Works.
>>
>> Subcommittee on Environmental Protection.
>>
>> Policy Options for Stabilizing Global
>>
>> Climate: Hearing. 101st Cong., 1st sess.
>>
>> Washington: GPO, 1989.

44. Map or Chart

Supply the item's title, identify it as a map or chart, and add the publication information.

> Southeastern United States. Map. Chicago: Rand,
>
>> 1993.

45. Cartoon

Provide the cartoonist's name and the title of the cartoon, if one is given. Include the word *Cartoon* and the publication information.

> Koren. Cartoon. New Yorker 17 May 1993: 48.
>
> Guisewite, Cathy. "Cathy." Cartoon. Providence
>
>> Sunday Journal 23 July 1995: F3.

46. Advertisement

Begin with the name of the subject of the advertisement (product, company, organization). Then include the word *Advertisement* and the appropriate publication information.

> Acura Integra. Advertisement. Elle Dec. 1995:
>
>> 134-135.

47. Unpublished Interview

Give the name of the person interviewed. Then indicate the type of interview: *Personal interview* (you did the interview in person), *Telephone interview* (you talked to the person over the telephone), or *Interview* (someone else conducted the interview). Then give the date of the interview, or give appropriation citation information with the date of publication or broadcast.

```
Danesh, Hasan. Personal interview. 7 Oct. 1994.

Novak, Robert. Interview with Charlie Rose. The

     Charlie Rose Show. PBS. WGBH, Boston. 29

     Nov. 1993.
```

48. Unpublished Letter

Give the author's name, a brief description (for example, *Letter to Jane Cote*), and the date. Identify letters addressed to you with the phrase *Letter to the author*. For letters exchanged between other people, give the name and location of any library or archive holding the letter in its collection. If the letter has an identifying number, give it before the name of the library.

```
Hall, Donald. Letter to the author. 24 January

     1990.
```

(For a letter in a published collection, see Entry 41.)

49. Surveys and Questionnaires

MLA does not specify a form for these field resources. When citing your own field research, you may wish to use the following form for surveys and questionnaires.

```
Thomsen, LaVonda. Survey of student attitudes

     on personal appearance. University of

     Rhode Island, Kingston, RI. 13-15 Nov.

     1995.
```

50. Observations

Because MLA does not specify a model for this type of field research, you may wish to use the following form to cite your notes on field observations of behaviors or events.

```
Sanchez, Darren. Observations of shoppers in a

     grocery store checkout line. Evergreen

     Park, IL. 22 Feb. 1994.
```

**46e
MLA**

51. Performance

Following the title of the play, concert, opera, or dance performance, supply the name of the director, the theater and city where the performance took place, and the date. When relevant to your purposes, include the names of actors or others involved in the production.

```
For Colored Girls Who Have Considered Suicide

    When the Rainbow Is Enuf. By Ntozake Shange.

    Dir. Ntozake Shange. New Federal Theater,

    New York. 20 July 1995.
```

(Entry 33 discussed the review form for a performance.)

52. Lecture

For a speech or an address, identify the speaker, the title (or type of presentation), and details about the meeting at which it was given, the group that sponsored the meeting, and where and when the presentation was made.

```
Dunkelman, Martha. "Images of Salome in Italian

    Renaissance Art." The Renaissance Woman, II,

    session. Sixteenth Century Studies Conf.

    Adam's Mark Hotel, St. Louis. 11 Dec. 1993.
```

4 Entries for media and electronic resources

For Internet and other electronic resources, the *MLA Style Manual and Guide to Scholarly Publishing* (1998) makes the following recommendations:

- **Publication Dates.** Give both the date when the material was initially posted to the Internet (or last revised or updated) and the date you accessed the source.
- **Uniform Resource Located (URL).** Provide a complete URL for the source preceded by an access-mode identifier (e.g., *http, gopher, telnet,* or *ftp*). Enclose the URL with angle brackets (< >). If you need more than one line for a URL, break only after a slash, and do not include a hyphen to mark the break.
- **Page Numbering.** If the source provides page or paragraph numbers, include them.

53. Film or Videotape

Alphabetize according to the title of the work. The director's name is usually necessary; include names of actors, producers, writers, musicians or others only if they are important to identifying the work or to your discussion. Include the company that distributes the film, the date, and other relevant information.

```
Rosencrantz and Guildenstern Are Dead. Dir. Tom

        Stoppard. Perf. Gary Oldman, Tim Roth, and

        Richard Dreyfuss. Cinecom Entertainment, 1990.
```

For a videotape, filmstrip, or similar resource, indicate the medium—videocassette, videodisc, and so forth. If the date of the original version is important, add this just before the description of the medium.

```
Rosencrantz and Guildenstern Are Dead. Dir. Tom

        Stoppard. Perf. Gary Oldman, Tim Roth, and

        Richard Dreyfuss. Videocassette. Buena Vista

        Home Video, 1990.
```

54. Television or Radio Program

Begin with the title of the episode, and use it to alphabetize. Give the program's name and include the names of the writer, director, actors, or others only if pertinent. Use abbreviations for their roles, for example, *Writ., Dir., Prod., Perf., Cond., Introd.,* or *Narr.*

```
"Louie and the Nice Girl." Taxi. Dir. James

        Burrows. ABC. 11 Sept. 1979.
```

55. Recording

Begin the entry with the title of the recording or the name of the person whose role you wish to emphasize, for example, the performer, the composer, the conductor, or the speaker. Underline the title of the compact disc, tape, or record. Put the work's name in quotation marks unless it is identified by key, form, or number, such as Symphony in A minor, no. 41. Continue with performers or others involved, manufacturer, and year the recording was issued. Indicate medium if other than a compact disc, e.g., *audiocassette* or *LP* (for a record).

```
Mozart, Wolfgang Amadeus. Symphony no. 40 in G

        minor. Vienna Philharmonic. Audiocassette.

        Cond. Leonard Bernstein. Deutsche Grammophon,

        1984.
```

56. Artwork

Give the artist's name, the work's, and it's location. Because many museum and gallery names are similar, indicate the city.

```
Uccello, Paolo. Saint George and the Dragon.

        National Gallery, London.
```

**46e
MLA**

57. Database, Scholarly Project, or Information Service

Databases containing information or texts are available online or on CD-ROM. Give the title of the database, project, or service; name of the editor; and online information (including date of access and URL) or CD-ROM publication information.

ONLINE SCHOLARLY PROJECT OR DATABASE

Jack London Collection. 1996. Berkeley Digital

    Library SunSITE. 25 Apr. 1998.

    <http://sunsite.berkeley.edu/London/>.

58. Online Book

Include the author's name and the title; the name(s) of any editor, compiler, or translator (if relevant); information about print publication (if any); electronic publication information, and date of access and URL.

ONLINE BOOK WITHIN A SCHOLARLY PROJECT

London, Jack. The Iron Steel. New York: Macmillan,

    1908. The Jack London Collection. 16 Oct.

    1996. Berkeley Digital Library SunSITE.

    1 May 1998.<http://sunsite.berkeley.edu/

    London/Writings/IronHeel/>.

59. Online Article

Give the author; title of article; name of periodical; details about the volume, issue, item number; and date of publication. Indicate page numbers, or give number of pages, paragraphs, or numbered sections (if any). Provide date of access and URL. (For articles on CD-ROM or diskette, see Entry 60.)

ARTICLE IN A SCHOLARLY JOURNAL

Lewis, Deanna L., and Ron Chepesuik. "The Inter-

    national Trade in Toxic Waste: A Selected

    Bibliography." Electronic Green Journal 1.2

    (1994) 29 Apr. 1996.

    ftp://ftp.uiadaho.edupub/docs/pub/

    publications/EGJ>.

ARTICLE IN A NEWSPAPER OR ON A NEWSWIRE

Warren, Jennifer. "Assembly Bill Requires

    Parental OK for Body Piercing." Los Angeles

46e
MLA

```
Times 28 May 1997 <http://www.aegis.com/
aegis/news/lat/ltl1997/lt970517.html>.
```

ARTICLE IN A MAGAZINE

```
Rickford, John R. "Suite for Ebony and Phonics."
Discover Dec. 1997. 25 Feb. 1998. <http://
www.discover.com/archive/index.html>.
```

60. Online or CD-ROM Abstract

ONLINE ABSTRACT

```
Prelow, Hazel., and charles A. Guarnaccia. "Ethnic
and Racial Differences in Life Stress Among
High School Adolescents." Journal of coun-
seling & Development 75.6 (1997). Abstract,
6 Apr. 1998 <http://www.counseling.org/
journals/jcdjul197.htm#Prelow>.
```

CD-ROM ABSTRACT (OR ARTICLE)

Give author's name; publication information for parallel printed source (title and date); database title; publication medium (CD-ROM, diskette); name of vendor; date of electronic publication.

61. Personal or Professional Site

```
Baron, Dennis. Dennis Baron. 5 May 1998 <http://
www.english.uiuc.edu/baron/index.htm>.
```

62. E-mail and Online Postings

Give writer's name, title (or type) of communication, and date.

```
Trimbur, John. E-mail to the author. 17 Sept. 1997.
```

ONLINE POSTINGS

If you can, aid readers by citing a stored version, perhaps a Web file. Label as appropriate, for example, *online posting* or *online debate*.

```
Woolly, Simon. "Re: Hooked on Ebonics?" 24 Dec.
1996. Online posting. Philadelphia Online:
Talk Show. 2 June 1998 <http://
interactive.phillynews.com/talk-show/
schools postings/199.html>.
```

Exercise

A.   Rewrite the following sentences to add MLA-style in-text citations.

1. After the fact, however, Johanson and Edey admitted, "Neither of us was prepared for the explosion of interest that followed the formal disclosure of *afarensis* in print."

    The quotation is from page 294 of Donald Johanson and Maitland Edey's book *Lucy: The Beginnings of Humankind* (New York: Simon and Schuster, 1990).

2. In Samoa during the 1930s, girls separated socially from their siblings at about age seven and began to form close and lasting relationships with other girls their age.

    The reference is to Margaret Mead's discussion in *Coming of Age in Samoa,* originally issued in 1928 and reprinted in 1961 by Morrow Publishers in their Morrow Quill paperback series. It cites the general discussion in Chapter 5, "The Girl and Her Age Group," on pages 59 through 73 of the 1961 edition.

B.   Create a list of works cited using MLA style, and include the following items.

1. An article reviewing books on Latin American families. The author is Elizabeth Anne Kuzenesof. Her review is titled "The History of the Family in Latin America." It appeared in the Spring 1989 issue of *Latin American Research Review* on pages 168–189 (paginated by issue). This issue of the journal was number 2 in volume 24.

2. An interview of Donald Davis published in the October 1992 edition (volume 67) of the *Wilson Library Bulletin.* The interviewer was Judith O'Malley, and the interview appeared on pages 52 and 53. The periodical appears monthly.

3. A book of 280 pages by Vera Rosenbluth titled *Keeping Family Stories Alive.* The subtitle is *A Creative Guide to Taping Your Family Life and Lore.* It was published in 1990 by Hartley and Marks, a publisher in Point Roberts, Washington.

4. A collection of the stories of Shalom Aleichem titled *Around the Table: Family Stories of Shalom Aleichem.* The collection was edited by Aliza Shevron and translated by her. The book was illustrated by Toby Gowing. Scribner Publishers in New York issued the book in 1991. It contains 364 pages.

5. A scholarly article by Beverly Whitaker Long and Charles H. Grant III in volume 41 of the journal *Communication Education.* Volume 41 is dated 1992, and the article runs from page 89 to page 108. The title of the article is "The 'Surprising Range of the Possible': Families Communicating in Fiction."

46e
MLA

C. Working with a partner or in a small group, compare answers to Exercises A and B. Correct any errors in your answers, using this handbook or your instructor's advice to resolve any differences of opinion.

46f Sample MLA paper

The following paper was written by a student using the MLA documentation style. The *MLA Handbook* recommends beginning a research paper with the first page of the text, using the format shown on Shane Hand's first page. Because his teacher required a title page and an outline as well, he prepared both of these, too. In the margin of the paper is a running commentary on the elements of the paper, from considerations of audience and purpose to organizational strategy, style, and format.

Place title one-third of the way down the page

Title catches readers' attention

Title page optional

Waste Disposal:

Have We Put Ourselves in Jeopardy?

Center and double-space all lines

by

Shane Hand

Double-space twice between groups of lines

Professor Charlotte Smith

English 1105

6 December 1991

Note form of date

46f
MLA

Heading for all pages: last name, one space, page number
(Roman numerals for outline, Arabic for paper) Hand i

Outline   *Center heading*
Outline optional; check with instructor   *Double-space below headi*

<u>Thesis statement</u>: Using landfills as a way to   *Keep th*
                                                              statem
dispose of solid and hazardous wastes is no longer *short—*

a valid option because we now know of the potential   *or*
                                                       sente
long-term dangers to our soil and groundwater that

landfills represent. We must both find new

technologies that safely dispose of waste and

reduce our own consumption.   *Outline uses*
                                               sentences (rather
                                               than topics or
   I. Mainly two types of waste pollute our   *phrases); ask*
      environment: solid and hazardous (toxic). *instructor's*
                                                 preference
      A. Most solid waste consists of packaging

         residues: aluminum cans, glass and plastic

         bottles, paperboard cartons, and wooden

         crates.

      B. Most hazardous waste consists of chemical

         toxins, by-products of manufacturing

         processes, or ingredients in a wide range of

         products.

  II. Americans are finally becoming aware of the

      problems with dumping wastes in landfills.

      A. Space is the most obvious problem--people do

         not want a landfill in their local area.

      B. Pollution of soil and groundwater is a more

         threatening problem.

Hand ii

III. The key to solving the waste disposal problem
is public commitment.

  A. People should take political action.

    1. They should urge politicians to pass
recycling regulations.

    2. They should force businesses to become

*Align all entries
of same level*   environmentally responsible.

    3. They should work to develop local and
national recycling programs.

  B. People should change their own consumer
habits.

IV. A poll shows that most people already have
changed their consumer habits.

 V. Along with public commitment, new waste
disposal technologies must also be developed.

  A. Currently, landfills with clay and plastic
linings reduce leakage into groundwater.

  B. Currently, incineration reduces the amounts
and toxicity of hazardous wastes.

46f
MLA

VI. New technology should not give anyone the
excuse not to change consumption habits.
Recycling is still the best approach to solving
this problem.

½" from top   Hand 1

1" from top of page

Shane Hand

Professor C. Smith   *Put information here if you do*
                          not include title page
1" margin
on each English 1105
side   *Double-space heading and paper*   *Opens*
        6 December 1991   *atten-*
                                                                   gettin
            Waste Disposal: Have We Put Ourselves in Jeopardy?   *device;*
                                                                  reader
Indent ¶ 1   A museum in New Jersey is dedicated to it. In *asks "*
five   California, artists use it to create high-priced   *is it?"*
spaces
             sculpture. But no one, absolutely no one, wants to

uses we to have garbage in his or her backyard. For decades we
identify
with   have buried it and hoped it would just disappear.
readers   But banishing it from sight did not get rid of it.

             Now our sins as a consumer society have come back to

             haunt us.

             2   There are many types of wastes polluting our
Presents
topic and   environment. Simply put, they include municipal
stance
             solid wastes and hazardous wastes. Both of these are

             a huge problem in the United States. They generally

             take up space or create a dangerous chemical

             imbalance. Sometimes both can happen, depending on

             the waste. Our soils are suffering from these

             pollutants, and we ourselves are in jeopardy.

             3   Solid waste, commonly known as garbage or
Elaborates
on ¶2   refuse, is what for years we have calmly thrown
Adds
definitions away, confidently believing that, by some miracle,

             it will be collected and will disappear.

             A significant portion of the solid waste problem

             stems from packaging residues, specifically

             containers. Aluminum cans, glass and plastic

             bottles, paperboard cartons, and wooden crates are

                    1" bottom margin

Hand 2

thrown away in massive numbers, never to be used
again. An average landfill today consists of six
main types of trash. Paper takes up about 50 percent *Adds*
by volume; plastic covers are close to 10 percent; *facts and*
statistics
metals take up 6 percent; glass holds 1 percent;
organic materials cover about 13 percent; and about
20 percent is miscellaneous substances (Rathje 116). *Cites*
author
These numbers may seem meaningless, but when we *and page*
think about the nation's daily output of these
materials (500,000 tons), it becomes clear that the
landfills are filling very quickly, so fast that our
soils cannot degrade the waste fast enough to
balance the space with the input. In fact, some
pollutants never degrade.

4   The average person assumes that hazardous
Defines
wastes account for a small percentage of today's *solid waste*
environmental problems. However, hazardous wastes *in larger*
context
are generated by almost all sectors of the economy.
These wastes are a general consequence of the
industrialized society in which we live. They

46f
MLA

reflect our need for packaging, appliances, cleaning
supplies, beauty aids, pharmaceuticals, and other
manufactured products. As with solid wastes, for
many years toxic wastes were considered safely gone
as soon as they were carted out of sight; as one
report reminds us, however, "As with other
environmental concerns, it is only within the past
twenty to thirty years that the possible adverse
environmental quality and health problems have been

Hand 3

Uses title in citation; author unknown

recognized and addressed" (<u>Hazardous Waste</u> 3). In
the past, hazardous waste disposal was accomplished
in the quickest and least costly manner, frequently
by open dumping and uncontrolled burning. These
practices have been found to present a hazard to
human health and the environment. The magnitude of
this problem can be best presented by totaling the
amount of hazardous wastes produced each year, which
the Office of Technology Assessment puts at about
250 million metric tons (5). As our industrial   *Cites source*
second time
society grows, finding ways to eliminate these   *page*
wastes while allowing the same or an improved   *number only*
standard of living should be an overall goal.

Uses   5   When the land was young, it was wide open and
generalization
to shift from unspoiled. Yet as the population grew, the spoilage
definitions to grew. But the problem has now reached such magnitude
argument
that Americans are finally becoming concerned about
what happens to their refuse. To some extent this
concern is due to some misconceptions about the

46f
MLA   viability of continued landfilling of municipal
solid wastes. One misconception is that the United
States is running out of landfill space. This does
not appear to be the case, as argued by a recent
study done on landfills. According to the study, "at
Uses expert source
the current rate of landfilling, all the MSW *Uses brackets*
to make key point   *to set off*
[municipal] solid waste] generated by the country *added*
over the next thousand years could easily be   *explanation*
contained within a 30-by-30 mile area using current
landfill technology" (Wiseman 9). However, this does
Long quotation might have been paraphr...

Hand 4

not resolve the problem since this idea is impractical. The space problem is distinctly regional, and no one region will consent to be the site for such a landfill. And where landfill siting is most a problem--along the northeastern seaboard, for instance--it is more often due to political opposition than to a lack of available space. This opposition goes back to the "not-in-my-backyard" syndrome.

6   Space is not the only problem these landfills have. There is a grave threat to the environment through the potential for surface water to percolate through landfills, releasing toxic constituents and heavy metals into soil and groundwater. They also have the potential to generate gases, including methane, that could have long-term environmentally destructive effects. A more immediate threat is that the gases could cause spontaneous explosions and fires. Even ordinary household items, once they are in landfills, can become hazardous wastes. A seemingly innocent bottle of nail polish puts more than six toxic chemicals into a landfill. All of these toxic constituents take hundreds and even thousands of years to disappear.

Moves from topic of space to topic of environmental damage

46f
MLA

Makes information "real" to readers

7   The key to solving the waste problem once and for all is public commitment. The public should urge the politicians to pass recycling regulations and force businesses to become environmentally responsible. Public action must be taken to develop and institute recycling programs on the local and

Presents one part of two-pronged proposal

Specifies public commitments

national level. Some may argue that recycling
programs are expensive and thus not practical, but
isn't our environment more important than a price
tag? In other countries, such as Germany, recycling
efforts have increased as much as 40 percent (Rathje
120). Funding for these programs comes from the
government with the approval of the taxpayers (121).
The public can also make a commitment even on a
small scale. As seen in the above breakdown of a
landfill's contents, at least 50 percent of a
landfill's space is occupied by items that can be
recycled. Reusing products and refusing to buy
products that are not recyclable or do not contain
recycled materials are two ways we as consumers can
bring about change. All of these ideas will help
control the space problem and relieve our soils.

8   With these ideas in mind, I turned to the
public to find out whether any of these ideas were
practiced or acceptable. I used a survey (Hand, see
appendix) which consisted of a series of questions
to find out people's habits and attitudes. My
results are based on a collection of roughly three
hundred responses. The participants in this survey
were either from the Virginia Tech area or from a
subdivision in Upper Marlboro, Maryland (my
hometown). Their ages ranged from about seventeen to
fifty years old, which provided a wide range for the
average consumer. Upon tabulating the responses, I
obtained the following results.

**46f
MLA**

*Places
complete
survey form
in appendix
so it does
not disrupt
argument*

Hand 6

Already Do

Use coffee mugs instead of polystyrene cups 55%

Reuse plastic wrap, foil, and plastic bags 64%

Recycle newspapers and magazines 46%

Recycle glass 57%

Recycle plastic containers 38%

Recycle aluminum cans 65%

Results could also be in a table or graph

Willing to Do

Take own bags to the store 66%

Shop at a store that's harder to get to
but carries biodegradable products 59%

Recycle plastic containers 59%

Pay more for products in low-waste
packaging 55%

Pay more for recycled paper 54%

9   It is important to remember that this survey
represents only a small region of the United States.
These results could be different in other parts of
the country. It is also possible that my respondents
wanted to make themselves out to be more
environmentally responsible citizens than they
really are. Still, I was favorably surprised by my
results. It seems that many people do take some
steps to preserve the environment and are willing to
take other steps once they are made aware of them.
This demonstrates how important it is to educate the
public about the environment.

**46f
MLA**

Caution about results helps make presentation seem balanced

Hand 7

Presents second part of proposal

10   Of course, along with public commitment, there must be technological improvement of waste disposal. Space and toxicity problems in landfills can be overcome or minimized by state-of-the-art landfill

Specifies technology that could be developed further

technology. Landfills lined with clay interposed between multiple layers of plastic sheeting greatly reduce the risk of contaminating the groundwater, especially if they are equipped with a system that collects and treats the substances that filter to the bottom of the landfill. Such a system does not need continuous removal of the substance since "landfills have an inherent capacity to lessen the toxicity of the substances introduced or generated in them" (Wiseman 9). This reduction in toxicity can also be accelerated by maintaining landfills as "biochemical" systems. As for the gases created, they can be collected and even marketed as fuel.

11   The preferred method for management of

Reconnects to first proposal

hazardous wastes is waste elimination. If wastes are not generated as the result of residential, commercial, and industrial actions, disposal is not necessary. If waste is not eliminated, then steps should be taken to reduce the amount generated. Due to extensive research efforts in the past few years,

Specifies another technology

more is known about incineration technology than any of the other waste management alternatives. For one, incineration provides the highest level of toxic control, and wastes destroyed by incineration do not need to be remanaged later. The by-product--ash--

Hand 8

takes up little space in a landfill and presents
little or no threat to the soil. Without a doubt,
incineration should play an increasing role in
hazardous waste management.

12 Still, though new advances in waste management
technology are moving toward resolving this
environmental problem, they do not give anybody the
excuse not to recycle since recycling is far more
beneficial to the environment than any technology.
We, as individuals, neighborhoods, and communities,
need to urge, by example and by political action,
the federal government to act now. Together, we can
clean up our garbage mess so our country can once
again be healthy and beautiful. We owe it to
ourselves as well as to future generations.

*Repeats
need to
change
habits in
conclusion*

*Uses we
and our to
strengthen
appeal to
readers*

**46f
MLA**

½" from top

Hand 9
Page numbers continue

I" from top of page

Works Cited   *Center heading*

First line of entry not indented
Additional lines indented five spaces

Hand, Shane. Questionnaire on consumer habits and

attitudes toward recycling. Blacksburg, VA and

List sources   Upper Marlboro, MD. 21-25 Nov. 1991.

mentioned in Hazardous Waste Incineration. New York: American

paper   Society of Mechanical Engineers, 1988.

Double-space Rathje, William L. "Once and Future Landfills."

National Geographic May 1991: 116-34.

Wiseman, Clark A. "Impediments to Economically

Efficient Solid Waste Management." Resources

105 (1991): 9-11.

46f
MLA

Hand 10

Works Consulted

Brown, Kirk W. Hazardous Waste and Treatment.

    Woburn: Butterworth, 1983.

Bugher, Robert D. Municipal Refuse Disposal.

    Danville: Interstate, 1970.

Flack, J. E. Man and the Quality of His Environment.

    Boulder: U of Colorado P, 1967.

Hand, Shane. Questionnaire on consumer habits and

    attitudes toward recycling. Blacksburg, VA and

    Upper Marlboro, MD. 21-25 Nov. 1991.

Hazardous Waste Incineration. New York: American

    Society of Mechanical Engineers, 1988.

Rathje, William L. "Once and Future Landfills."

    National Geographic May 1991: 116-34.

Van Tassel, Alfred J. Environmental Side Effects of

    Rising Industrial Output. Lexington, MA: Heath,

    1970.

Wiseman, Clark A. "Impediments to Economically

    Efficient Solid Waste Management." Resources

    105 (1991): 9-11.

Includes all works consulted even if not cited in the paper

46f
MLA

Hand 11

Appendix

Intro:

My name is Shane and I am taking a survey in order to study the habits of the average consumer. I am interested in seeing how your habits affect the environment. Please take a few moments to answer some questions.

Survey: *Includes clean copy of any survey,*
                           questionnaire, or other primary
Do you . . .   *research document*

Use coffee mugs instead of
     polystyrene cups?   Yes   No
Reuse plastic wrap, foil, and
     plastic bags?   Yes   No
Recycle newspapers and/or magazines?   Yes   No
Recycle glass?   Yes   No
Recycle plastic containers?   Yes   No
Recycle aluminum cans?   Yes   No

Are you willing to . . .

Take your own bags to the store?   Yes   No
Shop at a store that's harder to get to,
     but carries biodegradable products? Yes   No
Recycle plastic containers?   Yes   No
Pay more for products in low-waste
     packaging?   Yes   No
Pay more for recycled paper?   Yes   No

46g Using ACW guidelines for citing electronic sources

Because electronic resources are rapidly growing—both in number and in variety—the Alliance for Computers and Writing has endorsed a flexible style guide for documentation of electronic sources. This guide, MLA-Style Citations of Electronic Sources by Janice R. Walker, supplements MLA style, adapting its basic formats to accommodate a greater range of electronic resources and to pinpoint information about access. As a result, when you create your list of Works Cited, you should be able to integrate ACW entries for rapidly changing electronic sources with MLA entries for established print, field, and other resources. Ask your instructor for advice if you do not know how to document a particular source. Further information and updates of this guide are available electronically (http://www.cas.usf.edu/english/walker/mla.html). See also 44b-2 on using electronic databases and 44b-4 on using other electronic resources.

MODEL FORMAT FOR ELECTRONIC SOURCES

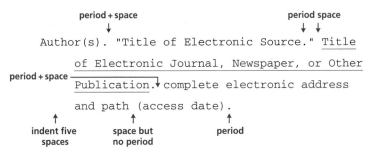

**46g
ACW**

- **Author(s).** Begin with the author's last name, and then supply the first name and any middle initial. For two or more authors or no author, see sample MLA entries 1 through 5 (pp. 659–660).
- **Title of Electronic Resource.** Give the full title of the specific resource in quotation marks, concluding with a period.
- **Title of Electronic Journal, Newspaper, or Other Publication.** Give the title of the publication, underlined and followed by a period. Add the original date of publication, if available.
- **Electronic Address.** Supply the complete, exact address needed to locate the site or file. Do not add a period at the end because this extra punctuation might be confused with the electronic address.
- **Access Date.** Supply in parentheses the date when you used the material, and then end the entry with a period.

1. Resource from the World Wide Web

Besides identifying the author, the resource title, and the publication title, supply the complete address (so that your reader can easily locate the material) and your date of access.

```
Poole, Jason. "On Borrowed Ground: Free

     African-American Life in Charleston, South

     Carolina 1810-61." Essays in History 36

     (1994). http://www.lib.virginia.edu/

     journals/EH/EH36/poole1.html

     (10 Mar. 1996).
```

See also MLA sample Entries 57–61 (pp. 676–677) which tell how to integrate print publication information into an entry for the electronic version of the same material.

2. Resource from a File Transfer Protocol (FTP) Site

Supply the complete address and path needed to locate the material.

```
Null, Christopher. "12 Monkeys: A Film Review

     by Christopher Null." 1996. ftp.nic.funet.

     fi/pub/culture/tv+film/reviews/

     12_Monkeys.452 (10 Mar. 1996).
```

3. Resource from a Telnet Site

Supply the complete address, including details needed to locate the resource itself.

```
Witmer, Robert, and James Robbins. "A

     Historical and Critical Survey of Recent

     Pedagogical Materials for the Teaching and

     Learning of Jazz." 1988. telnet

     mila.ps.uci.edu,#1,keyword: jazz,

     1988.Witmer.13517 (11 Mar. 1996).
```

4. Resource from a Gopher Site

Treat resources from a gopher, a local online information service, as you would material from any other online service.

```
de Armond, Paul. "Wise Use Moves into Electoral

     Politics." 1994. gopher/gopher.well.sf.
```

```
ca.us/Environmental Issues and Ideas/Wise
Use Movement as a Political Force (21 Nov.
1995).
```

See also the forms shown in MLA sample Entries 57 through 60 (pp. 676–677).

5. Resource from Interactive Communication

Identify the writer first and then the title or type of communication.

```
Slang. "Profession and Accountability." MOO.
    telnet purple-crayon.media.mit.edu
    8888/@GO NETORIC HEADQUARTERS (23 Apr.
    1996).
```

6. Resource from E-mail or a Newslist or Listserv Communication

Identify the writer, and supply the subject line, in quotation marks, as the resource title. Include a complete address and your date of access. If your source is a personal e-mail message, you may leave out the address.

```
Lemon, Alaina. "Germans Give Funds for Romani
    Church in Slovakia." omripub@omri.cz (6
    Mar. 1996).
Reynolds, Nedra. "Cultural Studies and Critical
    Studies." Personal e-mail (25 Feb. 1996).
```

46g
ACW

Documenting Sources: APA

Writers in the social sciences, including psychology, sociology, education, political science, economics, anthropology, and related fields often use the documentation system developed by the American Psychological Association (APA). In the social sciences, current research and theory often significantly alter the way scholars and others view a subject or a social problem. In addition, social science research often addresses current social, political, and cultural trends. For these reasons, readers are likely to be interested in the date a particular source was published. The **APA documentation style** makes the year of publication part of an in-text citation as in (Margolies, 1987), and gives the date right after the author's name in entries in a reference list.

> Margolies, H. (1987). Patterns, thinking, and
>
>   cognition: A theory of judgment. Chicago:
>
>   University of Chicago Press.

The discussions and examples in this chapter are designed to help you identify the most important formats and features for in-text citations and reference entries in the APA style. For any specialized formats not listed here, consult the *Publication Manual of the American Psychological Association* (4th ed., 1994). Some social science disciplines use documentation styles that vary somewhat from that set forth in the APA manual; others have alternative documentation styles of their own. Before you adopt the APA style, therefore, check with your instructor about the appropriate style of documentation.

47a Using in-text citations

The APA system provides parenthetical citations for quotations, paraphrases, summaries, and other information in the text of a paper. For advice on what to document and what not to document, see 46a. For an APA in-text citation, you include the author's name and the year of publication, separating these items with a comma. You may choose to name the author (and date) either within the parenthetical citation or within your text. When you are documenting the source of a quotation, follow the date with a comma, *p.* or *pp.,* and the page number on which the quoted material appears. Give the page number also if you wish to indicate the specific location of information or the source of paraphrased or summarized material.

PARENTHETICAL CITATION OF QUOTATION
One recent study points out that while "women radio news directors have exceeded the men in yearly salary, that may not be the case in other radio news positions" (Cramer, 1993, p. 161).

AUTHOR OF QUOTATION NAMED IN TEXT
As Cramer (1993) points out, "Although women radio news directors have exceeded the men in yearly salary, that may not be the case in other radio news positions" (p. 161).

PARENTHETICAL CITATION OF SUMMARY
In the mid-1960s, Tom Wolfe began writing unconventional and insight-filled essays about American popular culture. Despite his Ph.D. in American Studies from Yale, Wolfe and his work were at first ignored by most intellectuals, both inside and outside universities, who viewed serious or high-brow culture as far more important than popular culture (Aronowitz, 1993).

When you supply the author's name and the date in your text or an in-text citation, your readers will be able to identify a source in the list of references you provide at the end of your paper.

47b   Using content footnotes

Occasionally you may wish to expand information presented in the text or discuss a point further without making the main text of your paper more complicated or hard to follow. A content footnote allows you to do this, but you should use such footnotes sparingly because too many footnotes or long footnotes can distract your readers.

To prepare a content footnote, place a number slightly above the line of your text that relates to the footnote information. Make sure that you number the footnotes in your paper consecutively.

TEXT OF PAPER
I tape-recorded all the interviews and later transcribed the relevant portions.[1]

On a separate page at the end of your paper, below the centered heading "Footnotes," present the notes in the order in which they appear in your text. Begin each note with its number, placed slightly above the line. Indent five to seven spaces, the same as a paragraph, for the first line only of each footnote, and double-space all notes.

FOOTNOTE   [1]Most of the recordings had sections that were hard to hear and understand. Some of these were the result of problems with the tape recorder, and others were caused by background noises during the interviews. Despite these problems, gaps in the interviews did not substantially affect information needed for the study.

Your instructor may prefer that you type any footnote at the bottom of the page with the text reference.

Did You Know?

In addition to the MLA, APA, CBE, and CMS styles, academic and professional writing also employs a variety of other documentation systems. Here are a few.

CHEMISTRY   American Chemical Society, *The ACS Style Guide: A Manual for Authors and Editors,* 1986.

MATHEMATICS   American Mathematical Society, *A Manual for Authors of Mathematical Papers,* rev. ed., 1990.

MEDICINE   American Medical Association, *American Medical Association Manual of Style,* 8th ed., 1989.

PHYSICS   American Institute of Physics, *AIP Style Manual,* 4th ed., 1990.

47c
APA

47c Creating APA in-text citations

1. Work with One Author

When you cite a work with one author, supply the author's last name and the date of the publication in parentheses, separated by a comma and a space. If the author's name appears in the text, give only the date in parentheses. If both the name and the date are included in the text, no other information needs to be cited because the reader has enough information to locate the item in the list of references at the end of the paper.

Mallory's 1995 study of magnet schools confirmed several of the trends proposed earlier (Jacobson, 1989) and also updated the classification by Bailey (1991) based on district demographics.

Guide to APA Formats for In-Text Citations

1. **Work with One Author**
2. **Work with Two Authors**
3. **Work with Three to Five Authors**
4. **Work with Six or More Authors**
5. **Work with a Corporate or Group Author**
6. **Work with No Author Given**
7. **Work with a Specific Page or Section Cited**
8. **Work Cited More than Once**
9. **Authors with the Same Last Name**
10. **Personal Communications, Including Interviews**
11. **Two or More Sources in One Citation**

---

2. Work with Two Authors

For a work with two authors, include the names of both authors whenever you refer to the work. In a parenthetical reference, include both last names separated by an ampersand (&). If the names are mentioned in the text, however, use the word *and*.

> Part-time workers are usually paid an hourly wage rather than a salary (Mellor & Haugen, 1986). Durstan and Frank (1992) have reviewed the rates at which wages have increased in several major employment fields that include many part-timers.

3. Work with Three to Five Authors

For a work with three to five authors, include all of the authors' names, separated by commas, the first time you cite the work. Use an ampersand (&) before the last name in an in-text citation, but use *and* in the text itself.

> Most studies have found that the rate of forgetting is about the same as the rate of retention or remembering (Munn, Fernald, & Fernald, 1989).

In the second and other following references, include only the first author's name followed by *et al.* For instance, the next time you cite the source above, you would write (Munn et al., 1989).

4. Work with Six or More Authors

For a work with six or more authors, give the name of the first author followed by *et al.* (Albertini et al., 1986) in the first reference as well as any that follow. (In the reference list at the end of your paper, you will need to supply the names of all the authors.)

47c
APA

5. Work with a Corporate or Group Author

When a group such as a corporation, government agency, or association is the author of a work, cite the source with the spelled-out name of the group for the first entry. Then you may use an abbreviation for later entries if the name is long and awkward and the abbreviation will be clear to readers. If you wish to abbreviate a group author's name in this way, supply the abbreviation in brackets with the first entry.

FIRST ENTRY   Depression has a number of different causes, some psychological and some physiological or organic (National Institute of Mental Health [NIMH], 1981).

LATER ENTRY   The treatments for depressive disorders vary according to the duration and intensity of the condition (NIMH, 1981).

6. Work with No Author Given

When no author is named, cite the work by its title (or by the first few words of a long title). For example, *The Great Utopia: The Russian and Soviet Avant-Garde, 1915–1932* might appear in a citation as *Great Utopia.*

For most of the 1920s, art, architecture, and design in Russia mixed aesthetically startling images and arrangements with political themes and an endorsement of social change (*Great Utopia,* 1992).

7. Work with a Specific Page or Section Cited

Often, all you will want to cite is a specific section of a long study or a table, graph, or other figure from a work. If so, indicate what part of the work you are using. For one page, use the abbreviation *p.*; for a chapter, use *chap.*; for a figure, use *Figure.* Spell out any other words that may be confusing if abbreviated.

Teenagers who survive suicide attempts experience stages of recovery just as people who are told they are going to die go through stages of acceptance, and these stages of recovery have distinct symptoms (Mauk & Weber, 1991, Table 1).

8. Work Cited More than Once

If you cite the same source more than once in a paragraph, repeat the source as necessary to clarify a specific page reference or to show which information comes from one of several sources. If a second reference is clear, however, you do not need to repeat the date.

Piaget's view of the way sensory-motor experiences like holding a ball affect a child's mind is like "the immediate imprinting of a light sensitive film sheen exposed to a concretely present external event" (Feffer, 1988, p. 89). Having held a ball once, however, a child can later imagine holding it and playing with it in different situations. According to Feffer, one of the weaknesses in Piaget's work is his failure to take full account of such imaginative experiences.

By naming the author in the text for the second reference, the writer avoids interrupting the paragraph with an additional parenthetical citation.

9. Authors with the Same Last Name

When your reference list contains works by two different authors with the same last name, provide the author's initials for each in-text citation. Do this both for works with a single author and for works with several authors when the lead authors have the same last name. Giving the initials for potentially confusing references to authors will help your readers identify your sources and find them more quickly in your reference list.

Scholars have looked in depth at the development of African-American culture during slavery and reconstruction (E. Foner, 1988). The role of Frederick Douglass in this process has also been examined (P. Foner, 1950).

10. Personal Communications, Including Interviews

Cite letters, memos, interviews, e-mail, telephone conversations, and similar personal communications by the initials and last name of the person, the phrase *personal communication,* and the date. Because your readers probably will have no access to such sources, you need not include them in your reference list.

AUTHOR NAMED IN TEXT

According to J. M. Hostos, the state has begun cutting funding for social services duplicated by county agencies (personal communication, October 7, 1995).

PARENTHETICAL REFERENCE

The state has begun cutting funding for social services duplicated by county agencies (J. M. Hostos, personal communication, October 7, 1995).

11. Two or More Sources in One Citation

If you are summarizing information found in more than one source, include all the sources—names and years—within the citation. Separate the authors and years with commas, separate the sources with semicolons. List the sources in the same sequence that you use in your list of references, alphabetically by author and then oldest to most recent if you have used several sources by the same author.

Several researchers have found that work performance is affected by personality (Furnham, 1992; Gilmer, 1961, 1977).

47c
APA

47d Creating an APA reference list

Immediately after the last page of your paper, you need to provide a list of references to enable your readers to identify and consult the sources you have cited in the body of your paper. Begin your APA reference page by centering the word "References" at the top, and arrange the works alphabetically by author or by the first main word of the title if there is no author. Two or more works by the same author are arranged from the oldest to the most recent by year of publication. (See the References page at the end of the sample APA paper in 47e.)

47d
APA

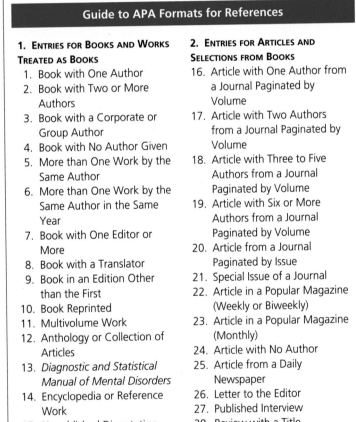

Guide to APA Formats for References

1. ENTRIES FOR BOOKS AND WORKS TREATED AS BOOKS

1. Book with One Author
2. Book with Two or More Authors
3. Book with a Corporate or Group Author
4. Book with No Author Given
5. More than One Work by the Same Author
6. More than One Work by the Same Author in the Same Year
7. Book with One Editor or More
8. Book with a Translator
9. Book in an Edition Other than the First
10. Book Reprinted
11. Multivolume Work
12. Anthology or Collection of Articles
13. *Diagnostic and Statistical Manual of Mental Disorders*
14. Encyclopedia or Reference Work
15. Unpublished Dissertation

2. ENTRIES FOR ARTICLES AND SELECTIONS FROM BOOKS

16. Article with One Author from a Journal Paginated by Volume
17. Article with Two Authors from a Journal Paginated by Volume
18. Article with Three to Five Authors from a Journal Paginated by Volume
19. Article with Six or More Authors from a Journal Paginated by Volume
20. Article from a Journal Paginated by Issue
21. Special Issue of a Journal
22. Article in a Popular Magazine (Weekly or Biweekly)
23. Article in a Popular Magazine (Monthly)
24. Article with No Author
25. Article from a Daily Newspaper
26. Letter to the Editor
27. Published Interview
28. Review with a Title
29. Review Without a Title

30. Article from an Encyclopedia or Reference Work
31. Chapter in an Edited Book or Selection from an Anthology
32. Dissertation Abstract

3. ENTRIES FOR OTHER PRINTED AND FIELD RESOURCES
33. Government Publication
34. Report
35. Unpublished Interview
36. Personal Communication
37. Paper Presented at a Meeting
38. Unpublished Raw Data

4. ENTRIES FOR MEDIA AND ELECTRONIC RESOURCES
39. Film or Videotape
40. Television or Radio Program
41. Recording
42. Database or Information Service
43. Online Book
44. Online Article
45. Online Abstract
46. CD-ROM Abstract
47. Computer Program

1 Entries for books and works treated as books

MODEL FORMAT FOR BOOKS AND WORKS TREATED AS BOOKS

period + space ↓   period + space ↓   period + space ↓

Author(s). (Date). <u>Title of work.</u> Place of

Publication: Publisher.

↑ indent 5–7 spaces   ↑ colon + space   ↑ period

- **Author(s).** Give the author's last name followed by a comma and the *initials only* of the first and middle names. Use the same inverted order for each author in a book with two or more authors. Separate the names of two authors with a comma and an ampersand (&); separate the names of three or more authors with commas, using an ampersand before the final name.
- **Date.** Provide the year of publication (in parentheses), followed by a period.
- **Title of Work.** Give the title followed by a period, and underline both the title and the period. Use a capital only for the first word of the main title, the first word of any subtitle, and any proper nouns.
- **Publication Information.** For U.S. publishers, give the city and state followed by a colon and a space; then supply the publisher's name leaving out unnecessary words such as *Inc.* or *Publishers*. Abbreviate the name of the state using the standard postal abbreviation. You do

47d APA

not need to name the state for the following familiar publishing locations: Baltimore, Boston, Chicago, Los Angeles, New York, Philadelphia, and San Francisco. For publishers outside the United States, give the city and the abbreviated name of the country. No country is needed for these familiar locations. Amsterdam, Jerusalem, London, Milan, Moscow, Paris, Rome, Stockholm, Tokyo, and Vienna.

- **Spacing.** Double-space all entries, and indent five to seven spaces, the same indentation that you choose for paragraphing, for the second and any additional lines. Note that APA style advises indenting the first line of a reference, not the following lines, if you are preparing a paper for publication. Then the publication will adjust the indentation in the printed version. We recommend indenting lines following the first in your course papers because readers then can easily see the alphabetical order of the references. Be sure to ask your instructor's preferences and follow any specific directions carefully.

1. Book with One Author

```
Corsaro, W. A. (1985). Friendship and peer
     culture in the early years. Norwood, NJ:
     Ablex.
```

2. Book with Two or More Authors

List each author's last name first, followed by first and middle initials. Separate the names with commas. Use an ampersand (&) for *and* in multiple-author works.

```
Munn, N. L., Fernald, L. D., Jr., & Fernald,
     P. S. (1989). Basic psychology. Boston:
     Houghton Mifflin.
```

47d
APA

3. Book with a Corporate or Group Author

Treat the organization or agency responsible for the work as you would an individual author, and alphabetize by the first main word.

```
Southern Anthropological Society. (1968). Urban
     anthropology: Research perspectives and
     strategies. Athens, GA: University of
     Georgia Press.
```

When the author and publisher are the same, give the word *Author* following the place of publication instead of repeating the name of the publisher (see Entry 13).

4. Book with No Author Given

The date of an anonymous work should come after, rather than before, the title. Use the first significant word of the title to alphabetize the entry.

Boas anniversary volume: Anthropological papers written in honor of Franz Boas. (1906). New York: Stechert.

5. More than One Work by the Same Author

List the works in chronological order by year of publication. Include the author's name in each entry.

Aronowitz, S. (1973). False promises: The shaping of the American working class. New York: McGraw-Hill.

Aronowitz, S. (1993). Roll over Beethoven: The return of cultural strife. Hanover, NH: Wesleyan University Press.

If the same lead author has works with different co-authors, alphabetize these entries based on the last names of the second authors.

6. More than One Work by the Same Author in the Same Year

When you list two or more works by the same author appearing in the same year, give them in alphabetical order by the first significant word in the title. Add lowercase letters after dates (e.g., 1992a, 1992b).

Gould, S. J. (1987a). Time's arrow, time's cycle: Myth and metaphor in the discovery of geological time. Cambridge, MA: Harvard University Press.

Gould, S. J. (1987b). An urchin in the storm: Essays about books and ideas. New York: Norton.

Alphabetized under *urchin* not *an.*

In your text, cite such works by providing both the date and the letter, for example, (Gould, 1987b).

7. Book with One Editor or More

Include (*Ed.*) or (*Eds.*) after the name(s) of the editors.

47d
APA

Claxton, G. (Ed.). (1986). Beyond therapy: The
impact of Eastern religions on
psychological theory and practice. London:
Wisdom.

8. Book with a Translator

Include the translator's name, in normal order, after the title, followed
by the capitalized abbreviation *Trans.*

Leontev, A. N. (1978). Activity, consciousness,
and personality (M. J. Hall, Trans.).
Englewood Cliffs, NJ: Prentice-Hall.

9. Book in an Edition Other than the First

Include information about a specific edition in parentheses after the
title (for example, *Rev. ed.* for "revised edition" or *3rd ed.* for "third edition").

Gilmer, B. (1975). Applied psychology:
Adjustments in living and work (Rev. ed.).
New York: McGraw-Hill.

10. Book Reprinted

Frankfort, H., Frankfort, H. A., Wilson, J. A.,
Jacobsen, T., & Irwin, W. A. (1977). The
intellectual adventure of ancient man: An
essay on speculative thought in the
ancient Near East. Chicago: University of
Chicago Press. (Original work published
1946)

11. Multivolume Work

Include the names of the editors or authors, making sure you indicate if they are editors. Then provide the inclusive years of publication. If the
work is a revised edition or has a translator, give this information after the
title. Then identify in parentheses the volumes you are using for your paper.

Strachey, J., Freud, A., Strachey, A., & Tyson,
A. (Eds.). (1966-1974). The standard
edition of the complete psychological
works of Sigmund Freud (J. Strachey et

al., Trans.) (Vols. 3-5). London: Hogarth
Press and the Institute of Psycho-Analysis.

12. Anthology or Collection of Articles

For an anthology or a collection of articles, give the name of the editor(s) first, followed by the abbreviation *Ed.* or *Eds.* in parentheses.

Lemert, C. C. (Ed.). (1991). Intellectuals and
politics: Social theory in a changing
world. Newbury Park, CA: Sage.

Ghosh, A., & Ingene, C. A. (Eds.). (1991).
Spatial analysis in marketing: Theory,
methods and applications. Greenwich, CT:
JAI.

13. *Diagnostic and Statistical Manual of Mental Disorders*

The manual known in short form as *DSM-IV* is widely cited in fields such as psychology, social work, and psychiatry because its definitions and guidelines often have legal force and determine patterns of treatment. Because of the volume's importance, the APA *Publication Manual* recommends the following specific form for the entry.

American Psychiatric Association. (1994).
Diagnostic and statistical manual of
mental disorders (4th ed.). Washington,
DC: Author.

In your text, following an initial full citation, you may use the standard abbreviations for this work: *DSM-III* (1980), *DSM-III-R* (1987), or *DSM-IV* (1994).

14. Encyclopedia or Reference Work

Kruskal, W. H., & Tanur, J. M. (1978).
International encyclopedia of statistics
(Vols. 1-2). New York: Free Press.

15. Unpublished Dissertation

Use the following reference format when you have consulted the dissertation itself. (See Entry 32 for a dissertation abstract.)

Yamada, H. (1989). American and Japanese topic
management strategies in business

47d
APA

```
conversations. Unpublished doctoral

dissertation, Georgetown University,

Washington, DC.
```

2 Entries for articles and selections from books

MODEL FORMAT FOR ARTICLES AND SELECTIONS

period +
space

period +
space

period +
space

↓

↓

↓

```
Author(s). (Date). Title of article. Title of

    Periodical, Volume Number, Page Numbers.
```

↑
indent
5–7 spaces

↑
number
underlined

↑
comma
underlined

- **Author(s).** Give the author's last name and initials followed by a period and a space.
- **Date.** Supply the date in parentheses followed by a period and a space.
- **Title of Article.** Give the article title, capitalizing only the first word (and the first word of any subtitle along with any proper names). Do not use quotation marks with the title. End with a period and a space.
- **Title of Journal, Periodical, or Book.** Give the journal title (underlined, with all main words capitalized), the volume number (also underlined), and the page numbers. Use commas to separate these, and underline the comma following the title.
- **Spacing.** Double-space all entries, and indent five to seven spaces, the same indentation that you choose for paragraphing, for the second and any additional lines (see p. 704).

**47d
APA**

16. Article with One Author from a Journal Paginated by Volume
When a journal is paginated by volume, you do not have to include the particular issue number because page numbers run continuously throughout the entire volume.

```
Lamphere, L. (1985). Deindustrialization and

    urban anthropology: What the future holds.

    Urban Anthropology, 14, 259-268.
```

17. Article with Two Authors from a Journal Paginated by Volume
```
Eisenberg, A. R., & Garvey, C. (1981).

    Children's use of verbal strategies in
```

```
resolving conflicts. Discourse Processes,
    4, 149-170.
```

18. Article with Three to Five Authors from a Journal Paginated by Volume

```
Iran-Nejad, A., McKeachie, W. J., & Berliner.
    D. C. (1990). The multisource nature of
    learning: An introduction. Review of
    Educational Research, 60, 509-515.
```

For entries with three to five authors, the first in-text reference should list all the authors; later references should give the name of the first author followed by *et al.*, as in (Iran-Nejad et al., 1990).

19. Article with Six or More Authors from a Journal Paginated by Volume

Supply the names of all the authors in the entry in the reference list. In-text references should give only the name of the first author followed by *et al.*, as in (Albertini et al., 1986).

20. Article from a Journal Paginated by Issue

When each issue of a journal begins with page 1, include the issue number in parentheses immediately (with no space) after the volume number. Do not underline the issue number.

```
Wurzbacher, K. V., Evans, E. D., & Moore, E. J.
    (1991). Effects of alternative street
    school on youth involved in prostitution.
    Journal of Adolescent Health, 12(7), 549-
    554.
```

47d
APA

21. Special Issue of a Journal

Begin with the special issue's editor (if other than the regular editor), then its title and the date. Place the title at the beginning before the date when no editor for the special issue is indicated. Indicate in brackets that it is a special issue. Since you are citing the entire issue, you need not include page numbers.

```
Balk, D. E. (Ed.). (1991). Death and adolescent
    bereavement [Special issue]. Journal of
    Adolescent Research, 6(1).
```

22. Article in a Popular Magazine (Weekly or Biweekly)

Supply the same information as you would for an article in a monthly magazine (see Entry 23), but add the specific date.

> Adler, J. (1995, July 31). The rise of the
>
> overclass. Newsweek, 126, 33-34, 39-40,
>
> 43, 45-46.

When an article is continued, list all the different pages, separated by commas.

23. Article in a Popular Magazine (Monthly)

Include the month of the magazine, along with the year. Spell out months. Add the volume number and pages. If there is no author, put the title first, before the date.

> Dajer, T. (1992, September). Divided selves.
>
> Discover, 13, 38-45.

24. Article with No Author

Begin the entry with the article's title, and alphabetize using the first main word in the title.

> True tales of false memories. (1993, July/
>
> August). Psychology Today, 26, 11-12.

25. Article from a Daily Newspaper

Use *p.* (page) or *pp.* to introduce the section and page numbers for newspaper articles. If there is no author, put the title first, as you would for a magazine article with no author listed.

> Gottlieb, A. (1995, September 24). Nontradi-
>
> tional methods yield results at Asbury.
>
> The Denver Post, pp. 1B, 7B.

26. Letter to the Editor

Treat a letter to the Editor like another newspaper article, but label it in brackets.

> Bryant, K. (1995, July 16). Lawyers should push
>
> for early settlements of lawsuits [Letter
>
> to the editor]. San Jose Mercury News, p.
>
> 6C.

27. Published Interview

Although APA does not specify a form for published interviews, you may wish to employ the following form, which is similar to other APA references. For a published interview, begin with the interviewer's name; provide the date of publication; then in brackets indicate that the selection is an interview and provide any other information to specify the source or occasion. Conclude with the publication information. If the interview has a title, give it following the date, as in a review (see Entry 28).

> Kosek, J. (1993). A different type of
>
> environmentalist: Ka-Kisht-Ke-Is (Chief
>
> Simon Lucas) [Interview]. Cultural
>
> Survival Quarterly, 17(1), 19-20.

28. Review with a Title

Following the title of the review, indicate the kind of work (book, film, video program, television program, and so on) and the title (underlined) of the work being reviewed. Enclose this information within brackets.

> Stolarz-Fantino, S., & Fantino, E. Cognition
>
> and behavior analysis [Review of the book
>
> Judgment, decision, and choice]. Journal
>
> of Experimental Analysis of Behavior, 54,
>
> 317-322.

29. Review Without a Title

Begin with the name of the reviewer. When the review article does not have a title, use a description in brackets in place of the title: follow the phrase *Review of* with the type of material and the title of the book, film, television show, or other topic of the review.

> Van Meter, E. J. (1994). [Review of the book
>
> Preparing tomorrow's school leaders:
>
> Alternative designs]. Educational
>
> Administration Quarterly, 30, 112-117.

30. Article from an Encyclopedia or Reference Work

For an article in an encyclopedia or other reference book, use *In* before the work's title, and follow it with the volume and page numbers. Begin with the title of the article if no author is identified.

> Chernoff, H. (1978). Decision theory. In
>
> International encyclopedia of statistics
>
> (Vol. 1, pp. 131-135). New York: Free
>
> Press.

31. Chapter in an Edited Book or Selection from an Anthology

If the work is a selection from an anthology, begin with the author's name, the year the book was published, and the title of the selection. Following the word *In,* cite the editors, the title of the collection, and the page numbers.

> Shepard, W. O. (1991). Child psychology:
>
> Identity and interaction. In J. H. Cantor,
>
> C. C. Spiker, & L. P. Lipsitt (Eds.),
>
> Child behavior and developmental training
>
> for diversity (pp. 236-257). Norwood, NJ:
>
> Ablex.

32. Dissertation Abstract

If you have consulted an abstract of a dissertation in *Dissertation Abstracts International,* use the following format. (See Entry 15 for an unpublished dissertation.)

> Yamada, H. (1989). American and Japanese topic
>
> management strategies in business
>
> conversations. Dissertation Abstracts
>
> International, 50(09), 2982B.

If you consult the dissertation on microfilm, give the University Microfilms number at the end of the entry in parentheses, for example (University Microfilms No. AAC—9004751).

3 Entries for other printed and field resources

33. Government Publication

> Select Committee on Aging, Subcommittee on
>
> Human Services, House of Representatives.
>
> (1991). Grandparents' rights: Preserving
>
> generational bonds (Com. Ref. No. 102-
>
> 833). Washington, DC: U.S. Government
>
> Printing Office.

34. Report

When the author is an individual, begin with that name. When a group or government agency is the author, give its name. If the agency also publishes the report, use the word *Author* in the publication information instead of repeating the group's name.

Drug Abuse and Mental Health Administration.

(1981). <u>Depressive disorders: Causes and</u>

<u>treatment.</u> Rockville, MD: U.S. Department

of Health and Human Services.

If the issuing agency has given a report a number, give the number in parentheses after the title with no punctuation between the title and parentheses. When several numbers are listed in the report, choose the one most likely to help readers obtain the document.

35. Unpublished Interview
To refer to an interview you have conducted yourself, provide the information only as part of an in-text citation such as the following: (R. Gelles, personal communication, September 14, 1993). (See p. 701.)

36. Personal Communication
Letters, e-mail, electronic bulletin board messages, telephone conversations, and similiar communications cannot be consulted by your readers, so do not include them in your reference list. Instead, cite them in text. (See p. 701 for examples.)

37. Paper Presented at a Meeting
For an unpublished paper presented at a conference or symposium, include the month as well as the year, and both the name and location of the meeting.

Nelson, J. S. (1993, August). <u>Political</u>

<u>argument in political science: A</u>

<u>meditation on the disappointment of</u>

<u>political theory.</u> Paper presented at the

annual meeting of the American Political

Science Association, Chicago.

38. Unpublished Raw Data
Field research generally produces raw data you can draw on when you prepare a paper. When you use data from field observations, a survey, or similar kinds of research, briefly describe the contents of the data within brackets following the date. Then conclude the entry with the phrase *Unpublished raw data.*

Williams, S. (1995). [Survey of student

attitudes toward increased library fees].

Unpublished raw data.

4 Entries for media and electronic resources

39. Film or Videotape

Begin with the name or names of the people primarily responsible for the work, and indicate each person's role (for example, director or producer) in parentheses following the name. Underline the title, and then indicate the medium (for example, film, videotape, or slides) in brackets. At the end of the entry, within parentheses, indicate the location and name of the distributor (for example, WGBH, Boston). If the distributor is not well known, supply the address so that your reader can locate the material.

```
Simon, T. (Producer), & LeBrun, N. (Writer).

     (1986). Atocha: Quest for treasure

     [videotape]. (Available from Columbia

     Tristar Home Video, 3400 Riverside Drive,

     Burbank, CA 91505-4627)
```

40. Television or Radio Program

Begin the entry for a series of programs with the name of the script writer, the producer, the director, or any other person whose role you wish to indicate. Give the title of the program or series (underlined). Conclude with the location and name of the network or channel responsible for the broadcast.

```
Moyers, B. (Executive Editor). (1993). Bill

     Moyers' journal. New York: WNET.
```
Television series.

For a specific episode in a series, indicate the director in parentheses immediately following the title, then indicate the producer before the title of the series.

```
Moyers, B. A. (1993). A life together (D.

     Grubin, Director). In D. Grubin

     (Producer), Bill Moyers' journal. New

     York: WNET.
```
Single episode of television series.

41. Recording

Begin by giving the name of the writer and the date of copyright (in parentheses). Following the song title, supply the recording artist in brackets, if this is someone other than the writer. Indicate the medium in brackets after the album title; include a number for the recording in the brackets if one is necessary for identifying the recording and obtaining a copy.

Freeman, R. (1994). Porscha [Recorded by R.
Freeman & The Rippingtons]. On <u>Sahara</u>
[CD]. New York: GRP Records.

42. Database or Information Service
Include the order number at the end of the citation.

Maher, F., & Tetreault, M. K. T. (1992). Inside
feminist classrooms: An ethnographic
approach. <u>New Directions for Teaching and</u>
<u>Learning, 49,</u> 57-74. (ERIC Document
Reproduction Service No. ED 443 234)

43. Online Book
Give the name(s) of the author(s), the date, the title, and the online
location. (Note that APA style spells *on-line* with a hyphen.)

Smith, R. L., & Smith, P. S. (1992). <u>Basic</u>
<u>techniques in marriage and family</u>
<u>counseling</u> [On-line]. Available: Internet:
Gopher AskERIC/Digests

44. Online Article
Begin with the author, the title, and the source. Then indicate the
medium and the publication information. Conclude with the availability
information needed to find the source.

Schroeder, E. (1988). Therapy for the
chemically dependent family. <u>Journal of</u>
<u>Chemical Dependency Treatment</u> [On-line],
<u>2</u>(1). Available: DIALOG File: Journal
Chemical Dependency

45. Online Abstract
For an abstract, give the source of the original work and the location
of the abstract.

Sack, K. (1995, July 14). House panel to draft
bill requiring AIDS tests of newborns
[On-line], <u>New York Times,</u> p. A15.
Abstract from: Lexis/News/CURNWS

47d
APA

46. CD-ROM Abstract

```
Schroeder, E. (1988). Therapy for the
     chemically dependent family [CD-ROM].
     Journal of Chemical Dependency, 2, 95-129.
     Abstract from: SilverPlatter File: PsycLIT
     Item: 76-37924
```

47. Computer Program

In brackets after the title, identify the source as a computer program, a computer programming language, or computer software. If the program's author owns specific rights to it, begin the entry with the author's name. Otherwise, begin with the name of the material. Give the location and name of the organization producing the program. Add any version number or retrieval information at the end in parentheses unless it is part of the title.

```
Family tree maker [Computer software]. (1993).
     Fremont, CA: Banner Blue Software.
     (Windows version)
```

Exercise

A. Turn to Exercise A in Chapter 46. Rewrite the sentences supplied there to add in-text citations in APA style.

B. Turn to Exercise B in Chapter 46. Rewrite the items supplied there to create a list of references in APA style.

C. Working with a partner or a small group, compare your answers to Exercise A and B above. Correct any errors in your answers, using your handbooks or your instructor's advice to resolve any differences of opinion.

47d
APA

47e Sample APA paper

*Number title page
and all others using
short title*

*Center title and all
other lines* Competitive Cyclists: Who Are They?

*Supply name and
institution* Steven King

University of Rhode Island

*Double-space
between lines*

*Ask your instructor
if instructor's name,
course name, and
date are necessary* Professor Hasan Danesh

Sociology 150

Section 10

November 24, 1993

*Supply abbreviated
title (50 characters
maximum) for
heading* Running head: CYCLISTS

47e
APA

Use short title Cyclists   2
Center heading   and page number

Supply one ¶ and do not indent

Abstract

Double-spac abstract a rest of pap

Cyclists at a race were asked to fill out a questionnaire about attitudes toward cycling, demographics, and self-perception of social status. Responses to the questionnaire provided general support for an initial hypothesis regarding the low level of women's participation in competitive cycling but not for a hypothesis regarding enjoyment of extreme physical exertion and pain as a reason for undertaking competitive cycling. In addition, the responses suggested further hypotheses concerning the relative lack of participation by cyclists under 25 years old and the likelihood that people of different ages, marital status, and levels of education undertake competitive cycling for different reasons.

Summariz paper i more than about words

Besides the abstract, typical sections in an APA paper are Introduction, Method, Results, and Discussion

47e
APA

first part is introduction
but no heading is used

1" top margin

Repeat and center title
Indent 9 five
to seven spaces;
Competitive Cyclists: Who Are They?

1   Bicycle riding is the third most popular
onsistent
participant sport in the United States, with an
or 9s and
references
estimated 55.3 million people riding a bike at
least once a year (Interbike, 1992). Another
report, from the Bicycle Institute of America
(1990), estimates that 25 million American adults
ride a bicycle an average of once a week. That
same survey indicates that 220,000 adults took
part in bicycle races during the year, or less
argin than 1% of those who ride frequently.
ch
de

2   In this paper I report on a group of people
who entered a particular bicycle race. I collected
data through a survey taken at the race. The
survey asked for demographic data as well as
information about level of commitment and
motivation. I then summarized and analyzed the
data. Although the purpose of my study was
primarily descriptive, I also was able to estimate
the kind of support available for two hypotheses I
developed before beginning the study. In addition,
the study suggested several more hypotheses useful
for further research.

[The introduction goes on to provide background information on
competitive cycling as a sport.]

Center section heading
Method

3   I gathered the data for this paper at a
bicycle race held in Westerly, Rhode Island, on
Sunday, September 27, 1992. Called "The First
Annual Charlestown 40 Kilometer Time Trial," the

1" bottom margin

Use introduction to present problem or subject, background information, and hypothesis or guiding question

Citation uses title; no author

47e
APA

Explains how the study was carried out

Follows general APA practice, discussing subjects, materials, and procedure for the study

event consisted of each entrant riding the course
individually "against the clock." The course was on
smoothly paved roads and was relatively flat. There
were 37 entrants, 34 male and 3 female.

4   The respondents filled out a survey (see *Supplies cross-*
reference t
Appendix) after they had completed the event and *survey in*
Appendi
were waiting for the results. I circulated through
the parking area and asked the entrants to go to the
registration table and complete the survey. My
original plan was to have the entrants complete the
survey prior to the race at registration. My goal
was a 100% response. As it worked out, I achieved an
88% response rate (32 of 36 possible respondents; I
was the 37th entrant).

5   The questionnaire requested basic demographic
information including a question regarding self-
perception of social status. It also asked
respondents to rate their cycling ability and
indicate how many years they had been active in
cycling competition. A question about the distance
traveled to get to the race was intended to provide
some indication of the level of commitment to
cycling competition. Traveling a substantial
distance to the race involves a considerable time
commitment and willingness to pay for transportation
and meals in addition to race entry fees. A final
open-ended question asked for three to five reasons
why the respondent entered competitive cycling
events.

47e
APA

Provides theoretical background for study and context for methods and conclusions; Literature Review section often follows Introduction

Literature Review

6 The factors motivating competitive cyclists do not appear to be a major issue in sociology or psychology at the present time. No journal articles that deal directly with the topic were found. Nonetheless, articles on body image, weight loss, and health risk-taking provide useful background for the present study.

7 In an article relating body image and exercise, David and Cowles (1991) make interesting comparisons between men and women and between younger and older men. Older men (over 25) and women of all ages are likely to desire to lose weight when asked to consider their own bodies. Women are far more dependent on dieting to lose weight than men, who seem more likely to exercise. Drewnowski and Yee (1987) also emphasize the tendency of women to turn to dieting and of men to turn to exercise in order to control weight. Schneider and Greenberg (1992) found that participants in individual sports such as swimming, jogging, tennis, and cycling tend to take fewer behavioral health risks in other aspects of their lives than do participants in team sports .

47e APA

8 A physiological study of the determinants of endurance in well-trained cyclists found that cyclists with 5 or more years of cycling experience had superior endurance compared to similarly trained

Cite up to five authors in first reference to a work

cyclists with 2 to 3 years of experience (Coyle, Coggan, Mopper, & Walters, 1988). This study suggests a link between performance and years of cycling experience. Because responses to the survey were anonymous, this study was unable to test the hypothesis by linking experience to performance in the race.

Hypotheses

Section added to discuss hypotheses in detail

9   This study was intended to be descriptive and to produce hypotheses for further research rather than test them. Nonetheless, I began the study with two tentative hypotheses designed to help interpret the data. On the basis of my experience with cycling, I predicted that the percentage of women entrants in the race would be approximately 10% and would not exceed 20%. In addition, on the basis of my experience and my reading about cycling (Matheny, 1986), I predicted that a common response to the survey question on motivation would be a half-humorous suggestion of "love of pain" or "love of suffering."

Results

Provides detailed summary of questionnaire responses

47e
APA

10   The gender split among respondents was 93.8% male and 6.3% female. This closely matches the overall registration proportion of 92.3% male and 7.7% female. The mean age of respondents was 36.6 years, ranging from a low of 16 to a high of 62. Only 1 entrant was under 25 while 5 were over 50. Just under half (46.9%) the respondents indicated they were married. No respondents indicated a household size of 6 or more. Education level was quite high middle class.

11   The question rating level of cycling ability brought about a respondent-created category. Three respondents felt so torn between the intermediate and advanced categories that they drew a large circle around both. If only one person had done this, I would have made an assignment based on other criteria, but with 3 out of 32 choosing this option, I decided to label it an additional category. There was also one crossed-out and re-circled response to this question, indicating that at least one more person had difficulty with the distinction between the two categories.

12   The mean number of seasons involved with competitive cycling was 4.2 years, ranging from 1 (5 cases) to 10 years (5 cases). Many of the athletes probably had experience in other aerobic sports prior to or overlapping with cycling. A high proportion (71.9%) of the respondents traveled over 50 miles one way to enter a race within the past year. Over two-thirds (69.2%) of those who traveled this distance did so with some frequency, four or more times during 1992.

Detailed information could be presented in table or chart

47e APA

13   The open-ended question regarding reasons for entering bicycle races produced 22 different responses. The most popular cluster was "like to compete" at 75%, followed by "enjoyment of training" at 59%, "friendship with other cyclists" at 40%, and "health benefits of cycling" at 31.3%.

Includes results that do not support hypothesis

Analyzes results and their implications   Cyclists   8

Discussion

14   In terms of the number of seasons of cycling experience, those respondents older than the mean of 36.6 years averaged exactly twice as many years experience as those younger than the mean (5.8 years to 2.9 years). Only one cyclist (7%) over age 36 was *Might be* in the first year of competition, while four (22.2%) *organized* age 36 or under were in the first year. More of *more clearly* the young riders traveled 50 miles to a race *to* *correspond* (77% to 64%), but the older riders who did travel did *with* so more frequently than their younger counterparts. *questionnaire* *items* Only 2 (11.2%) of the younger group traveled 7 or *or previous* more times, compared to 6 (42.8%) of the older group. *discussion* It seems that perhaps the older group is more committed one way or the other--to travel and compete regularly or to stay home.

15   Due to the low number of female entrants/ respondents, it is not appropriate to make statistical comparisons between male and female respondents. I will say, though, that the responses of the 2 women who completed the survey show little to distinguish them from the male respondents. It may be that this particular survey did not bring out gender-based differences, or it may be that the cycling experience transcends gender. The data are *Explores* too slim to support even a preliminary conclusion. *relationships* 16   Drawing on the results, I compared married *among answers,* respondents to all others. I found that married *suggesting* *tentative* racers tend to live in larger households, with 53.3% *conclusions and* living in households of 3 or more versus 17.6% of the *research issues*

47e
APA

nonmarried group. Of interest is that there are no
beginning-level cyclists among the married
respondents but 25% among the nonmarried group. It
is tempting to hypothesize that married people are
less likely to take up a new competitive sport such
as bicycle racing, but I'm restrained by personal
knowledge of many cyclists who have started
competing after being married. Married people also
mentioned "health benefits" as a reason for
competing more frequently than nonmarrieds (53.3% to
12.5%). Health benefits were also more important to
older cyclists (42%) than younger cyclists (22%).

17   There was no apparent relationship between age
and marital status. The mean age of the entire
sample (36.635) and the mean age of the married
cyclists (36.60) is within .035 years. When I
controlled for marital status (married) and

*Continues
discussion of
relationships
discovered
through analysis
of results*

household size (3 or more), I discovered a drop in
the percentage that travel from 66.7% to 50%. Both

**47e
APA**

respondents who mentioned cycling as a stress
release are married and in a larger household. By
the same token, there was almost perfect agreement
between these age and marital status subgroups and
the entire sample on the two most popular reasons
for competing, "like to compete" and "enjoyment of
the training process."

18   Splitting the group on the basis of level of
education showed that 90% of those with no college
degree traveled 50 miles to a race at least once.
But only 1 (10%) mentioned racing for "fun" and only

1 (10%) mentioned racing for "health benefits" while
40% mentioned competing to "achieve personal goals."
Health (40%) and fun (31%) were both more important
among those with a college degree while "achievement
of personal goals" was relatively less important
(13.6%).

[The discussion continues with a critique of the survey and its administration. The writer raises questions about the representativeness of the sample and the timing of the questionnaire's administration. He also discusses some problems with the phrasing of individual questions.]

Discusses whether the research supports hypotheses or answers guiding questions

Conclusions

19   This study had three goals: to describe the
group being studied, to test the viability of two
hypotheses, and to formulate additional hypotheses.
The survey responses provide a rough but interesting
description of competitive cyclists and suggest *Sums up goals of research and contributions to*
that the group deserves further study.

20   Of the two proposed hypotheses, the one *discussion of the subject*
regarding the level of women's participation seems
likely to be supported by further research. This
research also needs to look at the reasons for the
relatively low level of women's participation,
perhaps beginning with the literature suggesting
that women in general tend to depend on diet rather
than exercise to control weight. I suspect that
questions of body image and the difficulty of *Might consider whether family responsibilities limit women's participation*
cycling while overweight may also be worth
considering.

21   The second hypothesis regarding "love of pain"
as a reason for cycling received little support from

Suggests directions for further research

the data. This response was not even among the top 10 on the questionnaire.

22   Several new hypotheses emerged during the study. One deals with the low number of male competitors under 25 years of age. It may be the case that the health and weight concerns of men under 25 and the benefits of competitive cycling are contradictory. Some hypotheses regarding reasons for competing seem worth considering. It may be that people of different ages, marital status, and education levels have considerably different reasons for undertaking the same activity, in this case, racing a bicycle. These questions are certainly worth further study.

47e
APA

Center heading

Page numbers continue

References

Coyle, E. F., Coggan, A. R., Hopper, M. K., &

Double-space all entries   Walters, T. J. (1988). Determinants of

endurance in well-trained cyclists. Journal of

Applied Physiology, 64, 2622-2630.

David, C., & Cowles, M. (1991). Body image and

exercise. Sex Roles, 25, 33-34.

Drewnowski, A., & Yee, D. K. (1987). Men and body

image: Are males satisfied with their body

weight? Psychosomatic Medicine, 49, 626-634.

List source with no author by title   Interbike 1992 Directory. (1992). Costa Mesa, CA:

Primedia.

Matheny, F. (1986, February 5). Solo cycling. Volo

News, 157.

Schneider, D., & Greenberg, M. (1992). Choice of

exercise: A predictor of behavioral risks.

Research Quarterly for Exercise and Sport, 9,

231-245.

47e
APA

List sources alphabetically by last name of author

First line of entry not indented
Additional lines indented five spaces, like paragraphs, following instructor's directions

center heading and name of figure
material   *Page numbers*
dd A, B, and so on to heading   Appendix   *continue*
more than one appendix
                                Survey

Please take a minute or two to answer the following

questions for a University of Rhode Island study of

demographics and motivation of competitive athletes.

1. Sex (circle one) Male   Female   *Use clear material, retyped*
                                      or redrawn if necessary
2. Date of birth ___ / ___ / ___

3. Marital Status (circle one)

      Married Single Divorced Widowed Other

4. Number of people in your household (circle one)

      1 2 3 4 5 6 or more

5. Education level (circle one)

      Haven't finished high school

      High school or equivalency degree

      Associate degree

      Bachelor's degree

      Master's degree

      Doctoral degree

6. In regard to family income, attitudes, and

   values, how do you view your social status?

   (circle one)

      Lower class Lower middle class

      Middle middle class Upper middle class

      Upper class

7. How do you rate yourself as a competitive

   cyclist? (circle one)

      Beginner Intermediate Advanced Expert

8. How many years have you been involved in

   competitive cycling? _____

47e
APA

9. Have you traveled more than 50 miles one way to
    enter a bike race, triathlon, or biathlon
    during 1992? (circle one)   Yes   No
    If you answered yes to the above question,
    approximately how many times did you travel
    that far to enter an event? _____

10. Please list a few (3 to 5) reasons why you
    enter competitive cycling events (including
    biathlons and triathlons).

    I. _____

   II. _____

  III. _____

   IV. _____

    V. _____

    Thank you very much for completing this survey.

                    RIDE FAST!

47e
APA

CHAPTER

48

Documenting Sources: CBE

Papers written in the natural sciences (such as biology, chemistry, and geology) and related technical fields generally use documentation systems that differ in some significant ways from the documentation styles common in the humanities, history, and the arts (MLA and CMS styles, see Chapters 46 and 49) and from those common in the social sciences such as psychology and sociology (APA style, see Chapter 47). One typical and widely used form of documentation in the natural sciences is the Council of Biology Editors (CBE) style. This style tends to have more variations than the other styles, mainly because the papers written in the fields of natural science that employ **CBE documentation style** have different structural requirements. For this reason, it is important to check with your instructor to find out which variations to use. The following discussion covers the two most common variations of CBE style. For more detailed information, see *Scientific Style and Format: The CBE Manual for Authors, Editors, and Publishers* (6th ed., 1994).

48a Creating CBE in-text citations

You can use one of two methods for CBE in-text references, the name-and-year method or the number method.

1 Use the name-and-year method

With this method, you include the name of the author or authors along with the publication year of the text. If you do not mention the author's name in the paper itself, include both the name and year in parentheses; if you do mention the name, include only the year.

PARENTHETICAL REFERENCE

Decreases in the use of lead, cadmium, and zinc in industrial products have resulted in a "very large decrease in the large-scale pollution of the troposphere" (Boutron and others 1991, p 64).

AUTHOR NAMED IN TEXT
Boutron and others (1991) found that decreases in the use of lead, cadmium, and zinc in industrial products have resulted in a "very large decrease in the large-scale pollution of the troposphere" (p 64).

If you cite several works by the same author, all of which appeared in a single year, use letters (*a*, *b*, and so forth) after the date to distinguish them.

ONE OF SEVERAL APPEARING IN THE SAME YEAR
Decreases in the use of lead, cadmium, and zinc in industrial products have resulted in a "very large decrease in the large-scale pollution of the troposphere" (Boutron and others 1991a, p 64).

Did You Know

The CBE style manual traces the history of scientific names and symbols from the Sumerians and Egyptians, who divided the years into days and the days into hours, through the establishment of current standards and nomenclature in fields as widespread as astonomy, virology, and veterinary anatomy. Along the way, notable introductions included the period as a decimal point in 1617, the meter as a unit of measure in 1800, the time zones in the United States in 1883, and the first CBE manual in 1960.

Style Manual Committee, Council of Biology Editors, *Scientific Style and Format: The CBE Manual for Authors, Editors, and Publishers,* 6th ed. (New York: Cambridge UP, 1994), chap. 2.

48a
CBE

2 Use the number method

With this method, you use numbers instead of names of authors. The numbers can be placed in parentheses in the text or raised above the line as superscript figures. The numbers correspond to numbered works on your references page. There are two ways to use the number method. In one style, you number your in-text citations consecutively as they appear in your paper and arrange them accordingly on the references page.

Decreases in the use of lead, cadmium, and zinc in industrial products have reduced pollution in the troposphere (1).

In the second style, you alphabetize your references first, number them, and then refer to the corresponding number in your paper. Since only the number appears in your text, make sure you mention the author's name if it is important.

> Boutron and others found that decreases in the use of lead, cadmium, and zinc in industrial products have reduced pollution in the troposphere (3).

48b Creating a CBE reference list

You may use "Cited References" or just "References" as the heading for your references page. If your instructor asks you to supply references for all your sources, not just the ones cited in your text, prepare a second page called "Additional References," "Additional Reading," or "Bibliography."

The order of the entries in your reference list should correspond to the method you use to cite them within your paper. If you use the name-and-year method, for example, alphabetize the references according to the last name of the main author or by date of publication for works by the same author(s).

If you use the consecutive number method, the reference list will not be alphabetical but will be arranged according to which work comes first in your paper, which second, and so forth. If you use the alphabetized number method, arrange your list alphabetically, and then number the entries.

Following are some examples of the most commonly used formats for entries. Refer to *Scientific Style and Format: The CBE Manual* for further examples of documentation.

Guide to CBE Formats for References

1. ENTRIES FOR BOOKS AND WORKS TREATED AS BOOKS
1. Book with One Author
2. Book with Two or More Authors
3. Book with a Corporate or Group Author
4. Book with an Editor
5. Book with a Translator
6. Conference Proceedings
7. Technical Report

2. ENTRIES FOR ARTICLES AND SELECTIONS FROM BOOKS
8. Article from a Journal Paginated by Volume
9. Article from a Journal Paginated by Issue
10. Article with a Corporate or Group Author
11. Entire Issue of a Journal
12. Figure from an Article
13. Selection from an Anthology or Collection

3. ENTRIES FOR ELECTRONIC RESOURCES
14. Patent from a Database or Information Service
15. Online Article
16. Online Abstract
17. CD-ROM Abstract

48b
CBE

1. Entries for books and works treated as books

Formats for entries for the name-and-year method and the number method are the same except for the location of the year. The sample entries for a reference list follow the style for the number method, but model formats are shown for both methods.

MODEL FORMAT FOR BOOKS AND WORKS TREATED AS BOOKS

NAME-AND-YEAR METHOD

period + period +   period +
space   space   space
↓   ↓   ↓
Author(s). Date. Title of work. Place of

Publication: Publisher. Total Pages.
            ↑   ↑
      colon + space   period + space

NUMBER METHOD

period +   period +   period +
space   space   space
↓   ↓   ↓
1. Author(s). Title of work. Place of

    Publication: Publisher; Date. Total Pages.
                ↑   ↑   ↑
             colon   semicolon period +
             + space   + space   space

- **Author(s).** Give the author's name in inverted order, beginning with the last name and followed by *the initials only* (without periods or spaces) of the author's first and middle names, concluding with a period and a space. For more than one author, follow the same pattern for each author, and separate the names with a comma followed by a space. (Some scientific publications use full names for authors; check with your instructor if this style is required for your paper.) If no author is given, begin with the word *Anonymous* in brackets.
- **Title of Work.** Give the title followed by a period and a space. Do not underline the title, and capitalize only the first word and proper nouns or adjectives. Do not capitalize the subtitle following the colon in a title.
- **Publication Information.** Indicate the city, publisher, and date of publication. Put a colon after the city and a semicolon after the publisher. Conclude with a period. To avoid confusion between two cities with the same name or to identify cities likely to be unfamiliar, place a comma and a space after the city and include the abbreviated name of the state or the country.

- **Total Pages.** Supply the total number of pages in the work, including the index, but do not add in any preliminary pages with roman numerals.
- **Spacing.** Double-space your entries. For the name-and-year method do not indent any lines. For the number method, begin the second and any later lines underneath the beginning of the opening word in the first line. If your instructor gives you other spacing directions, follow these carefully.

1. Book with One Author

```
1. Simpson HN. Invisible armies: the impact of
   disease on American history. Indianapolis:
   Bobbs-Merrill; 1980. 239 p.
```

2. Book with Two or More Authors

List each author's last name first, and use commas to separate the authors.

```
2. Freeman JM, Kelly MT, Freeman JB. The
   epilepsy diet treatment: an introduction to
   the ketogenic diet. New York: Demo, 1994.
   180 p.
```

3. Book with a Corporate or Group Author

Treat an organization or government agency responsible for a work as you would an individual author. If the author is also the publisher, include the name in both places. You can use an organization's acronym in place of the author's name if the acronym is well known.

```
3. World Health Organization. Ataractic and
   hallucinogenic drugs in psychiatry: report
   of a study group. Geneva: World Health
   Organization; 1958. 179 p.
```

48b
CBE

4. Book with an Editor

Identify the editor(s) by including the word *editor*(s) (spelled out) right after the name.

```
4. Dolphin D, editor. Biomimetic chemistry.
   Washington: American Chemical Society;
   1980. 437 p.
```

5. Book with a Translator

Give the translator's name after the title followed by a comma and the word *translator*. If the work has an editor as well, place a semicolon after the word *translator* and then name the editor and conclude with the word *editor*. Give the original title at the end of the entry after the words *Translation of* and a colon.

```
5. Jacob F. The logic of life: a history of
   heredity. Spillmann BE, translator. New
   York: Pantheon Books; 1982. 348 p.
   Translation of: Logique du vivant.
```

6. Conference Proceedings

Begin with the name of the editor(s) and title of the publication. Indicate the name, year, and location of the conference, using semicolons to separate the information. Include the total number of pages at the end. You need not name the conference if the title does so.

```
6. Witt I, editor. Protein C: biochemical and
   medical aspects. Proceedings of the
   International Workshop; 1984 July 9-11;
   Titisee, Germany. Berlin: De Gruyter; 1985.
   195 p.
```

7. Technical Report

Treat a report as you would a book with an individual or corporate author, but include the total number of pages after the publication year. If the report is available through a particular agency—and it usually is—include the information a reader would need to order it. The report listed here can be obtained from the EPA department mentioned using the report number EPA/625/7–91/013. Enclose a widely accepted acronym for an agency in brackets following its name.

```
7. Environmental Protection Agency (US)
   [EPA]. Guides to pollution prevention:
   the automotive repair industry.
   Washington: US Environmental Protection
   Agency; 1991; 46 p. Available from: EPA
   Office of Research and Development;
   EPA/625/7-91/013.
```

2. Entries for articles and selections from books

MODEL FORMAT FOR ARTICLES AND SELECTIONS

NAME-AND-YEAR METHOD

period +   period +   period +
  space   space   space
  ↓   ↓   ↓

```
Author(s). Year. Title of article. Title of
Journal Volume Number:Pages.
         ↑                ↑
       space      colon + no space
```

NUMBER METHOD

period +   period +   period +
  space   space   space
  ↓   ↓   ↓

```
1. Author(s). Title of article. Title of
   Journal date;Volume Number:Pages.
        ↑     ↑                ↑
   space semicolon          colon +
      + no space            no space
```

- **Author(s).** Give the author's name in inverted order, beginning with the last name and followed by *the initials only* (without periods or spaces) of the author's first and middle names, concluding with a period and a single space. For more than one author, follow the same pattern for each author, and separate the names with a comma followed by a space. If no author is given, begin with *Anonymous,* placed in brackets.

- **Title of Article and Publication Information.** Give the article name, journal name, date, volume number and issue number (in parentheses), and page numbers. Do not enclose the article name in quotation marks or underline the journal title. Capitalize only the first word and any proper nouns in an article's title; do not capitalize the first word in a subtitle. For journal titles, follow regular capitalization rules, but use abbreviations standard in the field (see below). Conclude the title of the article with a period and a space. Place a space but no punctuation between the title of the journal and the date. Do not include a space before or after the colon separating the volume number from the page numbers or between volume and issue numbers.

- **Pages.** Include the specific pages of the article or chapter.

- **Journal Title (Abbreviated).** Always abbreviate a journal title unless

48b
CBE

it is a one-word title. To find out how to abbreviate titles, notice the abbreviations used in your sources and ask your instructor which book lists abbreviations for your field.

- **Spacing.** Double-space all entries. Do not indent the first line or any subsequent lines (name and year); align second and later lines under the beginning of the initial word of the first line.

8. Article from a Journal Paginated by Volume

```
8. Yousef YA, Yu LL. Potential contamination
   of groundwater from Cu, Pb, and Zn in wet
   detention ponds receiving highway runoff.
   J Environ Sci Hlth 1992;27:1033-44.
```

9. Article from a Journal Paginated by Issue

Give the issue number within parentheses immediately (with no space) after the volume number.

```
9. Boutron CF. Decrease in anthropogenic lead,
   cadmium and zinc in Greenland snows since
   the late 1960's. Nature 1991;353(6340):153-
   5, 160.
```

10. Article with a Corporate or Group Author

Treat the corporate or group author as you would any author. If a person's name is part of the corporation, as in this example, do not transpose the first and last names. Alphabetize by the first main word in the corporation name, even if it is a first name.

```
10. Derek Sims Associates. Why and how of
    acoustic testing. Environ Eng 1991;4(1):10-
    12.
```

11. Entire Issue of a Journal

Include the title of the main editor or compiler of the specific issue because this person will often be a guest editor.

```
11. Savage A, editor. Proceedings of the
    workshop on the zoo-university connection:
    collaborative efforts in the conservation
    of endangered primates. Zoo Biol
    1989;1(Suppl).
```

48b
CBE

12. Figure from an Article

Include the name of the figure (or table, chart, or diagram) and its number, as well as the page on which it appears. Use *p* in this context.

12. Kanaori Y, Kawakami SI, Yairi K. Space-time distribution patterns of destructive earthquakes in the inner belt of central Japan. Engng Geol 1991;31(3-4):209-30 (p 216, table 1).

13. Selection from an Anthology or Collection

The first name and title refer to the article; the second name and title refer to the book from which the article is taken. Include the page numbers of the article at the end of the citation.

13. Moro M. Supply and conservation efforts for nonhuman primates. In Gengozian N, Deinhardt F, editors. Marmosets in experimental medicine. Basel: S. Karger AG; 1978. p 37-40.

3. Entries for electronic resources

14. Patent from a Database or Information Service

The sample below, from the inventors' names through the date, illustrates how to cite a patent. In this instance, information about electronic access is added at the end.

14. Collins FS, Drumm ML, Dawson DC, Wilkinson DJ, inventors. Method of testing potential cystic fibrosis treating compounds using cells in culture. US patent 5,434,086. 1995 18 July. Available from: Lexis/Nexis/Lexpat library/ALL file.

15. Online Article

15. Grolmusz, V. On the weak mod m representation of Boolean functions. Chi J Theor Comp Sci [serial online] 1995 July 21;100-5. 2 screens. Available from:

```
http://www.csuchicago.edu/publication/cjtcs/
articles/1995/2/contents.html via the WORLD
WIDE WEB. Accessed 1996 May 3.
```

16. Online Abstract

Use a form similar to that for journal articles, but give the word *abstract* in brackets following the title.

```
16. Smithies O, Maeda N. Gene targeting
    approaches to complex genetic diseases:
    atherosclerosis and essential hypertension
    [abstract]. Proc Natl Acad Sci USA
    1995;92(12):5266-72. 1 screen. Available
    from: Lexis/Medline/ABST. Accessed 1996
    Jan 21.
```

17. CD-ROM Abstract

Indicate the medium (CD-ROM) in brackets following the title. Close the entry with the phrase *Available from*, followed by information about the source and retrieval number.

```
17. MacDonald R, Fleming MF, Barry KL. Risk
    factors associated with alcohol abuse in
    college students. Am J Drug and Alc Abuse
    [CD-ROM]; 17:439-49. Available from:
    SilverPlatter File: PsycLIT Item: 79-13172.
```

48b
CBE

Exercise

A. Turn to Exercise A in Chapter 46. Rewrite the sentences supplied there to add either form of in-text citations in CBE style. Prepare a corresponding list of references.

B. Turn to Exercise B in Chapter 46. Rewrite the items supplied there to create a list of references following either form used in CBE style.

C. Working with a partner or a small group, compare your answers to Exercises A and B above. Correct any errors in your answers, using your handbook or your instructor's advice to resolve any differences of opinion.

CHAPTER 49

Documenting Sources: CMS

Instead of the in-text references used in the MLA, APA, and CBE documentation styles (see Chapters 46 through 48), one of the documentation styles outlined in *The Chicago Manual of Style* (the CMS style) provides references in the form of endnotes or footnotes. Endnotes or footnotes are signaled by a superscript numeral in the text, for example,[1] and a correspondingly numbered reference note at the end of the paper (endnote) or, less often, at the bottom of the page (footnote). A bibliography at the end of the paper provides a list of all the sources in alphabetical order.

CMS documentation style is widely used in history and some other fields in the arts and sciences, and instructors in other courses may prefer its use of numbered notes to the parenthetical systems of the other documentation styles. Endnotes and footnotes are less compact than parenthetical references, yet they offer you a chance to cite a source in more specific detail and to include brief explanatory material. You need to resist the temptation to provide lengthy notes, however, because they can distract your reader's attention from the paper itself.

The CMS style is one of two systems of documentation outlined in *The Chicago Manual of Style* (14th edition, University of Chicago Press, 1993). The CMS style is also presented in detail in Kate L. Turabian's *A Manual for Writers of Term Papers, Theses, and Dissertations* (5th ed., rev. and exp. Bonnie Birtwistle Honigsblum [University of Chicago Press, 1987]). Because of the popularity of Turabian's manual, the CMS style is also widely referred to as "Turabian" or "Turabian style." You can consult either of these works for details of documentation not covered in this chapter.

49a Using endnotes and footnotes

To indicate a reference in the body of your text, insert a number slightly above the line,[2] making sure you number the references consecutively. Insert a number to indicate a reference to the source of a quotation, to alert readers to specific information and ideas borrowed from a source, or to specify the source of paraphrased or summarized material. At the end of the paper (in an endnote) or at the bottom of the page (in a footnote), provide detailed information about the source.

TEXT OF PAPER   To emphasize how isolated and impoverished his childhood neighborhood was, Wideman describes it as being not simply on "the wrong side of the tracks," but actually *under the tracks, if the truth be told—in a deep hollow between Penn and the abrupt rise of Bruston Hill.*"[1]

NOTE   1. John Edgar Wideman, Brothers and Keepers (New York: Penguin Books, 1984), 39.

1 Select endnotes or footnotes

Positioning footnotes between the body of the text and the bottom margin can be quite difficult and time-consuming. For this reason, even though it may be a bit easier for readers to look at the bottom of the page for a note than to turn to the end of the paper, you should generally employ endnotes. Most readers mark the page containing the endnotes so they can refer to notes with a minimum of disruption. Because readers may sometimes skip consulting a note unless they are particularly interested in your sources, you should make sure that you place all information necessary for understanding your argument or explanation in the body of your paper and not in the notes.

2 Consider content and explanatory notes

At times you may wish to supplement your text with material that may interest only a few readers. Notes are an appropriate place to do this, but don't make notes so detailed that they distract readers from the main text of the paper. You can also combine explanation with a source reference, though you need to make sure that a long and detailed discussion does not obscure the reference.

TEXT OF PAPER   Another potential source of conflict, or at least misunderstanding, in the contemporary workplace comes from differences in the ways men commonly give orders (directly) and the ways women give orders (indirectly, often in the form of requests or questions).[2]

NOTE   2. Deborah Tannen, "How to Give Orders Like a Man," New York Times Magazine, 18 August 1994, 46. It is sometimes easy to oversimplify the differences between the ways men and women use language. Tannen provides a detailed and balanced discussion in Talking from 9 to 5 (New York: William Morrow, 1994).

Did You Know?

The Chicago Manual of Style began as a single sheet of directions drawn up by a proofreader. It was first issued by the University of Chicago Press as a short volume titled "Style Book: Adapted and In Use for University Publications." Now in its four-teenth edition, the manual is an authoritative source consulted regularly by writers, editors, copy editors and proofreaders.

49b Creating CMS notes

After you have placed a number slightly above the line of text[3] to indicate the presence of an endnote or footnote and have made sure that your numbering system maintains consecutive order, you need to prepare the note. A typical note provides the author's name in regular order, the title of the work being cited, publication information, and the page number(s).

Place endnotes at the end of a paper, after appendixes but before a bibliography. Supply notes on a separate page with the centered heading "Notes." Indent the first line six spaces. Start the note with the number, fol-

Guide to CMS Formats for Notes

1. ENTRIES FOR BOOKS AND WORKS TREATED AS BOOKS
 1. Book with One Author
 2. Book with Two or Three Authors
 3. Book with Four or More Authors
 4. Book with No Author Given
 5. Book with an Editor
 6. Book in an Edition Other than the First
 7. Multivolume Work

2. ENTRIES FOR ARTICLES AND SELECTIONS FROM BOOKS
 8. Article from a Journal Paginated by Volume
 9. Article from a Journal Paginated by Issue
10. Article from a Popular Magazine
11. Article from a Daily Newspaper
12. Chapter in a Book or Selection from an Anthology

3. ENTRIES FOR OTHER PRINTED AND FIELD RESOURCES
13. Unpublished Interview

4. ENTRIES FOR MEDIA AND ELECTRONIC RESOURCES
14. Audio or Video Recording
15. Electronic Sources

5. ENTRIES FOR MULTIPLE SOURCES AND SOURCE CITED IN PRIOR NOTES
16. Multiple Sources
17. Book or Article Cited More than Once

49b CMS

lowed by a period and a space. Do not indent the second line or any others that follow. CMS suggests single-spacing all notes, but we advise double-spacing for ease of reading. (Check with your instructor.)

1. Entries for books and works treated as books

MODEL FORMAT FOR BOOKS AND WORKS TREATED AS BOOKS

<table>
<tr><td>note
number
↓</td><td>comma
+ space
↓</td><td>space
↓</td></tr>
</table>

1. Author(s), <u>Title</u> (Place of Publication: Publisher, Year), Page Number(s).

↑
comma + space

- **Author(s).** Give the name of the author(s) in regular order followed by a comma and a space.
- **Title.** Give the title of the work being cited. Underline the title of a book and follow the title with a space. (See 37b-2 on capitalization of titles.)
- **Publication Information.** Give all publication information within parentheses. Start with the city of publication, followed by a comma and an abbreviation for the state or country if this information is necessary to avoid confusion between two cities with the same name or to identify little-known places. Add a colon and a space; then give the publisher's name followed by a comma, a space, and the date of publication. Place a comma followed by a space after the closing parenthesis mark.
- **Page Number(s).** Conclude with the specific page numbers containing the information being cited or the passage being quoted, paraphrased, or summarized.

1. Book with One Author

1. Ruth Macklin, <u>Mortal Choices: Ethical Dilemmas in Modern Medicine</u> (Boston: Houghton Mifflin, 1987), 154.

2. Book with Two or Three Authors

Separate the names of two authors with *and*. Separate those of three authors with commas as well as *and* before the name of the third author.

2. Mary Knapp and Herbert Knapp, <u>One Potato, Two Potato . . .: The Secret Education of American Children</u> (New York: W. W. Norton, 1978), 144.

2. Michael Wood, Bruce Cole, and Adelheid Gealt, <u>Art of the Western World</u> (New York: Summit Books, 1989), 206-10.

3. Book with Four or More Authors

For works with more than three authors, give the name of the first author followed by *and others*. (Generally, all the names are supplied in the corresponding bibliography entry.)

3. Anthony Slide and others, <u>The American Film Industry: A Historical Dictionary</u> (New York: Greenwood Press, 1986), 124.

4. Book with No Author Given

If the author is not known, begin the entry with the title.

4. <u>The Great Utopia: 1915-1932</u> (New York: Guggenheim Museum, 1992), 661.

5. Book with an Editor

When a work has an editor, translator, or compiler (or some combination of these), give the name or names after the title preceded by a comma and the appropriate abbreviation, for example, *ed.*, *trans.*, or *comp.*

5. Charles Dickens, <u>Bleak House</u>, ed. Norman Page (Harmondsworth, Eng.: Penguin Books, 1971), 49.

Dickens is the author, and Page has prepared the particular edition of the work.

49b
CMS

If you wish to emphasize the role of the editor, translator, or compiler, give his or her name at the beginning of the entry.

5. Donald M. Scott and Bernard Wishy, eds., <u>America's Families: A Documentary History</u> (New York: Harper & Row, 1982), 177.

The editors are responsible for assembling materials from a variety of sources.

5. Robert H. Ferrell, ed., <u>Dear Bess: The Letters from Harry to Bess Truman 1910-1959</u> (New York: W. W. Norton, 1983), 71-2.

The word *by* with the author's name (Harry S. Truman) would be appropriate following the title, but it is not necessary because the author's name appears in the title.

6. Book in an Edition Other than the First

Use an abbreviation following the title to indicate the particular edition, for example, *4th ed.* (fourth edition) or *rev. and enl. ed.* (revised and enlarged edition).

6. John D. La Plante, <u>Asian Art</u>, 3d ed.

(Dubuque, Iowa: Wm. C. Brown, 1992), 7.

For a work that has been reprinted or appears in a special paperback edition, give information about both the original publication and the reprint.

6. Henri Frankfort and others, <u>The</u>

<u>Intellectual Adventure of Ancient Man</u> (Chicago:

University of Chicago Press, 1946; reprint,

Chicago: University of Chicago Press, 1977),

202-4.

7. Multivolume Work

A multivolume work can consist of volumes all by a single author (sometimes with different titles for each) or of works by a variety of authors with an overall title after the title. If you are referring to the whole multivolume work, include the number of volumes after the title. To indicate volume and page number for a specific volume, use volume and page numbers separated by a colon and no space. Give the volume number and name for separately titled volumes after the main title and omit the volume number in the page reference.

7. Sigmund Freud, <u>The Standard Edition of</u>

<u>the Complete Psychological Works of Sigmund</u>

<u>Freud</u>, trans. James Strachey (London: Hogarth

Press, 1953), 11:180.

2. Entries for articles and selections from books

MODEL FORMAT FOR ARTICLES AND SELECTIONS

note number ↓	comma + space ↓	comma inside ↓

1. Author(s), "Title of Article," <u>Title of</u>

<u>Publication</u> Volume Number (Date): Page Numbers.

     ↑   ↑   ↑
    space   space   colon +
                             space

- **Author(s).** Give the author's name in regular order.
- **Title.** Put the title of the article or selection in quotation marks. Put a comma inside the closing quotation mark, and leave a space after the quotation mark.
- **Publication Information.** Next give the title of the journal or book, underlined, and leave a space after it with no punctuation. Supply the volume number and then the date of publication in parentheses, varying the information and style for different types of publications (see below). Place a colon after the final parenthesis, and leave a space.
- **Page Number(s).** Supply the page numbers for the pertinent part of the article or selection.

8. Article from a Journal Paginated by Volume

When the page numbers run continuously through the individual issues that make up a volume, give the volume number but do not include the month, season, or number of the individual issue containing the article. Give specific page numbers for the part of the article you are citing. If you wish to refer to the article as a whole, give inclusive page numbers for the entire article, for example, *98–114.*

> 8. C. Anita Tarr, "'A Man Can Stand Up': Johnny Tremain and the Rebel Pose," The Lion and the Unicorn: A Critical Journal of Children's Literature 18 (1994): 181.

9. Article from a Journal Paginated by Issue

If each issue of a journal begins with page 1, give the volume number followed by a comma, the abbreviation *no.* (for number), and the issue number. If the issue is instead identified by month or season, include this information just before the year and within the same set of parentheses, for example, (*Winter 1994*) or (*February 1996*). Give page numbers for the specific part of the article you are citing or inclusive page numbers for the entire article if you are referring to it as a whole.

> 9. Peter Smagorinsky and Pamela K. Fly, "A New Perspective on Why Small Groups Do and Don't Work," English Journal 83, no. 5 (1994): 54–55.

**49b
CMS**

10. Article from a Popular Magazine

Follow the name of the magazine with a comma and the date. Use this order for the date if it includes the day: 25 November 1995. Place a comma at the end of the date before the page number, and give a page number for the specific part of the article you are citing or inclusive page numbers for the entire article if you are referring to it as a whole.

> 10. Deborah Tannen, "But What Do You Mean?" <u>Redbook</u>, October 1994, 57–58.

11. Article from a Daily Newspaper

Identify newspaper articles by date (rather than volume number) following the title of the article and the name of the newspaper. Present the date in this order: 4 February 1996. When the sections of a newspaper are separately paginated, provide the section number or letter and the page number—for example, *sec. B, p. 3*—using *p.* or *pp.* to introduce the page number(s).

> 11. Debra West, "Stalking Weeds of Spring for Traditional Meals," <u>New York Times</u>, 18 May 1995, sec. B, pp. 1, 7.

When an American newspaper's title does not include the city's name, give it at the start of the title (underlined). For less known newspapers, for those outside North America with the city not mentioned in the title, and for those from places easily confused with well-known cities, give the name of the state or country after the title or after the name of the city in the title: *Westerly (R.I.) Sun, Times* (London).

12. Chapter in a Book or Selection from an Anthology

For a selection from an anthology or for a book chapter, give the name of the selection or chapter in quotation marks followed by *in* and the name of book. If the book has an editor, follow the book's title with *ed.* and the editor's name.

> 12. Fred Pfeil, "'Makin' Flippy-Floppy': Postmodernism and the Baby-Boom PMC," in <u>Another Tale to Tell: Politics and Narrative in Postmodern Culture</u> (London: Verso, 1990), 107.

Chapter in a book.

> 12. W. E. B. Du Bois, "The Call of Kansas," in <u>W. E. B. Du Bois: A Reader</u>, ed. David Levering Lewis (New York: Henry Holt, 1995), 173.

Selection from an edited collection of one writer's works.

12. Julie D'Acci, "Defining Women: The Case of <u>Cagney and Lacey</u>," in <u>Private Screenings: Television and the Female Consumer</u>, ed. Lynn Spigel and Denise Mann (Minneapolis: University of Minnesota Press, 1992), 169.
<small>Chapter in an edited collection of essays.</small>

3. Entries for other printed and field resources

13. Unpublished Interview

For unpublished interviews done by someone else, begin with the name of the person interviewed followed by a comma, then give the phrase *interview by*, the name of the interviewer, the date (in this order: 2 May 1978), any file number, the medium (*tape recording* or *transcript,* for example), and the place where the interview is stored (such as *Erie County Historical Society, Buffalo, New York*).

For interviews you conduct, provide the name of the person interviewed, the phrase *interview by author*, a description of the kind of interview, the medium, and the place and date of the interview.

13. Shawon Kelley, interview by author, tape recording, Los Angeles, Calif., 2 May 1995.

13. Morton Kosko, telephone interview by author, transcript, Scottsdale, Ariz., 22 January 1996.

49b
CMS

4. Entries for media and electronic resources

14. Audio or Video Recording

Start with the work's title unless the recording features a particular performer, composer, director, or writer. Give names and roles (if appropriate) of performers or others whose participation needs to be noted. Indicate length of recording (video), company responsible, the recording number (audio), date, and medium (for example, audiocassette or videocassette).

14. <u>James Baldwin,</u> prod. and dir. Karen Thorsen, 87 min., Resolution Inc./California Newsreel, 1990, videocassette.

15. Electronic Sources

For information and text you gather through an electronic information service, use whatever format would be appropriate for similar material
available in printed form, but at the end of the entry provide the name of the
service (such as Dialog or ERIC), the name of the vendor, and the accession
or identifying numbers used by the service.

> 15. Mark Miller, "Two Beaked Whales Wash
> Up on Beach," <u>Daytona Beach News-Journal</u>, 20
> January 1994, in Newsbank [database online],
> ENV 3, G6.

5. Entries for multiple sources and source cited in prior notes

16. Multiple Sources

When you wish to cite more than one source in a note, separate the
references with semicolons and give the entries in the order in which they
were cited in the text.

> 16. See Greil Marcus, <u>Mystery Train:</u>
> <u>Images of America in Rock 'n Roll Music</u> (New
> York: E. P. Dutton, 1975), 119; Susan Orlean,
> "All Mixed Up," <u>New Yorker,</u> 22 June 1992, 90;
> and Cornel West, "Learning to Talk of Race,"
> <u>New York Times Magazine</u>, 2 August 1992, 24.

17. Book or Article Cited More than Once

The first time you provide a reference to a work, you need to provide
full information about the source in the note. In later notes you need to provide only the last name of the author(s), a shortened title, and the page(s).
Separate these elements with commas.

> 17. Macklin, <u>Mortal</u>, 161.
>
> 17. Wood, Cole, and Gealt, <u>Art</u>, 207.

If one note refers to the same source as the note before, you can use
a traditional scholarly abbreviation, *ibid.* (from the Latin for "in the same
place"), for the second note. *Ibid.* means that the entire reference is identical, but if you add a new page reference, the addition shows that the specific
page is different.

```
18. Tarr, "'A Man,'" 183.

19. Ibid.

20. Ibid., 186.
```

49c Creating a CMS bibliography

At the end of your paper you need to provide readers with an alphabetical list of the sources cited in your notes. CMS style calls for this list to be titled "Selected Bibliography" or "Sources Consulted" if it includes all the works you consulted. If you want to limit the list to the works appearing in your notes, you might call it "Works Cited," "References," or a similar title.

Place your bibliography on a separate page at the end of your paper, and center the title two inches below the upper edge. Continue the page numbering used for the text. CMS calls for single-spacing; we suggest double-spacing entries in student papers for ease of reading. Check with your instructor. Double-space each entry. Do not indent the first line, but indent the second line and any subsequent lines five spaces. Alphabetize the entries according to the authors' last names or the first word of the title, excluding *A* and *The,* if the author is unknown.

Guide to CMS Formats for Bibliography Entries

1. ENTRIES FOR BOOKS AND WORKS TREATED AS BOOKS
 1. Book with One Author
 2. Book with Two or Three Authors
 3. Book with Four or More Authors
 4. Book with No Author Given
 5. Book with an Editor
 6. Book in an Edition Other than the First
 7. Multivolume Work

2. ENTRIES FOR ARTICLES AND SELECTIONS FROM BOOKS
 8. Article from a Journal Paginated by Volume
 9. Article from a Journal Paginated by Issue
 10. Article from a Popular Magazine
 11. Article from a Daily Newspaper
 12. Chapter in a Book or Selection from an Anthology

3. ENTRIES FOR OTHER PRINTED AND FIELD RESOURCES
 13. Unpublished Interview

4. ENTRIES FOR MEDIA AND ELECTRONIC RESOURCES
 14. Audio or Video Recording
 15. Electronic Sources

5. ENTRY FOR MULTIPLE SOURCES
 16. Multiple Sources

**49c
CMS**

1. Entries for books and works treated as books

MODEL FORMAT FOR BOOKS AND WORKS TREATED AS BOOKS

```
            period +    period +                 colon +
             space       space                    space
               ↓           ↓                        ↓
Author(s).  Title.  Place of Publication:

      Publisher,  Date.
   ↑                ↑
 indent      comma + space
 5 spaces
```

- **Author(s).** Give the author's last name, followed by a comma, then the first and any middle names or initials, followed by a period and a space.
- **Title.** Give the title of the work, underlined, ending with a period and space and capitalize the main words of the title and any subtitle. Do not capitalize *a, an, the,* coordinating conjunctions (e.g., *and, or,* and *but*), and prepositions. Always capitalize the first and last words of any title or subtitle
- **Place of Publication.** Give the city where the work was published, followed by a comma and an abbreviation for the state or country if necessary to avoid confusion between cities with the same name or to identify little-known places. End with a colon and a space.
- **Publisher.** Give the publisher's name followed by a comma and a single space.
- **Date.** Give the date of publication followed by a period.

1. Book with One Author

> Macklin, Ruth. <u>Mortal Choices: Ethical Dilemmas
>   in Modern Medicine</u>. Boston: Houghton
>   Mifflin, 1987.

2. Book with Two or Three Authors

> Knapp, Mary, and Herbert Knapp. <u>One Potato, Two
>   Potato . . . : The Secret Education of
>   American Children</u>. New York: W. W. Norton,
>   1978.

> Wood, Michael, Bruce Cole, and Adelheid Gealt.
>   <u>Art of the Western World</u>. New York: Summit
>   Books, 1989.

3. Book with Four or More Authors

Slide, Anthony, Val Almen Darez, Robert Gitt,
and Susan Perez Prichard. The American
Film Industry: A Historical Dictionary.
New York: Greenwood Press, 1986.

4. Book with No Author Given

The Great Utopia: 1915-1932. New York:
Guggenheim Museum, 1992.

5. Book with an Editor

Dickens, Charles. Bleak House. Edited by Norman
Page. Harmondsworth, England: Penguin
Books, 1971.

Ferrell, Robert H., ed. Dear Bess: The Letters
from Harry to Bess Truman 1910-1959. New
York: W. W. Norton, 1983.

Scott, Donald M., and Bernard Wishy, eds.
America's Families: A Documentary History.
New York: Harper & Row, 1982.

6. Book in an Edition Other than the First

Frankfort, Henri, H. A. Frankfort, John A.
Wilson, Thorkild Jacobsen, and William A.
Irving. The Intellectual Adventure of
Ancient Man. Chicago: University of
Chicago Press, 1946. Reprint, Chicago:
University of Chicago Press, 1977.

La Plante, John D. Asian Art. 3d ed. Dubuque,
Iowa: Wm. C. Brown, 1992.

49c
CMS

7. Multivolume Work

Freud, Sigmund. The Standard Edition of the
Complete Psychological Works of Sigmund
Freud. Translated by James Strachey. Vol.
11. London: Hogarth Press, 1953.

2. Entries for articles and selections from books

MODEL FORMAT FOR ARTICLES AND SELECTIONS FROM BOOKS

period + space   period inside   space   space
↓   ↓   ↓   ↓

Author(s). "Title." <u>Name of Publication</u> Volume

(Date): Pages.

↑
colon + space

- **Author(s).** Give the author's last name followed by a comma, then the first and any middle names or initials followed by a period and a space.
- **Title.** Give the title of the article within quotation marks, and capitalize the main words of the title and of any subtitle. Do not capitalize *a, an, the,* coordinating conjunctions (e.g., *and* and *or*), and any prepositions. Always capitalize the first and last words of any title or subtitle. If the article's title contains the title of a work that needs to be italicized or underlined, use underlining; if it contains a title that requires quotation marks, use single quotation marks to enclose the interior title.
- **Name of Publication.** Give the title of the journal or magazine containing the article, and underline it.
- **Volume.** Give the volume number of the periodical; separate it from the name of the publication by a space without a comma or any other punctuation. Include the issue number only for certain kinds of publications (see below).
- **Date.** Provide the year in which the article was published (within parentheses), but indicate the month or season only for certain kinds of publications (see below).
- **Pages.** Follow the parentheses containing the date with a colon and a space, then give the inclusive pages on which the article appears.

8. Article from a Journal Paginated by Volume

Tarr, Anita C. "'A Man Can Stand Up': Johnny

    Tremain and the Rebel Pose." <u>The Lion and</u>

    <u>the Unicorn: A Critical Journal of</u>

    <u>Children's Literature</u> 18 (1994): 178–189.

9. Article from a Journal Paginated by Issue

Smagorinsky, Peter, and Pamela K. Fly. "A New

    Perspective on Why Small Groups Do and

Don't Work." English Journal 83, no. 5
(1994): 54-58.

10. Article from a Popular Magazine

Tannen, Deborah. "But What Do You Mean?"
Redbook, October 1994, 57-58.

11. Article from a Daily Newspaper

West, Debra. "Stalking Weeds of Spring for
Traditional Meals." New York Times, 18 May
1995, sec. B, pp. 1, 7.

12. Chapter in a Book or Selection from an Anthology

D'Acci, Julia. "Defining Women: The Case of
Cagney and Lacey." In Private Screenings:
Television and the Female Consumer, edited
by Lynn Spigel and Denise Mann, 169-201.
Minneapolis: University of Minnesota
Press, 1992.

Du Bois, W. E. B. "The Call of Kansas." In
W. E. B. Du Bois: A Reader, edited by
David Levering Lewis, 101-121. New York:
Henry Holt, 1995.

Pfeil, Fred. "'Makin' Flippy-Floppy':
Postmodernism and the Baby-Boom PMC."
Chap. in Another Tale to Tell: Politics
and Narrative in Postmodern Culture.
London: Verso, 1990.

3. Entries for other printed and field resources

13. Unpublished Interview

Kelley, Shawon. Interview by author. Tape
recording. Los Angeles, Calif., 2 May 1995.

```
Kosko, Morton. Telephone interview by the
     author. Transcript. Scottsdale, Ariz.,
     22 January 1996.
```

4. Entries for media and electronic resources

14. Audio or Video Recording

```
James Baldwin. Produced and directed by Karen
     Thorsen. 87 min. Resolution
     Inc./California Newsreel, 1990.
     Videocassette.
```

15. Electronic Sources

```
Miller, Mark. "Two Beaked Whales Wash Up on
     Beach." Daytona Beach News-Journal, 20
     January 1994. In Newsbank [database
     online], ENV 3, G6.
```

5. Entry for multiple sources

16. Multiple Sources

When a note lists more than one source, list each one separately in your bibliography, presenting them in alphabetical order among your other sources.

Exercise

A. Turn to Exercise A in Chapter 46. Rewrite the sentences supplied there to add note numbers in CMS style. Then prepare the corresponding notes for these items.

B. Turn to Exercise B in Chapter 46. Rewrite the items supplied there to create a list of works cited in CMS style.

C. Working with a partner or a small group, compare your answers to Exercises A and B above. Correct any errors in your answers, using your handbooks or your instructor's advice to resolve any differences of opinion.

CHAPTER

50

Writing Argumentative Papers Across the Disciplines

Some of the most common writing assignments in college courses, especially in the humanities and social sciences, are those that ask you to articulate and support a position or point of view. Such writing, including all forms of argument, is **point-driven writing.** Unlike purely informative writing, in which you play a neutral role and try to present information in an organized, objective, and readable way (see Chapter 52), **argumentative writing** is evaluative: it takes a stand. In argumentative writing, your own voice, attitudes, opinions, and values play an important role. As a result, you must attend carefully to the relationship between your ideas and your readers' potential responses.

Obviously, argumentative writing can't be separated entirely from informative writing. A grant proposal may need to educate a committee about existing research in the area being funded while it is also trying to persuade that committee to honor the financial request. But the *primary* goal of argumentative writing is to advance the writer's point of view, or to suggest a course of action to solve a problem. You want to say to your reader, rhetorically, "Try to see it my way," or "Here's a way to think about this, and here's why." In informative writing, you're more likely to imply, "Here's some new and interesting knowledge for you, but I'm just a reporter; don't confuse the message with the messenger."

This chapter presents some strategies for producing successful argumentative and other point-driven writing. The chapter also presents some sample argumentative papers written by college students, papers that take different approaches to persuading readers. Though the papers are effective, they also show how the writers struggled to meet the special demands of their assignments and what strategies of point-driven writing those assignments required. These sample papers also draw on a variety of sources for evidence that explains and supports the writer's perspective.

As you consider the Strategies for point-driven writing described and modeled in this chapter, remember that most writing is not formulaic. Do not think that to produce it you just need to remember a few rules. Even the simplest forms will vary according to your purpose, audience, and context.

50a   Developing argumentative writing

In many classes you may be asked to write a short argumentative paper, often documented with outside sources. Unlike a full-scale "objective" research paper, this kind of writing documents and supports your own opinion, usually on one specific aspect of a particular topic. Because you must limit yourself to a narrow focus and get right to the point, you have to construct your argument carefully and efficiently.

1 Identify an issue

Your feelings about some things may be so strong that you want to argue with anyone who disagrees with your position. But what if no one really disagrees? What if no one thinks the subject is worth arguing about? To have an argument in a formal sense, you must begin with an **issue,** a subject about which there are two (or more) clearly differing opinions. No one, for example, is willing to say that driving while intoxicated is a good thing; anyone who tried to advance this opinion would be considered foolish, at best. Drunk driving is not an issue. However, reasonable people disagree about what policies are most likely to discourage people from driving while intoxicated—strict laws, harsh punishments, roadblocks, advertising campaigns, door-to-door public information programs, programs for high school students, and so on. For most readers this question is certainly an issue, and they would probably be glad to listen to differing opinions in hopes of discovering the best way to deal with the problem.

Use the following questions to help you determine whether you have chosen an issue worth pursuing in your writing.

50a
arg

1. *Is the issue clearly debatable?* A fact is something about which there can be no debate ("The world is round," "Mice are rodents," "President John F. Kennedy was assassinated on November 22, 1963"). The only facts that can be debated are those that might be reasonably challenged *as* facts. For example, it was widely held as "fact" that peptic ulcers were caused by excess acidity in the diet, and for years treatment involved changes in eating habits, antacids, or acid-inhibiting drugs. New evidence, however, now supports a theory that ulcers are caused by a bacterium able to be treated with antibiotics. The question "Are peptic ulcers caused by diet?" is, in light of this information, a much more debatable issue than the question "Does the earth have a moon?"

2. *Can you explore the issue with something more than pure speculation?* Claims that can't be verified often make for interesting philosophical

discussion, but they don't lend themselves fully to argument. The question "Where do we go when we die?" is impossible to answer conclusively and therefore hard develop into an arguable issue. Statements for which there is only tentative supporting evidence ("There may be life on other planets") also make difficult choices for argumentative writing.

3. *Is the issue more than a matter of pure taste or preference?* An author's own values and beliefs need to be supported in argumentative writing with sound reasoning or evidence. Statements such as "I hate anything with tomatoes in it" can't be supported with anything more than circular reasoning ("because I hate tomatoes"). However, evaluative statements based on comparisons or analyses, such as those found in reviews (see 50f), can become reasonable supporting evidence for a broader assertion ("The food at Alfredo's Restaurant is highly overrated").

4. *Does the issue avoid assumptions that are so deeply or universally held that they cannot be argued?* Although some of the most important social and political issues of our time seem like good topics for argumentative writing, they may seriously frustrate your writing process. Arguments about topics such as the right to die and capital punishment may invoke systems of belief, including religious belief, that can't be logically debated. Debates between nonreligious students and their fundamentalist peers rarely end in resolution or change—interesting or confrontational though the discussions may be. When you choose a topic, ask yourself whether and how it can be explored through the use of sound reasoning and evidence.

Strategy

50a
arg

Here are three ways to identify an issue of interest to you and of significance to your readers.

- In your journal or on a piece of paper, "talk" to yourself about problems, controversies, trends, or ideas that concern you or that affect the ways we all live. Try making a list, adding to each item a short (one- or two-sentence) summary of at least two different opinions on the subject.

- Interview friends and family about questions and problems that concern them and that inspire strong opinions. Keep a list of their responses, and add your own ideas. Identify subjects about which there are at least two reasonable and differing opinions. (If many of the issues you discover seem of limited or local concern—such as campus parking policies or a controversy over a garbage-fired incinerator—remember that a focused subject is often a better choice for writing than an overly broad one, even one of global concern.)

- Leaf through newsmagazines and opinion magazines (such as *The*

New Republic and *National Review*); look at editorials in local and national newspapers (available in your library); and consult periodical indexes or databases like *Newsbank,* which provides newspaper editorials from the entire country (see 44b-2). List the issues that interest you, and write down any opposing opinions.

Exercise 1

A. Examine the following five issue statements. Decide which of the issues could be developed into argumentative papers and which would not lend themselves to such development. Explain why.

1. Permitting fast-food franchises to do business in the student union
2. The taste of fresh orange juice
3. The sale of pharmaceuticals (aspirin, sunscreen, condoms, tampons) in campus vending machines
4. Belief in the sacredness of cows
5. The reinstitution of chain gangs (prisoners shackled together at the legs) to do highway work

B. In a small group, compare your analysis of the items in Exercise 1A. Collectively choose two issue statements that would make good argumentative papers.

---

2 Articulate your stance

An **argument** is an attempt to resolve disagreement, not to defeat everyone who has an opinion other than yours. A good argument is positive: you attempt to persuade people to accept your opinion, but you don't attack them for having another point of view. In order to argue effectively, you first need a clear idea of your own opinion and the reasons why you hold it.

It is often easy to voice opinions in a lively discussion among friends— if another person disagrees, you can immediately defend or clarify what you have said or challenge the person with another point. In written argument, however, you don't have this luxury. Since your readers aren't responding to you "live," you need to anticipate their reactions and counterarguments.

Strategy

Here are several steps you can follow to begin articulating your stance and developing your arguments.

- Write informally (perhaps in your journal) about your intuitive reaction to your chosen issue. Does the issue make you feel scornful, pitying, fearful, or outraged? If the issue angers you, exactly what about it makes you angry?

- List the specific elements of the issue to which you have responded emotionally, and briefly summarize your responses. Add to this list other points that you may not react to emotionally but which, on an intellectual level, support your first reaction.

- Begin identifying facts, examples, and ideas that support your opinions. Also begin thinking about objections to your point of view. If you need to go outside your experience to provide support or to deal with opposing opinions, make a preliminary research plan identifying the kinds of information and ideas you may need to gather.

There are many other ways you can pinpoint your stance—for example, reading about the subject, talking with others, and listening to debates in person, on television, or on the radio. What is crucial, however, is that you make *writing* part of your attempt to develop your stand, not only because your final argument will be written but also because the act of writing pushes your thinking and reasoning.

Writer's Tip: Using a Computer

Electronic list servers, chat lines, bulletin boards, and conferences are excellent resources that can help you identify and formulate opinions and then test them on a receptive audience. "Cruising" the Internet will inevitably lead you into controversial discussions. You can also initiate a discussion to gauge interest in a topic or solicit informal responses to an idea or opinion. Such informal electronic chatting is relatively risk-free, like a conversation. The responses can be very useful as you craft your formal paper on a controversial issue.

If you haven't used the Internet before, consult a knowledgeable computer user or a librarian to see how to log on. To reach a wide audience, you might try the national-level Internet chat lines; these are also accessible through commercial systems like CompuServe and America Online. For more local audiences, your school may sponsor chat lines and other interactive networks. Discussions over such networks often focus on specific issues related to local policies and events.

**50a
arg**

3 Focus on a purpose and a thesis

As you begin identifying your point of view, try to limit the scope of your argument. If your issue is too broad, you will have a hard time covering it in a reasonable space and an equally difficult time persuading readers to agree with you. One good way to focus your effort is to ask yourself what kind of opinion you want to argue for. Do you want to argue that an activity, belief, or arrangement is good or bad (effective or ineffective, healthful or harmful, desirable or undesirable, and so on)? If so, you are asking readers to agree with a **value judgment.** Do you want to persuade readers that a particular course of action ought to be undertaken or avoided? If so, you are asking readers to agree with a particular **policy.** Do you want readers to agree that a particular explanation is correct or incorrect? If so, you are asking readers to endorse or reject an **interpretation.**

To construct an effective argument, you need to recognize your specific purpose for arguing and to focus on this purpose. For example, you may believe that stopping all cars on a highway to search for drunk drivers is a violation of civil liberties, so roadblocks should be replaced with another technique for keeping intoxicated people from driving. You need to recognize that this opinion commits you to arguing for both a value judgment (roadblocks violate civil liberties) and a policy (another technique for enforcing laws against drunk driving), so that your writing does not blur these points and the reasoning and evidence you use to support them.

Strategy

To organize your writing and to help readers focus on your opinion (and the evidence supporting it), state your outlook as a **proposition,** that is, as a thesis statement (see 5c) offering an opinion you want readers to adopt.

When you are planning and drafting a position paper, treat your proposition as a tentative thesis you will revise as you explore your reasoning in writing or as you identify supporting evidence and contrary arguments (see 5c-4). Check whether your tentative thesis blurs your specific purposes for arguing or is illogical.

BLURRED AND ILLOGICAL   Police should stop conducting unconstitutional roadblocks and substitute more frequent visual checks of erratic driving to identify people who are driving while intoxicated.

The value judgment and policy proposal are blurred in this thesis statement. In addition, the thesis is potentially illogical because the writer seems to assume that the roadblocks are unconstitutional and does not acknowledge that this value judgment needs to be argued (see "Begging the Question," 50c-5).

Make sure that your thesis either focuses on a single proposition or identifies two related propositions you will argue in an appropriate order.

SINGLE PROPOSITIONS   Roadblocks used to identify drunk drivers are unconstitutional.

Police should make more frequent visual checks of erratic driving to identify people who are driving while intoxicated.

**RELATED
PROPOSITIONS**   The current practice of using roadblocks to identify drunk drivers is unconstitutional; therefore, police should use an alternative procedure such as instituting more frequent visual checks of erratic driving behavior.

Exercise 2

A. Examine the following propositions as possible thesis statements for argumentative essays. Decide whether each example provides an adequate thesis, and explain your judgments.

1. The United States should deregulate all mail service in order to increase competition and improve the quality of service.
2. Rap music, which is violent, vulgar, and sexist, should be banned from public consumption, and fines should be imposed on anyone listening to it in public places.
3. The demands for "computer literacy" (knowledge of how to use computers on the job, at home, and in all aspects of public life) will keep increasing with each generation; therefore, public schools should be required to have courses in computer literacy for all students.
4. All Americans select and wear their attire on the basis of a discriminatory class system which, in the schools, distracts students from their education; therefore, we should pass a federal law requiring all students in public schools to wear identical uniforms.
5. Arson is not a crime; it is a mental disease and should be treated as such.
6. If children read when they are growing up, they will become literate.
7. Orange juice tastes better than cranberry juice.
8. Recirculating the hot air from your clothes drier into your basement during the cold winter months can significantly reduce your heating costs.
9. Humanity's woes began when Eve tasted the forbidden fruit in the Garden of Eden.
10. The telephone resulted in a society less prone to writing, but e-mail will likely lead us right back into the written word as a primary form of communication.

B. In a small group, compare your responses to Exercise 2A. For any propositions that you all agree are inadequate, collaboratively draft a revised proposition that would make an acceptable thesis statement for a short argumentative paper.

**50a
arg**

4 Develop supporting evidence

As you think about an issue or do research on it, be alert for the different kinds of **supporting evidence,** including examples from your personal experience, examples from other people's experiences, quotations and ideas from recognized authorities on a subject, technical information and statistics, data from surveys and interviews (from your own research or someone else's), background and historical information, and comparisons to similar situations or problems.

As you collect evidence in support of an assertion, also examine the balance of different types of evidence. If all your evidence comes from your own experience, your reader might argue that because other people don't share those experiences, your argument is not entirely valid. Try to achieve a balance of facts and statistics, quotations from experts, and personal knowledge. Avoid relying too much on beliefs, especially from religious scripture, as supporting evidence.

Examples. Examples drawn from your own experience or from the experiences of others can be among the most persuasive kinds of evidence you can use for support. Events, people, ideas, objects, feelings, stories, images, and texts—all these and similar "instances" can be turned into examples to support a thesis and encourage readers to share your point of view.

Relying on examples is something we and our readers do every day. When we are trying to make a decision or form an opinion, we often call to mind our own experiences or those we have read or heard about. Almost without thinking, we then try to decide whether the experiences are representative or unique and whether they apply to the issue or situation we are considering.

In choosing to provide examples in support of an argument, therefore, you need to keep in mind both the readiness of readers to be persuaded by examples and the likelihood that they will approach examples critically. Remember, too, that the power of examples to persuade often rests in the concrete detail a writer provides. Detail serves to illustrate and explain the point being made as well as to support the writer's conclusions.

A fully developed example uses explanation to provide readers with the information they need if they are to come to agree with an opinion or judgment. It uses specific details to help persuade readers of the ethical or emotional importance of a proposition and of its relevance to the reader and to other people. The following extended example does these things by drawing on the writer's experiences.

**50a
arg**

> I am afraid to grow old—we're all afraid. In fact, the fear of growing old is so great that every aged person is an insult and a threat to the society. They remind us of our own death, that our body won't always remain smooth and responsive, but will someday betray us by aging, wrinkling, faltering, failing. The ideal way to age would be to grow slowly invisible, gradually disappearing, without causing

worry or discomfort to the young. In some ways that does happen. Sitting in a small park across from a nursing home one day, I noticed that the young mothers and their children gathered on one side, and the old people from the home on the other. Whenever a youngster would run over to the "wrong" side, chasing a ball or just trying to cover all the available space, the old people would lean forward and smile. But before any communication could be established, the mother would take her child back to the "young" side.

— SHARON CURTIN, *Nobody Ever Died of Old Age*

Brief examples often serve more to explain than support, but by providing several related examples, you can often create a cluster of instances with considerable persuasive force, as in the following passage.

The era of the modern family system had come to an end, and few could feel sanguine about the post-modern family condition that had succeeded it. Unaccustomed to a state of normative instability and definitional crisis, the populace split its behavior from its beliefs. Many who contributed actively to such postmodern family statistics as divorce, remarriage, blended families, single parenthood, joint custody, abortion, domestic partnership, two-career households, and the like still yearned nostalgically for the *Father Knows Best* world they had lost. — JUDITH STACEY, "The Family Values Fable"

Quotations and Ideas from Authorities. By turning to the words or ideas of a recognized authority on a subject or issue, you can add to the reasons for readers to agree with your point of view. After all, we identify people as experts or authorities because we believe that they know more about a subject than we do, and the idea of expertise includes a general willingness to agree with the expert's opinion.

Most readers are nonetheless likely to maintain an intelligently critical attitude toward your use of ideas and quotations from experts. They will expect you to cite generally recognized authorities or to indicate why the person you are citing should be viewed as an authority. They may also reject the perspective of someone whose biases suggest a lack of fairness or balance, particularly if these biases differ from their own. As a result, you may need to present the words or ideas you are citing in ways that make clear that your source is both fair and authoritative, just as the writer of the following passage does.

Another role of the [African-American] family is to pass along different kinds of successful coping strategies against racism. One strategy, the heightened sensitivity to the potential for exploitation by white persons, has been referred to by Grier and Cobbs in *Black Rage* as cultural paranoia. While this heightened sensitivity often has been pathologized by the dominant culture, it is a realistic and adaptive

50a
arg

way of approaching situations that have frequently been antagonistic. Hopson and Hopson in *Different and Wonderful* suggest that another important coping strategy and a major source of psychological resilience is reflected in the sharing of African cultural derivatives with children while encouraging them to take pride in their ancestry. In *Long Memory,* Mary Berry and John Blassingame note that each generation of African Americans prepares the next for survival in a society that devalues them by passing along "searing vignettes" about what has preceded them. They view this process as a long collective memory that is in and of itself an instrument of survival.

— BEVERLY GREENE, "African American Families:
A Legacy of Vulnerability and Resilience"

Do not expect an authority to do all the work for you. After all, you cite an authority simply to add weight to your own thesis and perspective. You encourage readers to agree with you by pointing out that someone whose opinion carries considerable weight already agrees with you. For this process to be effective, you need to make sure that your words appear along with those of your source. This is important even when you include a quotation because you feel that your source makes a particular point more effectively and persuasively than you can. In the following paragraph, for example, the writer uses the final sentence to make sure readers see how the information he is citing fits his argument.

Accompanying this modern view of the nuclear family were the sentiments that enlivened it. The first of these was the sentiment, as described by Edward Shorter in *The Making of the Modern Family,* of *romantic love.* Beginning with nineteenth-century individualism, the belief arose that for each of us there is one other individual who was created as our perfect mate. Once we encountered that person, we would know it instantly and proceed to spend the rest of our lives forever "happily-ever-aftering." An essential condition of this romantic ideal was that a young woman would "save" herself for her fated partner. In this romantic context, [her] virginity was a valuable commodity that could be exchanged for a lifelong commitment to the relationship. Romantic love worked to keep couples together even when they were unhappy. **While this ideal was unfortunate for parents in unrewarding relationships, it often benefited children because parents stayed together and usually did not blame the children for the failure of the marriage.**

— DAVID ELKIND, "The Family in the Postmodern World"

As you search for examples to support your points, remember the importance of your own writing. No matter how well written your source, readers will ultimately be persuaded by what your own words say rather than by selected statements from someone else.

Detailed Information. The range of detailed information available to you on most issues is wide, including statistics, technical information, the results of surveys and interviews, background information, and historical detail. Which of these sources you choose and the role each plays in your writing will depend on the particular issue you are addressing, your point of view, and the views or knowledge of your intended readers. Be alert to these kinds of information as you think about an issue and undertake research, and consider the many different ways you can use the information to support your argument. Here are some examples of different kinds of detailed information used to support an author's thesis.

> Meanwhile, young people find it harder and harder to form or sustain families. According to an Associated Press report of April 25, 1995, the median income of men aged twenty-five to thirty-four fell by 26 percent between 1972 and 1994, while the proportion of such men with earnings below the poverty level for a family of four more than doubled to 32 percent. The figures are even worse for African American and Latino men. Poor individuals are twice as likely to divorce as more affluent ones, three to four times less likely to marry in the first place, and five to seven times more likely to have a child out of wedlock. — STEPHANIE COONTZ, "The Way We Weren't"

Comparisons. One important way to arrive at a judgment is to compare a particular issue, problem, policy, or situation about which you are uncertain to one about which you are more certain. In trying to decide whether to expand a local recycling program, for example, you might reasonably look at the success of current efforts. In arguing for restrictions on television programs or for wider access to technical information gathered by governments or corporations, you might look at the success or failure of such practices in other countries.

Comparisons can be particularly useful when you are arguing for a particular policy. Your readers will be concerned about the consequences of a policy and its likelihood for success or failure. No one can predict the future, of course, but comparisons can help you persuade because they point to the probability of certain outcomes.

At the same time, you should expect readers to approach comparisons critically, being skeptical of those that are far-fetched or unreasonable and judging whether the comparison speaks directly to the issue at hand. Instead of asking a comparison to stand on its own, therefore, spend some time pointing out its applicability and answering possible objections to it. The author of the following passage, for example, uses comparison to argue for two-parent, child-centered families even though he acknowledges that one-parent families can raise children successfully.

> Infants and children need, at minimum, one adult to care for them. Yet, given the complexities of the task, childrearing in all soci-

50a
arg

eties until recent years has been shared by many adults. The institutional bond of marriage between biological parents, with the essential function of tying the father to the mother and child, is found in virtually every society. Marriage is the most universal social institution known; in no society has nonmarital childbirth, or the single parent, been the cultural norm. In all societies the biological father is identified where possible, and in almost all societies he plays an important role in his children's upbringing, even though his primary task is often that of protector and breadwinner.

— DAVID POPENOE, "The American Family Crisis"

Strategy

Develop a list of questions that can guide your search for facts, ideas, and experiences that support your proposition. Here are some possible questions.

What are some good or bad consequences of this policy?
What do experts say about solutions to the problem?
What religious or moral values support my position on this issue?
Are there any comparisons that might help readers understand my perspective?

Trying to answer these questions can help you decide whether you can use your own knowledge to support an assertion or whether you need additional facts, opinions, and information.

5 Recognize and respond to counterarguments

50a
arg

Traditional argumentation is like debate: you imagine an adversary, someone who doesn't go along with your ideas, and try to undermine that adversary's points or **counterarguments.** Most contemporary approaches to argument aren't quite as battle-like. Your point should be not so much to "win" as to acknowledge other people's perspectives yet still try to convince them of the validity of your views. With either kind of argument, however, you need to anticipate your readers' reactions.

Strategy

Divide a sheet of paper into three columns. On the left, list the main points supporting your opinion. Write opposing points in the middle column. Put yourself wholly into the other position's point of view when you are listing opposing points. Pretend you are a person diametrically opposed to your original stance. Try to find weaknesses in the points in the left-hand column. Be as critical as possible.

In the rightmost column, list the possible defenses to the counterarguments you listed in the middle column. List any known or potential outside sources that would support your argument.

▶◀

Sometimes it may be difficult to imagine any point of view other than your own. The process of inventing counterarguments may need to move beyond your own frame of reference and beliefs. This is where taking your thesis or position into a more public forum can help. Use various audiences as a "test" for your assertions. Put the idea forward tentatively, so that you will be seen as searching openly for differences of opinion. You might, for example, ask some friends or acquaintances, "What do you think about this issue?" or "Do you think that we ought to do X to solve Y?" Then listen carefully, and take note of the responses. You might gently extend your friends' reasoning by raising a subsidiary issue or counterargument: "But what about the fact that . . . ?" Again, listen.

Exercise 3

A. Using the Strategy described in 50a-3, develop a workable thesis statement. List at least three pieces of supporting evidence or arguments for your assertion.

B. In a small group, use the Strategy in 50a-5 to create a list of counterarguments against each member's main supporting arguments. In a discussion of each thesis statement, try collectively to respond to those counterarguments in ways that weaken the objections to the original arguments.

50b Developing a point: Argument in progress

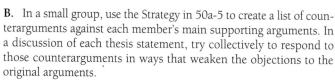

50b
arg

Knowing that he had to begin writing a short argumentative paper, Zachary Carter began jotting ideas in his journal. As he walked through the student union on his way to a class, he noticed a group of students crowding around a table where several members of the Coalition on Animal Rights sat. Large posters on the wall showed cruelties allegedly inflicted on monkeys, dogs, and other animals as a result of medical experiments. The students and the Coalition members were carrying on a lively debate about the animal experiments. As Zachary listened, he knew that he had stumbled on an idea for his paper. He grabbed some leaflets and hurried to class.

1 Identify an issue

At lunch, Zachary glanced through the leaflets he had taken. He couldn't help feeling that they turned an enormous, undefined topic ("animal rights") into something very specific by focusing on only one issue (the morality of performing medical experiments on animals). He started writing about his own feelings on this subject in his journal.

> One day when I was little, I came across some neighborhood kids taunting a frog they'd found. They were kicking it, tossing it to each other, rolling it down the sidewalk. I was horrified, but the kids were a lot bigger than I was, so I just stood a few yards away, ready to run to my house if they turned on me. I found the frog's bashed-up body in the grass the next day.
>
> Animal rights. Maybe this violation was outrageous because there was no purpose but a sick pleasure for the kids. Experiments inflict pain, too, but we're supposed to think it's all for the good of human beings. I don't know. A frog, some experiments. These seem so small. The problem is so much bigger than this. It's humans as a species, multiplying, taking over the planet and pushing out other creatures.

On his way to class, Zachary continued to puzzle over the question of animal rights. The experimentation problem seemed like a complex argument, since people can claim that animal experiments have led to cures for dozens of diseases and thus made our lives better. At the same time, it seemed manageably narrow, since experiments can be studied, monitored, and controlled. But what about other aspects of animal rights? What about the destruction of rain forests, the wiping out of entire species by human development, pollution killing off organisms by the thousands?

50b arg

2 Investigate an issue

The day after his encounter with the animal rights group, Zachary was checking his e-mail messages on his computer when he decided to try out his thoughts on his local university chat line.

> Hi, people. I've been thinking about animal rights. (I'm sure you saw the table in the student union.) I guess I'm more worried now than before about what happens to animals in experiments. But I keep thinking that the lab issue is missing the point. It seems so small compared to the huge injustices we keep doing to animals on the whole planet. If we stopped all the experiments in the world, animals still would have no rights because of what we are doing to their environment. What do you think?

Within a day, Zachary had about a dozen responses on the local chat line. Several students offered sensible replies and even suggested where Zachary could get more information.

In response to Zachary Carter's message: Take a situation like human hunger. Big problem, right? So some people create a food-shelf program in one city, and it helps a few dozen families. It doesn't get rid of the problem, but it's a start. Same with taking care of our environment.

Zach Carter: Check out Richard Wagner's book <u>Environment and Man</u>, and while you're at it, Al Gore's <u>Earth in the Balance</u>.

3 Articulate a stance

After thinking about the e-mail responses, Zachary knew that he had to work to articulate his stance. Was he concerned primarily about animal experiments? Or was his point more solution-based—that we should do something more fundamental about animal rights? But what was that something? Returning to his journal, he wrote a page exploring his ideas.

A day later, Zachary had narrowed his opinion into something approaching a thesis or proposition. In his brainstorming, he realized that he wanted to take a broader view of animal rights, and he settled on a tentative proposition for his paper.

> In considering the rights of animals, we must begin shifting our focus from small controversies such as animal experiments or the survival of a single species to the true injustice, the large-scale destruction of animals' habitat by humans.

Zachary felt generally satisfied with his focus but also knew that he really didn't have an argument, just a way of thinking about a problem. What exactly was he proposing—just that we should think more broadly, or that we should take some sort of action?

4 Find supporting evidence

Taking the advice of one of the e-mail respondents, Zachary went to the library in search of the books by Wagner and Gore. He found that they dealt broadly with the issue of the environment. As he read, he was drawn again and again to passages dealing with the issue of human overpopulation. Was there a way to link animal rights to human overpopulation? Searching the electronic databases in his library, he located a series of books by Edward Abbey dealing with the environment. The anthology in his composition course also included a useful article titled "The End of Nature." There was plenty here, he thought, to help him support his ideas. He started jotting down some useful quotations.

> "Global warming, ozone depletion, the loss of living species, deforestation—they all have a common cause: the relationship between human civilization and the earth's natural balance." (Albert Gore, <u>Earth in the Balance</u>, p. 31)

**50b
arg**

Especially powerful for his paper were various proposals for reducing the human population, or at least keeping it from growing out of control. This one main argument, Zachary thought, could lay the foundation for an approach to animal rights in which the earth would be balanced between humans and animals in a harmonious ecosystem.

5 Recognize counterarguments

Because Zachary had already received some e-mail objections to his original thoughts about animal rights, he decided to do most of his work on counterarguments by himself, trying to put himself in the shoes of people (including some of his friends) who would object to the idea. Using a listing strategy (see 50a-5), he divided a piece of paper into three columns, wrote down key supporting points, then imagined what people would say against his supporting points. After trying to come up with valid counterarguments, he looked for ways to defend his original supporting points. The result was a chart of ideas that he could develop in his paper.

Tentative thesis: In considering the rights of animals, we must begin shifting our focus from small controversies such as animal experiments or the survival of a single species to the true injustice, the large-scale destruction of animals' habitat by the overpopulation of humans

Supporting Points	Opposing Points	Defenses
Humans are pushing the balance of nature askew with their ever-increasing population.	We haven't yet mined the earth for all its resources, so we could support many more people in the future.	Mining all the earth's resources will inevitably destroy the existing ecosystem.
Large-scale tips in the balance of nature will cause a domino effect as interdependent species die off.	Entire species have gone extinct without major effects on ecology.	In the past, extinction has happened slowly and naturally because of changing conditions.
More humans need more water, leading to more dams, in turn leading to the destruction of submerged habitat.	Dams create lakes, which create new opportunities for plant and animal life.	Dams like the Glen Canyon Dam upset fragile ecosystems miles downstream.
Male sterilization can effectively curb overpopulation, as shown in Barbados, etc.	Sterilized men may change their minds about fathering children and then be unable to do so.	Semen can be collected prior to sterilization for later use in artificial insemination.

**50b
arg**

After creating this list, Zachary felt he was ready to begin more formal work on the structure of his paper in preparation for a preliminary draft. Note how he develops a complex argument that includes a definition of his key terms, adequate quotations from his sources to support his points, and a clear, crisp, readable style to engage his readers.

Animal Rights: The Big Picture

by Zachary Carter

1   The issue of animal rights is a multifaceted one, and, upon examination, it tends to make one follow a circle of logic which leads from one conclusion to the next, without the benefit of a final outcome or decision. But there is a way out of this circle, and that is to shift the focus of the issue away from small controversies such as animal experiments or the survival of a single species of tiny fish to the true injustice, the large-scale destruction of animals' habitat by the overpopulation of humans. Upon exploration, this particular avenue yields astonishing and interesting--even horrifying--results. Clearly an intense effort must be made to preserve the rights of animals (as defined later in this essay) for the benefit of every species involved, including the human race.

2   In order to examine this issue thoroughly, we must find a definition of both "animal" and "rights" and stick to them. So, for the purpose of this essay, "animal" will be defined as any creature that belongs to the kingdom Animalia, which includes reptiles, birds, insects, amphibians, and mammals (even humans). As for a concept of "rights," one must first look at what is most important for the whole of nature. The earth is a vast, spinning

50b
arg

ecosystem, teeming with countless forms of life, all
in diverse conflict and chaos. Yet amid all the
confusion there is an order, a balance, an
underlying simplicity. The food chain,
photosynthesis, the Krebs cycle, the water cycle,
migratory patterns--all these things indicate the
presence of an underlying balance, a large-scale
cooperation of organisms, the purpose of which is to
promote life.

3   Al Gore tells of this in his book <u>Earth in the
Balance</u>: "All its parts exist in a delicate balance
of interdependency" (50). This balance is important
to the continuation of life as we know it on earth
because "any interruption of this natural process
can have a magnified impact" (51). A large-scale tip
in this balance can result in devastating effects on
the lives of all creatures, <u>Homo sapiens</u> and other
species alike. It is apparent that the preservation
of this balance must be the paramount concern of any
society because all members in any society are
integral parts of nature. If the situation is viewed
in this light, then it becomes not only humanity's
right and every other species' right, but our duty
as well, for the very preservation of life and
nature as we know it, to live peacefully within the
balance of nature. Consequently, we arrive at the
most fundamental definition of "rights": the right
to exist within the balance of nature.

4   And now we come to the problem. Humans, driven
by natural instinct, are slowly pushing the balance
askew and, in the process, trampling on the rights

of other species to exist inside the balance. Because of the population boom, humans have spread across every continent, developing, settling, industrializing, mining, setting up agriculture, and so forth. Gore speaks of human intrusion into the balance: "Global warming, ozone depletion, the loss of living species, deforestation--they all have a common cause: the new relationship between human civilization and the earth's natural balance" (31).

5   The human race has destroyed vast areas of native habitat and cut down billions of trees which-- at that volume--are virtually irreplaceable. As Gore notes, "when we scrape the forests away, we destroy these crucial habitats along with the living species that depend on them" (116). Predatory species such as the wolf, coyote, and mountain lion, which are an important part of the ecosystem (because they dwell at the apex of the food chain), have been virtually wiped out in many areas. Deer and elk feel this loss through their subsequent boom in population, which in turn causes a demand for food which cannot be met. As a result, there are millions of starving deer and elk, all because of the destruction of a few predators.

50b arg

6   These examples of habitat destruction and the killing of species are clearly a violation of animals' rights to exist within the balance. Another type of disruption is the damming of rivers, which not only submerges vast areas of habitat, but also upsets the fragile river ecology for hundreds of miles downstream. A prime example of this is the

former Glen Canyon in Utah, now under Lake Powell, a result of the construction of Glen Canyon Dam. In South America, huge amounts of the Amazon rain forest are being burned, leaving billions, perhaps trillions, of animals homeless if not killed. Extinctions are on the rise: "living species of animals and plants are now vanishing in the world at a rate <u>one thousand times faster</u> than at any time in the past 65 million years" (Gore 25). The destruction of an entire species is an example of another clear violation of the rights of animals to exist within the balance. And there are more subtle and terrifying problems than these: global warming, the greenhouse effect, the rising of the oceans. These, in the words of Bill McKibben, can lead us "if not straight to hell, then straight to a place with a comparable 'temperature'" (274). But the underlying cause of all this injustice, the mother of all problems, is overpopulation.

7   We face a future in which there is no longer physical space on the earth for the human race, much less the billions of other species that inhabit the planet. In the words of Edward Abbey:

> The sea will be farmed, all deserts irrigated, whole mountains pulverized, the last forests turned to pulpwood plantations, in order to satisfy the ever-growing needs (no doubt as desperate as in the past) of a human population much larger than at present. (<u>Down the River</u> 117)

50b
arg

Richard Wagner, author of <u>Environment and Man,</u>
states that "adding four billion more [people]
staggers the imagination, for the earth is barely
able to support its present population" (553). He
also says that "overpopulation is one problem the
entire world must share" (538). Clearly the
population explosion must be stopped. This is the
only way to make room for all species to have
their rightful place within the balance, for the
benefit of human beings and the whole of the
natural world.

8   First, a move must be made to prevent future
development of similar problems, and the only way
to do this is to curb the population explosion.
Several things can be used to this end. Abortion,
while morally objectionable to many people, is a
natural form of population reduction. Rabbits in
the wild, for example, will abort their unborn
fetuses if the local environment is insufficient
for survival. If moral imperatives preclude the
use of this method, then there are other equally
effective chemical and mechanical methods, "but
the most reliable method is sterilization" (Wagner
547). A simple operation performed on a man
renders him unable to conceive offspring, and this
does not affect sexual impulses. The
irreversibility of this method can be combated by
taking samples of semen before the operation.
Then, at any time, the partner can be artificially
inseminated (Wagner 547). A reduction in
population <u>can</u> be achieved. This is demonstrated

**50b
arg**

by the efforts of "Barbados, Taiwan, Mauritius, Hong Kong, Tunisia, Singapore, Costa Rica, Egypt, Chile, and South Korea," which have achieved a reduction (Wagner 554). This proposed reduction in population will help to prevent further encroachment upon the natural habitat of animal species by human expansion and exploitation.

9   As for the present, efforts should be made to develop new and streamline old technology in order to make more efficient use of resources. Gore says, "It is now an axiom in many fields of science that more new and important discoveries have taken place in the last ten years than in the entire previous history of science" (31). This trend is expected to continue, and, if so, efficiency of production and use of natural resources should be steered in that direction. Subsequently, waste disposal, energy production, and manufacturing should be improved significantly. Gore also says that "the transformation of the way we relate to the earth will of course involve new technologies, but the key changes will involve new ways of thinking about the relationship [between people and nature] itself" (35).

10   The first and most important imperative is that all individuals make a conscious effort to improve this relationship to the balance of nature, for the sake of animal rights, themselves, and their children. Without this effort to preserve the balance, all members of the human

race are on a collision course with destruction,
taking millions of innocent species along with them:

> ...developers were bulldozing the last
> hundred acres of untouched forest in the
> entire area. As the woods fell away to
> make way for more concrete, more
> buildings, parking lots, and streets, the
> wild things that lived there were forced
> to flee. Most of the deer were hit by
> cars; other creatures--like the pheasant
> that darted into my neighbor's backyard--
> made it a little further. (Gore 25)

11   An effort to curb these injustices is in order
immediately, for the sake of the balance. For "the
earth, like the sun, like the air, belongs to
everyone--and to no one" (Abbey, Journey 88). And if
no effort is made...very well then...let the
world rot.

Works Cited

Abbey, Edward. "The Damnation of a Canyon." Beyond
    the Wall. New York: Holt, 1984.

---. Down the River. New York: Plume, 1991.

---. The Journey Home. New York: Plume, 1991.

Gore, Albert. Earth in the Balance: Ecology and the
    Human Spirit. New York: Houghton, 1992.

McKibben, Bill. "The End of Nature." The Informed
    Argument. Ed. Robert K. Miller. New York:
    Harcourt, 1992. 264-74.

Wagner, Richard H. Environment and Man. New York:
    Norton, 1978.

**50b
arg**

50c Using critical thinking to strengthen your argument

When you plan and draft a position paper, try to assemble your opinions and supporting evidence in an order that reflects a chain of reasoning supporting your proposition (thesis statement). Some of the most effective ways to do this are using different strategies of argument (logical, emotional, imaginative, and ethical) and using data-warrant-claim (Toulmin) reasoning.

1 Build logical strategies

When you employ **logical strategies** for argument, you arrange your ideas and evidence in ways that correspond with patterns of thought that most people accept as reasonable and convincing. You do not have to provide absolute proof for your opinion; if you could, there would be no real need to argue. After all, arguments help to resolve disagreements precisely because an absolutely correct position cannot always be identified. In such a case, an argument helps readers choose among opinions that are reasonable alternatives.

Here are four of the most commonly used logical strategies.

Reasoning from consequences. You argue for or against an action, outlook, or interpretation, basing your argument on real or likely consequences (good or bad).

Reasoning from comparisons. You argue for or against a policy or point of view, basing your argument on similar situations, problems, or actions.

Reasoning from authority and testimony. You draw ideas and evidence to support your outlook from recognized experts or from people whose experience makes them trustworthy witnesses.

Reasoning from examples and statistics. You draw on events, situations, and problems presented as illustrations (examples) or in summarized, numerical form (statistics) to support your point of view.

Induction and deduction are other commonly used logical strategies. A **deductive argument** begins with an explicitly stated **premise** (or assertion or claim) and then goes on to support that premise. It uses **syllogistic reasoning** as the basic logical format. A **syllogism** includes a **major premise, a minor premise,** and a **conclusion.** Here is a simple truthful syllogism.

MAJOR PREMISE   All landowners in Clarksville must pay taxes.

MINOR PREMISE   Fred Hammil owns land in Clarksville.

CONCLUSION   Therefore, Fred Hammil must pay taxes.

Faulty syllogistic reasoning is easily illustrated in a flawed syllogism.

MAJOR PREMISE   All Ferraris are fast.

MINOR PREMISE   That car is fast.

CONCLUSION   Therefore, that car is a Ferarri.

In a complex argument, of course, these truthful and faulty kinds of reasoning are much more elaborate. You might begin an argumentative paper, for example, by saying something that your readers would generally hold to be true, go on to show that specific examples of that assertion must also be true, and end with your argumentative assertion. This basic sequence can be used to shape each paragraph as well as to frame the paper as a whole.

In contrast, an **inductive argument** does not explicitly state the premise; rather, it leads readers through an accumulation of evidence until they conclude what the writer wants them to. Such arguments usually begin with a **hypothesis,** which differs from an assertion in being tentative, an idea that the writer wants to consider but as yet has not reached any hard-and-fast conclusion about. Of course, in a finished written argument, this hypothesis is somewhat disingenuous since the writer *does* have a conclusion but withholds it until the readers are convinced by reading through all the supporting points.

This form of argument is effective when you are taking a controversial stand on an issue. If you asserted your stand explicitly at the beginning of the paper, you might put many of your readers on the defensive, ready to criticize your argument right from the start. However, if you hold off your assertion, your readers may also hold off their judgment.

50c
arg

Exercise 4

A. Compose a simple proposition or thesis, and then try to support it with each of the four logical strategies described in 50c-1 (reasoning from consequences, reasoning from comparisons, reasoning from authority or testimony, and reasoning from examples and statistics). Invent authoritative statements or statistics if you wish.

EXAMPLE

Simple proposition: The student senate's proposal to allow alcoholic beverages to be served in the student union should not be passed.

Reasoning from consequences: The consumption of alcohol will increase crime on campus, especially personal assaults, drunk driving, and rape.

Reasoning from comparisons: Easy availability of alcohol deters students from their academic work; when a bar opened briefly *three years ago near fraternity row, every fraternity experienced a drop in average grades.*

Reasoning from authority and testimony: Having alcohol so easily available on campus may subvert our college's mission by contributing not to students' growth but to their deterioration. According to research conducted by Legman and Witherall, a large percentage of alcoholics over the age of thirty reported that their college binge drinking set a strong pattern for their later addiction.

Reasoning from examples and statistics: Bars on campus draw students away from more beneficial activities. Two years after Carmon College opened a wine and beer hall on campus, participation in lectures and special events had dropped by 26 percent; attendance at the film series declined by 18 percent; and weekend library usage between 5 p.m. and midnight dropped by 43 percent.

B. In a small group, compare your theses and logical strategies. Discuss the strength of each strategy as it is used to support the thesis.

2 Draw on emotional strategies

In drawing on **emotional strategies,** you focus on the values, attitudes, systems of beliefs, and emotions that guide people's lives and that are central to any decision-making process.

Values and beliefs. You may present examples, ideas, or statements that confirm or contradict your readers' probable values.

Emotions and values. You may present examples or use language that draws emotional responses (positive or negative) from your readers ("The consequence of this policy will be an increase in the already horrifying flood of bruised, battered, undernourished two- and three-year-olds brought into emergency rooms by parents who deny even the most obvious evidence of abuse").

Be aware that readers often see emotional strategies as weaker support for a point than reason or logic. In an argument against the use of animals for research, for example, an emotional appeal about cruelty to animals could be countered by an emotional appeal about the need for research to cure terrible diseases. A general emotional appeal about animal suffering is not as strong as specific, verifiable accounts of animals being subjected to unbearable pain in the name of research. Often the most powerful emotional appeals will be those directly linked to other forms of logical support.

Did You Know?

Some people think that the purpose of argument is to win a battle or to discredit the views of people with whom they disagree. A society that relied on such a view of argument to deal with problems and differing points of view would be a rather hostile place to live, however. Belgian scholar Chaim Perelman offers a different view of the aim of argument: to encourage or convince your audience to adhere to your point of view. In other words, argument creates agreement by encouraging people to come together in their beliefs and actions.

Chaim Perelman and L. Olbrechts-Tyteca, *The New Rhetoric* (South Bend: U of Notre Dame P, 1979).

---

3 Use data-warrant-claim (Toulmin) reasoning

In *The Uses of Argument* (1964), Stephen Toulmin proposes **data-warrant-claim reasoning,** which draws on several kinds of statements reasonable people usually make when they argue (statements of data, claims, and warrants), highlighting a way of relating these statements in order to convince readers.

Data corresponds to your evidence and *claim* to your conclusion. *Warrant,* however, is a more complex term; it refers to the mental process by which a reader connects the data to the claim. It answers the question "How?" Another way to understand this is to think of data as the indisputable facts and the warrant as the probable facts and assertions. As in an inductive argument, you present the data that lead to your claim, but you also present the warrants, the probable facts and assertions that will encourage readers to accept the validity of your claim.

For instance, as data, you might have the results of a detailed study establishing the likelihood of injury in each of the many different models of cars currently on the market. You could make a number of interpretive statements about the data (warrants) and point out patterns you see (probable facts—warrants) in order to provide reasoning that links the data to your claim: for the average consumer, buying a large car is a good way to reduce the likelihood of being injured in an accident.

To argue effectively, you need to show your readers *how* the data and the claim are connected. To warrant such a claim, you could say that there are small, medium, and large cars in the ratings and extend this warrant by pointing out that the large cars have a higher safety rating. To back up this warrant, you point out that although some of the smaller cars on each list are quite safe, in general, the large cars are the safest. You could extend the argument by citing further statistics (data) about safety along with arguments and reasoning from other sources (warrants).

50c
arg

DATA

Ratings of each car model according to likelihood of injury to driver and passenger (scale: 1 = low to 10 = high)

WARRANT

←——The cars in the ratings fall into three easily recognized groups: small, medium, and large.
Probable fact

WARRANT

←——The large cars as a group have a lower average likelihood of injury to passengers than either of the other groups.
Probable fact

WARRANT

←——Though some of the small and medium-sized cars have low likelihood of injury to passengers, almost all of the large cars seem quite safe.
Assertion and probable fact

WARRANT

←——Relatively few consumers will spend the time going over the crash ratings to determine which particular models get good or poor scores.
Assertion

CLAIM

For the average consumer, buying a large car is a good way to reduce the likelihood of being injured in an accident.

**50c
arg**

The data-warrant-claim approach to constructing an argument does not assume that an argument can provide absolute proof of a proposition. It aims instead at showing readers that an opinion or proposed action is plausible, grounded on good evidence and reasons, and worth their endorsement. Arguments that employ this kind of reasoning may sometimes seem more like purposeful dialogues than debates. If you employ this approach, you should take the attitude that your argument is open to other viewpoints, to compromise, and to negotiation.

4 Consider your audience and purpose

Remember that you won't write an effective argument if all you do is stridently voice your opinion on an issue. An argument is effective only if it's part of a relationship between you and your reader. Defining who your readers are, how you want them to perceive you, and what you want to convince them of is the essential first step to constructing an argument (see Chapter 6).

Your audience is partly determined by your topic and by your own stance. If you are writing about the abortion issue, for example, you need to be clear in your own mind whom you are addressing. Argument papers on this topic are often not well written because the audience is usually a vague "the other side." Remember, it is a fallacy to divide an issue into only two sides (see the discussion of the either/or fallacy in 50c-5). Likewise, it is ineffective to think of your readers as belonging to only one of two camps.

Rogerian argument, based on the theories of psychologist and group therapist Carl Rogers, provides a useful perspective for considering the responses of your audience. Rogers argued that people can more easily be changed when their opponent seems like an ally instead of an enemy. A highly combative or adversarial approach immediately puts a reader on the defensive, thus setting up a barrier to your ideas. The reader's psychological reaction is "Oh yeah? Well, let me tell you something, buster!" rather than "Hmmm, that's an interesting point worth considering."

Identifying Alternative Views. To practice Rogerian strategies, imagine for a moment that you share the views of someone who is opposed to your actual position or solution. What is your opponent's frame of reference? What assumptions might have led him or her to these views? Giving, for the moment, a charitable response that acknowledges someone else's right to hold an opinion you disagree with, what validity can you see in anything your opponent might say?

Rogers also found that a good way to understand someone's view is to try restating it rather than immediately countering it. When participants in a discussion negotiate their positions, sentences often begin not with statements of judgment or reaction ("Well, I think . . ." or "That point doesn't hold water."), but with statements of reflection and repetition: "What I hear you saying is . . . ," or "It sounds to me like you're trying to . . . ." This allows not only for mutual understanding of each person's points but for mutual respect for differences of opinion once those points are clearly articulated.

50c
arg

Making a Concession. When you understand your opponent's ideas, you may be prepared to work a **concession** into your argument. You make a concession when you acknowledge or consider a view opposed to one you are arguing. A concession does not have to be so strong that it undermines your entire argument. But placed strategically, it can help your reader to see that you have, in fact, tried to be fair-minded. A reader who recognizes that attitude will be more likely to trust your judgment and listen to you.

Concessions may appear briefly, embedded in the structure of a sentence, or they may be elaborate, sometimes taking one or more paragraphs to describe. Concessions embedded in single sentences often involve words like *although, while, while it may be true that, of course,* or *but.*

In a letter to the editor bemoaning the extinction of local, family-run hardware stores in the shadow of huge, warehouse-sized lumber centers, Angie Krastaat made an extended concession that consumers may be attracted by the lower prices and large selection at the lumber centers, but then countered it with an anecdote that led to a generalization.

> Of course, the lumber centers do have their draws: paint in every color, discounted power tools, and items too large to fit into most small stores. But what they gain in selection and pricing they sorely lack in their robot-like relationship with their customers. Where else can you get a single nut, bolt or nail—just one—than a loca hardware store? What large lumber center will replace that torn screen or broken window while you wait? Where can you find someone at Mega-Hardware who will work with you in the store to repair something, using ingenuity and bins full of single items?

Strategy

To make your argument on "hot" issues more effective, try limiting your audience to a particular group of people concerned about the issue—on abortion, for example, focus on reaching sexually active teens, unmarried mothers, or the people who protest at abortion clinics. Also consider your image as an arguer. How do you want your readers to perceive you? Do you want to be perceived as erudite, rational, and coolly objective; as passionate and moving; as outraged; as reflective and forgiving?

5 Recognize misleading and illogical reasoning

A **fallacy** is a flaw in the reasoning of any persuasive work, whether it's an argumentative essay, an interpretation of a literary work, a report of the results of a study, or a review. Fallacies often show up in advertisements, stated directly in the copy and implied in the visual images. An ad for beer that shows attractive, bikini-clad women and muscular, handsome men romping on a California beach implies (illogically) that drinking the beer will get you that life-style. This example of faulty cause-effect reasoning implies that *because* you drink the beer, you'll be like the people in the ad. The same fallacy can be a problem in academic and professional writing as well but may not be as blatant. For instance, if you read an article that says legalizing marijuana will result in a dangerous increase in cocaine use, you ought to question how the writer demonstrates that cause-effect relationship and supplies evidence linking marijuana use to cocaine use.

Faulty Cause-Effect Relationship. This problem is also called *post hoc, ergo propter hoc* (Latin for "after this, therefore because of this") or just a **post hoc fallacy.** This flawed reasoning attempts to persuade you that just because one event happens after the other, the first event causes the second.

FAULTY CAUSE-EFFECT
The increase in explicit violence on television is making the crime rate soar.

READER'S RESPONSE: This *may* be true, but no evidence is presented here linking the two situations.

False Analogy. **Analogies** are comparisons between two things, often on the basis of shared characteristics. In a **false analogy,** the things may at first glance seem to be comparable but really are not. (See the discussion of the red herring and *ad populum* fallacies in this section.)

FALSE ANALOGY
Raising the national speed limit is like offering free cocktails at a meeting of recovering alcoholics.

READER'S RESPONSE: I don't see the connection. Most drivers aren't recovering from an addiction to high-speed driving, and a legal limit is not the same thing as self-restraint.

Misleading Language/Misleading Evidence. This fallacy is also called **equivocation** and **slanted statistics.** A writer can use **misleading language** by beginning with one definition of a term (usually one everyone agrees with), then shifting to another sense of the word, one that supports the writer's argument but that not all readers may agree with.

MISLEADING LANGUAGE
Everyone has the right of free speech, so censoring films by rating them Triple X is against one's constitutional rights.

READER'S RESPONSE: This tries to pass off the *rating* of films as censorship (which it is not) and assumes that *free speech* and *censorship* are directly opposite terms (which they are not necessarily).

Misleading evidence includes statistics, survey results, and expert opinions stacked up in favor of only one side of the argument. For instance, someone who used an opinion poll to argue for the preservation of the spotted owl but polled only people at an environmental rally would have overwhelmingly favorable but misleading evidence.

50c arg

Red Herring. Similar to misleading evidence is the **red herring** fallacy. A red herring is something that distracts readers from the real argument.

RED HERRING
Gun control laws need to be passed as soon as possible to decrease the rate of domestic violence and home firearms accidents. The people who think guns should not be controlled are probably criminals themselves.

READER'S RESPONSE: The second sentence doesn't logically follow from the first; it just attacks the people who would oppose the writer's argument instead of supporting the initial assertion.

Ad Populum. *Ad populum* means "to the people" and refers to an argument that appeals to the audience's biases instead of using rational support.

AD POPULUM All doctors should be tested for AIDS and should not allowed to practice if they test HIV positive, so they don't spread the disease to their patients. Do you want to be one of those patients?

READER'S RESPONSE: This writer is obviously trying to invoke my fear of getting AIDS. The claim that HIV-positive doctors will pass on the disease to patients is not founded on valid research.

Ad Hominem. Another faulty argument based on audience biases is the **ad hominem** fallacy, which means "to the man." This is a personal attack on the opponent rather than a debate on the issue.

AD HOMINEM Of course Walt Smith would support a bill to provide financial assistance to farmers—he owns several large farms in the Midwest. Besides, how can he be a good senator after cheating on his wife?

READER'S RESPONSE: I'd like to hear reactions to Walt Smith's ideas, please. I don't really care whether he had an affair fifteen years ago.

Bandwagon. This fallacy is also called *consensus gentium,* "consensus of the people." A **bandwagon argument** is one that tries to convince you everyone else agrees with the idea already, so you ought to join in.

BANDWAGON Each year an increasing number of people are quitting smoking, so you ought to quit, too.

READER'S RESPONSE: This writer is trying to convince me to quit by saying that other people are doing it. Even though the assertion may be valid, the support is not.

Begging the Question. This fallacy also is called **overgeneralization** or **hasty generalization.** An argument is **begging the question** when it presents assumptions as if they were facts, sometimes using words and phrases like *obviously, certainly, clearly, people always/never,* and even the seemingly innocuous *some people say.*

50c arg

BEGGING THE QUESTION Most people these days are trying to be more physically fit; obviously, they are afraid of getting old.

READER'S RESPONSE: No evidence is presented for either the claim that most people are trying to be more fit or the claim that they are afraid of getting old. On what basis are these stated as facts?

Either/Or. An **either/or strategy** oversimplifies an issue, making it seem as if it has only two sides.

EITHER/OR On the matter of abortion, there are two positions: either we support a human's right to life, or we allow women to have complete control over their bodies.

READER'S RESPONSE: Why can't someone endorse protecting life while also supporting the right to choose what happens to one's body?

Circular Reasoning. Circular reasoning, also called **tautology,** is an attempt to support an assertion with the assertion itself.

CIRCULAR
REASONING

> The university should increase funding of intramural sports because it has a responsibility to back its sports programs financially.
>
> **READER'S RESPONSE:** All this really says is that the university should fund sports because it should fund sports.

Exercise 5

A. Choose a controversial topic you know something about—gun control, abortion, the death penalty, the right to die. Now choose any three of the fallacies described in 50c-5, and write one example of each fallacy to make claims about your topic. (Don't identify the names of the fallacies in your response.)

B. In a small group, exchange copies of the fallacious arguments you wrote for Exercise 5A. Discuss each set of fallacies, trying to identify the logical problems and to suggest revisions or identify specific kinds of support needed.

C. Work through your argumentative paper in progress, searching for cases of fallacies. Consider your supporting points for your argument—do any of them match these fallacies? Rework any flawed points.

Did You Know?

In a study of students who wrote dialogue journals (they swapped journal entries and responded to each other's ideas informally), researchers found the presence of considerable argument. But because the partners thought of themselves as carrying on a sustained conversation that required them to maintain their social link through the entries, they appeared to consider each other's views and present themselves in a nonconfrontational way.

Chris M. Anson and Richard Beach, "Argument in Peer Dialogue Journals," in Deborah Berrill, ed., *New Perspectives on Written Argument* (Cresskill, NJ: Hampton Press, 1995) 139–169.

**50d
arg**

50d The position paper

The short, often documented, **position paper** defines its issue, considers its audience, and draws on evidence and logical strategies to make its point.

1 Sample position paper

In the following paper, note how the writer frames her argument with an opening reference to the daily struggle of many people throughout the world to protect their limited food supply against spoilage and contamination. As you read, consider who the writer's audience is, what the main argument is, and how she constructs the support for the argument. What are the counterarguments, and how does she address them? What kind of support, if any, is missing? What fallacies, if any, do you detect?

Food Irradiation: An Idea Whose Time Has Come

by Stephanie Lewis

1   In almost every part of the world people struggle daily to protect their vital food supplies from spoilage. For most Americans, the threats of heat, damp, insect infestation, bacterial contamination, and rot may seem distant. Yet while there is no precise information on just how much of the world's food supply is lost to spoilage, it is clear that the losses are enormous, especially in less developed countries that can least afford the waste. In addition, many of these countries have warm climates that encourage the growth of organisms causing spoilage and that speed up the normal deterioration process (Thorne). Because the world's population is growing at a rapid pace, we need to find viable solutions to the problem of waste and decay.

2   The loss of edible food is only one part of the problem, however. Food-borne diseases are also some of the most common threats to human health. In particular, a fairly high percentage of raw animal meat is contaminated by bacteria, resulting in high levels of food-borne illness in most countries (Thorne).

Opens with background examples

Uses example plus authority

50d
arg

3   Efforts to reduce the price the public pays for food wastage and food-borne disease began many years ago. The first methods for the preservation of food were sun drying, salting, smoking, canning, and cooking. (For people in developed countries, these are now often techniques of gourmet cooking.) Recently, however, scientists have developed a new method for food preservation, irradiation. In this method, food is exposed to measured amounts of ionizing radiation. Scientists have discovered that this form of food preservation can slow spoilage, reduce insect infestation, and prevent contamination by other harmful organisms that cause food-borne diseases (<u>Food Safety</u>). Food irradiation is a particularly promising way to help reduce the worldwide problems of waste and disease.

Supplies specific examples

Supplies detailed information plus authority

4   Nonetheless, the public in this country has not fully accepted the concept of food irradiation (Lamb). Because of a decades-long fear of thermonuclear war and well-publicized accidents involving nuclear power (Three Mile Island and Chernobyl), many people fear anything associated with radiation. This fear persists even if the radiation is used for a nonthreatening purpose such as the preservation of food. Often this feeling of apprehensiveness is due to a lack of knowledge and information on the subject of food irradiation. This is also due to some confusion between the phenomenon of radioactive contamination and the process of irradiation used in food preservation.

Supplies examples

50d arg

5   One main reason why food irradiation is not used widely is that governments are still unsure about consumer acceptance of irradiated products. Without such acceptance, food irradiation will be neglected in developing countries as well as in the developed world. Even though about thirty-four countries have given approval for the radiation process of some thirty products, the use of radiation has been slow to materialize. Nonetheless, there is clear evidence that food irradiation is safe and that it effectively controls spoilage. In addition, there is strong proof of its cost-effectiveness in controlling the organisms and bacteria that contribute to waste and reduced shelf life or storage time for food (Lamb).

Presents statistics and detail information

Cites authority

6   Even though radiation has been an aid to health in diagnosing and treating diseases and in sterilizing medical equipment and pharmaceutical products, many people are sincerely scared of anything that appears to raise the risk of radiation exposure. Perhaps the best way to deal with these fears is to address them directly.

50d
arg

7   Is irradiated food safe? The answer to this question is a clear <u>yes</u>. Irradiated food is not harmful because the treatment does not alter the food in any way that would be detrimental to people's health. Are irradiated foods still nutritious? <u>Yes</u>. Even though, as with all methods of food processing, the level of nutrients is lowered by irradiation, the food is still nutritious. It is important to remember that even storing food at room temperature after harvesting can reduce its nutritional value. Moreover, the loss of nutrients is generally unmeasurable or insignificant at low

Supplies detailed information

doses of radiation. So not only has it been
demonstrated that food irradiation is a safe form of
food preservation, it is also a method of preserving
the nutrition in food (Blumenthal).   *Cites*
                                        authority
8   Food irradiation could reduce the amount of
waste due to spoilage of the world's food supply.
With the world's population expected to double
during the next century, this form of food
preservation could aid in feeding this growing
number of people in a safe and healthful way at low
cost. This technology could improve the world we
live in and change for the better the lives of
millions of people.

[The paper ends with a list of works cited.]

2 Commentary on Stephanie Lewis's position paper

Lewis's focus is clear through most of the paper, even though she
waits until the end of paragraph 3 to offer a thesis statement clearly presenting her proposition. She acknowledges sympathetically the fears many
people have about food irradiation and offers some scientific evidence of its
safety, but she might have offered even more. In her conclusion she speaks
of the low cost of food irradiation, but she touches on this matter only indirectly earlier in the paper. Her paper would benefit from revision in these
areas; nonetheless, it argues effectively in many ways.

50e
arg

50e The critique

A formal critique consists of two parts—a summary of the work being
discussed, and a critical reaction to the work. The summary should objectively
condense the whole work, including all of its main ideas. The critical response
is your subjective reaction to the work, but this does not necessarily mean a
negative reaction. Many students think a critique should tear a work apart,
pointing out all its faults, but this is not true. A good critique attempts to
explain *how* and *why* a work is written, although questioning both is often an
important part of the critique. In writing a critique, you are first understanding a body of knowledge and opinion, then making a point about it
that helps your reader to interpret it and see it from new perspectives.

1 Sample critique

This selection from a sample critique illustrates how the writer begins with an objective summary of Ortiz's speech and then adds his subjective reaction to Ortiz's ideas. Note the shift in tone as the student moves from summary to critique. Look for sentences that explain how and why Ortiz wrote the speech and for sentences that question Ortiz's ideas.

A Summary and Critique of Alfonso Ortiz's "Some Concerns Central to the Writing of Indian History"

by Reid Nelson

1   In the speech "Some Concerns Central to the Writing of Indian History," Alfonso Ortiz addresses the inadequacies created when non-Native American historians write Native American histories. Ortiz feels there is a need for historians to develop "greater sensitivity toward, and respect for, tribal traditions, and of learning Indian languages" (20).

2   Ortiz says Indians place the significance of past traditions in the place where they originally occurred. Indians therefore think of the past as occurrences relating to a space and not as events that took place at a certain time as historians do. This makes specific dates in the past unimportant to Indians. Ortiz feels that this way of thinking is illustrated by the Pueblo peoples' saying "'When it has been four times,'" which unites a sense of time and space simultaneously by noting when a "distance of four days travel has passed" or "when a time span of four days has passed" (19).

3   Ortiz's dissatisfaction with historians is deepened by their tendency to change occurrences that happened in a particular space into events that took place at a certain time, a practice which does quite the opposite of that which Indians do.

50e
arg

Furthermore, some historians feel that Indian attempts to represent history in terms of space and to use metaphors to describe this history are only a process of mythologization. Ortiz feels that this is an unfortunate and inaccurate judgment because it precludes the possibility to better understand Native American cultures.

[The writer continues with three more paragraphs summarizing Ortiz's points.]

7   In this speech Ortiz is both informing and persuading. Ortiz informs historians about the problems with the way they record Native American history and attempts to persuade them that their approach is detrimental to a better understanding of Native Americans.

8   Ortiz has presented his captive audience of historians with a very straightforward and simple argument. His speech utilizes neither complex theorizing nor bewildering vocabulary. Ortiz tells the audience the negative consequences that do occur when the situation goes unchanged, which are the continued misunderstanding of Native Americans and poor relations between the two groups, and strengthens this point by repeating it several times. The reception these ideas receive will depend on two things. It depends first on whether historians agree that there is a problem in the way they write history and second on whether they agree that Ortiz's proposals will benefit non-Native Americans' understanding of Indian history.

50e arg

[The writer concludes with a summary paragraph and a full reference to the printed source for the speech.]

2 Elements of a critique

An effective critique includes the following elements.

- It does not confuse objective summary with subjective opinion.
- It summarizes all the text's main ideas and important subpoints.
- It expresses a critical opinion of the text fairly, stressing how and why the text works and balancing positive and negative points.
- It gives the reader a clear picture of the text's content, its writer's stance, and the strengths and weaknesses of its argument.

3 Commentary on Reid Nelson's critique

Nelson encountered a common problem with writing critiques—making the summary concise yet understandable. He tries to include everything in Ortiz's speech, which results in giving equal priority to every point. He could explain the main argument of the speech in more detail in the first paragraph; this would orient the reader more clearly. Nelson could be more concise by cutting out some of the lead-in phrases such as *Ortiz says* and *Ortiz feels* and by using active instead of passive voice. In the critique section, Nelson could more explicitly state the problems with Ortiz's ideas.

50f The review

A common academic writing assignment is the review. A **review** is a critical appraisal of an event, object, or phenomenon, such as an art show, a concert, a restaurant, or a book. People read reviews either to help them make a decision about attending or experiencing whatever is being reviewed or to test their own judgments of it against those of another person (usually an expert). When you write a review, you describe, analyze, and evaluate your subject from an informed but clearly opinionated perspective.

Reviews come in many forms and are written from many points of view, from fairly objective and descriptive to very judgmental. The most common reviews are those that describe and evaluate an artistic work or performance: a book, a movie, a concert, a ballet, an opera, an album or CD, an art exhibit, or a play. Reviews can also describe and evaluate objects, such as a new car, a computer program, or a stereo system; events, such as the gala opening of a store or a fashion show; or experiences, such as dining at a restaurant or touring an amusement park. You can review almost anything that can be experienced by others, although your choice of what to review may depend on the interests of your intended audience.

Reviews typically both describe and evaluate, but there is no formula for how to include these two perspectives. Some reviews use a simple two-part structure, with a description followed by an evaluation. Many reviews, however, begin with an evaluative point in a kind of thesis statement: such-and-such was or is a success or failure, good in these areas but poor in these, worth experiencing or a waste of time and money.

Despite the different formats for reviews, however, some important principles tie reviews together as one kind of point-driven writing. First, good reviews are *considered.* They don't just state an opinion but support it with specific information and details. Second, good reviews are *authoritative;* most professional reviewers have experienced whatever they review hundreds of times. In writing your own reviews, for example, try to choose something you have experienced before, such as a movie, book, or CD.

1 Sample review

This book review assignment asked the students to develop a thesis based on the book's contents; the thesis could agree or disagree with the book's author if the book took a position on an issue. As you read the review, note how the writer supports her evaluation with facts and details. Note also how her writing gives the impression that she is reasonably familiar with the topic of deaf culture and communication, adding to her credibility.

<u>Laurent Clerc</u>:

The Issue of Early Deaf Literacy

by Amy Braegelman

1   The preservation of a language, though the community that uses it may be small, is crucially important. Language is not just a communicative amenity--it is a reflection of (and an influence on) a specific culture. Not only does a language allow a culture to flourish, but it allows the people within that culture to flourish. In some cases, a language is particularly well suited to a specific culture because it is all that allows its users to function in society. To allow or force a language so tailored to die is to leave the culture with no effective means of communication, only whatever its people have managed to acquire, usually by bare necessity, of the surrounding, dominant language.

2   Cathryn Carroll's book <u>Laurent Clerc: The Story of His Early Years</u> (Washington, D.C.: Kendall Green Publications, 1991) gives the reader a broader

50f arg

platform on which to base these convictions. Set in the early nineteenth century, Clerc examines the beliefs, stereotypes, and attitudes surrounding the deaf and their language. Like any culture that does not function within the mainstream, the deaf were heavily stigmatized historically; they were believed to be physically sick, mentally ill, or of low intelligence.

3   Of particular interest in Carroll's book is the account of Clerc's time at the Royal National Institute for the Deaf in Paris. The sadistic Dr. Itard, on the staff at the Institute during the first decades of the nineteenth century, dedicated all of his time and surgical background to the misguided endeavor of finding a cure for deafness. As Carroll points out, the school's students were the doctor's unfortunate subjects, and the consequences were "waste, folly, and pain" (86). Itard is a chilling representation of public sentiment at the time; the deaf were "sick" and needed to be cured. The cure, we know, was not available, and in Clerc we see how the deaf who were not used in experiments and were not part of the select few lucky enough to attend the Royal National Institute were treated: sent to live in filth in poorhouses, institutionalized in sanitariums, shunned as subhumans.

4   In this dramatic chronicle of deaf experience, Carroll goes on to show that even in the environment of the Royal National Institute, home and haven to men like Jean Massieu and Laurent Clerc--geniuses by any standards--the deaf were treated like an

50f
arg

attraction. Presentations were given to influential politicians and heads of state to display the talents of these deaf men and gain funding for the school. Audiences were free to ask Massieu and Clerc, positioned on stage like performers, any questions they liked. "What is eternity?" they asked, as if to test the relationship between the ears and the mind. "What is hope?" "Does God reason?"

5   Carroll's portrayal shows that among themselves, where they could be natural and talk freely, the deaf students at the Institute showed an open-minded insight that the hearing, for the most part, lacked at the time. Sign language allowed these students to form a community and a web of support in the hearing world. As Clerc recounts, "I wasn't only alone, I was deficient" (35), but in the deaf world, he finds he is not alone. Clerc illustrates the principle of literacy as power and control. On a trip to England, for example, Massieu and Clerc are accompanied by a hearing person, Abbé Sicard. Clerc recounts that "surrounded by people who spoke a language very different from his, our dear Abbé was completely at a loss. Massieu and I had no trouble getting around...we know how to use our bodies to ask for things." Carroll describes Sicard as a pompous, self-important man who thrives on the control he feels he can exert over the deaf, always under the guise of helpfulness. In England, where he cannot use his own language, he is powerless and is reduced to petty criticisms of the English language. Massieu and Clerc are used to

being surrounded by people who don't speak their language, and they adapt easily, feeling in control.

6   Carroll also devotes much of her book to explaining why the deaf were ostracized because of their lack of literacy and why it was often priests who undertook their education. Greater society felt that because the deaf could not learn about God, they were sinners and savages--and were damned. As Clerc puts it, "Abbé Sicard said we were savages. . . . He said we were children with no thoughts, no feelings, no nothing. We were like statues until he, the great Abbé Sicard, woke us in his classroom. . . . He said that deafness doomed us to darkness and to hell" (75).

7   Carroll's fascinating book illustrates the folly of expecting one mode of communication, one language, to suffice for every member of society. Her book portrays the struggle of the deaf to gain equal standing in a greater society that had so much trouble accepting them. It is, finally, a grand illustration that not only does literacy enable us to function in society, it shapes the way that other people view us. The deaf students at the Royal National Institute for the Deaf were intelligent children, fully capable of functioning in society; many displayed potential to make valuable contributions to science, art, and literature. However, because they could not communicate with their mouths, it was socially acceptable to confine them to asylums and poorhouses rather than giving their language the status it deserved and elevating the deaf beyond the realm of human silence.

50f
arg

2 Elements of a review

An effective review includes the following elements.

- It clearly describes the subject of the review at the start, providing all the information a reader would need to share in the experience (if it is repeatable) or to know when and where it happened (if it was a "one-time" experience such as a one-night-only performance).
- It has a clear organization. Reviews of experiences and events (plays, movies, and so on) are sometimes chronologically arranged, whereas reviews of static objects such as books or art exhibits may focus on different aspects of the work in order of their importance.
- It offers a reasoned, supported evaluation of the subject's main elements. Movie reviews, for example, may evaluate the filming, acting, costuming, directing, special effects, script, plot, casting, length, or stunt work, or the adaptation of another work such as a novel.
- It is authoritative. A reviewer who discusses an actor's performance should probably know something about the actor's other work. A restaurant reviewer who judges the quality of the curry in an Indian restaurant should have some prior experience with Indian food.
- It is generally verifiable by its intended readers; that is, they should be able to see how one might arrive at the evaluation in the review, even though they may not entirely agree with that evaluation.

3 Commentary on Amy Braegelman's review

Amy's paper is a good example of a point-driven review, one that develops a thesis early on and then extends and supports that thesis with reference to the material found, in this case, in a nonfiction book. Her paper artfully treats the issue of deaf literacy, but its description of the book itself is sparse. Amy might have synthesized the book at the start or worked through its contents from beginning to end.

50g
arg

50g The point-driven essay exam

In many of your classes, teachers will use **essay exams** to evaluate your skills as a synthesizer of information and as a critical thinker, skills that cannot be seen from a true/false or multiple-choice test. Thus, merely listing information, facts, and quotes without discussing their significance or making connections among them is not acceptable. When you study for essay exams, you will need to move beyond memorization to thinking about what the information means and how it fits into a larger context. Writing these thoughts down in a journal will help you prepare. (See also 52h.)

When you begin the exam, *first read the question(s) carefully*. You have only a short time in which to write, even with a take-home exam. You need to write quickly and concisely, answering the question specifically and with as much support as possible. It is crucial to understand what kind of answer the teacher expects and to plan the essay before actually writing.

Next, decide what position you want to take or what point you will make in the essay. This will become your working thesis or proposition—a perspective or interpretation that you will support with evidence. Try creating a brief outline for your answer, even just a few lines or items listed on the facing page of the test booklet. Working from an outline will help you make your paper more focused, point-driven, and clearly organized.

1 Sample essay exam

This exam asked the student to identify and discuss a common theme running through a survey course in American literature and to show this theme in two stories. The students were allowed to use their books in class in order to find quotations. As you read selections from this answer, note how the writer focuses on one theme. Note, too, how he incorporates quotations to illustrate the theme.

```
        Moral Perfection in "Young Goodman Brown"
                   and "The Birthmark"
                      by Ted Wolfe
1     Hawthorne's "Young Goodman Brown" explores the
conflict between good and evil. Young Goodman Brown
has his religious faith tested during a journey into
the woods. In what may or may not have been a dream,
he is shown by the devil that everyone he believed
to be good is evil.... When the devil is about to
baptize him, Brown calls out for Faith, his wife,
telling her to resist the temptation. He is really
calling out for faith, as in faith in God. When he
does this, the hellish vision passes, and he is
alone in the woods. From this, I think we can
conclude that Hawthorne believes that people should
try to resist temptation and live moral lives.
2     But Goodman Brown is never the same after the
experience, be it dream or reality. He becomes "a
stern, a sad, a darkly meditative, if not a
```

desperate man." In his heart he doubts the goodness of Faith/faith, Deacon Gookin, Goody Cloyse, and everyone else. . . . Symbolically, the experience in the woods caused him to give up his faith. The overriding message that Hawthorne is trying to convey is that one should try to keep one's faith, to believe in others' inherent goodness, and to try to live morally. If one doesn't, life becomes as barren and miserable as it became for Goodman Brown.

3   Hawthorne's "The Birthmark" also addresses the issue of morality. . . .

[The answer continues with supporting detail from the second story.]

4   . . . Hawthorne's point is that one should not get so caught up in trying to be morally perfect that it ruins one's life. People must learn to "find the perfect future in the present."

2 Elements of a point-driven essay exam

Although the specific criteria for an effective essay exam will vary from teacher to teacher and from course to course, an effective essay exam that makes and defends a point includes the following general elements.

- It addresses the exam question directly, taking into account all parts of the question.
- It uses references—quotes, facts, and other information—efficiently, supplying enough to illustrate or back up the writer's point without overloading the essay.
- It synthesizes material, makes connections among references, and discusses the significance of the material; it does not merely list information but interprets it and uses it to illustrate or document a point.

3 Commentary on Ted Wolfe's essay exam

Although Wolfe titles his essay "Moral Perfection," he digresses slightly to the themes of good and evil, faith, and living morally. These themes are all related to "moral perfection," but Ted could make the relationship clearer. His use of quotes is effective and using specific phrases rather than long passages conserved his time.

Reading and Writing
About Literature

When you read a novel, see a play, or read (or listen to) a poem, you are encountering literature, or, more precisely, imaginative literature. The word *literature* has other meanings as well, some of them used in this book. The literature of a subject of academic study, for example, consists of all the things scholars have written about it. In addition, people often use the term *literature* to distinguish novels and plays that are well written, enjoyable, and worth taking seriously.

In most college courses, however, the term *literature* is applied to certain kinds of texts—fiction, poetry, and drama—that are meant to be read in a manner different from the way we read texts like biographies, histories, reports, scientific papers, or magazine articles. To read a work as literature means to pay attention both to the various meanings it conveys (its insights into human relationships, for example) and to the artistry with which these insights are conveyed (a lively and convincing portrait of a character, for example, or a passage whose vivid and original language evokes a strong emotional response or brings a scene to life in a reader's mind).

It is possible to read almost any kind of text with this dual attention. For instance, you might read a newspaper editorial with a simultaneous focus on the author's point of view and on the persuasive and artful way it is presented. Yet in those works regarded as imaginative literature, the author generally calls special attention to the techniques of presentation, techniques such as characterization, plot, symbolism, and figurative uses of language. In addition, imaginative literature often conveys its meanings through a fictional representation of some setting or human activity: the events of a story, a confrontation between characters, a monologue revealing thoughts and emotions, or a scene in which events take place. To understand the meaning of such texts, you need to read them with a different kind of attention than you give to other kinds of writing. Likewise, to present in writing your interpretation of and responses to literary texts, you need to employ some special strategies of explanation and support.

51a Reading literary texts

When you read a novel, short story, or poem or view a drama or a film, you need to pay attention to both meaning and artistic technique. In doing this, however, you should be aware that there are many different strategies for reading and interpreting such works. Your choice of a reading strategy can determine the way you interpret a work's meaning and the way you respond to the writer's forms of expression. Your focus in reading can also dictate the strategies you should use in presenting your responses to a work. Your goal as a reader and writer concerned with meaning is to develop and present interpretations that your readers will consider insightful and convincing.

1 Read for meaning

For many critics and students of literature, to read for meaning is to read for theme. You can view **theme** as an idea, perspective, insight, or cluster of feelings that a work conveys or that permeates a work, organizing the relationships among its parts. Or you can view theme as the responses and insights readers are likely to derive from their experience of reading a work. In reading for meaning, therefore, you need to pay attention to theme, both as it is developed in a work and as it develops in your responses to the work.

Strategy

As you read, write down any ideas, perspectives, insights or clusters of feelings the work seems to focus on. Pay attention to the various techniques writers generally employ for conveying meaning (see 51a-2): characterization and dialogue, events and conflicts, descriptions or scenes, and discussions of ideas and emotions (either by characters, the speaker, or the writer addressing readers directly). Write down potentially important ideas or themes in the margins (if you own the book), on a sheet of paper, or in a journal you keep while you read. You need not explore potential themes in depth; for a first reading, at least, an informal list can be very valuable.

Look especially for repetition and contrast as a key to importance. Repeated words and ideas, contrasting characters or events, and patterns of images can signal themes worth noticing.

In the following marginal notes on Anson Gonzalez's short poem "Little Rosebud Girl," for example, Sevon Randolf, a college student, indicates some repetitions and contrasts that reveal an important cluster of feelings and ideas (a theme) that she thinks the poem conveys.

51a
lit

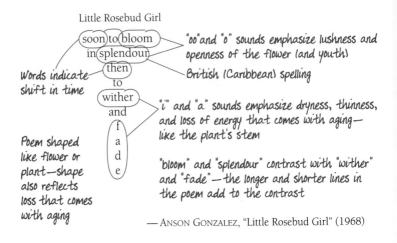

Little Rosebud Girl

— ANSON GONZALEZ, "Little Rosebud Girl" (1968)

The perspective you take as you read may suggest meanings and interpretations. If you know something about psychology, for instance, you might notice that the characters in a novel embody different psychological types or that the main character's actions can be explained as an attempt to overcome feelings of abandonment as a child. If you know something about history or political theory, you might be able to explain the events in a play as a reflection of an attempt to resolve contradictions affecting a particular society or culture. For example, you might be able to show that Shakespeare's *Macbeth* and his *Henry IV* plays deal with questions of power and the proper form of government, major concerns in Elizabethan England. Finally, if you are familiar with contemporary feminist thought, you might note that the psychological and social portraits in a work seem to follow recognizable patterns of dominance and oppression and that the work seems to be designed as a commentary on the ways society has often distorted the lives of women. (Jennifer O'Berry's paper on "The Yellow Wallpaper" on pp. 817–822 draws on several such approaches.)

2 Read for technique

When you read for meaning, you inevitably read for technique. A writer cannot create events, portray characters, represent scenes, or elicit a reader's reactions without using techniques of characterization, plot, setting, or imaginative language. Nonetheless, because these techniques are such an important feature of every literary text, you may wish to focus on them as you read, either to understand a writer's artistry or to cite the writer's use of the techniques as evidence for your discussion of a work's meaning.

As you read, pay particular attention to the following elements of a novel, short story, poem, or drama and to the techniques the writer uses in creating these elements.

51a
lit

Did You Know?

If you look to contemporary literary critics for ways to analyze texts, you may notice that their work follows one or more "schools" of criticism. Some critics emphasize the formal techniques in a work (new criticism); others look for the way a text contradicts or undermines its explicit purposes (deconstruction). Still others pay attention to the historical context, either to explain a work's meaning (historicism) or to interpret it as a product of a specific social formation (new historicism). Some critics look at the many ways readers respond to a text (reader-response criticism); others are more concerned with the writer's mind or the way a text probes human psychology (psychological criticism). And some pay special attention to the role of gender in the reading and writing of literary texts (feminist criticism).

Steven Lynn, *Texts and Contexts: Writing About Literature with Critical Theory* (New York: HarperCollins, 1994).

Character. Identify the major and minor characters and their personality traits. Are they represented in depth with a variety of traits, even contradictions, or are they one-dimensional? Observe how the characters change and develop—or fail to change—in response to events. Note how self-aware the characters are. Which ones are presented positively, which negatively? Consider which characters, if any, represent values that the work (and the writer) seem to endorse.

Plot. Identify the order of events. Is it chronological, or have events been rearranged in some way? Decide what role conflicts play in developing the plot. Ask whether the events spring from the characters' personalities or serve primarily to reveal character traits. Is there a main conflict, a chain of conflicts, or a climax to which the work builds? Weigh the possibility that not all events are to be taken at face value. Watch for subplots alongside the main plot. Is the meaning of events clear to characters (and readers) from the start or only later? Pay attention to techniques of foreshadowing and suspense.

**51a
lit**

Setting. Note the time and place in which the events occur, along with any extended descriptions or background information relating to the place and time. Does the setting help explain the character's actions or reactions? Does it convey a mood that shapes the readers' reactions or the work's meaning? If the work is from an earlier period, check for elements in the setting that require historical explanation.

Point of View. For novels and stories, decide who is telling the story. Stories can be narrated in the first person (*I*) either by a character in the narrative or by a narrative voice (sometimes representing the author). They can also be told in the third person by a narrator who speaks of the characters as *he* and *she* but does not identify himself or herself as *I*. Narrators may be limited in what they know, be omniscient (knowing and seeing things the characters cannot), or combine both in some way. Narrators may be reliable and truthful, be unreliable and deceptive, or mix these and other traits. The speaker in a poem may be a character or may be a persona, a voice that speaks for the poet.

Language. Look for special uses of language: similes, metaphors, understatement, paradoxes, ironic comments, and the like. Pay attention to vivid descriptive language that creates scenes and images (sight, sound, and the like). Look for unusual word choice and striking or emphatic arrangements of words. Be alert for rhythms in the wording and for patterns of sound and rhyme.

Genre. Pay attention to **genre**—the specific form or kind of work: novel, short story, poem, drama, or film. Be especially alert to the techniques and conventions characteristic of each form, and note how writers use these conventions to convey meanings and shape readers' reactions. Note instances in which the writer varies or alters conventions, perhaps by undermining them or developing them in unusual directions.

Strategy

As you read a literary text, make notes on the large-scale techniques the writer uses to shape the work (genre, plot, and point of view, for example) and also on the smaller-scale techniques that appear to be important in a particular passage (language and character, for example). If you make your notes in the margins of your book, you can highlight passages you may wish to cite later in a paper. If you make notes in your journal, however, you will have more room to explore your responses and the ideas you may wish to develop in a paper. (Your journal entries also should note important passages for later use.)

Whenever possible, relate your observations on technique to your perceptions of a work's meaning. This will help you understand the purposes behind the techniques. It will also help you identify evidence for your interpretations of a work.

Note how T. J. Corini's marginal notes on the opening paragraph of John Edgar Wideman's novel *Philadelphia Fire* identify techniques and link them to meaning in a way that points toward a paper he might write.

51a lit

What's going on?

On a day like this the big toe of Zivanias had failed him. Zivanias named for the moonshine his grandfather cooked, best white lightning on the island. Cudjoe had listened to the story of the name many times. Was slightly envious. He would like to be named for something his father or grandfather had done well. A name celebrating a deed. A name to stamp him, guide him. They'd shared a meal once. Zivanias crunching fried fish like Rice Krispies. Laughing at Cudjoe. Pointing to Cudjoe's heap of cast-off crust and bones, his own clean platter. Zivanias had lived up to his name. Deserted a flock of goats, a wife and three sons up in the hills, scavenged work on the waterfront till he talked himself onto one of the launches jitneying tourists around the island. A captain soon. Then captain of captains. Best pilot, lover, drinker, dancer, storyteller of them all. He said so. No one said different. On a day like this when nobody else dared leave port, he drove a boatload of bootleg whiskey to the bottom of the ocean. Never a trace. Not a bottle or bone. *Whole ¶ presents contrasts of character, attitude, perspective, and detail*

Marginal annotations:
- *st character— hero? an outlaw?*
- *: bones symbolize the past*
- *s actions make m seem verbal, self-assured*
- *etition and allelism help phasize his ing legend*
- *2nd character Cudjoe uncertain of his manliness? Admires Z.?*
- *Z. self-sufficient? Sure of himself? Characterization —Z.'s actions and attitudes contrast w/C.'s.*
- *contrast*
- *Contrast*

Exercise 1

A. Choose a short text or part of a text you are planning to write about. Read it, making notes on the meaning and technique in the margins or in a journal.

B. Ask a classmate to read the same text and make the same kind of notes that you made in Exercise 1A. (Return the favor by reading and annotating a text for your classmate.) Compare your notes, looking for points of agreement. Discuss any annotations or interpretations that need explanation or support.

C. Complete the preparation for your paper by writing notes for any part of the text you have not annotated. Jot down ideas and observations you think may be worth developing in your paper.

51b Writing about literary texts

When you write about a literary text, you interpret and analyze an author's words and techniques. To do so, you must arrive at conclusions—

judgments and observations—with which another reader may agree or disagree. Consequently, you need to convince readers that your conclusions are both reasonable and well-founded. You can generally do this by offering evidence from the text or from secondary sources.

1 Write about meaning

In writing about the meaning of a literary work, you may explain and support your conclusions about its theme. Or you may focus on insights you develop by applying a particular perspective to the work (a historical perspective or a feminist perspective, for example).

Developing a Thesis. If you are writing about a work's theme, you need to make sure readers can easily identify your statement of the theme. Presenting your conclusion about the theme early in your paper in a thesis statement is a particularly effective strategy. In addition, if you develop a working thesis early in your drafting, you can revise it and use it to help focus your supporting paragraphs.

Selecting Evidence. Suppose you developed the following working thesis for a paper.

> In "Young Goodman Brown," Hawthorne focuses on the dangers to human relationships and community posed by excessive concern with the self.

For supporting evidence, you can turn to passages in the text itself, either those that seem to state this theme or those you can analyze and explain in ways that support your conclusion. Simply quoting passages from the work is not enough. You need to discuss and analyze them in detail in order to show readers why the passages support your interpretation. You can also cite or summarize other elements of a work, such as events, characters, and symbols, analyzing them in detail to show that the text and the techniques it employs are consistent with your interpretation. Finally, you can turn to the writing of critics and scholars, using it to support your thesis and your view of specific parts of a work.

51b lit

Organizing. Because a paper about meaning focuses on your view of a text's theme or on your interpretation of all or part of the work, you need to organize the paper to explain and defend your perspective. There are two general ways to do this (with many variations, of course). One way is to separate your thesis into parts and take up each part in a different section of your paper. In writing about Hawthorne's "Young Goodman Brown," for instance, you might first demonstrate that the story deals with a character obsessed with the self, then look at what the story says about the consequences of this behavior. The other way to organize your paper is to divide it into parts corresponding to different segments of the work (beginning, middle, end) or different elements (characters, language, symbols), then show in sections of your paper how the particular part or element supports your thesis.

Writer's Tip

Follow these conventions for writing about literature.

- Use the present tense when summarizing literary texts ("In the next section of the play, Falstaff *acts* in a manner that calls into question the kind of morality he represents").
- Use the present tense for discussing what a writer does in a particular work or group of works ("Dickens *uses* descriptive passages in *Bleak House* to develop symbols that comment on the action and the characters").
- Use the past tense for discussing a work in historical context ("During the Vietnam War, Levertov's poetry *took* on a distinctly political tone").

---

2 Write about technique

In writing about technique, you explain the choices the author has made from the resources available for creating fiction, poetry, or drama. You also try to highlight the author's variations on the techniques, if any. Finally, you draw conclusions about the roles the techniques play in shaping the work's meaning and the likely responses of readers.

51b
lit

Developing a Thesis. Since your purpose in this kind of paper is to describe and analyze one or several techniques and then relate technique to meaning, your thesis statement should reflect this dual emphasis. In writing about the story "Young Goodman Brown," for example, you might say, "Hawthorne uses ambiguity in setting, symbolism, and characterization to suggest how excessive concern with the self can alter one's perception of everyday events."

Selecting Evidence. The primary evidence in a paper about technique is the text itself, presented either through quotations or through paraphrase and summary. But details from a text are not enough on their own to support your conclusions. You need to discuss the evidence, explaining the particular ways a technique is used and pointing out how this use supports your conclusions about the text's meaning. (The work of critics and scholars can also provide supporting evidence.)

Organizing. If you are examining a single technique, consider dividing your essay into parts corresponding to different sections of the work, demonstrating how the technique is employed in each section and for what purpose. (For a short work such as a poem, you might examine the work line by line or sentence by sentence, creating an **explication.**) If you examine more than one technique, you can divide your paper into parts, each concerned with the way a different technique is employed. Or you can take up each section of a work in turn, looking at the various techniques used there.

Writer's Tip

Stating your point in a thesis is a good start, but many promising papers still get bogged down in details, losing focus and losing the reader. One way to avoid this problem is to remind readers of your overall thesis each time you move to a new part of your essay, letting them know what section or technique you will discuss next and what you plan to conclude about it. This strategy can guide your drafting and your revision, helping you check the focus of your essay and pay attention to the needs of your readers.

Exercise 2

A. Choose a work you plan to write about. Read it, and write out a tentative thesis statement presenting your conclusions about the work's meaning and technique. Then prepare a list of particular passages or sections of the work you plan to use as evidence in your paper. Finally, create a rough outline or some other kind of plan for this paper.

51c
lit

B. Present your tentative thesis, list of evidence, and plan to a group of writers working on the same project. Discuss each writer's material, offering criticisms and suggestions to help each other prepare a draft. Draft your paper, and then share it with the same group for advice about revision. Take the group's advice into account as you revise and prepare the final draft.

51c The text analysis

A **text analysis** is a frequent assignment in many courses across the college curriculum. The first of the three examples here focuses on literary techniques in a poem. The second focuses on meaning in a short story. The third discusses visual strategies in a film.

1 Sample text analysis: Focus on technique

As you read the following paper, note how the writer goes through the poem line by line, accounting for nearly every image and phrase. This form of analysis is often called explication.

"Under Stars": A Portrait
by Chantele Giles

Under Stars
Tess Gallagher

The sleep of this night deepens
because I have walked coatless from the house
carrying the white envelope.
All night it will say one name
in its little tin house by the roadside.

I have raised the metal flag
so its shadow under the roadlamp
leaves an imprint on the rain-heavy bushes.
Now I will walk back
thinking of the few lights still on
in the town a mile away.

In the yellowed light of a kitchen
the millworker has finished his coffee,
his wife has laid out the white slices of bread
on the counter. Now while the bed they have left
is still warm, I will think of you, you
who are so far away
you have caused me to look up at stars.

51c
lit

Tonight they have not moved
from childhood, those games played after dark.
Again I walk into the wet grass
toward the starry voices. Again, I
am the found one, intimate, returned
by all I touch on the way.

                                        1978

1   With the use of visual imagery in the poem
"Under Stars," Tess Gallagher paints a romantic, yet
lonely portrait of the relationship between the
speaker of the poem and her long-distance lover.
Although the speaker's emotional state is plagued
with images of loneliness, she projects the long-
distance romance as a positive relationship that is
warm and caring.

2   As Gallagher brushes "The sleep of this night
deepens" of the first stanza onto her canvas, her
poetry begins to take shape. The word "sleep"
implies that the relationship with her lover is
peaceful. Since the "night" personifies the
relationship, the phrase implies further that the
relationship is past the early stages and is
deepening with the "sleep" of the night. In the next
lines the speaker is walking "coatless from the
house / carrying the white envelope." She walks
"coatless" because she does not need to cloak the
relationship; she is neither afraid nor ashamed.
Since the "white envelope" connotes purity,
goodness, and truth, it symbolizes the relationship
as being true. The word "coatless" implies not only
that the speaker has nothing to hide, but that the

51c
lit

affiliation is warm and caring. If it were cold and dysfunctional, the speaker would not be without a coat.

3   In the last two lines, Gallagher applies the final strokes to the first stanza. The first of the two lines implies that the speaker is consumed with thoughts of her lover. With the image of the "little tin house by the roadside," Gallagher suggests that the speaker's lover is some distance away, which implies that the speaker is trying to bridge the distance between the two of them. She accomplishes this by composing a letter and placing it in the "little tin house."

4   Since the second stanza exposes the inadequacies of the relationship, Gallagher applies a darker paint to her canvas. The "metal flag" suggests the cold reality of a long-distance relationship, since metal is cold to the touch; the flag's "shadow" implies that the relationship cannot be touched by the speaker. The association with her lover leaves only a lonely "imprint" on the speaker's heart, which is symbolized by the "rain-heavy bushes." The final three lines are painted a lighter color. With these lines, the speaker implies that the "shadow" of loneliness is not permanent. Since the "town a mile away" symbolizes the future, the speaker implies that the future is close at hand. The "few lights" of the town suggest that there is hope in the near future.

5   Gallagher allows the readers into the realm of the speaker's fantasy, as she begins the third stanza. The "millworker" and "his wife" represent her fantasy relationship. The warm atmosphere created by

51c
lit

the "yellowed light" implies that the speaker's fantasy is cheerful and bright. In this relationship, the couple reside and share their meals together. The "white slices of bread" connote food, nourishment, and sustenance. Since the "wife has laid out the white slices of bread" for the "millworker," the speaker implies that not only does she want to be her lover's sustenance, but she also wants to be consumed by him (the way the "millworker" will consume the "bread").

6   The last lines of the third stanza illustrate the speaker's need for closeness. Since the lover is "so far away" and the speaker looks "up at the stars," the speaker feels closer to her lover because of the possibility that the lover may be looking "up at the stars" also. This possibility creates a connection between the speaker and her lover. In the fourth stanza, Gallagher strokes onto her portrait "Tonight they have not moved / from childhood, those games played after dark." These lines suggest that the distance between the speaker and her lover has done little to change the affection she feels for her lover. "Those games played after dark" may refer to romantic liaisons; since these liaisons involve intense feelings, the speaker implies that the intensity of her feelings "have not moved from [the] childhood" of the relationship. Therefore, the speaker's connection to her lover is permanent.

7   With "Again I walk into the wet grass," Gallagher demonstrates that the speaker looks "up at the stars" on a regular basis, thus reinforcing the

51c
lit

various images of the poem such as walking coatless and the "rain-heavy bushes." The "starry voices" recall the images set forth in the third stanza and the first part of the fourth stanza. This line reinforces the images of the speaker's heavenly fantasy, as well as the feelings of permanence.

8   In the last lines, Gallagher displays the speaker's final analysis of the relationship. It is long-lasting and can survive the long-distance barrier. Since she considers herself to be "the found one," she implies that her lover is her one and only true love. She says further that her love is "returned by all" she touches, implying that their love is a powerful, all-encompassing natural force.

9   Tess Gallagher creates a gentle but stirring portrait of true love. Although the images suggest that the speaker endures the heartache of the separation, she does not succumb to the depression usually associated with it. Instead, she embraces the negative aspects of the situation and disempowers them through her fantasies and stargazing.

**51c
lit**

2 Sample text analysis: Focus on meaning

As you read, note how the writer backs up her interpretation with quotations from the story but does not let the quotations dominate the paper. If you have read this short story, consider other ways it could be interpreted; if you have not read the story, consider other ways the quotations used in this sample could be interpreted.

Images of Self in "The Yellow Wallpaper"

by Jennifer O'Berry

1   During the 1800s the idea of the "new woman" was appearing. Women began to realize that they were seen only as their husbands' and society's "property."

They began to pursue their independence and create their own identities. In Charlotte Perkins Gilman's short story "The Yellow Wallpaper," a nameless woman is searching for her personal identity and freedom from the oppressive childlike treatment inflicted on her by her doctor/husband. Gilman presents an elaborate metaphor about the images seen by the woman within the wallpaper found in her nursery/bedroom. This metaphor and the images the woman finds in the wallpaper play a significant role in the woman's achievement of finding her true self. Her state of insanity at the end of the story serves as a safe mask for her newly found freedom from alienation and oppression.

2   Gilman presents the woman in her story as a somewhat unstable character who believes that she is sick, although John, her doctor/husband, believes that she is only suffering from a "slight hysterical tendency" (416). This characterization seems intentional on the part of Gilman because it makes the reader see clearly that the woman's ideas are oppressed, even from the beginning, by her husband. John thinks that all his wife needs is a strict rest schedule in which she is "absolutely forbidden to 'work'" (416) until she is "well" again. Gilman seems to suggest, by putting <u>work</u> in quotes, that the duties of the woman, and all women at that time, were not truly considered work. She was forbidden to write and to have visitors. Early in the story, when the "rules" for her recovery are stated, the woman begins to comment on her disagreement with her husband, but she stops abruptly, as if she does not

dare to have such thoughts. She believes that she would more quickly recover if, instead of being quarantined and forbidden from such pleasures as her writing, she "had less opposition and more society and stimulus" (416).

3   The woman tells the reader that "Mary is so good with the baby" (417), implying that she herself does not want to spend time with the baby. The child is also never mentioned by the woman as being with her or spending time with her. This seems to suggest that she may actually be experiencing a type of postpartum depression, causing her to want to abandon her child. The thoughts that lead her to feel that she may be ill may actually be due to her desire to abandon her role of wife and mother which was so rigidly demanded by society at that time. She gets "unreasonably angry" (416) about the condition of things sometimes, but she blames this anger on her "nervous condition" (416). She tries to dismiss these thoughts because she feels that they are not proper. Therefore, she feels that she must be ill.

**51c
lit**

4   Gilman uses many images to enlighten the reader about the childlike treatment of the woman by her husband. The woman is directed by her husband to rest in a bedroom that used to serve as a nursery. Gilman chooses this room to show how John thinks of his wife. When referring to his wife, John commonly chooses names such as "blessed little goose" (418), "blessed child" (420), and "little girl" (421). This shows that he does not see his wife as an equal but rather as a helpless child who is solely dependent on him. As the woman begins to realize that she has

been a subject of this type of oppression, she begins to be "a little afraid of John" (422) and to "wish he would take another room" (424), which exhibits her awareness of this treatment and the desire to be free from it, and from him.

5   Because of her rigid rest schedule, the woman is forced to spend most of her time in her nursery/bedroom, where she begins to explore the "worst [wall]paper" (417) she has ever seen in her life. Since she is not allowed to do much else, she commits herself to "follow that pointless pattern to some sort of conclusion" (419). She finds many images in the pattern, all of which aid in her "improvement" (423) "because of the wallpaper" (423) out of her mother/wife roles. She describes the pattern as images that will "plunge off at outrageous angles, [and] destroy themselves in unheard-of contradiction" (417). These "contradictions" seem to be referring to the contradictory treatment of her by her husband and society's contradictory expectations of her to be the perfect wife and mother. She becomes entranced by the wallpaper and "follows the pattern about by the hour" (419). With each second, the images become more numerous and complex. She begins to see "a broken neck and two bulbous eyes" (418), a woman behind the pattern in wallpaper. This woman "is all the time trying to climb through . . . but nobody could climb through . . . it strangles so" (424). She begins to identify with the woman and decides that she will stop at nothing until the woman is released from her entrapment.

6   At the end of the story, the woman is simultaneously on the brink of self-identity and insanity. On the last night she is to stay in the house, she is left alone in the room where she finally frees the woman in the wallpaper. When the woman in the wallpaper begins to "crawl and shake the pattern" (425), the main character "[runs] to help her" (425). Through the night, the two women pull and shake the bars and are able to "peel off yards of that paper" (425). She breaks down some of these cultural bars with the help from the woman in the wallpaper. When morning arrives, there is only one woman—the two have merged, and the woman's true identity has been found. In the remaining wallpaper are "many of those creeping women" (426). This symbolically represents the great number of women who also desire to be freed from the bars put up by society. She wonders if those women will ever "come out of the wallpaper as [she] did" (426). This shows her symbolic escape and her desire for other women to experience this personal freedom.

7   John returns at the end of the story to discover his wife in a state of insanity. When he sees her as the woman in the wallpaper, creeping around the room, he faints. She "had to creep over him" (426) because he was blocking her path. This strongly symbolizes the conquering of her husband because of her dominant position over him. She tells him that he cannot "put [her] back" (426) because she is finally free. Her creeping, which is like that of an infant, seems to represent a birth of her new self. At the same time, she has become

completely insane. It is rather ironic that she must move into this state in order to be free from oppression. This seems to represent society's view of a liberated and self-identified woman. John believes that his wife is not ill before she begins her pursuit of self-discovery. When this discovery is complete, he sees her as insane. The opposite is true for the woman herself. She sees herself as ill before her process of identification and fully healthy afterward.

8   The woman in Gilman's short story uses the yellow wallpaper as a tool to find her true self. The color of the wallpaper itself seems to represent the brightness and hope of a new horizon, yet at the same time, it is a reminder of the "old, foul, bad yellow things" (423), like a fungus that grows and decays. This is representative of the woman's life. She can never truly be free, because society's views and ideas will never acknowledge that a liberated woman can achieve her own identity.

3 Sample text analysis: Focus on technique (film)

As you read, notice how the writer organizes his paper and uses details from the film to illustrate and support his points.

Realism and Visual Effect in Educating Rita

by Jason Fester

1   Educating Rita is a realistic film. It depicts an older woman hairdresser who returns to college to become educated. As a realistic film it presents itself very conventionally with authentic sets, vernacular dialogue, and routine eye-level shots with conversations consisting of medium two-shots

and close-ups. Since the film concentrates on
language and the interaction of characters, the
other elements of cinematic technique seem
secondary, and as a realistic film, this seems
appropriate. "Realists . . . try to preserve the
illusion that their film world is unmanipulated; an
objective mirror of the actual world" (Giannetti 3).
But the director inconspicuously uses color to
parallel character development and contribute to the
theme of his movie.

2   When Rita is first seen, she is light-skinned
and has bleached blonde hair. She wears red
lipstick, a thin white shirt, high heels, and a
tight hot-pink skirt. The next time she is seen, she
wears a white shirt, a bright red skirt, high heels,
dangling silver earrings, and this time pink
highlights adorning her hair. Rita is a vivacious,
vivid woman, and the colors of her wardrobe reflect
this. Her appearance presents her as sexual and
corporeal.

3   The university, however, is a dull, colorless
place. The building's walls are dirty white and gray
stone. Frank's office is a dungeon of brown
curtains, olive walls, and a drab red carpet, all
bordered by a montage of tan, matte yellow, earth
brown, and olive drab books. Everything associated
with the university is plain, colorless, and somber.
Frank's house continues the decorum of his office
with brown curtains, muted yellow, and olive drab
wallpaper. Frank wears suits exclusively in varying
tones of tan; his friend exists in the same gray
suit throughout the movie, and even Julia limits her

51c
lit

wardrobe to red-browns. There is no vividness to any of these places or people. Everything, except Frank, is sober.

4   This is the world to which Rita commits herself, regardless of Frank's warning that she will have to "suppress, perhaps even abandon altogether, [her] uniqueness." Thus it is appropriate that at the stage of her development when she has chosen to commit to her education, saying "I want to change," she is wearing a tan jacket with a brown skirt.

5   With the advent of spring comes the next phase of Rita's transformation: summer school. Here her apparel consists of the light blues and greens of the fertile season, suggesting that Rita herself is flourishing and growing. Upon her return to Cambridge, she responds to a compliment on her appearance with "I got a whole new wardrobe." Her appearance is now quite different from when she was first introduced. Her hair is now her natural brown; she is unadorned with jewelry or makeup; and she is clothed in a blue blazer, loose-fitting white pants, and a long white scarf. These neutral, asexual colors and styles continue throughout this period of her activities: light blues, greens, and soft grays cause her to blend with the garments of her student peers and the lusterlessness of the college.

6   Exceptions to this pattern are the retrogressive Roaring Twenties outfits Rita wears for the bistro. They consist of hot pinks, turquoise, pink and blue leopard skins, and lime greens arrayed in clashing ensembles. But these serve to mock her original style, for when she

jokingly displays one outfit to Frank, he humourlessly replies, "Why can't you just be yourself?"

7   The end of the movie presents a Rita vastly different from the one introduced at the beginning. Rita is now merely Susan, a confused, unfulfilled woman. She is dressed in blue jeans, common and ordinary. She wears no makeup. Her long brown hair hangs limply on her shoulders. As she walks along, her blue clothes merge with the dreary blues and grays of the wet rained-on streets. She doesn't know where she's going; she doesn't know what she wants to do.

8   The director uses the colors of Rita's clothes contrasted against the colors of her environment to further express the character changes she undergoes. Even though this is a realistic film, the director surreptitiously manipulates one technique, color, in a way that affects the emotions and responses of the viewer.

51c
lit

Work Cited

Giannetti, Louis D. Understanding Movies. 6th ed.
     Englewood Cliffs: Prentice, 1993.

4 Elements of a text analysis

An effective text analysis includes the following elements.

- It presents a unified interpretation that attempts to convince its readers of one specific way of reading the text.
- It accounts for every idea, argument, image, or allusion; it does not overlook elements that don't fit into the interpretation.
- It does not try to hide behind a facade of objectivity, presenting opinions as absolute truths, but neither does it resort to the relativist plea that "one person's opinion is just as valid as another's."

- It attempts to add a new way of reading the text to the existing ways; it does not merely repeat what has already been written about the text.
- It assumes a dialogue with the reader.

5 Commentary on students' papers

Chantele Giles was faced with the problem typical of writing explications of poetry, that of making the explication as lively and as engaging as the poem itself. Knowing that she must account for every line and image of the poem, she starts at the beginning and moves line by line to the end. To add interest, she frames the explication with an analogy of the poet to a painter, but her prose still sounds too dry. She could enliven her paper by varying the organization, perhaps by using the analogy as a frame to begin and end the paper rather than to begin each paragraph. She could also alternate the line-by-line approach with an occasional comment on the overall meaning of the poem. And she could move beyond discussing the meaning of the poem to other ways of looking at it, such as analyzing its effect on her or other readers or comparing it to other poems.

Jennifer O'Berry uses quotations from the text well; she seems to have an intuitive sense of what is significant about them and how they relate to each other. She could improve the paper by discussing these quotations in more depth, explaining why they are significant in understanding how this story illustrates the ways women were oppressed. As the paper is now, the significance of the quotations is a bit unclear, mainly because Jennifer does not define the terms that she uses to explain their significance (terms such as *self-identity, true self, insanity,* and *oppression*). Defining these terms would help strengthen the connection between the quotations and the discussion.

Jason Fester assumes that readers will be familiar with the film he is discussing, and as a result, he does not adequately identify some of the characters, scenes, and relationships he discusses. At the same time, however, his discussion of Rita's appearance and its relationship to her character is especially clear. He organizes his discussion so that it follows the chronological order of the film. This is particularly appropriate not only because the organization aids him in demonstrating the pattern in Rita's changing dress but also because it allows him to draw parallels with Rita's changes in character and the themes developed through these changes. He also presents detailed evidence about the film's techniques so that he is able to show convincingly how the evidence supports his interpretations of the director's work.

51c
lit

Writing Informative Papers Across the Disciplines

In many situations, your job as a writer may be primarily to convey information in a manner that is as clear, economical, and balanced as you can, serving the needs, interests, and curiosity of your readers. College writing assignments may ask you to gather and convey information—knowledge that you, as a student, have gained and are ready to convey to others. Unlike argument or other point-driven writing (see Chapter 50), **informative writing** doesn't aim primarily at supporting your opinion or your critical insights. Instead, informative writing asks you to adopt the stance of a careful reporter or an informed synthesizer.

Informative writing can describe a process or tell how to do something. It can report what others think about a topic or synthesize research findings. You can employ the strategies of informative writing to describe the components or structure of a natural object, to provide information that enables readers to arrive at informed judgments, or to record events.

Informative writing plays essential roles in business, government, research, and education. Most journalistic writing is also informative; reporters try to "tell it like it is" (or was). This chapter introduces some common uses for informative writing in college courses, and it outlines strategies you can employ in your informative writing in college and beyond.

52a info

52a Developing and presenting informative writing

Informative writing relies on thorough gathering of information, careful analysis and synthesis, and presentation shaped by both the subject matter and the readers' needs. Instead of thinking of readers as people to persuade, as in argumentative writing, you might think of them as clients who need information that you can supply in thoughtful, clear, and creative ways.

First, you need to offer your readers accurate information that is new, interesting, or useful to them. Your own values, attitudes, and opinions are less important than this information and its clarity and fairness. Though you, as a writer, are present everywhere in the text, as a source of personal opinions you may move to the background to let your readers focus on the details, ideas, and events that are your subject. Explanations of complicated ideas and phenomena may challenge readers, but the reading experience itself should be free from complications such as poor organization, inappropriate wording, or hard-to-follow sentences.

1 Analyze your readers' needs

To provide an effective base for your informative writing, try to identify your readers and their purposes for wanting information. In academic settings, you can usually assume that you are providing a teacher and classmates with information related to the course work. Your classmates probably know relatively little about your topic; your teacher may have a fuller background but is reading both to learn something new and to discover what the presentation reveals about your knowledge and your insights.

Strategy

Here are some ways to identify your readers' needs before you begin collecting and presenting information.

- In your journal or on a piece of paper, analyze your readers. How much background do they have in your subject? Are they experts, or do they represent a general, educated audience with no specialized knowledge? Are they merely curious about the topic, or will they do something with the knowledge (such as repair something, think differently about a subject, or seek more information)? (See also Chapter 6.)
- Find out what a friend or another trusted person would like to know about your topic, and list these questions or concerns.
- List information you already know about the topic. Then list questions you want to answer. If you ask and try to answer interesting questions, you are likely to share your involvement in the topic.

2 Collect information

Collecting expert material for an informative paper may involve probing your own memory or prior experiences; doing library research (see Chapters 43 and 44); doing field research through interviews, observations, surveys, or questionnaires; or collecting physical material for analysis. For a complex paper, you may need information from several different sources, organized in a sequence so that each stage of such work can inform the others.

Strategy

Here are some planning tips for informative writing. (See Chapter 44 for important guidelines for library and field research.)

- Create a list of possible information sources, and then order the sources in different possible sequences. In each sequence, note what information will likely come from each source and how it might affect the use of the next source. Also include notes about any practical issues in the collection of information. Choose the possible sequence that seems the most practical. Here is a sequence one writer chose for a paper on recent biological research in the South American rain forests.

1. Interview with Prof. James ⟶ help me focus on which Amazonian areas are most relevant for my paper, and suggest possible sources
2. General library research ⟶ background on rain forest research
3. Biology library research ⟶ information on medicinal discoveries from rain forest plants
4. Interview with Susan Shoulder ⟶ what she felt when discovering plants that have never been classified

- Keep copious and accurate notes. If you are observing, write down only what you are sure you are seeing. If you are conducting an interview, take accurate notes or use a tape recorder. If you feel you are reaching a conclusion during the interview, don't mix your conclusions into the notes as if they came from the person being interviewed. Instead, ask your interviewee whether your conclusion is justified.

52a
info

- Go back to your source, if possible, to verify or extend your data. If you *think* you saw a picture of a controversial activist on the office wall of the mayor you interviewed, see if you can verify its presence before mentioning it in your paper. You might even ask the mayor about its significance. If something in your library research is unclear, go back for more information to clarify the issue or fill the gap.
- Remember that your readers expect you to be fair to your subject and its various interpretations. Begin with what you know to be true, based on facts and evidence; don't leap to unsupported interpretations. Represent accurately what you *see* in your observations and what you *hear* in your interviews. If you cannot be balanced in your research or presentation, change subjects, or change to a kind of writing (argument, for instance) that allows you to take a position.

3 Synthesize and "chunk" information

Informative writing relies on careful internal logic that helps readers to process and understand information. If you shift topics without an obvious plan, for example, readers will have trouble organizing information in their own minds and integrating it into their existing knowledge. In a paper about the relationship between diet and colon cancer in the United States, for instance, readers will be able to process the information more easily if you present it in logical categories rather than jumbling up disparate facts about colon cancer, the American diet, and the basic food groups.

Strategy

To find an internal logic to your information, try some informal grouping and outlining techniques (see also Chapter 4).

- **Chunks.** List the main areas your paper will cover. All the information you have gathered should fit into these "chunks." If something does not fit, reconsider your list. Perhaps you can create an additional category for this item (and for others already listed elsewhere).
- **Patterns.** Look for patterns in your information. For example, if you are **comparing** or **contrasting** two objects or phenomena, then your work will involve two main groups of details or ideas—perhaps dividing your paper into two large sections or into a number of subtopics, each discussed in terms of your two main subjects. If you use **classification,** however, you will organize your information in terms of groups, categories, or parts, each presented in its own section. (See also 10b on patterns in paragraphs.)

  Also consider a **sequential order** (organizing information in a pattern within a particular perspective or focus) such as a *spatial sequence* (describing physical features in relationship to each other), a *chronological sequence* (describing events in a series to explain a history or the stages in a process), or a *hierarchical sequence* (describing relationships and the relative importance of a subject's features or parts).

  In a complex paper, you may need to use more than one form of organization. A fairly long research paper about an artist might include chronological sequences about the artist's life and the development of his or her work, spatial sequences to describe and discuss specific works, and a hierarchical sequence in moving from least to most important works.

**52a
info**

Exercise 1

A. Choose a topic of interest to you. On the basis of your existing knowledge, select a potential organizing strategy to present some background information about the topic. Create a simple outline.

EXAMPLE   Topic: Building a deck
Organizing strategy: Sequential
Outline:
1. Planning the location and style
2. Determining and obtaining the materials
3. Setting concrete piers
4. Building a supporting frame
5. Laying deck boards
6. Building stairs and rails
7. Finishing and trimming the deck

 B.   Share your outlines in a small group. As you discuss the outlines, try to imagine an alternative organizing strategy based on the collective knowledge of the group.

4 Balance description with analysis or synthesis

In many kinds of informative writing, you will need to present information as a function of a careful **analysis** or **synthesis.** To analyze means to break a subject into its components and study the relationship among these parts—how they affect or relate to each other, how they work together, how they fit within a larger system, or how they are in turn divided into smaller systems. When you analyze, you look for connections, patterns, and relationships within the larger whole—for example, the "system" in a classroom rather than just the details describing it. On the other hand, synthesis involves combining separate elements into a unified whole, for example, bringing order to a "trend analysis" through an overview or general conclusion based on disparate studies or data.

►◄ Strategy

Try the following ways to find a balance, when appropriate, among analysis, synthesis, and description.

- Collect as much descriptive or factual information as you can. Then look for connections and relationships in the factual information. Such relationships may be *causal* (*A* causes *B*), *sequential* (*A* comes before *B*), or *hierarchical* (*A, B,* and *C* are really parts of *X*). (Try some of the Strategies in Chapter 4 to help you see beyond simple facts.)
- Ask yourself whether your description or facts alone are enough to give your readers insight into your subject. Recounting the events in a homicide may be enough for a newspaper report, but a simple list of facts about oil consumption in the United States may not interest readers as much as a careful, objective analysis of the likely consequences of these facts.

52a
info

5 Check your stance

While conveying information fairly may seem like an easy task, don't be deceived; even journalists acknowledge that it is very difficult to report anything without subtly conveying a "point" or opinion. Consequently, it is important for you to think carefully about your own stance in relation to your subject, one in which you are not invested in a particular finding, conclusion, or set of facts. If you decide in advance that you can't write in a balanced way about your subject, don't deceive your readers into believing that you are being nonjudgmental in your treatment.

Strategy

- After writing a draft of an informative paper, ask yourself whether you are being true to the full range of information you discovered in your research. Ask yourself if you have left out information that might show your subject in a different and equally reasonable light. Responsible informative writing does not slant information but instead presents alternatives for readers to consider.
- Look carefully at any language in your draft that suggests an interpretation, such as *thus, therefore, as a result, consequently, it seems that,* or similar wording. Then ask whether that interpretation represents a fair conclusion in light of the information you gathered or whether it represents your particular opinion or bias.
- Locate and consider eliminating statements that carry strong personal opinions or judgments (such as *in my opinion, in my view, I believe,* or *I think*). Expletives like *it is clear that* and *there is evidence that* can also help convey values and opinions (see 11b). You need not eliminate all of your conclusions or opinions, but make sure they are identifiable as your own and do not unfairly shape the information you present.
- The personal pronoun *I* is more commonly used now in informative writing than in the past but may signal a stance that is too subjective or biased. Look carefully at any personal pronouns, and ask whether they help give a personal touch to your writing without adding bias.

52a
info

Exercise 2

A. Indicate whether the following statements suggest a fair or biased stance on the topic. Write out a brief explanation of your conclusion.

EXAMPLE

After talking with about twenty mall shoppers, I am more convinced than ever that people who frequent malls are not avid readers.

Analysis: Suggests bias through the implication that the writer was convinced of the stated relationship before conducting the survey ("I am more convinced than ever").

1. These sixteen independent research reports indicate that people who live in the midst of suburban sprawl are just as likely to suffer from geographically related stress as people who live within city limits.

2. Although rural residents were not studied, I believe it is obvious that they are less stressed than urban and suburban residents.

3. Several studies showed conclusively that urban residents who spent at least one weekend a month at a rural retreat, such as a lakeside cabin, suffered from less stress than their counterparts who did not leave the city.

4. The results of most studies imply a lot about the relationship of stress to people's wealth. After all, if you're rich, you can afford to relieve your stress.

5. Three research studies also found that able people without jobs who lived in urban areas had less stress than their working counterparts. This fact shows that we must consider laziness when we think about stress.

B. In a small group, compare your responses to Exercise 2A. Collectively revise any sentences that the group agrees imply a biased treatment of the subject.

C. Apply the Strategies in 52a-4 and 52a-5 to your paper in progress, revising any phrases, sentences, or paragraphs that suggest a biased or imbalanced approach to your subject.

6 Present information clearly

Informative writing is highly sensitive to the ways readers understand and retain information. When you are working with many facts or statistics, for example, your readers may become confused, bored, or frustrated if you try to present all these in sentence form.

52a
info

Strategy

To help your readers learn efficiently from your informative writing without confusion or frustration, try employing the following strategies if they are appropriate for your subject and your audience.

- Use graphs, charts, tables, and figures. You can set off numerical data or words and short phrases elegantly in columns or boxes.
- Use section markers. Longer informative papers can benefit from sections organized by numbers or subtitles.
- Use graphic devices such as boldface, italics, or varied fonts (type styles) to help readers attend to specific terms or ideas that may be new. But be careful not to overuse such devices; too many different fonts, for example, can confuse readers more than help them.

Use white space on the page. Too dense a text can tire your readers when you present a lot of information in long blocks. Break a discussion into shorter paragraphs, or use illustrations and tables.

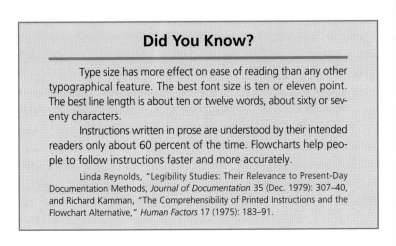

Did You Know?

Type size has more effect on ease of reading than any other typographical feature. The best font size is ten or eleven point. The best line length is about ten or twelve words, about sixty or seventy characters.

Instructions written in prose are understood by their intended readers only about 60 percent of the time. Flowcharts help people to follow instructions faster and more accurately.

Linda Reynolds, "Legibility Studies: Their Relevance to Present-Day Documentation Methods, *Journal of Documentation* 35 (Dec. 1979): 307–40, and Richard Kamman, "The Comprehensibility of Printed Instructions and the Flowchart Alternative," *Human Factors* 17 (1975): 183–91.

Exercise 3

A. Examine a chapter from one of your textbooks in a course such as psychology or biology. Write a brief informal description of strategies used in the textbook to make the information easy to learn and retain. Look for section markers, graphic devices, tables and charts, illustrations, and the use of white space to help "chunk" the text. Make a photocopy of one page to attach to your description.

B. In a small group, compare textbook analyses. Observe any especially effective strategies for the presentation of information. Discuss how ineffective books or sections could be improved through the use of such strategies.

C. Examine your paper in progress for any ways you can make your information easier to learn and retain, using the Strategy described in 52a-6 as well as any others that improve your paper.

52b   Developing an interview paper: Informative writing in progress

In his anthropology class, Brian Schwegler was assigned to write a paper about an interesting person, focusing particularly on the person's occupation. Examples his teacher offered were a mortician, a sky diver, and a woman construction worker. The purpose of the assignment was to practice gathering information from sources other than library materials and to organize that information into an interesting, informative paper.

Brian remembered a performer at the boardwalk amusement area in a coastal resort town near his university campus. He decided that Dave "The Guesser" Glovsky would be a good subject. This person operated a guessing booth located near a striker hammer game. As a "guesser," Dave offers to guess people's ages, weights, occupations, and similar matters. When Dave agreed to give Brian an interview for his paper, Brian sketched this preliminary list of questions that could inform his final paper.

1. How do you guess? What do you do when you guess?
2. Do you do anything else besides guessing?
3. How did you get into this business?
4. What are some of your best guesses?
5. What types of people come to get guessed?

Arriving at the boardwalk armed with his questions and a tape recorder, Brian realized that he might be able to observe Dave at work as well as interview him. After spending about an hour with Dave doing both, Brian went home and began the long process of transcribing the tape-recorded session so he could accurately use quotations and details.

Below are the first few minutes of Brian's interview. Note how his list of preliminary questions helped to shape his interview without entirely controlling it. Also observe how accurately Brian created his transcript, even when other sounds on the tape drowned out a word or two.

52b
info

```
                  Dave Glovsky

       Palace Playland: Dave's Guessing Stand

                   July 8, 1994

                 Brian Schwegler

(Sound of game, "The Striker" hammer swing in

background for all of tape)

     First interchange between Brian Schwegler and

Dave Glovsky is inaudible, due to background noise.

BS: So, Dave, can you tell me a little something

about how you guess? Can you tell me how you guess?

DG: Ages? I read the lower lids. I read the lower

lid. It deteriorates as we get older. The more it
```

gets darker, they get older. Even children of sixteen can fool me with the deterioration under the eyes. They can have beautiful skin, but I don't check the skin, I check the lower lid of their eyes.

BS: How about weight?

DG: Weight, well I just guess on the weight. You know, I feel the arm, I feel the stomach. Not women though, I don't touch the women. I just guess....

[The interview contines until a customer arrives.]

DG: Hey come on in, have fun. What do you want me to guess?

Female cust: My age.

DG: All right, that's a dollar. (Holds up one-dollar bill) A hundred-dollar bill. Step into the office here. (Points to a patch of pavement) Are you going to tell me the truth?

Cust: Yeah.

DG: You wouldn't lie to me. You promise truly, yeah. Smile, is that your father here. (Points to male companion of similar age). I'm gonna say, look at the beautiful girl. Look at the face on her. Let's see if you are married. (Looks at hand to check for rings) Nope, not married. Holy Cow! (Writes 22 on pad) How old are you?

Cust: Eighteen.

DG: You got me, I got twenty-two.

Cust: Huh, yeah right.

DG: Well, the lower lid, the lower lid. What do you want me to guess on now? (To female companion of previous customer, who looks noticeably younger)

Cust 2: Age.

Cust: Twenty-two, I thought that you were going to
say twelve.

DG: Can't get them all. Smile. . . .

At the end of the interview, Dave invited Brian to his home the next
morning to talk further. Brian also wondered what other workers thought
about Dave, so he returned to Palace Playland as well.

As he analyzed the transcript, it occurred to Brian that Dave's success
as a guesser may depend on establishing the right social relationship with
his customers, getting them to offer information or behave in a way that
reveals something about their ages or other characteristics. Instead of making Dave's technique obvious to readers, Brian chose to present Dave's methods without detailed commentary. This approach would allow his paper to
be true to the facts but point readers to an analysis of those facts without
forcing them to accept any particular conclusion.

Brian decided to organize his essay in sequential order, using a
"blended" chronological sequence that weaves details about Dave's life (past)
with details of events occurring during the interview (present). Brian also
planned to use some spatial sequences throughout the paper in describing
Dave's surroundings. But as he wrote, Brian realized that he had three main
sources of information—the original interview and observation, his brief
interviews with other fair workers, and his visit to Dave's house. Not wanting to explain too much in his paper about the various interviews, he decided
to "chunk" the two interviews with Dave into a single temporal sequence. Here
is how he diagramed the sequence in his planning notes.

Day 1: Interview and observation session ⟶ blend in workers'
        comments ⟶ Dave's invitation to come to his house
Day 2: Dave's house

52b
info

Following are the first several pages of Brian's rough draft. Notice
how Brian is able to maintain an objective, informative stance while still
injecting some style and human interest into his account. Note also the artful balance of interview material and observational data, seamlessly blending information about Dave's life with the ongoing events in the present.

First Draft: Dave the Guesser

by Brian Schwegler

1   "Come on in, have some fun with the famous
guesser of Old Orchard," says Dave "The Guesser"
Glovsky. Relying on his voice and personality to

attract customers, he seems out of place in this mechanized wonderland. Hand-painted signs covered with cramped writing are his advertisement. I peer at them and try to decipher the writing that is more anxious than able.

> The Guesser Has Experience
>
>   Sex Appeal
>
>   Personality   Try him, you'll
>   enjoy his humor
>   and guessing skill.

Palace Playland's World Famous Guess Station: Come in, fill up with fun--You'll be glad you did.

2   As I stand in front of his stand and read his signs, a young woman approaches Dave.

3   "Hey, come on in, have fun. What do you want me to guess?" Dave asks.

4   "My age," says the young woman.

5   "All right, that's a dollar." Holding up the dollar bill that the woman gives him, Dave examines it the way a jeweler examines a precious stone. "A hundred dollar bill." Pointing to a space on the pavement, Dave says, "Step into the office here." Dave checks her out from all angles, looking for the clue that will let him know her age within two years, his margin of error. "Smile," he says while peering into her face. Pointing to her boyfriend, Dave asks, "Is that your father here?" Her face erupts into a smile, and Dave has gotten some of the information he needs to make his guess. "Let's see if you are married," he says, looking for a wedding ring. Seeing none, he smiles and winks at me. He

52b info

pulls a rumpled pad out of his pocket and a pen out of nowhere and writes his guess on the paper. "How old are you?"

6   "Eighteen."

7   "You got me, I got twenty-two." Turning to her girlfriend, he says, "Can't get them all. Smile...."

8   Guessing is Dave's life, his living, his love. While at his stand, he is an actor on a stage. He not only wants to take people's money, he wants to entertain his customers. A former Portland comedian, Dave once put on a show for Edwin Muskie while Muskie was governor. Talking about the people that he guesses, Dave says, "They like the fun that I give them. . . . I make them laugh." There doesn't seem to be much of a difference, to Dave, between being an actor and being a guesser. "I was a comedian anyways," he says with a shrug that tells me that is all that guessing is about.

[The next two paragraphs further explain how Dave relates to people.]

11   Dave's guessing is a talent that he has worked on over the years. He has a system worked out for guessing the person's age. He relies on his knowledge of the human face, clinical knowledge tempered by forty-five years of experience. He explains it to me during a lull in our visit. I feel a kind of rush, excited to learn the secrets of the trade.

12   "Whellp, the way I guess ages, they don't realize that I check the lower lid of their eyes. And it's effective with eighty-five percent of the people. The eyes on the bottom deteriorate as we

52b info

age. It gets darker and darker and wrinklier, and then at the age of, beginning at the age of thirty-nine, it starts to get a, getting a line up here, (on side of face). And then it gets deeper and deeper and deeper, and when it gets way up here (at top of cheeks), I really got to guess, fifty or sixty. And in the sixties, they start getting these things (loose skin on neck). So, through all of these years, I have accumulated all the knowledge of the human face."

[The next four paragraphs explain Dave's other types of guesses and his impact on customers.]

17   Other workers at Palace Playland recognize the role that Dave plays at the park. Chris McArthur, owner of Palace Groundz, a coffee stand, says, "There's a lot of people that come in here just to see him. And I've noticed people walk by and go, 'Oh my God, he's still alive, he's still here. I remember him when I was a little kid.'" . . .

[The paper continues for five more pages.]

52c
info

52c   The short informative documented paper

In many courses, you may be asked to write an informative paper that draws on a few outside sources, most often those you have located in modest library research. Such papers do not argue a point but present information on a focused topic.

1 Sample short informative documented paper

As you read the following passages from David Aharonian's paper, note that even though it is informative, citing facts and statistics from four articles, it is not a paper without a thesis. Unlike an argumentative thesis (see 50a-3), however, David's thesis presents a conclusion based on his synthesis of research studies. Note, too, that his paper does not recommend a course of action, which would require taking a position; instead, it stops short of argument, allowing the reader to take the next step based on a considered response to the information David presents.

Desperate Times for Teachers

by David Aharonian

1   There is a major controversy regarding teacher salaries presently in this country. Many people feel that teachers are overpaid because they have summers off from work. They feel that teachers do not truly work year round and therefore are either getting a fair rate of pay or getting too much. Many teachers, however, disagree with this assessment. They feel that they are underpaid for the work that they do. Most teachers find it very difficult just to make ends meet on a teacher's salary, and often they resort to moonlighting.

2   Moonlighting means that a person holds another job in addition to his or her career....

[The next four paragraphs supply information and statistics on moonlighting teachers from two sources.]

7   But there really are no easy solutions to the problem. One obvious answer would be to increase teacher salaries (Alley 21). This would lead to less moonlighting and allow teachers to concentrate more on their primary occupation. But there are still plenty of people who oppose raising teacher salaries. Many times teachers may go two or three years without any raise in their pay. Then when the teachers do get their raises, it may only be 2 or 4 percent. This certainly lowers the morale of the teachers and can cause the teacher to become frustrated (Henderson 12). As one teacher in Oklahoma put it, "It's hard to look across the hall

52c
info

and see a teacher who's taught 14 years, making only
$4,000 more than you are" (Wisniewski and Kleine 1).

[This paper ends with a list of works cited]

2 Elements of a short informative documented paper

An effective short informative documented paper includes the following elements.

- It concisely summarizes or synthesizes the views, research results, or positions of other writers.
- It presents information in the writer's own words but does so fairly, without bias.
- It may provide conclusions based on a reasoned consideration of the work it cites but usually allows the reader to decide what these conclusions mean for a course of action, set of beliefs, and the like.
- It is well organized and easy to read.

3 Commentary on David Aharonian's short informative documented paper

The writer does a good job of pulling together various research studies in an interesting short paper. His way of integrating the references into his own writing works nicely. If his paper had cited statistics more heavily, he could have presented them in a less narrative form, perhaps creating a box or chart. Although it ends with a direct quotation from a teacher, his paper seems to stop abruptly; he could have included a short paragraph summing up the material he cites. (For more information on research papers, see Chapters 43–45.)

**52d
info**

52d The literature review

The **literature review,** also sometimes called a survey paper or a review of the literature, is usually one section of a longer paper but may be assigned as a paper in itself. In a psychology paper reporting the results of an experiment, for instance, the literature review is the first section after the introduction. The purpose of a literature review is to synthesize the existing research on your topic—to describe the main points of comparison and disagreement in others' studies. As the first section of a longer paper presenting your own research, it provides a backdrop for your study. Your study generally would not repeat what another study has already done but might test the hypothesis or the methods of an earlier study, examine an aspect overlooked by previous researchers, or study a related aspect of the topic

---

Did You Know?

College instructors often look for a thesis statement at the beginning of an academic paper as a guide to the line of reasoning and the kinds of evidence and arguments the student will present. Just as important for most instructors, however, are topic sentences and other statements in the body of a paper that guide readers through the steps in the reasoning and serve as reminders of the paper's overall purpose and direction. Students who do not include such reminders as they write may lose track of their own reasoning and produce disorganized papers. Even a well-organized paper can be hard to follow, however, if the writer does not provide readers with guidance throughout.

Linda K. Shamoon and Robert A. Schwegler, "Sociologists Reading Student Texts: Expectations and Perceptions," *Writing Instructor* 8 (Winter 1988): 71–84.

---

in order to add to the accumulated knowledge. A literature review, then, establishes a context for your own research.

Most literature reviews try to present the findings of others in a fair and balanced manner. Two or more studies may reveal major disagreements in a field, but your job in a literature review is to document those disagreements without judging the studies themselves, at least initially. Some kinds of literature reviews do judge the works being summarized; for example, an author of a medical research article may present the findings of previous studies while criticizing their methods. Such a review tends to be more point-driven (see Chapter 50) because the writer is laying the groundwork for a claim that his or her own methods are superior. In most general college courses requiring a literature review, however, you will be asked to summarize the literature instead of critique it. Your reviews will be informative, aiming at summary and synthesis.

52d
info

1 Sample literature review

Turn to the research paper in 47e for a sample literature review in the context of a longer paper. As you read this sample, note how the writer connects his sources to each other and to his own study.

2 Elements of a literature review

An effective literature review includes the following elements.

- It accurately and concisely summarizes the results of other researchers.

- It synthesizes these other studies, combining results where they overlap, while giving credit to each researcher.
- It includes major points of disagreement among the other studies.
- It establishes a context for your own study.

52e The lab report

If you take courses in subjects like biology, chemistry, physics, or engineering, you may find yourself writing lab reports. Your teacher will want to read, quickly, what you did in an experiment, and you will need to make your report as concise and as clear as possible. Although the format of a lab report can help you organize the information clearly, you will still need to avoid ambiguous language and unclear references.

The **lab report** represents a kind of informative writing in its sharp focus on the objective description of causes and effects. It requires just the right balance between too little and too much detail. If certain aspects of an experiment or procedure are irrelevant to the cause-effect relationship, you need not include them. However, it is important to describe very clearly just what was done in the experiment and what happened as a result. The color of the counter in the lab is irrelevant information, but the size of the beaker used may be important both to the replication of the experiment and to the nature of the processes involved.

Lab reports follow different formats, depending on the discipline in which they are written and even the requirements of individual teachers. Some teachers value conciseness and require all lab reports to be no longer than two double-spaced pages. Others expect more detail and may stretch the length to five or ten pages. Check with your teacher about the format, style, and other requirements of the report, such as specific section numbers and headings. A typical structure begins with an overview or *abstract* of the experiment, including its focus or goal (why it was done), an *introduction* to the problem or principles involved (what it shows), a description of the *methods* used (how it was done), an explanation of the *results* (what happened), a *discussion* of the outcomes (what the results mean), and a *conclusion* (what the experiment shows). See the sample paper in 47e for a similar presentation of research results in the social sciences.

1 Sample lab report

Speed of Sound in Water

by Michael Perry

I. <u>Abstract</u>. This experiment was designed to measure the speed of sound in water and determine how changes in the properties of the water affect

the speed of sound. First, the speed of sound in
water at room temperature was measured using a "time
of flight" method. Then the speed of sound was
measured at different temperatures to determine the
change in the speed with varying temperature. The
speed of sound from part 1 of the experiment was
1479.7 m/s. In part 2 the speed of sound was found
to vary from 1419.75 m/s at 10.8°C to 1581.03 m/s at
33.10°C.

   II. <u>Introduction</u>. A wave traveling through a
material causes quick compressions and expansions of
the material. The pressure and density oscillate
where these compressions and expansions take place.
The speed of the wave is determined by how much the
density changes with a given pressure change. Water
is a liquid and is therefore less compressible than
a gas, for example, air. So it takes a greater
pressure in water to change density a given amount.
We can therefore expect the speed of sound in water
to be greater than that in air. . . .

   [The paper continues with the following sections: III Experimental, IV
Results, V Discussion, and VI Conclusion.]

**52e
info**

2 Elements of a lab report

   An effective lab report includes the following elements.

- It strictly follows the lab report format required by your teacher.
- It does not digress into unnecessary commentary on the experiment.
- It uses specific terminology and unambiguous language.
- It presents data and results accurately, without distortion.

3 Commentary on Michael Perry's lab report

   Some of the terms are specialized for the field, but this report is written to an audience that understands the jargon. Perry's report is for the most

part clear and concise; however, he could have explained why the time of flight method was not accurate.

52f The abstract

Teachers may often ask you to submit an abstract along with your lab report, study, or other research paper. An abstract is a concise summary—one paragraph, usually no more than three hundred words—of your paper. It is entirely objective, restating the content of the paper without extraneous commentary. An abstract for a scientific study must include, at a minimum, a summary of the hypothesis, the method, the results, and the discussion sections of your paper. An abstract of the review of the literature might be needed as well. The reader of your abstract, with no familiarity with your paper, should be able to understand not only the gist of the paper but your method, stance (your theory or opinion), and conclusions.

1 Sample abstract

See the abstract in 52e, introducing a lab report, or in 47e, preceding a research study.

2 Elements of an abstract

An effective abstract includes the following elements.

- It summarizes all the important sections of your paper.
- It defines any key terms used in unique or unusual ways.
- It is concise; all unnecessary words and phrases are eliminated.

52g info

52g The annotated bibliography

An **annotated bibliography** is just like a regular bibliography (see Chapters 46–49) except that each entry includes an annotation describing the aim, purpose, or content of the work cited. Its purpose is to provide a useful resource for readers who want to find out what has been written about a topic or to consult specific works themselves. Annotated bibliographies are also commonly assigned in college courses either to help students to survey and report on a body of scholarship or to help them prepare for a longer research paper.

Usually you begin with a brief introduction to the topic, perhaps highlighting the kinds of works covered in your bibliography. You then cite each work and follow it with an annotation, usually in a short paragraph or two. Annotations sometimes employ an abbreviated sentence structure like this: Summarizes research on the development of the Cherokee syllabary.

1 Sample annotations

The annotation below has been taken from Ian Preston's annotated bibliography, which consisted of an introduction to the topic followed by twelve entries. He prepared his bibliography for a writing class focusing on language and bilingualism in the United States.

```
          Annotated Bibliography on Bilingualism

                      by Ian Preston

Glazer, Nathan. "Where Is Multiculturalism Leading

     Us?" Phi Delta Kappan 75 (1993): 319-24.

This article describes the Center for the Study of

Books in Spanish for Children and Adolescents, an

organization that promotes the positive aspects of

bilingualism. Unlike other organizations that

portray their ethnic groups as victims, the Center,

Glazer argues, ought to be followed as a model of a

bilingual program.
```

2 Elements of an annotated bibliography

Effective annotated bibliographies usually include the following elements.

- An introduction which orients readers to the topic being covered in several paragraphs or pages, depending upon the complexity of the topic or the range of the citations.
- A list of references to the literature cited, each followed by a clear précis or summary of the work that briefly but accurately represents the work.
- Accurate references which readers often use to locate the works listed. (See Chapters 46 through 49 for help with accurate bibliographical entries.)
- An emphasis on summary in order to provide readers with an accurate depiction of what the work says or does, without unnecessary detail.
- Alphabetical organization, generally by the authors' last names. Long or complex annotated bibliographies are often organized into sections, sometimes chronologically ("Nineteenth-Century Studies," "Twentieth-Century Studies"), sometimes by general topic or focus ("Studies Using Quantitative Research Methods," "Studies Using Qualitative Research Methods"), but still alphabetically within each section.

52g
info

3 Commentary on Ian Preston's entries

Preston successfully captures the gist of the work cited. Notice how he includes both the topic of the article and its author's point of view.

52h The informative essay exam

Essay exams can be divided into those in which you illustrate and defend a claim or point (see 50g) and those in which you provide clear and objective information. The latter, the informative essay exam, can be relatively short—a paragraph or two describing a phenomenon, for example—or longer, involving more elaborate descriptions and data.

Informative essay exams must be carefully organized, clearly written, and detailed. After receiving your exam question, spend a few minutes developing a simple outline; even a three- or five-paragraph structure can help you to chunk your information and move from point to point logically so that a teacher can quickly see whether the essay reflects adequate knowledge of the subject.

1 Sample informative essay exam

The short informative essay exam that follows was written in a general biology course in response to this assignment: "Define the concept of natural selection, being sure to explain its main features and how it affects behavior." Students were given thirty minutes to craft their answers.

```
          Natural Selection Essay Exam
                by Nicholas Branahan
        Natural selection is a process in which the
characteristics of an organism that best promote its
ability to reproduce are selected and the
characteristics which hinder it are weeded out. As
random gene mutations form new characteristics,
natural selection will select those that enhance the
organism's ability to reproduce. Ability to
reproduce depends on adaptability to the weather,
ability to find food, avoidance of predators, and
other aspects of survival.
```

[The answer continues in two more paragraphs.]

2 Elements of effective informative essay exams

An effective informative essay exam includes the following.

- It answers the question directly, without unnecessary padding.
- It is organized clearly and logically, with each paragraph focusing on a different aspect of the topic or question.
- It avoids obscure language or uninterpretable statements as a strategy for covering up an inability to answer the question.
- It includes, as possible, brief examples, cases, and references.

3 Commentary on Nicholas Branahan's informative essay exam

Branahan's essay shows that he understands the concept of natural selection. The first paragraph provides a general definition of the concept of natural selection. The second paragraph answers the question about the ways in which natural selection may affect behavior. The third paragraph extends the concept by considering what happens to the organism when the environment changes. The writing is clear, concise, and error-free, but adding one or two brief examples would make the answer less abstract.

52h
info

CHAPTER

53

Developing Business Writing

In spite of all the new technology, most business decisions are still made by people, and communication between individuals becomes the critical factor in most business negotiations. Your personal success and the success of your work depend largely on how you represent yourself and communicate orally and in writing. Effective writers rapidly gain the respect and admiration of their colleagues, and writing ability often plays a role in professional advancement.

A complete discussion of business writing would take a book in itself. This chapter has a more modest goal: to acquaint you with some standard business writing styles and practices. Think of it as a preliminary guide to successful business writing. As you become more involved in professional activities during college you should add a complete business writing guide to your personal library. Such books offer sound advice on accepted business writing styles and present models of a number of business documents, such as letters, memos, proposals, reports, and résumés.

53a bus

53a Using general strategies for successful business writing

Business writing is reader-centered: you're writing to persuade, inform, or meet the needs of your audience (see Chapter 6). Focus your effort on making your writing and the design of your document easily accessible to your readers. Keep in mind the general advice for writing found throughout Part I of this book, and pay special attention to the following composing strategies.

1 Plan to meet your readers' needs

Your main focus while planning business writing will be the relationship between your information and your audience. Sometimes your audience will be made up of different readers in different positions (for

---

Writer's Tip

Business documents should have a "friendly" design and layout, inviting the reader to read and to continue to read. Is there enough white space in your document to make it look uncluttered? Are your margins sufficient? What does the spacing of your document look like—are sections squeezed together, or have you left enough space to show blocks of information? Remember that a readable document is attractive and inviting, not tight and cluttered.

---

example, someone in the marketing department and someone else who handles shipments from the warehouse). Be sensitive to the needs and perspectives of your various intended readers.

Because your readers are likely to be busy and impatient—whether they are other people at work or members of the general public to whom you are writing in a professional capacity—you need to be especially careful in organizing your information.

Strategy 1

Using the audience continuum in 6a, spend a few minutes writing about your intended readers. What do they know about the topic? How will they use the document? What do you know about their technical background, their level of education, their interest in the topic, and their need for what you have to offer?

Strategy 2

Write a precise outline of your information before you draft your document. In business writing, your reader should know what your document contains from the start, and its contents should have a logical and preconceived design. Outlines are especially effective (see Chapter 4).

**53a
bus**

2 Draft as clearly as possible

As you draft, remember to emphasize clarity. Effective business writing is easy to read—unambiguous, uncluttered, and direct.

Strategy

Instead of drafting with an eye to style, try to write the essential information as baldly and directly as you can. As you write, concentrate on exactly what you want to say. You can revise for a smoother and more appealing style after you've presented the main information directly.

---

3 Be sure to revise and edit

In some business settings you may be under pressure to write a document quickly—even more quickly, for example, than a paper due in two days for your composition class. Under these circumstances, it's easy to skip the revising process. Be especially careful not to fall into this trap. Reread *all* your documents. Plan your work so you have at least some time for revision and editing. Even a single badly chosen word, one garbled sentence, or a lone case of misinformation can be embarrassing.

In addition, set specific goals for your revising. Plan, for example, to eliminate wordy passages, extraneous information, and irrelevant facts. Or aim to avoid clichés, exaggeration, passive voice, and overly technical language. Try to choose vocabulary appropriate for your audience's level of expertise, and revise accordingly.

> ### Writer's Tip
>
> Business writing often makes use of graphics to present information clearly and concisely. When you use graphics, label them carefully, and mention them in the text of your document before they actually appear in the text.

53b Writing business letters

53b
bus

Good business letters follow some standard practices and established formats. Most business letters are presented in either block format or modified block format. In **modified block format,** which is often used for longer letters, the return address and the closing and signature are centered on the page, but the paragraphs are not indented from the left margin. (For an example, see 53g). In **block format,** often used for short letters, all paragraphs (including the greeting and signature) are flush at the left margin. In both styles, notations following the signature are flush left including initials for the writer and typist (RL: gw), *Enc.* or *Enclosure,* or *cc: Nancy Harris* (the name of a person sent a copy). Follow these additional guidelines for business correspondence.

- **Stationery.** The best is 25 percent or 50 percent white cotton bond paper. Avoid colors and fancy paper styles.
- **Print quality.** Check that your typewriter or word processor is in good repair. Use a laser printer or a letter-quality impact printer. Your

credibility will be damaged and your readers may be frustrated by fuzzy or light print. Avoid nonstandard or stylized print styles—they are often hard to read.

- **Salutations.** Use the first name of your recipient only if you are already on a first-name basis. Use the full name if you don't know the person's gender. Avoid male-specific salutations such as "Dear Sir" or "Gentlemen"; they are no longer appropriate. If you do not know exactly to whom you are writing, use salutations such as these.

    Dear Accounts Department:

    Dear Credit Manager:

- **Longer letters.** Use plain paper of the same weight as the first page. Use letterhead stationery only for the first page.

- **Envelope.** Envelope paper should be the same color and weight as the letter, and the type style should match that of the letter. (See the sample envelope below for placement of information.)

```
Charisma Publishing, Inc.
757 First Street
Huntington, VA 24066



                    Mr. Elliott P. Buchanan
                    Driving Dynamics, Inc.
                    34 Westover Avenue
                    Lexington, MA 19046
```

53c Writing agendas

An **agenda** is a plan of action for a business meeting. Agendas are usually circulated in advance to those who will attend the meeting; however, occasionally an agenda may be presented at the start of a meeting to show the attendees how the meeting will be structured. Consider the following points when you create an agenda.

- List the date, location, time, and topic of the meeting at the top of the agenda.
- Clearly define the goals of the meeting.
- List in a logical order the issues to be discussed at the meeting; clearly show how the meeting will proceed.
- List any items to be discussed or introduced by specific individuals.

AGENDA

Executive Committee
February 5, 1996
Conference Room B

1. Approve minutes of Jan. 8, 1996, meeting

2. President's report

3. Old business
   a. Fleet report (Ted Lakeland)
   b. Manufacturing division update (Rona Schwartz)
   c. Annual retreat (Tom Good)

4. Sales division report on expansion of sales
   territory

5. New committee and task force assignments
   a. Task force on sexual harassment
   b. Personnel committee

6. Recycling committee report (Kristen Danforth)

7. New business

8. Summary

53d Writing meeting minutes

Meeting minutes are a major form of organizational communication and often serve as a corporate "memory." You may also need to keep minutes for various school organizations and committees that are run in a businesslike manner. Minutes should be an impartial record of what occurred at a meeting, most of which will be dialogue and reports from attendees. Minutes may also describe visuals used at the meeting or documents circulated to participants.

For routine meetings, minutes can be brief, noting only the most important topics presented or discussed. In other cases, when significant topics are discussed in detail or when important individuals who did not attend the meeting will read the minutes and perhaps even make decisions based on their contents, more detailed minutes are required. Sometimes it is desirable to tape-record a meeting in order to write more detailed minutes. If you decide to tape a meeting, notify participants before the meeting starts.

Meeting minutes should conform to the following guidelines.

- Consider who will be reading the minutes and for what purpose before determining how detailed the minutes should be.
- Carefully note the date, time, and location of the meeting.

- List the individuals who have participated in the meeting and, if it is not common knowledge, their positions in the organization or roles at the meeting. Note also those individuals whose attendance was expected but who did not attend. Always note who is chairing the meeting and who is taking minutes. The person taking the minutes should sign or initial the minutes next to his or her name. This person may be identified by *minutes* or by the term *secretary* or *recorder*.
- Always identify who said what, but *summarize* this information; include the most important points as accurately as you can. Try not to misquote or misinterpret anyone's remarks.
- Be impartial. Record as objectively as possible what transpired at the meeting. Editorializing in minutes is unprofessional.

Meeting identified by title

```
Driving Dynamics, Inc., Executive Committee Meeting

              Minutes for January 8, 1996 Date, location, and
                 Boardroom, 9:00-10:05      time

Present: E. Buchanan (Chair), B. Kramer, M. Sun,
L. Whitlock, L. Hammond, E. Parker (minutes),
T. Perez, P. Straley, R. Allison, Mary Travis (state
police officer)           Person taking minutes

Absent: P. Pelligrino, L. Rosenberg

The next meeting of the executive committee will be
on Monday, February 5, at 4 p.m. in the boardroom.

Publicity--Publicity chairperson Tony Perez reported
that the new radio spots are nearly ready for
airing. Ads will be heard on WSPT-FM and WCAR-AM
four times each day starting January 23.

Hiring--Executive Committee chair Elliott Buchanan
announced that, beginning May 1, he will take a one-
year leave of absence from Driving Dynamics in order
to complete a book on driving safety for which he
has contracted with a major publisher.

Recycling--Recycling Committee chair Lynn Rosenberg
sent in a written report. Company efforts to improve
recycling have been successful. New receptacles for
aluminum cans and glass bottles have been installed
in all lounge areas and in the main front and rear
entrance vestibules. Rosenberg suggested that more
efforts are needed for plain-paper recycling. The
Recycling Committee will investigate this issue and
give a report at the next meeting.

Because of lack of further business, the meeting
adjourned at 10:05.
```

53d
bus

Did You Know?

Many businesses now carry on much of their internal correspondence through computer networks. Once employees are linked by computer, they can quickly and efficiently send announcements and reminders, minutes, reports, memos, and other documents. This also saves greatly on the use of paper. If someone wants to take a document out of the office, the document can always be printed, creating what is called a hard copy. Because computer networks tend to encourage informal, "talky" prose, however, some people find they must work extra-hard to maintain a professional style when they write on the network.

53e Writing memos

Although some organizations provide employees with printed forms, you should know how to write your own **memos.** These internal documents rarely circulate outside an organization. The organization's name and logo, or letterhead, may appear at the top of the memo, but no address is needed.

The words *to, from, subject,* and *date* appear on all memos, often in this order. (The order is sometimes based on the filing system used in the organization or business.) Spacing, notations for enclosures, additional pages, and copies all follow the same pattern as in letters.

53e
bus

```
              Reliable Book Wholesalers


To:      Executive Committee members

From:    Marilyn Caperton

Subject: Selection of new executive vice president

Date:    January 29, 1996


   A meeting of the executive committee will be held
on February 4 to discuss the resignation of our
current vice president, Tracy Langer, and the
selection of a new vice president.

   Ms. Langer has taken a position with Rank,
Incorporated, of San Francisco and will leave her
position with us on March 15.
```

We have several applications on file, and we need to discuss the procedures we will follow to advertise the position and hire a new vice president.

Please come to the meeting with ideas or suggestions for possible candidates.

Executive Committee Meeting
Presidential Boardroom
Friday, February 2, 3:30 p.m.

53f Writing résumés

Résumés and letters of application are the most important sales documents you will write; the "product" is, after all, yourself and everything you have accomplished. There are countless "right" ways to prepare these documents. This section offers some guidelines for the content, design, and construction of a résumé and letter of application. Take the time to write, revise, and edit your résumé so it will be attractive to a potential employer. Also be sure to visit your college placement service for help on résumé construction.

The purpose of a résumé and application letter is to get an interview, not a job. Few employers hire using only the information contained in a résumé and letter. When constructing your résumé and letter, concentrate on trying to create a professional identity for yourself. Don't brag, but highlight your skills or achievements clearly and objectively.

Potential employers favor job candidates who are motivated, mature, and responsible. You can't simply state these things; your résumé and letter must exemplify these traits. For instance, employers like applicants who know how to start and finish a project without help and who are self-motivated, capable, and willing to face challenges confidently. Describe your experiences not only in terms of what you have actually done but in terms of what you learned from the experiences and how they will help you in the future.

**53f
bus**

1 Begin with a résumé preparation checklist

Before you start to prepare your résumé, you need to reflect about both your career goals and your own qualifications and background.

Strategy

Write informally in response to the following questions. Jot down your ideas and as many examples from your background as you can remember. Later you can select the best ideas and examples for your purposes.

1. What kind of work do you want to do? What kind of job do you want?

2. What are your career goals?
3. What jobs have you held?
4. What volunteer positions have you held?
5. What are your skills, abilities, or interests, even if you have not been formally educated in these things?
6. What are the main features of your educational background? Consider the following points.
   a. College major, minor, and concentrations.
   b. Special projects or research
   c. Honors and awards
   d. Memberships and offices in organizations
   e. Volunteer positions
   f. Special skills
   g. Grade point average (overall and in major)
7. What other awards or special honors, if any, have you received (from work, volunteer efforts, or community organizations)?
8. Who might supply a good reference for you? Try to identify at least one former or current professor, one former job supervisor or employer, and one personal reference.
9. What makes you different from other applicants? Why should a prospective employer hire you rather than someone else?

2 Use categories to construct your résumé

After you've collected the information for your résumé, your task is one of construction—placing the information into appropriate categories, phrasing it concisely, and arranging it in a visually appealing way. Use the following advice as you work.

Career Objective. When you write your career objective, avoid empty phrases like *position of responsibility with a fast-growing firm*. Consider tailoring your objective to each position for which you apply.

Job Experience. When you get ready to describe your job experience, list all the duties you had, and then choose the ones you think might be most similar to those of the job you want. If you have had many jobs, don't list them all in your résumé. List only the ones you held the longest, the ones that are most similar to the job for which you are applying, or the ones that demonstrate your most employable characteristics. If you think that you have little job experience that relates to the job you seek, highlight other desirable job skills, such as handling responsibility, supervising others, working alone, or writing and public speaking. Don't simply state that you have these skills; provide examples from your experience.

Volunteer Experience. If you've held volunteer positions that may be attractive to a potential employer, list them; they're often considered impor-

Carol E. Westermeyer   *Don't use "Résumé" here*

College Address   *Full name,*   Home Address

Apt. 23 College Park   *address,*   7562 Galsworth Road
Greenville, Virginia 20205   *and*   Squires, Texas 30303
(804)555-3345   *phone*   (512)555-7912

Brief job
OBJECTIVE   Entry-level position as a mechanical engineer   *objective*

EDUCATION   B.S. Mechanical Engineering, May 1994   *Concise*
Virginia Polytechnic Institute and State   *statement of*
University, Blacksburg, Virginia 24060   *education*
G.P.A.: 3.18/4.0 Minor: Economics

Reverse chronological order Dates and addresses included
EXPERIENCE   Technician/Assembler, May 1991–September 1991
Experience   Communications Technology, Inc., Fairview, Virginia
organized to   - Developed cost analysis and designed prototype
show skills   wireless communication products for Masters
                   Mountain Laboratories.
Job titles   - Built and tested various AF and RF products:
underlined   transmitters, receivers, headsets, amplifiers,
                   and antenna networks.
Past tense   - Served as company representative to demonstrate
for job duties   new generation of wireless radios at Atlanta
                   National Radio Conference.

Interoffice Administrator (part time), 1989-present
Bergland Technology Associates, Lakeview, Virginia
- Updated and reorganized shop inventory control
  using office IBM software and hardware.

PROJECT   Member, Design Team for Formula Car, 1991-92
Virginia Tech Department of Mechanical
Engineering
- Drive train group duties included testing,
  tuning, and modeling constant velocity
  transmission (CVT) and coordinating data
  acquisition for CVT.

**53f
bus**

SKILLS   Computer: Finite Element (FEPC), Personal
              Simulation Language (PSL)
Optional   Personal: Public speaking, technical writing

ACTIVITIES   President, Student Society of Engineers; Student
Engineering Council; Society of Automotive
Engineers; Gymnastics Club; The Voice (student
newspaper)

References available upon request
Centered

tant experience. Note that the position was voluntary, but handle the rest of the information just as you would for any other job. Don't use an apologetic tone here; the fact that you were not paid for the job doesn't mean it was not serious work that gave you valuable experience.

Sequence of Experience. Typically, jobs are listed in reverse chronological order (with your most recent job first). If your most important job experience is not your most recent, however, list that one first, and then list the others in chronological order.

References. Unless the employer asks for specific references, use the general statement *References available upon request.* Few employers will want to look at your references unless they wish to interview you. You should have your references available, and you can print a separate page listing the names and addresses of three or four references to send out if you are so asked. (*Always* ask permission to use someone as a reference.) Most colleges have student placement services that will send out dossiers that include confidential references.

Writer's Tip: Using a Computer

Programs are now available for creating résumés on computers. Most such programs include several different formats for standard résumés as well as options for custom-made résumés. The program prompts you for information in various categories. Once you've typed in this information, it is formatted according to the type of résumé you've selected. Résumé programs allow you to spend your time focusing on your background and accomplishments rather than spacing and layout. Try out several résumé formats to see which one will be the most appealing for the kind of job you want.

**53g
bus**

53g Writing letters of application

Your résumé and your application letter should be related documents; the topics named in both should be related and should work as a unit to make you appear organized and professional. Letters of application offer you a chance to discuss or highlight skills or experiences mentioned in your résumé or to add information not in your résumé. Your application letter should be concise—just a few well-written paragraphs. Remember that your readers may be considering many applicants and thus need to focus quickly on your main accomplishments and abilities. Wading through lots of irrelevant prose to locate this information will only frustrate them and compromise your application.

1½" top margin

Uses business letter format

Apt. 23 College Park
Greenville, Virginia 20205
February 10, 1994

Writer's complete address

Dr. Grace Penland, Director
PKL Design, Inc.
232 Sturbridge Avenue
Fairfax, Virginia 20949

Recipient's complete address

Dear Dr. Penland: *Dear and name*

Identifies job

I am interested in applying for a position as an entry-level
mechanical engineer at PKL Design, Inc. I found the position
advertised at the placement office at Virginia Tech. I will
graduate in May 1994 with a degree in mechanical engineering
and hope to start my career at that time.

Highlights job experience

Single-space text

During the past four years I have had a good deal of academic
experience in communications technology. As an active member
of the Formula Car drive train group, I learned much about the
practical challenges mechanical engineers face each day, and
about the complexities of collaborating and strategizing with
fellow team members. In my position with Communications
Technology, I was able to test and sharpen the skills I was
learning at school and use them on a regular basis. In
addition to the responsibilities noted in my résumé, I
designed an innovative software program that compiles data
used by other firms and interprets the results for the sales
division at Communications Technology.

Double-space ¶s

My experience working with others has given me confidence
in my interpersonal skills and decision-making abilities,
particularly in the area of effective communication and
intellectual compromise. Making a contribution to an effort
goes much further than simply possessing skills; one must
have the ability to work toward a consensus everyone can
live with.

Tells how to reach applicant

I am available for an interview given a week's notice. I can
be reached by phone at (512)555-7912 between 3 p.m. and 5 p.m.
daily. Thank you for your time and consideration.

Sincerely,

Carol C. Westermeyer

Carol E. Westermeyer

Enclosure   *Enclosure with letter noted*

**53g
bus**

Credits

We thank the following student writers for permission to reprint their work:
David Aharonian, Elizabeth A. Bowden, Alexis Brady, Amy K. Braegelman, Carey Braun, Sara Brilliant, Jeanne Brown, Amy L. Burns, Zachary Carter, Elizabeth Cuddy, Kimlee Cunningham, Timothy J. Dunbar, Jason W. Fester, Chantele D. Giles, Shane Hand, Andrea K. Herrmann, Anita N. Jackson, Steven L. King, Fredza Léger, Stephanie E. Lewis, Kris Lundell, Jennifer L. O'Berry, Paula A. Fry Post, Rachel E. Ritchie, Megan Tubridy, Douglas T. Vander Linden, Ted Wolfe.

From *Anatomy of Anti-Communism*. New York: Hill and Wang, 1969, p. 118.

From The Holy Bible, Authorized King James Version. London: Oxford University Press, p. 397.

"Bodybuilding" entry from *InfoTrac Academic Index*. Reprinted by permission of Information Access Co.

"Bodybuilding" entry from *1991 Reader's Guide to Periodical Literature*, p. 271. Copyright © 1992. Reprinted by permission of H. W. Wilson Company.

"Darwin's Notebooks on Transmutation of Species" from *Bulletin of British Museum* (Natural History), Zoology, Historical Series, 11, 1960. Reprinted by permission of Trustees of The Natural History Museum, London.

From *The English Language*. London: Penguin Books, 1988, p. 69.

"Exercise" entry from *1992 Reader's Guide to Periodical Literature*, p. 763. Copyright © 1993. Reprinted by permission of H. W. Wilson Company.

"Exercise" entry from *1993 Social Sciences Index*, pp. 592–593. Copyright © 1993. Reprinted by permission of H. W. Wilson Company.

From *Merriam-Webster's Collegiate Dictionary*. Copyright © 1995 by Merriam-Webster Inc. By permission.

"Sizing Up the Sexes" from *Time*, January 20, 1992. Copyright © 1992 by Time, Inc. Reprinted by permission.

"The Stock Account" from *Prospectus*, College Retirement Equities Fund for Individual Retirement and Tax-Deferred Variable Annuity Certificates, March 1, 1990. Reprinted by permission.

From *Treasures of Tutankhamun*. National Gallery of Art, p. 13.

From Edward Abbey, *Beyond the Wall*. New York: Holt, Rinehart & Winston, 1971, pp. 97, 98.

From Edward Abbey, *Down the River*. New York: Dutton, 1982, p. 117.

From Edward Abbey, *The Journey Home*. New York: Dutton, 1977, p. 88.

From Robert A. Apostal and Carol Helland, "Commitment to and Role Changes in Dual Career Families." *Journal of Career Development*, Volume 20, Winter 1993, p. 123. Reprinted by permission of Plenum Publishing Corp. and the author.

Francis Bacon, *Essays, Civil and Moral and the New Atlantis*. New York: P. F. Collier & Son, 1937, p. 122.

From Hanson W. Baldwin, "R.M.S. Titanic." *Harper's* Magazine, 1933.

From Albert C. Baugh and Thomas Cable, *A History of the English Language*, 3rd ed. Englewood Cliffs, NJ: Prentice Hall, 1978, p. 243.

From John Berendt, "Class Acts." *Esquire*, 1991.

From Wendell Berry, *What Are People For?* Berkeley, CA: North Point Press, 1990.

From Wm. Bingham, *A.M., a Grammar of the English Language*. Philadelphia: E. H. Butler & Co., 1867, p. 98

From H. G. Bissinger, *Friday Night Lights*. Reading, MA: Addison-Wesley, 1990, pp. 176–177.

From Louise Bogan, "Old Countryside" from *The Blue Estuaries: Poems 1923–1968*. Copyright © 1968 by Louise Bogan. Reprinted by permission of Farrar, Straus & Giroux, Inc.

From Claude F. Boutron et al., "Decrease in anthropogenic lead, cadmium and zinc in Greenland snows since the late 1960s." *Nature*, 1991.

From Fredson Bowers, *The History of Tom Jones: A Foundling*. Middletown, CT: Wesleyan University Press, 1975.

From James Finney Boylan, "The Bean Card Method."

From Michael Bright, *Animal Language*. Ithaca, NY: Cornell University Press, 1984.

From J. Bronowski, *The Ascent of Man*. Boston: Little, Brown, p. 213.

Excerpt from Beverly Green, "African American Families." *National Forum: The Phi Kappa Phi Journal*, Volume 75, Number 3 (Summer 1995). Copyright © by Beverly Green. By permission of the publishers.

From Gerald Gross, *Editors on Editing*. New York: Harper & Row, 1962, pp. 79, 81.

From John Haines, *The Stars, the Snow, the Fire*. New York: Simon & Schuster, 1977.

Donald Hall, "A Small Fig Tree" from *Old and New Poems*. Copyright © 1990 by Donald Hall. Reprinted by permission of Ticknor & Fields/Houghton Mifflin Co. All rights reserved.

From Donald Hall, *String Too Short to Be Saved*. Boston: Nonpareil Books, 1979.

From Pete Hamill, "The Neverglades." Reprinted by permission of Janklow & Nesbit.

From Thomas Harvey, A.M., *a New English Grammar for Schools*. New York: American Book Company, 1900, p. 244.

Nathaniel Hawthorne, *Young Goodman Brown* and *The Birthmark*.

From "Hazardous Waste Incineration." American Society of Mechanical Engineers, 1988.

From Ernest Hemingway, *The Old Man and the Sea*. New York: Scribner's, 1952, p. 136.

From E. Mavis Hetherington, "Effects of father absence." *Developmental Psychology*, 1972.

From Lewis Hill, *Fetched-Up Yankee*. Chester, CT: The Globe Pequot Press, 1990.

From Maureen Honey, *Creating Rosie the Riveter*. Amherst: University of Massachusetts Press, 1984, p. 135.

From J. N. Hook, *The Appropriate Word*. Reading, MA: Addison-Wesley, 1990, pp. 34, 180.

From Robert Jastrow, *The Enchanted Loom*. New York: Simon & Schuster, 1981.

From Robert Jastrow, *Journey to the Stars*. New York: Bantam Books, 1989, p. 91.

From Donald Johnson and Maitland A. Edey, *Lucy: The Beginnings of Humankind*. New York: Simon & Schuster, 1981, p. 294.

From Lawrence E. Joseph, "The Scoop on Ice Cream." *Discover*, 1992.

From Simon Kerl, A.M., *a Common-School Grammar of the English Language*. New York: Ivison, Blakeman, Taylor & Company, 1871, p. 337.

From Maxine Hong Kingston, *The Woman Warrior*. New York: Knopf, 1976, p. 8.

From William Severini Kowinski, *The Malling of America*. New York: Morrow, 1985.

From Ann J. Lane, *The Charlotte Perkins Gilman Reader*. New York: Pantheon Books, 1980.

From Marsha Lesowitz et al., "School-based developmental facilitation groups for children of divorce." *Psychotherapy*, 1987.

From Michael Lewis, *Liar's Poker*. New York: Penguin Books, 1989.

From James J. Y. Liu, *Chinese Theories of Literature*. Chicago: University of Chicago Press, 1975.

From Barry Lopez, *Crossing Open Ground*. New York: Random House, 1988.

From James Lundquist, *Chester Himes*. New York: Frederick Ungar, 1976.

From T. R. Mayers, "(snap)shots." Reprinted by permission of author.

From Thomas R. McDonough, "Is Anyone Out There?" *Discover*, November 1992. Copyright © 1992 by The Walt Disney Company. Reprinted with permission of Discover Magazine.

From M. A. J. McKenna, "Film provides 'Beauty'-ful role models." *Boston Herald*, 1991.

From Bill McKibben, *The End of Nature*. New York: Random House, 1989.

From Ruth Macklin, *Mortal Choices*. Boston: Houghton Mifflin, 1987, p. 4.

From Margaret Mead, *Male and Female*. New York: Morrow, 1949, p. 251.

From Hugh Merrill, *The Blues Route*. New York: Morrow, 1990, p. 13.

From Alfred Metraux, *Haiti: Black Peasants and Their Religion*. London: Harrap, 1960.

From Kinereth Meyer, "'It Is Written': Tom Stoppard and the Drama of the Intertext." *Comparative Drama*, 1989.

From Mark Crispin Miller, *Seeing Through Movies*. New York: Random House, 1990.

From Margaret Mitchell, *Gone with the Wind*.

From Desmond Morris, *Bodywatching*. New York: Crown, 1985, p. 39.

From Paul Mungo and Bryan Clough, "The Bulgarian Connection."

From Ross C. Murfin, *Joseph Conrad* Heart of Darkness *A Case Study in Contemporary Criticism*. New York: St. Martin's Press, 1989, p. 84.

From Edward R. Murrow, *In Search of Light*. New York: Knopf, 1967, p. 36.

From Bill Neal, "How to Call a Pig." *Esquire*, 1991.

From Kesaya Noda, "Growing Up Asian in America," as appeared in *Making Waves* by Asian Women United. Reprinted by permission of the author.

From Susan Orlean, *Saturday Night*. New York: Random House, 1990.

From Alfonso Ortiz, "Some Concerns Central to the Writing of 'Indian' History." *The Indian Historian*.

From Phil Patton, "How a ridiculous idea mutated into a marketing star." *Smithsonian*, 1992.

From Noel Perrin, "About Men: The Androgynous Man." *The New York Times Magazine*, February 5, 1984. Copyright © 1984 by The New York Times Company. Reprinted by permission.

From Brenda Peterson, *Nature and Other Mothers*. New York: HarperCollins, 1992.

From George Plimpton, "Bonding with the Grateful Dead." Copyright © 1993 by George Plimpton.

Esquire, February 1993. Reprinted by permission of Russell & Volkening as agents for the author.

Alexander Pope, *Alexander Pope: Selected Poetry & Prose.* Orlando, FL: Holt, Rinehart & Winston, p. 78.

Excerpt from David Popenoe, "The American Family Crisis." *National Forum: The Phi Kappa Phi Journal,* Volume 75, Number 3 (Summer 1995). Copyright © by David Popenoe. By permission of the publishers.

From Neil Postman, *Amusing Ourselves to Death.* New York: Penguin Books, 1985.

From Anna Quindlen, *Thinking Out Loud.* New York: Random House.

From Adrienne Rich, *On Lies, Secrets, and Silence.* New York: Norton, 1979, p. 13.

Mary Roach, "Sunstruck" excerpted from an article by Mary Roach. *Health,* © 1992.

From Richard Rodriguez, *Hunger of Memory.* Boston: David R. Godine, 1983.

From Scott Rosenberg, "The Genie-us of 'Aladdin.'" *San Francisco Examiner*, 1992.

From Hubert Saal, "Dylan Is Back." *Newsweek,* 1968.

From Mari Sandoz, *Hostiles and Friendlies.* Lincoln: University of Nebraska Press, 1959.

From Juliet B. Schor, *The Overworked American.* New York: HarperCollins, 1991.

Brian Schwegler, "Character Development Sketch: Dave 'The Guesser.'" *Salt* Magazine, August 1994. Reprinted by permission of the author and SALT Center for Documentary Field Studies.

From Mina P. Shaughnessy, *Errors and Expectations: A Guide for the Teacher of Basic Writing.* New York: Oxford University Press, 1977, p. 7.

Philip Sidney, "His Lady's Cruelty" from *The Oxford Book of English Verse 1250–1918.* London: Oxford University Press, 1973, p. 143.

From Robert G. Sprackland, Jr., *All About Lizards.* Neptune City, NJ: TFH Publications, 1977, p. 11.

Excerpt from Judith Stacey, "The Family Values Fable." *National Forum: The Phi Kappa Phi Journal,* Volume 75, Number 3 (Summer 1995). Copyright © by Judith Stacey. By permission of the publishers.

From Elsie Myers Stainton, *The Fine Art of Copyediting.* New York: Columbia University Press, 1991.

From Jane Stern and Michael Stern, *Roadfood.* New York: HarperCollins, 1992.

From William Strauss and Neil Howe, *Generations.* New York: Morrow, 1991.

From Andrew Sullivan, "Muscleheads." *The New Republic*, 1986.

From Deborah Tannen, *You Just Don't Understand: Women and Men in Conversation.* New York: Morrow, 1990.

From Deborah Tannen, *You Just Don't Understand: Women and Men in Conversation.* New York: Morrow, 1990, p. 293.

From Carol Tavris, *The Mismeasure of Woman.* New York: Simon & Schuster, 1992.

From Lewis Thomas, *Late Night Thoughts on Listening to Mahler's Ninth.* New York: Penguin, 1982.

From Larry A. Tucker, "Effect of Weight Training on Self-Concept: A Profile of Those Influenced Most." *Research Quarterly for Exercise and Sport,* 1983.

From Mark Twain, *Adventures of Huckleberry Finn.* New York: HarperCollins, 1987.

From Richard H. Wagner, *Environment and Man.* New York: Norton, 1971, pp. 451, 454, 460.

From *Webster's Third New International Dictionary.* Copyright © 1993 by Merriam-Webster Inc., publisher of the Merriam-Webster dictionaries. By permission.

From Eudora Welty, *One Writer's Beginnings.* Cambridge, MA: Harvard University Press, 1984.

Excerpt from E. B. White, "Late August" from *Writings from* The New Yorker *1927–1976.* Copyright 1949, © 1977 E. B. White. New York: HarperCollins.

Walt Whitman, "Song of Myself" from *Leaves of Grass.* New York: Norton, 1973, p. 28.

From John Edgar Wideman, *Brothers and Keepers.* New York: Random House, 1984.

From John Edgar Wideman, *Philadelphia Fire.* New York: Henry Holt, 1990, p. 3.

From Ellen Willis, "Rock, Etc." *The New Yorker*, 1974.

From Clark A. Wiseman, "Impediments to economically efficient solid waste management." *Resources for the Future,* 1991.

From Richard Wisniewski and Paul Kleine, "Teacher Moonlighting: An Unstudied Phenomenon." *ERIC,* 1983.

From P. G. Wodehouse, *The Mating Season.* New York: HarperCollins, 1949, p. 7.

From Carl Zimmer, "The Body Electric." *Discover*, February 1993. Copyright © 1992 by The Walt Disney Company. Reprinted with permission of Discover Magazine.

Glossary of Usage and Terms

Three kinds of entries are found in this glossary: grammatical terms (such as *irregular verb*), rhetorical terms (such as *freewriting*), and words that writers frequently find confusing or difficult (such as *farther* and *further*). The latter entries, which deal with matters of usage, are indicated by an arrow (→).

→ **a, an** When the word that follows the article *a* or *an* begins with a vowel, use *an: an apple, an outrageous film.* Use *a* before consonants: *a banana, a shocking film.* (*See* 14-a)

abridged dictionary Any type of abbreviated dictionary that does not aim to be exhaustive in its treatment of English vocabulary. (*See* 28a)

absolute phrase A phrase consisting of a noun, a pronoun, or a word group acting as a noun followed by a present or past participle and any modifiers; it is used to modify a noun or an entire clause. (*See* 14c-2, 22d)

> **Their lungs burning from the acrid smoke,** the fire fighters pressed ahead into the burning building.

abstract A concise summary of a paper, sometimes used as an overview or preface at the beginning of the paper itself. (*See* 44b, 52f)

academic journal An exploratory journal kept in an academic setting for the purpose of thinking, learning, and improving one's writing by focusing on course content or ideas for papers. (*See* Chapter 2)

→ **accept, except** Use *accept* to mean "to take or receive." Use *except* to mean "excluding."

> She **accepted** the invitation.
> Everyone finished the race **except** Larry.

acronym An abbreviation whose letters begin some or all of the words in the full version: *NASA* (National Aeronautics and Space Administration), *AIDS* (acquired immune deficiency syndrome). (*See* 41a-2)

action statement In a writing assignment, the directions that specify the processes the writer should go through in completing the assignment. (*See* 5a-2)

action verb A verb that indicates an action or activity: *swim, analyze, dig, turn, negotiate.* (*See* 14a-3; *compare* **linking verb**)

active voice The form of a verb in a sentence in which the doer (or agent) takes the position of the main subject, before the main verb. (*See* 11c, 14a-3, 16d, 23c, 29a-2; *compare* **passive voice**)

gloss

ad hominem   A **fallacy** in which an argument is based upon personal attack rather than rational support and evidence. (*See 50c-5*)

ad populum   A **fallacy** in which an argument appeals to an audience's biases instead of using rational support. (*See 50c-5*)

adaptation   The principle of adjusting writing style, organization, and language to the expectations of readers in particular settings. (*See 1b-2*)

adjective   A word that modifies a noun, pronoun, or word group acting as a noun by answering such questions as "How many?" "What kind?" or "Which one?" (*See 14a-5, 18a, 18b*)

adjective clause   (*See* **relative clause**)

adjective phrase   A phrase that modifies a noun. (*See 14c-5*)

adverb   A word that modifies a verb, an adjective, an adverb, or an entire sentence by answering such questions as "When?" "Where?" "Why?" "How often?" "Which direction?" "What conditions?" and "What degree?" (*See 14a-6, 18a, 18b*)

adverb clause   A clause that acts as an adverb. (*See 14c-5*)

→ **adverse, averse**   Someone opposed to something is *averse* to it; if conditions stand in opposition to achieving a goal, they are *adverse.*

Bill wasn't **averse** to going on the ski trip unless the warm temperature would be **adverse** to good skiing conditions.

→ **advice, advise**   *Advice* is a noun meaning "counsel" or "recommendations." *Advise* is a verb meaning "to give counsel or recommendations."

Professor Raul wanted to **advise** his students, but they believed they needed no **advice.**

→ **affect, effect**   *Affect* is a verb meaning "to influence." *Effect* is a noun meaning "a result." More rarely, *effect* is a verb meaning "to cause something to happen."

It is thought that CFCs **affect** the deterioration of the ozone layer. The **effect** of that deterioration on global warming is uncertain. Lawmakers need to **effect** changes in public attitudes toward our environment.

agenda   A plan of action for a business meeting. (*See 53c*)

→ **aggravate, irritate**   *Aggravate* means "to worsen"; *irritate* means "to bother or pester."

He was **irritated** that the hotel had no humidifiers because the dry air **aggravated** his skin condition.

gloss

agreement   The correct matching, in **person, number,** and **gender,** of subjects and verbs or pronouns and their antecedents. (*See Chapter 17*)

| SUBJECT-VERB AGREEMENT | *The dog and the boy* **are running** in the field. |
| | *The dog* **is running** in the field. |

| PRONOUN-ANTECEDENT AGREEMENT | *A memo* should address the needs of **its** audience. |
| | *Memos* should address the needs of **their** audience. |

→ **ain't** Although widely used colloquially, *ain't* is inappropriate in formal writing. Use *am not, is not,* or *are not;* the contracted forms *aren't* and *isn't* are more acceptable than *ain't* but may still be too informal in some contexts.

all-purpose modifier A modifier such as *very, totally, major,* or *central* that adds little or no meaning to a sentence and often can be cut. (*See 29a-1*)

all-purpose word A filler word that carries little or no meaning and often can be cut: *factor, aspect, field, thing, kind.* (*See 29a-1*)

→ **all ready, already** *All ready* means "prepared for"; *already* means "by that time."

Sam was **all ready** for the kickoff, but when he had climbed to his bleacher, the game had **already** started.

→ **all right** This expression is always spelled as two words, not as *alright.*

→ **all together, altogether** Use *all together* to mean "everyone"; use *altogether* to mean "completely."

We were **all together** on our decision to climb the cliff, but it was **altogether** too hard for us to leave Jennie behind.

→ **allude, elude** Use *allude* to mean "hint at" or "refer to indirectly"; use *elude* to mean "escape."

Francis **alluded** to the time the refrigerator broke when he was on vacation; the rotten smell had **eluded** the house sitter, who never thought to open the refrigerator.

→ **allusion, illusion** An *allusion* is a reference to something; an *illusion* is a vision or false belief.

Peter found an interesting **allusion** to UFOs in a government document. It turned out that the UFOs were just an **illusion.**

→ **a lot** This expression is always spelled as two words, not as *alot.* Even when spelled correctly, *a lot* may be too informal for some academic writing. Use *many, much,* or some other modifier instead.

→ **a.m., p.m.** These abbreviations may be capital or lowercase letters. (*See 41a-3*)

ambiguous reference A sentence in which a reader cannot identify a pronoun with its **antecedent.** (*See 21a-1*)

→ **among, between** Use *between* to describe something involving two people, things, or ideas; use *among* to refer to three or more people, things, or ideas.

gloss

A fight broke out **between** the umpire and the catcher; then there was a discussion **among** the catcher, the umpire, and the team managers.

→ **amount, number** Use *amount* to refer to a quantity of something that can't be divided into separate units. Use *number* when you want to refer to countable objects.

A large **number** of spices may be used in Thai dishes. This recipe calls for a small **amount** of coconut milk.

→ **an, a** (*See* **a, an**)

analogy A comparison between two things, often on the basis of shared characteristics. (*See 50c-5; see also* **false analogy**)

analysis Writing that analyzes or "takes apart" a topic, often looking at how the parts relate to one another. (*See 52a-4*)

analyze To divide or break something up into its constituent parts to examine their relationships. (*See 5a-2*)

→ **and etc.** (*See* **etc.**)

→ **and/or** Although widely used, *and/or* is usually imprecise and may distract your reader. Choose one of the words, or revise your sentence.

IMPRECISE	The police **and/or** the fire department will usually arrive first when someone calls 911.
EDITED	The police **or** the fire department will usually arrive first when someone calls 911.

anecdote A brief story or account of a personal experience, often used in an introductory paragraph to spark a reader's interest. (*See 10c-1*)

annotated bibliography A **bibliography** that includes annotations (short descriptions of each entry, sometimes with accompanying evaluative comments). (*See 52g*)

annotations Notes written about (or sometimes directly on) a draft or a published text. Annotations can include **interpretations,** questions, **counterarguments**, restatements, or **evaluations.** (*See 3a-3*)

→ **ante-, anti-** Use *ante-* as a prefix to mean "before" or "predating"; use *anti-* to mean "against" or "opposed."

Some people experience strong **anti-racist** feelings when touring the slave quarters of **antebellum** Southern plantations that survived the Civil War.

antecedent The noun or pronoun to which another word (usually a **pronoun**) refers. (*See 14a-2, 17c, Chapter 21*)

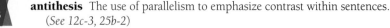

antecedent   pronoun
Jean presented **her** proposal to the committee.

antithesis The use of parallelism to emphasize contrast within sentences. (*See 12c-3, 25b-2*)

antonym A word opposite in meaning to another word: *hot* and *cold.* (*See 28a; see also* **thesaurus**)

→ **anyone, any one** *Anyone* as one word is an indefinite pronoun. Occasionally you may want to use *any* to modify *one,* in the sense of "any individual thing or person." (The same distinction applies to **everyone, every one;** *somebody, some body;* and *someone, some one.*)

Anyone can learn to parachute without fear. But the instructors are told not to spend too much time with **any one** person.

→ **anyplace** Avoid using this term in formal writing; instead, use *anywhere* or revise your sentence.

→ **anyways, anywheres** Avoid these incorrect versions of *anyway* and *anywhere.*

APA documentation style The style of documentation suggested by the American Psychological Association and described in its guide. (*See Chapter 47*)

application letter A brief letter of application for a job, usually accompanied by a **résumé.** (*See 53g*)

appositive A noun or pronoun that renames or stands for a preceding noun (*See 31c-3*)

appositive phrase A phrase consisting of an appositive (usually a noun) along with its modifiers, used to rename a noun in order to add information to a sentence. (*See 14c-3, 15a-4, 31c-3*)

Ken Choi and Stephanie Almagno, **my classmates,** won an award for their innovative packaging design.

→ **apt, likely, liable** Use *apt* to mean "a tendency to." Use *likely* to mean "probable." Use *liable* only to imply risk, or, in a legal context, an obligation or responsibility.

Claude was **apt** to ski the most treacherous slopes when he was young, but he will **likely** keep to the moderate slopes now because he is **liable** to hurt himself again if he skis the expert slopes. The ski resort was **liable** for Claude's injuries because it did not mark the location of the cliff.

archaic word A word that is no longer in general use or is in the process of dropping from the language, such as *save* in the sense of "except." (*See 27b-4*)

argue To prove a point or persuade a reader to accept or entertain a particular position. (*See 5a-2; see also* **argument; argumentative writing**)

argument Not a disagreement, but the reasons, evidence, and explanations used in an attempt to resolve a disagreement by encouraging readers (listeners) to agree with the writer (speaker). (*See Chapter 50*)

argumentative writing Writing that presents and defends a position or point of view. (*See Chapter 50*)

article One of three words that precede a noun: *a, an,* or *the.* An *indefinite article* (*a* or *an*) precedes a general noun (one that does not refer to a specific thing). The *definite article the* precedes a specific noun. (*See 14-a*)

gloss

→ **as, like** Used as a preposition, *as* indicates a precise comparison. *Like* indicates a resemblance or similarity.

Remembered **as** a man of habit, Kant would take his walk at exactly the same time each day. He was **like** many other philosophers: brooding, thoughtful, and at times intense.

→ **as to** *As to* is considered informal in many academic contexts and should be avoided.

INFORMAL	The media had many speculations **as to** the skater's involvement in the attack against her rival.
EDITED	The media had many speculations **about** the skater's involvement in the attack against her rival.

→ **assure, ensure, insure** Use *assure* to imply a promise; use *ensure* to imply a certain outcome. Use *insure* only when you imply something legal or financial.

The surgeon **assured** the world-renowned pianist that his fingers would heal in time for the performance. To **ensure** that, the pianist could not practice for three weeks. In case of an even worse accident, the pianist had **insured** his hands with Lloyd's of London.

→ **at** In any writing, avoid using *at* in direct and indirect questions.

COLLOQUIAL	Jones wondered where his attorney was **at.**
EDITED	Jones wondered where his attorney **was.**

atlas A book containing maps and related information. (*See 44b-1*)
audience The implied or intended readers for a particular piece of writing. (*See Chapter 6, 45c-1, 50b-4, 52a-1*)
audiovisual collection A library collection of videotapes, films, audio recordings, and similar resources. (*See 44b-3*)
auxiliary verb (*See* **helping verb**)
→ **awful, awfully** Use *awful* as an adjective modifying a noun; use *awfully* as an adverb in verbal structures.

Sanders played **awfully** at the U.S. Open Golf Tournament. On the sixth hole, an **awful** shot landed his ball in the pond.

→ **awhile, a while** *Awhile* (as one word) functions as an adverb; it is not preceded by a preposition. *A while* functions as a noun (preceded by *a, an* article) and is often used in prepositional phrases.

The shelter suggested that the homeless family stay **awhile.** It turned out that the children had not eaten for **a while.**

→ **bad, badly** Use *bad* as an adjective that modifies nouns or with a linking verb expressing feelings. Use *badly* as an adverb.

The summit was scheduled at a **bad** time of year for some delegates. The British prime minister felt **bad** that some countries weren't represented. Several heads of state spoke **badly** of East-West relations.

balanced sentence A sentence built around pairs of parallel phrases and clauses, used to create emphasis. (*See 25b-2*)

bandwagon argument A **fallacy** in argumentative writing in which the writer tries to convince the reader that everyone else feels a particular way about a topic and that the reader ought to as well. (*See 50c-5*)

base form The present tense form of a verb. (*See* **tense;** *see 16a*)

→ **because, since** In general, avoid using *since* in place of *because,* which is more formal and precise. Use *since* to indicate time, not causality.

INFORMAL **Since** the meeting was canceled, Sam gave his nonrefundable plane tickets to a friend.

EDITED **Because** the meeting was canceled, Sam gave his nonrefundable plane tickets to a friend.

CORRECT **Since** then, Sam has avoided buying nonrefundable tickets for meetings.

begging the question In argument, a **fallacy** in which assumptions are presented as facts, sometimes using words like *obviously* or *clearly*. (Also known as *overgeneralization* or *hasty generalization*.) (*See 50c-5*)

→ **being as, being that** Avoid using *being as* or *being that* in academic and other formal writing when you mean *because*.

→ **beside, besides** Use *beside* as a preposition to mean "next to." Use *besides* as an adverb meaning "also" or an adjective meaning "except."

Betsy placed the documents **beside** Mr. Klein. **Besides** being the best lawyer at the firm, Klein was also the most cautious.

→ **better, had better** Avoid using *better* or *had better* in place of *ought to* or *should* in formal writing.

COLLOQUIAL Fast-food chains **better** realize that Americans are more health-conscious today.

EDITED Fast-food chains **ought to** realize that Americans are more health-conscious today.

→ **between, among** (*See* **among, between**)

bibliographic sources Lists of resources you can consult in your research. **Bibliographies,** indexes, electronic databases, and catalogs all provide information about possible sources. (*See 44a-3*)

bibliographies Lists of library or other resources available in specific subject areas. (*See 44b-1*)

bibliography A list of the sources used by the writer of a research paper, an article, or a book, prepared so that a reader can easily find the same materials. (*See, for instance, the formats in Chapters 46–49; see also* **annotated bibliography**)

biographical sources Source materials that supply information about the lives and times of important people. (*See 44b-1*)

block format A format for short letters in which all the paragraphs are flush at the left margin. (*See 53b; compare* **modified block format**)

gloss

block quotation   A quotation of sufficient length to justify separating it from the body of a text in an indented block of prose. (*See 34b, 45b-5*)

body   The main section of a paper or written document. It is preceded by an **introduction** and followed by a **conclusion.** (*See 7a-2*)

boundary statement   A sentence at the start of a paragraph that acts as a bridge from the paragraph before. (*See 9c-2*)

brainstorming   A technique for generating material for possible use in a written document. Brainstorming involves concentrating on a topic, thinking associatively, and finding connections among different ideas. (*See 2c-2, Chapter 3*)

→ **bring, take**   *Bring* implies a movement from somewhere else to close at hand; *take* implies a movement in the opposite direction.

   Please **bring** me a coffee refill, and **take** away these leftover muffins.

broad pronoun reference   Using a pronoun to refer to an entire idea rather than a specific **antecedent.** (*See 21b-1*)

→ **broke**   *Broke* is the past tense of *break*; avoid using it as the past participle.

INCORRECT	The computer was **broke.**
EDITED	The computer was **broken.**

→ **burst, bursted**   *Burst* implies an outward explosion. Do not use the form *bursted* for the past tense.

CORRECT	The gang of boys **burst** the balloon.

→ **bust, busted**   Avoid the use of *bust* or *busted* to mean "broke."

COLLOQUIAL	The senator's limousine **bust** down on the trip to Washington.
EDITED	The senator's limousine **broke** down on the trip to Washington.

→ **but however, but yet**   These are **redundant pairs;** choose one word of each pair, not both.

INCORRECT	The medfly was a nuisance, **but yet** the state of California was finally able to control it.
EDITED	The medfly was a nuisance, **but** the state of California was finally able to control it.

→ **calculate, figure, reckon**   These three terms are sometimes used informally to mean "imagine" or "think." When in doubt, avoid them.

INFORMAL	John **figured** he had never seen such a large pike.
EDITED	John **thought** he had never seen such a large pike.

→ **can, may**   *Can* implies ability; *may* implies permission or uncertainty.

gloss

Bart **can** drive now, but his parents **may** not lend him their new car.

→ **can't hardly, can't scarcely** Use these pairs positively, not negatively: *can hardly* and *can scarcely,* or simply *can't.*

→ **capital, capitol** *Capital* refers to a government center or to money; *capitol* refers to a government building.

Madison is the **capital** of Wisconsin.

card catalog A file of printed cards listing a library's books and other holdings. An individual work usually has several cards that list it by author, title, and subject area(s). (*See 44b-2; see also* **online catalog**)

case The grammatical role that a pronoun or noun plays in a sentence (as subject, object, direct object, and the like). *Subjective case* refers to the role played as the subject of a sentence. *Objective case* refers to the role played as the object of a sentence. *Possessive case* refers to the role played in a sentence to indicate possession or ownership. (*See 14a-2, 15a*)

CBE documentation style The style of documentation suggested by the Council of Biology Editors and described in its guide. (*See Chapter 48*)

→ **censor, censure** *Censor* means the act of shielding something from the public eye, such as a book or movie. *Censure* implies a punishment or critical labeling.

The school board **censored** *Catcher in the Rye,* but a group of parents **censured** the school by naming it on a list of "anti-intellectual" schools in the area.

→ **center around** Something can't center *around* something else. Use *center on* or *focus on* instead, or reword as *revolve around.*

→ **chairman, chairperson, chair** The use of *chairman* is now considered sexist. *Chairperson* is an awkward but acceptable substitute. *Chair* is now a common nonsexist alternative.

SEXIST	Gayle is now **chairman** of the provost's academic standards council.
EDITED	Gayle is now **chair** of the provost's academic standards council.

character Any person, usually fictional, in a work of literature. (*See 51a-2*)

→ **choose, chose** Incorrect use of these terms often has its source in a simple spelling error. Use *choose* for the present tense form of the verb; use *chose* for the past tense form.

chronological order A pattern for structuring writing in which elements of an event are presented in the order in which they happened. (*See 9b-5*)

circular reasoning In argumentative writing, a **fallacy** in which an assertion is supported with the assertion itself. (Also known as *tautology.*) (*See 50c-5*)

gloss

→ **cite, site** *Cite* means to acknowledge someone else's work; *site* means a place or location.

Phil decided to **cite** Chomsky's theory of syntax as evidence for his thesis.

We chose the perfect **site** to pitch our tent.

claim (*See* **data-warrant-claim reasoning**)
clarifying sentence (*See* **limiting sentence**)
classification The organization of information into groups, categories, or parts. (*See 52a-3*)
classification paragraph A paragraph in which several subjects are sorted into groups based on their similarities or relationships. (*See 10b-5*)
cliché An overused or trite word or expression: *startling discovery, today's modern world, turn you on.* (*See 29b-1*)
→ **climactic, climatic** *Climactic* refers to the culmination of something; *climatic* refers to the weather conditions.
climactic sentence order A sentence structured to build to a climax, often through the use of elements in a series. (*See 12a-4*)

What every truly modern home has, she said, is a dishwasher, a gas grill, a Jacuzzi, and a divorce.

clustering A planning strategy in which groups of ideas are related graphically to a kernel topic. (*See 4b-1*)
CMS documentation style The style of documentation described in *The Chicago Manual of Style.* (*See Chapter 49*)
coherence Writing in which each sentence or paragraph follows clearly from the one before and leads clearly to the next in a recognizable, easy-to-understand arrangement. (*See 9b*)
collaborative revision The process of working with one or more people in order to revise writing drafts. (*See 8c*)
collective noun A kind of noun that refers to a unit composed of more than one individual or thing: *group, board of directors, family.* Such nouns generally take a singular form even though they refer to more than one thing. (*See 14a, 17b, 17c, see also* **noun; count noun; mass noun**)
colloquialism A word or expression that is used informally (often in specific regions or among specific groups) but is not usually considered appropriate in formal and academic prose. (*See 27a-1*)
comma splice Two or more sentences (independent or main clauses) incorrectly joined with a comma. (*See Chapter 20, 31a; compare* **fused sentence**)

gloss

COMMA SPLICE The human eye is not like that of the cat, it has many more color-sensitive cells.

EDITED The human eye is not like that of the cat; it has many more color-sensitive cells.

common adjective Any adjective that is not a **proper adjective.** (*See 37b*)

common noun Any noun that is not a **proper noun.** (*See 14a-1, 37b*)

comparative form One of three forms taken by an adjective or adverb to indicate whether the noun or verb modified is being compared to something else. The comparative form adds -*er* or *more* to the adjective or adverb. (*See 18c; compare* **positive form** *and* **superlative form**)

ADJECTIVE　　This oven is **cleaner** than mine.
　　　　　　　She is the **more imaginative** designer of the two.

ADVERB　　　Sometimes you can travel **faster** in Manhattan by foot than by car.
　　　　　　　Peggy designs **more imaginatively** than Horace.

→ **compare to, compare with** Use *compare to* when you want to imply similarities between two things—the phrase is close in meaning to *liken to.* Use *compare with* when you want to imply both similarities and differences.

CORRECT　　　To help the little boy understand his virus, the doctor **compared** it **to** a tiny army in his body.

CORRECT　　　**Compared with** his last illness, this one was mild.

comparing and contrasting A technique for organizing an entire paper or for developing individual paragraphs or sentences. Opinions, characteristics, or objects are compared for similarities and differences, which often are presented in alternating form. (*See 10b-3, 51a-2; see 25b-2 on* **parallelism;** *see also* **point-by-point organization** *and* **subject-by-subject organization**)

complement A word (noun, pronoun, or adjective) or phrase tied by a linking verb to a subject. (*See 14b-2, 15a-2, 18b-2*) A *subject complement* "completes" the linking verb by describing the subject or renaming it. An *object complement* renames or describes the *direct object.*

→ **complement, compliment** *Complement* means "an accompaniment"; *compliment* means "words of praise."

The diplomats **complimented** the ambassador on her choice of opera. The theater's grand ceiling **complemented** the theme of the opera perfectly.

complete predicate (*See* **predicate**)

complete sentence A sentence that contains both a subject and a complete predicate and is therefore grammatical. (*See Chapter 19; compare* **sentence fragment**)

complete subject (*See* **subject**)

complex sentence A sentence with one **main clause** and one or more **subordinate clauses.** (*See 14d-1, 26b-1; compare* **compound sentence; compound-complex sentence; simple sentence**)

compound antecedent A group of words to which a pronoun or noun refers. (*See 21a; see also* **antecedent**)

gloss

compound-complex sentence A sentence with two or more **main clauses** and one or more **subordinate clauses.** (*See 14d-1; compare* **compound sentence; complex sentence; simple sentence**)

compound predicate A predicate that contains two or more complete verbs, usually connected with *and.* (*See 19c-1*)

The car **struck and injured** the bystander.

compound sentence A sentence with two or more **main clauses** and no **subordinate clauses.** (*See 14d-1, 26a; compare* **complex sentence; compound-complex sentence; simple sentence**)

compound subject Two or more subjects joined with *and* or *both...and.* (*See 17b-1*)

Jim and the rest of the Boy Scouts were responsible for the rescue.

conclusion The ending section of a paper, preceded by the **introduction** and **body** (*see 7a-2*); also the necessary consequence of a line of reasoning, especially in **deductive argument.** (*See 50c-1*)

conditional statement A sentence that expresses something improbable or hypothetical, often beginning with *if.* Conditional statements use the *subjunctive* form of the verb. (*See 16b-3*)

conjunction A word that joins two elements in a sentence. (*See 14a-8, 17b, 25b-2, 31a*) Coordinating conjunctions (*and, but, or, nor, for, yet, and so*) link grammatically equal elements such as parts of compound subjects, verbs, objects, and modifiers.

We analyzed **and** discussed the theory in class.
Fresh orange juice **or** grapefruit juice contain citric acid.

Subordinating conjunctions (*because, although, while, if, or since*) create a **subordinate** (or *modifying*) **clause.**

<u>**Because** they were tired,</u> they did not notice that the pot was boiling over.

conjunctive adverb An adverb such as *however, moreover, thus,* or *therefore* that joins sentences or elements within sentences and indicates a logical relationship between them. (*See 14a-6, 31b-3, 32a-2*)

connotation The associative or affective "shades of meaning" conveyed by a word, as opposed to its literal meaning. If someone is said to have *retreated* from a gathering, the word connotes that the person was feeling attacked or bewildered. (*See 27b-2*)

→ **consensus of opinion** Avoid this redundancy by using *consensus.*

content The specific ideas or information presented in a piece of writing. (*See 6c-1*)

→ **continual, continuous** *Continual* implies that something is recurring; *continuous* implies that something is constant and unceasing.

The **continual** noise of landing jets didn't bother the homeowners as

gloss

much as the foul odor that drifted **continuously** from the landfill near the airport.

contraction A form in which two words are brought together, usually by eliminating one or more letters and adding an apostrophe to mark the omission(s): *it's, they're, can't.* (*See 33b-1*)

controlling idea (*See* **thesis statement**)

coordinate adjectives A pair of adjectives, each modifying a noun on its own and therefore separated by a comma. In *noncoordinate adjectives,* which are not separated by commas, the first adjective modifies the second, which modifies the noun. (*See 31f*)

coordinating conjunction (*See* **conjunction**)

coordination A sentence structure that links and equally weights main clauses using *coordinating conjunctions.* (*See 26a; compare* **subordination**)

> COORDINATE   These drawings present a **quick, simple** solution to the drainage problem.

> NONCOORDINATE   We can use **flexible plastic** pipe to carry water away from the building.

correlative conjunctions Pairs of conjunctions (*not only . . . but also; either . . . or; neither . . . nor; both . . . and; whether . . . or*) that join sentence elements that are grammatically equal. (*See 14a-8; see 25b-2 on* **parallelism**)

→ **could of, would of** These incorrect pairs are common because they are often pronounced as if they are spelled this way. Use the correct verb forms *could have* and *would have.*

> INCORRECT   I **could of** majored in psychology.

> EDITED   I **could have** majored in psychology.

count noun A type of noun that refers to individual ("countable") items: *chair, bean, cup.* A count noun can be made plural by the addition of an *-s.* (*See 14a-1; see also* **noun; collective noun; mass noun**)

counterargument A claim or opinion opposed to the one being supported in an argumentative paper. (*See 50a-5*)

→ **couple, couple of** These terms are used colloquially; in formal writing, use *a few* or *two* instead.

> COLLOQUIAL   Watson took a **couple of** days to examine the data.

> EDITED   Watson took **a few** days to examine the data.

> EDITED   Watson took **two or three** days to examine the data.

→ **criteria** *Criteria* is the plural form of *criterion.* Make sure your verbs agree in number with this noun.

> SINGULAR   One **criterion** for winning the bonus was selling ten cars in two weeks.

> PLURAL   The **criteria** were too strict to follow.

gloss

critique A paper that summarizes and presents a critical reaction to a specific work, such as a speech or book. (*See 50e*)

cumulative sentence A sentence that begins with the main clause and then adds details and statements in the form of modifying phrases, clauses, and words. (*See 12a-4*)

→ **curriculum** *Curriculum* is the singular form of this noun. For the plural, use either *curricula* or *curriculums*, but be consistent.

dangling modifier A sentence that contains no **headword** or **phrase** to which a modifier can be correctly linked. (*See Chapter 22; compare* **disruptive modifier** *and* **misplaced modifier**)

> DANGLING   Staring from his study, **Paul's stomach** tied itself into knots.

> EDITED   Staring from his study, **Paul** felt his stomach tying itself into knots.

→ **data** Although now widely used for both the singular and plural, *data* technically is a plural noun; *datum* refers to a single piece of data. If in doubt, use the more formal distinction between the two, and make sure your verbs agree in number.

> SINGULAR   This one **datum** is astonishing.

> PLURAL   These **data** are not very revealing.

data-warrant-claim reasoning A reasoning or argumentative strategy in which data (indisputable facts) lead to a claim (or conclusion) through a mental process involving probable facts and assertions (warrants). Also called Toulmin reasoning. (*See 50c-3*)

database A computerized (CD-ROM or online) collection of resources available to researchers. Databases contain a wide variety of materials such as articles, graphics, bibliographies, and statistics and usually focus on a particular area of study or a particular topic. (*See 44b-2*)

declarative sentence A type of sentence that makes a statement. (*See 12b-2, 14d-2; compare* **exclamatory sentence; imperative sentence; interrogative sentence**)

The motor is making a rattling noise.

deductive argument An argument that begins with an explicitly stated **premise** and goes on to support that premise, using **syllogism** as the basic logical format. (*See 50c-1; compare* **inductive argument**)

definite article (*See* **article**)

demonstrative adjective (*See* **demonstrative pronoun**)

demonstrative pronoun A pronoun (*this, that, these,* or *those*), that points out or highlights an antecedent. (*See 14a-2, 17c-3*)

dependent clause (*See* **subordinate clause**)

description A kind of writing and a means of developing paragraphs that uses specific details to evoke images of places, objects, characters, or feelings. (*See 10b-3; see also* **objective description** and **subjective description**)

desk dictionary A midsized dictionary suitable for most professional and academic contexts. (*See 28a*)

detailing list A prewriting and revision strategy for creating more detailed prose. (*See 4a-4*)

dialogue journal A kind of collaborative journal in which partners swap journal entries and respond to each other's ideas, often about readings or other course material. (*See 3b, 4a-6*) An *internal dialogue* (*see 4a-6*) can be created when writing by oneself.

diction The choice of words and phrases in a piece of writing. (*See Chapter 27*)

→ **different from, different than** The subtle difference between these two phrases is marked by what follows them: use *different from* when an object follows, and use *different than* when an entire clause follows.

Jack's quiche recipe is **different from** Marlene's, but his cooking method is **different** now **than** when he was an apprentice.

direct object (*See* **object**)

direct quotation A quotation that presents a speaker's or writer's ideas and feelings in the same words the speaker used, set off by quotation marks. (*See 23b-2, 23d*)

directions One type of process explanation in which the writer gives a step-by-step guide for assembling or creating something or for following a procedure. (*See 10b-4*)

→ **discreet, discrete** *Discreet* means "reserved or cautious"; *discrete* means "distinctive, different, or explicit."

Emmons was as **discreet** as an anthropologist could be, but he violated some of the **discrete** codes of research when he lived among the tribe.

discriminatory language Language that implies or reinforces racist or discriminatory views toward other cultures or groups. (*See 30b*)

discuss To provide an intelligent, focused commentary in a paper. (*See 5a-2*)

→ **disinterested, uninterested** *Uninterested* implies boredom or lack of interest; *disinterested* implies impartiality or objectivity.

It wasn't that Reagan was **uninterested** in environmental issues; he was simply a **disinterested** party when it came to special-interest groups.

disruptive modifier A sentence in which two closely connected elements such as a noun and a verb are inappropriately disrupted by a modifier. (*See 22c; compare* **dangling modifier** and **misplaced modifier**)

DISRUPTIVE   The engineer, **even though he could have lost his life if he had become trapped in the burning plant,** was able to shut off the gas valve and prevent millions of dollars in damage.

gloss

EDITED	**Even though he could have lost his life if he had become trapped in the burning plant,** the engineer was able to shut off the gas valve and prevent millions of dollars in damage.

division paragraph A paragraph in which a subject is split into its constituent parts so that the relationship between these parts can be highlighted or explained. (*See 10b-5*)

documentation The process of citing the source or reference for an idea, sentence, passage, or text in a research paper. (*See Chapters 46 through 49*)

→ **done** Avoid using *done* as a simple past tense; it is a *past participle*. (*See 16b-1*)

INCORRECT	The skater **done** the best she could at the Olympics.
EDITED	The skater **did** the best she could at the Olympics.

→ **don't, doesn't** These and other contractions may strike some academic readers as too informal. Check with your reader, or err on the side of formality (*do not, does not*) when in doubt.

double negative Avoid the incorrect use of two negative forms. (*See 18d*)

INCORRECT	The state **hasn't** done **nothing** about it.
EDITED	The state **has** done **nothing** about it.
EDITED	The state **hasn't** done **anything** about it.

drafting The process of creating a preliminary but readable version of an essay or other text. (*See Chapter 7*)

draft thesis statement (*See* **tentative thesis statement**)

→ **due to** When meaning "because," use *due to* only after some form of the verb *be*. Avoid *due to the fact that,* which is wordy.

INCORRECT	The mayor collapsed **due to** campaign fatigue.
EDITED	The mayor's collapse <u>was</u> **due to** campaign fatigue.
EDITED	The mayor collapsed **because** of campaign fatigue.

editing The process of fine tuning a rough draft for problems in grammar, wording, style, sentence rhythm or length, and other details. (*See Chapter 13; compare* **proofreading** *and* **revising**)

→ **effect, affect** (*See* **affect, effect**)

→ **e.g.** From a Latin term meaning "for example," this abbreviation is common in much writing but should be avoided when possible.

AWKWARD	Her positions on major issues, **e.g.,** gun control, abortion, and the death penalty, are very liberal.
EDITED	Her positions on major issues **such as** gun control, abortion, and the death penalty are very liberal.

gloss

either/or strategy In argumentative writing, a **fallacy** in which an issue is oversimplified, usually into two sides or positions. (*See 50c-5*)

e-journals Scholarly journals published (or distributed) through electronic computer networks. (*See 44b-4*)

electronic indexes Computerized (CD-ROM or online) indexes to articles in magazines, newspapers, or scholarly journals. Indexes enable researchers to identify possible sources. (*See 44b-2; see also* **printed indexes**)

electronic research Research conducted using electronic media or technology, such as CD-ROM databases, online resources, or electronic card catalogs. (*See 44c; see also* **research**)

ellipsis A series of three or four evenly spaced periods telling a reader that something has been left out of a quotation. (*See 36d*)

As Fielding describes it, Squire Allworthy's house had "an Air of Grandeur in it, that struck you with awe **. . .** and it was as commodious within, as venerable without."

elliptical construction The omission of an otherwise repeated element in a sentence; appropriate omissions are not misleading or confusing. (*See 24b-2*)

| LEFT IN | Some car owners invest lots of time caring for their cars; others **invest little time caring for their cars.** |
| OMITTED BUT CLEAR | Some car owners invest lots of time caring for their cars; **others invest little.** |

e-mail Mail exchanged through electronic computer networks. (*See 44b-4*)

→ **emigrate from, immigrate to** Foreigners *emigrate from* one country and *immigrate to* another. *Migrate* implies moving around (as in *migrant workers*) or settling temporarily.

emotional strategy In argumentative writing, a focus on the values, attitudes, systems of beliefs, and emotions that guide people's lives and are central to most decision-making processes. (*See 50c-2*)

empty phrase A phrase that adds little or no meaning to a sentence and can be cut or reduced: *at this point in time, due to the fact that, each and every.* (*See 29a-1*)

e-newsletters Scholarly or professional newsletters containing current information and announcements, published (or distributed) through electronic computer networks. (*See 44b-4*)

→ **ensure, assure, insure** (*See* **assure, ensure, insure**)

→ **enthused** Avoid *enthused* to mean *enthusiastic* in formal writing.

equivocation (*See* **misleading language/misleading evidence**)

→ **especially, specially** *Especially* implies "in particular"; *specially* means "for a specific purpose."

It was **especially** important that Nakita follow the workouts **specially** designed by her coach.

essay exam A test written out in essay form, either during a timed, in-class session or at home between class sessions. (*See 50g, 52h*)

gloss

→ **etc.** Avoid this abbreviation in formal writing by supplying a complete list of items or by using a phrase like *so forth*.

> **INFORMAL**   The Washington march was a disaster: it was cold and rainy, the protesters had no food, **etc.**

> **EDITED**   The Washington march was a disaster: the protesters were cold, wet, and hungry.

etymology The history of a word, including its source(s) and the changes it has undergone. (*See 28a*)

etymological dictionary (*See* **etymology**)

evaluation The process of deciding the relative worth of a source, phenomenon, or opinion, including the credibility or authority of a researched source. (*See 5a-2, 45a-3*)

evaluative summary (*See* **summary**)

→ **eventually, ultimately** Use *eventually* to imply that an outcome follows a series of events or a lapse of events. Use *ultimately* to imply that a final or culminating act ends a series of events.

> **Eventually,** the rescue team managed to pull the last of the survivors from the wreck, and **ultimately** there were no casualties.

→ **everyday, every day** *Everyday* is an adjective that modifies a noun. *Every day* is a noun modified by *every*.

> **Every day** in the Peace Corps, Monique faced the **everyday** task of boiling her drinking water.

→ **everyone, every one** *Everyone* is a pronoun; *every one* is an adjective followed by a noun. (*See also* **anyone, any one**)

> **Everyone** was tantalized by **every one** of the items on the dessert menu.

→ **exam** In formal writing, some readers may be bothered by this abbreviation of the word *examination*.

→ **except, accept** (*See* **accept, except**)

exclamatory sentence A type of sentence that expresses something emphatically. (*See 12b-2, 14d-2; compare* **declarative sentence; imperative sentence; interrogative sentence**)

> The car is on fire!

explanation A kind of writing that provides details on how a mechanism or procedure works. (*See 10b-4*)

expletive construction In indirect sentences, the use of opening expletives such as *there is, there are,* or *it is* to delay the actual subject until further into the sentence. (*See 11b, 29a-2*)

> **This is** the case in which the man bit the dog.

gloss

explication A line-by-line analysis of a text. (*See 51b-2*)

→ **explicit, implicit** *Explicit* means that something is outwardly or openly stated; *implicit* means that it is implied or suggested.

> The conductors **explicitly** assured the passengers that they were traveling to a comfortable new life, but **implicit** in their voices was the Nazi menace that the Jews had come to recognize.

exploratory sources (*See* **preliminary sources**)

extend In writing assignments, to take an idea or concept and apply it more extensively. (*See 5a-2*)

fallacy Any flaw in reasoning, particularly in the context of persuasive or argumentative writing. (*See 50c-5*)

false analogy A **fallacy** in which two things that are presented as comparable are actually not. (*See 50c-5*)

→ **farther, further** *Farther* implies a measurable distance; *further* implies something that cannot be measured.

> The **farther** they trekked into the wilderness, the **further** their relationship deteriorated.

faulty cause-effect relationship A **fallacy** in which one event is assumed or implied to have caused another event. (*See 50c-5*)

faulty parallelism (*See* **parallelism**)

faulty predication A sentence in which the second part comments on or names a topic different from the one announced in the first part. (*See 24a; see* **shift**)

FAULTY	The **presence** of ozone in smog is **the chemical** that causes eye irritation.
EDITED	The **ozone** in smog is the **chemical** that causes eye irritation.

→ **female, male** Use these terms only when you want to call attention to gender specifically, as in a research report. Otherwise, use the simpler *man* and *woman* or *boy* and *girl,* unless such usage is sexist. (*See Chapter 30*)

→ **fewer, less** Use *fewer* for things that can be counted, and use *less* for quantities that cannot be divided.

> Bush had **fewer** supporters for the bill than before, but there was much **less** media coverage this time.

field research (*See* **research**)

field resources Original documents, interviews, surveys, questionnaires, and personal observations gathered during the process of **research.** (*See 44g*)

figure, calculate, reckon (*See* **calculate, figure, reckon**)

→ **finalize** Some readers object to adjectives and nouns that are turned into

gloss

verbs ending in *-ize* (*finalize, prioritize, objectivize*). When in doubt, use *make final* or some other construction.

→ **firstly** Use *first, second, third,* and so forth when enumerating points in writing.

INAPPROPRIATE	**Firstly,** I will compare Sartre's and Camus's versions of existentialism.
EDITED	**First,** I will compare Sartre's and Camus's versions of existentialism.

first person (*See* **person**)

five-paragraph theme A kind of academic paper that has a simple, clearly defined structure including an **introduction,** a **body** of three paragraphs each starting with a **topic sentence,** and a **conclusion.** (*See 5c-3*)

focus-imagine-choose strategy A strategy for choosing the correct case of pronouns: focus on the pronoun, imagine each possible choice, and choose the correct form. (*See 15a*)

focused freewriting Writing quickly, without stopping, about a particular idea or topic. (*See 4a-2; see also* **freewriting**)

focused paragraph (*See* **paragraph**)

→ **former, latter** *Former* means "the one before" and *latter* means "the one after." They can be used only when referring to two things.

fragment (*See* **sentence fragment**)

freewriting A technique involving writing as quickly as possible without concern for style or grammar. Freewriting is often used to avoid writer's block, to "warm up" for more formal writing, or to generate ideas for a paper. (*See 4a-1; see also* **focused freewriting**)

→ **freshman, freshmen** Many readers consider these terms sexist and archaic. Unless you are citing an established term or group (such as the Freshman Colloquium at Midwest University), use *first-year student* instead.

further, farther (*See* **farther, further**)

fused sentence Two or more complete sentences incorrectly joined without any punctuation. (*See Chapter 20; compare* **comma splice**)

FUSED	Frank Lloyd Wright's Robie House is a good example of his architectural principles it embodies the idea of "space, not mass."
EDITED	Frank Lloyd Wright's Robie House is a good example of his architectural principles; it embodies the idea of "space, not mass."

gloss

future perfect tense (*See* **perfect tense**)
future progressive tense (*See* **progressive tense**)
future tense (*See* **tense**)
gazetteer A dictionary of geographical places and cities. (*See 44b-1*)
gender Labeling of nouns and pronouns according to whether they are

masculine, feminine, or neuter. Pronouns must agree in gender with the nouns to which they refer. (*See 14a-2, 15a, 17a*)

Harry put on **his** shirt.

general academic writing Writing typically found in introductory courses across the college curriculum, including term papers, essay exams, short reports, abstracts, summaries, and argumentative analyses. (*See 1b-2*)

general reference A reference to the main ideas in a source or to information presented throughout the work, not in a single place. (*See 46b; compare* **informational reference** *and* **specific reference**)

general sources Books, indexes, databases, and nonspecialized periodicals used for background and to point the way to **specialized sources.** (*See 44a-3, 44b-1*)

general-to-specific pattern (*See* **logical order**)

genre The form, or category of discourse, to which a work conforms (e.g., poem, play, novel, novella, film). (*See 51a-2*)

gerund An -*ing* form of a verb that acts as a noun. (*See 14a-4, 14c-2, 15b-6; see also* **verbal phrase**)

Running can be enjoyable.

→ **get** Avoid imprecise or frequent use of *get* in formal writing; use more specific verbs instead.

INFORMAL	Martin Luther King had a premonition that he would **get** shot; his sermons and speeches before his death **got** nostalgic at times.
EDITED	Martin Luther King had a premonition that he would **be** shot; his sermons and speeches before his death **waxed** nostalgic at times.

→ **go, say** In very informal contexts, some speakers use *go* and *goes* colloquially to mean *say* and *says*. This usage is considered inappropriate in all writing.

INAPPROPRIATE	Hjalmar **goes** to Gregers, "I thought it best to make a clean break."
EDITED	Hjalmar **says** to Gregers, "I thought it best to make a clean break."

→ **gone, went** Do not use *went* (the past tense of *go*) in place of the past participle form *gone*.

INCORRECT	The players **should have went** to their captain.
EDITED	The players **should have gone** to their captain.

gloss

→ **good and** This is a colloquial term when used to mean "very" (*good and* tired; *good and* hot). Avoid it in formal writing.

→ **good, well** *Good* is an adjective meaning "favorable" (a *good* trip). *Well* is an adverb meaning "done favorably." Avoid colloquial uses of *good* for *well*.

COLLOQUIAL   The Vikings played real **good** in the playoffs.

CORRECT   A **good** shot in the game of golf is not a hard-hit shot but a shot that is placed **well.**

→ **got to** Avoid the colloquial use of *got* or *got to* in place of *must* or *have to*.

COLLOQUIAL   I **got to** improve my ratings in the opinion polls.

EDITED   I **must** improve my ratings in the opinion polls.

government documents Archives of congressional reports and documents issued by federal agencies as well as state and local governments. (*See* 44b-3)

→ **great** In formal writing, avoid using *great* as an adjective meaning "wonderful." Use *great* in the sense of "large" or "monumental."

INFORMAL   Our trip to Stone Mountain was **great.**

APPROPRIATE   As you approach Stone Mountain, a **great** carving appears on the rock face.

guiding question In research, a specific question that helps to determine the kinds of sources to consult, the process of locating sources, and the possibilities for organizing the paper. (*See* 43b, 43c)

→ **hanged, hung** Although the distinction between these terms is disappearing, some readers may expect you to use *hanged* exclusively to mean execution by hanging and *hung* to refer to anything else.

The convict was **hanged** at dawn.

The farmer **hung** the dead pheasant upside down for a day before cooking it.

hasty generalization (*See* **begging the question**)

→ **have, got** (*See* **got to**)

→ **have, of** (*See* **could of, would of**)

→ **he, she, he or she, his/her** When you use gender-specific pronouns, be careful not to privilege the male versions. Look for ways to avoid awkward alternations of *he* and *she* or *his* and *her* by revising structures that require them. (*See* 30a-3)

headword The word a modifier refers to. (*See* Chapter 22)

helping verb The different forms of *be, do,* and *have* that link to main verbs and create complex verb forms. Helping verbs are sometimes called **auxiliary verbs** or **modal auxiliaries.** (*See* 14a-3, 16b, 17b-1)

> helping   main
> verb   verb

The tourist agency is planning to make a video of the local attractions.

highlight paragraph A transition paragraph used to call attention to important ideas and information. (*See 9c-3*)

homophones Words that sound like each other but are spelled differently (*accept/except; assent/ascent; principal/principle; stationary/stationery*). (*See 42b-4*)

→ **hopefully** Although the word is widely used to modify entire clauses (as in "Hopefully, her condition will improve"), some readers may object. When in doubt, use *hopefully* only to mean "feeling hopeful."

Bystanders watched **hopefully** as the workers dug their way to the trapped spelunkers.

→ **however, yet, but** (*See* **but however, but yet**)

→ **hung, hanged** (*See* **hanged, hung**)

hyphenated noun A single noun that consists of two or more words linked by hyphens: *father-in-law*. (*See 33a-3*)

hypothesis A tentative assertion to be explored in an argument. (*See 50c-1*)

idiom A common expression that typically means something different from its literal interpretation (e.g., *kick the bucket*). (*See 27b-5*)

→ **if, whether** Use *if* before a specific outcome (either stated or implied); use *whether* when you are considering alternatives.

If holographic technology can be perfected, we may soon be watching three-dimensional television. But **whether** any of us will be able to afford it is another question.

illogical comparison (*See* **incomplete sentence**)

→ **illusion, allusion** (*See* **allusion, illusion**)

→ **immigrate to, emigrate from** (*See* **emigrate from, immigrate to**)

imperative mood (*See* **mood**)

imperative sentence A type of sentence that makes a request or command. (*See 12b-2, 14d-2; compare* **declarative sentence; exclamatory sentence; interrogative sentence**)

Do your chores immediately.

→ **implicit, explicit** (*See* **explicit, implicit**)

incomplete comparison (*See* **incomplete sentence**)

incomplete sentence A sentence that fails to complete an expected logical or grammatical pattern. An *incomplete comparison* leaves out the element to which something is being compared. An *illogical comparison* is worded so that it seems to be comparing things that cannot be reasonably compared. (*See 24b*)

gloss

INCOMPLETE COMPARISON	The sound quality of the new digital audiotapes is much better.
EDITED	The sound quality of the new digital audiotapes is much better **than that of the old analog tapes.**

indefinite article (*See* **article**)

indefinite pronoun A pronoun that refers to people, things, or ideas in general rather than to specific antecedents. Indefinite pronouns include *all, another, any, anybody, anyone, anything, both, each, every,* and *everyone.* (*See 14a-2, 15a, 17c-3*)

independent clause (*See* **main clause**)

indicative mood (*See* **mood**)

indirect object (*See* **object**)

indirect question A sentence whose main clause is a statement and whose embedded clause asks a question. Such sentences usually behave as statements, not as questions. (*See 23b-2, 35b-1*)

Phil wondered whether it would be too much work to take on an additional course.

indirect quotation A quotation in which a writer reports the substance of someone's words but not the exact words the person used. Quotation marks are not needed. (*See 23b-2, 23d*)

inductive argument An argument that does not explicitly state a premise but leads the reader through an accumulating body of evidence to a conclusion. (*See 50c-1; compare* **deductive argument**)

infinitive The "root," tenseless form of a verb. In English, infinitives are preceded by *to: to live, to perform, to abolish.* (*See 14a-4, 14c-4; see also* **split infinitive** and **verbal phrase**)

inform In a writing assignment, to tell the reader about some facts, views, or phenomena. (*See 5a-2*)

informational reference A reference that provides background information or material potentially useful for readers but too cumbersome to include in the text itself. (*See 46b; compare* **general reference** and **specific reference**)

informative writing Writing whose content and strategies are shaped by the purpose of conveying, explaining, or analyzing information (*See 43h-1, Chapter 52; see also* **point-driven writing**)

→ **in regard to** Although it may sound sophisticated, *in regard to* is wordy and unnecessary. Use *about* instead.

gloss

WORDY	The cruise company was adamant **in regard to** its docking rights at Christiansted.
EDITED	The cruise company was adamant **about** its docking rights at Christiansted.

→ **inside of, outside of** When you use *inside* or *outside* to mark locations, do not pair them with *of*.

> **INAPPROPRIATE** **Inside of** the hut was a large stock of rootwater.

> **EDITED** **Inside** the hut was a large stock of rootwater.

→ **insure, assure, ensure** (*See* **assure, ensure, insure**)

intensifying phrase A phrase that is meant to make a sentence more forceful but carries little or no additional meaning: *for all intents and purposes, in my opinion, all things considered*. (*See 29a-1*)

intensive pronoun A **reflexive pronoun** used to give emphasis to, or intensify, a sentence. (*See 14a-2, 15b-7*)

> He was able to move the heavy refrigerator **himself.**
> She **herself** was responsible for the mismanagement of the firm.

intentional fragment (*See* **partial sentence**)

interjection An emphatic word or phrase used to convey a strong reaction or emotion, such as surprise (*Hey!*) or disappointment (*Oh no!*). (*See 14a-9*)

interlibrary loans Systems that allow for the exchange of books, articles, and other resources between libraries to serve users of a library that does not have an item in its own holdings. (*See 44b-3*)

internal dialogue (*See* **dialogue journal**)

interpolation The introduction of your own words, marked with brackets, into a verbatim quotation from someone else. (*See 36b-1*)

> Kent said, "Captain Sims **[the boat's owner]** has chosen a special place within two hours of Key West."

interpretation The process of reading into or adding your own understandings to a source, concept, or phenomenon. (*See 45a-2, 50a-3*)

interrogative pronoun The pronouns *who* and *which* when these are used to introduce questions. (*See 14a-2, 15a, 15c-2*)

interrogative sentence A type of sentence that poses a question. (*See 12b-2, 14d-2; compare* **declarative sentence; exclamatory sentence; imperative sentence**)

interrupters Parenthetical remarks such as *in fact* or *more importantly*. (*See 31d*)

in-text citation In research writing, a citation that is placed within the text of the paper rather than at the end in a works cited page or bibliography. (*See 46b*)

intransitive verb A verb that is not followed by an **object** or **complement.** (*See 14b-2; compare* **transitive verb**)

>   verb   no object
> The president **dreamed.**

gloss

introduction The first part of a paper or other document, often leading up to or containing a **thesis.** (*See 7a-2*)

invention A term from classical rhetoric referring to the process of generating and exploring ideas before writing a draft. (*See Chapter 4; see also* **brainstorming; planning; prewriting strategies**)

inverted sentence order A sentence in which the normal subject-verb-object/complement word order is shifted by placing a subsidiary element at the beginning of the sentence in order to call attention to it. (*See 12a-4*)

NORMAL	**The director's voice thundered** from the darkness near the rear of the auditorium with criticisms of our acting.
INVERTED	**From the darkness near the rear of the auditorium thundered the director's voice** with criticisms of our acting.

→ **irregardless** Avoid this erroneous form of the word *regardless,* commonly used because *regardless* and *irrespective* are often used synonymously.

irregular verb A verb that does not follow the usual pattern for distinguishing forms for the present, past, and past participle. (*See 16a*)

	Present	Past	Past participle
REGULAR VERB	bake	baked	baked
IRREGULAR VERB	swim	swam	swum

→ **irritate, aggravate** (*See* **aggravate, irritate**)

issue A subject about which there are two (or more) clearly differing opinions. (*See 50a-1*)

italic type Type that *slants to the right* and is the equivalent of <u>underlining</u> for emphasis or for some titles. (*See Chapter 38*)

→ **its, it's** Use *its* as a possessive pronoun and *it's* as a contraction of *it* and *is.* (Some readers may also object to *it's* for *it is* in formal writing.) (*See 33b*)

The porcupine raised **its** quills threateningly. **It's** a shame that dogs must learn about porcupines the hard way.

→ **-ize, -wise** Some readers object to the process of turning nouns or adjectives into verbs by adding *-ize* at the end (*finalize, itemize, computerize*). When in doubt, opt for different verbs. Also avoid adding the suffix *-wise* to words, as in "Weather-*wise,* it will be a chilly night all over the region."

journalist's questions A set of questions (*who? what? when? where? why? how?*) used during the planning or prewriting process to generate or explore ideas or existing material. (*See 4a-5*)

key words Most **database** resources and other electronic sources of information such as an **online catalog** or **electronic indexes** allow researchers to retrieve information and listings by typing in important (key) words identifying the subject or some important ideas or details related to the subject. (*See 44b-2*)

→ **kind, sort, type** These words are singular nouns; precede them with *this*, not *these*. In general, use more precise words.

→ **kind of, sort of** Considered by most readers to be informal, these phrases should be avoided in academic and professional writing.

lab report A paper that summarizes the methods and results of a laboratory experiment. (*See 52e*)

→ **latter, former** (*See* **former, latter**)

→ **lay, lie** *Lay* is a transitive verb requiring a direct object (but not the self). *Lie,* when used to mean "place in a resting position," refers to the self but takes the form *lay* in the past tense. (*See 16e-1*)

INCORRECT   I was going to **lay** down for a while.

EDITED   I was going to **lie** down for a while.

→ **less, fewer** (*See* **fewer, less**)

→ **liable** (*See* **apt, likely, liable**)

library research (*See* **research**)

→ **lie, lay** (*See* **lay, lie**)

→ **like, as** (*See* **as, like**)

→ **likely, apt, liable** (*See* **apt, likely, liable**)

limiting modifier A **modifier** such as *only, almost, hardly, just, scarcely, merely, simply, exactly,* or *even* that limits or qualifies a word, usually the one that follows it. (*See 22a-2*)

limiting sentence A sentence that limits, or narrows, the focus of a **topic sentence.** (*See 9a-2*)

linking verb Verbs that express a state of being or an occurrence: *is, seems, becomes, grows.* Also known as **state-of-being verbs.** (*See 14a-3, 14b-2, 17b-2*)

listing A technique for exploring ideas by making a list of points, usually in preparation for writing a formal paper. (*See 4a-3*)

→ **literally** Avoid using *literally* in a figurative statement (one that is not true to fact). Even when used correctly, *literally* is redundant because the statement will be taken as fact anyway.

INCORRECT   The visiting scholars **literally** died when they saw their accommodations.

REDUNDANT   The visiting scholars **literally gasped** when they saw their accommodations.

EDITED   The visiting scholars gasped when they saw their accommodations.

literature review A paper or part of a paper that provides a **synthesis** of existing literature or research on a specific topic. (*See 52d*)

gloss

logical order   A pattern for paragraph development in which details and generalizations are arranged according to a *question-answer pattern,* a *problem-solution pattern,* a *general-to-specific pattern,* or a *specific-to-general pattern,* suggesting an internal logic to the flow of sentences and ideas. (*See 9b-5*)

logical strategies   The arrangement of ideas and evidence in ways that correspond with patterns of thought that most people accept as reasonable and convincing. (*See 50c-1*)

looping   A technique involving successively **freewriting,** reviewing the material produced from freewriting in order to find new ideas or concepts, and then freewriting on those ideas or concepts. (*See 4a-2*)

→ **loose, lose**   Commonly misspelled, these words are pronounced differently. *Loose* (rhyming with *moose*) is an adjective meaning "not tight." *Lose* (rhyming with *snooze*) is a present tense verb meaning "to misplace."

I was afraid that I would **lose** my ring because it was very **loose.**

→ **lots, lots of, a lot of**   (*See* **a lot**)

main clause   A word group that contains a subject and a verb and can act as a complete sentence. Also called an *independent clause.* (*See 14c; compare* **phrase**)

main verb   The central or main verb (word showing action or state of being) in a sentence; it can stand alone or be accompanied by one or more **helping verbs.** (*See 14a-3*)

major premise   (*See* **premise**)

major revision   (*See* **revision**)

→ **man, mankind**   For many readers, these terms represent sexist usage when they refer to all humans. Use *people, humans, humanity,* or some other substitute. (*See Chapter 30*)

→ **may, can**   (*See* **can, may**)

→ **maybe, may be**   *Maybe* means *possibly; may be* is part of a verb structure.

The President **may be** addressing the nation tonight, so **maybe** we should turn on the news.

mass noun   A kind of noun that refers to material that cannot be "counted," or divided into separate units to form a usual plural. (*See 14a-1; see also* **noun; collective noun; count noun**)

COUNT NOUNS	chair+s, cake+s, shadow+s, pea+s
NONCOUNT NOUNS	flour, rice, sugar, steel, sunlight, earth, water

gloss

→ **media, medium**   Technically, *media* is a plural noun requiring a verb that agrees in number. Many people now use *media* as a singular noun when referring to the press.

The **media** <u>is</u> not covering the story accurately.

Medium generally refers to a conduit or method of transmission.

The telephone was not a good **medium** for reviewing all the budget figures.

meeting minutes A report of the items discussed during a business meeting. (*See 53d*)

memo A short, usually internal, note between or among people working in a business. (*See 53e*)

microfiche A flat sheet of **microfilm,** on which printed materials have been placed to save space. (*See* **microform collection**)

microfilm A type of film on which printed materials are recorded to save space. (*See* **microform collection**)

microform collection A library collection containing books, **periodicals,** newspapers, and unpublished documents in the form of **microfilm** or **microfiche.** (*See 44b-3*)

→ **might of, may of** (*See* **could of, would of**)

→ **mighty** Avoid this adjective in formal writing.

INFORMAL   It was a **mighty** proud moment for NASA.

EDITED   It was a **very** proud moment for NASA.

minor premise (*See* **premise**)
minor revision (*See* **revision**)
minutes (*See* **meeting minutes**)
misleading language/misleading evidence A **fallacy** in which a writer deceives a reader through the use of language or information. Using misleading language, the writer shifts the meaning of a term from one sense to another but still gives the erroneous impression of supporting the argument. Using misleading evidence, the writer uses faulty statistics, survey results, and other material slanted in favor of only one side of an argument. (*See 50c-5*)

misplaced modifier A modifier incorrectly placed relative to its intended **headword,** giving the impression that it modifies something else. (*See Chapter 22; compare* **dangling modifier and disruptive modifier**)

MISPLACED   In *Walden,* Thoreau describes how he **simply** lived, conserving his resources.

EDITED   In *Walden,* Thoreau describes how he lived **simply,** conserving his resources.

gloss

mixed sentence A sentence with mismatched topics or with a shifted grammatical structure. (*See 24a; see* **faulty predication**)

MLA documentation style The style of **documentation** suggested by the Modern Language Association and described in its guide. (*See Chapter 46*)

mnemonic An aid to memorization, for example, of correct spellings. (*See 42c-1*)

modal auxiliary verbs (*See* **helping verbs**)

modified block format A format for longer letters in which the return address and the closing and signature are indented but paragraphs are not. (*See 53b; compare* **block format**)

modifier A word or word group, functioning as an adjective or adverb, that qualifies or adds to a noun or verb. (*See Chapter 22*)

mood The verb form that indicates the speaker's attitude in a sentence. *Indicative mood* characterizes statements intended as truthful or factual. *Imperative mood* characterizes statements that function as commands. *Subjunctive mood* characterizes statements expressing uncertainty. Many **conditional sentences** require the subjunctive mood. (*See 14a-3, 16b-3, 23b-3*)

INDICATIVE MOOD	It will rain today.
IMPERATIVE MOOD	Beware of lightning!
SUBJUNCTIVE MOOD	Were it to rain, we would not play golf.

→ **Ms.** To avoid the sexist labeling of women as "married" or "unmarried" (a condition not marked in men's titles), use *Ms.* unless you have reason to use *Miss* or *Mrs.* (for example, when giving the name of a character such as *Mrs. Dalloway*). Use professional titles when appropriate (*Dr., Professor, Senator, Mayor*). (*See Chapter 30*).

multiple-word noun A noun consisting of two or more words that are treated as a single unit when marking plurality or possession. (*See 33a-3*)

The **union leaders'** negotiations fell through.

→ **must of, must have** (*See* **could of, would of**)

narrative A type of writing, or **genre,** in which the writer usually traces events in the past, present, or imagined future. Narratives tell stories about people, places, or events, often from the writer's own experience. (*See 10a-1*)

narrowing The process of taking a more specific perspective on a chosen topic. (*See 5c-1*)

neologism A word that has entered into general use very recently, sometimes not yet having been put into any dictionaries. (*See 27b-4*)

nominalization A sentence in which a verb or adjective is (sometimes inappropriately) turned into a noun: *completion* (noun) from *complete* (verb), *happiness* (noun) from *happy* (adjective). (*See 11a-2, 29a-2*)

noncoordinate adjectives (*See* **coordinate adjectives**)

noncount noun (*See* **mass noun**)

nonrestrictive clause (*See* **restrictive modifier**)

nonrestrictive modifier (*See* **restrictive modifier**)

gloss

→ **nor, or** Use *nor* in negative constructions and *or* in positive ones.

    NEGATIVE   Neither rain **nor** snow will slow the team.

    POSITIVE   Either rain **or** snow may delay the game.

→ **nothing like, nowhere near** These are considered informal phases when used to compare two things (as in "Gibbon's position is **nowhere near** as justified as Carlyle's"). Avoid them in formal writing.

noun A word that names a person, place, or thing and is often preceded by an **article** (*a, an,* or *the*). (*See 14a; see also* **collective noun; count noun; mass noun**)

noun clause A clause that functions as a noun. (*See 14c-5*)

noun string A string of nouns used as modifiers (usually adjectives) of a main noun. Such strings are grammatically correct but may seem overly abstract or technical. (*See 11a-4*)

The **area computer network downlink access program** failed.

→ **nowheres** Use *nowhere* instead.

number A grammatical concept referring to whether a noun or pronoun is singular or plural. Pronouns must agree in number with the nouns they modify, and subjects and verbs must also agree in number. (*See 14a-2, 14a-3, 15a, 16a, 17a*)

→ **number, amount** (*See* **amount, number**)

object A noun, pronoun, or group of words functioning as a noun to which the action of a verb applies. *Direct objects* receive the action of **transitive verbs;** *indirect objects* are affected indirectly by the action of a transitive verb. (*See 14b-2; see also* **complement**)

object complement (*See* **complement**)

object of a preposition The noun or pronoun that follows a preposition. (*See 14b-2, 14c-1*)

object pronoun A pronoun that is the **object** of a verb. (*See 14c-5*)

objective case (*See* **case**)

objective description Description that emphasizes physical details. (*See 10b-2; compare* **subjective description**)

objective summary (*See* **summary**)

→ **of, have** (*See* **could of, would of**)

→ **off of** Use simply *off* instead.

→ **OK** When you write formally, use *OK* only in dialogue. If you mean "good" or "acceptable," use one of these terms.

→ **on account of** Avoid this expression in formal writing. Use *because* instead.

online catalog A computerized listing of books, magazines, and other holdings in a library. A researcher can retrieve individual listings by author, title, or subject area. Many online catalogs list resources in more than one library and can be accessed through computer networks as well as by terminals in a library. (*See 44b-2; see also* **card catalog**)

gloss

outline A list, usually hierarchical, showing the main contents of a paper. (*See 4b-6*) A *working outline* shows the general sequence of information in a paper and the relationships between the segments of information. (*See 45c-4*)

→ **outside of, inside of** (*See* **inside of, outside of**)

overblown language **Diction** that is too formal or technical for the writer's purpose and audience, often used out of a misguided attempt to impress the reader. (*See 29b-2*)

overgeneralization (*See* **begging the question**)

paragraph A unit of prose marked by an indent at the left margin and consisting of a **topic** and its **development.** A *focused paragraph* is one in which the topic, main idea, or perspective is evident and is maintained throughout the paragraph. A *unified paragraph* contains sentences that are clearly and directly related to the main idea. (*See Chapter 9*)

paragraph development The examples, facts, concrete details, explanatory statements, or supporting arguments that make a paragraph informative and give it a sense of structure. (*See Chapter 10*)

parallelism The expression of similar or related ideas in similar grammatical form. *Faulty parallelism* occurs when elements in parallel are given incorrect or unequal grammatical form (*see Chapter 25*). In paragraphs, parallelism refers to a technique in which grammatical structures are repeated in order to highlight similar or related ideas. (*See 9b-4*)

paraphrase A rewriting of an original sentence or passage in your own words, preserving the essence and level of detail of the original. (*See 34b-2, 44f-2, 45f*)

partial sentence An effective sentence fragment used for emphasis. (*See 19d*)

participle The form a verb takes when it is linked to a helping verb. Verbs can take two participial forms, the *present participle* and the *past participle*. (*See 14a-4, 14c-4, 16b*)

particle (*See* **phrasal verb**)

passive voice The form of a verb in a sentence in which the doer (or agent) takes the position of the direct object. (*See 11c, 14a-3, 16d, 23c, 29a-2; compare* **active voice**)

    subject   verb   object
The ball was caught by the outfielder.

gloss

past participle (*See* **participle**)

past perfect tense (*See* **perfect tense**)

past progressive tense (*See* **progressive tense**)

past tense (*See* **tense**)

peer group A group of fellow writers, usually in a classroom, who participate in collaborative writing activities. (*See 6d-3*)

→ **per** Use *per* only to mean "by the," as in *per hour* or *per day*. Avoid using it to mean "according to," as in "*per* your instructions."

→ **percent, percentage** Use *percent* only with numerical data. Use *percentage* to imply a statistical part of something.

INCORRECT	A **percentage** of my commute is through Tomkins State Park.
CORRECT	Ten **percent** of the sample returned the questionnaire.
CORRECT	A large **percentage** of the revenue from the parking meters was stolen.

perfect tense A tense used to indicate that something happens before something else happens. Three perfect tenses can be marked in verb phrases: present perfect, past perfect, and future perfect. (*See 16b-2*)

PRESENT PERFECT	**I have reported** the fire already.
PAST PERFECT	The fires **had burned** for an hour before the brigade arrived.
FUTURE PERFECT	Nancy **will have finished** by the time the dentist is ready.

periodic sentence A sentence structured so that subsidiary phrases, clauses, or other elements are piled up at the beginning, delaying the sentence's main clause. (*See 12a-4*)

Because she knows that inspired designs often spring from hard work, because she loves perfection yet fears failure, and because she believes that risk-taking ought to be accompanied by attention to detail, Janelle is working up to eighteen hours a day on the clothing for her fall collection.

periodical A recurring publication that contains articles by different authors. Periodicals include magazines, scholarly journals, and newspapers. (*See 44b-2*)

person The form that a noun or a pronoun takes to identify the subject of a sentence. *First person* is someone speaking (*I, we*); *second person* is someone spoken to (*you*); *third person* is someone being spoken about (*he, she, it, they*). Verbs must agree in person with their subjects. (*See 14a-3, 15a, 16a, 17a, 23a*)

persona The way a writer chooses to characterize himself or herself through the choice of words and phrases, voice, and other devices. (*See 27a-3, 45c-1*)

personal pronoun A pronoun that designates persons or things. (*See 14a, 15a*)

SINGULAR	I, me, you, he, him, she, her, it
PLURAL	we, us, you, they, them

personal voice In writing, the use of stylistic devices (such as personal

gloss

pronouns, narration, or the expression of beliefs and opinions) that convey a strong sense of the writer's self. (*See 2d-1*)

phrasal verb   A verb plus a closely associated word (**particle**) that looks like a **preposition** (*run down, burn up, call up, clear out*). Unlike prepositions, particles can be moved from a position after the verb to a position after a direct object. (*See 14a-3*)

BEFORE OBJECT   Mr. Sims **burned up** all the wood.

AFTER OBJECT   Mr. Sims **burned** all the wood **up.**

phrase   A word group lacking one or more elements (such as a subject or predicate) that would make it a complete sentence. (*See 14c; compare* **main clause**)

plagiarism   The unethical practice of claiming that another writer's words or text are your own, or citing another person's words or text without credit, thereby giving the illusion that that person's words are your own. (*See 45d*)

planning   A set of writing strategies through which the writer generates material and makes decisions about the content, organization, and style of a piece of formal writing. (*See Chapter 4; see also* **brainstorming; prewriting; invention**)

planning paragraph   A kind of transition paragraph used near the beginning of an essay or section of an essay in order to help readers understand the arrangement of a discussion. (*See 9c-3*)

plot   The chain of events in a work of fiction. (*See 51a-2*)

→ **plus**   Avoid using *plus* as a conjunction joining two independent clauses.

INFORMAL   The school saved money through its "lights off" campaign, **plus** it generated income by recycling aluminum cans.

EDITED   The school saved money through its "lights off" campaign and also generated income by recycling aluminum cans.

Use *plus* only to mean "in addition to."

ACCEPTABLE   The wearisome reelection campaign, **plus** the pressures from the media, exhausted the senator.

→ **p.m., a.m.**   (*See* **a.m., p.m.**)

pocket dictionary   An abbreviated or abridged dictionary useful for quick checks on spelling or definitions. (*See 28a*)

point-by-point organization   A strategy for arranging paragraphs that make use of **comparing and contrasting.** Comparable features of two different or opposed subjects are described one by one. (*See 10b-3; compare* **subject-by-subject organization**)

point-driven writing   Writing whose content and strategies are shaped by the purpose of explaining the writer's ideas, interpretations, and perspectives and providing support for them. (*See Chapter 50; see also* **informative writing**)

point of view The perspective from which something (particularly a work of fiction) is told. (*See 51a-2; see also* **person** and **persona**)

policy In argumentative writing, a position that a particular course of action is one that should be undertaken or avoided. (*See 50a-3*)

position paper A short, often documented paper that defines an issue, considers an audience, and draws on evidence and logical strategies to make its point. (*See 50c*)

positive form One of three forms taken by an adjective or adverb to indicate whether the noun or verb modified is being compared to something else. The positive form is used when no comparison is indicated. (*See 18c; compare* **comparative form** and **superlative form**)

ADJECTIVE	This is a **clean** oven.
	She is an **imaginative** designer.
ADVERB	You can travel **fast** in Manhattan by foot.
	Peggy designs **imaginatively.**

possessive case (*See* **case**)

possessive noun A noun that expresses ownership. Possession is usually marked with an apostrophe to distinguish the form from a plural. (*See 33a*)

The bird's call is becoming fainter.

possessive pronoun A pronoun that shows ownership. (*See 14a*)

| SINGULAR | my, mine, your, yours, her, hers, his, its |
| PLURAL | our, ours, your, yours, their, theirs |

***post hoc* fallacy** (*See* **faulty cause-effect relationship**)

→ **precede, proceed** *Precede* means "come before"; *proceed* means "go ahead."

The Mickey Mouse float **preceded** the mayor's car. The parade **proceeded** down Fifth Avenue.

predicate In a sentence, the word or words indicating an action, a relationship, consequences, or conditions. A predicate typically takes the form of a **verb phrase** preceded by the subject of the sentence. A *simple predicate* consists only of a verb or verb phrase; a *complete predicate* consists of a verb or verb phrase plus any modifiers and other words that receive action or complete the verb. (*See 14b-1, 14b-2*)

prefix An affix, such as *un-* in *unforgiving* placed before a word. (*See 42b-3*)

preliminary sources Reference works (such as encyclopedias) or electronic sites (such as mail lists or bulletin boards) that you can consult early in a research project for background information or for issues and

gloss

questions of current interest. Preliminary (or *exploratory*) sources help you explore broad topics and identify areas for further, more intensive research. (*See 44a-3*)

premise   A claim or assertion that serves as the foundation of an argument. **Syllogistic reasoning** includes both *major* and *minor premises*—assertions or *claims* on which conclusions can be based. (*See 50c-1*)

preposition   A word that indicates a location, direction, or time (for example, *to, from, with, under, in, over*). (*See 14a-7; see also* **object of a preposition**)

prepositional phrase   A phrase, created from a preposition plus a noun phrase, that can add information to a sentence or make it more precise or detailed. (*See 14a-7*)

A faint smell **of grilled onions** came **through the window.**

prereading strategies   A set of reading strategies in which the reader previews, skims, and samples a reading before working through it more formally. (*See 3a*)

present participle (*See* **participle**)
present perfect tense (*See* **perfect tense**)
present progressive tense (*See* **progressive tense**)
present tense (*See* **tense**)

→ **pretty**   Avoid using *pretty* (as in *pretty good, pretty hungry, pretty sad*) to mean "somewhat" or "rather." Use *pretty* in the sense of "attractive."

prewriting strategies   A set of writing strategies used to explore ideas and information in order to generate material for a formal paper. (*See Chapter 4; see also* **brainstorming; invention; planning**)

primary sources (*See* **research**)

→ **principal, principle**   *Principal* is a noun meaning "an authority" or "head of a school" or an adjective meaning "leading" ("a *principal* objection to the testimony"). *Principle* is a noun meaning "belief or conviction."

printed indexes   Books listing articles that appear in magazines, newspapers, or scholarly journals. Indexes help researchers locate useful sources. (*See 44b-2; see also* **electronic indexes**)

problem-solution grid   A planning strategy through which a variety of hypothetical solutions are generated to solve a specific problem. (*See 4b-4*)

problem-solution sequence   A piece of writing in which a problem is presented followed by a proposal for one or more solutions, perhaps with their advantages and disadvantages. (*See 4b-4*)

→ **proceed, precede** (*See* **precede, proceed**)

progressive tense   A tense used to show an ongoing action in progress at some point in time. Verb forms can show three types of progressive tense: *present progressive, past progressive,* and *future progressive.* (*See 16b-2*)

PRESENT PROGRESSIVE   The carousel **is turning** too quickly.

PAST PROGRESSIVE   The horses **were bobbing** up and down.

FUTURE PROGRESSIVE   The children **will be laughing.**

pronoun A word that takes the place of a noun, such as *them, his, she,* and *it.* Pronouns are often used to avoid repeating the nouns used in the sentence. (*See 14a-2, 17c*)

Jim changed **his shirt** after spilling gravy on **it.**

pronoun-antecedent agreement (*See* **agreement**)

pronoun reference The connection between a pronoun (*its, him, them,* etc.) and its **antecedent,** or the noun or person to which it refers. (*See Chapter 21*)

proofreading The process of reading a draft in order to identify and correct distracting and usually minor errors in spelling, punctuation, incorrect hyphenation, and word division. (*See 13d, Chapters 37 through 42, 45e-3; compare* **editing**)

proper adjective An adjective derived from a proper noun, used to modify a noun: *Brazilian music, Dickensian portrait.* (*See 37b-1*)

proper noun A noun that refers to specific people, places, titles, or things and is capitalized: *Miss America, New Orleans, Xerox Corporation.* (*See 14a-1, 37b-1*)

proposition A **thesis statement** offering an opinion or conclusion that the writer wishes readers to accept or agree with. A proposition is supported or made convincing by an **argument.** (*See 50a-3*)

purpose The writer's rhetorical goals or aim for a piece of writing. (*See Chapter 5, 27a-2, 45c-2, 50b-3*)

purpose structure A series of statements briefly describing the function of each paragraph or section of a paper. (*See 5b-1, 45c-2*)

quantifier A word like *each, one,* or *many* that indicates the quantity of a subject. (*See 17b-1*)

question-answer pattern (*See* **logical order**)

→ **quote, quotation** Formally, *quote* is a verb and *quotation* is a noun. *Quote* is sometimes used as a short version of the noun *quotation,* but this may bother some readers. Use *quotation* instead.

→ **raise, rise** *Raise* is a transitive verb meaning "to lift up." *Rise* is an intransitive verb (it takes no object) meaning "to get up or move up."

He **raised** his head from the newspaper and watched the fog **rise** from the lake.

→ **rarely ever** Use *rarely* alone, not paired with *ever.*

REDUNDANT   He **rarely ever** spoke about the gulag.

EDITED   He **rarely** spoke about the gulag.

reader The intended or imagined **audience** for a piece of writing. (*See Chapter 6*)

gloss

→ **real, really** Use *real* as an adjective modifying a noun; use *really* as an adverb.

> Emmons drove **really** well in the race because for once she was in a **real** stock car.

→ **reason is because, reason is that** Avoid these phrases in formal writing; they are wordy and awkward.

reciprocal pronoun A pronoun (*one another, each other*) that enables a writer to refer to individual parts of a plural antecedent. (*See 14a-2*)

> The two kinds of birds compete for territory by destroying **each other's** nests.

→ **reckon, calculate, figure** (see **calculate, figure, reckon**)

red herring A **fallacy** in which some fact or information distracts a reader from the real argument. (*See 50c-5*)

redrafting Part of the revision process that involves writing unworkable material over again. (*See* **revision**)

redundancy The use of unnecessary or repeated words and phrases that can be reduced through **editing** (see 8a-4). *Redundant pairs* are two words used when only one is needed: *aid and abet, one and only, part and parcel, kith and kin. Redundant phrases* say the same thing twice: *each individual, fresh news, free gifts.* (*See 29a-1*)

redundant pair (*See* **redundancy**)

redundant phrase (*See* **redundancy**)

reference chain A chain of pronouns whose antecedent is stated in the opening sentence of a passage. Reference chains can help to guide readers through a passage and remind them of the controlling topic. (*See 21a-3*)

reflexive pronoun A pronoun that enables a subject or doer of an action also to be the receiver of the action. (*See 14a-2, 15b-7*)

> **He** paid **himself** for the work.

→ **regarding, in regard, with regard to** (*See* **in regard to**)
→ **regardless, irregardless** (*See* **irregardless**)

relative clause An adjective-like clause that modifies a noun or pronoun and begins with a **relative pronoun.** (*See 14a-2, 14c-5, 15c-1*)

> **Who** bought the new minivan?
> I reminisced about all the shellfish **that** I had bought in Seattle.

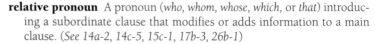

gloss

relative pronoun A pronoun (*who, whom, whose, which,* or *that*) introducing a subordinate clause that modifies or adds information to a main clause. (*See 14a-2, 14c-5, 15c-1, 17b-3, 26b-1*)

remote reference Placing a **pronoun** at a distance from its **antecedent.** (*See 21a-2*)

rereading The process of going back over a reading in order to review, summarize, or understand it. (*See 3a-3*)

research The process of investigating a topic, either through *primary sources* such as interviews or observations or through *secondary sources* such as other writers' books and articles on the same topic. *Library research* is conducted primarily using the print and electronic materials in libraries; *field research* is conducted in settings where the subject of the research can be found in primary form. (*See Chapter 43, 44a-1*)

research plan An anticipated sequence of activities that guides the work of a research paper. (*See 43d*)

→ **respectfully, respectively** *Respectfully* means "with respect"; *respectively* implies a certain order for events or things.

The senior class **respectfully** submitted the planning document. The administration considered items 3, 6, and 10, **respectively.**

restrictive clause (*See* **restrictive modifier**)

restrictive modifier A midsentence clause that presents information essential to the meaning of a passage. In contrast, a *nonrestrictive modifier* adds information that is useful or interesting but not essential to the sentence's meaning. (*See 26b-1, 31c*)

RESTRICTIVE MODIFIER   The charts **drawn by hand** were hard to read.

NONRESTRICTIVE MODIFIER   The charts, **drawn by hand,** were hard to read.

résumé A synthesis (in one or two pages) of one's education and employment history, usually prepared for the purpose of applying for a job. (*See 53f*)

resumptive modifier A modifying clause or phrase used to extend a sentence that appears to have ended, adding new information or twists of thought. (*See 12c-2*)

People who are careful about what they eat may lead healthier lives, **healthier, though not necessarily longer.**

review A critical appraisal of an event, object, or phenomenon, such as an art show, a concert, or a book. Most reviews are both descriptive and evaluative. (*See 50f*)

revision The process of improving rough or preliminary versions of a document by making large-scale changes, additions, or deletions in the material. *Major revision* involves redrafting, reorganizing, adding, or deleting significant material; *minor revision* involves changes within paragraphs, often at the sentence level. (*See Chapter 8, 45e; see also* **editing** and **proofreading**)

rhetorical purpose (*See* **purpose**)

rhetorical question A question asked not in expectation of an answer but for the purpose of providing the answer. (*See 12b-2*)

rhyming dictionary A dictionary that gives rhymes for words. (*See 28a*)

→ **rise, raise** (*See* **raise, rise**)

Rogerian argument A strategy for argument that calls for acknowledging

gloss

the reasonableness of the opposing point(s) of view rather than strong opposition to alternative perspectives. (*See 50c-4*)

rough draft A preliminary version of a paper which will later undergo **revision.** (*See Chapter 7*)

run-in list A list whose items aren't placed on separate lines. Such lists can present items in full or partial sentences. (*See 37a-5; compare* **vertical list**)

run-on sentence (*See* **fused sentence**)

→ **says, goes** (*See* **goes, says**)

search strategy A strategy for research papers in which you identify the type of research you are conducting, the sources you might consult, and the tasks you need to perform. (*See 44a*)

second person (*See* **person**)

secondary sources (*See* **research**)

semidrafting While creating a **rough draft,** the process of writing out full sentences interspersed with *etc.* or other words indicating that something needs to be added later. (*See 7b-3*)

sentence A group of words containing a complete subject and predicate. (*See also* **compound sentence; compound-complex sentence; declarative sentence; exclamatory sentence; imperative sentence; interrogative sentence; simple sentence**)

sentence cluster A group of sentences that develop related ideas or information, often arranged using **parallelism.** (*See 25c*)

sentence fragment A part of a sentence incorrectly treated as a complete sentence with a capital letter at the beginning and a period at the end. (*See Chapter 19*)

FRAGMENT	They were able to get the pump started again. **By replacing the gas filter.**
EDITED	They were able to get the pump started again by replacing the gas filter.
	By replacing the gas filter, they were able to get the pump started again.

sequential order The organization of information into a specific sequence, such as *spatial* (the relationship of physical features), *chronological* (events in a series), or *hierarchical* (most to least important features). (*See 50-a3*)

→ **set, sit** *Set* means "to place"; *sit* means "to place oneself." (*See 16e-2*)

gloss

The research assistant **set** the sample near the centrifuge and then **sat** down on the stool.

setting The physical and temporal context of a work of fiction. (*See 51a-2*)

sexist language Language that implies or reinforces unfair, misleading, or discriminatory stereotypes on the basis of gender. (*See 30a*)

shift An incorrect or inappropriate switch in **person, number, mood, tense,** or **topic.** (*See Chapter 23, 24a*)

→ **should of** (*See* **could of, would of**)

show In a writing assignment, to demonstrate or provide evidence for something. (*See 5a-2*)

signal paragraph A type of transition paragraph used to alert readers to a major change in direction or the start of a new section of the discussion. (*See 9c-3*)

simple predicate (*See* **predicate**)

simple sentence A sentence with one main (independent) clause and no subordinate (dependent) clauses. (*See 14d-1; compare* **complex sentence; compound sentence; compound-complex sentence**)

simple subject (*See* **subject**)

→ **since, because** (*See* **because, since**)

→ **sit, set** (*See* **set, sit**)

→ **site, cite** (*See* **cite, site**)

slanted statistics (*See* **misleading language/misleading evidence**)

→ **so** Some readers object to the use of *so* in place of *very*.

| INFORMAL | The filmmaker is **so** thoughtful about giving his films distinct themes. |
| EDITED | The filmmaker is **very** thoughtful about giving his films distinct themes. |

social context The social, cultural, generational, or economic circumstances of a writer; of an intended **audience;** or of a piece of writing. (*See 6b*)

→ **somebody, some body** (*See* **anybody, any body**)

→ **someone, some one** (*See* **anybody, any body**)

→ **sometime, some time, sometimes** *Sometime* refers to an indistinct time in the future; *sometimes* means "every once in a while." *Some time* is an adjective (*some*) modifying a noun (*time*).

The probe will reach the nebula **sometime** in the next decade. **Sometimes** such probes fail to send back any data. It takes **some time** before images will come back to us from Neptune.

→ **sort, kind** (*See* **kind, sort**)

spatial order In paragraph development, a pattern for arranging descriptive sentences based on the spatial or visual arrangement of a scene, work of art, person, mechanism, or phenomenon (left to right, top to bottom, and so on). (*See 9b-5*)

special collections Library collections that include rare books, manuscripts, and documents, including those of local historical interest. (*See 44b-3*)

specialized dictionary Dictionary that lists terms from a particular field or about a specific topic. (*See 44b-1*)

specialized sources Focused, often complex or technical resources for research that provide detailed information on narrow topics and often

gloss

include the latest scholarly findings. Sources of this kind include research reports, scholarly articles, specialized electronic databases, and interviews with experts. (*See 44a-3*)

→ **specially, especially** (*See* **especially, specially**)

specific pronoun reference Using pronouns to clearly specify the relationships between statements. (*See 21b*)

specific reference A reference that documents the exact location of a word, idea, or fact in a source (for example, on a specific page or in a chart or drawing). (*See 46b; compare* **general reference** and **informational reference**)

specific-to-general pattern (*See* **logical order**)

speculative writing Writing that explores and considers a topic without taking a position on it. (*See 43h-4*)

spelling dictionary A dictionary that gives the spellings of words but not their definitions or etymologies. (*See 28a*)

split infinitive An **infinitive** in which a word separates *to* from the verb. Some readers object to split infinitives. (*See 22c-3*)

SPLIT INFINITIVE	The office designer tried **to** respectively **address** each of the workers' concerns.
EDITED	The office designer tried **to address** each of the workers' concerns respectively.

squinting modifier A modifier that incorrectly appears to modify both the word or phrase that comes before it and the one that comes after it. (*See 22a-3*)

SQUINTING	Those who smoke **seldom** seem concerned about the potential health hazards.
EDITED	Those who **seldom** smoke seem concerned about the potential health hazards.

state-of-being verb (*See* **linking verb**)

→ **stationary, stationery** *Stationary* means "standing still"; *stationery* refers to writing paper.

structure The arrangement of ideas, sections, or paragraphs in a paper or other text. (*See 6c-2; see also* **outline** and **purpose structure**)

structured observation Carefully planned and focused observation of events, people, or situations intended to produce research data from which conclusions can be drawn. (*See 44g-4*)

style The distinctive choice of words (**diction**), sentence structures, and **persona** in a piece of writing. (*See 6c-3*)

subject In a sentence, the doer or the thing talked about—typically the first noun phrase followed by a verb phrase. A *simple subject* consists of one or more nouns (or pronouns) naming the doer or the topic. A *complete subject* consists of the simple subject plus all its modifying words or phrases. (*See 14b-1*)

gloss

subject-by-subject organization A strategy for arranging paragraphs that make use of **comparing and contrasting.** The writer considers one subject in its entirety and then the other, instead of presenting one point for both and then the next point. (*See 10b-3; compare* **point-by-point organization**)

subject complement (*See* **complement**)

subject pronoun A pronoun that is the subject of a clause. (*See 14c-5*)

subjective case (*See* **case**)

subjective description Description that emphasizes the emotional impact of events or phenomena. (*See 10b-2; compare* **objective description**)

subject-verb agreement (*See* **agreement**)

subjunctive mood (*See* **mood**)

subordinate clause A word group that contains both a subject and a predicate but cannot stand on its own as a sentence because it begins with a subordinating word such as *because, since, although, which,* or *that.* Also called a *dependent clause.* (*See 14a-8, 14c-5, 26b-1, 26b-2, 31b-1*)

subordinating conjunction (*See* **conjunction**)

subordination A sentence structure in which one clause modifies another, helping readers perceive the links between ideas and understand the relative importance of information. The **main clause** is accompanied by a **subordinate clause** that modifies, qualifies, or comments on the ideas or the information in the main clause. (*See 26b; compare* **coordination**)

→ **such** Some academic readers will expect you to avoid using *such* without *that.*

INFORMAL Anne Frank had **such** a difficult time living the life of a normal young girl.

EDITED Anne Frank had **such** a difficult time growing up **that** her diary writing became her only solace.

suffix An affix added to the end of a word in order to form a derived word (*bold+ness*) or to provide a grammatical inflection (*talk+ing*). (*See 42b-3*)

summarize (*See* **summary**)

summary A précis in your own words of an original passage, preserving the essence of the original but boiling it down to its essential points. An *objective summary* focuses on the content of the original passage, without any authorial judgment or commentary. An *evaluative summary* contains the author's opinions and comments on the passage. (*See 34b-2, 44f-3, 45d*)

summary paragraph A transitional or concluding paragraph used to mark the end of a discussion or to help readers remember main points. (*See 9c-3*)

summative modifier A modifying phrase or clause that summarizes the preceding part of a sentence and then takes the sentence on a new course. (*See 12c-1*)

To protect your vegetables against harmful insects, you can use soap sprays, scatter insect-repelling plants among the beds, or introduce

gloss

"friendly" insects like ladybugs and praying mantises—**three techniques** that will not leave a harmful chemical residue on the food you grow.

superlative form   One of the three forms taken by adjectives and adverbs to indicate whether the noun or verb modified is being compared to something else. The superlative form adds -*est* or -*most* to the adjective or adverb and indicates a comparison of three or more objects or actions. (*See 18c; compare* **comparative form** and **positive form**)

ADJECTIVE	This is the **leanest** oven I've seen.
	She is the **most imaginative** designer of the three.
ADVERB	You can travel **fastest** in Manhattan if you ride a bicycle.
	Peggy designs **most imaginatively** of the three.

supporting evidence   Material that supports a central claim or **thesis**, including examples from personal experience, examples from other people's experience, quotations and ideas from recognized authorities, technical information and statistics, data from surveys and interviews, background and historical information, and comparisons to similar situations and problems. (*See 50a-4*)

supporting idea   Material that supports an assertion or **thesis**. (*See 5c-4; see also* **supporting evidence**)

→ **suppose to, supposed to**   The correct form of this phrase is *supposed to*; the -*d* is sometimes mistakenly left off because it is not always heard in pronunciation.

→ **sure, surely**   In formal writing, use *sure* to mean "certain." *Surely* is an adverb; don't use *sure* in its place.

He is **sure** to pass the exam.
He has **surely** studied hard for the exam.

→ **sure and, try and**   *And* is sometimes used in place of *to* with *sure* and *try*. Write *sure to* and *try to* instead.

INCORRECT	We will be *sure and* bring our rackets.
CORRECT	Bob will *try to* win the match.

suspended hyphen   A hyphen used at the end of the first of two parallel modifiers (from which the noun is deleted). (*See 39b-3*)

The process is equally effective with **oil-** and **water-based** compounds.

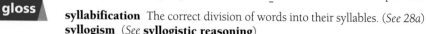

syllabification   The correct division of words into their syllables. (*See 28a*)
syllogism   (*See* **syllogistic reasoning**)
syllogistic reasoning   A kind of logical reasoning that includes a *major premise*, a *minor premise*, and a conclusion. (*See 50c-1; see* **premise**)

MAJOR PREMISE	All landowners in Clarksville must pay taxes.
MINOR PREMISE	Fred Hammil owns land in Clarksville.

| CONCLUSION | Therefore, Fred Hammil must pay taxes. |

synonym A word that is identical or nearly identical in meaning to another word: *ill* and *sick, large* and *big.* (See 27b-2; see **thesaurus**)

synthesis The combining or distilling of separate elements into a single, unified entity. Synthesizing source material for a research paper involves combining concepts and details from a variety of sources to form a unified discussion of a topic. (See 5a-2, 45a-1, 52a-4)

→ **take, bring** (See **bring, take**)

tautology (See **circular reasoning**)

tense The form a verb takes to indicate time—whether the verb's action occurred in the past (*past tense*) or the present (*present tense*). The present tense form is also called the **base form** of the verb. *Future tense* is marked with the use of **helping verbs.** (See 14a-3, 16a, 16b, 23b-1, 23b-2)

PAST	Her grandmother **made** possum stew.
PRESENT	Her friends **stop** to pick up "road kill."
FUTURE	Her children **will find** these old customs offensive.

tense sequence The pattern of tenses in a piece of writing. Incorrect tense shifts can annoy a reader. (See 16c)

tentative thesis statement A preliminary statement of your key ideas and purposes used to help focus planning for the drafting of a paper. (See 44c-3)

text analysis A paper that provides a close, analytical reading of a particular text, often a work of literature. The analysis can focus on elements of the text such as technique or meaning. (See 51c)

→ **than, then** *Than* is a word used to compare something; *then* implies a sequence of events or a causal relationship.

Gregorian chants are more lugubrious **than** other vocal music from that period. As a result, we were lulled by the Gregorian chants, but **then** the organ recital started.

→ **that, which** Although the distinction between *that* and *which* is weakening in many contexts, formal academic writing often requires you to know the difference. Use *that* in a clause that is essential to the meaning of a sentence (**restrictive modifier**); use *which* with a clause that does not provide essential information (*nonrestrictive modifier*).

| THAT | He has the report **that** will vindicate Clareson. |
| WHICH | He has a penchant for emotionalism, **which** may help him win the jury's favor. |

gloss

→ **theirself, theirselves, themself** All these forms are incorrect; use *themselves* to refer to more than one person, and *himself* or *herself* to refer to one person.

→ **them** Avoid using *them* as a subject or to modify a subject, as in "Them are delicious" or "*Them* apples are very crisp."

theme In literary works, an idea, perspective, or cluster of feelings and insights conveyed to a reader through various fictional devices. (*See 51a-1*)

→ **then, than** (see **than, then**)

→ **there, their, they're** These forms are often confused in spelling because they all sound alike. *There* indicates location; *their* is a possessive pronoun; *they're* is a contraction of *they* and *are*.

THERE	Look **over there.**
THEIR	**Their** car ran out of gas.
THEY'RE	**They're** not eager to hike to the nearest gas station.

thesaurus A dictionary of **synonyms** and **antonyms**—words similar or opposite in meaning to each other. (*See 27c-2, 28a*)

thesis or **thesis statement** A sentence, often at the conclusion of an essay's first paragraph, that establishes the point, main argument, or direction of a paper, giving the reader a sense of purpose and an understanding of the essay's contents. (*See 5c, 45c-3, 50a-3*)

third person (*See* **person**)

→ **thusly** Avoid this term; use *thus* or *therefore* instead.

→ **till, until, 'til** Some readers will find *'til* and *till* too informal; use *until*.

time sequence A planning strategy, particularly for papers involving chronological or temporal structures, in which events are labeled along a timeline. (*See 4b-3*)

→ **to, at** (*See* **at, to**)

→ **to, too, two** Because these words sound the same, they may be confused. *To* is a preposition indicating location. *Too* means "also." *Two* is a number.

The Birdsalls went **to** their lake cabin. They invited the Corbetts **too.** That made **two** trips so far this season.

topic The focus or subject of a piece of writing. (*See 5a-1*)

topic sentence A sentence, usually located at the beginning of a paragraph, which announces its main idea or perspective. (*See 5c-3, 9a-2*)

topic shift (*See* **faulty predication, shift**)

→ **toward, towards** Prefer *toward* in formal writing. (You may see *towards* used in England and Canada.)

trace In a writing assignment, mapping out a history or chronology or identifying the origins of something. (*See 5a-2*)

transition (*See* **transitional expression**)

transitional expression Words or phrases (*in addition to, on the other hand, therefore, without a doubt*) that link one idea, sentence, or paragraph to the next, helping readers to see relationships among ideas by connecting them logically. (*See 9b-3, 31b-3, 32a-2*)

transitive verb A verb followed by an **object** or **complement.** (*See 14b-2; compare* **intransitive verb**)

transitive verb   object
The President **called** the British Prime Minister.

tree diagram A planning strategy in which a central idea (or trunk) generates many subsidiary or associative ideas (branches), which can branch off into even more subsidiary twigs. (*See 4b-2; compare* **clustering**)

→ **try and, try to, sure and** (*See* **sure and, try and**)

→ **ultimately, eventually** (*See* **eventually, ultimately**)

unabridged dictionary A full-size reference dictionary, generally available in a library, that has not been abbreviated to save space. (*See 28a*)

uncountable noun (*See* **noncount noun**)

unified paragraph (*See* **paragraph**)

→ **uninterested, disinterested** (*See* **disinterested, uninterested**)

→ **unique** Use *unique* alone; don't write *most unique* or *more unique* since the word indicates an absolute condition.

→ **until, till** (*See* **till, until, 'til**)

→ **use to, used to** Like *supposed to,* this phrase may be mistakenly written as *use to* because the *-d* is not always clearly pronounced. Write *used to.*

vague generalization A sentence or passage that offers so little specific information that it is not meaningful. (*See 29b-1*)

vague pronoun reference Using pronouns that refer to antecedents that are implied rather than stated, or pronouns that are not connected explicitly to a specific antecedent. (*See 21b*)

value judgment An argument that an activity, belief, or arrangement is desirable or undesirable. (*See 50a-3*)

verb The word in a sentence that indicates the action that has occurred, is occurring, or will occur. (*See 14a*)

verb phrase A phrase that consists of a main verb plus a helping verb. (*See 14a-3, 16b*)

verbals Verbs or parts of verb phrases that are used to function as nouns, adjectives, or adverbs. The three kinds of verbals are **infinitives, participles,** and **gerunds.** (*See 14a-4, 14c-4*)

verbal phrase A verbal plus its modifiers, object, or complements. (*See 14c-4*)

vertical file A library file of clippings, pamphlets, and other useful materials. (*See 44b-3*)

vertical list A list whose items are placed on separate lines. (*See 37a-5; compare* **run-in list**)

voice (*See* **active voice, passive voice**)

→ **wait for, wait on** Use *wait on* only to refer to a clerk's or server's job; use *wait for* to mean "to await someone's arrival."

Julie **waited on** the customers while she **waited for** Melissa to arrive.

warrant (*See* **data-warrant-claim reasoning**)

→ **well, good** (*See* **good, well**)

→ **went, gone** (*See* **gone, went**)

gloss

→ **were, we're** *Were* is the past plural form of the verb *was*; *we're* is a contraction of *we* and *are*.

We're going to the ruins where the fiercest battles **were.**

→ **where . . . at** (*See* **at**)
→ **whether, if** (*See* **if, whether**)
→ **which, that** (*See* **that, which**)
→ **who, whom** Although the distinction between these words is slowly disappearing from the language, many readers will expect you to use *whom* in the objective case. When in doubt, err on the side of formality. (Sometimes editing can eliminate the need to choose.) (*See 15c*)

QUESTIONABLE	The person **who** we chose to be the next board president was Harland Clasgow.
EDITED	The person **whom** we chose to be the next board president was Harland Clasgow.
EDITED	We chose Harland Clasgow to be the next board president.

→ **who's, whose** *Who's* is the contracted form of *who* and *is*. *Whose* indicates possession.

The man **who's** going to Frankfurt tried to find the man **whose** bag he mistakenly took at the airport.

→ **wise, -ize** (*See* **-ize, -wise**)
  wordiness Use of too many words. (*See Chapter 29*)
  working bibliography An in-progress bibliography or list of references kept during the **research** process. (*See 44d*)
  working outline (*See* **outline**)
  working thesis A statement of the major ideas to be covered in a paper, used to guide further planning and drafting. A working thesis often appears in a draft but is usually revised by the final version. (*See 45c-3*)
  works cited List of the works to which the writer makes reference in the body of a research paper, either through in-text (parenthetical) citations or through footnotes or endnotes. (*See 46b*)
→ **would of, could of** (*See* **could of, would of**)
  writer's commentary A writer's direct address of the reader or reference to himself or herself in prose that is not intended to convey personal feelings. (*See 29b-3*)
→ **yet, however, but** (*See* **but however, but yet**)
→ **your, you're** *Your* is a possessive pronoun; *you're* is a contraction of *you* and *are*.

If **you're** going to take physics, you'd better know **your** math.

gloss

**A Guide to Using
Computer Resources
at UIC
(http://www.uic.edu/depts/engl/online.html)**

Keith Dorwick and Elli Shellist

Introduction:

Students and teachers alike will find that their studies at the
University of Illinois at Chicago will benefit from the great
range of computing resources available to members of the UIC
community. These include: basic computer resources (such as
e-mail), the use of the public labs, and the ability to connect to
the UIC system from home. SCAILAB (Student Computer
Assisted Instruction Laboratory) is specifically available to
students of the Tutorium in Intensive English and to students
taking English courses whether those courses are composition
courses, literature courses, or upper level writing courses.

Where to Get More Information:

The best source for more information about the kinds of
technology available at UIC is the university's web site, which
includes a link to the home page of the Academic Data
Network (ADN), which supplies computer technology to the
entire UIC community. Many of these pages will be of interest
to you, so here are some of the web addresses for these pages:

ADN Home Page:

http://www.uic.edu/depts/adn/

On this page, you can click on the word "Students" in the
graphic at the top for more information and additional links,
some of which are detailed below:

Creating a Student Computer Account:

http://www.uic.edu/depts/adn/new_account.html

Building a Web Page:

http://www.uic.edu/depts/adn/www_publish/

TimeTable:

The complete TimeTable (the list of courses offered each semester) is available online at

gopher://gopher.uic.edu/11/classroo/mtt00000

Gopher, by the way, though often considered dated and old-fashioned by many web users, is a precursor to the World Wide Web which offers its readers text-based information, such as potential classes you might take. There are still lots of gopher sites out there that have useful information; however, both the Web and Gopher can contain information that appears relevant and exciting, but is so dated or inaccurate as to be useless. In the case of the Time Table, the Gopher version is often far more up to date than the print version you can obtain from the campus bookstore, since it directly reflects the changes made to it as courses are added or dropped.

It's always worth taking a look at Gopher before you try registering for a class that no longer exists!

Class Scheduling Assistant, a program which helps you plan your schedule for classes each semester, a very helpful tool:

http://www.uic.edu/htbin/csa/

Finding the Public Labs:

You may not have a computer with Internet access of your own. If so, you might not know how you can get to the

World Wide Web, a huge collection of texts, graphics, sounds, and games, in which case the list of web sites listed above may not seem very useful! For its students, staff, and faculty, UIC maintains a number of public labs; several are listed below. At the end of this section you'll also find an URL (Uniform Resource Locator, the address of a given web page or other Internet resource) that lists all the labs and their schedules. Since the schedules are subject to change, and new labs are continually being opened, the best way to keep up with these changes is to go to the main web site (http://www.uic.edu). You can also read (or "surf") the web in Scailab.

Locations of Selected Labs:

* Benjamin Goldberg Research Center, located at 1940 West Taylor St.
* Behavioral Science Building, located at 1007 West Harrison.
* SCAILAB, located at 700 South Halsted
* Student Residence and Commons, located at 700 South Halsted

Getting a Netid (Network Identification):

Very few resources are accessible without a netid, which is a unique form of identification that links you to all of the computer resources to which you have access, such as e-mail and certain library resources. All students at UIC are assigned netids automatically, but they require activation before you can use them. To do so, go to one of the Public Labs and use the account creation procedure at http://www.uic.edu/depts/adn/new_account.html

Connecting from Home:

Students and teachers who wish to connect to UIC systems such as the library, the university web pages (which themselves include a number of resources for composition students), and e-mail should obtain a copy of the Network

Services Kit from the ADN (Academic Data Network) which is available on CD-ROM. To find out how to order a NS-Kit, e-mail consult@uic.edu. Include your name, address, netid, platform (Windows or Macintosh), and whether you want to pick up the kit at BSB, SEL (east side labs), or BGRC (west side labs). There is a small charge.

You can download the kit for free from on-campus machines from our UIC FTP (File Transfer Protocol) site. See http://www.uic.edu/depts/adn/nsk.html for more information.

Using the Library:

Some research materials are only available online; the UIC library is the place to access electronic journals, databases, and password protected web sites. Even the card catalog is now completely online. Increasingly, the library's web pages will enable you to find and use resources you need. See http://www.uic.edu/depts/lib/ for current information about library holdings.

Don't Panic!

If you are feeling overwhelmed by the strange acronyms and technical terms above, don't worry. While words like "URL" and "netid" may be unfamiliar to you, the technology is quite accessible. There are many orientation programs available, and the labs are staffed with knowledgeable people who would be glad to show you the ropes. There's a good chance your English instructor will bring you by SCAILAB to get your feet wet, so to speak. If you want to do it on your own, check out the free seminars offered by UIC's Instructional Technology Lab (http://www.uic.edu/depts/adn/cso/seminars/index.html/).

Index

Revision and Editing Symbols

abbrev	incorrect abbreviation, **41**		**no ¶**	no new paragraph, **10**
agr	error in subject-verb or pronoun-antecedent agreement, **17**		**p**	error in punctuation, **31–36**
			punc	error in punctuation, **31–36**
			⌢	comma, **31a–31i**
apos	lack of (or incorrect) possessive apostrophe, **33**		**no** ⌢	no comma, **31j**
art	article used incorrectly, **14a**		;	semicolon, **32a**
awk	awkward construction		:	colon, **32b**
cap	capital letter needed, **37**		℣	apostrophe, **33**
case	incorrect pronoun case, **15**		" "	quotation marks, **34**
clear	clearer sentence needed, **11**		.	period, **35a**
coh	paragraph or essay coherence needed, **9b**		?	question mark, **35b**
			!	exclamation point, **35c**
cs	comma splice, **20**		( ) [ ] —	parentheses, brackets, dashes,
coord	faulty coordination, **26a**		. . . /	ellipses, slashes, **36**
dev	paragraph or essay development needed, **10**		**prep**	preposition error, **14a**
			pr ref	pronoun reference error, **21**
discrm	sexist or discriminatory language, **30**		**ref**	pronoun reference error, **21**
			rep	repetitious, **29**
dm	dangling modifier, **22b**		**sent**	sentence revision needed, **12**
dneg	double negative, **18d**		**shift**	shift, **23**
emph	emphasis needed, **12a**		**sp**	word spelled incorrectly, **42**
foc	paragraph or essay focus needed, **9a**		**spell**	word spelled incorrectly, **42**
			sub	faulty subordination, **26b**
frag	sentence fragment, **19**		**t**	wrong verb tense, **16a, 16b**
fs	fused sentence, **20**		**tense**	wrong verb tense, **16a, 16b**
hyph	hyphen (-) needed, **39**		**trans**	transition needed, **9b, 9c**
inc	incomplete sentence, **24b**		**und**	underlining (italics), **38**
ital	italics (underlining), **38**		**us**	error in usage, **Glossary**
lc	lowercase letter needed, **37**		**var**	sentence variety needed, **12b**
link	paragraph linkage needed, **9c**		**verb**	incorrect verb form, **16**
log	faulty reasoning, **50c**		**wc**	faulty word choice, **27a**
mixed	grammatically mixed sentence, **24a**		**wordy**	too many words, **29**
			ww	wrong word, **27**
mm	misplaced modifier, **22a**		⌃	insert
modif	incorrect adjective or adverb, **18b, 18d**		ℐ	delete
			◡	close up space
num	incorrect number, **40**		⁓	transpose letters or words
//	parallel elements needed, **25**		#	add a space
¶	new paragraph, **10**		×	obvious error

Recognize and Revise
Ten Serious Problems

Recognize	Revise
1. The heavy rain turned the parking area to mud. *Which meant that thousands of cars would get stuck.*	**fragment, 19**
2. The promoters called *the insurance company they discovered* their coverage for accidents was limited.	**fused sentence, 20**
3. After talking with the grounds keeper, the security chief said *he* would not be responsible for the safety of the crowd.	**unclear pronoun reference, 21**
4. The local authorities *hadn't scarcely* enough resources to cope with the flooding.	**double negative, 18d**
5. The mayor *was worried, she urged* the promoters to cancel the event.	**comma splice, 20**
6. *After announcing the cancellation from the stage, the crowd* began complaining to the promoters.	**dangling modifier, 22b**
7. Even the *promoters promise* to reschedule and honor tickets did little to stop the *crowds complaints.*	**lack of possessive apostrophe, 33a**
8. The mayor *who was newly elected* asked people to leave in an orderly manner.	**comma missing in nonrestrictive modifier, 31c**
9. Turning away from the crowd, the mayor said, "I hope either the security chief or the promoters *has* a plan to help all these people leave safely."	**subject-verb agreement, 17a, 17b**
10. *Although,* the muddy parking area caused problems, all the cars and *people, left* the grounds without incident.	**unnecessary commas, 31j**

Reader Response Symbols

(Shortcuts for Responding to Another Writer or Analyzing Your Own Work)

lease add	I would like more information or detail. (8a-3)
ompress	You could say the same thing in less space. (8b-3)
ontradict	This contradicts what you say elsewhere.
ut?	I think this is unnecessary. (8a-4)
ap?	I'm confused—information or an explanation is missing. (8a-3)
erge [with ppropriate arrows]	Consider consolidating this material.
roof (+, OK, -, ?)	You provide strong (+), adequate (OK), weak (-), or inadequate (?) support for your conclusions.
eorganize/structure 1 x–x)	I think you need to reorganize the paper or these paragraphs. (6c-2)
nse?	I can't make sense of this passage, *or* This passage seems to have more than one meaning, and I don't know which to choose. (8b-1)
tyle (+, , -, ?)	The way you say this is effective (+), is adequate ( ), lacks vitality (-), or is hard to follow (?). [Bracket the passage.] (8b-2)
	Is this an error in grammar, sentence structure, wording, punctuation, or mechanics? [Add a correction symbol or reference to the appropriate section of the handbook.] (13b)
	Could you explain this more clearly? What are you trying to accomplish? (8a, 8b-1)
errific, fun, triguing, uching, etc.	I like this; your writing here really works. [Choose your own terms to describe your reactions accurately.]